Property Appraisal and Assessment Administration

Property Appraisal and Assessment Administration

General editor
Joseph K. Eckert, Ph.D.

Senior technical editors
Robert J. Gloudemans
Richard R. Almy

**The International Association
of Assessing Officers**

Library of Congress Catalog Card Number:
90-84144

ISBN Number: cloth, 088329-080-4
              paper, 088329-081-2

Printed in the United States of America

Table of Contents

Figures

Tables

Preface

In 1985, the International Association of Assessing Officers' (IAAO's) Education Committee sought the Executive Board's approval to plan a new comprehensive textbook. Rapid technological developments in the late seventies and eighties made possible improved methods of valuation and administration. Computer-assisted mass appraisal and mapping and statistical techniques for quality control, in particular, have dramatically changed the operation of assessment offices and made their ties to other parts of government stronger.

The Education Committee felt that these technological changes, along with changes in administrative policy at the state and provincial level, required an updating of IAAO's two existing textbooks, *Property Assessment Valuation* (1977) and *Improving Real Property Assessment* (1978). Policies that emphasized market-value-based assessment, short appraisal cycles, and use of modern quality control techniques led to the view that basic appraisal, mass appraisal, and administrative skills are all crucial for the successful functioning of the property tax professional.

Mass appraisal skills are needed for the production of initial values as part of a revaluation effort. Basic appraisal skills are needed to appraise special-purpose properties and to defend assessed values. Administrative skills are needed to manage the human and physical resources of the assessment office and assure quality at every stage of the mass appraisal process. The committee felt that these subjects needed to be brought together in a basic text that would support IAAO courses and provide a reference work for assessors, appraisers, and appeal boards. In 1986, the Executive Board approved the appointment of a broadly representative ad hoc committee to refine the concept and write the general outline.

Scope

This book presents the first comprehensive treatment of all the bodies of knowledge important in assessment administration. The material on valuation begins with a thorough treatment of the economic principles important in real estate appraisal. The appraisal process is characterized as applied economic analysis. The purpose of this analysis is to identify the best use of land via a broad study of trends in consumer demand and related demographic data, investigate the supply and demand forces in the market for the identified best use, and develop a valuation model that predicts the most probable selling price of property within that market. The economic framework defines single-property appraisal and mass appraisal as complementary methods, a view not always understood in the past.

This book also provides the first full treatment of mass appraisal. The material on model specification and calibration will be particularly relevant to jurisdictions wishing to develop and maintain their own in-house, computer-assisted mass appraisal system.

The comprehensive administrative material in the book includes a treatment of features that should be included in the legal and administrative structures governing assessment at the state, provincial, and national levels. The material on modern management theory and practice as it relates to all aspects of assessment will be valuable to jurisdictions of any size. Special emphasis is given to mapping system management, revaluation planning, computer resource management, data management, and quality control.

Organization

The textbook is divided into twenty-one chapters organized into six subject areas. Chapters 1 and 2 introduce the text and provide basic information on the organization of the ad valorem tax system and how valuation is handled within that system. Chapters 3 and 4 deal with the economic basis of appraisal and the relationships between mass appraisal and single-property appraisal. Chapter 5 deals with the management of information within the assessment office. Chapters 6–12 deal with single-property appraisal, chapter 7 with the appraisal of land, and chapters 6 and 8–12 with the sales comparison, cost, and income approaches to valuation. Chapters 13–15 deal with mass appraisal theory, model specification, and model calibration.

Chapters 16–21 treat administration of the assessment office. Chapter 16 describes general principles of management. Each of the remaining chapters on administration discusses management of a particular area: mapping, revaluation, computers, performance evaluation, quality assurance, and appeals.

This book may be used in several ways. It may be read from beginning to end for an overview of assessment. It may be used as a reference manual. The index, glossary, references, and list of equations will help readers find material on specific topics. Finally, this book supports all IAAO courses and workshops. Course manuals list specific reading assignments and develop the material by case studies, problems, and more detailed discussion of some topics.

Acknowledgments

Property Appraisal and Assessment Administration is a product of the labor and dedication of a large community of professionals. My special thanks go to Robert J. Gloudemans and Richard R. Almy. Bob wrote more than a third of the text and served as a senior technical editor. Rich provided continual encouragement and support during his tenure as executive director of the International Association of Assessing Officers (IAAO), wrote parts of the text, and served as a senior technical editor. Special thanks go also to the IAAO Executive Board and the IAAO Education Committee, which have supported the development of this text during the past five years.

Many others contributed to one or more stages in the writing and review of the text. Although some repetition of names is involved, I have listed the contributors to each stage of the book's development.

Joseph K. Eckert, Ph.D.; Joseph E. Hunt, CAE; Bernard W. Saler, CAE; and Bruce W. Sauter wrote the chapter outlines.

The text was written by Richard Almy; Annie Aubrey, Ph.D.; James F. Coffman, Ph.D.; Alan S. Dornfest; Joseph Eckert; Jack P. Friedman, Ph.D.; Glenn W. Fisher, Ph.D.;

Roger L. Gilliam, CAE; Robert Gloudemans; Joseph Hunt; Michael W. Ireland, CAE; Thomas L. Jacobs; Gregory J. Landretti; Anders Müller; Janet O. Philips, CPM, Ph.D.; and John F. Thompson, Jr.

Richard Almy and Robert Gloudemans served as senior technical editors. Annie Aubrey, C. Kurt Barrow, CAE, Frederick M. Chmura, Robert C. Denne, Glenn Fisher, Michael Ireland, Gregory Landretti, Ian W. McClung, Dean A. McQuown, Janet Philips, J. Scott Renne, CAE, Bernard Saler, and Bruce Sauter served as global editors.

The individual chapter reviews and content contributions of Linda L. Adams; Diane M. Ange, CAE; W. Chris Ballmer; Sheldon Bluestein; Richard A. Borst; Charles C. Cook; John C. Crissey, Jr., CAE; C. A. Daw; Jack Eichenbaum, Ph.D.; Jewette Farley, CAE; Robert J. Flanagan, CAE; Jerome C. German; Morgan B. Gilreath, Jr.; William S. Goodyear; Austin J. Jaffe; David L. Jensen; Bruce A. Kolacny, CAE; Gregory J. Lafakis, CAE; Patrick M. O'Connor; Fran Pearl; Thomas K. Tegarden, CAE; Richard D. Ward, Ph.D., CAE; Hector M. Wilks; and Arlo Woolery, CAE, are also gratefully acknowledged. Greg Landretti's detailed comments on each chapter are particularly appreciated.

When the global review was completed, Annie Aubrey, Roberta A. Hilleman, and Janet Philips edited the manuscript.

Beatrice Owen and Janet Philips coordinated the chapter reviews. Rhonda Hedge typed the preliminary manuscript, Ruth C. Duncan typed the final manuscript, Eleanore H. Law proofread at every stage, and Audrey Kozera Brady designed the book.

I am grateful to all of the above for the sacrifices they have made to ensure the publication of this book.

Joseph K. Eckert, Ph.D.
General Editor
August 5, 1990

Introduction

Good administration of the ad valorem tax system is essential for adequate funding of local government services. The first section of this text sets forth the framework for a well-administered, efficient assessment system. Chapter 1 provides a history of the property tax in North America and a brief overview of its use in other parts of the world. This chapter also defines the role of the assessor and the important legal and administrative features of a model assessment administration system.

The view of appraisal presented in this text integrates single-property appraisal and mass appraisal and shows appraisal to be firmly rooted in economic analysis. Chapter 2 introduces the economic concepts and appraisal principles elaborated later in the text.

The Ad Valorem Tax System

I

Property assessment administration is a complex and technical profession vital to the financial health of local government. Assessors are responsible for administering the ad valorem tax system, and their chief task is to identify and appraise all property in their jurisdictions.

An ad valorem tax is based on the principle that the amount of tax paid should depend on the value of property owned. The property tax was once regarded as the fairest possible tax and was the major source of government revenue in the United States and Canada. Today, sales and income taxes are more important as revenue sources; nonetheless, the property tax remains a major source of local government revenue.

Adequate local services and the survival of healthy local government depend on proper assessment administration. In most communities, the property tax is the major source of revenue generated from within the community for financing local government services such as parks, fire protection, police, schools, public works, and public health. The property tax may be a revenue source for city government, county government, the school district, a separate park district, or other units of local government.

The assessor is, therefore, a key person in local government. Appraised values used for tax purposes must be accurate so that the tax burden will be distributed fairly and the public will have confidence in local tax administration. Without such confidence, funding of local services may shift away from the local property tax and no longer be subject to local control.

This textbook presents the technical and administrative prerequisites for a well-administered assessment system. If assessors master the techniques presented here and are given the resources to apply them, the quality of appraisal for tax purposes will improve.

A Brief History of the Property Tax in the United States and Canada

The property tax was known in ancient times, and several different forms of property taxation were used in Europe even before the settlement of America. In the British colonies of North America, five types of taxes were in common use. Poll (capitation or head) taxes were flat rate taxes, usually levied on all adult males and sometimes on slaves of either sex. Property taxes were often specific taxes, levied at fixed rates, rather than according to value, on items enumerated in the statute, but some attempts were made to tax property according to its value. Faculty taxes were levied on the "faculty," or earning capacity, of persons practicing certain trades or having certain skills. Unlike income taxes, faculty taxes were levied not on income actually earned, but on estimated ability to earn. Imposts were levied on goods imported or exported from a colony. Excises were levied on enumerated items of consumption goods, especially liquor.

The mix of taxes varied from colony to colony, depending on conditions in the colony and the power of various groups. Tax laws usually overburdened the politically weak and favored the politically powerful, especially the landed classes. In some colonies, frequent shifts in power from one faction to another resulted in frequent changes in the tax system. In others, control by large landowners or planters minimized taxes on plantations or large wilderness tracts held for speculation.

With the coming of the Revolutionary War, rapid increases in taxes to finance the war highlighted inequities and multiplied complaints. Legislators in some of the new states, uncertain of public loyalty and knowing taxes were disliked, borrowed heavily; nonetheless, taxes rose, precipitating armed resistance to assessors and tax collectors in several states. There was some movement toward more equal taxation. In their constitutions, a few states provided for taxation based on the value of property.

As the United States broke away from England, Loyalists headed north to Canada. Already accustomed to local self-rule through elected bodies, Loyalists expected the same rights in Canada. Local taxation to raise revenue and provide local services naturally followed. Issues of equality and fairness arose in Canada as property taxation became more common.

By the beginning of the nineteenth century, the idea of a uniform tax based on the value of all property owned was widespread. The first constitution of the state of Illinois, adopted in 1818, contained a "bill of rights" provision that each person should pay a tax "in proportion to the value of property that he or she has in his or her possession." Although Illinois ignored the provision for twenty years, the idea spread, and most state constitutions adopted or revised in the nineteenth century required uniform ad valorem taxation.

What little discussion of these provisions has been preserved makes clear that ownership of property was seen as a measure of ability to pay taxes. All property, tangible and intangible, was to be included in the tax base, and the property tax was to be the major source of revenue for state and local governments.

Administering the general property tax turned out to be difficult, especially when more complex forms of wealth and ownership and varied types of property developed. Taxing intangible property was a problem. Although some kinds of intangibles are wealth, which should be taxed, other kinds are merely rights over taxable tangible property. It was argued, for example, that a farm mortgage is a property right with value to its owner, but it is not economic wealth separate from the farm. Taxation of both farm and mortgage is double taxation of wealth. Various ways of dealing with this problem were tried, such as allowing the farm owner to deduct the value of the mortgage, but administrative difficulties were compounded by the ease with which intangible property could be hidden and by complicated questions of tax jurisdiction.

Early legislators and tax administrators struggled unsuccessfully with such problems. The growing complexity of property rights made the problem even more difficult and led most states to abandon the ad valorem taxation of intangible property.

Tangible personal property (movables) presented problems of discovery and valuation. Some personal property can be hidden from the assessor or moved out of the jurisdiction on assessment day. Even in the colonial period, there were stories of cattle being driven into the wilderness to avoid taxation. One of Abraham Lincoln's first cases is said to have dealt with the taxation of a ferryboat that was tied up on the opposite side of the river on assessment day. Such problems multiplied as personal property became more complicated, specialized, and mobile. Some taxing jurisdictions still include personal property in the tax base, more often in the United States than in Canada.

Real estate is, by definition, immobile, and ownership must be registered in official records. As a result, discovery and listing of taxable real estate is not difficult, but valuation is fraught with problems. Early property tax laws established small assessment districts, such as the ward or township, and provided for election or appointment of part-time assessors. In Canada, assessors were appointed by the local governing body. It was assumed that these individuals would be well acquainted with the area and with local values and could easily list and appraise the property in their communities.

The part-time local assessors were in a difficult position. Because the amount of county and state tax paid by a locality was determined by the values assigned to properties in the district, assessors had a strong incentive to please their neighbors by keeping values low. Assessors became aware that their counterparts in other districts were also un-dervaluing property, which led to competitive undervaluation.

Eventually, state and provincial action was necessary. Boards of equalization were established, with the authority to change aggregate local assessments to compensate for inequities. These boards, or separate boards of review, were also given power to review individual assessments. Unfortunately, boards of equalization or review seldom had the skill or information necessary to equalize assessments, and complaints about unequal assessments multiplied. Later, many states established tax commissions and gave them power to train and supervise local assessors, as well as responsibility to equalize and review assessments. Resulting improvements in the quality of assessment were sometimes temporary if political pressures weakened the authority of the tax commissions.

In the United States today, administration and regulation of assessment are the responsibility of state government. In many states, however, state powers are limited. Local governing bodies are usually responsible for carrying out assessment, although most states monitor the quality and consistency of assessments performed at the local level.

In 1986, 2,500 county, 1,800 municipal, 8,900 township, and a few other units of government, including the state jurisdiction of Maryland, were responsible for carrying out the assessment function in the United States. In almost all states, local assessors were supervised by a state agency.

In Canada, on the other hand, assessment is administered and regulated centrally in all provinces and usually carried out by provincial governments—in six provinces by provincially appointed independent assessment bodies. In four provinces, local jurisdictions both regulate and carry out assessment, although the provinces usually are responsible for assessment in sparsely populated areas.

At the beginning of the twentieth century, the property tax remained the major form of revenue in both the United States and Canada, but it was apparent that the dream of a uniform tax on all wealth had not been achieved. Criticism of the tax was widespread. It was attacked as being unsound in theory and in practice. Tax administrators and academic experts suggested that the attempt to tax all kinds of property be abandoned and that states seek other sources of revenue, leaving the property tax to local governments. Other suggestions included new administrative organizations and new methods of assessment. There was no immediate rush to follow this advice, but over the years many changes have been made in administrative practices, and most states and provinces have abandoned the property tax as a source of revenue.

The idea of taxing all wealth uniformly has also been abandoned. Many kinds of tangible and intangible personal property have been exempted from taxation, although some exempted property has been subjected to *in lieu* taxes not based on value. Exemptions have also been granted to achieve social ends such as encouraging economic development or benefiting the poor. Several states and provinces have adopted comprehensive classification systems in which different kinds of property are assessed at different percentages of value.

Property tax administration has improved. Early in this century, many jurisdictions adopted systematic methods of appraisal that used land value maps and manuals based on construction cost data. Property owners were often satisfied that all property was being treated alike.

By about 1910, economists and appraisers had developed the outlines of appraisal theory as it is known today. The three approaches to value—the cost, income, and sales comparison approaches—had been developed. Some assessors began to apply them systematically, and they are still the standard approaches used.

In 1934, the National Association of Assessing Officers was formed to improve assessment. This organization, now known as the International Association of Assessing Officers (IAAO), prepares educational materials, conducts classes, and provides technical assistance to assessors and governmental bodies. Many jurisdictions use IAAO courses and materials for staff training. An IAAO designation program allows assessors to earn certification of their qualifications to appraise for tax purposes. Some states and local governments recognize IAAO designations with increased salaries. Other states have adopted their own systems for testing and certifying the competence of assessing personnel.

Techniques for mass appraisal (appraisal of a group of properties, not just a single property) have improved the efficiency of assessment offices. Modern mapping techniques and low-cost computers have made mass appraisal procedures more sophisticated and efficient.

An Overview of the Property Tax around the World

A tax on property exists in about 130 countries, but its importance varies. In most countries, property tax revenue is from 1 to 3 percent of the total tax revenue for all levels of government. In the United States, this figure is nearer 9 percent. Some other English-speaking countries also rely heavily on the tax.

Some countries have reduced the importance of the tax. In the United Kingdom, the tax on residential property has been replaced by a poll tax (tax per person) called the community charge. Other countries have increased the importance of the property tax. Portugal, Spain, and Indonesia have recently instituted major reforms of the property tax.

In many developing countries, assessment administration needs to be modernized and improved. Revenue is desperately needed to maintain and expand the infrastructure in fast-growing urban areas, yet collection is hampered because many properties are not listed on the tax roll, and revenue is lost because recorded values are below true market value.

In many countries, computers have been introduced during the past few decades to support property tax administration. Collection and printing of tax bills has been computerized, and some countries have successfully used computers in the time-consuming process of estimating value.

Comparison of the policies and practices of different countries can be useful to governments planning reforms or modernization. On the other hand, the property tax and its administration differ from country to country. A solution that works well in one country might be disastrous in another. The tax base, what is being taxed, the person responsible for payment, the governmental level controlling the system, the degree of integration of assessment administration with other agencies in government, and administrative capabilities are different from country to country.

Tax Base

The tax base — the object being taxed — can vary, and some countries have several different taxes on property, each with a different base. In some countries, land and improvements are taxed; in other countries, only land. The value taxed may be market value (the highest price a property will bring in a competitive and open market) or annual rental value.

The United States and Canada have one property tax, and the tax base is the market value of land and improvements. The United Kingdom has one property tax, called "the rates," with the annual rental value of land and buildings as the base. France has three different property taxes, all based on annual rental values. Denmark has a land tax, based on the market value of the land alone and supplemented by a service tax based on the market value of buildings used for commercial or administrative purposes. Japan uses market value as a base and taxes both land and improvements.

A few countries use square meters of land or buildings as a surrogate for value and then levy the tax as an amount per square meter for different types of properties. In The Netherlands, municipalities can elect to use either area or market value as a basis for taxation, although most use market value. In South Africa, only the market value of land (not improvements) is taxed, but when land is developed, owners of land granted a zoning variance for higher density use pay a development contribution to pay for city services. Argentina has a land value tax based on the productive potential of farmland. Taiwan has three property taxes: a house tax on improvements, a land value tax on the current market value of land, and a land value increment tax, paid when land is sold at a profit. Israel uses both market value and rental value as bases. Besides the property tax itself, Israel has a land betterment tax, a land increased value tax, and a land registration rate.

Opinions about which tax base is best—annual rental or market value, land and improvements, or only land—differ. The choice between annual rental and market values may not make a big difference. The key issue in choosing is the kind of market evidence available—rent information or sales prices. However, annual rental values do not include the value of future development, and vacant land is not usually taxed when the annual rental value is the tax base. Market value is, thus, the best tax base in countries where speculative hoarding of urban land is common (for example, many developing countries). Changing the tax base is a major operation. Recent property tax reforms in Indonesia and Portugal, however, have included a change of the tax base from annual to market values.

Whether improvements should be included in the tax base has been the subject of heated debate. In the nineteenth century, an American economist, Henry George, formulated his theory of the "single tax." He argued that only one tax was needed, and by far the best and fairest would be a tax on land value only. The tax should be high enough to equal the economic rent of the land attributable to society and not to the effort of the owner. These ideas have inspired other economists, who argue that a land tax would encourage urban development. Some countries (such as Denmark, Australia, and New Zealand) do have land taxes, but the benefits of a land tax as compared to a tax on both land and improvements are not clear.

When the tax base is market value, the usual standard is that properties should be valued at their highest and best (most profitable) economic use, yet many exceptions to this rule exist. Some countries value all properties at current use; others reserve that standard for certain types of property only, such as agricultural land.

Exemptions also affect the tax base. Many countries exempt charities, public areas, educational and religious institutions, governmental bodies, and the like. Some countries exempt major property classes, for example, agricultural land in the United Kingdom and The Netherlands and owner-occupied houses in Portugal and Thailand. This can result in a narrow tax base.

Responsibility for Payment

Responsibility for payment of the property tax also differs from country to country. In the United States, Canada, and many other countries, assigning the owner responsibility for payment is usually combined with the government's right to seize the property and sell it if the tax is not paid. If this right is exercised, tax collection will usually function well. In the United Kingdom and many developing countries, the occupier is responsible for payment, which can make collection difficult. If sanctions against the occupier who does not pay have been rarely used, it is politically difficult to step up enforcement. Many developing countries with weak enforcement experience serious problems in collection of the property tax.

Local vs. Central Administration

In the United States, the property tax is used for services of local governments (school districts, municipalities, counties). Local jurisdictions administer the tax, and states often monitor their performance. In most other countries, the property tax is also local, but higher levels of government often have a stronger role in its administration. The central government is often responsible for valuation (as in France, Germany, the United Kingdom, Sweden, and Denmark) or coordinates it. Central government may also collect the local property tax (France, Sweden, and The Netherlands). Central control of assessment promotes uniformity of administrative procedures. Computer systems are either centralized or uniform local systems.

Integration of Assessment Administration

The extent to which property assessment administration is integrated with administration of other taxes and with other activities based on land information varies from country to country.

In the United States, the property tax is usually administered independently of other administrative offices. All information about properties is gathered by the assessor, who often also produces cadastral (assessment) maps. The assessed values are used only for the property tax. Usually, cooperation has been established with the land registrar, from whom the assessor receives information about sales prices and changes of ownership.

Other countries have established more integration. If a national cadastre (inventory of land by ownership, description, and value) exists, its cadastral maps and parcel identification numbers can be used for the property tax, and the building authority can supply information about the buildings. City planners and other officials can use information gathered by assessment administrators. Other taxes related to property may be based on assessed values, for example, a net wealth tax or an income tax on the imputed rent of owner-occupied homes.

One country with extensive coordination along these lines is Denmark, where a network of computerized multipurpose land information systems, using parcel numbers and street addresses as cross references, has been operating since the 1970s. An extensively computerized valuation system produces values that are used as the basis for the property tax, net wealth tax, and income tax of the imputed rent of owner-occupied homes.

Administrative Policies and Capabilities

The quality of valuations can be affected by administrative policy and technological sophistication. For example, a policy of high transfer tax rates may deter buyers and sellers from recording transfers or stating accurate sales prices.

In the United States, the transfer tax, on average, is only 0.1 percent of declared value. Several other countries have low transfer tax rates, but most have high rates (France, 14 percent; Portugal, 10 percent; Bangladesh, 15 percent). One consequence of high rates may be that declared sales prices are unreliable and will not be good indicators of market value. This situation in many countries—especially developing countries—makes it difficult to achieve accurate valuations.

In an ideal system, a reappraisal, an updating of values for all properties in a jurisdiction, would be done annually. Frequent reappraisal, especially where property values are changing rapidly, may be essential to fair distribution of the property tax. In most countries, the law requires a reappraisal at specified intervals, usually every three, four, or five years. In some countries, however, reappraisal has been delayed for a long period. In the years between reappraisals, some countries index property values by computer according to price trends for different types of properties (France, Denmark).

The quality of valuation is high in the United States. Reappraisals are usually frequent and accurate, especially where sophisticated computer systems are available. Valuation accuracy is expected in the United States, and there is a willingness to use resources to achieve it, perhaps as a consequence of the high effective rates that make accuracy more important. Also, property tax administration in the United States is less subject to budget cuts because it is local.

In developing countries, little money is available for administrative improvements, and administration often functions poorly for reasons that cannot be remedied by a higher level of technology. A common problem is that civil servants are underpaid. This makes administration open to corruption or forces the staff to hold second jobs.

Developing countries setting goals for improvement of assessment administration should focus on the accurate estimation of market values, not on sophisticated systems and models. Because declared sales prices are often unreliable, an attainable goal might be to develop simple valuation models based on common sense, cost figures, traditions, and sporadically reliable sales prices. Using these models in the valuation process will improve its quality and equity even if the resulting values do not equal true market values. Only a few land and building attributes that are inexpensive to gather and update and easy to verify should be included in the model. Characteristics visible from the street or information available from independent sources fit these criteria. Finally, in many developing countries improvement of tax collection and expansion of the tax roll to include all taxable properties are as important as improving valuation procedures.

The Role of the Property Tax

The United States

In the United States at the beginning of this century, local government was fiscally the most significant level of government. Except in time of war, the federal government's activities were limited, and few internal federal taxes were imposed. Tariffs, levied to protect manufacturing from foreign competition, and the sale of public lands financed most peacetime federal activities.

State governments were fiscally less important than local governments. In 1902, state governments collected $190,000,000 in revenue, but local governments collected $854,000,000. Forty-three percent of the state total was from property taxes, 39 percent from other taxes. The remainder came from charges, miscellaneous revenues, and a very small amount of federal aid. Seventy-three percent of local revenue came from the property tax and only 9 percent from other taxes. Charges, miscellaneous revenue, and state aid accounted for the remaining local revenue.

Figures 1 and 2 show how the situation changed. The percentage of total general revenues received from property taxation by

Figure 1. Sources of State Government Revenue: Selected Years, 1902-1988

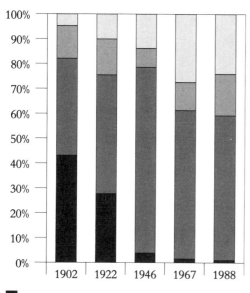

- ■ Property taxes
- ■ Other taxes
- ▨ Charges and miscellaneous revenue
- ▢ Intergovernmental

state governments declined from 43 percent in 1902 to about 1 percent in 1988. In the latter year, state governments received 58 percent of general revenue from taxes other than the property tax, 16.5 percent from charges and miscellaneous revenue, and 23 percent from the federal government.

The decline in the percentage of local revenue from the property tax results, in part, from the increased amount of federal and state aid and from increased amounts of revenue from charges and other miscellaneous sources. In 1988, only 29 percent of local *revenue* was from the property tax, but 74 percent of local *tax revenue* was from that source.

The large amounts received from state and local government bring with them various

restrictions and limitations, and charges and miscellaneous revenue are not suitable sources of revenue for some government functions. For these reasons, many believe that the independence and autonomy of local governments are closely related to the health of the property tax.

Figure 2. Sources of Local Government Revenue: Selected Years, 1902-1988

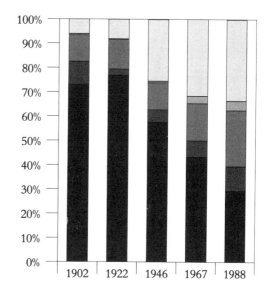

- ■ Property taxes
- ■ Other taxes
- ▨ Charges and miscellaneous revenue
- ▨ From federal government
- ▢ From state government

Other evidence of the change in the role of the property tax is provided by figure 3, which shows property tax collections as a percentage of personal income in the United States. In 1934, in the depths of the economic depression, property tax collections were equal to 7 percent of personal income. Be-

Figure 3. Property Taxes as Percent of Income: Selected Years, 1934–1988

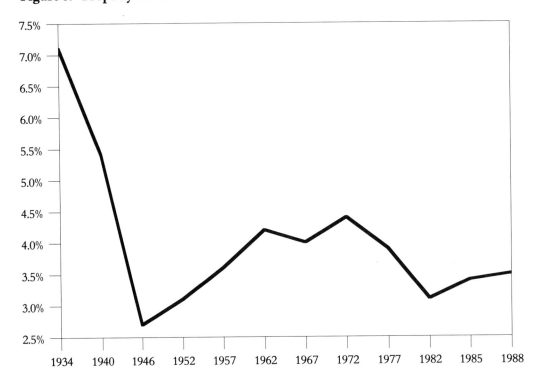

cause the activities of state and local government were curtailed during World War II, this dropped to less than 3 percent by 1946, before rising to about 4.5 percent in 1972. In 1988, the percentage was 3.5, about half what it was in 1934.

Property taxation is not equally important to all types of local governments. Figure 4 shows the major sources of revenue for five types of United States local government in 1988. County governments (of which there are 3,000) received 28 percent of their revenue from property taxes, compared with 36.4 percent from intergovernmental sources. Municipalities (of which there are 19,200)

received almost as much from sales and other taxes as from property taxes, and, like counties, received more from intergovernmental grants than from the property tax. Townships (of which there are 16,700) received more than half their revenue from the property taxes. Special districts (of which there are 12,200 authorized to levy property taxes) received more than half their revenue from charges and miscellaneous sources, and only 12.2 percent from the property tax.

More than half the revenue received by school districts (of which there are 14,700) came from intergovernmental sources, chiefly from the state. Substantial sums were received from charges for such things as school lunches and textbook rental, and from miscellaneous sources. The property tax is the only significant source of direct tax revenue for school districts. The magnitude of school property taxes is indicated by the fact that school districts received $54.6 billion (36.6 percent of all property taxes) in fiscal year 1988.

The importance of the property tax to local governments goes beyond its importance as a source of revenue. Most of the general obligation bonds issued by local government to finance streets, public buildings, and other

Figure 4. Revenue Sources for Various Types of Local Government in 1988 (percent of total)

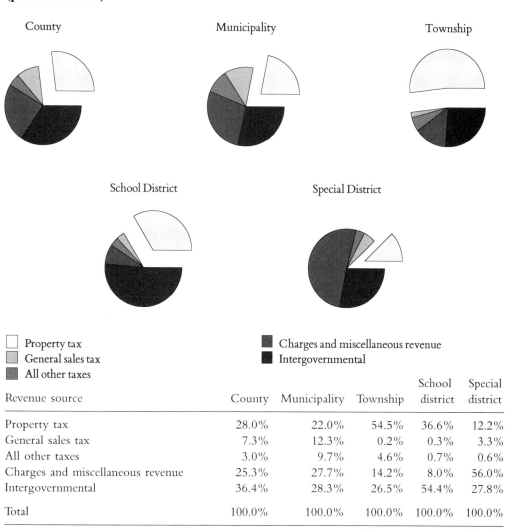

Revenue source	County	Municipality	Township	School district	Special district
Property tax	28.0%	22.0%	54.5%	36.6%	12.2%
General sales tax	7.3%	12.3%	0.2%	0.3%	3.3%
All other taxes	3.0%	9.7%	4.6%	0.7%	0.6%
Charges and miscellaneous revenue	25.3%	27.7%	14.2%	8.0%	56.0%
Intergovernmental	36.4%	28.3%	26.5%	54.4%	27.8%
Total	100.0%	100.0%	100.0%	100.0%	100.0%

Source: United States Census of Government Reports

public works are backed by pledges to levy property taxes to pay the principal and interest. Sometimes this pledge is included even though it is intended that other sources of revenue will be used to make the payments. Bond rating agencies evaluating the fiscal capacity of local governments place considerable importance on assessed value and assessment practice. The ratings assigned by these agencies affect the marketability of local government bonds and the interest rate paid.

Assessed value is often used to limit taxing and borrowing by local governments. For example, the amount of bonds that a local government may issue is often limited by the state to a percentage of assessed value. It is also common for states to limit the property tax that may be levied for a particular purpose to a specified percentage of the assessed value. These limitations played a role in the development of the fund system of accounting, which assures that taxes collected for a certain purpose are actually budgeted and spent for that purpose.

The property tax also plays an important role in the distribution of federal and state aid to local governments. Sometimes total assessed values or total property taxes levied are used as a measure of fiscal capacity in determining the share of state aid given to local units.

Canada

In Canada, local taxing authorities are unable to levy, collect, or share directly in revenues from taxes such as sales and income taxes — sources of revenue closely guarded by provincial and federal governments. Municipal taxation powers are limited to property taxation. After property taxes, the second most important source of general revenues for many Canadian municipalities is fines and fees for permits, licenses, inspections, and the like. Canadian municipalities also receive funding from the provincial and federal governments in the form of conditional and unconditional grants.

Revenues from sources other than property taxes often fluctuate, preventing local governments in Canada from relying on them to sustain a consistent level of local services. Thus, property taxes are an important source of revenue because they provide a stable and predictable supply of funds.

More than 40 percent of local governmental expenditures in Canada go for primary and secondary education. Typical local government functions such as roads, health, recreation, public safety, and the environment account for most of the rest.

Property Tax Assessments, Levies, and Rates

Underlying the diverse laws and regulations governing the property tax is a common structure, reflected in the use of terms such as tax levy, assessment, and tax rate. Within this structure is a clear and consistent delineation of responsibilities for valuing property, determining the total amount of property taxes to be raised, computing the amount of property tax to be paid on a single parcel of property, and collecting taxes.

The assessment function and the role of the assessor are integral parts of a property tax structure. To understand assessment administration, it is first necessary to understand the relationships among appraised value, assessed value, tax levies, and tax rates.

The *appraised value* of a property is an appraiser's judgment as to the full market value on a specific appraisal date. It is the responsibility of assessors to determine the appraised value of each parcel of property in their jurisdictions.

The terms *assessment* and *assessed value* are often interchangeable. Assessment may refer to the assessed value of a single parcel of property, the total assessed value of all properties within the boundaries of the tax jurisdiction, or the assessed value of any group of properties.

Assessed values are usually based on the appraised value of property. The term *appraised value* distinguishes full value from assessed value when the assessed value is a proportion of full value. According to various laws, the assessed value of property for tax purposes must represent either the full fair market, or cash, value of the property or a specified percentage of such value. Whether assessments are at full value or a proportion thereof is usually a constitutional or legislative policy decision, not an administrative one.

A *property tax levy* is the total amount of money to be raised from the property tax, as set forth in the budget for the local government or tax jurisdiction. This levy, whether higher or lower than the preceding year, is determined by the budget-making authority of the local government. It is usually recommended by an administrator (for example, a mayor or school superintendent) and adopted by the local legislative body (city council, county board, or board of education).

The nominal *tax rate* is simply a mathematical expression of the relationship between the tax levy and the total assessment for the jurisdiction: the levy amount is divided by the assessment amount to give the nominal tax rate.

The tax rate is usually expressed as dollars per $100, mills per dollar, or dollars per $1,000 of assessed value. The tax for each parcel is calculated by multiplying the parcel's assessed value by the nominal tax rate for the jurisdiction so that the tax for each parcel is at the same percentage of assessed value; the tax is, therefore, a tax according to value.

The *effective* tax rate, although mathematically related to the nominal tax rate, is not directly used in the calculation of property taxes. It is the proportion of tax dollars to full, or market, value and may be calculated for all properties, a single parcel, or any group or stratum of properties (for example, residential property). If variations exist in the levels of assessment for different classes of property, effective tax rates will also vary among the classes. The effective tax rate is the only way to compare the effect of the property tax across jurisdictions. To calculate the effective tax rate, divide the property tax by market value. For example, the effective tax rate of a property with a market value of $100,000 and a property tax of $1,200 is

$$\$1{,}200/\$100{,}000 \ = \ 0.012 \ = \ 1.2 \text{ percent.}$$

If properties are appraised at market value, the effective tax rate can also be calculated by multiplying the nominal tax rate by the assessment ratio or assessment level (proportion of assessed to appraised value) for the property in question. For example, if a property is appraised at its full market value, the assessment ratio is .50, and the nominal tax rate is 2.6 percent, then the effective tax rate is

$$0.50 \times .026 = 1.3 \text{ percent.}$$

The Role of the Assessor

It is hard to overstate the importance of assessors to the administration of the property tax and, indirectly, the vitality of local governments. Appraised values, as the basis of assessed values, determine the distribution of property tax levies among taxpayers. Only if these values are correct will tax limits, debt limits, and the distribution of state aid to localities be as the legislature intended. Boards of review and boards of equalization can never fully correct poor initial assessments.

The assessing officer is known officially by a variety of names—valuator, assessor, appraiser, or assessment commissioner—but the term *assessor* is probably the most commonly used in the United States and Canada. It is the assessor's duty to list all taxable property and estimate values in accordance with the laws that govern the jurisdiction.

Assessors may be elected or appointed. They may administer jurisdictions as small as a township or village or as large as a state or province. Many aspects of the assessor's work are spelled out in statutes. The statutes may also define value, list the information to be included on the assessment roll, and provide a timetable for completing various duties.

These duties are carried out within an administrative and political system that includes many other elected or appointed officers. The assessor may work closely with a clerk who is responsible for preparing forms and computing the tax bills and a treasurer who collects the taxes. Other units of local government need timely information about assessed values.

Other branches of government oversee the assessor's work. A governing board or a superior officer of the jurisdiction reviews and approves budgets prepared and defended by the assessor. State, provincial, or federal agencies may also supervise assessors.

Valuations are subject to appeal to a quasi-judicial board of review. Taxpayers always have the right to appeal assessment procedure to the courts, and in some jurisdictions courts may be asked to review assessed values.

Real Property Assessment Systems

A real property assessment system organizes resources to carry out the primary assessment responsibilities of discovery, listing, and valuing properties in accordance with property tax policy. Figure 5 is an overview of such a system. Responsibilities related to assessment, often carried out by agencies other than the assessment office, include supervision, handling of appeals, appraisal review, and equalization.

Supervision describes a variety of oversight or coordination activities, including fact-finding and analysis, providing appraisal tools and equipment, providing technical and professional services, educating and certifying appraisal personnel, and enforcing laws, regulations, and standards.

Appeal refers to the process whereby taxpayers may challenge their assessments.

Appraisal review describes the examination of appraised values by a governmental agency

Figure 5. Major Elements of a Real Property Assessment System

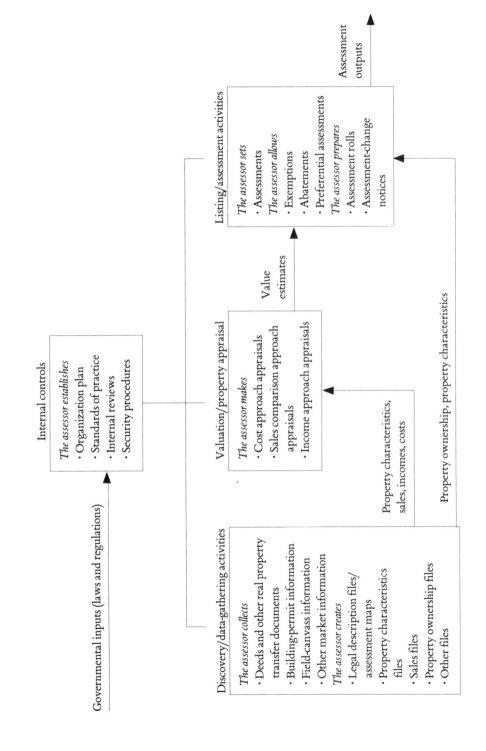

that has power to alter individual appraisals on its own initiative in order to correct clerical errors, assess previously omitted property, exempt property that was assessed in error, and correct appraisal inequities. Administrative appeal bodies often have the power to review appraisal values.

Equalization describes the process by which an agency with authority over two or more assessment districts makes adjustments to the total appraised values (or assessments) of the districts (interjurisdictional equalization) or of classes of property within the districts (intrajurisdictional equalization), or both, so that the total appraised (or assessed) values within the agency's jurisdiction all bear the same relationship to total market value.

The primary tasks performed by assessors working toward completion of an assessment roll are

1. *Locating and identifying all taxable property in the jurisdiction.* An accurate set of cadastral maps that plot every parcel of land is the assessor's major tool for identifying and locating taxable real property. If personal property must be assessed, the laws usually prescribe administrative procedures to locate and identify it. For example, the taxpayer may be required to file a return listing taxable personal property with the assessor, who then audits the return.

2. *Making an inventory of the quantity, quality, and important characteristics of all taxable property.* An inventory is essential to the accurate valuation of properties and to the assurance of equity in the taxation of similar properties. An on-site inspection is almost always necessary to complete an inventory.

3. *Estimating the value of each taxable property.* Assessors use all appropriate appraisal techniques to estimate value. The quality of their estimations is critical to the equitable distribution of the tax burden. Assessors use three basic approaches to estimating value: the cost approach, the sales comparison approach, and the income approach. Historically, properties have been appraised one at a time. Increasingly, properties are appraised in groups (mass appraisal).

4. *Determining the extent of taxability of each property.* To determine the extent of taxability of each property, the assessor must review legislation affecting the taxable status of properties and property owners in the jurisdiction. A thorough review must include not only the general taxable and exempt provisions of legislation, but also provisions of local legislation affecting individual property or property owners. Some legislation will provide that properties exempt from taxation must, nonetheless, be assessed; other legislation will provide exemption from assessment as well as taxation. The assessor must also research case law that may have interpreted the legal meaning of a specific legislative provision relating to the taxability of a particular type of property—a difficult task unless the assessor keeps up with legal interpretations as they occur. Recognized case reporting systems, such as the IAAO's *Assessment and Valuation Legal Reporter*, are a useful tool.

5. *Calculating the assessed value of each property.* The property tax rate of each tax district in which a property lies is applied to its *assessed value*, the value appearing on the

assessment roll, to determine the amount of the property tax.

An increasing number of jurisdictions have established by law a percentage of market value at which the assessed value is to be set. Several have defined classes of property and assigned percentage factors to each. For example, single-family residential properties might be assessed at 12 percent of market value, and industrial properties at 16 percent. The percentage factor is then applied to the market value of all properties within each class to generate assessed value. Other jurisdictions have weakened this already tenuous link between assessed value and estimated market value by imposing limits on assessment increases—a practice that the IAAO opposes.

6. *Preparing and certifying the assessment roll of the entire jurisdiction.* The assessor lists all properties in the assessment jurisdiction, usually on a printed form satisfying legislative requirements for preparation of the assessment roll. Then the assessor prepares a certificate (usually in a form regulated by statute) attesting to the sufficiency of the roll and to compliance with the statutory provisions for its preparation. Preparation may be done by computer, Addressograph, typewriter, or hand. The assessment roll is then presented to the appropriate agency by the statutory date set for its delivery. The roll is reviewed, taxes computed, and tax bills sent out. Monies are usually collected by another agency.

7. *Notifying owners of the assessed value of their properties.* Legislation usually requires that owners of properties be notified of the appraised and assessed values of their properties at the same time as, or immediately before, the date set for the return of the assessment roll. In some jurisdictions, tenants must also be notified. In several jurisdictions, notification is required only when a change has been made from the previous assessment. The formal notification is called a valuation or assessment notice.

8. *Defending value estimates and valuation methods during appeals by taxpayers.* All assessment legislation provides taxpayers with the right to appeal appraised values. Assessors should be thoroughly familiar with the pertinent legislation and with the operating procedures of the appeal body. Assessors are responsible for the assessment roll, whether they themselves, or staff members, or contract appraisers made the appraisals. Assessors, therefore, should be prepared to justify all valuations and methods to the satisfaction of the appeal body and, ideally, to the satisfaction of the taxpayer.

9. *Calculation of rates and tax bills.* The calculation of individual property tax bills is the last in a series of actions taken by local government revenue officers (see figure 6).

Most state and provincial assessment legislation requires that assessment rolls be prepared annually, because local property taxes are levied annually and must be based on ownership and property value information that is accurate as of a specified date. Thus, all of the activities of the assessor should be repeated annually or as is otherwise necessary to ensure that all property is appraised based on its market value.

The above activities sound deceptively simple. In reality, assessment is more complex. To understand assessment operations and the recommendations made in this book, the following characteristics of assessment must be appreciated:

- Because appraisal and taxation cycles are not necessarily of the same length, ineq-

nature of properties change. The very imposition of a tax causes changes: capital investment may be discouraged or encouraged; tax burdens may cause owners to sell or abandon their properties; and the capitalization of new taxes changes

Figure 6. Determining Tax Rates and Bills

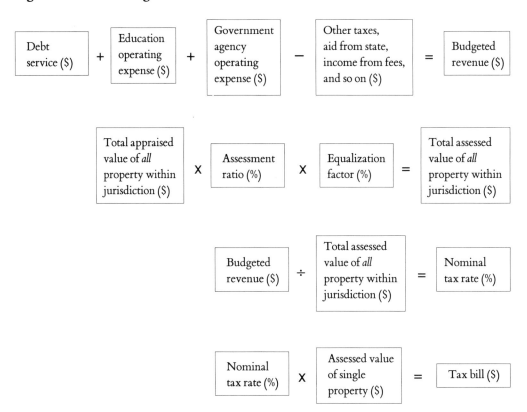

uitable distribution of the property tax burden may occur. Taxation occurs annually, but in many jurisdictions appraisal does not (whether by law or common practice).

- Assessment activities are continuous and cause changes. Owners, values, and the

market values. Appraisals should reflect these changes accurately.

- Assessment tasks are performed simultaneously and are interrelated. The processing of deeds, for example, provides information needed in discovery (size, shape, and location of the sold parcel), listing (name and address of the new owner), and valuation (price paid and information about financing).

- Assessment is a shared responsibility. Legislatures establish assessment policy. National, state, provincial, and sometimes county agencies supervise, maintain equalization, and sometimes share in assessment work. Administrative and judicial review and appeal agencies resolve disputes.
- Assessment tasks are varied, complex, numerous, and difficult. The challenge is compounded by the need to appraise large numbers of properties inexpensively as of a single date.

Assessment takes place in an economic and political environment in which both the public and the private sectors are acting, reacting, and interacting. Assessors need to be especially aware of the political activities that change property tax policy and of the land-use and development activities of participants in the real estate market. The influences of these activities on assessment are shown in figure 7.

Policy and Administrative Features of an Effective Assessment System

Empirical research conducted by the IAAO and others shows that the principal features of an effective assessment system are

- Legal support
- Annual reappraisal
- Periodic ratio studies that measure the relationship between appraised values and independent estimates of market values (usually sales prices)
- Adequate budget

- Competent staff
- Effective training programs
- Effective internal controls
- Complete maps and property data
- Accurate sales data
- Modern data processing
- Effective valuation techniques
- Active public relations

Legal Support

An effective assessment system requires legal support as well as good administrative practices. A strong legal framework includes a full market value assessment standard and requires annual reappraisals. Laws should also (1) mandate the disclosure to assessors of such market data as sales prices and terms, rents, and operating expenses; (2) establish effective assessment notification, review, and appeal; (3) provide warranted property tax relief through tax abatements and credits rather than through reductions in assessed values; and (4) require public notice of, and controls on, increases in tax levies made possible by reappraisals.

The law may require assessments to be either at full (100 percent) market value or a specified fraction of that value. Increasing the legal level of assessment (the ratio between a parcel's assessed value and its market value) to 100 percent is a cost-free reform that can improve uniformity, demystify assessments, and make it easier for a taxpayer to identify errors. Nonetheless, fractional assessment systems are common.

The property tax organization and administration plan should ensure a strong, effective partnership with clearly delineated roles among agencies and tiers of government involved in the assessment function. Laws should not undercut the market value

Figure 7. The Assessment Environment

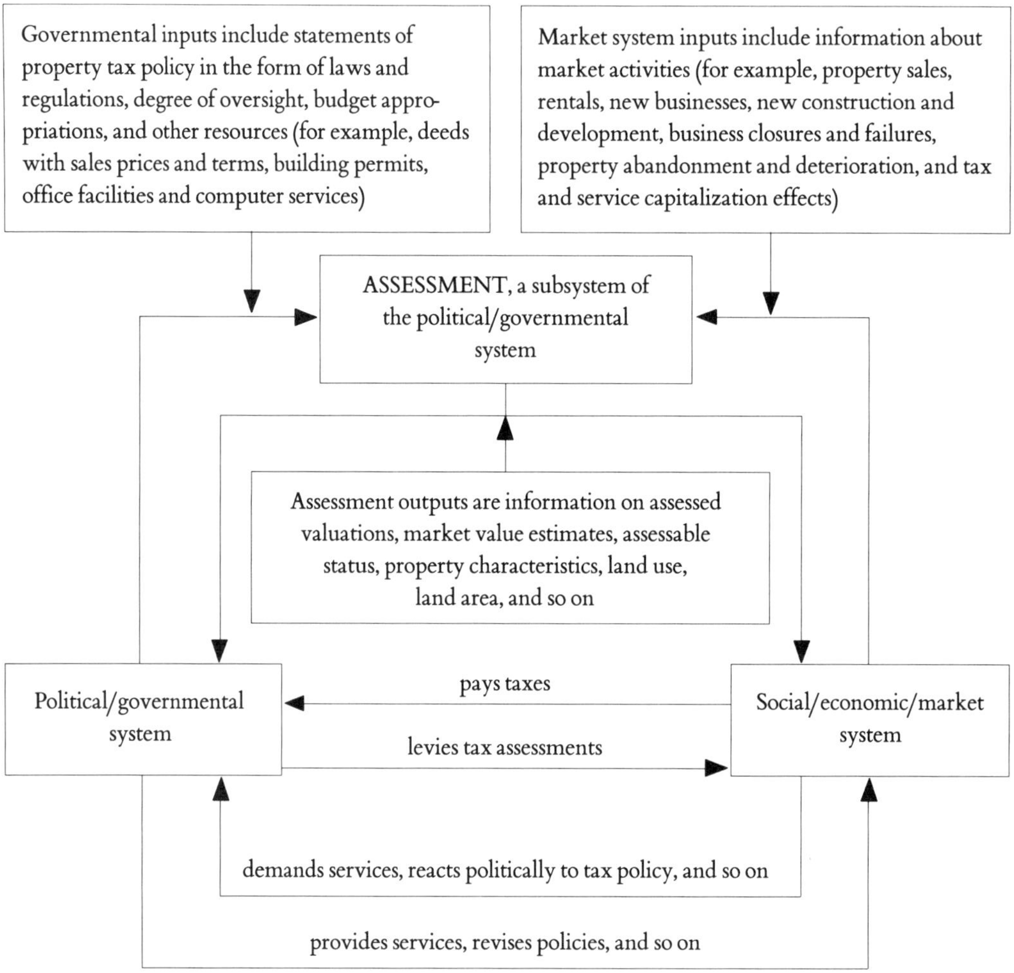

Governmental inputs include statements of property tax policy in the form of laws and regulations, degree of oversight, budget appropriations, and other resources (for example, deeds with sales prices and terms, building permits, office facilities and computer services)

Market system inputs include information about market activities (for example, property sales, rentals, new businesses, new construction and development, business closures and failures, property abandonment and deterioration, and tax and service capitalization effects)

ASSESSMENT, a subsystem of the political/governmental system

Assessment outputs are information on assessed valuations, market value estimates, assessable status, property characteristics, land use, land area, and so on

Political/governmental system

Social/economic/market system

pays taxes

levies tax assessments

demands services, reacts politically to tax policy, and so on

provides services, revises policies, and so on

standard by limiting assessment increases or by instructing assessors to ignore inflation, to consider only the current use to which property is put, to deduct the ordinary costs of sales, or to do anything else that produces distorted estimates of market values. Incentives for competitive underassessment should be removed by, for example, distributing in-

tergovernmental transfer payments on *equalized* assessed values.

Assessors work within the laws that govern the property tax in their jurisdictions. Even if the legal framework is less than ideal, assessors usually can establish administratively many of the features of a model assessment system.

Annual Reappraisal

Reappraisal may be annual or at longer intervals. Legally sanctioned reappraisal periods generally range from one to ten years. Three-, four-, or six-year periods are most common. If reappraisal is annual, the assessor attempts to maintain all appraised values at current market levels as of each assessment date. If reappraisal is at longer intervals, the assessor attempts to bring appraisals on all properties or a specified subset to market value at the end of each period or to reappraise a fraction of the properties each year.

Periodic Ratio Studies

A sales ratio is the ratio between a parcel's appraised or assessed value and its estimated market value as represented by an open-market, arm's-length sale (an expert appraisal is sometimes used as a proxy for market value). In the past, ratio studies were usually made after appraisals were completed. Today, the collection and analysis of sales data for purposes of internal quality control are integral parts of the local assessment process.

Oversight agencies also conduct ratio studies. Findings may be used to audit the quality of the local assessor's work, to equalize the distribution of taxes and financial aid among assessment districts, and to compute the full value of property for collateral purposes such as economic research or determining a bond rating.

In the United States, ratio studies are frequently used by state boards of equalization to determine the true aggregate value of property in a given area. Many local governments lie in more than one assessment district, and state boards have the responsibility for preventing unequal taxation resulting from these overlaps.

Many formulas for the distribution of aid to local governments take account of the equalized value of taxable property. In many school equalization plans, more aid is given to districts with fewer dollars in taxable property per inhabitant or per pupil. In other cases, the value of taxable property is used as one element in a measure of the "size" of a district. Federal legislation now prohibits taxation of railroad and some other kinds of transportation property at levels higher than other commercial and industrial property and specifies that ratio studies are to be used to determine whether inequities exist. Personal property ratio studies may also be required to comply with federal legislation (see appendix 1-1).

Ratio data are analyzed in two ways to measure the quality of appraisals. Measures of central tendency, such as the arithmetic mean (average) or the median (middle value), provide a measure of the general level of appraisal in a given geographic area or for a given type of property. Measures of central tendency, however, reveal nothing about appraisal quality within a class or area. Statisticians have developed other measures of such variation; the one usually used in ratio studies is the coefficient of dispersion (COD) (see chapter 20). It measures the average percentage by which individual ratios vary from the median ratio. A low COD indicates that appraisals within the area or class of property are uniform; a high COD indicates that properties are being appraised at inconsistent percentages of market value.

The COD and a measure of central tendency, taken together, can provide much information about the quality of appraisal performance. A measure of central tendency near 1.00 is evidence that properties are usually being appraised near market value.

Similar measures of central tendency for different areas and classes of property are evidence that the tax burden will be uniformly distributed among areas or classes of property. A low COD for an area or class of property is evidence that the property within that area or class is appraised uniformly.

It is possible to use ratio studies to make detailed analyses of the quality of appraisals. For example, it is possible to compute a coefficient that indicates whether the level of appraisal is equal for low-value and high-value properties. Statistical analysis can also detect other biases in the assessment process.

Adequate Budget

An assessor's budget is an expression of the political support for accurate and equitable assessments. Budgeting procedures vary from government to government, but in most cases assessors are responsible for submitting a budget request in a standard format to a superior officer or governing board. It is the assessor's responsibility to ask for the funds needed to carry out the assessing function and defend that request if necessary.

Salaries are the most important part of an assessor's budget, often making up 80 to 90 percent of the budget. Cash expenditures and indirect expenses such as equipment maintenance and employee fringe benefits must also be budgeted.

The cost of a good assessment system is often underestimated, especially when a reappraisal is undertaken or quality has to be improved. It costs less to maintain a good system than to develop one or improve an inadequate one. Chapter 16 discusses budgeting and chapter 18 shows how to calculate costs and gives examples of costs incurred in specific situations.

Competent Staff

Assessors and their staffs should be familiar with traditional appraisal methods, real estate markets, capital markets, and local conditions. Other technical and professional skills are needed as well: statistical skills for building and applying statistical models; management skills for recruiting, training, and directing staff; data processing skills for designing and maintaining computer programs; and public relations skills for dealing with the media and the public. Employees in smaller offices usually fill several roles. Larger offices usually hire specialists.

The ideal office will have employees with skills in administration, mass appraisal, and single-property appraisal so that appraised values of all properties can be developed in house and defended successfully at every level of appeal.

Effective Training Programs

Training programs can be developed within the assessment office or elsewhere in local government. The program should be planned well in advance; employees can be encouraged to participate by appropriate increases in salaries and responsibilities. The budget should include funds for training and, if necessary, provide for temporary staff to carry out the regular responsibilities of persons absent for training.

Effective Internal Controls

Planning and quality assurance programs ensure that laws and regulations are met, standards of appraisal accuracy are maintained, work is finished on time, and staff and resources are used wisely. Internal controls are an important part of a quality assurance program. The larger the staff, the more extensive and formal the documentation of internal controls should be. In large offices, an assessment standards officer or an assessment standards department, reporting directly to the assessor, should help develop and maintain internal controls.

State, provincial, and local laws establish the framework within which the assessor should operate, for example, lien and tax dates, valuation bases, fractional assessment ratios, exemptions, and personnel qualifications. Laws also may prescribe appraisal cycles, capitalization rates, cost factors, and other valuation criteria. The assessor should understand the relevant statutes and take them into account when establishing internal controls. Figure 8 shows major types of internal controls and their functions.

Organization Plan An organization plan controls the allocation of staff time and the division of responsibility. A plan's purpose is to allocate duties to qualified persons and avoid duplication of work. The plan should include an organization chart and statements of duties and responsibilities. This information should be discussed with all employees.

Standards of Practice Standards of practice may incorporate or be contained in laws, regulations, policy memoranda, procedural manuals and guidelines, appraisal manuals and schedules, standard treatises on property appraisal and taxation, and forms. Repeated tasks, particularly those done by more than one person, should be described in guidelines or manuals. There should be a procedure for establishing standards of practice and maintaining them (for example, updating manuals). Explanations of standards should be part of training programs.

Monitoring Activities Reviews of progress and performance contribute to effective and efficient operations. Procedures are necessary for monitoring the quality of assessments, editing data, reviewing appraisals, and reporting time and productivity.

Monitoring the Quality of Assessments Ratio studies should be conducted at least annually according to the standards outlined in chapter 20.

Data and Procedural Edits Staff should understand the importance of accurate data and be instructed to review each record for completeness and accuracy as it is processed. Edits, manual or automated, monitor the completeness and reasonableness of data.

Supervisory Reviews of Appraisals As an alternative method of evaluating appraisal accuracy, supervisors can review work for conformance with appraisal standards. Supervisors should review exceptionally difficult appraisals and the appraisals of trainees.

Time and Productivity Reports Records of the time spent on a task and the number of production units completed (for example, properties inspected) help supervisors gauge progress and schedule and budget future work.

Security Procedures Security procedures must protect both paper and computer records with a direct effect on assessed values from destruction, removal, or unauthorized changes. Moreover, audit trails should be left after all changes in the data base. In computer-assisted systems, the secrecy of passwords should be preserved. Security measures in addition to passwords and check

Figure 8. Internal Controls: Elements and Their Functions

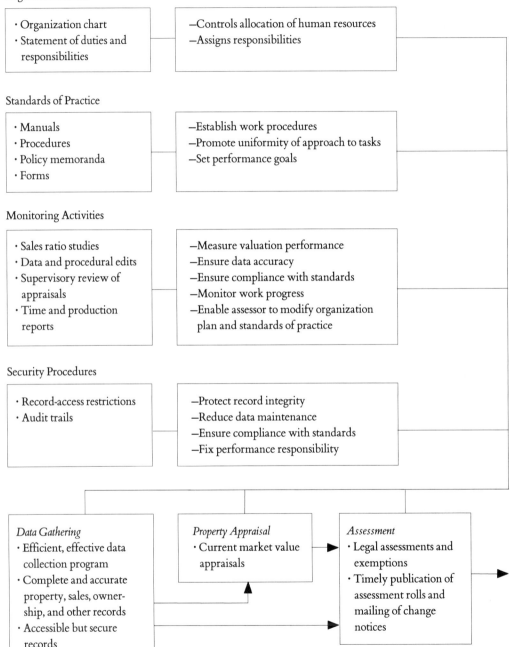

Organization Plan

· Organization chart
· Statement of duties and
  responsibilities

—Controls allocation of human resources
—Assigns responsibilities

Standards of Practice

· Manuals
· Procedures
· Policy memoranda
· Forms

—Establish work procedures
—Promote uniformity of approach to tasks
—Set performance goals

Monitoring Activities

· Sales ratio studies
· Data and procedural edits
· Supervisory review of
  appraisals
· Time and production
  reports

—Measure valuation performance
—Ensure data accuracy
—Ensure compliance with standards
—Monitor work progress
—Enable assessor to modify organization
  plan and standards of practice

Security Procedures

· Record-access restrictions
· Audit trails

—Protect record integrity
—Reduce data maintenance
—Ensure compliance with standards
—Fix performance responsibility

Data Gathering
· Efficient, effective data
  collection program
· Complete and accurate
  property, sales, owner-
  ship, and other records
· Accessible but secure
  records

Property Appraisal
· Current market value
  appraisals

Assessment
· Legal assessments and
  exemptions
· Timely publication of
  assessment rolls and
  mailing of change
  notices

digits might include periodic reporting of all audit trails and read-only versus read-and-write access to data files.

Complete Maps and Property Data

To assess real estate correctly, the assessor must have complete maps of all property in the jurisdiction, updated regularly to show changes in parcel boundaries or other physical characteristics. Map sheets should be indexed so that it is easy to locate the correct sheet. Each parcel should be assigned a unique parcel identification number that will link all records containing data on that parcel.

An assessment office also needs property record files that include dates of appraisals and sales; street address and legal description; a description of the site, buildings, or other improvements; and information about the use of the property. The records should also include information about sales, income and expenses for income-producing property, changes in assessed value, information about assessment appeals, ownership information (including the owner's mailing address), and codes showing the governmental units having jurisdiction to tax the property. Building permits and other public records will alert the office to addition or demolition of improvements, but the office should not rely completely on such sources.

Accurate Market Data

All the approaches to estimating value depend in some way on market information. The assessor's records must contain complete and accurate information about the sales prices and conditions of properties sold in the jurisdiction. Real estate transfer documents are usually the primary sources of information. Ideally, the law would require

buyers and sellers to send the assessor an affidavit containing the required information. Affidavits should show date of sale, full consideration paid, name and address of buyer and seller, and parcel identification number, legal description, and address.

It is important to know whether the transaction was arm's length (between unrelated parties or parties not under abnormal pressure from each other) or resulted from foreclosure, condemnation, or other circumstances in which price was not representative of the market. It is also important to know the type of financing and whether any personal property was included in the transaction. If information is missing, buyers or sellers should be sent questionnaires, called, or interviewed. Third-party sources such as real estate listing services, title companies, and banks also may provide information.

Transactions that are not clearly arm's length should be coded so that they are not used in ratio studies or the appraisal process unless the appraiser is informed. Sales that included personal property or that involved unusual financing, such as seller financing or assumption of an existing mortgage, should also be eliminated or the price appropriately adjusted.

The law should also require the owners of income-producing property to file affidavits of rental property income and expenses. Affidavits of building and construction costs also should be required.

Modern Data Processing

The computer has made it possible for any jurisdiction to record and retrieve more information more quickly. With recent developments in microcomputer technology, even the smallest jurisdiction can now use computers. The computer system should provide for storage and rapid retrieval of property and sales data. It should be possible to link many kinds of data for a single parcel, compute summary measures, adjust data, and value properties using computer-assisted mass appraisal techniques. Advances in computerized mapping make it possible to link appraisal data with mapping files and other data in geographic information systems. If maps are not computerized, parcel information in the computer should be coded so that it can be linked to a map.

Designers of data processing systems for assessors should consider the needs of other users. Local government computer systems are often designed to integrate assessment, preparation of tax bills, and tax collection. Property information may be used by departments of planning, transportation, or other public or private agencies. The system should make data sharing as efficient as possible but safeguard computer files from unauthorized disclosure or alteration.

Effective Valuation Techniques

Modern assessors must learn computer-assisted mass appraisal techniques in order to develop valuation models that replicate the local real estate market as a whole. Because most assessment is done by mass appraisal, appraisal methods necessarily differ from those of single-property appraisers. The obligation to assign values to all property in the jurisdiction limits the time given to appraisal of any one property, but it also makes feasible techniques not practical for single-property appraisal. Data on properties that have sold can be used to develop valuation models for estimating the values of unsold properties. Among the advantages of such

models are the large data bases, the availability of statistical tests of reliability, and the ease with which new information can be added when values are updated. Assessors must master single-property appraisal skills to appraise unusual and special-purpose properties and to defend values. Both mass appraisal and single-property appraisal are treated in detail in later chapters of this book.

Active Public Relations Program

A good public relations program helps the public understand the assessor's job and the importance of the property tax. A good program will reach out to the public, not just respond to angry taxpayers or investigative reporters. Public relations are especially important during major changes, such as a reappraisal or the adoption of a new appraisal system.

The first step in public relations, however, is good assessment. A public relations program that attempts to cover up poor performance or lack of concern will ultimately fail. Good public relations include talking to the public and the news media, providing printed information, sending correspondence, and creating easy-to-use forms. Chapter 21 discusses the details of a good public relations program.

The Future of the Property Tax

Ownership of property has long been considered a good measure of wealth. Uniformity provisions were put into many constitutions in an effort to ensure that the property tax would be the basic source of revenue. The dream of tax equality through property taxation was never achieved, but a modified form of the property tax remains an important source of revenue for local governments in the United States, Canada, and elsewhere.

In spite of dramatic improvements in appraisal methods, efficiency, and equity, assessors are often not given the resources and freedom from political interference that they need to put into practice the best appraisal methods. This lack of support can have important implications for the future of local government. No other tax can produce such large revenues—especially for smaller units of government. If the property tax continues to decline in fiscal importance, local governments are likely to become more and more dependent on state-collected revenues, or will have to be reorganized into larger units that can collect income or sales taxes.

Improvements in assessment quality and public support will occur only if assessors are well trained, provided with adequate budgets, and encouraged to do their jobs well, and if laws and administrative procedures include the policies and administrative structures that promote equity.

A Framework for Valuation

2

Real property appraisal is applied economic analysis. Basic economic principles are as important to understanding property appraisal as they are to understanding the selling of breakfast cereal or automobiles. This brief chapter introduces basic economic concepts as they apply to real estate—value, price, supply, demand, markets, equilibrium, anticipation, substitution, model specification, and model calibration. The three approaches to value—cost, income, and sales comparison—are defined, and distinctions between mass appraisal and single-property appraisal are outlined. Later chapters develop and explain fully all of these concepts.

Economic Analysis in Real Property Appraisal

Rights and Value

The appraiser's first task is to identify *what* is being appraised. A physical description of the property accomplishes only part of that task. The other part is identifying the rights being valued. For example, unless appraisers establish what rights have been sold, they will be unable to judge the comparability of sales as indicators of value for a subject property.

There are six basic rights associated with the private ownership of property: (1) the right to use, (2) the right to sell, (3) the right to lease or rent, (4) the right to enter or leave (real property), (5) the right to give away, and (6) the right to refuse to do any of these.

These rights are included in what is known as the *bundle of rights*, which is the ownership of all the legal rights obtained with fee simple title. The bundle of rights may be compared to a bundle of sticks, each representing ownership of one property right. Property ownership is transferred in many circumstances without the exchange of the full bundle of rights.

Highest and Best Use

Real property appraisal is based on an economic analysis that has two steps. In the first step, the appraiser who is appraising a parcel of land does a broad study of the workings of the regional and local economy. The result of this study is an understanding of the *highest and best use* of the land, that is, its most profitable use at a specific time, given legal, physical, and financial limitations. The appraiser tries to analyze how land (a factor of production) is best used given the total pattern of consumer preferences.

Highest and best use is not always actual use. For example, in a midwestern city, a riverfront area easily accessible from downtown is occupied by small factories. The surrounding neighborhood, however, is residential and has become fashionable because of its solid housing stock and proximity to downtown. *Demand* for riverfront residences has, therefore, increased. As some factories along the river have gone out of business, developers have converted the buildings to elegant condominiums and upscale shopping malls. The remaining factories are still thriving, but new factories to produce the same products more efficiently are being built on the West Coast. What is the highest and best use of these old riverfront factories? Of the land under the factories?

Potential buyers and sellers, as well as appraisers, must analyze the economic forces at work in the area and the nation to answer these questions. Buyers anticipating a certain use for the property do such an analysis to decide how much they are willing to pay. Some developers might see these properties as a site for a high-rise office complex. The price such a use could justify might be reduced by the risk of not being able to get the right zoning, by the cost of demolishing the existing structure, or by predicted instability in future rental markets. Other developers might want to convert existing structures to residential or retail use. Yet others might see the structures as adaptable to new manufacturing uses. City planners have a long-range plan to turn the riverfront into parks, arguing that parks would increase the value of surrounding property and the attractions of the city. The potential sellers of the factories will consider the income they can expect from continued present use. They might analyze expected demand for their product, environmental law, and the possibility of new factories competing with them. The owners might be unwilling to sell at a price attractive to any of the developers.

Appraisers must understand the thinking of buyers and sellers, and the appraiser's analysis of highest and best use should reflect the market realities that affect buyers and sellers for the many competing uses of the land being appraised.

The first step of the appraiser's economic analysis, finding the highest and best use of the land, is similar to *general equilibrium analysis* in economic theory. (When there is no intention to demolish the existing improvement, the analysis is similar to *partial equilibrium analysis*.) Both kinds of analysis trace how consumer preferences are translated through the price system into demand for goods and services and then to demand for the *factors of production*.

Equilibrium, a central concept in economics, describes a point of rest, or equilibrium, where the factors of production—land, labor, capital, and management—are used in the production of an array of consumer goods that maximize consumer welfare. It is in this sense that resources are used most productively, that is, in their highest and best use. Equilibrium, however, is rarely attained in the marketplace because the forces affecting supply and demand are constantly changing.

Modeling of the Market

Suppose the appraiser in our example concludes that high-rise residential development is the highest and best use of the riverfront land. The appraiser is then ready for the second step of the economic analysis, study of supply and demand in the market for the identified highest and best use. The purpose of such an analysis is to develop a *model* that represents the behavior at a particular time of the supply and demand factors in the market being analyzed. A model is a simplified or generalized pattern for thinking about something. Appraisers use models whenever they value a property. All appraisal models estimate the present value of the future benefits of a piece of property. In this sense, models represent the workings of an efficient market.

The term *model* is often used as a synonym for *equation* or *formula*, but a model could also be a statement. For example, the statement, "The value of a property with a new building is the sum of the land value and the improvement value," is a model. In fact, it is the simplest form of a model expressing one approach to valuation, the *cost* approach. Expressed as an equation, this model becomes

$$V = LV + IV, \tag{1}$$

where V is the estimated value of a property with a new building, LV is the value of the land, and IV is the improvement value. The formal development of a model in a statement or equation is called *model specification*.

Appraisers apply models every time they appraise a property. As they move from junior to senior positions, appraisers are called upon to develop models to express their methods for appraising properties.

Often a simple model needs to have terms added or other modifications made to express how value is determined in the market. For example, many readers will see that the simple model for the cost approach is adequate only for new improvements — it represents the supply side of the market. A valuation model for improvements in general would need a depreciation term. The new model expressed as a statement is, "The value of a property is the sum of the land value and

of the improvement value less depreciation (D)," or

$$V = LV + (IV - D), \tag{2}$$

where V is the value of a property, LV is land value, IV is improvement value, and D is depreciation.

A simple model for another approach to value, the *income approach*, is

$$V = I / R, \tag{3}$$

where V is the value of a property, I is the income it produces, and R is a capitalization rate. In simplest terms, someone figuring out what to pay for an income-producing property might say, "This property produces $50,000 a year in income, so if I can get a 10 percent return on competing investments, then the property's value can be no more than $500,000."

Models used by sophisticated appraisers have a great many more terms reflecting the complexities and components of the more general terms in the simplest models. Depreciation, for example, can be broken down into various kinds of loss in value, each of which must be determined separately: physical deterioration, functional obsolescence, and economic obsolescence. Appraisers will have an easier time understanding a complex equation if they remember the simple underlying model and see the complexities as representing refinements that make the model a better representation of how the market operates.

Three Approaches to Value

Historically, there have been three approaches to specifying valuation models that represent the market. Two of these, the cost approach and the income approach, have been mentioned. The third is the *sales comparison approach*.

A basic model for the sales comparison approach is, "The market value of a subject property is equal to the sale price of a comparable property plus adjustments to the sale price for differences between the attributes of the comparable and subject properties." Expressed as an equation, the model is,

$$MV = S_c + ADJ_c, \qquad (4)$$

where *MV* is the estimated market value of the subject property, S_c is the sale price of a comparable property, and ADJ_c is the total dollar amount of adjustments to the sale price of the comparable property. In practice, appraisers use three to five comparable properties to estimate the market value of a subject property. Appraisers also refine the basic model by listing the attributes considered and giving each a value according to its contribution in estimating value. A refined, but still simple, sales comparison model might look like this:

$$MV = b_0 + b_1 SFLA + b_2 \#BATHS, \quad (5)$$

where b_0 is a basic dollar amount, and b_1 and b_2 are adjustments, or coefficients, assigned to the attributes *SFLA* (square feet of living area) and *#BATHS* (number of baths), respectively.

The adjustments, or coefficients, are determined through analysis of sales data in a process called *calibration*. Analysis of sales data might reveal, for example, that $32 is the value of each square foot of living area (b_1) is then $32. Calibration of cost and income approaches involves finding values for

costs, rates, incomes, and so on from analysis of market data.

Supply and Demand in the Three Approaches to Value

The common element in all three approaches is that they must contain terms that represent the workings of both the supply and demand sides of the market. Each approach, however, uses different sources of data to represent supply and demand.

The sales comparison approach uses sales prices as evidence of the value of similar properties. The price at which a property sells is the price at which supply and demand meet at the time of sale.

The income approach uses income and expense data to represent supply and demand. The principles of *anticipation* and *substitution* are recognized in the income approach. Buyers want property because they anticipate a future stream of income. However, the availability of other investments, which can be substituted for real estate investment, influences both the demand for and supply of income-producing property. If an investor or developer can get better returns from gold and bank certificates of deposit, then they become better investments than real estate. The appraiser, estimating a property's value with the income model defined earlier,

$$V = I/R, \qquad (3)$$

estimates the income stream that would be produced in the highest and best use of the property under typical management. Then the appraiser finds the rate of return that compensates for the risk of ownership of that property. The rate will be influenced by the relative risks and returns of other investments.

The cost approach assumes that the value of an existing improvement is the cost of constructing an equally desirable substitute. An investor has the option of buying an existing improvement or constructing a new one with equal utility. To estimate the value of an existing improvement, the appraiser calculates what it would cost to construct a functionally equivalent improvement and subtracts from the cost an estimate of depreciation in the existing improvement. Market data on the costs of each element of the property and on components of depreciation represent supply and demand, respectively.

Mass Appraisal vs. Single-Property Appraisal

Both mass appraisal and single-property appraisal are systematic methods for arriving at estimates of value. They differ only in scope. Mass appraisal models have more terms because they attempt to replicate the market for one or more land uses across a wide geographic area. Single-property models, on the other hand, represent the market for one kind of land use in a limited area.

Quality is measured differently in mass appraisal and single-property appraisal. The quality of a single-property appraisal is measured against a small number of comparable properties that have sold. The quality of mass appraisals is measured with statistics developed from a sample of sales in the entire area appraised by the model.

Value in Appraisal

The Nature of Value

The term *value* has been used repeatedly in this chapter without definition. Because its definition depends on context, value is often used with a qualifying term: *market* value, *assessed* value, *use* value, and so on. The idea of value is essential to appraisal. The purpose of most appraisals is to estimate market value, which is usually defined by statute. Generally, market value is the cash price a property would bring in a competitive and open market. In such a market, sufficient time has been allowed for a sale, the buyer and seller are not subject to undue pressure, and both are well informed. Market value may not be the same as price. Prices are historical facts. Values are opinions, or hypothetical prices, which are often based on actual prices, particularly when the comparable properties have sold in a competitive and open market. Market value can also be viewed as the present value of future benefits. This view of market value is the basis of the income approach to valuation.

Two kinds of value distinguished in economic theory are *value in use* and *value in exchange*. A sapphire has little value in use but high value in exchange. Bread is very useful but has little value in exchange, unless there are serious food shortages. Assessors are concerned primarily with value in exchange because this value reflects the behavior of buyers, sellers, and investors.

The Imperfection of Real Estate Markets

When markets are in long-run equilibrium, and there are many well-informed buyers and sellers under no coercion to buy or sell (a perfect market), then market value, market price, and value in exchange are identical. When these conditions are not met (an imperfect market), then value and price may be different.

Real estate markets are imperfect by the standards of market perfection in economic theory. For example, a perfect market requires homogeneity of the objects traded, but every parcel of real estate is unique at least with respect to location. There also are relatively few buyers and sellers, and market participants possess less than full knowledge. In addition, real estate markets are highly localized and segmented according to type of property. Finally, the supply of land is relatively fixed, whereas the demand for land can be quite volatile. For these reasons, *actual sales prices*, which are historical facts, and *estimates of values*, which are hypothetical prices, cannot be expected to be equal. In other words, the terms *price* and *value*, as used in real property appraisal, are not synonymous, although they are frequently used as if they were. Prices are indicators of values. One task of appraisers is to determine the degree to which the market is competitive so they can judge how reliable sales prices are as indicators of value.

Summary

The task of appraisal, estimating the market value of property, in the simplest terms requires the following: identification of *what* is being appraised (the nature of the property and the rights being valued), identification of the *market* in which value is determined (highest and best use), an understanding of the *economic forces and principles* within that market, and the ability to represent the market in a *model* (model specification and calibration).

Creating a working understanding of the task of appraisal in its full complexity is one of the aims of the remainder of this book.

Economic Theory

Appraisal is rooted in economic theory. This section of the text addresses the elements of economic theory that explain and support appraisal. Chapter 3 outlines the evolution of economic thought related to the problem of value. The chapter deals with the microeconomic issues of supply and demand analysis, the theory of production and cost, and resource pricing within a general equilibrium framework. The macroeconomic issues related to the determinants of aggregate demand for goods and services are also explained. The roles of monetary policy and of real estate as an investment good in this framework are addressed in some detail.

Chapter 4 integrates single-property appraisal and mass appraisal within a legal and economic framework. This framework characterizes appraisal as applied economic analysis, the purpose of which is to identify the highest and best use of a property, investigate the supply and demand forces in the market for the identified best use, and develop a valuation model that predicts the most probable sale price.

The Economics of Real Property Appraisal

3

Economic Theories of Value and Real Property Appraisal

Many methods and concepts used by appraisers have developed from the work of economists trying to define and explain value. Data collected by assessment offices for valuation are often analyzed and interpreted using models developed by economists. Appraisers should, therefore, master basic economic principles.

An economic system is the infrastructure that determines what commodities are produced and services rendered, how these are allocated, and how and what resources are used to produce the goods and services. Economic systems are studied as either the operation of the economy as a whole (macroeconomics) or the behavior of people, groups, firms, and organizations in a specific market (microeconomics). Real property valuation is principally a microeconomic activity because appraisers are looking at the interaction between buyers and sellers in a single market in order to estimate the value of real estate in that market.

However, appraisers must also understand macroeconomics, which shows them how aggregate demand for goods and services is determined and influenced by government fiscal and monetary policies and ultimately translated into the demand for resources, par-

ticularly land. A thorough understanding of basic macro- and microeconomic principles will help the appraiser understand appraisal, which is applied economic analysis.

Modern economic thought began to take shape with the increase in commerce and manufacturing brought about by the Industrial Revolution. Ever since, economists have wrestled with questions posed by the nature of capitalism, the prevailing economic system. What is value? What are its components? To what extent does each component affect total value?

The Labor Theory of Value

In the first English-language economics book, *An Inquiry into the Nature and Causes of the Wealth of Nations* (1776), Adam Smith noted that some life-sustaining necessities such as water were either free or inexpensive, but diamonds—"the greatest of all superfluities"—were precious. This led him to distinguish between value in use and value in exchange: The water is very useful but worth little in exchange for other items; the diamond, on the other hand, has greater value in exchange than in use.

Real property, similarly, may have different values for use and for exchange. For example, a particular property placed on the market may not command much of a value in exchange due to poor location or a deteriorated physical condition. However, it may have value in use to its owner, who lives in it and likes its amenities. On the other hand, a similar property may not be suitable for its owner to live in and thus will lack value in use as a residence, yet it will have value in exchange to an investor or a buyer willing to make the needed repairs. Economists puzzled over this paradox for almost one hundred years until Alfred Marshall combined several streams of economic thought into supply–demand analysis, the cornerstone of modern economic theory.

Smith, however, concentrated on explaining value in exchange. He developed a labor theory of value, measuring exchange value by the amount of labor a commodity can command. However, certain items clearly have an exchange value not the same as the labor required for their production. For example, a capitalist might hire workers to produce commodities and sell them for more than the pay given to the workers. Smith concluded that the true value of a commodity includes wages, paid for labor; capital, which permits the purchase of resources and is compensated by a return on the investment; profit, paid for risk taking and management; and rent, paid for land. Smith's analysis of the components making up the value of a commodity has evolved into what is known in market economics as the four factors of production: land, labor, capital, and management.

A later economist, David Ricardo (1772–1823), recognized the issues left unresolved by Smith's labor theory of value. Ricardo believed that for a commodity to command value in exchange it must first possess utility, defined as the ability to excite desire for possession and thus satisfy a need. He noted that the scarcity of nonreproducible commodities (such as rare statues and paintings) contributes to their value in exchange, but he dismissed such cases as unusual and thus unimportant. He concentrated instead on the value in exchange of reproducible items and advocated the use of Smith's labor theory of value.

Smith had maintained that the quantity of labor necessary to produce a commodity was equivalent to its value in exchange. Ricardo attempted to reconcile the fact that wages can be less than the price at which goods sell by theorizing that the return to the capitalist is a return for past labor as embodied in tools, buildings, and other objects associated with production.

He noted, as did Smith, that as agricultural activities increased, it became necessary to use poor land due to the limited availability of good land. More labor is then needed to produce the same output. In consequence, the cost of labor also increases. This observation was the basis for the economic principle of increasing and decreasing returns: when successive increments of one agent of production are added to fixed amounts of the other agents, future net benefits (income or amenities) will increase up to a certain point (point of diminishing returns), after which successive increments will decrease future net benefits.

Karl Marx (1818–1883) claimed to have resolved the inconsistencies in the labor theory of value as developed by Smith and Ricardo. Marx combined this theory with a social and political theory based on a struggle among capitalists, middle class, and working class. He argued that the value in exchange of a commodity over and above the quantity of labor needed to produce the item is surplus value. This surplus value was created by the labor of the working class and illegitimately appropriated by the capitalist. This exploitation was Marx's main justification for a revolution that he predicted would destroy the capitalist system.

The Marginal Utility Theory

A number of economists were dissatisfied with the labor theory of value. Jean Baptiste Say (1767–1832), a French economist, claimed to be a follower of Adam Smith, but his book, *Traité d'économie politique*, emphasized utility as the determinant of value. He borrowed from Abbe Condillac, who had published a book in the same year as Smith's *Wealth of Nations*. Condillac considered utility to be a determinant of value, but also regarded land, labor, and capital as partners in the productive process.

Working independently, William Stanley Jevons (1835–1882), Carl Menger (1840–1921), and Leon Walras (1834–1910), developed the marginal utility concept as a central part of value theory. They argued that the value of a commodity depends on the utility, or usefulness, of the *marginal* unit. This solved the problem raised by Smith of how water could have less exchange value than diamonds. The "first" unit of water, necessary to sustain life, would have a high utility and would command a high price if it were the only unit available. Because water is usually available in large quantities, however, the marginal unit has less utility and would command a much lower price (figure 1). Because all units are identical, the marginal unit determines the market price.

The marginal utility theory provides a reasonable explanation of the demand side

Figure 1. Declining Marginal Utility

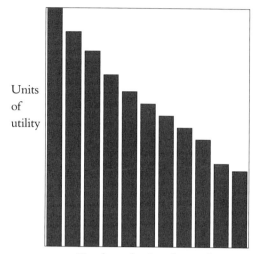

Units of utility

Number of units of a good

of the market. It explains the demand for a consumer good and shows how consumers allocate income among the various goods available. A simple example will help make this clear. Table 1 shows the units of utility that a particular consumer ascribes to successive increments of goods A and B. The price of good A is $1.00 and of good B, $2.00. The "marginal utility per dollar" columns show the number of units of utility that could be obtained for $1.00 at each level of consumption.

A consumer with only one dollar to spend on the two goods could maximize utility by purchasing one unit of good A. The second dollar spent on the same good would provide 40 units of utility. The third dollar would be spent to buy one-half unit of good B because one dollar's worth of that good would produce 39 units of utility, whereas the third unit of A would provide only 28. (In the illustration it is assumed that it is pos-

Table 1. Consumer Utility

	Good A		Good B	
Quantity	Marginal utility	Marginal utility per $	Marginal utility	Marginal utility per $
1	50	50	78	39
2	40	40	68	34
3	28	28	58	29
4	25	25	38	19
5	20	20	38	19

sible to purchase one-half of a unit and that the marginal utility of the first and second half is the same. Economists avoid this problem in theoretical works by using continuous mathematical functions, which assume infinite divisibility of goods and productive services.) Table 2 shows the amount of each good that would be purchased at various levels of expenditure.

Table 2. Expenditures on Goods A and B

Expenditure	Good A	Good B
$1.00	1	0
2.00	2	0
3.00	2	½
4.00	2	1
5.00	3	1

Consumer equilibrium exists when all consumers have adjusted their expenditure patterns to achieve the maximum amount of utility from their incomes—with saving included as a good. Equilibrium is upset whenever the price of any consumer good changes, consumer preferences change, or consumer income changes. For example, if the price of good A decreases, consumers will be able to improve their positions (maximize utility) by buying more of good A and less of good B because the marginal utility per dollar for good A would increase.

This analysis is the basis of the concept that price and quantity demanded are inversely related and demonstrates the principle that demand for a good is also determined in part by the price of substitutes. In this case, demand for B would decrease because the price of A has decreased. This insight into the dynamics of demand is the basis for the appraisal principle of substitution discussed later in this chapter. Likewise, a change in a consumer's tastes and preferences would cause the marginal utility measure and the way income is allocated among goods (see box) to change. An increase in income would make it possible for the consumer to purchase more of both goods. Modern price theory (discussed in the next section) developed a more rigorous explanation of the determinants of demand from these insights.

Finally, although marginal utility theory provides an explanation of the demand side of the market, it does not explain the quantities of a good available for sale at various prices; that is, it does not explain the supply side of the market. One might attribute the relative scarcity of diamonds and the large supply of water to nature, but that explanation becomes less satisfactory when the commodities in question are produced by man.

Consumer Equilibrium

The principle that a consumer attempts to maximize the utility from goods consumed can be expressed mathematically as follows:

$$\frac{MU_a}{P_a} = \frac{MU_b}{P_b}$$

where MU is marginal utility, P is price, and a and b are consumer goods.

This equation states that a consumer will distribute expenditure on goods a and b in such a way that the utility received from the last dollar spent on each product will be equal. It applies to two products, a and b, but could be expanded into a system of equations stating that every consumer equalizes the marginal utility per dollar of every potential consumer good.

Modern Price Theory (Microeconomics)

Alfred Marshall (1842–1924) and a group of English economists originated modern price theory by combining the marginal utility concept with a concept of supply based on the cost of producing a commodity. The result was a logically consistent explanation of how price is determined in a market economy. Modern price theory can also be used as the basis for explaining how total income is shared among those who provide the labor, capital, and land used to produce goods. With the development of modern price theory, many economists began to distinguish between *price* as an objectively determined fact, and *value*, a term with ethical and political connotations outside the province of economics.

The basic concept of modern price theory is that in any given market price will equalize the amount of a good produced and offered for sale and the amount of that good purchased. The schedule of amounts that will be offered for sale at various prices is called the supply schedule; the schedule of amounts that will be purchased at various prices is called the demand schedule.

Demand Underlying the theory of demand are several assumptions: that individual consumers have information concerning the general ends they desire, that consumers have information about how various goods can contribute to achieving these ends, and that consumers use the information to maximize attainment of the desired ends.

Five factors determine whether a consumer is willing and able to purchase a given quantity of a commodity within a given unit of time. The quantity demanded, that is, depends on price, the consumer's income, the price of related commodities, the consumer's expectations, and the consumer's taste and preferences.

The Price of the Commodity Quantity is inversely related to price.
EXAMPLE: If residential houses in a given area fall in price, the quantity demanded will increase.

The Consumer's Income Higher incomes usually mean that more units of a good will be purchased, but sometimes the opposite is true. Some goods, called inferior goods, serve as substitutes for more desirable goods, and rising income may cause a consumer to reduce purchases of the inferior good. For example, purchases of extremely cheap cuts of meat may decrease as income rises.

EXAMPLE: An increase in income may mean that persons leasing apartments now purchase two-bedroom houses, leading to a decline in the rental market. On the other hand, a decrease in income may lead to a decrease in the purchase of two-bedroom houses and an increased demand for apartments.

The Price of Related Commodities Commodities that are related are either substitute commodities or complementary commodities. If goods are substitutes, one commodity may be replaced by another because both have similar characteristics and equal utility. An increase in the price of one of these commodities will tend to decrease the quantity demanded and increase the quantity demanded of the other commodity. This is the basis of the appraisal principle of substitution.

In accordance with the principle of substitution, the value of a property will not exceed that of its replacement. A prudent buyer will pay no more for a property than the purchase price of a similar and equally desirable one. This principle is basic to the approaches to valuation of property to be discussed later in the text.

Complementary commodities are goods utilized in association with each other. An increase in the price of a commodity will decrease the quantity demanded and therefore also the quantity demanded of associated commodities.

EXAMPLE: If the price of kitchen sinks increases, the quantity demanded will decrease. The quantity demanded of equipment, such as faucets, that usually accompanies the purchase of sinks will also decrease.

Consumer Expectations The quantity demanded of a commodity depends on the expected price of the commodity in the future. Consumers who expect the price of a commodity to increase will make their purchases sooner. Those who expect a price decrease will postpone purchases.

EXAMPLE 1: The lack of new construction in a particular region will create a shortage of one-family houses within the next year. This will increase the price of available one-family houses. Consumers will, therefore, purchase houses as quickly as possible.

EXAMPLE 2: Because of overbuilding, the price of one-family houses in a particular region is expected to decrease within the next year. Consumers will, therefore, postpone purchasing until that time.

The appraisal principle of anticipation follows directly from the role of consumer expectation in generating demand. Buyer and seller expectations about real estate market conditions and future benefits of ownership are directly related to current property values, so the principle of anticipation is important in the valuing of property.

Consumer Taste and Preference Perceived utility of goods and services is in part determined by social factors such as age, location, peer group, occupation, cultural background, and educational background. Taste and preference shift periodically or even change instantaneously as they do in music and clothing fashions. Preferences may also evolve slowly, however, as they do in the home-furnishing and residential housing industries.

Changes in technology, the environment, and locational patterns continually influence the value of individual properties, neighborhoods, cities, regions, and even countries. The appraisal principle of change is a result of the influence of consumer taste and preference on demand.

Demand Schedules Demand for a good can be illustrated by constructing and graphing a demand schedule. Such a schedule shows the relationship between various prices and the quantity of a commodity that an individual consumer, or groups of consumers, is able and willing to purchase within a given unit of time. A demand schedule assumes that nonprice determinants of demand are held constant.

As shown in table 3, a demand schedule lists the different quantities of a commodity that consumers will purchase at various prices per unit of time. For typical goods, there is an inverse relationship between price and quantity demanded because, as price increases, the perceived utility of the good per dollar decreases.

Table 3. Demand Schedule for Two-Bedroom Houses Purchased within a Six-Month Period

Price	Quantity per unit of time
$ 60,000	14
70,000	9
80,000	7
90,000	6
100,000	5
110,000	3
120,000	1

A second way of illustrating consumer demand is by plotting a demand curve. A specific quantity and its corresponding price listed in a demand schedule can be plotted. It is customary to show price on the vertical (y) axis and quantity on the horizontal (x) axis.

In the demand curve shown in figure 2, seven points derived from the demand schedule in table 3 are connected to form a curve. The demand curve, like the demand schedule, shows the quantity of the commodity (two-bedroom houses) that consumers were able and willing to purchase at varying prices ($60,000 to $120,000) per unit of time (six months).

Demand for a good can change in two ways. A change in price causes the quantity demanded to change. The increase in consumer demand at lower prices is reflected in the downward slope of the curve. Conversely, as prices increase, the quantity demanded will decrease.

When one of the determinants of demand other than the price changes, it is said that there is a *change in the demand* at every price. This is reflected in a shift in the demand curve. For example, the demand curve in figure 2 is shown as curve A in figure 3. Curve A represents demand in a neighborhood before a manufacturing plant that employed 45 percent of the local population closed. The result of the closing is a decrease in the average income of those residents most likely to purchase two-bedroom houses. Demand curve A′ in figure 3 illustrates the quantity of the commodity (two-bedroom houses) purchased at varying prices after income, a determinant of demand, has changed.

A market demand schedule is produced by adding the quantities that would be pur-

Figure 2. Demand Curve for Two-Bedroom Houses

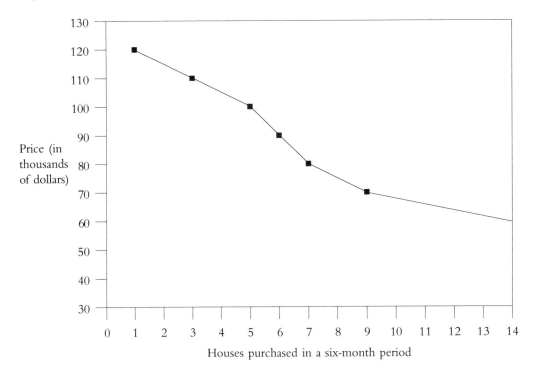

chased by all individuals in the market area. If the good in question is used by businesses in the process of producing other goods, the amount that would be purchased for this purpose would be added to the amount that would be purchased by consumers at each price to obtain the market demand schedule.

Supply Underlying the theory of supply are assumptions similar to those affecting demand: that producers have information on products that will maximize profit and that they know how inputs can be combined to produce these goods efficiently. These assumptions will be explained in detail later in this chapter in the section on production costs and the supply curve.

Once the producers have assembled this information, three factors determine the quantity of goods each producer will supply. The first is the price of the good; more will be produced as prices increase. The second is the availability and cost of land, labor, capital, and management. More will be produced as these are more available or decrease in price. The third factor is the technology available for producing the good in question. Improvements in technology increase the supply of a good. For real property, relevant supply factors would be housing prices, the size of the standing housing stock, and construction costs and techniques.

Figure 3. Demand Curves for Two-Bedroom Houses before and after a Change in Income

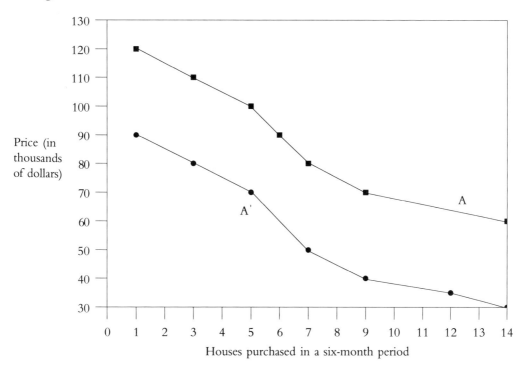

Price (in thousands of dollars)

Houses purchased in a six-month period

A supply schedule illustrates the relationship between the quantity of a good that an individual supplier, or groups of suppliers, is able and willing to produce at various prices within a given unit of time. Like a demand schedule, a supply schedule assumes that the only determinant of supply that changes is price. The remaining determinants of supply (production techniques, the cost of inputs, the price of related goods, and the expected future price of the good) are held constant. An increase in price of a particular good means that suppliers will increase their income by producing more of that good and less of others. The quantity supplied will, therefore, usually be more at higher prices. As shown in table 4, a supply schedule lists the different quantities of a good that a supplier will provide at various prices per unit of time.

A supply curve is a second way of illustrating supply. This curve plots the information in a supply schedule with price on the vertical (y) axis and quantity on the horizontal (x) axis. Figure 4 shows a supply curve that plots the supply schedule in table 4.

Supply may also change because a determinant of supply other than price has changed. In this case, it is said that there is a *change in the supply at every price*. This change in supply is responsible for a *shift* in the supply curve. For example, the supply curve in figure 4 is shown as curve B in figure 5. Curve B represents supply in a neighbor-

Figure 4. Supply Curve for Two-Bedroom Houses

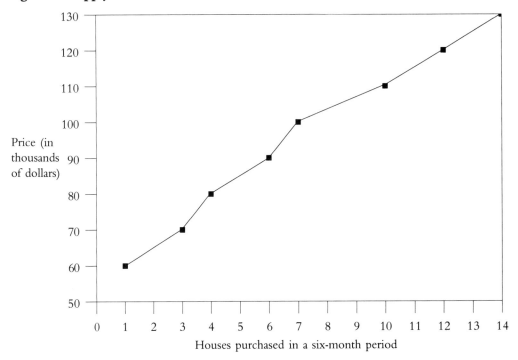

hood before a shortage of manual laborers causes the regional construction industry to increase its wages to attract employees. The wage increase will increase the cost of one of the factors of production, labor. The increased cost of labor causes the supply curve of houses to shift to the left (curve B′), showing that fewer houses are available for sale at every price.

Market Price   Figure 6, a typical supply and demand diagram, illustrates the interplay of the demand and supply forces operating in a typical market. Price and quantity purchased are determined at the point where the supply curve and demand curve intersect (point A). The price P and quantity Q are called the equilibrium price and quantity. At price P, the quantity of two-bedroom houses

offered for sale (supplied) and the amount of such houses purchased (demanded) are equal. Any movement away from this equilibrium point would be resisted by the automatic workings of the market.

Table 4.   Supply Schedule for Two-Bedroom Houses Constructed in a Six-Month Period

Price	Quantity per unit of time
$ 60,000	1
70,000	3
80,000	4
90,000	6
100,000	7
110,000	10
120,000	12
130,000	14

Figure 5. A Shift in the Supply Curve for Two-Bedroom Houses

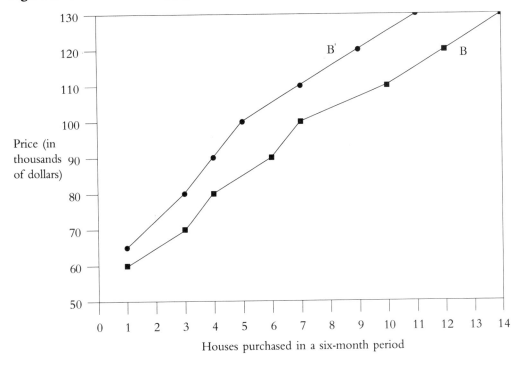

Figure 6. Typical Supply and Demand Diagram

If the price were fixed at P′, the amount demanded would fall to Q′, but producers would be willing to sell the larger amount Q″ at that price. This situation would not be stable. There would be a glut, or oversupply, and producers would lower their prices until the price P was established. If the higher price had been established by government order, the government would probably find it necessary to decide how much each producer would be allowed to sell at the fixed price, or an illegal market would develop in which prices were lower than the price fixed by government. A similar disequilibrium would occur if the price were fixed at an amount lower than P, but now the amount

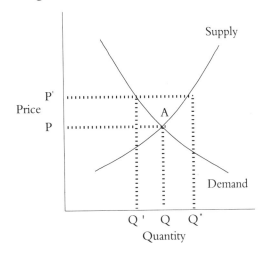

demanded would be greater than the amount supplied, and the price would have to rise to create an equilibrium.

The equilibrium price changes whenever supply or demand changes. Figure 7 illustrates how changes in demand might affect the price of a good—perhaps a certain type of residential property. The intersection of supply curve s and demand curve d at point A indicates that the equilibrium price is P and that the amount sold is Q. Demand curve d' is a new, reduced demand curve. Smaller quantities of the good are demanded at every possible price. Such a shift could occur because one of the five determinants of demand changed. Perhaps the incomes of potential buyers declined because of wage reductions or reductions of overtime in the community's major industry, or potential consumers believed that the prices of the houses would decline and decided to hold off purchases. The new equilibrium is at point B. The new price would be P' and the new quantity sold would be Q'.

Figure 7. Change in Demand

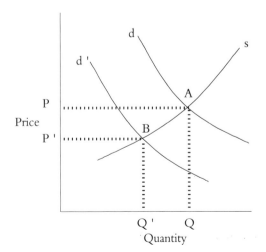

Figure 8 illustrates the effects of an increase in supply. Perhaps new production techniques or a decrease in interest rates made it cheaper to produce new houses. Producers are willing to supply a larger number at each price. The result is a new supply curve, s', and a new equilibrium, indicated by point B.

Figure 8. Change in Supply

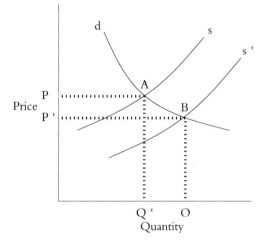

In an unchanging world of perfect knowledge, the price corresponding to the intersection of supply and demand would be established quickly and be stable. The price would be in equilibrium because the forces would be in balance. In real estate markets, the nonprice determinants of demand change frequently, causing shifts in the demand curve. Changes in techniques and production costs result in frequent shifts in the supply curve. Prices and quantities sold are seldom stable for long. Equilibrium is not attained for long, but is a constantly changing point toward which the system is always moving. This tendency for markets to reach a new equilibrium after a change in one of the determinants of supply or demand is the basis for the appraisal principle of balance.

Value and Markets

Market Structure and Competition

A market can be represented by supply and demand diagrams, but it is really the "place" in which buyers and sellers interact. The buyers and sellers may be in the same physical place, as at an auction, or they may be connected by a worldwide communication network, as in the securities market. It is in markets that price is determined.

Economists have found it necessary to be precise in defining the various kinds of competition that exist in a market. The study of economics usually starts with the study of *pure competition*. The four conditions necessary for pure competition are:

1. *Homogeneity of product.* The units of the product must be identical, or at least the buyers and sellers must so believe.

2. *Buyers and sellers too small to have a measurable effect on the price.* Individual wheat farmers, for example, do not perceive that their output or the output of a particular neighbor will affect the price received for the wheat. They will not be concerned that their increased production will lower the price.

3. *Absence of artificial restraints.* It is necessary that the market in question be free of price or output fixing by government, producers' associations, labor unions, or other agencies.

4. *Mobility.* Goods and productive services must be free to move to receive the greatest return. Buyers must be free to buy where the price is lowest.

Sometimes economists distinguish between pure and *perfect* competition. Perfect competition requires all of the above conditions and the condition that all buyers and sellers possess complete knowledge of the market. No delays will then occur while market participants become informed about changes in the economy.

These restrictions make it difficult to cite an example of perfect competition. Nevertheless, the concepts are important. The assumption that markets are perfect makes it possible to construct mathematical models of the economy that illustrate interactions within it. Without these restrictions, it would be necessary to allow for essentially unpredictable actions such as price fixing by groups of producers, government price supports, or labor union action. The restrictions do approximate conditions in some parts of the economy, and the model of perfect competition is often used as a norm against which the performance of the economy is checked. For example, antitrust laws and the regulation of public utilities are attempts to ensure price and output closer to those that would prevail under perfect competition.

Not all economic analysis assumes pure competition. Models have been developed that describe the pricing and output policies that would be followed by a monopolist (one who controls the entire output of a product) or a monopsonist (one who is the sole buyer of a product). Various other degrees of competition, such as oligopoly (few sellers) and imperfect competition (several sellers of slightly different products) have been described and analyzed. Although these models often lack the precision of the pure competition models, they do give insight into the process of price determination under various market conditions.

Real estate markets differ from perfectly competitive markets in several ways. Among the differences are the following:

1. Goods or services in a perfectly competitive market are homogeneous and can be substituted for each other. In a real estate market, each parcel is unique. Residences in a newly developed subdivision may be good, but not perfect, substitutes for each other; many parcels of industrial or commercial property may be reasonable substitutes for each other.

2. A perfectly competitive market will have a large number of buyers and sellers, no one of whom can measurably affect price. A real estate market may have only a few buyers and sellers in a particular price range at a particular time.

3. A perfectly competitive market must be free of artificial restraints or incentives. Real estate markets are affected by a variety of state and local government regulations. Federal government policy affects interest rates, and various government programs provide financing for real estate transactions. Federal income tax laws and regulations affect the demand for real estate. Uncertainty is introduced by frequent and unpredictable changes in government programs.

4. In a perfectly competitive market, goods and productive resources must be free to move to the place where they receive the largest return or the price is the highest, and buyers must be free to buy where the price is the lowest. Real property is immobile and must be used or consumed in its present location. The demand for real property is greatly affected by events in the neighborhood. Changes in employment opportunities or in the environment may make a parcel more or less desirable, even though the parcel itself has not changed.

5. In a perfectly competitive market, buyers and sellers are knowledgeable and informed about market conditions. Buyers and sellers of real estate often are poorly informed. Many of them buy or sell infrequently and are not familiar with market procedures.

Although real estate markets are not perfectly competitive, the forces of competition are important in determining the price of real estate. Parcels may not be identical but often they are close substitutes. The buyer of residential real estate may prefer a particular location or type of house but will substitute another type or location if the price is right. Buyers of commercial and industrial real estate may not be bound to one location, and real estate developers and builders move from market to market in response to profit opportunities.

Price and Value

The study of *value* and its determination has always been a principal concern of economists. Value theory is often listed as a major branch of economic theory. However, the term value has almost disappeared from economic textbooks, in part because of historical developments and in part because value has so many different meanings.

Because early Marxists used the labor theory of value as a justification for revolution, the term value acquired political and ethical connotations that Marshall and his followers attempted to avoid. They demonstrated how price would be determined in particular market situations but generally avoided labeling any of these prices as the value.

Concepts of Value   The theory of price determination discussed above implied that for a good to have value it must have *utility*, it must be *scarce*, and there must be a *desire* for it. An object that lacks utility cannot have value, because utility arouses desire for possession and has the power to give satisfaction.

Utility and scarcity do not by themselves confer value on an object; desire by the purchaser must also be present. Desire must be backed up by purchasing power (the ability to pay) in order to constitute effective demand, and potential purchasers must be able to participate in the market to satisfy their desires. If these conditions are met, the price of a good determined in a market can be considered as the net present value of the future benefit of owning the good.

Kinds of Value   Adam Smith's distinction between *value in use* and *value in exchange* is important. A property may have one value in use and a significantly different value in exchange. Value in use embodies the premise that an object's value is related to its current use. For example, an obsolete, but functioning, oil refinery may still have considerable use value to its owners. Value in exchange, however, is determined by the market. Value in exchange is a relative value in that the good must be compared to other substitute goods and services in a competitive, open market.

Market Price vs. Market Value   *Market price*, or value in exchange, is represented by the equilibrium price determined by supply and demand in a market. Market price is the amount actually paid in a particular transaction. The type of competition prevailing in the market is ignored in this definition. For example, no allowance is made for knowledge or prudent conduct on the part of buyer or seller, degree and type of stimulus motivating either or both, financing terms,

the use for which the property is best suited or is to be put, or length of time the property is exposed to the market. Market price can, and often does, result from caprice, carelessness, desperation, egotism, ignorance, pressure, sentiment, social ambition, whim, and many other factors.

Market value is a hypothetical, or estimated, sale price, such as would result from the careful consideration by the buyer and seller of all data, with primary reliance on those data that reflect the actions of responsible, prudent buyers and sellers under conditions of a fair sale. The definition of market value is concerned with the type of competition prevailing in the market. Although the definition does not require adherence to all the features of pure competition, it incorporates many of them. It principally leaves out the requirement that goods be exact substitutes for each other. Market value, as defined here, is what the appraiser is trying to estimate in the appraisal process.

Market price approximates market value and value in exchange under the following assumptions:

1. No coercion or undue influence over the buyer or seller in an attempt to force the purchase or sale
2. Well-informed buyers and sellers acting in their own best interests
3. A reasonable time for the transaction to take place
4. Payment in cash or its equivalent

Equilibrium and Time Periods

Equilibrium is central to economics. The concept is borrowed from Newtonian physics, where it describes a system in a state of rest. No forces exist within the system that tend to bring about further change. Supply and demand are in equilibrium when the amount supplied and the amount demanded at an established price are equal during a specified period. Nothing within the system will bring about a change in price, amount supplied, or amount demanded.

Equilibrium is disturbed when some critical elements change. If, for example, preferences for a good increase, the increase in demand will upset the equilibrium. The amount of the good being supplied will not be sufficient to meet the demand at the current price. Buyers will offer to pay more, and sellers will raise prices. Existing levels of production will not be sufficient, and producers will attempt to raise output by increasing the use of the factors of production (land, labor, capital, and management).

Some factors, such as factories and arable land, are relatively fixed, that is, their quantities cannot easily be changed. Others, such as hours worked and seeds planted, are called variable because their quantities can be changed easily. Because it is not possible to increase the amount of the fixed input immediately, in the short run production can be increased only by increasing the quantity of the variable input. As a result, the cost of producing the marginal unit will rise, and the supply curve will shift. Over a longer period, it will be possible to increase the amount of the fixed input. For example, new manufacturing plants will be built. If there are no further external changes, the system will again attain equilibrium. The amount supplied and the amount demanded will be equal at a stable price. In practice, of course, equilibrium is rarely achieved. It is a constantly changing target toward which the system is moving rather than a state that is maintained. The fixed supply of land and the long life of im-

provements to land make it particularly difficult to attain equilibrium in real estate markets.

Some changes within the system, such as the building (or the wearing out) of manufacturing plants or apartment houses, require a long time. While these changes occur, other conditions, such as the demand for the good, techniques for producing the good, and prices of productive services, may change. To analyze these changes more systematically, economists often specify the periods involved. The *market* period is a short period in which the only items offered for sale are those already produced. In a livestock auction, for example, prices are established by the supply of livestock in the sale barn and demand from the potential buyers present at the auction.

The term *short run* describes a period long enough for new production to occur but too short to permit the fixed factors of production to be increased. The plants in existence can be operated for more or fewer hours per week, workers can be discharged or added, and so forth, but no new plants can be built. The short run is not a definite calendar period and may be short or long depending on the time required to increase or decrease the variable service. The short run is apt to be longer in a real estate market than in the market for small, quickly produced items. The *long run* is a period long enough to permit alterations of all services.

It is common for equilibrium to exist in one period and not in another. For example, the amount supplied and the amount demanded may be equal at a price that is stable in the short run, but if the price of a fixed input, such as a manufacturing plant, has changed, long-run equilibrium may not exist. If the cost of replacing the plant has risen, the plants that wear out may not be replaced until the price of the product rises. Conversely, if the price of the fixed input has fallen or technology has improved, new, more efficient plants may be built before existing plants are worn out. When the new plants are completed, the price of the product will fall.

This example illustrates an important aspect of how the price of a product is determined. Past, or "sunk," costs are irrelevant to price determination, and there is no guarantee of a return to a fixed service. A factory building may be well maintained and productive, but, when a cheaper method of production becomes available, the historical cost of the older factory is irrelevant to the long-run price of the product being produced. As soon as the new method of production can be placed in operation, the price will fall, and the older factory will continue to operate only if it can cover variable costs plus something more. The price at which the older factory will sell is determined by the amount of the "something more," not by the factory's historic cost. Because of the durable nature of most real estate, this principle is especially important in real property appraisal.

Economic Rent

The time required to adjust the mix of productive services gives rise to the phenomenon of economic rent, or surplus productivity. In the short run, certain productive factors are fixed and the quantity used cannot be expanded. If a shift in productive techniques or an increase in the demand for the good produced causes an increase in the demand for a particular productive service,

the good's price will rise above its long-run equilibrium price. The result is that during the period of adjustment owners of the service will receive more than the normal long-run return. This excess return is called economic rent, quasi rent, or, sometimes, pure profits.

The same kind of analysis explains fluctuations in the price of land. Land, as defined by economists, is the resource provided by nature—it does not include any improvements such as buildings, drainage, irrigation, or terracing. The supply of land so defined cannot be increased. A price must be paid to the owners of land to obtain its use, but it is not a compensation necessary to overcome real costs. This price is known as land rent or, to economists, simply as rent. Land rent, like any price, is determined by the intersection of supply and demand. The difference is that the amount supplied is fixed by nature. The supply curve is a vertical line on a supply-demand diagram (see figure 9). If the demand for land increases, as shown by the shift from curve d to d', price will increase from P to P'. The amount supplied will remain the same.

Because of the importance of location to many business and commercial activities, the demand for a particular parcel of land may be very high compared with the demand for land located in a less desirable place. This, combined with the vertical supply curve, and the sometimes imperfect land market, may result in rapid fluctuations in the price of land in desirable locations. It also may result in land prices that are much higher than those for land located only a short distance away. Thus, appraising land, particularly in commercial and industrial uses, is one of the most challenging tasks faced by appraisers.

Figure 9. Supply and Demand for Land

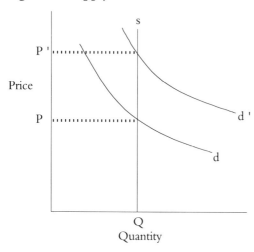

External Economies and Diseconomies

The cost of producing a good is influenced not only by the way productive services are combined within a firm but also by events outside the firm. If an industry uses a large portion of the available quantities of a resource, its price may rise as the industry expands. Each firm then pays higher costs even if it does not expand output, and the supply curve is shifted upward. An industry that faces increasing costs as output expands is said to be an increasing cost industry. Of course, such external diseconomies can also result from forces outside the industry, such as pollution from one industry increasing cleanup or purification costs to another industry.

External economies work in the other direction. Sometimes the presence of several firms in an area will encourage suppliers to locate there or will lead to development of a pool of specialized labor that reduces the costs to firms in the industry. The cost of ex-panding real estate developments into thinly populated areas may be reduced as the area becomes developed and the cost of supplying infrastructure such as street and utility connections declines. In this case, the long-run industry cost curve declines.

Production Costs and the Supply Curve

Modern price theory extended the concept of marginal utility to the supply side of the market by recognizing that a profit-maximizing individual will compare the cost of producing an additional unit of a product with the additional return from producing that unit. As long as the marginal return is higher than the marginal cost, total profit will be increased by additional production. This will not result in the highest average profit per unit produced, but in the highest possible total profit. In order to understand supply-side economics and how a supply curve is determined, it is necessary to understand production principles and the related costs of production.

The Production Function The term *production function* refers to the physical relationship between a firm's inputs of productive services and its output of goods or consumer services. Firms can usually vary the proportions of resources combined to produce a good or service. Inputs can be substituted for one another, and a firm can choose the combination of inputs it will use. The law of diminishing returns, sometimes called the law of variable proportions, states: When the quantity of one production input is increased by equal increments (with the quantities of another production input remaining fixed), the resulting output of product will, at some point, begin to decrease.

The law of diminishing returns is a technical principle concerning the relationship between inputs of productive services, such as hours of labor and acres of land, and physical output, such as bushels of corn. The units of variable input are assumed to be homogeneous. If labor is the variable input and acres of land the fixed input, the output of corn per worker will decline, not because less efficient laborers are employed, but because each laborer has less land with which to work.

A numerical example will clarify the significance of the law of diminishing returns. Table 5 has been constructed on the assumption that a firm has a fixed quantity of a production input, such as land or manufacturing plant. Various quantities of another production input, such as labor, can be used with the fixed input to produce output (column 2), measured in physical units such as bushels of corn or number of refrigerators.

In table 5, the total product increases as units of the variable input are added until total product reaches 35, when 7 units of the

Table 5. Diminishing Marginal Product

Units of variable input (1)	Total product (2)	Average product (3)	Marginal product (4)
0	0	0	0
1	3	3	3
2	8	4	5
3	15	5	7
4	23	5 3/4	8
5	30	6	7
6	34	5 2/3	4
7	35	5	1
8	35	4 3/8	0

variable input are employed. The addition of the eighth unit of variable input adds nothing to output. Possibly, the addition of a ninth would reduce total output. If, for example, the variable input is labor, it is possible that the additional worker would be in the way and impede work. Column 3 shows the average output per unit of variable input (computed by dividing total product by number of units of the variable input). Column 4 shows the marginal, or added, product resulting from employing one additional unit of the variable input.

The marginal product is important because a profit-maximizing producer must compare the cost of adding a marginal unit with the return from selling the product of that additional unit. The relationships among the total, average, and marginal products are seen more clearly in figure 10.

Certain mathematical relationships always exist among the curves shown. For example, the marginal product curve always cuts the average product curve from above at its highest point (maximum average product). This must be true because the addition of a unit of productive input that produces an added (marginal) product less than the previous average must always lower the average. Total product always reaches its maximum point at the same input at which marginal product reaches zero. This must be true because a negative marginal product reduces total output.

It is not possible to specify the most efficient combination of resources or level of output from data regarding physical input-output relationships, but it is possible to say that production will always be in stage 2. Clearly, it would be unwise to produce in stage 3 because total output would be

Figure 10. Total, Average, and Marginal Product Curves

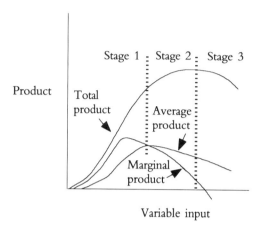

Variable input

reduced with each additional unit of the variable input. In stage 1, output per unit of variable input is not maximized. The producer can increase average output per unit of variable input by simply increasing the units of the variable input. Even if fixed inputs were free, the profit-maximizing producer would extend output into stage 2 as long as the marginal revenue per unit is greater than the per unit cost of the variable input. To determine exactly where within stage 2 a profit-maximizing producer should operate, it is necessary to know the relative cost of the fixed and variable services. That subject is considered in the next section.

Costs and the Supply Curve   Economists define cost in terms of alternative use of resources. The *opportunity cost* principle states that the cost of a resource to a firm is its value in its best alternative use. To secure the services of a particular resource, such as lumber or labor to produce housing, a firm must pay as much as another firm would be willing to pay to use the resource to produce

some other good. If cash outlays must be made to obtain these resources, costs are explicit and are similar to what are commonly called expenses, but the economist's notion of cost includes the implicit costs of not employing the resources in alternative uses.

For example, the cost of producing a good includes the amount that the resources used in production could have earned in the most profitable alternative use. In an accounting statement, this return is income, including any profit. To an economist, however, any amount necessary to keep resources in their current use is cost, not profit. A return above the most profitable alternative use that results from a temporary situation or the existence of a monopoly is "pure profit," or economic rent.

Costs incurred by a firm in a period of time too short to permit variations in the amount of all resources used can be divided into fixed and variable costs. Fixed costs are those that cannot be varied during the period in question. For example, the firm may own a plant of fixed size. The costs of operating it are the same regardless of the level of output. It is possible to vary the amount of other resources, such as labor or materials, and therefore the level of output. Table 6 illustrates the relationships involved.

Table 6 assumes a fixed productive input, perhaps a manufacturing plant, that costs $50 per time period regardless of the output. Different amounts of variable input result in outputs varying from 1 to 10 units of finished product. The variable costs are shown in column 3 and the total of the variable and fixed costs in column 4. Although it is possible to compare total cost figures and total revenue figures to determine the most profitable output of a firm, it is more instruc-

Table 6. Fixed and Variable Costs for a Firm

Output (1)	Total fixed cost (2)	Total variable cost (3)	Total cost (4)
1	$50.00	$ 30.00	$ 80.00
2	50.00	37.00	87.00
3	50.00	43.00	93.00
4	50.00	50.00	100.00
5	50.00	60.00	110.00
6	50.00	72.00	122.00
7	50.00	87.00	137.00
8	50.00	106.00	156.00
9	50.00	131.00	181.00
10	50.00	161.00	211.00

tive to work with average and marginal cost figures. In table 7, the totals from table 6 have been converted to averages by dividing them by output. The last column shows the marginal costs of producing each additional unit of output.

In general, the average variable, average total, and marginal cost curves are all monetized versions of the corresponding variable, total, and marginal product curves and demonstrate the same economic relationships. For example, when average product is increasing, average cost is decreasing, and when marginal product is increasing, marginal cost is decreasing. In economic terms, both demonstrate increasing returns to scale, that is, movement toward an efficient use of variable and fixed resources.

Figure 11 shows typical average and marginal cost curves. The shape of the curves will vary from firm to firm and time to time, but some constant mathematical relationships exist. Careful study of figure 11 will reveal much about the nature of the costs that face a firm. For example, the marginal cost curve cuts the average cost curve from below at the lowest point on the average cost curve. This is always true. As long as the cost of producing one additional unit is lower than the average cost, the production of an additional unit will lower the average cost.

Table 7. Average Cost Schedule for a Firm

Output (1)	Average fixed cost (2)	Average variable cost (3)	Average total cost (4)	Marginal cost (5)
1	$50.00	$30.00	$80.00	$_____
2	25.00	18.50	43.50	7.00
3	16.67	14.33	31.00	6.00
4	12.50	12.50	25.00	7.00
5	10.00	12.00	22.00	10.00
6	8.33	12.00	20.33	12.00
7	7.14	12.43	19.57	15.00
8	6.25	13.25	19.50	19.00
9	5.56	14.56	20.11	25.00
10	5.00	16.10	21.10	30.00

It follows that the output of an operating, profit-maximizing firm will be no less than the output at which marginal cost equals average variable cost. If the price that a firm receives is not enough to cover the variable costs and pay something toward the fixed costs, it would be better for the firm not to operate. Likewise, the output at which marginal cost equals average variable costs is the output at which resources are used most efficiently. However, the firm may choose to operate at an output level above this if the expected marginal revenue (which is price in purely competitive markets) exceeds the marginal cost of producing the higher output.

In that case, it pays to produce the extra units even though resources are not used most efficiently, because net profit increases whenever the production and sale of an extra unit of production adds more to revenue than it does to cost. The firm will increase productivity until the marginal revenue of the extra output equals the marginal cost of producing it.

Figure 11. Typical Cost Curves

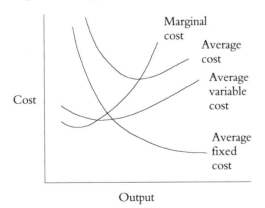

The marginal cost curve is a mirror image of the marginal product curve. Because the marginal productivity of additional units of the variable input falls, the marginal cost of the additional outputs produced by employing these additional inputs rises. (If there is a pure competition, the firm would be small enough that its purchases would have no influence on the price of the input being purchased. If the firm is large enough to influence the price, additional purchases would cause the price of the inputs to rise, and the marginal cost curve will rise even faster.)

The marginal cost curve, therefore, shows the amount of the good that the firm will supply at various prices. It is the supply curve for the firm. By adding the marginal cost curves of all the firms in the market, it is possible to construct an industrywide supply curve. Because the firm will always operate in the range in which marginal cost is rising, the supply curve will always slope upward.

For example, table 8 shows the cost data for a construction company producing single-family houses. If the firm believes it can sell its houses for $55,000, it will produce three houses. If it believes it can sell its houses for $60,000, it will produce six houses. If for $75,000, nine houses. As the potential selling price increases, output will increase until marginal cost equals the new marginal revenue (price). Figure 12 uses the above data to construct a supply curve for this firm. This example is simplified. It assumes purely competitive markets and only one fixed and one variable input (in practice, there may be many). The degree to which an input is fixed depends on the period. In the long run, few services are completely fixed.

Cost curves and equilibrium positions differ depending on the period.

Another thing to note, however, is that the firm may produce anywhere along the supply curve as long as marginal revenue exceeds or equals marginal cost *and* marginal revenue exceeds *average cost*. Only under these conditions would the firm be making profits. If it produced at an output level where marginal revenue (price) were equal to marginal cost but less than average revenue, it would be losing part or all of fixed, and possibly some variable, cost and could not stay in business in the long run. These insights pro-vide the rationale for appraisers to study unit costs as a basis for estimating market value. A firm will not stay in business unless price is at least equal to average total cost.

Appraisers using the cost approach esti-mate the cost of constructing a similar prop-erty and adjust for demand-side influences by subtracting an allowance for depreciation. If the property is newly constructed and ap-propriate for its location, this method is ex-cellent. New tract housing, for example, can be expected to sell for approximately the cost of producing it. Market prices above reproduction costs would cause potential

Table 8. A Firm's Construction Cost Table for Single-Family Houses

Variable input (labor)	$ Value of variable input (labor)	$ Value of the fixed input (management)	=	Total input (total cost)	Commodity (houses)
5	$ 50,000	$80,000		$130,000	1
11	100,000	80,000		180,000	2
17	155,000	80,000		235,000	3
23	210,000	80,000		290,000	4
30	270,000	80,000		350,000	5
37	330,000	80,000		410,000	6
45	395,000	80,000		475,000	7
55	465,000	80,000		545,000	8
66	540,000	80,000		620,000	9

Quantity (houses)	Average cost (cost per house)	Marginal cost
1	$130,000	$_____
2	90,000	50,000
3	78,333	55,000
4	72,500	55,000
5	70,000	60,000
6	68,333	60,000
7	67,857	65,000
8	68,125	70,000
9	68,888	75,000

Figure 12. Supply Curve for Single-Family Houses

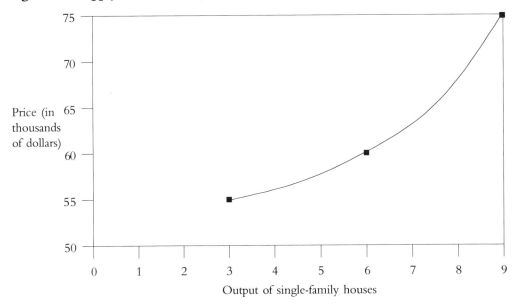

buyers to choose to build a new house; prices much below the cost of reproduction would attract buyers who had considered building.

Finally, another insight can be developed from a construction cost table such as table 8. Not only the number of houses that will be produced at various prices, but also the amount of variable resources that will be required to produce each output level can be determined. For example, at the $50,000 price, the firm will hire eleven workers to produce the two houses. At the $65,000 price, the firm will hire forty-five workers and produce seven houses. Thus the demand for labor depends on the demand for houses. Appraisers doing highest and best use analysis should understand this principle. The demand for resources will depend on the demand for final goods and services. Consequently, the appraiser will have to understand broadly the trends in consumer preferences in order to understand how land can be put to its best use in the long run.

Real Estate, Money, and Capital Markets (Macroeconomics)

The level of aggregate income (gross national product) of a country is the sum of consumer, investor, and government spending. Consumer spending is related to the amount of individual disposable income. Investment spending depends on the aggregate savings level and the cost of borrowing money (that is, the interest rate). Government spending depends on the tax yield and the amount of government debt. Governments in capitalistic countries attempt to fine-tune the economic activity of the country through fiscal and monetary policies. Fiscal policy relates to tax policy and government spending. Monetary policy works through interest rates to influence investment and consumer spending.

Government typically attempts to raise taxes or interest rates, or both together, when the economy is experiencing inflationary pressures. This reduces total consumption and investment spending and thus reduces demand-driven inflation. When the economy is depressed, the government reduces taxes and interest rates by intervening in money

---

Producer Equilibrium

Producers will attempt to improve their positions by varying the mix of productive factors used in the productive process. They will increase the use of a productive service if the additional output (marginal physical product) produced by using one dollar's worth of that factor is greater than the output resulting from using one dollar's worth of another factor. The process of substitution will end and equilibrium will be achieved when

$$\frac{MPP_a}{P_a} = \frac{MPP_b}{P_b},$$

where MPP is the marginal physical product, P is the price of a productive service, and a and b are productive services such as labor or land.

MPP/P for any factor is the physical amount of the good produced as the result of employing one additional dollar's worth of the productive service. The inverse, P/MPP, is the cost of producing one additional unit, that is, the marginal cost of the product being produced. A profit-maximizing producer will produce at the output at which the price of the good is equal to the marginal cost of the good.

In equilibrium, for good A,

$$\frac{MPP_x}{P_x} = \frac{MPP_y}{P_y} = \frac{1}{MC_a} = \frac{1}{P_a};$$

for good B,

$$\frac{MPP_x}{P_x} = \frac{MPP_y}{P_y} = \frac{1}{MC_b} = \frac{1}{P_b};$$

where MC_a and MC_b are the marginal cost for goods A and B, respectively, and x and y are any factors.

The illustration involves only two productive services and two goods. However, the system of equations could be expanded to include more goods and productive services.

The system of equations indicates that in equilibrium the value of the product produced by employing the marginal unit of each productive service is equal, and the marginal cost of each good is equal to its price. Producers are in equilibrium because no producer has any incentive to change the method of production, mix of productive services used, or level of output. In the terminology of appraisal theory, each productive service is employed in its highest and best use.

markets to stimulate consumption and investment spending. Over time, this raises the level of aggregate income and employment.

Aggregate investment spending is in part composed of spending to develop new or existing real estate. As a consequence, government policies aimed at influencing money markets and the interest rate affect real estate markets.

In fact, real estate markets are greatly influenced by conditions in money and capital markets for two reasons: First, real estate transactions are usually large in relation to the assets of buyers and sellers and are usually financed in part with borrowed funds. Availability of funds and interest rates are important factors in the decision to purchase real estate. Second, much real estate is purchased as an investment. The potential investor compares the various real estate alternatives, but also considers other investments in the capital market as alternatives to real estate investment.

Money Markets

Money is the medium of exchange. Interest is a price for the use of money, expressed as an annual percentage. The money supply is often defined as currency and coin in circulation plus the total demand deposits (checking account deposits) in banks. The widespread use of bank accounts that combine features of savings and checking accounts and of several forms of investment quickly available for spending have made this definition less accurate. As a result, other definitions of monetary aggregates are also used. Some key features of the money and capital markets are described below for the United States. Similar arrangements may be found in other economies.

The *money market* is the interaction of buyers and sellers as they buy and sell short-term credit instruments, such as short-term notes. The *capital market* is the interaction of buyers and sellers as they buy and sell long-term financial instruments, such as mortgages, bonds, and stocks. Short-term is often defined arbitrarily as one year, but the line between money and capital markets is not distinct. Buyers and sellers often shift back and forth between short-term and long-term instruments as conditions and investors' judgments about the future change.

Money Market Instruments   Although real estate purchases are usually financed in the capital, rather than money, markets, short-term money market instruments are important because they are used by developers to finance new construction and to provide "bridge loans" to finance purchases of property while arrangements for permanent financing are completed. Short-term, or money market, interest rates are also important because of the relationship between these rates and capital market rates. Investors often shift between short- and long-term instruments as rates of return vary. Among the most important money market instruments in the United States are federal funds, Treasury bills, repurchase agreements, certificates of deposit, commercial paper and bankers' acceptances, and municipal notes or warrants.

Federal Funds   Banks attempt to maximize profits by loaning as much as possible, but day-to-day fluctuations in loans and deposits may cause a bank's reserves at the Federal Reserve to fall below the required amount. This shortfall may be met by borrowing excess reserves from other commercial banks. Such borrowing is for a short period, sometimes overnight. The rate at which such borrowing occurs is a key rate, closely watched by those who study and predict market rates.

Treasury Bills Treasury bills are short-term obligations of the United States Treasury. They are issued in three-, six-, and twelve-month maturities in denominations of $10,000 or more. The Treasury sells bills frequently at auction. The bills are sold at a discount, which means that there are no interest coupons. Bidders state the rate at which they are willing to discount a bill of a given maturity. For example, if the winning bid on a twelve-month bill is 6 percent, the bidder would pay $9,400 for a $10,000 bill and would receive the face amount upon maturity, earning $600 interest on a $9,400 investment, for a true return of 6.383 percent. The Treasury bill rate, like the federal funds rate, is an important indicator of prevailing interest rates, and trends are studied carefully.

Repurchase Agreements Repurchase agreements are short-term financing arrangements whereby those needing funds for a short period sell securities but agree to repurchase them at a fixed price at a specific time.

Certificates of Deposit Certificates of deposit are time deposits in a bank or savings institution. They carry a fixed rate of interest and a penalty for withdrawal before maturity. Some are negotiable, that is, they can be sold to another lender.

Commercial Paper and Bankers' Acceptances Commercial paper is a short-term promise to pay issued by a corporation. Because it is backed only by the unsecured credit of the issuer, commercial paper is most likely to be issued by large, well-known corporations. A banker's acceptance is similar, but has been "accepted" or guaranteed by a bank. Acceptances are principally used in foreign trade.

Municipal Notes or Warrants Local governments sometimes issue short-term promises to pay, known as municipal notes or tax anticipation warrants. They may be issued pending collection of property taxes or special assessments or as temporary financing of capital projects. Interest on most municipal obligations is exempt from federal income taxes; therefore, these securities pay a lower rate of interest.

Monetary Policy and the Interest Rate

Interest rates, like other prices, are determined by supply and demand, but the money market has unique features. The interest rate and the supply of money greatly influence the general price level and the economic health of the country. Large supplies of money and low interest rates are inflationary. Conversely, small supplies of money and high interest rates are deflationary and may precipitate high unemployment and recession.

Because of the crucial importance of the money market, the United States Constitution and federal statutes assign the federal government an important role in the regulation of the money supply. Congress has established a system of fractional reserves permitting the amount of money in the banking system to expand or contract by a multiple of new deposits. Borrowers usually deposit new loan amounts in their own accounts or write checks to other individuals or firms, who deposit them in their accounts. These new deposits, less the required reserve, may become the basis of loans which, in turn, are deposited in other bank accounts. These, less the required reserve, may be the basis of still other loans.

The total amount of new money (bank deposits) created by a single new loan is determined by the reserve requirements established by the Federal Reserve System and by the willingness of the banks to lend. Of course, the process can work in reverse. The money supply contracts when a bank reduces the amount of its loans.

The United States Federal Reserve is an independent regulatory agency with responsibility for maintaining the health of the economy through its regulation of the money supply and the rate of interest. Members of the Federal Reserve Board are appointed by the president, with the consent of the Senate, for fourteen-year terms. The long terms are an attempt to give board members a degree of independence from the current administration. The Federal Reserve has three main instruments for affecting the money supply and the interest rate: reserve requirements, the federal discount rate, and open-market operations.

Reserve Requirements   Within limits imposed in the statutes, the Federal Reserve Board can establish the amount of reserves that member banks must maintain. A commercial bank that is a member of the Federal Reserve System must keep deposits in the Federal Reserve Bank of its region equal to an established percentage of its deposits. By increasing the percentage, the board can reduce the amount of loans that can be made by member banks. In practice, reserve requirements are rarely changed.

Federal Discount Rate   Commercial banks that are members of the Federal Reserve System are allowed to borrow funds, which they can lend to customers. By changing the rate (of-

ten called the re-discount rate) at which member banks can borrow, the Federal Reserve can encourage or discourage borrowing and lending by commercial banks. Changes in the discount rate are often regarded as an indication that the Federal Reserve Board sees a need for a change in policy. The "announcement" effect of such a change may be as important as the change itself.

Open-Market Operations   The most widely used instrument of monetary control is the purchase or sale of government securities on the open market. Purchase of a government security by the Federal Reserve is paid for by a check, which will be deposited in a Federal Reserve Bank, increasing the reserves of the member bank. This will support an increase in lending equal to five or six times the amount of the increase in reserve (depending on the reserve ratio). The sale of a government security by the Federal Reserve to a member bank will have the opposite effect. A member bank's reserve will be reduced by the amount paid for the security, and the amount of money in the system will be reduced by a multiple of that amount.

Figure 13 illustrates the effect of an increase in the money supply on the interest rate. The intersection of supply and demand at point A results in equilibrium interest rate R. Federal reserve purchase of bonds would increase the supply of loanable funds in the hands of banks or the general public, resulting in a new supply curve such as s′. This would result in a new equilibrium point B and the new interest rate of R′, which is lower than the original rate. The lower rate of interest would increase the demand for housing, as shown in figure 14. The new demand curve d′ intersects the supply curve at point B, and the new equilibrium price of this type of housing would rise from P to P′.

If the Federal Reserve were to sell securities, they would be paid for with money currently in the hands of banks or the general public. This would shift the supply-of-money curve to the left, and the new equilibrium rate of interest would be higher than the original. This would reduce the demand for housing and lower prices, exactly the reverse of the sequence of events shown in figures 13 and 14.

Monetary and Fiscal Policy and Real Estate

The availability of money and credit is the lifeblood of real estate activity. As a general rule, when the real interest rate is low, real estate activity is strong. The reverse, high real interest rates, causes a reduction in real estate activities. However, there have been periods with exceptions.

Business and Real Estate Cycles The peaks and troughs of the real estate cycle usually demonstrate more volatility than does the general business cycle. At one time, economists believed that the real estate and business cycles acted in the opposite directions. They believed that when the general economy is strong, there would be little money or labor available for building activity because of business and government borrowing for expansion. When the economy weakens, money and labor become available to allow construction at an affordable price. This countercyclical concept has been eroded considerably in recent years as real estate has become procyclical. That is, real estate activity has increased with improved general economic conditions. Regardless of the relationship between the real estate and business cycles, the following is a description of how cycles seem to occur.

Bottom At the bottom of a business cycle, the unemployment rate is high. Many peo-

Figure 13. Supply and Demand for Loanable Funds

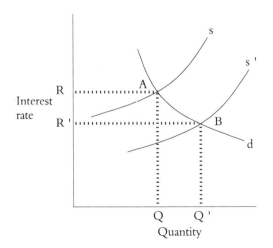

Figure 14. Supply and Demand for Residences

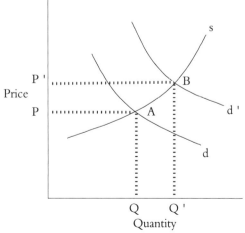

ple have to share housing because of the economic situation. Prices seem to be low — prices of raw materials have been declining because of inadequate consumer and business demand. Both groups, consumers and businesses, have been spending conservatively. They are reluctant to commit to long-term borrowing or investing, wary that the recession might affect them more severely. Government policies are expansionary: real interest rates are low, and income tax incentives are offered to those who provide new jobs (job credits) and buy new equipment (investment tax credits, depreciation allowances). Some take advantage of the situation because they are optimistic about the future, and the after-tax cost of purchases is low.

Recovery   Then more consumers and businesses begin to sense an improvement in economic conditions and believe that the time is right to start buying. As employees feel more comfortable about their jobs and others regain their positions, they become more relaxed about spending. Vacant single-family houses and apartments are again occupied as people leave shared housing. As this feeling of security spreads, the pent-up demands for "big-ticket" items — cars, houses, furniture, and appliances — are heard. Interest rates are low, so many can afford installment payments. Economic recovery is well under way.

All this activity increases the demand for money. Interest rates inch up. Businesses expand their plans. They increase inventories and hold more receivables from the sale of goods. As interest rates rise, businesses tend to have a priority on loanable funds. That is, they will pay a higher interest rate for money than consumers. Still, there is plenty of credit available for consumers.

Peak   Prices of goods rise in response to the increased production costs (which now reflect overtime wages and higher interest rates) and consumer demand. Real estate activity increases as people, now enjoying prosperity, carry out their wishes for improved housing. Employment increases and there is a scarcity of skilled workers. The economy is in full swing. Prices continue to rise as the demand for goods and services exceeds the supply. Consumers seem eager to buy now. Postponement may only result in higher prices later. Investors notice that fixed income deposits — savings accounts, bonds, mortgages — have lost ground in terms of purchasing power. Tangibles have appreciated with inflation. Investors switch some of their assets to tangible investments such as art, real estate, rare coins and stamps, precious metals and gemstones, and other collectibles. These are perceived as a hedge against inflation. The federal government, noting some poverty in the face of prosperity, expands social programs with the feeling that they are easily affordable by taxpayers. Deficit spending continues.

The government, notably the Federal Reserve Board, soon becomes concerned over the rising inflation rate. Job and investment tax credits are removed because the economy no longer needs stimulation. Government deficits are attacked as inflationary. Suggestions to cut back spending are voiced. The country's currency is much weaker on foreign exchange markets. Prices of imports rise, particularly of energy-related products. The Federal Reserve Board tightens up on the money supply in an effort to curb inflation. Interest rates are driven up. The government, the largest borrower in the nation, is easily able to borrow what it needs because it has the highest credit rating. Businesses come next, although they begin to feel crowded out of the money market. Last in priority is the consumer. Small loans are still available at high rates, but mortgage loans are scarce because investors fear their erosion by inflation.

Savings and loan institutions, the primary source of home mortgage money, are being affected by removal of funds by depositors who invest their money in opportunities with higher yields. Therefore, these institutions have no new money to lend for mortgages. Indeed, many must sell some of their assets to remain liquid. Mortgage bankers are able to find some money for mortgage loans, although the rates are high. Some home buyers are willing to pay the price, but most cannot afford loans at high rates. Real estate and construction activity moderates. Construction workers begin to get laid off as activity declines and proposed projects are aborted. Some projects that were committed to earlier continue to completion.

Recession   For a while, the high interest rates cause prices to rise further as manufacturers seek to pass along the higher rates to customers via higher prices. Consumers are willing to pay. Inflation is assailed as the nation's number one enemy. The Federal Reserve Board becomes alarmed. It tightens the money supply further in an effort to control inflation. Businesses are unable to use borrowed money profitably. The interest rate is too high. Business expansion plans are postponed. Companies that built machines to produce consumer goods find that orders are cancelled. Workers are laid off. With fewer employed than before, there is less demand for goods. High prices and interest rates

cause many consumers to forgo big-ticket purchases. As demand for such items tapers off, unemployment increases. Price increases moderate. Prices for some raw materials fall.

As inflation seems checked, curbing the rapidly increasing unemployment becomes the nation's first economic priority. The national government puts pressure on the Federal Reserve Board to loosen the purse strings. Still concerned about inflation, the board reluctantly concedes. Although interest rates decline, the real rate (nominal rate less inflation) is high. Borrowers are few. Businesses curtail expansion plans. Consumers stay out of the market for big-ticket items.

As unemployment worsens, the government carries out various job programs to put the nation's labor force back to work. Although its tax revenues are declining, government increases its spending in an effort at stimulation. It again offers tax incentives for those who are buying machines and creating jobs. Optimistic risk-takers in the private sector see opportunities. If things work as planned, the economy is stimulated and the economic recovery begins.

To conclude, the availability of money and credit significantly affects real estate activity. Tools of the Federal Reserve System (open-market operations, reserve requirements, and discount rates) have a pronounced effect on the monetary system. When the Federal Reserve Board loosens the money supply, real estate activity increases; tightening has the reverse effect. The Federal Reserve Board adjusts the money supply in an effort to keep the economy in balance. However, this causes real estate, which gets the residual money available (after government and businesses borrow what they need) to incur cycles that are more exaggerated than the general business cycle.

Fiscal Policy The interest rate and general price level are affected not only by the monetary policy pursued by the Federal Reserve, but also by fiscal policy—that is, by the taxing, spending, and borrowing of governments. Deficit spending is inflationary. A government surplus means more is being taken in taxes than is reintroduced into the economy by government spending and, therefore, is deflationary.

Fiscal and monetary policy are closely related. The Federal Reserve can offset the inflationary tendencies of a government deficit by a restrictive monetary policy, but this results in higher interest rates, which reduce investment and consumer purchases and lead to reduced employment and perhaps a recession. Real estate prices are affected as higher interest rates and scarcity of mortgage funds reduce a buyer's ability to finance. The attempts that government makes to coordinate fiscal and monetary policy to maintain a stable economy may have a greater effect on real estate markets than on other markets. Consequently, the appraiser must understand and monitor the government's monetary and fiscal policies in order to understand what is happening in real estate markets.

Capital for Real Estate Financing

Real estate is financed by two types of capital: equity and debt. Equity is the owner's interest in property beyond the claims of debtors. The equity owner takes the most risk, but equity return is not limited to a fixed rate. The investor who provides debt financing is in a more secure position but has no possibility of a return beyond the receipt of interest and return of the capital. In the residential real estate market, the owner's equity investment is usually the down payment. Debt financing is provided by a lender (mortgagee) that takes a mortgage on the property from the borrower (mortgagor) to secure payment of principal and interest.

Financing of large commercial and industrial properties often involves more complicated arrangements that include use of several kinds of capital instruments and numerous equity and debt owners. In recent years, unsettled conditions in the real estate market, tax considerations, and changes in the structure of financial institutions have led to many variations—even in the residential market.

Sources of Equity Capital The equity of a home buyer usually comes from funds saved for a down payment. Although corporations may make down payments on real estate from accumulated cash, such equity capital frequently comes from investors. An investor may provide equity capital to purchase a parcel for lease or resale, or enter any of a number of arrangements whereby several investors pool funds to take an equity interest. In this way, investors can diversify risk, which makes it easier to finance large projects beyond the capacity of a single investor.

Trusts are often used to assemble equity funds for real estate investment. Trusts can be organized so that the earnings are passed through and taxed to the individual investor and, at the same time, investors receive the immunity from liability for the trust's actions that is characteristic of corporations. Real estate investment trusts (REITs) sell shares to small investors and use the proceeds to acquire real estate.

Partnerships are also used to pool funds for real estate investment. Limited partnerships permit the general partner to be the manager and to assume responsibility for partnership debt; limited partners provide funds but take no active part in the management. Limited partnerships were widely marketed as tax shelters in the early 1980s, but their attractiveness was reduced when Congress limited the extent to which losses from such partnerships could be used to shelter other income from taxation.

Joint ventures are often organized to construct large projects, with a financial institution supplying most of the capital and other partners supplying construction or other expertise. Joint ventures may take the form of a partnership, but one intended to continue only for a limited time.

Pension funds and life insurance companies have traditionally invested in bonds and stocks. The growth of these institutions and concern about the effect of inflation on the return from fixed-rate investments such as bonds has led to more real estate equity investments.

The unfavorable balance of international payments and high United States interest rates have resulted in increasing ownership of land in the United States by foreigners. Japan, Western Europe, and the oil-rich Middle Eastern nations have been prominent suppliers of equity capital.

Debt Financing Because of the relative stability and permanence of real estate, debt plays a large part in real estate finance. Savings and loan associations have traditionally financed most residential real estate. These associations are financial intermediaries that receive deposits from savers and lend to those wishing to buy or build. Originally, savings and loan associations were local, nonprofit or mutual organizations. Now, many are

multistate, for-profit corporations borrowing funds on the national money market, lending for real estate and non-real-estate purposes, and originating mortgages for sale on the secondary market.

Mutual savings banks are similar to savings and loan associations. They enjoyed broad lending powers when savings and loan associations were still limited to making real estate loans. With the relaxation of these limits, the differences have decreased.

Commercial banks offer a variety of financial services. They have traditionally supplied construction and development loans to real estate developers who make other arrangements for long-term financing. Commercial banks make some mortgage loans.

Life insurance companies must invest for long terms and therefore have always been important suppliers of debt capital for the real estate market. They may make loans through their mortgage origination offices or purchase mortgages on the secondary market.

Secondary Mortgage Markets Mortgages may be bought and sold, and the originator of the mortgage may sell it to another investor. Often the terms of the sale will provide that the originating institution will continue to "service" the mortgage by collecting and remitting payments.

The United States government has been deeply engaged in the secondary mortgage markets as a means of encouraging housing and stabilizing the economy. A number of government corporations such as the Federal National Mortgage Association (Fannie Mae), the Federal Home Loan Mortgage Corporation (Freddie Mac), and the Government National Mortgage Association (Ginnie Mae) were established to finance residential construction and ownership. They express government policy in the field by buying or selling mortgages. The terms on which these sales or purchases are made affect the price and availability of mortgage funds. For example, the market can be tightened by a decision to require larger down payments on mortgages purchased.

In addition to the government-established corporations, there is a private secondary mortgage market. Indeed, some companies originate mortgages with the intention of selling them on the private market. Banks and insurance companies buy and sell mortgages as their investment needs and opportunities change. In recent years, there has been interest in collateralized mortgage bonds, backed by a package of mortgages much as mutual funds shares are backed by stocks or bonds.

General Equilibrium

Much economic analysis is concerned with prices and outputs of particular goods or particular productive services. This is known as *partial equilibrium* analysis because it deals with isolated sectors of the economy. For example, in analyzing the price of a consumer good, one might ignore the price of all other goods except those that are close substitutes or that are complementary to the good being analyzed. For many purposes, this is sufficiently accurate. In analyzing the price of a residence, it may make little difference that the price of a loaf of bread has risen.

To gain an adequate understanding of the functioning of the entire economy, it is necessary to realize that interactions exist throughout the economy and are often too important to be ignored. The prices of goods are affected by the cost of the productive services used to produce them, and the prices of productive services are affected by the price of the various goods in whose production they are used. Because of these interconnections, a single change may have wide repercussions. For example, a change in the demand for housing will change the demand for construction labor and lumber. This will change the price of labor and lumber and the cost of producing any good that requires them. Changes spread throughout the economy like ripples in a pond—becoming smaller at each stage but having some effect on the price of every good and service.

Other changes occur because most incomes are derived from the sale of productive services such as labor, land, or mineral resources. A change in demand for a good or productive service affects the prices of productive resources and thus the distribution of income in the economy. This, in turn, affects the demand for various kinds of goods.

It may seem tempting to say that everything depends on everything else and that any attempt to solve the problem involves circular reasoning. This is not the case. General equilibrium theorists have shown that a system of equations can be developed to estimate the quantity and prices of goods demanded as well as the quantity of productive services expended and their prices under equilibrium. Theorists have shown that the number of unknowns, the number of equations, and the form of the equations constitute a solvable system. The number of equations and the amount of data required would be very large, but the system is theoretically solvable. Simplified versions have been employed to create input-output models that provide quantitative information

General Equilibrium

Earlier in the chapter it was pointed out that consumer equilibrium exists when consumers have adjusted their purchases so that the marginal utility of each good purchased is proportional to the price, that is

$$\frac{MU_a}{P_a} = \frac{MU_b}{P_b},$$

where MU_a and MU_b are the marginal utility for goods A and B, respectively.

Producer equilibrium exists when producers have adjusted their purchases of productive services and their productive methods so that equal returns are received from additional units of each productive service and the marginal cost of producing each good is equal to the price at which it can be sold.

$$\frac{MPP_x}{P_x} = \frac{MPP_y}{P_y} = \frac{1}{MC_a} = \frac{1}{P_a},$$

where MPP is the marginal physical product, x and y are any factors, and P is price.

An additional equation is necessary to indicate the connection between the production sector and the consumer sector.

$$\frac{MU_a}{MU_b} = \frac{P_a}{P_b} = \frac{MC_a}{MC_b},$$

where MC is the marginal cost.

These equations tell us that producers and consumers have adjusted their behavior to be consistent, given existing consumer preferences and techniques of production.

about relationships among sectors of the economy.

A detailed description of general equilibrium analysis is beyond the scope of this chapter, but the concept is important. An important point for the real estate appraiser to remember is that in equilibrium productive services, such as parcels of real estate, will be employed in their most productive use. If equilibrium does not exist, some resources will be employed in less productive uses. Eventually, someone will employ such resources in more productive uses. This is the basis of the appraisal principle that real estate should be assessed at its "highest and best use." In a dynamic, competitive economy there will be frequent changes in prices and in the way productive resources are employed and in the price or market value of goods and services, particularly of real estate. An appraiser must recognize when real estate would obtain a larger return in some use other than the one to which it is currently put.

Summary

This chapter has discussed the economic principles of value, marginal utility, price, supply and demand, and equilibrium. Appraisers who master these principles will have a good foundation for understanding appraisal models and principles. Chapter 4 discusses how economic principles and appraisal principles are alike and different. It discusses the relationships between economic principles and important concepts in appraisal such as market value and highest and best use. Chapter 4 also shows how supply and demand factors are incorporated into appraisal models for the cost, income, and sales comparison approaches.

Appraisal Theory: Mass Appraisal and Single-Property Appraisal

4

Appraisal Theory

Appraisal, the act of estimating the price at which a parcel of real estate would sell, is an application of economic theory. Many concepts used by appraisers are economic concepts, with some differences. The developers of appraisal theory were not always trained economists. Some reinvented economic concepts and gave them different names. Sometimes the necessity of making an appraisal in difficult circumstances forced appraisers to deal with practical problems that theoretical economists were able to ignore.

As a result, economic theory and appraisal theory, although parallel in many ways, are different. For example, the model of price determination developed by economists and explained in chapter 3 is a highly developed, internally consistent model that contributes to understanding how prices are determined, how markets work, and how the product of the economy is distributed. Terms are defined precisely and the model can be reduced to mathematical terms. This permits checks for internal consistency and determination of how changes in one quantity affect other quantities. However, the entire model is based on a set of definitions and assumptions that do not correspond to conditions as they exist in a given market. In contrast, appraisal theory is directed toward specific applications and is not as tightly reasoned as economic theory.

The Concept of Property

Property is a cultural concept of the relationship between people and things. In our culture, people can gain the right to possess, use, enjoy, and dispose of things. Governments authorize and protect those rights. Hence, property has a legal dimension. Property also has a physical dimension: the things we can gain rights over may be tangible or intangible. The economic dimension of property is its value: property is an element of wealth. Appraisers need to know both the legal and physical nature of the properties they appraise. Assessors need to follow the law governing the taxation of property.

Property Law The legal dimension of property is reflected in the principles embodied in treatises, statutes, and cases. This section presents an overview of some of the more important legal concepts concerning property rights. The definitions contained in the following section on the physical nature of property also are encompassed in property law.

Property rights can be divided and shared. This has led to the concept of a "bundle of rights." Each of the rights related to the ability to possess, use, enjoy, and dispose of a thing is visualized as a stick in the bundle of rights. Some of the rights can be acquired in the open market. Others are reserved to government. The six basic rights associated with the private ownership of property are the right to use, sell, rent or lease, enter or leave, give away, and refuse to do any of these. This collection of rights is known as *fee simple absolute*, a term that often is shortened to "fee simple" or "the fee." Real property rights reserved to government include police power and taxation. These are important in property tax administration and will be discussed further in a later section. Two other governmental rights, eminent domain (the power to take private property for public use) and escheat (which reverts property to the state when there are no heirs), have little direct effect on appraisal.

Property rights, whether fee simple or not, may be separated, as when air or mineral rights are owned separately from surface rights. Rights may be individual or divided among several owners in partnerships, joint tenancy, tenancy in common, time-sharing, condominiums, cooperatives, and so forth. A lease transfers certain rights to the lessee (tenant), including possession, but fee ownership remains with the lessor (landlord). The lessee has a leasehold estate; the lessor owns the leased fee interest.

Real and Personal Property Physically, property falls into two broad categories: real property and personal property. Real property is the rights, interests, and benefits connected with *real estate*. Real estate is the physical parcel of land, improvements to the land (such as clearing and grading), improvements attached to the land (such as paving and buildings), and appurtenances (such as easements that cross the parcel or give access to the parcel). Personal property is defined by exception: property that is not real is personal. The salient characteristic of personal property is its movability without damage either to itself or to the real estate to which it is attached. Hence personal property is known sometimes as *movables* and real property, as *immovables* (other synonyms for real and personal property are *realty* and *personalty*). Personal property falls into two broad categories: tangibles and intangibles.

The fact that personal property often is exempt from property taxation gives rise to questions about whether a given item is real property and is taxable or is personal property and is exempt. Statutes and cases provide some guidance, but not in every instance. Items that were movable and are now permanently attached to the real estate —sinks, bathtubs, and the like—are called fixtures and considered part of the real estate. However, attached items used in the conduct of business, such as barber chairs, bowling alleys, and so on, are called trade fixtures and treated as personal property. Industrial machinery and equipment, pipelines, and the like may be considered personal property, even when permanently attached.

Intangible personal property includes rights over tangible real and personal property, but not rights of use and possession. For example, a mortgage is the right to take possession of real estate if the borrower fails to fulfill a contract to pay principal and interest; a share of stock in a corporation represents certain rights over its real and personal property.

Effects of Property Rights on Value Both the physical and legal dimensions of a property must be specified in an appraisal and identified in the analysis of a sale. Otherwise, erroneous conclusions about value are likely. Private and governmental rights sometimes have profound effects on value.

The effect of the police power of governments on property values is particularly extensive. Police power is the right of governments to protect the health, safety, and welfare of the public by promulgating and enforcing zoning ordinances and fire, health, building, and environmental codes. Zoning, as a limit on the use of property, may prevent construction of certain improvements. The effect on property values can be substantial. Value estimates should be based on existing zoning requirements. Fire, health, and building codes require safe and sanitary structures. Unless there are substantial code variations among communities, or changes in code requirements have occurred, only minor adjustments should be needed for comparable properties. On occasion, however, both site and improvement values may be affected. Environmental protection requirements may have the same effect; the time and effort of compliance will in themselves create added costs.

Rent controls imposed by government limit the owner's control over use of a property, effectively restricting the appraiser from valuing the property at its highest and best use. The effects on value of the right of governments to tax property will be discussed later.

Property rights may be limited by private encumbrances that affect value and sale price. Such encumbrances include easements, condominium controls, deed or subdivision restrictions, and financial obligations (liens) such as tax, mortgage, and mechanic's liens. Court judgments against a property, including enforcement of liens, must be satisfied—by a foreclosure sale if necessary. The possibility of imminent foreclosure is likely to cause a reduction in property value.

Easements are the right to use property owned by another for a specific purpose, for example, placement of billboards, installation of utility transmission lines, or access to another property. Easements may increase value when they generate income (such as billboard space rent) or attract desired services. They may decrease value when they represent nuisances (unsightly utility wires) or prevent alternative profitable property uses. Appraisers should ascertain the effect of easements on the property being considered.

The common areas of an office or apartment condominium may require use restrictions. Common areas, such as corridors of a building, access roads, parking areas, elevators, swimming pool, and tennis courts, are owned by all individual owners through an association. Rules for use and the sharing of maintenance expenses are usually established by the association in accordance with law. When estimating the value of an office condominium, for example, an appraiser should consider not only the area owned but also the common areas in terms of amenities and their related expenses.

Deed restrictions may limit or prohibit certain property uses. Examples are restrictions that prohibit businesses on the property from being open on Sundays or selling alcoholic beverages, or covenants specifying that businesses on the property may not compete with certain enterprises. If a restriction is upheld in court, property may not be freely developed to its highest and best use, and value may be affected.

Subdivision restrictions are usually imposed before construction of improvements to ensure harmonious use of the lots within a subdivision. Examples are minimum house size requirements and specification of architectural styles. A restriction to prohibit business establishments, although intended to maintain the subdivision's integrity, may also prevent alternative profitable uses, for example, of lots on busy intersections that would be more valuable as commercial property. Thus restrictions may increase the value of some lots within a subdivision and decrease the value of others.

Restrictions may be set by grant, deed, or will. The use of property for a park, school, or other purpose will limit its value in the open market, yet may add to the value of surrounding property.

Lien position may affect value. Taxes are usually in the first lien position by law. Subsequent lien positions are often determined by the order of recordation. Placing a lien at a lower priority is termed subordination.

A mortgage is a pledge of property as collateral for a debt. Because most mortgages are recorded immediately after the closing, they are likely to be in the best lien position after taxes, although statutes sometimes give the mechanic's lien a more advantageous position. The mortgage loan with first claim on the property is called a first mortgage. The equity owner may borrow additional amounts with junior mortgages, also called second or third mortgages, depending on the priority of claim. Upon default and a foreclosure sale, the holder of the first mortgage is repaid in full before junior mortgages are honored.

Other factors affect value, for example, encroachments by neighboring properties, a license granted for specific activities on the property, or the nature of the rights to (and profits from) annual crops (emblements) growing on the land.

Appraisal of Partial Rights Appraisers usually value all rights that may legally be owned, that is, fee simple title with value not affected by encumbrances and the like. Most property tax statutes require the assessor to assign all value-contributing rights to the title owner of the land. Sometimes, however, the lessee's interests must be separated. A complete discussion is beyond the scope of this book, but examples of significant issues are given below.

Wherever oil, gas, coal, or other mineral industries are important, mineral rights are likely to be owned or leased separately from other property rights. If so, the appraiser should know the value of these rights and how the value of other rights in the same property is affected because they are not included. For example, appraisers in Oklahoma using the sales comparison approach to value residential properties with separately owned mineral rights should be sure to use similar properties as comparables.

Leasehold interests — the value to lessees of favorable leases — are of interest in the jurisdictions that permit assessment of rentals on exempt properties. Leasehold interests in exempt properties are known as possessory interests. For example, a university student center, exempt from ad valorem taxation because the owner is an educational institution, may house a drugstore, ice-cream parlor, and fast-food chain restaurant. The leasehold rights held by these profit-making businesses may be taxable, so the assessor may need to value them. Usually, the longer the lease, the greater the value. Examples of partial interests that affect income-producing properties are presented in chapter 11.

Situs and Legal Description The assessor should identify all property by situs and legal description. Assessment of property at its legal situs and in its proper taxing jurisdiction is essential for a legal assessment.

The situs of real estate is its physical location. Because personal property is by definition movable, the issue of tax situs (where the item should be taxed) often arises. Situs is usually defined as the place the property is permanently located. If this cannot be determined, personal property may be assessed at the domicile or headquarters of its owner. Estimating value may also be complicated by the existence of intangible rights having a situs elsewhere.

Real estate is identified by legal description. The three forms most common in the United States are lot and block, metes and bounds, and government (rectangular) survey. Monuments were used in earlier days. (See chapter 17.)

The Legal Definition of Market Value

Although the term *value* remains difficult to define, the term *market value* is well defined. The constitutions and statutes of states, provinces, and nations have precise, but different, definitions of market value. The assessor should refer to the definition of market value found in the statutes and court decisions of the state or province in which the jurisdiction is located.

Neither the United States Supreme Court nor the United States Circuit Court of Appeals has defined market value of real property in an ad valorem tax case. The Supreme Court, however, provided a definition of market value for personal property in an 1865 case involving ad valorem duties upon imports. In this case, the Supreme Court approved the trial judge's instructions to the jury, as follows:

The market value of goods is the price at which the owner of the goods, or the producer, holds them for sale; the price at which they are freely offered in the market to all the world; such prices as dealers in the goods are willing to receive, and purchasers are made to pay, when the goods are bought and sold in the ordinary course of trade. You will perceive, therefore, that the actual cost of the goods is not the standard. (Cliquot's Champagne, 70 U. S. 125 [1865]).

For a definition of market value as it relates to real property, we must borrow from the field of eminent domain cases. In a 1934 case, the United States Supreme Court said:

In respect of each item of property that value may be deemed to be the sum which, considering all the circumstances, could have been obtained for it; that is, the amount that in all probability would have been arrived at by fair negotiations between an owner willing to sell and a purchaser desiring to buy. In making that estimate there should be taken into account all considerations that fairly might be brought forward and reasonably be given substantial weight in such bargaining. The determination is to be made in the light of all facts affecting the market value that are shown by the evidence taken in connection with those of such general notoriety as not to require proof. Elements affecting value that depend upon events or combinations of occurrences which, while within the realm of possibility, are not fairly shown to be reasonably probable, should be excluded from consideration, for that would be to allow mere speculation and conjecture to become a guide for the ascertainment of value. (Olson v. United States, 292 U. S. 257 [1934]).

In an eminent domain case decided in 1878, the United States Supreme Court stated that market value does not depend on current use:

In determining the value of land appropriated for public purposes, the same considerations are to be regarded as in a sale of property between private parties. The inquiry in such cases must be what is the property worth in the market, viewed not merely with reference to the uses to which it is at the time applied, but with reference to the uses to which it is plainly adapted; that is to say, what it is worth from its availability for valuable uses. Property is not to be deemed worthless because the owner allows it to go to waste, or to be regarded as valueless because he is unable to put it to any use. Others may be able to use it. (Boom Co. v. Patterson, 98 U. S. 307 [1878]).

Two definitions of market value implied by these rulings may be restated as follows:

- *Personal property* Market value is the price that dealers in the goods are willing to receive and purchasers are willing to pay when goods are bought and sold in the ordinary course of trade.
- *Real property* Market value is the amount of money that probably would be arrived at through fair negotiations between a willing seller and a willing buyer, taking into consideration the uses to which the property may be put.

The following characteristics of market value should be noted: Market value

- is the most probable price, not the highest, lowest, or average price
- is expressed in terms of money
- implies a reasonable time for exposure to the market
- implies that both buyer and seller are informed of the uses to which the property may be put
- assumes an arm's-length transaction in the open market
- assumes a willing buyer and a willing seller, with no advantage being taken by either buyer or seller
- recognizes both the present use and the potential use of the property

These characteristics may be restated in a definition: Market value is the most probable price expressed in terms of money that a property would bring if exposed for sale in the open market in an arm's-length trans-

action between a willing seller and a willing buyer, both of whom are knowledgeable concerning all the uses to which the property is adapted and for which it is capable of being used.

This definition is much like the definition of market value that economists use when describing value in exchange in competitive markets (see chapter 3). Compare this definition with the one handed down in 1892 by the Supreme Court of Kansas:

The market value means the fair value of the property as between one who wants to purchase and one who wants to sell, not what could be obtained under peculiar circumstances when a greater than its fair price could be obtained, nor its speculative value; not a value obtained from the necessities of another; nor, on the other hand, is it to be limited to that price which the property would bring when forced off at auction under the hammer. It is what it would bring at a fair public sale, when one party wanted to sell and the other to buy. (Kansas City, W & NWR Co. v. Fisher, 49 Kans. 18 [1892]).

Highest and Best Use

The way in which property is used plays an essential role in its value. Chapter 3 describes the economic basis for this by demonstrating that the demand for resources depends on the pattern of demand for final consumer goods. There is a legal basis for this principle that incorporates many of the same economic notions. In 1894, the United States Supreme Court stated:

The value of property results from the use to which it is put and varies with the profitableness of that use, present and prospective, actual and anticipated. There is no pecuniary value outside of that which results from such use. (Cleveland, C.C. and St. Louis Railway Co. v. Backus, 154 U. S. 445 [1894]).

Almost all property is subject to competing uses. Rural land is subject to the competition between farming and grazing. Urban land is subject to many competing uses: a single parcel of land may be sought as the site for a store, gas station, apartment building, or office building. When one is estimating market value, it is necessary to determine which of the competing uses is the highest and best use.

One definition of highest and best use is that use which will generate the highest net return to the property over a period of time. The highest and best use must be a legal use. This means not only that the use cannot be criminal but also that it must be permitted under local administrative regulations, such as zoning. Assuming that zoning regulations are strictly enforced, the highest and best use may be limited. If it is easy to obtain a change or variance in zoning, uses not permitted by current regulations must be considered along with the probability that the zoning will be changed. The use also must not be prohibited by enforceable restrictions contained in the chain of title to the property.

The use must be a probable use and not an unlikely or speculative one. There must be a demand for the use either in the present or in the near future, as determined by the market.

With time, the highest and best use of property may change. Changes in the character of a neighborhood may create demands for different uses. The appraiser periodically reviews and revises conclusions as to highest and best use. The highest and best use may be the present use or an entirely different one. It may even be a combination of uses over a period of time. Imagine, for example, a site in a good downtown location on which stands a three-story store with a 75 percent vacancy factor. Assume that the site could be developed with a modern fifteen-story office building. However, because there is currently too much unrented office space on the market, the highest and best use of the property might be as a parking lot for the next five years. Once the excess office space is absorbed, highest and best use could be as an office building.

Properties in transition present a difficult appraisal problem. Not only must a future highest and best use be specified for the property, but an estimate must be made as to when the property will begin the new use. Occasionally, there will be an interim use before the future highest and best use. In order to estimate the value of these consecutive uses, the benefits must be identified, valued, and summed. The total value is the sum of the present worth of the income stream from the interim use for the period of that use, less the cost of erecting any additional interim improvements; the salvage value of the interim improvements, less eventual removal costs; and the income stream from the future use, less the cost of erecting the future improvements.

The highest and best use will be a complementary rather than a competitive use. For example, if there are gas stations on three of four corners, a fourth gas station will reduce the customers that are available to all four stations. However, suppose that on the fourth corner a fast-food restaurant were established. The restaurant would draw business from the gas stations' customers, and the gas stations would draw business from the restaurant's customers.

The highest and best use must be the most profitable for the entire property—land, buildings, and other improvements—because the market deals with the total property unit, and land and buildings usually are not sold separately. Also, when estimating highest and best use, the appraiser should not combine under common ownership parcels that are used independently for different purposes.

The highest and best use generates the highest net return over a reasonable period of time. A use that yields a very high immediate income, but one of short duration, may not be as valuable as a use that results in a lower, but more prolonged, income stream.

Approaches to Appraisal

Since about 1910, three approaches to estimating market value have been evident in the literature of appraisal: sales comparison, cost, and income. All have been refined through the years and variations developed for specific appraisal problems. Chapters 6 and 8–12 treat the three approaches in detail.

Sales Comparison Approach The sales comparison approach uses sales prices as evidence of the value of similar properties. The price at which a particular property sells is the price at which the supply and demand curves intersect at the time of sale. If competitive market conditions were approximated, and conditions have not changed greatly, a similar property would sell at approximately the same price.

Because no two real properties are ever exactly alike, systematic methods must be used to adjust the prices of sold properties, known as comparison properties, or comparables. The known prices are adjusted by adding or subtracting the amount which a given feature appears to add to, or subtract from, the price of the comparison property. If, for ex-

ample, a comparison house has a two-car garage, and the subject house has only a one-car garage, an appropriate sum would be subtracted from the price at which the comparison house sold. Adjustments may also be made for time and terms of sale. For example, if the comparison property was sold two years ago, and real estate prices in the community have been increasing, an inflation adjustment might be made to the price of the comparison house. If the adjusted prices turn out to be similar, the appraiser has good evidence as to the value of the subject property. The price of similar houses is one of the factors affecting the demand for a house. Buyers are unlikely to pay more than they would have to pay for a similar house. If the prices of similar houses rise, a seller knows that demand has risen.

Figure 1 shows a supply and demand curve for a particular type of house. The supply and demand curves intersect at point A. The price is P and the number of houses sold is Q. A rise in the price of other types of houses will cause an increase in demand as shown by demand curve d'. The intersection of the supply curve and the new demand curve (point B) will be the new equilibrium point. The price will now be P' and the number of this type of house sold will be Q'.

The sales comparison approach is most suitable when there are frequent sales of similar property. It is widely used in the appraisal of single-family residential property and vacant land, and sometimes in the appraisal of multifamily or commercial properties.

The Cost Approach The cost approach is sometimes called the summation, engineering, or brick and mortar approach. The cost approach is based on the idea that the value

Figure 1. Change in Demand for Houses

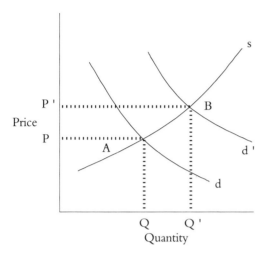

of an existing property is the value of the land plus the replacement cost of the improvements less depreciation (not accounting depreciation, based on the number of years used, but the loss of value caused by physical deterioration, functional obsolescence, or changes in the economy or neighborhood). The appraiser determines the replacement cost of a new property functionally equivalent to the subject property, not necessarily an exact replica. If, for example, the subject property is a large building with high ceilings and many windows placed to provide cross-ventilation in hot weather, it might be replaced with a low-ceilinged, air-conditioned building that has equal utility.

Sometimes the cost of the replacement building is determined stick by stick, that is, by an actual engineering calculation of the cost. More often, estimates are made using tables that show the per square foot values of constructing various types and styles of buildings. These tables may be prepared lo-

cally or purchased from firms that specialize in providing such information.

The cost approach is based on the principle of substitution. The potential owner of a real estate improvement has the option of purchasing an existing building or constructing a new one. If the existing building is new, construction may be a good substitute for purchase, and the price of the existing building would be almost identical to the cost of construction—with perhaps some allowance for the time needed for construction. If the building is older, depreciation measures the extent to which the older building is not a perfect substitute for a new one. The cost approach is easiest to apply when the building or other improvement is new and appropriately located so that adjustments for depreciation are small.

The Income Approach The income approach requires the appraiser to estimate the income from a property and capitalize the income into an estimate of current value. The approach recognizes that potential buyers demand property because they anticipate a future stream of income. Traditionally, appraisers have referred to this as the principle of anticipation.

The principle of substitution is also important in the income approach. Investors are interested in the size, certainty, and timing of the income flow, but usually they have little preference as to the source. Real estate investment can readily be substituted for other kinds of investments, and the demand for income-producing real property is strongly influenced by the return on alternative investments. A rise in interest rates or in the expected earnings in non-real-estate enterprises will reduce the demand for income-earning real estate.

The formula that relates income to value is

$$I = R \times V, \qquad (1)$$

where I is income, R is a capitalization rate, and V is value. This formula can be rewritten

$$V = \frac{I}{R}. \qquad (2)$$

A property expected to provide a perpetual income of $10,000 per year when the rate of return on investments of similar safety is 10 percent (0.10) will have a value of $10,000/.10, or $100,000. An offer to sell the property for less than $100,000 may result in many buyers offering to buy it; a higher price may lead investors to prefer another investment.

The appraiser estimates the income stream that would be produced in the highest and best use under typical management. The property, not current management, is being valued; therefore, it is proper to assume that the potential investors would use the property for its most profitable legal use, and the buyer would employ typical rather than extraordinary management.

To apply the income approach, appraisers estimate a capitalization rate. The appraiser estimates the rate by collecting information from the market about the rate investors are receiving on investments of similar risk. Investors buying properties with uncertain income prospects demand rates of return higher than the return available from risk-free investments such as government bonds. Estimating a rate is sometimes done directly by computing the rate of return received by investors in similar properties.

The income approach is most suitable for types of properties frequently purchased and held for the purpose of producing income, such as apartments, commercial buildings, and office buildings. It could be applied to single-family residential properties in communities with a large rental market for such properties, but expensive single-family residences are seldom rented, and factors such as pride of ownership, personal preferences, and income tax considerations affect the residential housing market in ways that make it difficult to apply the income approach even when rental data are available. It is also difficult to apply to properties such as factory buildings that are integrated into complex business operations and seldom leased.

Appraisal Models

Appraisal models are systematic ways of thinking. They are useful because they help an appraiser systematically state a problem and identify the data needed to solve it. Models may be simple verbal or algebraic statements, or they may be elaborate systems of mathematical equations that can be used to handle quantities of data that could not be analyzed in another way. The models presented in this chapter are simple general models, but such models can be elaborated as the need, availability of data, and skills of the user change. (Chapters 14 and 15 address specification and calibration of mass appraisal models in more detail.)

Mathematical models that once would not have been feasible are now used on computers that process large amounts of data. This development is especially important in mass appraisal, because many properties are appraised, and large quantities of data analyzed.

Most of the models used in real estate appraisal are based on one of the three approaches to value. The models do not require that complete supply and demand curves be plotted, but all have as their objective the estimation of the point at which the supply and demand curves cross. Consequently, each model must include terms that represent both the supply and demand side of the market.

Modeling the Sales Comparison Approach In the sales comparison approach, sales prices of comparison properties are adjusted to reflect differences between them and the subject property.

Expressed algebraically, such a model might appear as follows:

$$AP = S + BA + BeA + GA \\ + IA + CA + NA, \qquad (3)$$

where AP is the adjusted price of a comparison property, S is the sale price of the comparison property, BA is the adjustment for differences in number of baths, BeA is an adjustment for differences in number of bedrooms, GA is an adjustment for difference in garage, IA is an adjustment for inflation since date of sale, CA is an adjustment for difference in condition, and NA is an adjustment for differences in neighborhood.

These adjustments could add or subtract dollars and be expressed as lump sums or percentages. For example, the inflation adjustment might be further defined as:

$$IA = ti(S), \qquad (4)$$

where t is the time since sale, in months, and i is the annual rate of inflation in local real estate prices.

The above equations do not constitute a complete model but merely adjust the sale price for a single comparison property. A complete model would include systematic methods of obtaining all adjustments, such

as the equation for calculating the inflation adjustment. Another equation would be needed to compute a single value from the adjusted prices of several comparison properties.

Modeling the Cost Approach A simple cost model is:

$$V = LV + BV, \qquad (5)$$

where V is value, LV is total land value, and BV is total cost of constructing a building.

The terms in this equation can be defined as:

$$LV = SL \times L, \qquad (6)$$

and

$$BV = SB \times M, \qquad (7)$$

where SL is square feet of land, SB is square feet of building area, L is typical land value per square foot, and M is the typical building cost per square foot shown in a cost manual.

By substitution, the model would become

$$V = (SL \times L) + (SB \times M). \qquad (8)$$

Any number of enhancements can be made to the model as conditions and available data permit. For example, M could be multiplied by an inflation adjustment to allow for construction cost increases after publication date of the cost manual, or an adjustment could be made to L to reflect an irregular shape or a favorable view.

Modeling the Income Approach Alfred Marshall pointed out that value is the present worth of future income. From this insight, two categories of valuation models that represent different ways to find the present value of an income stream developed: yield capitalization models and direct capitalization models.

Yield models are based on the discounted cash flow formula,

$$V = \frac{I_1}{1 + R} + \frac{I_2}{(1 + R)^2}$$

$$+ \frac{I_3}{(1 + R)^3} + \ldots + \frac{I_n}{(1 + R)^n}, \quad (9)$$

where V is the present value, I is the income or cash flow, R is the interest or discount rate, and n is the number of periods.

To apply this model, an estimate of the income to be received in each period is necessary. In effect, this requires that the supply and demand for the property in each future period be estimated. The income of the final period should include the resale value of the property, which may be either more or less than current value. If it is projected that the property will be held over its entire remaining economic life, only salvage value will exist, which could be negative if there is expected to be a net cost of disposing of the property.

The discounted cash flow formula (equation 9) is versatile and widely used in investment analysis. Allowance can be made for the varying tax situations and financial alternatives available to potential buyers. It is also possible to use different discount rates and a variety of assumptions about inflation and other factors that might increase the flow of income, even as the property is physically depreciating.

Direct models are simpler to apply. Typically, only first-year income is used in a direct model, and there is no need to estimate reversion value (the sum that might be realized by a sale at the end of the ownership period). A rate is developed, from the sales of like properties, that contains a provision for both return *on* capital and return *of* capital (recapture).

Relation of Appraisal Models to Economic Models   None of the models commonly used by appraisers represents complete supply and demand schedules, but all require market data. The sales comparison approach begins with actual sales prices, that is, with the prices at which supply and demand curves have intersected. Sales that took place in an open, competitive market and were arm's-length sales involving knowledgeable buyers and sellers are very good evidence of the price at which a similar property would sell. Adjusting the sales prices of comparison properties is intended to allow for differences between properties or markets. The resulting adjusted sales prices provide evidence of the price at which the subject property would sell.

Cost models emphasize the *supply side* of the market. They reveal the prices at which new buildings with certain specifications would be supplied. The usefulness of cost data depends on assumptions or data about *demand*. If the subject property is new, and similar property is being constructed and sold, as in a new subdivision, it can safely be assumed that there is a demand for the property at a price equal to cost. The replacement cost of older property must be adjusted for physical deterioration and functional and economic obsolescence. Adjustments for obsolescence are adjustments for demand in the market because functional and economic obsolescence reflect changes that have occurred in the market for a good.

Income models focus on the *demand side* of the economic equation. Investors' demand for property depends on the income stream and the associated rate of return on investment. This does not mean that supply plays no role. In addition to estimating future income, appraisers estimate current discount rates, which means that they consider supply as well.

Definitions for Real Property Appraisers

Economists and appraisers deal with similar subject matter, but differences in terminology sometimes hinder communication. The following terms are among the important ones used in one or both professions:

Supply Supply is a schedule showing the amount of a good or productive service that would be offered for sale at various prices during a given period. A supply schedule expressed graphically is a supply curve. Supply curves usually slope upward, indicating that more will be supplied at higher prices.

Demand Demand is a schedule showing the amount of a good or productive service that would be purchased at various prices during a given period. A demand schedule expressed graphically is a demand curve. Demand curves usually slope downward, indicating that less will be purchased at higher prices.

Market Price Market price is determined by the intersection of supply and demand curves. It is the price a particular buyer and seller agree to in a particular transaction. Because few real estate transactions occur in a perfect market, price may not be equal to "normal price" or market value.

Competition Competition is basic to the economist's analysis of price. When the amount of property of a certain type offered for sale is large in relation to demand, competition will reduce prices; competition will force prices up when the opposite situation prevails. Economists carefully define various degrees of competition. Legal definitions of value often include less rigorous descriptions of market conditions.

Market Value The purpose of most appraisals is to determine market value. Appraisals for property tax purposes must conform to the definitions in statutes, which usually define value as the dollar, or cash, price that would result if the property were sold in a competitive market with neither buyer nor seller being under undue pressure. Sometimes the statute spells out one or more aspects of a competitive market, such as well-informed buyers and sellers and exposure of the property for sale for a sufficient period. Market value is not the same as price but, if the market is reasonably competitive, prices can be strong evidence of market value.

Highest and Best Use Demand for a property depends on potential utility rather than utility in current use. In a well-functioning market, buyers and sellers are aware of the various uses to which a property could be put, and market value is based on its most profitable legal use. In equilibrium, all property will be in its highest and best use.

Use Value Use value is the value of a property for a specific purpose. In a number of jurisdictions, certain types of property, such as agricultural land, are assessed at value in a specific use, rather than at value in highest and best use.

Balance   Markets have a tendency to move toward equilibrium. Balance is a term used by appraisers to indicate that there is a proper mix of types and uses of property. When a real estate market is in balance, land values are maximized.

Substitution   A property's value tends to be set by the cost of acquiring an equally desirable substitute. This principle applies to all three approaches to value. In the cost approach, the cost of building a similar property will serve as a ceiling on the price of an existing property. The sales comparison approach assumes that the market price is set by the price of available substitutes. Rents and interest rates used in the income approach are strongly affected by the availability of other rental space and alternative investments. The economic concept *opportunity cost* is a closely related idea.

Contribution   Appraisers apply the principle of contribution to the parts of a property to determine the contribution of each part to the total value. Total value may not equal total cost of the individual parts. For example, adding a third bathroom to a small house will probably increase value less than the cost of the improvement. This principle is related to the economic concept of marginal productivity.

Anticipation   Market value is the present worth of all future benefits expected by market participants. The principle of anticipation is the basis of the income approach to value.

Surplus Productivity   Surplus productivity is income remaining after the costs of labor, capital, and management have been paid. It exists in the short run when the owner of a fixed productive service benefits from changed conditions. Because the supply of land is fixed, the owners of land may be the beneficiary of surplus productivity even in the long run. The economic concepts of quasi rents and land rents are closely related to surplus productivity.

Variable Proportions   The law of variable proportions, often called the law of decreasing returns or the law of proportionality, is an economic principle stating: When the quantity of one productive service is increased by equal increments, the quantities of other productive services remaining fixed, the resulting increment of product will decrease after a certain point. (See *contribution*). This principle explains, for example, why the value per square foot of residential lots usually decreases with size.

Mass Appraisal and Single-Property Appraisal

Introduction

Assessors need skills in both mass appraisal and single-property appraisal, skills in mass appraisal to produce the initial values in a reappraisal and in single-property appraisal to defend assessed values within the courts and to appraise special-purpose properties not easily valued by mass appraisal. Simply stated, single-property appraisal is the valuation of a particular property as of a given date; mass appraisal is the valuation of many properties as of a given date, using standard procedures and statistical testing. Both require market research. The principal differences are in scale and quality control.

The scale of mass appraisal often requires that many people work on the process. This requires synchronization of both tasks and appraisal judgments. In the single-property approach, only one person need perform all research tasks and make all appraisal judgments. Also, mass appraisal requires standardized procedures across many properties. Thus, valuation models developed for mass appraisal purposes must represent supply and demand patterns for groups of properties rather than a single property.

Quality is measured differently in mass and single-property appraisal. In mass appraisal, statistical methods are used to measure deviations of all sales in the population data base from their mass-appraised values. If most mass-appraised values for properties with sales fall within a predetermined average deviation from actual sales prices, work quality is considered good. The focus is not on the individual property. In single-property appraisal, quality can usually be judged by a comparison with comparable sales. Both mass and single-property appraisal can be judged by their adherence to professional standards.

Both mass and single-property appraisal are exercises in applied economic analysis. They represent logical, systematic methods for collecting, analyzing, and processing data to produce intelligent, well-reasoned value estimates. Figure 2 identifies five major steps common to mass and single-property appraisal. The five steps vary somewhat due to the differences in scale.

Definition of the Appraisal Problem

Four actions define the appraisal problem: identifying the property or properties to be appraised, determining the rights involved, defining the purpose and function of the appraisal, and specifying the date of appraisal.

Properties to Be Appraised The appraiser identifies the property or properties

Figure 2. The Appraisal Process

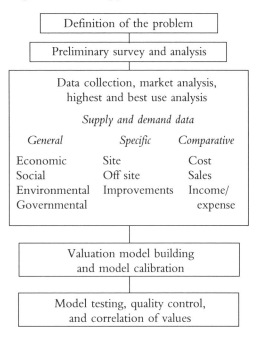

to be appraised. A property may be identified by street address, assessor's parcel identifier, or legal description. A good ownership mapping system is the foundation of a good property identification system. The mapping system may use simple drafting or sophisticated computerization.

The product of a mapping system is the identification and depiction of individual parcels and neighborhoods. A unique identifier (usually a number) may be assigned to each parcel and neighborhood to help locate each parcel on the map. When the mapping system is complex, it is common practice to use part of the number to identify each map and where to find it. Use of the street address of the property and its legal description make on-site inspection easier. The legal description is also used as a secondary identifier to keep the assessor's ownership records up-to-date.

Property Rights Involved   All rights that may legally be owned, that is, fee simple title, are usually appraised. Most property tax statutes require the assessor to assign all value-contributing rights to the title owner of the land. Sometimes, however, the assessor may have to identify and appraise partial ownership rights, such as leasehold interests or air, water, and mineral rights.

Purpose and Function of the Appraisal   The purpose of all appraisals is to estimate value, but the type of value sought must first be established. The assessor is usually most concerned with market value (value in exchange), although value in use may be estimated as well. (Other appraisal specialists use other types of value, such as insurance value, mortgage value, and condemnation value.) The function of the appraisal is the use to which it is put. The assessor usually appraises properties to establish a basis for property taxation.

Date of Appraisal   The estimate of value, strictly construed, is effective only on the date of the appraisal. This date is specified in the property tax laws of each jurisdiction and may also be referred to as the "assessment date" or the "lien date." As indicated by the economic principle of change (chapter 3), conditions, trends, and other factors that affect value may shift the supply and demand factors (sometimes substantially), even over a short time.

Data Collection, Market Analysis, and Highest and Best Use Analysis

Overview   The definition of the appraisal problem should lead to an inventory of the data to be collected and allocation of time and resources to accomplish the assignment.

Both single-property and mass appraisal problems require the gathering of information. The nature of the property or properties will determine the extent and type of data collection. At the same time, the dominant approach to value may present itself, usually as a result of the nature of the property and the available data. Assessors should prudently budget time and resources.

Developing correct appraisal models for both mass and single-property appraisal depends on collecting and analyzing market data, making a judgment as to highest and best use, and studying the supply and demand factors operating in the market for the identified highest and best use.

Highest and best use analysis determines what use will generate the highest present value to the property at the time of the appraisal. As outlined in chapter 3, the idea of highest and best use is based on the economic concept of general equilibrium: in the long run, economic resources will be allocated such that consumer preferences will be perfectly satisfied; producers of goods and services will maximize profits; and the raw materials of land, labor, and capital will be put to their most productive and profitable use.

To make this kind of broad economic analysis and develop appraisal models for the identified best use, data are collected and analyzed that represent the supply and demand for probable land uses in the market for the subject property. Historically, this kind of supply and demand data has been conceptualized as falling into three categories: general, site-specific, and comparative.

General data include social, governmental, economic, and environmental information needed to understand the general market. Site-specific data include information on the immediate land site, proximate off-site features, and all site improvements. Comparative data include information on cost, sales, income, and expenses.

For highest and best use analysis, the general data should be analyzed from a regional or city perspective to gain a broad understanding of the economic base, and from a neighborhood perspective to grasp how broad forces affect the subject property. A site analysis that looks at the land as if vacant, as well as improved, should be undertaken before highest and best use can be determined.

Once highest and best use is identified, the appraiser studies the market for the specific use and also identifies the important supply and demand variables to be included in value models that replicate the workings of that market. The appraiser must decide how the relevant supply and demand factors relate within the model. These are model building, or specification, tasks. Once a model is specified, the appraiser estimates how each factor included in the model affects value (model calibration).

Market Analysis Skills For highest and best use analysis, model building, and model calibration the appraiser needs to develop conceptual and statistical skills in market analysis. Certain conceptual skills enable appraisers to understand how social, economic, environmental, governmental, and site conditions relate to the determinants of supply and demand, and how changes in these determinants affect the market prices of land

and improvements. In particular, appraisers must understand the supply and demand factors that affect market value and the effect of shifts in these factors on price. Changes in the demand-side determinants of income, housing preferences, size of market, price of substitutes, and future expectations of price change will shift the demand schedule to the right or left, resulting in a new equilibrium price. Figure 3 shows this.

Figure 3. Supply and Demand for Housing

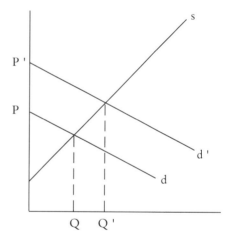

Suppose income, one of the determinants of demand, increased in a region. This trend is represented in the graph by a shift to the right in the demand curve for housing. This shift from d to d′ would cause a housing price increase from P to P′ and also increase the number of units sold. A decrease in income would have the reverse effect.

Likewise, if factors affecting the supply determinants of land, labor, and capital change, the supply curve will shift, causing a change in equilibrium prices. For example, if construction costs increase, supply will decrease at every price. This is represented by a shift of the supply curve to the left, from s to s' (figure 4). Prices will rise from P to P', and the quantity of housing units sold will decrease from Q to Q'.

Figure 4. Supply and Demand Curve for Land, Labor, and Capital

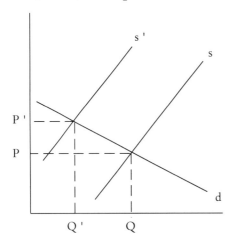

The principle of substitution can also be illustrated by this supply and demand format (figure 5). For example, an increase in the price of substitute housing from P to P' because of a shift in demand for the substitute will cause the demand for housing for the subject property to shift to the right, increasing price from P to P'. The shift in demand occurs because the price of substitutes is one of the demand factors in the demand curve for the subject property.

Likewise, an expected change in prices of housing will affect prices now (figure 6). Expected price increases will cause the demand for housing now to shift to the right from d to d', causing prices to rise from P to P'. This illustrates the principle of anticipation.

Some factors are more difficult to analyze because they affect the determinants of both supply and demand. For example, an increase in interest rates will affect affordability on the demand side (the size of the market) and on the supply side (the availability of capital for construction purposes), so demand and sup-

Figure 5. Supply and Demand Curves Illustrating Substitution

Substitute

Subject

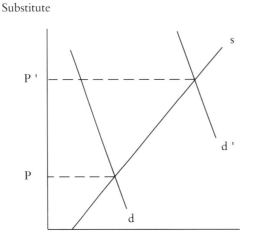

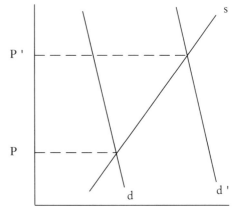

ply will decrease at every price. Consequently, these effects can be expressed by a simultaneous shift of the supply and demand curves to the left (figure 7).

The effects of these two simultaneous shifts in supply and demand on equilibrium prices may be difficult to predict. The shift in the demand curve alone would tend to decrease prices; the shift in the supply curve alone would tend to increase prices. The combined effects partially offset each other, leaving equilibrium prices in the above example slightly increased from P to P′.

Finally, the principles of change and balance are illustrated by all of the above examples. Shifts in supply and demand curves in response to changes in factors that affect their determinants illustrate the principle of change in the market place. A new equilibrium price after a supply or demand curve has shifted illustrates the principle of balance working in the marketplace.

Table 1 summarizes how changes in social, economic, environmental, and governmental factors affect supply and demand for owner-occupied housing. The table assumes that a change in an individual factor occurs while other factors remain constant. When a change in a factor affects both the supply and demand side of the market the effect on price tends to be offset. Likewise, when more than one factor changes at the same time, the effects on prices may reinforce or offset each other. Data analysis techniques, like multiple regression analysis, useful for measuring the direction and responsiveness of price changes to factor changes of this kind can provide the appraiser with estimates of the effects on prices when many factors change simultaneously.

Appraisers also use statistical skills to analyze the direction of trends in social, economic, governmental, and environmental data, the relationships between supply and

Figure 6. Supply and Demand Curve Illustrating Principle of Anticipation

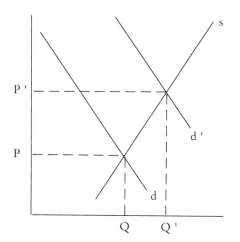

Figure 7. Supply and Demand Curves Illustrating Effects of Increased Interest Rates

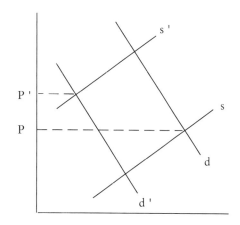

Table 1.   Effects of Changes in Economic, Social, Governmental, and Environmental Factors on Determinants of Supply and Demand for Owner-Occupied Housing

	Supply side	Shift to	Effect on price	Demand side	Shift to	Effect on price
Economic factors						
Income Trends				x		
increases					Right	Increase
decreases					Left	Decrease
Interest Rates	x			x		
increases		Left	Increase		Left	Decrease
decreases		Right	Decrease		Right	Increase
Lending Policies and Availability						
of Lending Funds	x			x		
restrictive		Left	Increase		Left	Decrease
liberal		Right	Increase		Right	Increase
Construction Costs	x					
increases		Left	Increase			
decreases		Right	Decrease			
Availability of Vacant Land	x					
increases		Right	Decrease			
decreases		Left	Increase			
Rental Rates				x		
increases					Right	Increase
decreases					Left	Decrease
Housing Prices				x		
increases					Right	Increase
decreases					Left	Decrease
Social factors						
Population Trends				x		
increases					Right	Increase
decreases					Left	Decrease
Family Size				x		
increases					Right	Increase
decreases					Left	Decrease
Education Trends				x		
more education					Right	Increase
less education					Left	Decrease
Crime Rates				x		
increases					Left	Decrease
decreases					Right	Increase

Table 1. (cont.)

	Supply side	Shift to	Effect on price	Demand side	Shift to	Effect on price
Age Distribution				x		
trend to younger					Right	Increase
trend to older					Left	Decrease
Governmental factors						
Zoning	x			x		
restrictive		Left	Increase		Left	Decrease
liberal		Right	Decrease		Right	Increase
Building Codes	x					
restrictive		Left	Increase			
liberal		Right	Decrease			
Municipal Services				x		
more					Right	Increase
less					Left	Decrease
Community Effective Tax Rate				x		
higher than average					Left	Decrease
lower than average					Right	Increase
Environmental factors						
Topography				x		
poor					Left	Decrease
good					Right	Increase
Lot Shape				x		
standard					Right	Increase
irregular					Left	Decrease
Soil Conditions	x			x		
standard		Right	Decrease		Right	Increase
poor		Left	Increase		Left	Decrease
Access to:						
Parks				x	Right	Increase
Stores				x	Right	Increase
Schools				x	Right	Increase
Churches				x	Right	Increase
Employment				x	Right	Increase
Public transportation				x	Right	Increase
Service establishments				x	Right	Increase

demand factors, and their relationship to value. A number of statistical and data analysis tools are helpful: one-way data profiles, two-way analysis, three-way analysis, correlation analysis, and multivariate analysis.

One-Way Analysis　The simplest data analysis arrays a sequence of data and then computes associated statistics like the mean, median, minimum, maximum, range, and coefficient of dispersion. (See chapters 14 and 20 for a review and examples of this kind of analysis.) Arrays are useful for understanding small data sets. One-way analysis is particularly useful for understanding average values and dispersions of quantitative data such as square footage, effective age, and sales prices. Qualitative data such as grade and condition should be analyzed using frequency distributions, histograms, and polygons (see chapter 20). These tools are useful in summarizing measures of central tendency and dispersion by strata, which is how qualitative data are typically listed.

Two-Way Analysis　One-way analysis does not provide information about relationships between variables. Appraisal data must be analyzed along multiple dimensions to analyze trends as part of highest and best use analysis and to identify supply and demand factors that should be included in appraisal models. The simplest two-way analysis arrays data for one factor in an order implied by data for another factor. For example, trends in regional income or population can be examined by ordering historical data for these two factors by time. Table 2 shows an analysis of population trends.

Scatter diagrams display the relationship between two qualitative variables. Figure 8 shows a scatter diagram of the data listed in

Table 2.　Trends in Population over Time

Year	Population	Annual change (in percent)
1900	181,704	5.25
1910	277,094	5.25
1920	330,948	1.94
1930	385,019	1.63
1940	445,206	1.56
1950	612,128	3.75
1960	929,383	5.18
1965	1,082,515	3.3
1970	1,239,545	2.9
1975	1,412,800	2.8
1980	1,620,902	2.95
1985	1,815,050	2.4
1990	2,028,900	2.36
2000	2,340,800	1.54
2010	2,629,900	1.24

table 2. The factor being studied (for example, population) is usually located on the vertical axis of the graph, and the related factor (for example, time), on the horizontal axis.

Relationships between two qualitative variables can be evaluated using *cross-tabulations*. The relationship between a quantitative and a qualitative factor can be analyzed with a *breakdown analysis*, which shows statistics for the quantitative variable by levels of the qualitative variable. Table 3, for example, shows the average sale price in a jurisdiction by neighborhood.

Three-Way Analysis　Graphic and statistical techniques for examining the relationships among three variables are also available, for example, cross-tabulation software that allows the comparison of two variables to the mean of a third variable. Table 4 shows mean sale price by neighborhood and neighborhood grade. Two-dimensional graphic pro-

Figure 8. Scatter Diagram of Population by Time

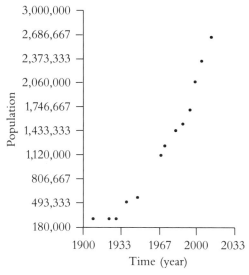

grams that allow the data points to be represented by a color or geometric shape can depict three and four dimensions (figure 9). Software is also available that can produce three-dimensional graphs directly (figure 10). Figure 9 shows the distribution of sales ratios across a jurisdiction. Each shape represents a property type, the size of the shape represents the value range for the sales ratios, and the x and y coordinates represent location. Figure 10 shows the distribution of sales prices across a jurisdiction. The x dimension plots the x location coordinate, the y dimension plots the y location coordinate, and the z coordinate plots the sales prices.

Correlation Analysis The strength of linear relationships between two variables can be measured by the correlation coefficient r. This coefficient varies from -1.0 to $+1.0$. Two variables that have a perfect linear relationship will have an r of $+1$ or -1, depending on the direction of the relationship. Variables that have no linear relationship will have an r of 0.

Most statistical software will produce a correlation matrix, which shows the correlation coefficients between all variables in a data set. Table 5 shows the correlation between sale price and land and building area. In this table, building and land area are both strongly related to sale price; the other correlations are moderate.

Multivariate Analysis Data analysis using data profiles and graphic techniques is limited to analyzing three or four dimensions or variables at one time. The development of mass appraisal models requires multivariate statistical tools, such as multiple regression analysis and feedback (see chapter 15). These techniques help identify supply and demand factors that are not important determinants of value in a market and help measure the effect on value of changes in any of the important determinants.

Table 3. Breakdown Analysis of Average Sale Price by Neighborhood

Neighborhood number	Row weighted mean sale price
1	29,507.14
2	0.00
3	36,198.28
4	38,500.00
5	49,903.57
6	40,116.67
7	91,200.00
8	51,480.08
9	61,722.23
10	65,447.06
11	80,508.34

**Figure 9.   Three-Dimensional Graph Showing Distribution of Sales Ratios
by Location and Property Type**

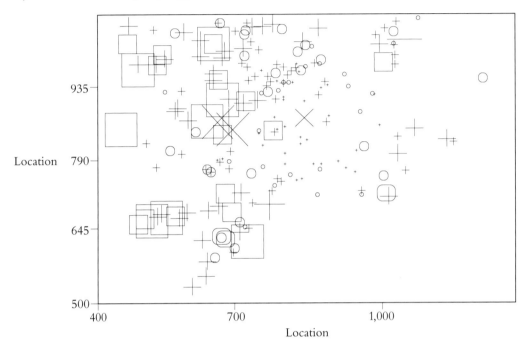

**Table 4.   Three-Way Analysis of Neighborhood Grade, Number,
and Mean Sale Price**

| Neighborhood number | Neighborhood grade | | | Weighted mean sale price |
	Improving	Static	Declining	
1	$ 0.00	$28,600.00	$22,250.00	$29,507.14
2	0.00	0.00	0.00	0.00
3	38,812.50	35,780.00	0.00	36,198.28
4	0.00	38,500.00	0.00	38,500.00
5	61,600.00	45,225.00	0.00	49,903.57
6	46,500.00	36,925.00	0.00	40,116.67
7	91,200.00	0.00	0.00	91,200.00
8	55,782.47	42,337.50	0.00	51,480.08
9	76,500.00	54,333.33	0.00	61,722,23
10	92,520.00	54,166.67	0.00	65,447.06
11	99,350.00	76,740.00	0.00	80,508.34

Figure 10. Three-Dimensional Graph Showing Distribution of Sale Price by Location

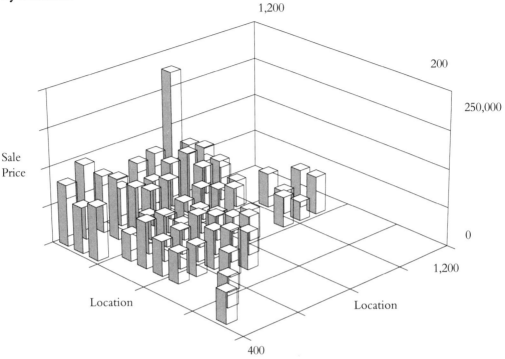

Table 5. Correlations between Sale Price, Building Size, and Lot Size

Variable	Sale price	Total SF*	Total lot size
Sale price	1.000	0.713	0.253
Total SF*		1.000	0.143
Total lot size			1.000

*Total finished square feet

Levels of Market Analysis Conceptual and statistical skills are used to analyze the economic base of a region by studying regional and neighborhood economic, social, governmental, and environmental forces. This analysis is followed by a complete site and improvement analysis.

City and Regional Analysis Data on regional *economic forces* affecting property values should be collected and monitored over several years. Economic trends operate through both the demand and supply sides of the market. For residential properties, macroeconomic factors affecting demand include employment and income patterns, general trends in real property prices and rents, ownership-tenant ratios, interest rate trends, and types and sources of mortgage financing. Factors affecting supply include the availability of vacant land, construction trends and costs, and interest rates.

Factors that relate to commercial property include the commercial/residential mix in the region as well as the direction of residential growth and distances from competing commercial sites. Factors that relate to industrial properties include wage rates, utility costs, and transportation costs, as well as industrial uses in the region, which should be comprehensively inventoried.

Social forces work primarily through the principle of change on the demand side of the market. Regional demographic trends in population growth, migration, rates of family formation, and population age distribution will be major determinants of land use.

Governmental forces also affect land use. Appraisers collect data on the level of public services; the extent of local zoning, building, and health codes; national, state, and local fiscal policies; and special legislation that might limit ownership rights, such as rent control or restrictions on condominiums. Any of these factors can affect both the supply and demand sides of the market.

Environmental forces are important in consumer preference formation and are principally considered demand-side characteristics. They relate to site characteristics such as topography, shape of lot, and type of improvement, as well as the broader regional location factors such as access to parks, stores, schools, churches, employment, cultural facilities, public transportation, service establishments, and so on.

In single-property appraisal, the information on these regional forces is incorporated into a written analysis that supports highest and best use analysis. Mass appraisal, in addition to using the data to determine highest and best use of groups of properties, quantifies the effects of regional forces as a set of adjustments and includes them as factors in the appraisal model.

Neighborhood Analysis   Social, environmental, economic, and governmental forces directly affect the subject property within a neighborhood. In single-property appraisal, neighborhood analysis should begin with the definition of a neighborhood and proceed to analyze and discuss the relevant forces influencing the subject property at this level. The neighborhood boundary should be described in detail and its historical significance explained.

A neighborhood has direct and immediate effects on value. A neighborhood is defined by natural, man-made, or political boundaries and is established by a commonality based on land uses, types and age of buildings or population, the desire for homogeneity, or similar factors.

Each neighborhood may be characterized as being in a stage of growth, stability, or decline. The growth period is a time of development and construction. In the period of stability, or equilibrium, the forces of supply and demand are about equal. The period of decline reflects diminishing demand or desirability. During decline, general property use may change. Declining neighborhoods may become economically desirable again and experience renewal, reorganization, rebuilding, or restoration, marked by modernization and increasing demand.

The appraiser must analyze whether a particular neighborhood is in a period of growth, stability, or decline and predict changes that will affect future use and value.

Neighborhood information also becomes part of a written report supporting highest and best use analysis in single-property appraisal. In mass appraisal applications, the information can be useful for comparing or combining neighborhoods or for developing neighborhood ratings, which are introduced as adjustments in mass appraisal models.

Site Analysis Site description and analysis provide a description of the subject property and an analysis of factors that affect the market value of the site. Site analysis also provides a basis for allocating values to land and improvements, for analyzing comparable sales to determine the highest and best use of the site, and for estimating locational obsolescence.

"Land" and "site" have different meanings. Land is undeveloped property. A site is land that has been improved to the extent that it is ready to be used for some purpose. The improvements may be either off-site, for example, roads, utilities, and access; or on-site, for example, buildings, driveways, and landscaping. Appraisals of improved property, by definition, involve the analysis and valuation of a site.

A site analysis is a study of the site description, in conjunction with the city and neighborhood analysis, from the perspective of utility, marketability, and, ultimately, market value. Comparisons are made with competing sites to build a foundation for the site valuation portion of the cost approach. All factors that create or destroy value should be considered.

Site analysis, site valuation, city and neighborhood analyses, highest and best use analysis, and estimation of locational obsolescence in the subject property are all related.

A typical site description may include
- dimensions, shape, area of site
- topography

- soil and subsoil conditions
- drainage
- utilities and services, including costs and comparisons of those costs with competing properties
- access
- identity
- off-site improvements such as streets, curbs, sidewalks
- on-site improvements such as landscaping, driveway, patio walks, septic system
- view
- proximity of hazards or nuisances
- zoning (a conforming use?), restrictions, easements, covenants, encroachments, and so forth
- units of comparison and market competition
- conformity or nonconformity with competing properties
- location and setting
- other locational factors that would affect market value

After the site is described, items in the description are related to one another and to their influence on supply and demand and, therefore, value. The site characteristics of the subject are compared to those of competing properties. The subject property is evaluated against neighborhood standards. Items that are significantly superior or inferior to those in competing properties are noted and considered in the site valuation.

Improvement Analysis Description of the subject building and other improvements provides a basis for analysis of comparable sales and rents; for the development of capitalization rates or multipliers; for highest and best use analysis of the site as improved;

and for estimation of reproduction or replacement cost new and physical and functional depreciation. The analysis should show how the factors relate to the utility and marketability of the subject property, and, ultimately, its market value. The improvement analysis and the neighborhood analysis bear on similar questions, for example, whether the improvements represent highest and best use and conform to the neighborhood.

Depending on the type of property, the description of improvements may include

- dimensions and area of total building and rooms or sections within the building
- room count
- quality and type of construction
- style, design, layout
- year of original construction, and years of remodelings or additions
- exterior construction and foundation
- roof
- interior (floors, walls, trim, ceilings, decorating)
- doors, windows, skylights, openings
- all mechanical systems (plumbing, electrical, heating and cooling) — condition and utility
- closets, cabinets, storage
- built-in equipment
- garages, decks, porches, or other structures
- siting of improvements on subject lot
- separation of long-life and short-life items (age, actual and effective, remaining economic life, condition)
- functional utility or disutility

The improvement analysis describes relationships among items and compares them to those in competing properties and to neighborhood standards. Items that will be treated as functional obsolescence in the cost approach need thorough analysis. The condition of

building components is particularly important because it provides the basis for estimates of effective age and remaining economic life.

Highest and Best Use Analysis   Highest and best use analysis is the culmination of regional and city, neighborhood, and site analysis. The purpose of all three is to help the appraiser understand the factors affecting property values in the market being analyzed and the most probable use of the site in long-run economic equilibrium.

Highest and best use is the reasonable and probable use that supports the highest present value as of the date of the appraisal. For improved properties, the highest and best use is determined for the site both as if vacant and as improved. The latter analysis assumes that the existing improvement will not be replaced, even though it may not be the best use of the site. Indeed, construction of a new improvement should not be assumed unless the return from the new use more than covers demolition and construction costs.

The highest and best use must be physically possible, legal, financially feasible, and productive to the maximum, that is, highest and best, use. The analysis should be done as of the date of appraisal. Just as real estate values change, so the highest and best use of a property may change over time.

The appraiser determines what use of the property will maximize income or utility in both the short and the long run. From an economic standpoint, the appraiser evaluating the highest and best current use is doing short-run, or partial, equilibrium analysis (as opposed to long-run equilibrium analysis, which assumes the site is vacant). In mass appraisal, the current highest and best use is usually considered to be the current use, that is, buildings will not be immediately demolished or replaced. However, this does not lessen the need to evaluate long-run highest and best use for different groups of properties before a general revaluation. Land values in particular will reflect the influence of long-run highest and best use if different from current use. If market value is the legal standard, such influences (which may reduce or increase value) should be recognized.

More detailed analysis may be needed for special complex or situations, for example, uses in transition, interim uses, nonconforming uses, multiple uses, speculative uses, excess land, and highest and best use of improved property that differs from the highest and best use of the land as if vacant.

Data Collection Strategies Data collection strategies vary with the type of data. In a site visit, information is usually collected on neighborhood characteristics, site characteristics, and improvement characteristics, including a judgment of effective age and construction grade.

Comparative data, which include cost, income and expense, and sales information, are usually collected by interview or questionnaire or from public records. Sales information should include the names and addresses of buyer and seller, legal description and parcel identifier, type of transfer, interests transferred, type of financing, personal property included in sale price, date of transfer, and sale price. Chapter 5 has a detailed discussion of sales collection, processing, and screening.

Cost data may be collected in a number of ways. Some jurisdictions survey the owners of property with new improvements. Cost questionnaires should request informa-

tion on site preparation and demolition costs, excavation costs, building and structure costs, landscaping and yard improvements, and indirect costs.

Contractors, builders, and developers are good sources of cost information. They can furnish detailed cost breakdowns for specific new buildings or average costs of standardized models of buildings such as tract housing. Appraisers may ask contractors to provide current cost breakdowns of benchmark properties with certain specifications. Cost services provide precomputed cost factors and adjustments, arranged in convenient schedules and updated regularly.

A cost index is a ratio of the price of a single building component or, more usually, the composite price of a set of components on a base date in one location, compared with the price or composite price of the same components on another date in the same location. Cost indexes are necessary to the updating of cost estimates and rates. The appraiser may also require location indexes for adjusting base costs to the jurisdiction or for making adjustments within the jurisdiction. Cost indexes are published by several cost services and in federal government publications. Chapter 6 in *Improving Real Property Assessment* (IAAO 1978) has additional information on developing and collecting cost data.

The income approach to value depends on adequate data. Gross income data are essential; expense data that allow determination of net incomes are desirable. In a full income and expense data collection effort, the appraiser seeks information on the number and type of rentals (units, apartments, square feet, and so on), per unit rents, vacancy rates, collection losses, miscellaneous income, and allowable expenses. Once collected, this information is used to estimate per unit market rents, potential gross rents, vacancy and collection loss rates, gross rents, gross incomes, expense ratios, and net incomes. There are at least five methods of gaining income and expense information: mail questionnaires, personal contact, telephone, assessment appeals, and published studies and other third-party sources.

Income and expense data for various businesses can be found in *Sources of Composite Financial Data: A Bibliography* (Robert Morris Associates, Philadelphia), a bibliography covering manufacturers, wholesalers, retailers, services, and contractors; *Income/Expense Analysis: Apartments, Condominiums, and Cooperatives* (Institute of Real Estate Management, Chicago); *NAPA Consolidated Jobber Operatives* (National Automotive Parts Association, Rosemont); *Operating Cost Percentages* (Associated Retail Bakers of America, Chicago); and *Table Service Restaurant Operation Report* (National Restaurant Association, Chicago). Chapter 8 of *Improving Real Property Assessment* (IAAO 1978) explains methods of collecting income and expense data, and Chapters 11 and 12 in this text describe the types of data needed.

In addition, the following background data should be collected in preparation for any appraisal, whether single-property or mass appraisal. General data, which include social, economic, governmental, and environmental information, were described above. They are collected by a combination of direct and indirect methods and will usually relate to the analysis of the economic base as part of highest and best use analysis and to the specific market for the subject property as identified by highest and best use analysis.

Local government data are usually easy to obtain. The assessor's colleagues in the building, planning, education, and other offices of government are good sources.

Social and economic data can be obtained from government agencies and the local chamber of commerce. Specific governmental sources are the United States Department of Census publications, *The Statistical Abstract of the United States, State and Metropolitan Area Data Book 1986*, and the *County and City Data Book 1988*. United States Department of Labor publications include the annual *Area Wage Survey*, the quarterly *Consumer Price Index*, and the monthly *Retail Prices and Index of Fuel and Electricity*. Other services include *Platts Oilgram*, a newsletter published by McGraw-Hill; and the Donnelly Markets Information Services, a Dun and Bradstreet subsidiary that will provide customized demographic and economic information for cities, states, or regions.

Data on environmental factors are usually collected by direct site inspection, augmented by information gathered at appropriate municipal local government offices. Planning and building departments can be particularly helpful.

Valuation

Model Specification and Model Calibration
The appraiser's task is to analyze market data using appropriate research methods in order to identify those supply and demand factors that best explain value for a specific property or for many properties in a specific market. This activity is called *model specification*. It is the process of designing models based on data analysis and appraisal theory.

Supply and Demand Factors   In chapter 3, demand for real property was described as depending on five factors: the price of real property, consumer income, consumer preferences, price of complementary and substitute goods, and expectations about future prices. Supply was described as depending on price, amount of the current stock, construction costs, and financing.

Chapter 3 pointed out that the interaction of supply and demand forces leads to a specific price and quantity demanded and supplied, graphically represented by the intersection of supply and demand curves. The intersection of supply and demand curves represents market equilibrium, which is the principle of balance in operation. Thus, housing prices depend on both supply and demand factors operating in the market. This insight provides direction for the specific kinds of information that need to be analyzed during the neighborhood and site analysis phases of model building.

Typical demand factors for residential properties are buyer preferences for site and improvement characteristics and the price of substitute properties. Examples of property characteristics important to buyers are effective age, location, condition, construction quality, and size. Supply factors include the availability of properties in terms of these various characteristics as well as such economic factors as construction costs and the cost of mortgage funds. For income properties, demand factors include rents and location; supply factors include expenses and financing rates.

Specifying and Calibrating Models The principal difference between single-property and mass appraisal models is complexity. Mass appraisal models are more complex because they attempt to replicate market operations in a broad geographic area. Models developed exclusively for single-property appraisal are more narrowly focused.

The forces of supply and demand cannot be completely replicated because measurable economic, physical, or site characteristics cannot be found to represent all market forces. However, once the implicit relationships between value and the *available* supply and demand factors have been identified using appraisal logic backed up by data analysis, then the actual effects on market value of the specific factors can be determined. This function is called *model calibration*.

The final result is a relationship between value and its determinants, expressed as a mathematical model. An example of a simple appraisal model for residential properties might be:

$$MV = IV + LV, \qquad (10)$$

where MV is market value, IV is improvement value, and LV is land value.

This model can be expanded to include the relationship of IV and LV to improvement and land size:

$$IV = P_I \times ISIZE; \qquad (11)$$

$$LV = P_L \times LSIZE, \qquad (12)$$

where P_I is the price per unit of improvement size, $ISIZE$ is improvement size, P_L is the price per unit of land size, and $LSIZE$ is land size.

Market value can then be expressed as improvement size times unit price plus land size times unit price:

$$MV = P_I \times ISIZE + P_L \times LSIZE. \quad (13)$$

This model is an additive linear model: it assumes improvement and land values grow in proportion to size. In this simple example, the choice of improvement size and land size as factors in the model is based on the principle of contribution: market value will increase as desired housing services increase. In this case, land size and improvement size are the data chosen to represent the amount of housing services.

The development of the unit prices P_I and P_L for improvement and land is an example of model calibration. The values of P_I and P_L are based partly on the principle of substitution, which says that the values of P_I and P_L will be no higher than the prices of alternative housing services of equal utility.

A complete appraisal model for residential property has many measurable supply and demand factors that the appraiser can identify, measure, and calibrate. Some of these are *additive factors* that describe the improvements. These factors, such as improvement size, have a linear relationship to value; other factors represent *qualitative judgments* that affect improvement value, land value, or both in a multiplicative manner. For example, topography is usually expressed as a percent adjustment to basic land value, and relative neighborhood value can be expressed as a percent adjustment to total value in the cost and market approaches.

Well-specified cost and sales comparison models will have a general structure that contains three kinds of terms: *additive terms* that represent the amount of improvements and land services, *qualitative terms* that affect either land or improvement value, and *general qualitative terms* that affect the sum of land and improvement value. Likewise, the general structure for income models will always contain terms that measure the income stream for the property and the capitalization rate (or income multiplier) to be applied to the income stream.

Both cost and sales comparison models should have the same supply and demand factors included in their model structures. In sales comparison models, the influence of supply and demand factors on value are calibrated with data from the local real estate market. In cost models, however, supply factors (represented as replacement cost new) are calibrated from the construction market, and the demand factors that relate to consumer preferences and depreciation are calibrated from the local real estate market.

One of the principal differences between the two kinds of income models—direct and yield capitalization models—rests on how the rates and income measures are calibrated. In direct capitalization models, the rates are usually calibrated from local real estate markets; residual capitalization and cash flow models use information from other capital markets as well.

Application of the Three Approaches to Value

Sales Comparison Approach The sales comparison approach is based on the concept of value in exchange (market value). This approach compares the property being appraised (the subject) to properties that have been sold in the recent past. In single-property appraisals, the market evidence from the sales is analyzed to determine which sold properties are similar to the subject property. Characteristics important in determining value are derived by market analysis, and dollar adjustments are estimated for each characteristic. The sales prices of comparable properties are then adjusted for differences between comparable and subject. The sales comparison approach may be used to value any type of property, improved or vacant, that is being exchanged periodically on the market. Chapters 6, 14, and 15 describe the application of the sales comparison approach in single-property and mass appraisal.

In single-property appraisal (mass appraisal works differently—see chapters 14 and 15), the sales comparison approach has the following steps:

- Discover and analyze the data.
- Determine the units of comparisons and the determinants of value.
- Develop a model that relates the units of comparison to the value determinants (model specification).
- Develop reasonable adjustments for the value determinants based on the market (model calibration).
- Apply the model to the comparable properties to arrive at adjusted sales prices for the comparable properties.
- Analyze the adjusted comparables to arrive at a value estimate for the subject property.

Cost Approach To the estimated value of the land, preferably derived from sales data (see chapter 7), is added the current depreciated reproduction or replacement cost of the improvements. The value estimate is the sum of the depreciated improvement cost and the site value. The cost, then, clearly applies the principle of substitution. Chapters 8, 14, and 15 will describe in further detail the application of the cost approach in single-property and mass appraisal.

The steps in the cost approach are:

- Develop a model to estimate the value of the land as if it were vacant and marketable (model specification).

- Develop the land value rates and site adjustments for the land model (model calibration).
- Develop a model that can estimate the reproduction or replacement cost of all improvements to land as of the date of appraisal (model specification).
- Develop the base rates and unit prices for the building model (model calibration).
- Develop a model that can estimate accrued depreciation from all causes and deduct this estimate from the estimate of reproduction or replacement cost (model specification).
- Develop the dollar or percentage adjustments for the depreciation model (model calibration).
- Add the current depreciated reproduction or replacement cost of all improvements to the estimated land value.

Income Approach Income-producing real property is usually purchased for the right to receive future income flow. The appraiser seeks to evaluate this income flow for quantity, quality, direction, and duration and then convert it by means of appropriate capitalization rates into an expression of present worth: market value. If expense data are available the steps in this approach are:

- Estimate gross or net income from market data.
- Select the appropriate capitalization method (model specification).
- Estimate a capitalization rate or income multiplier (model calibration).
- Compute value by capitalization.

The income approach (like the sales comparison approach) may be used to value both vacant and improved properties, provided that a sample of such properties are leased or rented in the market. The appraiser may use conventional or computerized analytical methods. Chapters 9 through 12 discuss in detail the theory and application of the income approach in single-property appraisal; chapters 14 and 15 discuss mass appraisal applications.

Not every approach is pertinent and useful for valuing all properties. For example, the income approach does not lend itself to the valuation of single-family residences, which are not usually purchased for their income-producing abilities. The cost approach is not applicable to the valuation of vacant land. The sales comparison approach is not helpful in the valuation of, for example, a zoo or a public library, because sales data will be lacking.

Reconciliation of Values, Model Testing, and Quality Control

In single-property appraisal, the final step in the appraisal process is reconciliation, the resolving of differences that result from the application of the three approaches to value. (Some appraisal authorities use the term "correlation.")

Reconciliation usually begins by stating the values estimated by the three approaches, reports the development of these values, and states an opinion as to the weight that should be placed on each approach. The type of property being appraised and the amount and quality of the data used in the development of each value estimate are noted. In general, the appraiser should use or give greatest weight to the approach that is most supportable given the available data.

A thorough reconciliation analysis reviews briefly the data developed and used, considers the quality and quantity of data, considers the relative strengths and weaknesses of each approach for valuation of the type of property, and considers the relevance of each approach to the subject property.

There are several things that reconciliation does *not* do. It does not check the work performed in each of the three approaches; this check should be done as part of each approach, until the appraiser is sure that everything reported within that particular approach is as correct as it can be. It does not simply average the three approaches under any method of arithmetic. It does not necessarily require that one of the three values is the final value. The purpose of most appraisals is to estimate market value, usually defined as "the most probable selling price," and this may not be the amount indicated by any one of the three approaches.

The appraiser looks carefully at each approach and considers *why* the value differences exist. These differences are then reconciled and a decision made as to which values and indicators should be given more weight. Sometimes one approach will produce the single best reflection of the most probable sale price of the subject—but not necessarily. Significant weight can be attached to all three approaches; a final conclusion at a point in between might then best represent market value.

In mass appraisal, model testing and measuring the quality of values are the final steps. Values generated from the mass appraisal models are compared with a representative sample of sales, preferably including some sales not used in the calibration phase of the model building process. A standard ratio study should be conducted and the results compared to the goals for appraisal level and dispersion.

The *Standard on Ratio Studies* (IAAO 1990) suggests that the level of appraisal in each stratum (group of like properties) should be within 5 percent of the overall appraisal ratio in the jurisdiction, and the overall appraisal level should be within 10 percent of the legal level. For residential properties, uniformity, as measured by the coefficient of dispersion, with respect to the median ratio, should be 15 percent or less generally and 10 percent or less in areas of newer and fairly similar residences. Uniformity within strata composed of income-producing properties requires a coefficient of dispersion of 15 percent or less in larger, urban areas, and 20 percent or less generally. Within all other strata, the coefficient of dispersion should be 20 percent or less.

Minimum quality standards are often not met when initial models are tested against a holdout sample. This leads to a process of refinement during which the model may be respecified or recalibrated several times before values generated from them meet preset appraisal standards. The refinement process can be aided by additional data analysis, such as scatterplots that relate sales ratios to various characteristics of the data base. For example, a scatter graph of sales ratios vs. sales

prices can identify patterns of inequalities related to value range (vertical inequities). A scatter graph that relates sales ratios to effective age can identify problems with depreciation schedules or the computation of effective age. Typically, several refinements to the mass appraisal models will be needed before they perform well enough to be used to generate values for assessment purposes. Chapters 14 and 20 discuss these quality control issues in detail.

Summary

This chapter has constructed a bridge from economic theory to the valuation of property. Economic theory and appraisal theory are closely related. Because appraisal deals with imperfect markets, it cannot be as consistent or tightly reasoned as economic theory. Legal definitions of market value recognize the imperfect nature of real estate markets.

Valuation of property requires the appraiser to understand and apply legal concepts of property, to perform market analysis, and to specify and calibrate models that reflect the workings of the market.

The most expensive and crucial part of valuation is data collection, which is treated in the next chapter. Subsequent chapters discuss land valuation and the three approaches to value in more detail.

Data Collection

Assessors, in addition to their role in the valuation of real and personal property for ad valorem tax purposes, manage information. The data bases they maintain are essential for valuation and are an important community resource. Chapter 5 develops in detail a framework for the collection and management of the data essential for proper assessment administration and other important community planning functions.

Data Collection and Management 5

Introduction

The word *data* refers to the many codes, words, numbers, and symbols recorded on field documents and entered into files. Data enable the appraiser to estimate the value of a property. A real property assessment system must have an inventory of all real properties, their uses, and their physical and locational characteristics. The investment in making this inventory can be 75 percent of the cost of a reappraisal. The cost can be amortized over a long period if the data are maintained and the data base can accommodate the data requirements of new appraisal techniques.

In mass appraisal, field inventory work is usually conducted by junior-level employees trained to measure and list certain types of property. Appraisers rely on such data to estimate value. If the data are wrong, the final estimate may be wrong. This is certainly true in a computer-assisted mass appraisal (CAMA) system, as the computer has no outside knowledge of the property, neighborhood, and market conditions. Most such errors can be avoided by proper planning, supervision, and quality control.

Methods for data inventory vary from jurisdiction to jurisdiction. Jurisdictions that have recently done a full field review of the property inventory are likely to know the adequacy and quality of their data. If data

have been reviewed in the last two to three years, and procedures are in place to keep track of changes in property inventory, the data are likely to be good. Jurisdictions that do not have a sufficiently accurate inventory can establish a better data base for the future by addressing the issue comprehensively.

Data collection requires a good set of current cadastral maps. Parcel identification numbers should incorporate the tax map identifier to provide a necessary control in accounting for properties during data collection and processing.

Property Characteristics Data

Determining Data Needs

Before redesigning a data inventory system, it is important to evaluate the quality and quantity of existing data. The designer should also consider the needs of users other than the assessor's office.

Quality is concerned with how accurately recorded information used to estimate values reflects the current status of the property. Information is often fairly accurate for properties that have been visited recently (for example, to verify new construction based on a building permit). But the information may be out of date for properties that have not been visited for five or more years.

A field study is effective for evaluating the quality of existing data. To conduct a field study: (1) Use a sample of properties from different areas and classes, representing a good cross section of the jurisdiction. (2) Take copies of existing property records to the field for verification. (3) Note corrections on the copies so statistical measures of the types and size of errors can be identified. Often errors can be categorized according to their effect on value (see chapter 21).

If time is not available for a field study, sales ratios can help indicate the quality of existing data. A high coefficient of dispersion is likely to be a result of poor data quality.

Quantity refers to how much data are currently available or need to be collected. Information on factors that affect value may be missing. Computerization may require new information such as computer sketches to support computerized valuation and record maintenance.

A survey of existing property record information often reveals that additional data should be collected. What data, and in what form, requires careful evaluation. Collecting insignificant or difficult-to-obtain information wastes limited resources.

A pilot study helps evaluate what to collect and how. In a pilot study, data are collected on a limited set of representative properties. Values may be estimated for these properties using several approaches and the resulting values analyzed to identify what factors contribute to value. Usually only a few factors are consistently significant. When factors are highly correlated, only a small subset is needed to explain most variation in value. To establish credibility, data on factors of marginal significance, but important to taxpayers, can be collected and used to explain and support values.

Describing and Coding Property Characteristics

Developing a scheme for accurate and efficient description and coding of property characteristics goes hand in hand with the determination of data needs. Once a characteristic has been identified as potentially useful, the following questions should be asked: How can this characteristic be described? How can this description be coded? What resources (chiefly labor) are required in the description and coding process? Is the effort likely to be worthwhile (cost-effective)?

Appraisers may describe a property characteristic in words or in a picture. They may draw sketches, take photographs, take measurements, make counts, compile lists, sort into classes, and assign ratings. The choice of technique depends on the nature of the characteristics and the purposes for which the data are being collected.

Coding reduces a description to a more manageable size through the use of letters, numbers, or symbols. In real property appraisal systems, descriptions of relevant property characteristics are ultimately reduced to numerical values so that mathematical calculations may be performed.

A description may be qualitative or quantitative. An appraiser may describe a house as a mansion because mansions are "large" and the house in question is the largest house around—a qualitative description. Or the appraiser may measure the ground-floor area of the house, say, 3,130 square feet—a quantitative description. Qualitative descriptions are often, but not always, subjective, and quantitative, objective. Qualitative descriptions are often based on objective criteria and observable characteristics delineated in a data collection manual.

Property characteristics may be continuous, discrete, or binary. A continuous characteristic or variable is one that is based on measurement. Building area, for example, is a continuous variable. A discrete variable, such as construction grade, can take on specific numerical values — usually, whole number values — within certain limits. The number of rooms in a dwelling is also a discrete variable, although half-room counts are sometimes used. A binary, or yes–no, variable is one for which only two values are possible. An example of a question that creates a yes–no variable is: "Does this site have lake frontage?" Binary variables are often called dummy variables.

Rating schemes are often used for discrete variables, such as construction quality and building condition. Construction grade, for example, may be defined in terms of categories ranging in half-point increments from 1.0 to 6.0. Building condition, or state of repair, for example, could be described on a scale of, say, 1 to 10, or as poor, fair, average, or good. For the purpose of calculating value, the ratings are scaled. For example, average may be given a value of 100 percent and the extremes of poor and good, 60 and 120 percent. Such discrete variables are called categorical variables. (Building condition could also be treated as a continuous variable if the "percent good" were allowed to assume any value between 0 and 100 percent.)

Rating schemes can be based on an absolute standard, one that applies to all properties in the system, or they can be based on a relative standard, one that changes from neighborhood to neighborhood or from one group of properties to another. If the rating standard is absolute, a building described as being in good condition in one location would also be good in any location. An example of a variable described by a relative standard is the typical or representative lot, the determination of which is based on lots in the neighborhood or area.

Coding and rating schemes should account for all possibilities (be exhaustive), and categories should be mutually exclusive. In addition, property characteristics should be described and coded in a consistent way.

Property characteristics may be objective or subjective. Objective characteristics are directly measurable or verifiable, for example, square feet of living space or year of construction. Subjective characteristics require a judgment; they are not directly measurable, observable, or verifiable. Examples include a location index, the quality of a view, and the condition of a structure. Guidelines for making judgments about subjective factors should be included in the data collection manual.

Designing the Property Record Form

The nature of the data and the valuation procedure will influence the design of the property record form, the choice of data elements to collect, and the form in which to collect them. Before designing a property record form, the assessor should look at standard forms available from oversight agencies or other sources. Many agencies supply appraisal manuals that provide property record forms and associated inventory procedures. Some agencies mandate that assessors use these manuals; others offer them as suggestions.

The assessor should also consider the intended use of the form. Some forms are designed solely as field data collection documents. After data have been recorded or verified in the field, they are entered in the computer. When needed, the data are printed directly from the computer file. In other operations, the form is used as a field worksheet and for value computations. It is then filed and used to explain the property's appraisal to taxpayers. These forms are periodically pulled from the files, values are updated, and the forms refiled; such forms must provide space for annual value summaries.

Factors often included on property record forms are listed in figure 1. A parcel identification number uniquely identifies each parcel and provides the essential link to other assessment files. Neighborhood codes are used to identify homogeneous market areas and provide geographic control for valuation. The items listed as optional may be recorded on the property record form or on supplementary forms.

Figure 1.   Typical Factors Included on a Property Record Form

Parcel identification number
Street address
Property use classification
Tax rate area code (tax district)
Neighborhood code
Legal description
Size and shape of parcel
Site characteristics
Improvement characteristics
Building perimeter sketch
Cost approach data

Optional items
  Building permit history
  Sales history
  Income and expense information
  Record of inspections and visits to
    the property
  Assessment history
  Appeals history

How the form is designed affects how data are coded and recorded. Both the data collector and the computer system require a clear and precise format. The order of information such as dwelling characteristics should match the order in which the data collector will be observing such information when approaching the house, questioning the owner, and measuring the house, additions, and outbuildings (see figure 2).

For convenience, information should be coded in a predefined format. In figure 3, for example, a checklist of wall material codes (left side) might be replaced by a more com-

Figure 2.   Sequencing of Dwelling Characteristics for Data Collection

Items observed in approaching the house
  Story height
  Style
  Roof type and material
  Wall type

Items to be obtained by questioning the property owner or conducting an interior inspection
  Year built/remodeled
  Number of rooms/bedrooms/family
    rooms
  Heating/cooling systems and fuel type
  Basement type and finish
  Attic finish
  Other features such as fireplaces and
    unfinished areas
  Miscellaneous other features
  Grade and condition

Measurements
  Perimeter of house and its additions
  Coding of additions for type and
    construction, such as open or
    enclosed porch, garage
  Outbuildings

prehensive set of codes, to be circled or entered (right side). For measurements and other quantitative fields, standard formats should be used and enough space provided to record the largest values and measurements.

The form should be laid out in a sequence that makes office use easier. Computer input screens should match the flow of information on the form, so the data entry clerk can follow the form efficiently. Fields to be entered into the computer can be screened or shaded as a guide for the data entry clerk and a reminder to the data collector. The form should have sufficient space so that most properties will fit onto one document. Figure 4 shows two sides of a well-designed residential property record form used to collect and enter data.

Designing Data Inventory Manuals

The data inventory manual defines the property characteristics and the format for collection. The manual should help data collectors be efficient, accurate, and consistent with one another. Explanations of the purpose of collecting items will help data collectors make decisions about unusual situations.

Definitions of terms ensure that each data collector evaluates items from the same frame of reference. Good definitions achieve a balance between consistency and the flexibility needed to accommodate unexpected circumstances. Distinctions between categories should be drawn carefully. For example, the definition of a raised ranch that is above ground should distinguish it from a two-story colonial.

If definitions are too simple, data collectors will be uncertain of how to apply them. Definitions that are too detailed, however, will be intimidating, cumbersome, and unworkable. A sketch or photograph often improves a definition. When detailed observations are required to describe an item, instructions, with examples, should specify each step.

Field Data Collection

Field data collection is often the major activity of a reappraisal project, especially one being done for the first time in several years. The data collection program therefore requires organization, planning, and close supervision. In-office preparation, selection and training of staff, entry and validation of

Figure 3. Comparison of Collection Formats

Checklist

Wall materials

____ Wood
____ Brick
____ Stone
____ Aluminum
____ Vinyl
____ Asbestos
____ Frame/masonry

____ _____

Code list

Wall Codes

01 Wood	06 Asbestos
02 Brick	07 Stucco
03 Stone	08 Cedar shake
04 Aluminum	09 Masonry and frame
05 Vinyl	10 Other

Circle or enter code _____

Figure 4. Residential Property Record Form

3

TOWN OF

PROPERTY ASSESSMENT RECORD   R-002

PLAT/LOT	TO2/016-08				
LOCATION	21 ELVIRA HEIGHTS	**ZONING** A-80	**NEIGHBORHOOD** 3-00	**STATE CODE** 1-3	

RECORD OF OWNERSHIP	BK	PG	SALE PRICE	CARD	1 OF 1
	0121	0060			**REMARKS**
					BRICK VENEER

BUILDING PERMIT RECORD				
DATE	TYPE	DESCRIPTION	#	AMOUNT

DATE 12/19/84   SALE PRICE 20000

PROPERTY FACTORS

STREET	IMPROVEMENTS	LAND ADJ.
paved	electric	
curb		

TOPOGRAPHY Level   **TREND** Improving

LAND VALUE COMPUTATION AND SUMMARY

		CLASSIFICATION	# SITES	ACRES	S.F.	RATE	VALUE	FACTOR	ADJ.	VALUE	RATIO	ASSESSMENT
INSPECTION DATA		BUILDING SITES	1	1.84	80000	44000	44000	1.000	0	44000	70	30800
	BY	DATE	EXCESS USEABLE									
MEAS.	SF	11/23/87	EXCESS REAR		0.16	6970	3000	480	1.000	0	500	70	350
LIST	SF	11/23/87	WASTE LAND									
REV.	SF	07/12/88	WATERFRONT									
PRICE	SMA	04/16/88	CERT. OPEN SPACE									
			CERT. FARM									
			CERT. FOREST									
			TOTAL LAND VALUE		2.00	87120					44500		31150
			TOTAL BLDG. VALUE								141500		99050
			TOTAL OTHER CARDS										
			TOTAL VALUE								186000		130200

BUILDING CHARACTERISTICS

OCCUPANCY	single family
ROOF TYPE	Hip
ROOF	Asphalt Shingles
EXT. WALLS	Vertical
FOUNDATION	Concrete
BASEMENT	Full
FRAMING	Wood Joists
# ROOMS	6
STYLE	Ranch
COLOR	brick
# BEDROOMS	3
INT. FLOORS	W-W Carpet
INT. WALLS	Drywall
ATTIC	None
FIN. BSMNT.	0
# BATHS	1 / 1 / 2
HEATING	Hot Water
INT. FINISH	Average
INT. COND.	Good
INT. LAYOUT	Good

BUILT-INS	REMODELED	DATE
dishwasher		

BUILDING COMPUTATIONS

STORY HEIGHT	1.00
BASE S.F.	1591
BASE PRICE	102717
STORY HT. ADJ.	1.00
SUBTOTAL	102717
BSMNT ADJ.	0
HEATING ADJ.	0
PLUMBING ADJ.	1200
ATTIC ADJ.	0
ADDNS. & PORCHES	16442
SUBTOTAL	120359
GRADE ADJ.	1.20
SUBTOTAL	144430
FEATURES	0
TOTAL	144430

DESCRIPTION OF OBSOL.

70 1SFR/B 8

32.5 24 FG 32

22 4 11.5 24

4 × 6 OP

HALF SCALE

ADDITIONS	S.F.	RATE	VALUE
Wood Deck	144	9.36	1348
Garage-Fra.	768	18.95	14554
Open Porch	24	22.50	540
TOTAL			16442

FEATURES	VALUE
TOTAL	

BUILDING SUMMARY

TYPE	CONSTRUCTION	SIZE	GRADE	RATE	AGE	COND.	REPL. COST	DEPRECIATION		VALUE	RATIO	ASSESSMENT
								NORM.	OBSOL.			
DWELLING	1.00stfr	1591	B —5		1986	E	144431	0.02	0.00	141500	70	99050

collected data, and quality control should all be carefully planned. In most cases, additional (usually temporary) staff must be hired and trained. Data collectors should be supervised closely so they meet the production schedule and standards.

Hiring Data Collectors In hiring data collectors, consider the schedule, the local labor market, and the caliber of people needed. These temporary employees not only are responsible for quality and production but also represent the assessor's office in an important contact with the public.

Suitable candidates may sometimes be difficult to attract. Qualifications include the physical ability to work in the field, basic observational and mathematical skills required to collect data and perform arithmetic computations, and communication skills. In-house programs can train the well-prepared person but will never compensate for a lack of basic skills. Some data collection programs have successfully used college students over a summer break. However, most programs last longer and will be staffed with people from a variety of backgrounds.

Pay is important. Some local governments may tie the labor classification for data collectors to low wages. The assessor may need to negotiate with local officials and try to establish a pay scale that will attract qualified applicants. Data collectors are often required to provide their own transportation to the field and can be reimbursed by mileage or a flat allowance.

Existing staff should supervise data collectors. If this is not possible, new staff with the requisite skills and experience should be hired and trained for supervisory roles. If data collection will go on for a long time, data collectors who demonstrate leadership and communication skills can be promoted to supervisory positions.

Training Programs for Data Collectors The training program should teach data collectors what data to collect, how to do it, and how to be courteous, businesslike, and helpful to the public. The program should prepare data collectors to answer questions and provide brochures with answers to standard questions and a phone number to call for additional information.

The training program should have classroom and field sessions. The classroom sessions should cover the following:

- General background information on property assessment and the purpose of the reappraisal program
- The data collector's role in the project
- Information to be collected and the data collection form, including organization of information, proper means of recording information, explanation of each field on the form, and procedures for sketching improvements
- The mechanics of data collection: organizing the day's work, getting to the field, approaching the property, contacting the property owner, interior inspection, exterior measurements and observations, estimating information, and turning work in to the supervisor
- Special observational skills: recognizing dwelling style, determining grade (quality of construction), and determining condition

The data inventory manual often contains a set of photographs representative of each architectural style. However, the data collector will encounter a wider variety and mixture of styles and grades in the field. A slide show with many slides of different types of properties from the community is an excellent base for developing skills in recognizing architectural styles.

Field training is necessary before data collectors meet the public and begin collecting data. An exercise can be developed to allow data collectors to practice techniques on representative properties.

Classroom and field training should be followed by closely supervised field data collection, in which a supervisor accompanies and observes the data collector. The supervisor should review each day's work and conduct follow-up visits to some of the properties visited by the data collector. Continuing feedback will correct problems and improve skills, reducing the supervision required in ensuing weeks.

Office Preparation of Property Record Forms Preparation of property record forms in the office will expedite field collection. This preparation includes entering parcel identification information (for example, parcel identification number, legal description, and owner name and address) on each property record, transfer of information (for example, building perimeter sketches) from previous forms, and arrangement of the forms for geographic routing.

If existing property records are to be a basis for data collection, preparatory work in the office can make production easier in the field. Information already in the computer can be printed on the new form and then other information, such as improvement sketches and measurements, transferred. The data collector can verify and correct measurements without having to make adjustments to the sketch, unless there are significant errors. If the data collector is un-able to gain entry, the availability of existing interior information will reduce the need for a return visit.

Routing organizes the forms geographically into manageable batches. The forms within each batch are organized in a sequence that simplifies field review for data collectors, group leaders reviewing the properties collected, and the appraisers who check data and use it for valuations. Routing requires a set of cadastral maps with parcel identification numbers. The forms for each map can be routed by a clerk. Routing parcels counterclockwise around the block makes a "drive-by" review easier. The map and routing number are recorded on the form and the routing numbers noted on a map to be included with each pack of forms. Each batch of forms can also have a control form that indicates how many parcels are in each pack.

When routing is done, land measurements, zoning, neighborhood identifications, development restrictions, and other related data from the cadastral maps should be listed on the form. If parcels are to be valued by front foot, the lot frontage and depth for rectangular lots are entered on the form. Irregular lots are broken down into a set of equivalent rectangles so size may be computed. If parcels are to be valued by square foot or acreage, the parcel area and breakdown by use (primary, secondary, and so forth) should be entered. Aerial photos may help identify land breakdowns, as well as multiple improvements, which require extra forms. Land size information on computer files can often be fed directly from administrative or cadastral map files into the CAMA record.

Field Visits Good public relations before data collectors are sent into the field is important. News releases, informational brochures, and public meetings should be used to explain the purpose of the reappraisal program and the importance of accurate data collection. Announcing where the data collectors will be working in the next few weeks is also helpful. Some jurisdictions have used a precollection notification to inform property owners of the upcoming visits. This notice can be either mailed or left as a brochure or door hanger at each property. Notices are usually distributed about two weeks before the scheduled data collection for the neighborhood.

Data collectors should carry proper identification, such as a picture identification card prepared by the police department. Identifying signs on vehicles and informational brochures confirm that the data collectors are from the assessor's office.

Requirements for interior inspection vary. In newer communities where construction is fairly standard there is usually little variation in interior features of the house. However, in older communities with predominantly older houses, often the critical characteristics affecting value are inside the house. The data collector cannot determine the extent of deterioration or renovation without gaining entrance.

Where interior inspection is essential, the property owner must be notified. Data collection is usually done during the working day, but often no one is at home during the day. Inspecting the property when someone is there may require a second or third visit in the evenings or on a Saturday. Door hangers allow property owners to mail in information (see figure 5). Door hangers can also provide a space for property owners to indicate times when they would like to have

inspections and a phone number to call for appointments (figure 6).

Exterior features and measurements can be recorded even if no one is at home. The data collector may be able to estimate interior characteristics from experience with similar properties in the same locale. The assessor will need to decide the extent to which such estimates are permitted. (The data collector should note on the form whether the information came from estimation or interior inspection.) Experienced data collectors may also confirm their estimates with neighbors, although this source should be used with discretion.

Quality Control The key to accurate data is quality control. Group leaders provide frontline quality control and should be personally accountable for the quantity and quality of work produced by those in their charge.

Good field supervision requires an adequate number of well-trained field supervisors who understand their accountability for the work done by data collectors. Each field supervisor or group leader should be responsible for no more than four or five data collectors.

The group leaders' responsibilities include
- Meeting the data collectors in the field at the beginning and end of the work day to distribute and collect work
- Reviewing work done by the data collectors, especially the coding of subjective items such as grade and condition
- Checking samples of the data collectors' work for quality by review and interviews with property owners
- Discussing problems with the group and individual data collectors and retraining or dismissing unsatisfactory employees

Figure 5. Door Hanger Including Mailer Card for Self-reporting

DEAR PROPERTY OWNER:

Sorry we missed you today!

A representative of the _____ Company was here to gather information for the _____ County property revaluation program. Under Ohio law, all property records must be updated every six years.

Please keep in mind that our field representatives are not appraising your property. They are basically recording current, updated information which is needed to determine the fair market value.

Please complete the self-addressed card with accurate data and return it as soon as possible. In the absence of such input from you, we will have to estimate the interior features.

We appreciate your cooperation.

Date card left at property: _____

TAX DISTRICT _____ **PARCEL NO.** _____

MAP NO. _____ / _____ / _____ **ROUTING NO.** _____ / _____

Street Address _____

STORY HEIGHT

One _____   One and a half _____   Two _____

Two and a half _____   Three _____   Three and a half _____

YEAR ERECTED: Dwelling _____   Garage _____

LIVING ACCOMMODATIONS

Total Rooms _____ (exclud. bathrooms)   Bedrooms _____   Family Rooms _____

Tub Baths _____   Shower Baths _____   Half Baths _____

Other Plumbing Fixtures _____   Please Describe _____

BASEMENT

Slab _____   Crawl _____   Partial _____   Full _____

Size _____ X _____

FINISHED BASEMENT AREA: Yes _____   Size _____ X _____
No _____

ATTIC

None _____   Unfinished _____   Finished _____

Number of Attic Rooms _____

HEATING

None / Space heaters _____   Central system _____

HEATING FUEL TYPE

Gas _____   Electric _____   Oil _____   Heat Pump _____   Solar _____

HEATING SYSTEM TYPE

Warm Air _____   Electric _____   Hot Water _____   Steam _____   Solar _____

Central Air Conditioning or Heat Pump   Yes _____   No _____

WOODBURNING FIREPLACES (no.) _____   Stacks _____   Openings _____

REMODELING AND MODERNIZATION

Exterior   19 ___ ___   Bathroom   19 ___ ___

Interior   19 ___ ___   Plumbing   19 ___ ___

Additions 19 ___ ___   Elect/Htg/A.C. 19 ___ ___

Remodeling Cost _____

INTERIOR CONDITION RELATIVE TO EXTERIOR

Better _____   Same _____   Poorer _____

DATE OF ACQUISITION: Property was purchased (Mo. & Yr.) ___ / ___ at a purchase price of $_____. New buildings have been erected (after or before) purchase date at a construction cost of $_____ for a (describe bldg. erected) _____ .

SIGNATURE:

Figure 6. Door Hanger Including Phone Number to Call for Appointment

PARCEL NUMBER

_____ − _____ − _____ | _ − _____ | __
Tax Dist.　Book　　Page　　　　Parcel

DEAR HOMEOWNER:

Sorry we missed you today. We called at your home to gather property information for the 1984 _____ County Revaluation Program being conducted by the _____ Company and as ordered by the Department of Tax Equalization under Secton 5713.01 of the Ohio Revised Code.

Should you desire an interior inspection please call _____ within 72 hours from the date indicated below to arrange an appointment. Appointments may be arranged for inspection only during normal working hours Monday thru Friday.

_____

Date　　　　　　**County Auditor**

- Completing production reports for each data collector
- Managing data collection assignments for the group
- Assuring consistency of data among data collectors

Quality control procedures ensure that data collection is uniformly monitored. These procedures include quality checks on specified percentages of each data collector's work in each area — as much as 25 percent during the first few weeks. As production increases and data collectors demonstrate adequate skills, sampling can be reduced to less than 5 percent. Each form that has been checked for quality should be marked.

Group leaders should also maintain a log for each data collector, noting the problems found and a current indication of the quality of work.

If desired, a predesigned form can be used to rate each aspect of a data collector's work (see figure 7). The rating forms can be entered and processed, using personal computer software, to produce a variety of statistical reports; based on these, retraining can be provided at a group level to correct pervasive problems or individuals can be singled out for specific retraining.

Logistics It is difficult to forecast production for a project when it is affected by so many factors — some outside the project manager's control. Nonetheless, planning and attention to critical elements at the start of a project can improve the chances for success. Actual production rates will be a function of parcel density (number of parcels and improvements per square mile), ease of getting to a particular part of the jurisdiction (and the policy with respect to data collectors being on-site in the field at the beginning of the work day), the weather, and other factors outside the project manager's control. Production rates and quality are also a function of the skills and ability of employees and the extent to which they are motivated to produce.

If interior inspection levels are to be maintained, time must be allotted for callbacks, or scheduled visits, to the property. These are usually made by the same data collector but can also be handled by a callback team.

For planning, use typical production rates. Production rates should allow for turnover and include time for replacement and retraining.

Figure 7.   Data Collector Evaluation Form

LISTER EVALUATION FORM

Lister _____ Checker _____ Date _____ Score _____
Client _____ Parcel ID _____ Routing No. _____ Card No. ___ of ___
Property Class _____ Date Listed _____ Field Supervisor _____

| UNSATISFACTORY—NO—UNACCEPTABLE |
| SATISFACTORY—YES—ACCEPTABLE |

PART I—Obtained From Property Contact

1. Did he/she properly identify him/herself? . . . . ☐ ☐
2. Did you understand why he/she was there and what he/she was doing? . . . . ☐ ☐
3. How would you describe his/her general personal appearance? . . . . ☐ ☐
4. Was he/she courteous. . .respectful. . .considerate? . . . . ☐ ☐
5. Did he/she appear to be conscientious about the work? . . . . ☐ ☐
6. What kind of inspection did he/she make? None ___ Partial ___ Thorough ___ . . . . ☐ ☐
7. Did he/she request all applicable. . .Costs ___ Sales ___ Remodeling ___ Rental ___ data? ☐ ☐

PART II—Obtained From Property Record Card

1. Was the information listed on the correct card? . . . . ☐ ☐
2. Were the property data listed accurately? . . . . ☐ ☐
   Address ___   Class ___   Card # ___   Land Use ___   Zoning ___   Property Factors ___
3. Were all the improvements listed? . . . . ☐ ☐
   Main Building ___   Additions ___   Out Buildings ___   Yard Items ___
4. Were the measurements accurate? . . . . ☐ ☐
5. Were the construction data listed accurately? Keypunch Items ___ Other ___ . . . . ☐ ☐
6. What was the condition of the card? Neat ___ Sloppy ___ Borderline ___ . . . . ☐ ☐

PART III—Economic Data (for commercial and industrial listers only) . . . . ☐ ☐

1. Applicable Data	Requested	Refused	Referral	Obtained	Complete	Accurate	
Cost . . . . ☐	yes no	yes no	yes no	yes no	yes no	yes no	
Sales . . . . ☐	yes no	yes no	yes no	yes no	yes no	yes no	
Remodeling . . . ☐	yes no	yes no	yes no	yes no	yes no	yes no	
I & E . . . . ☐	yes no	yes no	yes no	yes no	yes no	yes no	TOTAL ___

PART IV-Supplementary Data

1. Average daily production during the period when this property was listed _____
2. Type of listing: Relatively—Easy _____ Average _____ Difficult _____ Expected production _____
3. Type of commercial: CBD Fringe Strip Neighborhood Hyway-Svc Park Center Scattered
4. Grade Used? _____ Acceptable Range _____ Accurate _____ High _____ Low _____
5. Depreciation/CDU? _____ % Acceptable _____ % Accurate _____ Liberal _____ Conservative _____

PART V—Remarks: (If additional space is needed, use other side.)

_____

_____

_____

A formula for determining time required and production rates takes into account many factors (figure 8). The formula will show differences for different areas of a jurisdiction and also estimate an overall rate of production.

Figure 8.   Determining Field Production Rates

Parcels/day = Average data collection rate in field
× Parcel density factor
× Complexity factor
× Callback factor (1 − fraction of each day spent on callbacks)
× (1 − travel hours/work day hours)
× (1 − weather days/total work days)
× (1 − training days/average work days)

Hypothetical rates for suburban community of custom homes located in the snow belt:
Average data collection rate: 20 minutes per parcel (24/day)

Parcel density factor (less dense)	0.95
Complexity factor (custom houses)	0.90
Callback factor (2 hours per day)	0.75
Travel hours (0)	1.00
Weather days	
(10 per year; 5% of work days)	0.95
Training days (10, during a year)	0.95

Parcels/day = 24 × 0.95 × 0.90 × 0.75 × 1.00 × 0.95 × 0.95 = 13.89

Staffing requirements for data collectors and supervisors can also be calculated. Using the example in figure 8, which has an effective production rate of 14 per day, assume 60,000 residential parcels to collect in ten months (200 work days). A staff of

$$60,000/(200 \times 14) = 21.4 \text{ data collectors}$$

is required. The number of available work days should reflect holidays, vacation, personal, and sick days. In the above example, this was accomplished by assuming only 20 work days per month.

If 4 or 5 data collectors per group leader is the standard adopted, to start with 5 group leaders and 5 data collectors per group leader would allow for attrition during initial training. With 10,000 residential parcels to collect in six months (120 work days), a staff of

$$10,000/(120 \times 14) = 6 \text{ data collectors}$$

would be required, which would present the assessor with the choice of having 1 group leader supervise more than 5 data collectors or cutting back on the number of data collectors and managing their production carefully. If 7 or 8 data collectors were needed, it would be wise to have 2 group leaders.

When many data collectors are supervised during an extended collection period, hiring and training in stages has several advantages. One is a higher level of supervision for the first set of data collectors during the critical first weeks. Experience from early training sessions and field work can then be used to improve training programs and supervision techniques for subsequent collectors. Also, experienced data collectors with supervisory potential can be promoted to group leader positions.

Regional field offices are advantageous when a large data collection staff and several levels of field management are required. The regional manager can use the office for meetings with group leaders to distribute and collect work, and for counseling and retraining individual data collectors. The regional office can increase productivity by reducing travel time to the field.

Document Control in the Office

Field supervisors should be responsible for getting data collectors' work reviewed and back to the assessment office for additional review and processing. A control form, designed to provide control and summary information, or a similar procedure, should be used to log batches of property record forms as they are routed between data collectors, field supervisors, and the assessment office. Figure 9 is an example of a control form with the following blocks of information:

- Identification—the cadastral map or maps included in the batch
- Number of units—number of parcels, with a breakdown by property type
- Field and office functions—dates on which activities were completed, and the person responsible
- Commercial cards—each commercial property and its type
- Incomplete field—parcels still requiring field work
- Market data—parcels with recent sales
- Card temporarily pulled—control on property record cards pulled from the batch for field work

If properly maintained, the control forms for a location can also be used to locate sales or examples of a particular type of property for use in valuation and review.

A quality check of property record forms returned from the field should be ready to confirm the completeness and validity of critical information. This can be done during data entry, if data entry is done promptly in the reappraisal office. If an outside data entry service or employees unfamiliar with property record data are doing the data entry, a quality check should be performed in the reappraisal office before data entry to ensure that the forms are complete and can be entered correctly. This will minimize expensive corrections and additions. If data will not be entered in the computer, the values should be calculated and recorded on the property record form in preparation for field review.

Data Inventory Mailer

The data mailer (figure 10) contains a summary of property information and allows the owner to submit corrections to the assessment office. Returned mailers should be reviewed. Many will not need corrections. Others will need minor corrections or can be confirmed after a phone call to the property owner. A few will require field checks.

Collecting Property Characteristics Data for Commercial and Industrial Properties

Commercial and industrial properties are fewer in number than residential properties but more complex and more diverse in size and use. A separate data collection form (sometimes two or three forms) is used, one for each type of use, such as apartment, office or retail, and industrial (warehouse and manufacturing). Data collectors need more training and knowledge of the valuation process to collect data on commercial and industrial property. They encounter larger, more complex structures and list special features, some of which appear only rarely. They must differentiate between real and personal property; some features can be either real or personal, depending on specific use and the policy and laws of the jurisdiction.

Figure 9. Batch Control Form

CONTROL FORM   CLIENT _____   NO. _____

CARDS TEMPORARILY PULLED			REMARKS	01 IDENTIFICATION
CD NO	REASON	BY		TWP-6 Greenwood
34-35-36				MAP 10
10 cards	COMM listing (1-20-88) 32			(Black 1-20)
54				

	NUMBER OF UNITS		CARD NUMBERS OMITTED	CARD NUMBERS ADDED
02	54 LAST ROUTING NO.			
03	NO. OF PARCELS	54		
04	CARDS OMITTED	-0		
05	CARDS ADDED	+0	FIELD FUNCTION	
06	NO. OF SERIES CARDS	+5	MEASURE / LIST / REVIEW	
07	TOTAL CARDS	59		
08	DWELLINGS	30	011 · 29 · 10 (1-10-88 / 11-15-88) 011 · 29 · 10 (1-10-88 / 11-15-88) 012	0 / 1
09	COMMERCIALS	3	021 · 021 · 022	
10	APARTMENTS	3	021 · 021 · 022	
11	INDUSTRIAL-REPORTS	0	024 · 024 · 026	
12	INDUSTRIAL-CARDED	0	025 · 025 · 026	
13	FARMS	2	013 · 2 · 10 (1-10-88 / 11-15-88) 013 · 2 · 10 (1-10-88 / 11-15-88) 014	
14	AUXILIARY IMPVMTS.	3	3 (1-10-88 / 11-15-88) 3 · 10 (1-10-88 / 11-15-88)	
15	EXEMPTS	2	015 · 2 · 10 (1-10-88 / 11-15-88) 015 · 2 · 10 (1-10-88 / 11-15-88) 015	
16	PUBLIC UTILITIES	1	027 028 · 027 028 · 029	
17	VACANT LAND	15	15 · 10 (1-10-88 / 11-15-88) 15 · 10 (1-10-88 / 11-15-88)	

	OFFICE FUNCTION	ACT CODE	DATE	BY	CHK BY
18	ROUTING-LAST NO. USED 54	002	1-2-88	4	
19	LOT SIZES ENTERED	002	1-4-88	5	
20	SKETCHES DWG./FARM	002	12-10-88	3	
21	TRANSFERED COMM./IND.	002	12-10-88	3	
22	SQ. FT. AREA DWG./FARM	003			
23	COMPUTATION COMM./IND.	003			
24	DWELLING	003			
25	EXT. FEAT.	003			
26	PRICING FARM BLDGS.	003			
27	COMM./IND.	003			
28	PRE-REVIEW CHECK/Q.C.	003			
29	LAND PRICING	017			
30	LAND EXTENDED	004			
31	DWG./FARM	005			
32	FINAL CHECK COMM./IND.	005			
33					
34	DP ENCODED				
35	DP VERIFIED				
36	COPYBACK	009			
37					
38	100% COMPLETE-LOGGED				

COMMERCIAL CARDS		IND. CARDS		EX. CARDS	
CD NO	TYPE	CD NO	TYPE	CD NO	TYPE
34	Office			52	Church
35	Gas Sta.			53	School
36	Fast F.				

50	INCOMPL. FIELD WORK	
CD NO	REASON	
34-35-36	3 COMM - NOT LIST	
10	3 CARDS - NOT LIST	
54	P.U. - NOT LIST	
14	DWLG - UNDER CONST	

60	MARKET DATA				
CD NO	LAND ONLY	BLDG ONLY	LD & BLDG	YR	NOTE
13	5000	25000 (TB)		87	
23	6000			85	
30			61500	88	
31			34000	87	

Commercial data collectors should have experience in residential data collection and knowledge of commercial and industrial valuation procedures. More training and a higher level of supervision are required. To use the capabilities of the available staff more efficiently, work assignments may be broken down by major property use and complexity.

Commercial data collectors need to present themselves in a businesslike manner and be prepared to deal with a variety of circumstances. More time may be required to explain the reason for the visit and gain the confidence of the property owner. Often the owner is not present and the data collector's contact is with an agent or a tenant.

Figure 10.   Sample Data Mailer

RESIDENTIAL PROPERTY DESCRIPTION REPORT

JULY 8, 1987

THIS REPORT CONTAINS THE DESCRIPTION INFORMATION COLLECTED FOR YOUR PROPERTY. PLEASE REFER TO THE ENCLOSED NOTICE FOR INSTRUCTIONS AND DEFINITIONS.

MAKE CORRECTIONS BY MAIL ONLY

(MAIL ADDRESS)
ASSESSORS OFFICE
TOWN HALL

— —

IDENTIFICATION INFORMATION
TAX MAP NO.   363-1-25
ITEM NUMBER   205180
SCHOOL DIST.
LOCATION   814 SOUTHSIDE AVE.
PROPERTY TYPE   1 FAMILY RESIDENCE

01	SALE DATE		11/76	21 HEAT TYPE	HOT WATER
02	SALE PRICE		41000	FUEL TYPE	OIL
03	LOT SIZE	1	75×178	22 CENTRAL AIR	NO
04	NEIGHBORHOOD TYPE		RESIDENTIAL	23 NUMBER OF BEDROOMS	6
05	ZONING		A	24 NUMBER OF BATHROOMS	2.0
06	WATER		PUBLIC	25 TOTAL ROOMS	9
07	UTILITIES (GAS)		NO	26 BATHROOM QUALITY	NORMAL
08	ROAD		IMPROVED	27 KITCHEN QUALITY	NORMAL
09	TRAFFIC		LIGHT	28 BATH REMODELED	NO
10	VIEW		NONE	29 KITCHEN REMODELED	NO
11	SITE ELEVATION		LEVEL	30 INTERIOR CONDITION	NORMAL
12	DRIVEWAY		PAVED	31 EXTERIOR CONDITION	NORMAL
13	SITE COMPARABILITY		TYPICAL	32 DORMERS	NONE
14	ENTRANCE GAINED		YES	33 BASEMENT REC AREA	YES
15	STORY HEIGHT		2.0	34 FIREPLACES	NONE
16	STYLE		COLONIAL	35 BASEMENT GARAGE	NONE
17	WALL CONSTRUCTION		ALUM/VINYL	36 CONSTRUCTION QUALITY	AVERAGE
18	YEAR BUILT		1952	37 TOTAL LIVING AREA	1464
19	YEAR REMODELED		NONE	38 OTHER STRUCTURES	DET. GARAGE
20	BASEMENT		FULL		

FILL IN IF CORRECTION IS NEEDED

OCCUPANT
814 SOUTHSIDE AVE.
WEST ISLIP NY
11795

SIGNATURE _____

DATE   _____

PHONE   _____

MAKE CORRECTIONS BY MAIL ONLY

Data Maintenance

Once data have been collected, they must be kept up-to-date. Data maintenance is organized to minimize the number of trips to the field. Work is organized geographically and, if possible, scheduled close to the assessment date to eliminate repeat trips to check on partial construction.

Data collection does not stop when all of the properties in the jurisdiction have been visited. Periodic physical review (at least once every four to six years) is essential to maintain an accurate and current inventory. (See the IAAO *Standard on Mass Appraisal of Real Property* [1984].) Building permits do not catch all changes in property characteristics, especially important ones such as property condition. The review can be a careful drive-by of properties in the area to look for signs of change. Unreported improvements should be noted and the property owner contacted to bring assessment records up-to-date.

In areas that do not have effective building permit systems, aerial photographs are another way to spot new construction. Comparison of property records against aerial photographs can identify unreported improvements. It may even be feasible to determine type of structure and approximate square footage from the photographs. Aerial photographs are particularly effective in rural areas where improvements are hard to see from the road.

Land Information and Ownership Records

Assessors and cadastral mappers should understand constitutional, statutory, and common law governing parcel mapping and ownership determination and then develop policies to cover basic problems. They also need to communicate effectively and knowledgeably with grantees, grantors, and fellow land information professionals in the banking, surveying, real estate, and title insurance fields.

The Legal Framework

An understanding of property law, and an ability to communicate it, is essential for two reasons: because land is valuable and because land owners have emotional bonds with their properties and may react strongly when an assessor's office processes a conveyance and discovers problems with ownership or boundaries.

One major task is determining who should receive a parcel's assessment notice and tax bill. For many properties, where there is a continuous chain of title evidenced through recorded instruments, this is relatively simple. But many conveyances are not so straightforward. These typical problems arise: grantee not the owner of record; property appearing to overlap adjoining parcel; conveyances through complex divorce decrees, trust agreements, or decrees of distribution; properties involving vacated streets and alleys or abandoned railroads; and even multiple claimants to the same parcel, each holding an apparently valid title. In such situations, it may be necessary to carry multiple names on ownership rolls (just as it may be necessary to show multiple locations for corners and boundaries on a parcel map). Such an action should be explained to the affected persons and documented for future reference.

The transfer of ownership of real property, or of partial interests in real property, is usually done by means of a written instrument. The primary ones used to convey title are deeds, wills, contracts for deed, and unrecorded conveyances.

Deeds

A deed is a written agreement, in proper legal form, that conveys title to or an interest in real property. The purpose of the deed is to describe the land intended to be conveyed and identify it for title purposes, as protection for the purchaser. The most important parts of the deed are

1. *Names of parties.* The grantor is the seller and the grantee is the buyer. A deed may contain multiple grantors and grantees.
2. *Consideration (value exchange).* A consideration does not have to be money. "Love and affection" is often used. It is also common to have a nominal consideration such as "one dollar and other good and valuable consideration." However, some states require full disclosure of purchase price and terms in the deed. Others require the submission of an affidavit or transfer document if this information is not included in the deed.
3. *Granting clause.* A clause containing words of conveyance such as "grant, transfer, or convey."
4. *Habendum clause.* A clause such as "to have and to hold to said grantee, his heirs, successors, and assigns."
5. *Legal description.* The description of the property being conveyed. An inadequate description does not necessarily void a deed.
6. *Testimony clause.* The concluding clause, usually beginning "in witness whereof."
7. *Signature.* The signature of the grantor is required. The grantee's is usually not required.

8. *Witness.* The signature of those witnessing the signing. In some states this must be notarized.
9. *Date.* The date of execution of the signatures.

Most deeds are recorded, or entered into the public record. Although recording statutes vary, the deed is usually recorded in the county where the real estate is located. Recordation of property transfers is often mandatory. The act of recording provides notice to all the world of the existence of the transfer and the description of the property. Recording protects innocent purchasers who might be unaware of an unrecorded instrument, protects the grantee in the event that the instrument is lost or altered, gives legal priority to interests in order of recording, and gives evidence that the instrument has been delivered and is authentic.

Types of Deeds A warranty deed contains the most assurances for the grantee. In it the grantor warrants that he or she owns the property and has the right to sell it, and that there are no encumbrances against the property not specified in the deed. The grantor guarantees the title against defects arising both before and during the time he or she owned the land, agrees to bear the expense of defending the grantee's title if a third party asserts a rightful claim, and assures the grantee that he or she will perform any acts necessary to perfect the title.

A special warranty deed does not contain the above assurances. The grantor warrants the title only against defects arising during the period of his or her ownership of the property, not against defects existing before that time. A special warranty deed is often used by executors or trustees when conveying the property of a principal, as they usually have no authority to warrant against acts of their predecessors.

A quitclaim deed is one in which the grantor releases whatever interest he or she may have in the property. There are no warranties as to title or possession, and there is no assurance that the grantor even had any interest in the property. Quitclaim deeds are commonly used to resolve boundary disputes, title problems, and contract defaults, but may also be used simply for legal convenience.

A deed of correction is used to correct errors in a prior deed. For example, a mistake may be discovered later in a legal description.

A mineral or timber deed conveys only that specific ownership interest, not the entire real property. Mineral deeds may convey only one mineral, or one seam of a mineral.

Many other types of deeds are used; however, most property transfers are done with warranty deeds. Laws and customs as to property transfer by deed vary.

Wills

A will is a written document in which the testator (maker of the will) provides for the disposition of both real and personal property. A will takes legal effect only upon the testator's death; thus, it can be revoked or amended at any time before death. The testator must be of age and of sound mind, and must declare the writing to be his or her "last will and testament."

For a will to become operative, it must be filed in the proper court and admitted to probate. Creditors and other interested parties are thus notified to present their claims or show why the provisions of the will should not be enforced by the court. The executor

of an estate must file a final accounting to the court showing all income, expenses, and remaining assets. Depending on the complexity of the estate, the court may not release the executor and settle the estate for many years. During this time, the property is assessed to the "estate." Real property transfers as a result of a will can come in two forms. If the property must be sold to satisfy debts or to distribute the proceeds to the heirs, an executor's or administrator's deed may be filed. If the will passes the real property directly to one or more persons, no additional record is necessary.

Some laws recognize the interest a husband has in property owned by his wife at the time of her death (curtesy) and the interest a wife acquires in the property her husband held or acquired at any time during the marriage (dower). These rights do not become a legal interest in the property until the spouse's death. They give the surviving spouse a lifetime interest in the property, even if it has been willed to someone else.

A person who dies without a will or after leaving an invalid will is said to die intestate. Property passes to heirs or descendants according to the applicable laws of descent. If a person dies intestate and without heirs, the property transfers to the state through the process of escheat.

Contract for Deed and Unrecorded Conveyances

Contract for Deed   A contract for deed, also called a real estate contract or a land contract, is an agreement between the seller and buyer for the purchase of real property. The purchase price is paid in installments over the period of the contract, with the balance due at maturity. Usually the buyer is given possession of the property, and the seller retains the legal title. After the buyer completes the required payments, the seller is obliged to deliver legal title in the property through a deed.

Unrecorded Conveyances As a general rule, the law does not require a conveyance to be recorded in order for it to be considered a valid and legal transaction. Legally, the owner of the property is the party to whom title has passed, and deliverance of the deed constitutes transfer of title. However, it can be a local policy that a conveyance must be recorded before the assessor's office changes the ownership record.

Other Sources of Land Information and Ownership Records

Many local offices with various titles and responsibilities have records that provide land information and land ownership records. The responsibilities associated with recording and maintaining the land information base are recording, dividing, and transferring title; inventorying; valuing; assessing; and collecting property taxes.

The following are sources of information:
- Recorder of mortgages and liens
- Business promotion and regulation offices and agencies
- Law enforcement and public protection agencies
- Planning and zoning agencies
- Agricultural promotion and regulation agencies and offices
- Transportation, engineering, and surveying agencies
- Court records
- Historical archives
- Education and research institutions

- Federal and state land management agencies

Sales Data

Sales data are needed for specifying and calibrating valuation models and for sales ratio studies. The reliability of any valuation model or sales ratio study depends on the quantity and quality of its data. Sales data must be collected, edited, and adjusted to obtain valid indicators of market value. Ratio studies also require data on appraised (or assessed) values. Data on property characteristics are needed for stratification and the preparation of sales reports.

Useful Sales Data

The following sales data are useful for property appraisal and ratio studies and should be collected whenever possible:

1. *Sale price.* Sale price is the single most important information about any sale. Adjustments to the sale price, often necessary before a sale can be used, are only possible if the price has been identified.
2. *Names and addresses of buyer and seller.* These allow a current ownership record to be maintained, identify the parties to the transfer, and enable the assessor to request additional information on the sale.
3. *Relationship of buyer and seller.* Any blood or marital relationships between individuals or corporate relationships between businesses must be discovered, because sales between related parties may not reflect market value.
4. *Property address, parcel identifier, and legal description.* This information links the sale

to the assessor's records and identifies the property's location. Without careful matching of parcel identifier with legal description, the wrong appraised or assessed value may be used in a ratio study. The legal description also helps identify parcel splits, which are not usable in ratio studies unless separate values have been assigned to the new parcels. Finally, this information can be used to prevent sales from being included twice. An example is a sale of vacant land from a developer to a builder, followed six months later by a sale of the improved lot from the builder to a private individual. In such situations, the appraised value should be matched against whichever sale (if any) accurately reflects the parcel's status on the assessment date.

5. *Type of transfer and deed.* A sale used as a comparable or in a ratio study must meet the criteria of an arm's-length, open-market transaction. In such a sale, the seller is under no undue pressure to sell, but is willing to do so and seeks the highest possible price on the open market. Similarly, the buyer is not forced to buy, is knowledgeable, and seeks to pay the lowest possible price. The type of deed often indicates whether it is usable. A warranty deed, for example, is generally associated with a usable sale; gift and sheriff deeds are not.

6. *Interest transferred.* A transaction that conveys the full rights of ownership to a property is known as a "fee simple" transfer. Transfers that convey less than full interest are rarely usable in ratio studies without adjustment, unless the appraised value and sale price reflect the same ownership rights. Examples include sales involving life estates, encumbered leases, fractional interests, and mineral rights.

7. *Instrument number.* When recorded, each transaction is assigned a unique identification number, which identifies the sale and makes sales research easier.

8. *Personal property.* If significant personal property is included in the sale price, the value of the personal property must be estimated and subtracted from the price to determine the value of the real property transferred.

9. *Financing.* The financing of a transfer can affect the sale price. The information needed to determine whether an adjustment to the sale price is required (and, if so, by how much) includes amount of down payment, type of loan (fixed or variable), interest rate, amortization provisions, and the type and value of any trades.

10. *Date of transfer.* This is usually the date the sale was agreed to, as reflected in a signed contract or agreement. The date the deed or other document of transfer was filed or recorded can be used if there was only a short delay in recording the sale.

Obtaining Sales Data

Both the sales comparison approach and sales ratio studies require sufficient arm's-length, open market transfers. Three basic sources of sales data are real estate transfer documents, buyers and sellers, and third parties.

Real Estate Transfer Documents These include deeds, contracts or agreements of sale, and affidavits of property value. A real property transfer tax, if based on the full sale price, enables calculation of total price. Laws mandating full disclosure of sales data to assessment and equalization officials are the single most effective tool for the acquisition of sales data. Disclosure laws are especially important in rural areas, where every available sale is needed. At least thirty states require full disclosure of the sale price on transfer documents.

Buyers and Sellers When sales data are not available on transfer documents, are incomplete, or require verification, assessors can contact parties to the transaction, particularly buyers or sellers. Taxpayers are more likely to supply information if they understand why it is needed. Sales information is obtained from buyers and sellers by mail questionnaire, in a telephone interview, or in a face-to-face interview.

Mail Questionnaire The form should request information concisely. Clear questions will increase the number and accuracy of responses, and information received will be easier to analyze. The questionnaire should be accompanied by a signed cover letter on official stationery that explains why the information is requested and names a person to call in case of questions. The cover letter should specify a return date not more than two or three weeks from the mailing date. Postage paid return envelopes improve the response rate. If no response is received in three or four weeks, a second mailing should be made. If it is unsuccessful, another party to the sale can be contacted.

The questionnaire should include all necessary data items. Separate questionnaires can be developed for different property classes. Although mail questionnaires are relatively inexpensive, the assessment agency must plan for printing and mailing costs and for staff to review and process the data.

Telephone Interview Advantages of the telephone interview are quick response and the opportunity for immediate clarification. This is particularly useful with income-producing properties, the sales of which frequently include complex financial arrangements and substantial amounts of personal property. Disadvantages include an inability to prove the caller's identity, the need for trained staff, and the difficulty of reaching the party called. Accuracy of information tends to be lower than with a written and signed confirmation. A sales interview form, similar to the mail questionnaire, should be used to record the information.

Face-to-Face Interview Although often cost prohibitive, a face-to-face interview is the most effective way of obtaining sales information from buyers and sellers. Refusals are less frequent, the information is usually reliable, and unusual or special considerations about the sale may be revealed. The approach is particularly well suited to commercial and industrial sales. A qualified analyst or appraiser should conduct the field interviews.

Third-Party Sources Third-party sources constitute an additional source of sales data and are particularly important when transfer documents do not provide full disclosure or omit important data. In such cases, the assessor should seek a strong working relationship with third-party sources: real estate agents, multiple listing services, title companies, private appraisers, financial institutions, leasing agents, and certified property managers.

Local organizations that collect real estate data, usually for membership use or sale to interested parties, include real estate boards and multiple listing services, local tax assessing offices, credit bureaus, cadastral map reproduction firms, university research centers, and private brokerage or appraisal firms.

Metropolitan areas usually have a board of realtors, and often other broker groups, that sponsor multiple listing services. When property listed through a multiple listing service is sold, the broker must supply information about the completed transaction. Each property sold and its terms of sale are, therefore, available on computer or in a published book. Some boards provide information to members only; some share with other real estate organizations.

University research centers, many of which are sponsored by license fees paid by brokers and salespersons, may have brought together data on real estate transactions collected from other sources within the state or province. These data are often helpful in identifying trends by city for various types of property.

Many real estate appraisers and brokers retain data for property owned by their clients and others. They will often share information, usually for reciprocity rather than payment.

Sales Screening and Analysis

Sales must be screened to identify sales that require adjustment or are not indicative of market value. In general, sales fall into seven categories:

Market Value Sales (Single Parcel)   This group includes all single-parcel sales that appear to be arm's-length and representative of market value. They may require adjustments for financing, personal property, or time of sale before being used for ratio studies or the sales comparison approach.

Multiple-Parcel Sales Sales including more than one parcel are common, particularly in commercial, industrial, and agricultural categories. In general, these sales are as valid as single-parcel sales, but all parcels included in the sale must be identified. In sales ratio studies, the appraised or assessed values should be summed before they are divided by the sale price. The sale price should be adjusted for any plottage value, that is the value of the combined parcels in excess of the sum of their individual values.

Non-Arm's-Length Sales Such sales should not be used in ratio studies. Some typical examples are

- *Sales involving courts, governmental entities, or public utilities*. These are generally forced sales, such as condemnation or tax sales.
- *Sales involving charitable, religious, or educational institutions*. These are often full or partial gifts and thus not representative of market value.
- *Sales in which a financial institution is the buyer*. These sales are often made in lieu of a foreclosure and are not exposed to the open market. However, open-market sales in which a financial institution is a willing buyer, such as the purchase of vacant land for a branch bank, are likely to be valid. Sales in which a financial institution is the *seller* should be viewed cautiously but may be valid if made on the open market.
- *Sales between relatives or corporate affiliates*. These are not open-market sales and are usually made at prices favorable to the buyer. Relationships between buyers and

sellers are usually best identified by a direct question on the affidavit of value or sales questionnaire. (A difference in surnames is never a sufficient indication of no relationship.) Occasionally, sales between relatives do represent market value, particularly in rural areas where blood relationships among landowners are common. Corporate sales often require considerable research to determine legal relationships.

- *Sales of convenience.* Sales of this kind are made to change or correct the title or deed. The grantee and grantor may be the same, and the sale price is usually nominal. A review of the deed is usually the best method of identification.
- *Estate sales.* Sales in which the *buyer* is an executor or trustee are usually nonmarket sales at nominal consideration. Sales from an estate may be made to satisfy the debts of the deceased or the wishes of an heir; otherwise, sales in which an estate is the *seller* may well be valid arm's-length sales.

Partial Interest Sales Sales of partial interests require careful analysis to determine whether they are open-market, arm's-length sales. It may be possible to impute the value of the fee simple interest in a property, if the sum of partial interests sold at the same time equals 100 percent and all the sales were at arm's length. Plottage should be considered. However, these sales often involve related parties and may not represent full market value. Inclusion in a ratio study is only possible if a combination of sales conveying full interest occurs at one time. (Even in this rare situation, the sale should be used only if needed to produce an adequate sample.)

Land Contracts This is an installment sale in which the buyer initially pays only part

of the purchase price and agrees to make additional payments at stated intervals. Title does not transfer until the final payment is made. However, the date of sale is the date on which the contract was signed, not when the deed was recorded or title transferred. Because the contract itself is often not recorded, discovery of these sales is difficult until the deed is finally recorded. The sale then is likely to be too old to be used.

Trades A trade includes items of real or personal property as a portion of the price. The transaction should not be used if the items traded constitute the entire price. Otherwise, if the value of the traded items is stipulated, can be ascertained, or is small in comparison with the total price, the sale *can* be used by including the value of the items traded in the total purchase price. As a general rule, however, exclude sales involving trades if the full price cannot be reliably established and there is an otherwise adequate number of valid sales.

Outliers Outliers are properties with very high or low sales ratios. They may result from poor or outdated appraisals, non-arm's-length sales, or a mismatch between the property sold and the property appraised. Particularly when the sample is small, outliers can distort ratio studies and should be reviewed carefully. One reasonable approach is to flag for review all ratios that lie above or below selected cut-off points, say 0.25 and 2.00. Another approach is to review all ratios that fall more than two standard deviations from the mean ratio (usually about 5 percent of the ratios).

Table 1 contains an example of an outlier ratio, 2.200, associated with the tenth sale. If that sale is invalid, its elimination will improve the accuracy of ratio statistics calculated for the sample. When samples are large, outliers can be ignored or, preferably, automatically excluded by cut-off points set to exclude predominantly invalid sales.

Although sales screening and verification are necessary, their goal is to obtain an adequate number of valid sales, not to find reasons to exclude sales. Most sales are usable for the sales comparison approach and ratio studies, although many require adjustments. In large samples, the accidental inclusion of a few invalid sales will have little effect on ratio studies.

Adjustments for Personal Property

Many sales include significantly valuable personal property. If these sales are used in ratio studies or mass appraisal, the value of the personal property must be estimated and subtracted from the sale price to determine the price paid for the real property alone. Statutory and administrative definitions help determine what constitutes personal property. The preferred method of adjusting for personal property is to identify the personal

property items in each sale, obtain or make an estimate of their market value, and subtract it from the total purchase price. Personal property items often included in the purchase of residential property are rugs, curtains, draperies, furniture, above-ground swimming pools, and refrigerators and other movable appliances. In new residences, estimated value can usually be obtained from the buyer or builder. In older residences, personal property has usually depreciated, making an estimate more difficult. If the buyer or seller has furnished an estimate of personal property value that appears reasonable, the estimate can be accepted and subtracted from the sale price. If the items are listed and described without giving a value, an appraiser can make a reasonable estimate or, if the value appears trivial, assume zero value.

In commercial, industrial, and multifamily residential sales, personal property usually is more than a small percentage of the total sale price. A reasonable value for personal property must be estimated. Personal property usually included in such sales are machinery and equipment, trade fixtures, inventories, furnishings, and business licenses. Transfer documents and sales questionnaires can include questions that identify and obtain the estimated value of such items. A personal inspection may be required for unusual items or for sales in which the value of personal property is a large proportion of the sale price. When the amount of personal property is substantial and a reliable estimate of value cannot be obtained, the sale may be excluded.

When adequate data on personal property are not available, another procedure is to estimate reasonable percentage allowances by type of property. This is best done by

Table 1.   Example of Outlier Ratio

Sale number	Appraised value (A)	Sale price (S)	Ratio (A/S)
1	$15,000	$25,000	0.600
2	15,000	22,000	0.682
3	17,000	20,000	0.850
4	19,000	22,000	0.864
5	25,000	27,000	0.926
6	24,000	25,000	0.960
7	25,000	25,000	1.000
8	20,000	16,000	1.250
9	35,000	25,000	1.400
10	55,000	25,000	2.200

reviewing a sample of transfers for each type of property and determining the percentage of the purchase price usually attributable to personal property. Although not as accurate as an individual analysis of each sale, the procedure can be cost-effective and is preferred to ignoring personal property items completely or making an arbitrary across-the-board adjustment. When adequate personal property data have been obtained for some sales but not others, the technique can be used to make a reasonable, or typical, adjustment for sales lacking personal property data.

Adjustments for Financing

The market value of property is its most probable selling price in terms of cash or the equivalent. When financing reflects prevailing market practices and interest rates, sales prices can be considered equivalent to cash. Under such conditions, neither the buyer nor the seller gains any advantage as a result of the manner of financing; hence, there is no reason for the sale price to differ significantly from its cash value. Indeed, in such situations the seller usually receives all cash for the property, if not directly from the buyer, then from a bank or other third-party lender.

Appraisers have long recognized that nonmarket, or creative, financing tends to inflate sales prices, because creative financing usually involves below-market interest rates. Unless compensating adjustments are made to the sales prices of property so financed, using the sales in valuation models or ratio studies will produce distorted results. Values will be overstated. Ratios will be understated.

Except in periods of unusually tight money and high interest rates, most transfers will be financed at prevailing market terms and rates; thus they will *not* require financing adjustments. Adjustments are needed if (1) the seller and lender are the same party, (2) the buyer assumes an existing mortgage at a nonmarket interest rate, (3) the buyer assumes an existing lease, (4) the seller pays points, or (5) the buyer pays delinquent taxes. In general, sales prices should not be adjusted for real estate commissions or other closing costs, except for points paid by the seller.

As with the treatment of personal property, the preferred means of adjusting for financing is by individual parcel using compound interest tables. Appendix 5-1 describes methods of adjusting in these five situations. When individual parcel adjustments are impractical because data are not available, an alternative procedure, acceptable for ratio studies and mass appraisal, is to develop and apply percentage adjustments by type of property and, if known, type of financing. These adjustments can be based on a sample of sales for which the necessary financing data have been obtained.

Finally, the market may not recognize or capitalize the full amount of financing adjustments based on compound interest tables. This topic is discussed in appendix 5-2.

Adjustments for Time

When price levels are changing significantly, sales prices must be adjusted for time. Separate time-adjustment factors by type of property and geographic area may be necessary, as rates of change in real estate prices often vary with these factors. If practical, the target date to which sales prices are adjusted should be the assessment date. When the assessment date is a future date, sales prices should be adjusted as close to it as is possible.

Sales prices can be adjusted by either month or quarter; annual adjustments tend to be imprecise. Also, rates of value change can be derived and applied on either a compounding or constant (straight-line) basis. Although compounding may be more technically correct, the straight-line method is simpler. Except in cases of extreme inflation or deflation, the two methods produce similar results. Appendix 5-3 discusses methods of deriving time-adjustment factors from market data.

Cost and Income and Expense Data

Valuation by the cost approach requires data on construction costs. These and other market data are used to develop and update cost manuals. Cost manuals represent cost models in a format that allows the models to be applied easily. Developing a cost manual is both a model specification and a model calibration task. For that reason, the discussion of cost data appears in chapter 8 on the cost approach.

Valuation by the income approach requires information on income and expenses. Sources of market data for rental income and expense include national publications, local sources, and the property owner. National organizations collect information from owners and managers in major cities on local rents and operating expenses for various types of commercial property. An appraiser can use the information judiciously to determine whether the subject property appears consistent with experience reported nationally.

Obtaining Income and Expense Data

Income and expense data are not needed on each property, but sufficient data are needed to estimate typical income and expense figures for various types of income-producing properties. The assessor should seek information on the number and type of rental units (apartments, square feet, and so on), per unit rents, vacancy rates, collection losses (optional), miscellaneous income, and allowable expenses. Once collected, this information can be used to estimate normal unit rents, potential gross rents, normal vacancy and collection loss rates, normal gross rents, normal gross incomes, normal expenses, and normal net incomes. There are at least five methods of gathering income and expense information: (1) mail questionnaires, (2) personal interview, (3) telephone, (4) assessment appeals, and (5) published studies and other third-party sources.

Mail Questionnaires Many assessment jurisdictions have adopted the practice of mailing income and expense questionnaires before a reappraisal. The questionnaire should be as brief and clear as possible but request all essential information. The questionnaire should appear on official stationery or should be accompanied by a cover letter on official stationery. Either the questionnaire or the cover letter should briefly state the purpose and importance of the requested information, cite statutes if applicable, and bear the assessor's signature.

The questionnaire should provide a means to list each type of unit and actual and scheduled rents for each type. Types of units should be defined in the instructions so that responses will be uniform. Important questions to be answered about rentals are whether utilities or furnishings are included and whether there is seasonal variation in rents. Expenses should be listed by category. A three-year history of itemized other income, vacancy rates, and expenses is useful for normalizing income and expenses. Different forms for apartment buildings, hotels and motels, service stations, and shopping centers are usually necessary.

In addition to sending out income and expense questionnaires before a reappraisal, it can be highly desirable to do so when a sale occurs or a lease is negotiated. Questionnaires sent out as a result of sales will be very similar to those used in a reappraisal, except that information should be requested as of the sale date. Such information is useful in the development of capitalization rates.

Income and expense questionnaires mailed in response to newly negotiated leases aid the assessor in maintaining current record of lease information. The questionnaire should request information on the property included in the lease, the duration of the lease, annual rent, lessor and lessee's responsibility for various expenses, and renewal options.

Although questionnaires are an inexpensive way to gather information, response rates are poor. Chapter 8 of *Improving Real Property Administration* (IAAO 1978) has samples of questionnaires and a more detailed discussion.

Personal Interviews Personal interviews are another means of gathering information. In addition to a high response rate, personal interviews have the advantage of affording the opportunity to resolve unclear responses. The one obvious disadvantage is that personal visits require a good deal of professional staff time. The method is most efficient when it is combined with the collection of physical property data.

In gathering income and expense data in the field, it is important to use a form to record the most essential data. This ensures uniformity of collection procedures and helps the assessor to collect complete data. Copies of ledgers or other statements that the property owner or agent is willing to supply can be reviewed in the office.

Telephone In general, the telephone is not a good primary source of income and expense data. The property owner or agent may not be in, may not have time to talk, or may not have all the relevant information at hand. More important, there is generally a reluctance to supply such information over the phone. The phone is, however, an excellent supplementary source of income and expense data, particularly when returned questionnaires are unclear or incomplete. In such cases the owner or agent should remember answering the questionnaire and therefore should know the identity of the caller and the purpose of the call. The caller should have the relevant documents at hand and questions written out so the call can be completed quickly and efficiently.

Assessment Appeals A fourth possible source of income and expense data is assessment reviews and appeals. In some jurisdictions, property owners or agents questioning or appealing an assessment are requested to fill out an income and expense statement for the assessor's review. These statements are filed and used to supplement information obtained through other sources.

Published Studies and Other Third-Party Sources The annual *Building Experience Exchange Report* published by the Building Owners and Managers Association (BOMA)

International provides information on office building rental rates and operating expenses in major United States cities. Information is reported by BOMA members. The Urban Land Institute releases a new edition of *Dollars and Cents of Shopping Centers* every two years. The National Retail Merchants Association's *Department Store Lease Study* is another source of information on shopping centers.

The Institute of Real Estate Management (IREM) of the National Association of Realtors publishes annually *Income/Expense Analysis*, which provides information on office and apartment buildings. Several groups publish data on national and local trends in the hotel and motel industry: Laventhol & Horwath (*Lodging Industry*), Pannell Kerr Forster (*Trends in the Hotel Industry),* and Hospitality Valuation Services (*Hospitality Market Data Exchange* and *Rushmore on Hotel Valuation*).

In addition, reliable information may often be obtained from such local sources as real estate brokers, private appraisers, lenders, zoning and planning agencies, renters, and newspaper advertisements.

Data Management

Data management requires system controls. One such control is the accounting for every property within the jurisdiction. An up-to-date cadastral mapping program provides a clear means of identifying each property and its current owner(s). The parcel identification number should incorporate the map identification number for each property on the assessment roll. The computer file containing basic parcel and ownership information is the assessment administration file. In a CAMA system, a correspondence should be established between records in the assessment administration and property characteristics files. Skeletal records can be created in the property characteristics file for new records in the assessment administration file. The skeletal records can be used to produce reports showing those parcels for which inventory work must still be completed. This control mechanism assumes that both the assessment administration and property characteristics files use the parcel identification number as a key.

With proper controls in place, the ongoing addition and deletion of records from the assessment administration file due to splits and combinations should produce the same changes in the property characteristics files. These changes should be reported periodically to the data collection staff.

Source Document Control

Source documents are paper or hard copy records (such as property record forms, income and expense forms, deeds, and data transcription forms) that are the "source" of information stored and maintained in computer files.

Various mechanisms can be developed for controlling source documents. When many documents move between office and field (as they do during a reappraisal program) controls on the documents are important, especially when data entry takes place in a separate office. Control forms can be tailored to the project work plan and can track batches of source documents as they move from one phase of the operation to the next (see figure 9). In addition to control forms for each batch, a log book listing all batches and their current status is essential.

The creation of the property characteristics file should be done geographically, following the flow of the field work. If no field work is involved (for example, in conversion of existing manual records), doing this geographically is still a good idea, because work for a given area can be completed in phases. Source documents should be grouped according to map, usually in units of 50 to 100 property record forms, which will require several hours of data entry work.

Documents are sometimes misplaced or lost by careless employees who do not understand the cost of replacing the documents. Once data have been entered in the computer, the source document is replaceable to the extent that all significant information has been computerized.

Data Entry

Data entry is the process of getting the information on the source documents into the computer. With on-line computer processing, data entry is interactive. Computerized data are organized into "screens" of logically grouped sets of information. Formatted screens display the labels and the input areas for each piece of information to be entered (see figure 11). The computer programs can verify the validity of data as they are entered by requiring that only numbers be entered into a field containing numeric data. Entries can be checked against computerized lists and ranges of allowed values. Logical edits ensure that corresponding pieces of information are consistent. Perimeter sketch vectors can be edited, areas calculated, and perimeter sketches displayed. Well-formatted screens make visual verification easier. Manual checking of source documents may be combined with data entry. However, incomplete source documents must be returned to the data collector.

Because on-line computer programs can check information as it is entered and perform relatively complicated processing, it is cost-effective to train less skilled clerical employees for data entry.

Employees who enter data should understand the data they are entering and be able to recognize exceptions. During early stages of data input an appraiser, who can decide what should be entered, should be available to help the data entry staff.

Key verification and manual editing are sometimes necessary. If data entry is being done in a batch (noninteractive) mode, the data being entered cannot be immediately checked against existing information for the same property. In this case, manual screening and key verification of data will reduce errors. Batch edit programs should be written to detect remaining errors. With modern data entry, input data can be edited on-line and selected data elements can be key verified.

Batch data entry can be productive and cost-effective if the source documents are well designed for data entry and if controls in data collection and office checking procedures minimize errors in the documents. Experienced data entry operators key in more than 12,000 to 15,000 strokes per hour. A typical property record document requires 200 to 500 strokes. Entry of ownership information or sketch vector information, in addition to typical property characteristics data, requires many more strokes. Interruptions caused by source document errors reduce productivity. Documents with errors should be flagged and corrected before entry.

Data Management Systems

CAMA systems have a module for managing property records. The module creates

Figure 11.   Data Input Screen

```
CAMA   RES S5                                                        3/31/88
DISPLAY   DWELLING DATA—1                     PARCEL 041-02-0-20-15-111.00-0/01

500 PROPERTY INDICATOR      0
505 STORY HEIGHT            10
506 EXTERIOR WALLS          1
507 DWELLING STYLE          01
508 ROOF MATERIAL           01
510 AGE: YEAR BUILT 1       960    AGE   EST       REMODELED   1900
515 BSMT FOUNDATION WALL    1
520 BASEMENT DESCRIPTION    1
525 HEATING & COOLING       2
526 HEATING FUEL TYPE       2
527 HEATING SYSTEM TYPE     6
530 LIV ACOM: TOT RMS       07     BED RMS  03  FAM RMS  1
535 PLUMBING: FULL BATHS    0      HLF BTHS 0   ADDNL FXT  0   TOT FXT   00
540 ATTIC TYPE              1
541 FLOOR COVERING          1
542 INTERIOR WALLS          1
545 PHYSICAL CONDITION      1


PRESS CMD KEY 7 TO EXIT PARCEL                            NEXT FIELD 560
```

computer records to store information from the source documents, loads information into these records, edits the information for validity and consistency, and reports on maintenance activities. The data management system may be either batch or on-line.

Batch Data Management   Data entered from one or more batches of source documents are collected on a computer-readable medium, usually a magnetic tape. The data management system requires the data to be in a special format. Usually the following are included:

- record to be updated (usually identified by a parcel identification number)
- action to take (for example, load information for this record, change existing infor-

mation, remove existing information, or delete this record or parcel)

- effective date of the action (this can be used for sequencing multiple actions affecting the same parcel)
- type of information being loaded to or changed in the record
- information to be loaded

Other control information (the batch identifier and the date of entry) is usually included to aid in tracing back to the source documents if necessary.

Batch data management programs process information through a series of steps. First the information is sorted into the same sequence as the file it will be updating. The sort also puts the transactions for a given parcel or record into effective date sequence so they are applied to the file in the order of occurrence. Next the transactions may be processed through an edit routine that checks them for validity. Incomplete or otherwise invalid transactions are reported and only valid transactions are passed to update the master file.

An update program then processes the transactions against the master file, taking the appropriate actions and reporting the changes. The update program validates that the action is appropriate for the record affected by the change. If it is not, the transaction is rejected and reported on an error report.

The update program produces an audit trail showing all activity against the master file in the update run. Usually this audit trail will include a "from-to" report showing the information in each updated field before and after applying the transaction. A report should also show total number of records in the master file and a list of records by transaction status.

Finally, the batch data management process should include a master edit program that edits the information in each updated record for validity, completeness, and consistency.

On-line Data Management   In on-line operations, data management takes place interactively. Usually a screen will be displayed that solicits the record to be updated and the action to be taken (figure 12). After the operator enters the record's identification number and the action to be taken, the computer checks the master file for the record, validating that the action requested is consistent with the record's current status on the file. If it is not, an error message will be displayed

indicating the problem, and the user will need to correct the entry. If the record is on file, it is retrieved for updating.

Data screens display the information in the record and, based on the action indicated, prompt the user for modifications to the pertinent data fields within the record. As information is entered into individual data fields it may be checked for validity (for example, numeric characters in numeric fields). As screens of information are transmitted to the program, the input data can be edited against more sophisticated criteria including range and table checks. Logical consistency checks can be applied and derived values or results generated. For example, the computer-generated area computations and perimeter sketch shown in figure 13 were produced from the sketch vector input shown on the left side of the figure.

When the update activity is completed, the record may undergo additional checks and processing. Changes to the record may be logged by the program to an audit file that stores before-and-after information for each field updated as well as the time, date, operator, and action taken. This audit file is then used to report daily or weekly all of the updates made to the file (see figure 14). Data displayed on the computer screen should be visually checked against the information on the property record form by someone other than the data entry operator.

Edits

Edits improve the integrity of data in the computer file. They reduce input errors and identify data collection errors. Above all, edits help validate value calculations. Edits can be classified as "hard" or "soft." A hard edit is designed to catch a serious error and

Figure 12.   On-Line Data Management Menu Screen

```
CAMA    RES MM                                                      3/31/88
PARCEL  STATUS ACINA                        PARCEL 041-02-0-20-15-111.00-0/01

                        RESIDENTIAL ON-LINE MENU

          01—DISPLAY THIS RECORD'S DATA

          04—UPDATE THIS RECORD'S DATA
          05—UPDATE THIS RECORD'S APPRAISER REVIEW FIELDS

          07—GROUP DELETE DATA FROM THIS RECORD

          10—DELETE THE APPRAISAL DATA FROM THIS RECORD

                PLEASE ENTER YOUR MENU SELECTION: 00

PRESS CMD KEY 7 TO EXIT PARCEL                          NEXT FIELD 060
```

Figure 13.   On-line Data Management Screen for Displaying Computer Sketch

```
CAMA    RES S7                                                      3/31/88
DISPLAY         DWLG ADDTN & SKETCH             PARCEL 041-02-0-20-15-111.00-0/01
ADDN.    LWR   1ST   2ND   3RD    AREA
601             11                0370    4 – CB – 4
602       50    11                0070    + – 5 + – + – – 17 – – – +
603       50    16                0032    14  14                    |
604             16                0020    |  B |        A        20
605             16                0108    |   |                     |
606                               0000    6 – 5 +                   |
607                               0000    + + – – – 20 – – – + – +
608                               0000    |                         |
       – – – – – – – – – – – – – –        |                         |
651      A0CU30X20                        30                       30
652      A1U30R2CU6R5U14R17D20    |              *          |
653      L22                              |                         |
654      A2U36R2CU14X5                     |                         |
655      A3U50R2CU4X8                      |         E         |
656      A4N                              +6 – – – – 20 – – – –6 +
657      A5R1CR18X6H                       + – – – –18 – – – – +
658
659
660                              GFA MAIN AREA 00600

PRESS CMD KEY 7 TO EXIT PARCEL                          NEXT FIELD 701
```

Figure 14. Audit Trail Report Showing before and after Values for Each Data Item Updated

MAS760   03/31/88   13:58:41

APPRAISER'S CAMA AUDIT TRAIL

PARCEL ID	MAINT DATE	TIME	PRV MT DATE	TRAN CODE	OPER ID	FLD CD	FIELD DESCRIPTION	ORIGINAL FIELD	NEW FIELD
001010010100101001R	033188	13:51	032988	31	XY2	201	SALE-DATA	*00000000000000	**128710010600010
001010010100301A01R	033188	13:53	032488	31	XY2	202	SALE-DATA	*00000000000000	**12871000495001X
001010010100301A01R	033188	13:53	032488	31	XY2	450	PARKING	*222	**121
001010010100301A01R	033188	13:53	032488	31	XY2	553	FB-LV-AREA	*00 000	**14X020
001010010100301B01R	033188	13:55	030488	31	XY2	471	BLDG-PRMT	*0000000000000000000	**00551033088000050001
001010010100301B01R	033188	13:55	030488	31	XY2	565	GRADE-FACT	*D-	**D
001010010100301B01R	033188	13:55	030488	31	XY2	575	CDU	*PR	**FR
001010020200301001R	033188	13:58	110587	31	XY2	560	GFA	*01500	**01200
001010020200301001R	033188	13:58	110587	31	XY2	601	ADDITIONS	* 0000	* 11 0120
001010020200301001R	033188	13:58	110587	31	XY2	602	ADDITIONS	* 0000	** 19 0040
001010020200301001R	033188	13:58	110587	31	XY2	651	SKETCH-VEC	*NV	**A0CU40X30
001010020200301001R	033188	13:58	110587	31	XY2	652	SKETCH-VEC	*	**A1U30R30CR12X10
001010020200301001R	033188	13:58	110587	31	XY2	653	SKETCH-VEC	*	**A2R18CR10D4L10U4H

causes the information being edited to be rejected. A soft edit is designed to catch values that are probably wrong but may be correct in exceptional circumstances. Soft edits result in warning messages but not in the rejection of information. Hard edits are sometimes designed so they can be overridden by a user who enters an acceptance code.

A check digit serves as an internal edit on critical value fields such as the parcel identification number. Check digits catch minor errors such as transposition of two digits in the input sequence, that could result in accessing a different valid parcel identifier. Check digits can be calculated by assigning a numeric weight to each position of the parcel identifier and multiplying the number in that position by the weight. Nonnumeric characters can also be assigned a numerical value. One check digit scheme for eliminating transpositions alternately adds and subtracts the digits in each position. For example, for the identifier 100-134578-5 the check digit is

$$1 - 0 + 0 - 1 + 3 - 4 + 5 - 7 + 8 = 5.$$

If the 5 and 4 had been transposed (identifier 100-135478-3), the check digit would have been calculated as

$$1 - 0 + 0 - 1 + 3 - 5 + 4 - 7 + 8 = 3.$$

The check digit is usually appended to the field it is calculated against and is required to update the parcel.

The data type edit protects against nonnumeric data being entered in all numeric fields.

The range edit is usually performed on numeric data elements to determine if the values fall between a specified minimum and maximum value. For example, in a relatively new midwestern county, year built may be required to fall between 1930 and the current year. If the edit is to be a hard edit, and a few dwellings were built between 1880 and 1930, the range should be expanded or made subject to an override provision.

Value, or table, edits check the value against a list or table of allowable values. Values not on the list or table are rejected. Table edits are used for land use codes, zoning codes, and other items such as structure types and special features.

Cross edits involve "cross checks" between two or more related data elements. For example, finished basement area can be checked against basement code. If a finished basement area is entered but the basement code indicates "no basement," an error message informs the user of the inconsistency.

Ad hoc edits are user-developed in response to particular problems discovered during data collection. A data collection supervisor could, for example, request a report displaying selected information for two-story houses collected by data collector 023 in neighborhood 101A.

System Controls

Building and maintaining a computerized data base requires additional controls. Because the data base is used to determine values for ad valorem taxation, the system should provide basic accounting controls.

As mentioned earlier, any CAMA update activity should be reported on an audit report that shows what information was changed, when it was changed, who changed it, and the reason for the change. Changes in values should be totaled and reconciled. When values are posted from the property characteristics file to the assessment administration file, totals should be produced and balanced between the two files.

To maintain the integrity of the assessor's office, procedures should be established to ensure that employees are not responsible for collecting data or setting values on their own properties.

Multiyear system controls are also necessary. Due to the nature of the assessment cycle, significant overlaps between tax years may occur. A property's value is usually established for the year based upon its status as of the assessment date. Often a period of time after this date is required to establish final values, notify property owners, conduct informal reviews and assessment appeals, and put final values on the assessment and tax rolls. Meanwhile, changes occur that affect the next assessment date: parcels are split or subdivided; buildings are added, remodeled, or demolished; zoning changes affect land values; and so forth. It is necessary to identify the year for which these changes are effective. In early CAMA systems (and in manual operations), this problem was addressed by setting aside the changes for the next year until all current tax year work was done. Most contemporary CAMA systems make provisions for identifying the effective tax year for any data changes, so that data can be entered for the new tax year before work for the current year is completed.

New Developments in Data Collection

Improvements in hardware and software have introduced new products and methods for data inventory. Three of these are hand-held data entry devices, optical scanners, and video imagery.

Hand-held Data Entry Devices

During the early 1980s, several studies were done using hand-held data entry devices for direct input of property characteristics in the field. These devices, in effect, eliminated the paper property record form, replacing it by a small computer file stored in the hand-held computer. The hand-held computer is programmed to display a series of screens to accept data keyed in by the data collector through the device's keyboard. The system is programmed to perform many or all of the same edits on the input that a full CAMA system would perform, and it can also be programmed to carry out value computations. The screens on these systems are now much like those in a full CAMA system.

At the end of the day, the day's work can be transmitted to a central computer to update the master file, and work for the next day can be downloaded to the device. The benefits of such a system are a reduction in paper and elimination of errors of omission in the field and data input errors in the office.

Optical Scanning

Another way to get information into the computer is to design data collection forms to be computer readable. Several techniques are available, including "mark sense" and "optical character reading." With mark sense forms, a grid of "bubbles" corresponds to each character of each field to be entered. Usually the form includes a place to record the numbers above or beside the bubbles. The appropriate bubbles are marked with pencil. A mark sense reader scans the form, translating the location of the marked bubbles on the form into the appropriate characters for output onto a magnetic tape. This works best when all entries are numeric. There are other limitations: visual editing of the form is more difficult, and space limitations reduce the amount of data that can be put on a form because ten bubbles must be allotted for each digit to be recorded (twenty-six if alphabetic, thirty-six if alphanumeric).

Optical character recognition eliminates the need to fill in the bubbles by reading the characters written on the form. However, each character must be written in a precise form in a specific box in order to be read accurately. Optical scanning is usually limited to numbers, although great improvements in pattern recognition technology are being made.

In both mark sensing and optical scanning, rejected forms have to be checked manually and corrected as part of the initial conversion processing or through subsequent data entry.

Video Imagery

Video imagery also has significant implications for data inventory. A complete set of up-to-date video images of each property in the jurisdiction provides a resource that can reduce the need for subsequent field reviews. Even questions on subjective data elements such as grade of construction and condition can often be answered by looking at the video image of the property.

Video imagery provides essentially the same information as a photograph of each property. However, random access to video imagery improves productivity.

Appraisal

Section three deals with general appraisal principles as applied in single-property appraisal. The purposes of this section are to explain how the three approaches to value can be used to replicate the workings of the real estate market and to teach assessors the skills they will need to defend assessments at all levels of appeal.

Chapter 6 shows how the sales comparison approach can be applied to residential, industrial, and commercial properties. Methods of automating selection of comparables and the adjustment grid are also discussed.

Chapter 7 develops a theory of land valuation that integrates concepts from economics and geography. This chapter explains the use of the sales comparison approach and of indirect methods for appraising land. Chapter 7 also addresses development of land valuation models for mass appraisal. Chapter 8, on the cost approach, discusses traditional approaches to the development of cost models, accrued depreciation, the development of cost manuals, and methods of developing a formula-driven cost approach.

Chapters 9–12 deal with the income approach. The material in these chapters covers investment analysis as it relates to real estate, the development of income and expense estimates, lease analysis, and capitalization.

The Sales Comparison Approach

6

Introduction

Constitutions, statutes, and case law define a market value standard for assessment. In assessment litigation, under the "rules of evidence" a bona fide sale of the subject property is considered the best evidence of market value. In the absence of a sale of the subject, sales prices of comparable properties are usually considered the best evidence of market value. Consequently, the sales comparison approach is the preferred approach when sales data are available.

The sales comparison approach models the behavior of the market by comparing the properties being appraised (subjects) with similar properties that have recently sold (comparable properties) or for which offers to purchase have been made. Comparable properties are selected for similarity to the subject property. Their sales prices are then adjusted for their differences from the subject. Finally, a market value for the subject is estimated from the adjusted sales prices of the comparable properties.

The economic principles of supply and demand provide a framework for understanding how the market works. The interaction of supply and demand factors determines property prices. Supply depends on current inventories and, in the longer run, on the availability of human skills, material, and capital. Demand is influenced by population

levels, mortgage rates, income levels, local services, personal housing preferences, and the cost of substitutes. One demand factor is the cost of substitutes, which ensures that prudent consumers will pay no more for a piece of property than for comparable properties with equal utility, assuming no unreasonable delays. The principle of substitution implies that the market will recognize differences in utility between the subject and its best alternatives by a difference in price.

The sales comparison approach requires the following steps: definition of the appraisal problem, data collection, analysis of market data to develop units of comparison and select attributes for adjustment (model specification), development of reasonable adjustments (model calibration), application of the model to adjust the sales prices of comparables to the subject property, and analysis of the adjusted sales prices to estimate the value of the subject property. The entire valuation process depends on accurately defining the appraisal problem, because the nature of the problem determines the sources of information, methods of comparable selection, and adjustment techniques.

Defining the appraisal problem includes identifying the property, the rights to be appraised, the date of appraisal, the use, and the type of value to estimate. The rights to be valued can be a partial interest or fee simple absolute interest. Fee simple absolute interest is usually assumed for both the subject and comparable sales. The date of the appraisal, the "as of" date, is usually defined by statute. In narrative appraisals, the date of appraisal is identified on the valuation report. All comparables are adjusted to the "as of" date.

Collection of accurate data, described in chapter 5, is also essential to the sales comparison approach. The appraiser analyzes market data to identify important supply and demand factors and determine data needs.

Specifying the Sales Comparison Model

The sales comparison approach estimates the market value of a subject property by adjusting the sales prices of comparable properties for differences between the comparables and the subject. A general sales comparison model is:

$$MV = S_c + ADJ_c, \qquad (1)$$

where MV is a market value estimate, S_c is the sale price of a comparable property, and ADJ_c is the total dollar adjustment to the sale price of the comparable for quantitative and qualitative differences between attributes of the comparable and the subject property.

Selecting the Comparables
The Number of Comparables Appraisers use several sold properties as comparables. Three to five comparables are usually adequate, but a larger number improves confidence in the final estimate, increases the awareness of patterns of value, and stabilizes assessments over time. The sales comparison approach requires numerous adjustments for time, attribute differences, and other factors. The number of calculations required can be handled easily by a computer.

The Issue of Comparability Comparability is a measure of similarity between a sale and a subject. Sale and subject should be similar with respect to date of sale, economic conditions, physical attributes, and competitiveness in the same market. Of these, the most important is competitiveness. If the comparable and subject do not compete in the same market, they do not face the same supply and demand forces, so value inferences from comparable to subject may be misleading.

Units of Comparison
In the sales comparison approach, appraisers estimate a price per unit. The unit of comparison may be the property as a whole or some smaller measure of the size of the property. Converting the sale price to a price per unit makes it easier to compare and adjust properties that compete in the same market. In addition to the entire property, common units of comparison for the sales comparison approach are square feet of gross building area, square feet of net rentable area, apartment, and room. Table 1 shows units of comparison for various property uses.

The price per unit of comparison is the dependent variable—what is being estimated—in the valuation model. The value of the dependent variable is predicted by (or depends on) the values of other variables such as property attributes. The unit of comparison should never be the grounds for selecting comparables. Property attributes should be used instead.

Model Specification

Determining the Attributes   Attributes, the characteristics of a property, are such things as the age, size, number of bathrooms, and quality of construction. The sale price is a function of how buyers and sellers perceive the utility of important property attributes. The importance of an attribute is known only after the data have been analyzed (see chapter 20 for a discussion of analytical

Table 1.   Units of Comparison by Property Type

Property type	Unit of comparison
Agricultural land	Yield per acre
Apartment buildings	Square feet, apartment, room; gross rent multiplier
Apartment sites	Acre, square feet, site
Auto agencies	Square feet
Boat docks	Slip, frontage feet
Bowling alleys	Square feet, lane
Churches	Square feet
Coal or lumber yards	Square feet
Commercial sites	Acre, square feet, potential site
Condominiums	Square feet, room, condominium unit; gross rent multiplier
Drive-ins	Car stall
Duplexes	Square feet, room, unit; gross rent multiplier
Funeral homes	Square feet
Golf courses	Hole, green, fairway
Grain elevators	Bushel
Hospitals	Square feet, bed
Hotels and motels	Square feet, room
Industrial sites	Acre, square feet, potential site
Loft buildings	Square feet
Office buildings	Square feet; gross rent multiplier
Parking garages	Car space
Parking lots	Square feet, car space
Raw acreage	Acre, square feet; potential site, buildable unit
Residential sites	Square feet; gross rent multiplier
Retail stores	Square feet
Schools	Square feet
Scrap yards	Square feet
Service stations	Square feet, bay
Single-family residences	Parcel, square feet, room; gross rental multiplier
Ski hills	Run, lift, foot of drop
Storage tank farms	Gallon
Supermarkets	Square feet
Theatres	Square feet, seat
Truck terminals	Square feet, bay
Warehouses	Square feet, cubic feet

techniques). Therefore, more attributes are usually collected than are needed for valuation. After deciding which attributes to collect, the appraiser decides which will be used for selecting and adjusting comparables. The selected attributes must reflect the important supply and demand variables in the market at the time of the appraisal.

Table 2 lists property attributes that have been found to be important in estimating value. Also listed is the kind of variable (quantitative or qualitative—see chapter 5) and the type of property to which the attribute usually applies. Although the list is not complete, it illustrates many of the important attributes in today's marketplace. As illustrated, attribute inclusion varies with the class of property and the conditions of the market. Attributes can represent both supply and demand sides of the market. In general, attributes that are qualitative represent demand because they measure utility. Quantitative attributes that measure the range of housing services available usually represent supply, but may represent demand as well. Qualitative attributes are usually adjusted with percentages, quantitative attributes with dollar amounts.

Relationships among Adjustments and Attributes

Two kinds of relationships must be specified: (1) How the attributes (and, therefore, adjustments) relate to one another. Are the adjustments to be added together to form a total adjustment or are they to be multiplied, or some combination of the two? (2) How changes in quality and size of an attribute relate to changes in value. Does every square foot added to the size of a property make the same marginal contribution to value? Does

a second bathroom make the same marginal contribution to value as the first?

If each unit added, whether a square foot or a bathroom, adds the same value, there is a *linear* relationship between size or quality and contribution to value. The relationship is *nonlinear* if additional units add less (or more) value than previous units. For example, the contribution to value for each square foot of a residential property up to 1,500 may be $35.00. Demand for larger residences may be lower, so a 1,600 square foot residence will command only $33.00 per square foot for the area greater than 1,500 square feet. An 1,800 square foot residence might command only $31.00 per square foot for the area greater than 1,600 square feet. In a computer-assisted mass appraisal program, nonlinear functions can be part of the adjustment equation. Nonlinear relationships cannot easily be analyzed in single-property appraisal. Chapters 14 and 15 discuss in more detail how to determine functional relationships among attributes.

Calibrating the Sales Comparison Model

Determining Adjustment Amounts

During model specification, the appraiser determines the significant attributes and the relationships among the attributes. The adjustment amounts (coefficients) are determined during model calibration. Paired sales analysis, multiple regression analysis, adaptive estimation procedure, and the cost method are often used to calibrate sales comparison models.

Paired Sales   Paired sales analysis is the foundation of single-property appraisal by the sales comparison approach. Paired sales

Table 2. Major Property Attributes by Type and Class

Attribute	Kind of variable	Represents supply (s) or demand (d)	Property type
Building size	Quantitative	s	Residential, agricultural, commercial, industrial
Site/location	Qualitative	d	Residential, commercial, industrial
Land area	Quantitative	s	Residential, commercial, industrial
Building features			
Number of bathrooms	Quantitative	s, d	Residential, commercial
Garage	Quantitative	s, d	Residential
Air conditioning	Qualitative	s, d	Residential, commercial, industrial
Number of bedrooms	Quantitative	s, d	Residential
Number of rooms	Quantitative	s, d	Residential
Porches	Quantitative	s, d	Residential
Additions	Quantitative	s, d	Residential
Swimming pools	Quantitative or qualitative	s, d	Residential
Family rooms	Quantitative	s, d	Residential
Finished basement	Quantitative	s, d	Residential
Fireplaces	Quantitative or qualitative	s, d	Residential
Plumbing fixtures	Quantitative	s, d	Residential, commercial, industrial
Construction quality	Qualitative	d	Residential, commercial, industrial
Year built	Quantitative	d	Residential, commercial, industrial
Condition	Qualitative	d	Residential, commercial, industrial
Date of sale	Quantitative	s, d	Residential, commercial, industrial
Design	Qualitative	s, d	Residential
Story height	Quantitative	s, d	Commercial, industrial
Fire protection	Qualitative	d	Commercial, industrial
Rail or road access	Qualitative	d	Industrial
Storage	Qualitative	s, d	Commercial, industrial
Soil type	Qualitative	d	Agricultural
Topography	Qualitative	d	Residential, agricultural, commercial, industrial

analysis requires that sales properties be identical in all attributes except the attribute being measured or that adjustments have already been made for the other attributes. The assessor compares these sales and isolates the value contribution for the desired attribute.

Calibrating with paired sales analysis is usually impractical in mass appraisal because it is difficult to find sales that meet this condition. Even more unreasonable is the expectation that sales are available to measure all the attributes needed in the sales comparison approach. In addition, it is difficult, if not impossible, to determine rates of change using this method, for example, when the contribution for additional square feet decreases as the size of the property increases. However, paired sales analysis can be useful when many homogeneous sales are available; for example, in some residential neighborhoods it can be used to determine both time and attribute adjustments.

An analysis of resales using paired sales analysis, as illustrated in table 3, is one method of determining time adjustments. It is necessary to use properties that have had no changes between the sale dates. The steps are to (1) list the sales, (2) calculate the percent change between the first sale price and the resale price, (3) divide the percent change by the number of months, and (4) estimate a time adjustment from the results. Chapter 20 discusses other time-adjustment methods that are more appropriate in mass appraisal.

As with any data, the level of confidence in the estimate is a function of the recency, amount, variance, and reliability of the data. Proper functional fit to a well-specified model is also essential to good estimates. The above example assumes a linear function, which may not be the case, and shows a constant rate of 5.2 percent per year. Without graphic display, and perhaps additional data, it is difficult to identify the true pattern or amount of the adjustment.

When an adequate volume of sales is available, the appraiser can use paired sales to estimate qualitative and quantitative adjustments. Again, the analysis requires that attributes other than the one being measured remain constant. Table 4 shows an example of using paired sales to measure the marginal contribution of an additional bathroom. This process differs from estimating the time ad-

justment because resales are not required (the sales should occur at the same time or have already been adjusted for time). In paired sales analysis, the appraiser must determine benchmark properties for measurement purposes. In this case, the benchmarks are properties with one bath. Comparable 1 is identical to comparables 2, 3, and 4 in all respects except the number of bathrooms. Comparable 5 is identical to comparables 6 and 7 in all respects except the number of bathrooms. Sales prices of the benchmark properties are subtracted from each comparable to obtain an estimate for the presence of a second bath.

This example illustrates the principle of using paired sales to derive an adjustment from the market. The paired sales method can be used for any adjustment, including size, style, garage, basement, or location. The greater the number of sales, the greater the level of confidence in the adjustments.

Multiple Regression Analysis Multiple regression analysis can be used to calibrate sales comparison models for single-property appraisal. Unlike paired sales analysis, regression does not require strict similarity between parcels. The same conditions and assumptions required for developing market models with multiple regression analysis (see chapter 14) are required for calibration with multiple regression analysis.

Additive linear models can be used to calibrate the sales comparison approach. This process identifies the degree of importance in each of the variables and shows how well the model itself performs as an estimating device. However, the adjustments derived from these models represent a fixed marginal contribution to value and do not recognize interaction among the variables.

Table 3. Time Adjustment with Paired Sales

	First sale	Second sale	Percent change	Months between sales	Percent per month
Comparable 1	$65,000	$67,800	4.3	10	0.43
Comparable 2	$73,400	$81,800	11.4	24	0.48
Comparable 3	$58,000	$63,500	9.5	21	0.45
Comparable 4	$59,500	$61,100	2.7	7	0.39
Comparable 5	$62,700	$65,500	4.5	12	0.38

Average percent per month, 0.43%
Average percent per year,   5.2%

Table 4. Additional Bath Adjustment with Paired Sales

	Number of baths	Sale price	Dollar difference
Benchmark properties: Comparables 1 and 5			
Comparable 1	One bath	$67,800	
Compared to:			
Comparable 2	Two baths	$69,700	$1,900
Comparable 3	Two baths	$70,100	$2,300
Comparable 4	Two baths	$69,900	$2,100
Comparable 5	One bath	$56,300	
Compared to:			
Comparable 6	Two baths	$58,300	$2,000
Comparable 7	Two baths	$58,500	$2,200
Average contribution for extra bath			$2,100

Nonlinear, rather than linear, models are often better for calibrating the sales comparison approach because nonlinear functions address the interactions among variables and recognize that the marginal contribution to sale price changes as the attribute changes. For example, the contribution for each square foot of area decreases as the number of square feet increases.

Adaptive Estimation Procedure Adaptive estimation procedure (AEP, or feedback) can also be used to determine the adjustments in the sales comparison approach. Before AEP is used, attributes must be classified as either qualitative or quantitative and as applicable to land or improvements. AEP estimates the value contribution (coefficient) for each attribute using an error reducing technique (multiple regression analysis uses a minimizing technique). However, unlike regression, AEP does not produce test statistics about the quality of the coefficients.

Cost Method In the absence of other methods, the appraiser can use the cost of reproduction or replacement to calibrate the sales comparison approach. However, cost methods suffer from the fundamental weakness that cost amounts often do not reflect the supply and demand relationships found in the sales market. Nor do buyers usually think in terms of depreciated cost when making purchase decisions. The relationship between cost-derived and sales-derived coefficients is seldom consistent. In some situations, purchasers will be willing to pay more than the cost new of a component. In others, a relatively expensive component may contribute nothing or may even decrease sale price.

Confidence in the Adjustments

Although it is important for the appraiser to determine the appropriate attributes and their contributions to value, it is equally important to know the level of confidence in the adjustments. The level of confidence in the attributes and adjustments determines the level of confidence in the final estimate of value. Calibration techniques, such as multiple regression analysis, that produce confidence measures are more useful when explaining and defending values than those that do not. Whatever calibration method is used, appraisers who know the market, understand the principles of economics and appraisal, have adequate data, and can explain variance in the data can feel confident about adjustments.

Applying the Model

Once the attributes have been selected and the adjustment amounts determined, the ap-praiser can apply the sales comparison model. The appraiser first describes subject and comparables in a comparative attribute display, then selects an adjustment method and adjusts each comparable to the subject. The adjustment process should answer the question, "How much would the comparable sell for if it had the same attributes as the subject on the date of appraisal?"

Methods of Adjusting Comparables

Comparative Attribute Sales Adjustment Grid Types The sales comparison approach uses a column and row format to organize the data for comparison. There are several methods of adjusting comparables: lump-sum, cumulative percentage, multiplicative percentage, and hybrid methods. These methods are part of model specification. The following text, including tables 6 through 9, illustrates each method using the same residential subject and sales properties (table 5). However, the adjustment amounts vary according to the method selected. The objective of each method is to adjust each comparable to the subject property in every respect. The adjustment process applies the marginal contribution to value against the differences between subject and comparable for each attribute.

The sequence of adjustments depends on the method of adjustment selected. However, comparables should be adjusted first to terms of cash and then for time to a common date. The time adjustment provides a common starting point from which to make all other adjustments. There are four methods of deriving time-adjustment factors from market data. These include paired sales analysis, resale analysis, sales ratio trend analysis, and

Table 5. Comparative Attribute Display of Sales Data

	Subject	Sale 1	Sale 2	Sale 3
Sale price	—	$96,300	$82,400	$83,400
Date of sale	—	24 months	18 months	18 months
Age of improvement	10 years	10 years	12 years	8 years
Condition	Good	Average	Good	Average
Lot size	50′ × 140′	70′ × 200′	50′ × 150′	60′ × 175′
Floor area (in square feet)	1,500	1,700	1,600	1,500
Garage	Attached	Attached	Detached	Attached
Quality	Good	Good	Good	Average

multiple regression analysis (see chapter 20 and appendix 5-3).

Lump-Sum Adjustments Lump-sum adjustments are dollar amounts representing the difference between subject and comparable. The assumption here is that the adjustments, or coefficients, have been derived using the entire property as the unit of measure. Table 6 shows three sales (the comparables) adjusted with dollar amount adjustments derived from market analysis.

Time. It has been 24 months since the date of sale for sale 1 to the valuation date. The adjustment amount for time is $500 per month times 24 months, or $12,000. Therefore, the positive adjustment of $12,000 would make Sale 1 equivalent to the subject in terms of sale date. Sales prices for sales 2 and 3 are also adjusted upward for the 18 months from the time of sale to the valuation date.

Age. The market analysis indicates that consumers expect to pay $1,600 less for every year of age of the property. Sale 1, like the subject, is 10 years old so there is no adjustment. Sale 2 was 12 years old at the time of sale. If it had been the same age as the subject (10 years), its market price would have

been higher by $3,200 (2 years times lump-sum annual adjustment of $1,600). The appraiser, therefore, adds $3,200 to the sale price of sale 2 to show what its sale price would have been if it were the same age as the subject. To make Sale 3 equivalent to the subject, it must be made "older" by 2 years. The adjustment of 2 years times $1,600 per year, or $3,200, should be subtracted from the sale price of Sale 3.

Condition. The market analysis indicates a $4,800 difference between each condition rating; that is, $4,800 between average and good, $4,800 between good and excellent, and so on. Because Sales 1 and 3 are in average condition, but the subject is in good condition, the sales prices of Sales 1 and 3 need to be adjusted upward by $4,800 to reflect the same condition as the subject. Sale 2 requires no adjustment because it is in the same condition as the subject.

Lot size. The adjustment for lot size is $5,000 per size rating. The size ratings for this neighborhood have been defined as small (50 front feet), average (60 front feet), large (70 front feet), and very large (80 front feet)—no adjustment is required for depth. The subject is a small lot, Sale 1 is large, and Sale 3 is average. The sale price of Sale 1 is

Table 6. Comparative Attribute Sales Adjustment Grid: Lump-Sum Adjustments

	Subject	Sale 1	Sale 2	Sale 3
Sale price	—	$96,300	$79,400	$83,400
Time adjustment	—	+ 12,000	+ 9,000	+ 9,000
Time-adjusted sale price		$108,300	$88,400	$92,400
Age	10 years		+ 3,200	− 3,200
Condition	Good	+ 4,800	0	+ 4,800
Lot size	50′ × 140′	− 10,000	0	− 5,000
Floor area (in square feet)	1,500	− 9,600	− 4,800	0
Garage	Attached	0	+ 800	0
Quality	Good	0	0	+ 4,000
Net adjustment	− 14,800	− 800	600	
Adjusted sale price	$93,500	$87,600	$93,000	

Adjustments

Time	$500 per month
Age	$1,600 per year
Condition	$4,800 between average and good
Lot size	$5,000 between each size variation
Floor area	$48.00 per square foot
Garage	$800 less for detached
Quality	$4,000 between average and good

adjusted downward by $10,000 and the sale price of Sale 3 is adjusted downward by $5,000 to make them both equivalent to the subject.

Floor area. The market analysis indicates $48 per square foot for the size adjustment. Sale 1 is 200 square feet larger than the subject, so the sale price of Sale 1 requires an adjustment of −$9,600, but Sale 3 is only 100 square feet larger, so its sale price requires an adjustment of −$4,800.

Size adjustments can be confusing. If the unit of comparison is the entire property, as in this example, then the adjustment for a sale with more square feet than the subject is negative. Sale price increases as square feet increase, so the price of the comparable will have to be adjusted downward. However, if the unit of comparison is square feet, the adjustment for a sale with more square feet than the subject can be positive. Sale price per square foot usually decreases as square feet increase, so the price of the comparable may be adjusted upward.

Garage. The market shows that properties with attached garages sell for $800 more than those with detached garages. Sale 2 has a detached garage and therefore requires an adjustment of +$800 to make it equivalent to the subject.

Quality. The market indicates a $4,000 difference between each quality rating. Sale 3 is of average quality, but the subject is considered good quality. Therefore, Sale 3 is adjusted by +$4,000 to make it equivalent to the subject.

Cumulative Percentage Adjustments   Percentage adjustments represent the difference between subject and comparable in terms of percentages rather than dollar amounts. These percentages are either summed (in the cumulative method) or multiplied (in the multiplicative method) to determine the net adjustment to the comparable. The net adjustment is then applied against the time-adjusted sale price to yield a value estimator.

Table 7 shows an application of the cumulative percentage method using adjustments derived from the market. First, a time-adjusted sale price is developed for each comparable to bring all sales to a common date. Other percentage adjustments are summed to give a net adjustment, which is applied to the time-adjusted sale price. The adjustments are applied with the same signs as in the lump-sum example. The only difference is that the total adjustments are not presented as whole dollar amounts, although it would be easy enough to do so. The percentage adjustments are added together to produce a total adjustment by which to multiply the time-adjusted sale price. This dollar amount is added to or subtracted from the time-adjusted sale price to give an estimate of value. The adjustments for time, age, and condition are described below to illustrate the

process, which is similar to the lump-sum process.

Time. It has been 24 months since the date of sale for Sale 1, so the adjustment for time is 0.5% times 24 months, or 12%. Therefore, the positive adjustment of 12% would make Sale 1 equivalent to the subject in terms of selling date. Sales 2 and 3 are also adjusted upward for the 18 months from the time of sale to the valuation date.

Age. Market analysis shows that consumers expect to pay 2% less for every year of age of the property. Sale 1 is identical to the subject so there is no adjustment. Sale 2 was 12 years old at the time of sale. If it had been the same age as the subject (10 years old), Sale 2's price would have been higher by 4% (2 years times the annual percentage adjustments of 2%). The time-adjusted sale price of Sale 2 is adjusted upward by 4%. Sale 3 was 8 years old at the time of sale, so the time-adjusted sale price for Sale 3 is adjusted downward by 4%.

Condition. Market analysis shows that the difference between condition levels is 5% per level. Because Sale 1 is in average condition and the subject is in good condition, the price of Sale 1 must be adjusted upward. Therefore, 5% is added to the time-adjusted sale price of Sale 1 for condition. The direction of adjustments is the same as in the lump-sum process.

Multiplicative Percentage Adjustments   Multiplicative percentage adjustments recognize interrelationships among factors. The individual adjustments are multiplied by one another, rather than added, to produce a total percentage adjustment. This method should be used cautiously and only after market analysis determines the true relationships among variables. Table 8 shows an ap-

Table 7.   Comparative Attribute Sales Adjustment Grid: Cumulative Percentage Adjustments

	Subject	Sale 1	Sale 2	Sale 3
Sale price	—	$96,300	$80,400	$83,400
Time adjustment	—	+12%	+9%	+9%
Time-adjusted sale price	—	$107,856	$87,636	$90,906
Age	10 years	0	+4%	−4%
Condition	Good	+5%	0	+5%
Lot size	50' × 140'	−10%	0	−5%
Floor area (in square feet)	1,500	−10%	−5%	0
Garage	Attached	0	+3%	0
Quality	Good	0	0	+5%
Net adjustment	—	−15%	+2%	+1%
Adjusted sale price (to nearest $100)	—	$91,700	$89,400	$91,800

Adjustments

Time	0.5% per month
Age	2.0% per year
Condition	5% between average and good
Lot size	5% between each rating
Floor area	5% per 100 square foot
Garage	3% less for detached
Quality	5% between average and good

plication of the multiplicative percentage method using adjustments derived from market analysis.

Again, the direction of the adjustments is the same as in the previous example. In this method, however, the adjustments are presented as factors around 100%. Negative adjustments are less than 100% and positive adjustments, greater. For example, the 12% adjustment for time for Sale 1 is presented as 1.12 and the −5% age adjustment for Sale 3 is presented as 0.95.

The Hybrid Adjustment Method The hybrid adjustment method uses both additive (dollar amounts) and multiplicative (percentages) adjustments and more accurately reflects the behavior of the market. Table 9 shows how percentage and dollar adjustments derived from the market are applied.

The hybrid adjustment method classifies attributes as quantitative or qualitative. Quantitative attributes are usually additive and can easily be expressed as dollar amounts; qualitative attributes are usually

Table 8. Comparative Attribute Sales Adjustment Grid: Multiplicative Percentage Adjustments

	Subject	Sale 1	Sale 2	Sale 3
Sale price	—	$96,300	$80,400	$83,400
Time adjustment	—	1.12	1.09	1.09
Time-adjusted sale price		$107,856	$87,636	$90,906
Age	10 years	0	1.04	.95
Condition	Good	1.05	0	1.05
Lot size	50′ × 140′	0.90	0	0.95
Floor area (in square feet)	1,500	0.90	0.95	0
Garage	Attached	0	1.03	0
Quality	Good	0	0	1.05
Net adjustment	—	0.851	1.018	1.005
Adjusted sale price (to nearest $100)	—	$91,800	$89,200	$91,400

Adjustments

Time	0.5% per month
Age	2.0% per year
Condition	5% between average and good
Lot size	5% between each rating
Floor area	5% per 100 square foot
Garage	3% less for detached
Quality	5% between average and good

expressed as percentages and can be either additive or multiplicative. Defining relationships among attributes requires statistical analysis with an advanced analytical method such as AEP or multiple regression analysis. Note that time is an overall qualitative (percentage) adjustment, although it is shown here in its traditional position for consistency with the other models.

Grid for an Income Property Apartment Building In the sales comparison approach, procedures are similar but the units of comparison and attributes selected are different for different property types. Table 10 shows an attribute comparison grid for five apartment building sales, and table 11 uses the data to extract market value indicators.

From the analysis of value indicators, the appraiser selects a unit of measurement that most clearly reflects purchasers' behavior in the marketplace. As a general rule, the best market indicator is the one with the lowest variance, as shown by the coefficient of variation. In the example in table 11, price per apartment appears to be the best indicator, although price per room could work as well.

Table 9.   Comparative Attribute Sales Adjustment Grid: Hybrid Adjustments

	Subject	Sale 1	Sale 2	Sale 3
Sale price	—	$96,300	$80,400	$83,400
Time adjustment	—	1.12	1.09	1.09
Time-adjusted sale price	—	$107,856	$87,636	$90,906
Quantitative				
Lot size	50′ × 140′	−7,000	−500	−3,500
Floor area (in square feet)	1,500	−9,600	−4,800	0
Garage	Attached	0	+800	0
Total quantitative	—	−16,600	−4,500	−3,500
Adjusted sale price	—	$91,256	$83,136	$87,406
Qualitative				
Age	10 years	0	1.04	.96
Condition	Good	1.05	0	1.05
Quality	Good	0	0	1.04
Total qualitative	—	1.05	1.04	1.048
Adjusted sales prices (to nearest $100)	—	$95,800	$86,500	$91,600

Adjustments

Time	0.5% per month
Age	2% per year
Condition	good = 1.05; average = 1.00
Lot size	$1.00 per square foot
Floor area	$48 per square foot
Garage	$800
Quality	good = 1.04; average = 1.00

The unit of measurement chosen is used as the starting point for adjustments to a sales comparison model.

The next step is market analysis to select the attributes to be adjusted and the size of the adjustments. Adjustments can then be made by the methods described in the residential example.

Grid for a General-Purpose Commercial Property   Table 12 is a comparable attribute display for a general-purpose facility used for storage or light industry and several comparable properties.

The attributes in table 12 are either physical characteristics or are described in terms of utility. Utility is evaluated in terms of

Table 10.   Comparative Attribute Display of Sales Data for an Apartment Building with Sixteen or More Units

	Subject	Sale 1	Sale 2	Sale 3	Sale 4	Sale 5
Sale price	—	$361,200	$338,900	$358,000	$333,000	$384,900
Months from date of sale	—	8	10	15	15	24
Age of improvement (in years)	10	12	15	8	18	10
Land area (square feet)	51,200	51,200	49,000	53,000	53,000	55,000
Number of stories	2	2	2	2	2	2
Floor area (square feet)	12,800	12,800	10,640	13,120	13,400	14,400
Number of units	16	16	14	16	16	18
Number of rooms	64	64	56	64	64	72
Condition	Average	Average	Good	Average	Average	Below average
Quality	Average	Average	Average	Below average	Average	Average
Location	Good	Average	Good	Good	Good	Average
Air conditioning	Yes	None	Yes	None	None	Yes
Carpeting	Yes	Yes	Yes	Yes	None	Yes

Table 11.   Extraction of Market Value Indicators for an Apartment Building with Sixteen or More Units

Sale number	Time-adjusted sale price	Square feet	Number of Apartments	Rooms	Adjusted sale price per Square foot	Apartment	Room
1	$361,200	12,800	16	64	$28.22	$22,575	$5,644
2	$338,900	10,640	14	56	$31.85	$24,207	$6,052
3	$358,000	13,120	16	64	$27.29	$22,375	$5,594
4	$333,000	13,400	16	64	$24.85	$20,813	$5,203
5	$384,900	14,400	18	72	$26.73	$21,383	$5,346
		Averages			$27.79	$22,271	$5,568
		Standard deviations			2.58	1,301	325
		Coefficient of variation			9%	6%	6%

Table 12. Comparative Attribute Display of a General-Purpose Commercial Building

	Subject	Sale 1	Sale 2	Sale 3	Sale 4	Sale 5
Sale price	—	$330,000	$361,000	$270,000	$265,000	$395,000
Months from date of sale	—	1	5	10	10	14
Age of improvement (years)	18	15	20	17	20	14
Land area (acres)	2.5	2.2	2.5	2.7	2.3	2.5
Number of stories	1	1	1	1	1	1
Floor area (square feet)	18,000	16,500	19,000	15,000	22,000	17,500
Condition	Average	Average	Below average	Average	Below average	Good
Quality	Average	Average	Average	Average	Average	Average
Location	Good	Good	Good	Average	Good	Very Good
Load docks	Adequate	Adequate	Adequate	Adequate	Adequate	Adequate
Height (feet)	16	15	18	17	18	18
Fire protection	Full	Full	Full	Full	Full	Full
Lighting	Adequate	Adequate	Adequate	Adequate	Adequate	Adequate
Heating	Adequate	Adequate	Adequate	Adequate	Adequate	Adequate
Plumbing	Adequate	Adequate	Adequate	Adequate	Adequate	Adequate
Frame	Steel	Steel	Preengineered steel	Steel	Steel	Steel
Walls	Concrete block	Concrete block	Steel	Concrete block	Concrete block	Concrete block

equivalent utility. Is fluorescent lighting of 2 watts per square foot equivalent to high-pressure sodium lighting of 2 watts per square foot? Is gas-fired unit heat equivalent to gas-fired radiant heat? The grid in table 12 uses the product of such an analysis. Equivalent utility is measured from the perspective of the typical purchaser in the context of the highest and best use of the property and is best done by a combination of user interviews and statistical analysis.

The appraiser should interview the users of, and agents for, commercial and industrial space—buyers, sellers, brokers, the suppliers of capital, development authorities, planners, and trade associations. Interviews help identify the needs and constraints of real estate purchasers and determine comparable selection criteria and adjustment methods.

Statistical analysis is then used to verify (or make) judgments about equivalent utility. Correlation and multiple regression analysis help explain the significance of attributes and their relationship to one another. These findings are used for model specification in the adjustment grid.

Sale price per square foot is usually selected as the unit of comparison because users of general-purpose commercial space derive utility from the space itself. The adjustments selected on the basis of interviews and statistical analysis are then applied to comparables using the methods described for residential properties.

Special-Purpose Property Grid Property use can be described on a continuum from general purpose to special purpose. General-purpose properties have many different uses; special-purpose properties, only a few. Single-purpose properties have only one use. The sales comparison approach is difficult to use with special-purpose properties because comparables are few. Because it is difficult to determine equivalent utilities for properties designed to produce different goods, the level of confidence in the adjustments is reduced. Therefore, selecting sales having similar uses is important because similar uses imply that the sales compete in the same market as the subject. For the sales comparison approach, it is useful to define the property's purpose and the degree to which its uses are limited.

For properties such as golf courses, tank farms, and ski hills, the only legitimate comparables are sales having the same use. However, use is not the only factor that makes a property unique. Uniqueness is also defined by such factors as size and number of stories. Although some properties are not unique in use or purpose, they may still have to compete in a "special" market. Examples include preengineered steel buildings, very large general-purpose properties, and extremely high bay structures.

The sales comparison approach can be used however complex the property. However, the many different motives for purchasing special-purpose property result in higher variance in

the unit of comparison for special-purpose property (as measured by the coefficient of variation) than for general-purpose property. Low sales volume means that comparables are more difficult to find. Limited market data means that adjustments are more difficult to determine.

The following example describes the sales comparison approach for large, urban industrial facilities. The comparables all have more than 100,000 square feet and compete in the same large-facility industrial market as the subject. The subject is classified as special purpose because of its size. Alternative uses are few. Table 13 is a comparable attribute display for the subject and several comparables.

As for the commercial example, equivalent utility of some attributes needs to be determined. The appraiser interviews users of industrial space to determine the motivations of purchasers, to define the qualitative terms, and to determine the units of comparison. Although the example has five comparables, as few as two or three are acceptable if sales data are not available. The unit of comparison can be related to the use of the property. Sale price per unit or output per square foot are common choices for industrial properties. In this example, the sale price per square foot is selected as the unit of comparison.

After displaying the attributes of the subject and the comparables, the appraiser selects the attributes to be used and the size of adjustments through statistical analysis and market interviews. The diverse motivations of buyers and sellers in this market often lead to wide variation in adjustment amounts. The adjustments are then applied to the differences between the comparables and the subject using the methods described for residential properties.

Table 13. Comparative Attribute Display of a Special-Purpose Industrial Building

	Subject	Sale 1	Sale 2	Sale 3	Sale 4	Sale 5
Sale price (dollars)	—	2,000,000	2,250,000	1,855,000	1,720,000	2,005,000
Months from date of sale	—	8	12	14	20	22
Age of improvement (years)	20	18	20	14	28	22
Land area (acres)	6	6	8	7	5	5
Number of stories	1	1	1	1	1	1
Floor area (square feet)	125,000	135,000	120,000	118,000	128,000	140,000
Percent office	10	9	10	12	10	8
Percent general manufacturing	70	67	60	73	67	68
Percent storage	20	24	30	15	23	24
Condition	Average	Good	Good	Average	Below average	Average
Location	Average	Average	Good	Good	Average	Good
Load docks	Adequate	Adequate	Adequate	Adequate	Adequate	Adequate
Height (feet)	16	20	17	16	16	16
Fire protection	Full	Full	Full	Full	Full	Full
Lighting	Adequate	Adequate	Adequate	Adequate	Poor	Adequate
Heating	Adequate	Adequate	Adequate	Adequate	Below average	Adequate
Plumbing	Adequate	Adequate	Adequate	Adequate	Adequate	Adequate
Frame	Steel	Steel	Steel/concrete	Steel	Steel	Mixed
Walls	Concrete block	Concrete block	Wood/steel	Concrete block	Concrete block	Concrete block
Parking	Adequate	Adequate	Adequate	Below average	Adequate	Below average
Rail	Yes	Yes	No	No	No	No
Utilities	All	All	All	All	All	All
Functional obsolescence	Slight	Slight	Slight	Slight	Slight	Slight
Economic obsolescence	None	None	None	None	None	None

Measures of Confidence

The estimated sale price of each adjusted sale is an intermediate product of the sales comparison approach. Each comparable is adjusted for all differences between it and the subject, with the adjustment in the direction of making the comparables equivalent to the subject. The adjusted sale price for each comparable is an estimate of the amount that the property would have sold for had it been the subject.

From the information produced by the sales comparison approach, the appraiser can construct statements of confidence about the final estimate of value. Statistics to measure confidence in the approach can be calculated for each sale and for the group of sales. Measures for each sale include the number of individual adjustments and the absolute gross adjustment. A measure for the group of sales is the variance of the individual estimates.

Measures of Confidence for Individual Comparables The measures for individual comparables indicate how good each is as an estimator. The measures are valid only when comparing sales that compete in the same market.

The Number of Adjustments The number of adjustments required to make a sale appear equivalent to the subject is a measure of comparability. Generally, the greater the number of adjustments, the less comparable the sale, as illustrated in table 14. In terms of the number of adjustments, Sale 4 is the most comparable with only one adjustment. It is followed by Sales 1 and 2, both with two adjustments, Sale 3 with four adjustments, and Sale 5 with five adjustments.

In general, fewer adjustments mean a lower probability of error in the estimate. This does not mean that the appraiser should hesitate to apply indicated adjustments. When there is evidence to show that many adjustments are appropriate, applying these adjustments will improve the reliability of the final estimate.

The Absolute Gross Adjustment This measure can be produced for each comparable. It is the sum of the absolute value of each adjustment. The adjustments can be expressed as either dollars or percentages, but the two cannot be mixed. This statistic measures the differences between the sale and subject in terms of the market contribution for each at-

tribute. (Thus, the statistic could be used as a selection measure [or metric] to locate the best comparables for the subject).

The use of absolute gross percentage adjustment is illustrated in table 14. Although Sale 3 has a large number of adjustments, it has the lowest absolute gross adjustment, indicating the greatest "overall" similarity to the subject. Again, confidence in Sale 3 depends on the certainty of the adjustment attributes and the accuracy of the adjustment amounts. The absolute gross adjustment deserves consideration because the adjustments are weighted market factors. That is, the adjustment amounts represent the actual substitution preferences of the market. They are market-derived measures of similarity. For a multiplicative adjustment grid, subtract one from each adjustment factor to obtain percentage adjustments before taking absolute values. For example, the absolute gross adjustment for the factors 0.95 and 1.10 is 0.05 plus 0.10, or 0.15.

The net adjustment is an intermediate figure needed only to calculate the final estimate. This number should not be used as a measure of confidence. A net adjustment of 2 percent can just as easily arise from gross adjustments of 0 percent and 2 percent (high confidence) as from 100 percent and −98 percent (low confidence).

Measures of Confidence for the Comparables as a Group Even if a subject and a group of comparables provide too few observations for a statistically adequate sample, the coefficient of variation can be a useful measure in the sales comparison approach. The coefficient of variation is defined as the standard deviation divided by the mean, times 100. This statistic can be calculated for

Table 14. Sales Comparison Approach: Comparative Number of Adjustments

Attribute	Sale 1	Sale 2	Sale 3	Sale 4	Sale 5
1	+5%	0	+5%	0	+5%
2	0	+10%	+2%	0	−1%
3	+10%	0	−2%	−15%	−2%
4	0	−2%	+1%	0	+6%
5	0	0	0	0	+3%
Number of adjustments	2	2	4	1	5
Absolute gross adjustment	15%	12%	10%	15%	17%
Net adjustment	+15%	+8%	+6%	−15%	+11%

Table 15. Sales Comparison Approach: Adjusted Sales Prices per Square Foot and Associated Standard Deviations and Coefficients of Variation (COVs) for Six Appraisals

	Comparable 1	Comparable 2	Comparable 3	Mean	Standard deviation	Coefficient of variation (percent)
Appraisal U	14.00	14.00	14.00	14.00	0	0
Appraisal V	13.50	14.00	14.50	14.00	.50	3.57
Appraisal W	13.00	14.00	15.00	14.00	1.00	7.14
Appraisal X	12.00	14.00	16.00	14.00	2.00	14.29
Appraisal Y	10.00	14.00	18.00	14.00	4.00	28.57
Appraisal Z	7.00	14.00	21.00	14.00	7.00	50.00

the adjusted sale price for each comparable.

The use of the coefficient of variation in measuring the variation of the group of sales prices for adjusted comparables is illustrated in table 15.

It is more difficult to estimate value as the variation in adjusted sales prices increases. For instance, there is no question about the $14.00 per square foot value estimate in Appraisal U. There is no variation in the three adjusted sales prices. However, Appraisal Z has considerable variation and the best estimate is unclear (without other evidence).

Variations among the adjusted sales prices could result from many sources, including an erroneous sale price, an irrational market, a poorly specified model, selection of the wrong unit of comparison, or erroneously calibrated adjustments. A high coefficient of variation serves as a suggestion to review the data to attempt to reduce further the variation in adjusted sales prices.

Automated Comparable Selection

Mass appraisal applications of the sales comparison approach are practical using computers. Automated sales comparison is used for the defense of assessment appeals, in the appraisal of benchmark properties, and in evaluating the reliability of other methods. Automated techniques, although conceptually more complex, have advantages over manual selection. Manual selection requires simultaneous comparison of many properties. A high volume of sales renders consistent selection virtually impossible. Automated methods increase the speed of selection, standardize the selection attributes, and produce measures of comparability. Selected sales listings, iterative search routines, and dissimilarity functions are three methods that vary in complexity, user control, and ability to select sales.

Selected Sales Listings

Selected sales listings are lists of sales using predefined sorting criteria. The appraiser defines a limited number of sort attributes such as neighborhood, size, or age. If the volume of sales is high, it is useful to stratify by a control attribute such as neighborhood. A listing of sales is ranked in either ascending or descending order of the sort attributes. Although this method is easy and inexpensive, it does not ensure comparability. Comparability requires sales to be compared in terms of each attribute's contribution to value. Sales listings do not consider this contribution. Even though sales listings are not the best alternative for sales selection, they serve a useful purpose for market analysis and administrative processes.

Iterative Search Routines

An iterative process modifies and repeats itself until a solution is obtained. The appraiser specifies the number of sales desired and the attributes to be compared. The computer searches the sales file and selects the speci-fied number of sales. Two routines are possible. One technique culls the entire sales file until only the specified number of sales remains. The other builds the specified number of sales by means of successive passes through the file. The efficiency of iterative search routines depends on the number of passes required to yield the desired solution.

Iterative search routines select the desired number of sales and eliminate the need to analyze a large sales file. However, the cost of computer time may be high because many iterations are necessary for each subject. The major disadvantage is that the technique does not consider the marginal contribution to value for attribute differences in the selection process. Even though the desired number of sales is selected, they may not be the best choices.

Dissimilarity Functions

A dissimilarity function is a comparison algorithm. It is used to assign an index of dissimilarity (or similarity) to properties compared to the subject. The lower the calculated dissimilarity index, the more comparable the sale. Of the many indexes available, the Euclidean distance metric and the Minkowski metric are most frequently used in appraisal. The Euclidean distance metric is defined as

$$\sum_{j=1}^{k} = [w_j\ (x_{sj}\ -\ x_{ij}\ /\ \sigma_j)]^2\ , \qquad (2)$$

where x_{sj} is the value of the jth attribute of the subject property, x_{ij} is the value of the jth attribute of property i, σ_j is the standard deviation of the jth attribute, w_j is a weight assigned by the user to the jth attribute, and k is the number of attributes for which comparability is defined.

Table 16. Automated Sales Comparison Approach: Computation of the Euclidean Distance Metric—A Dissimilarity Index

Attribute	Subject property	Sale property	Difference	Standard deviation	Standardized difference	Appraiser-assigned weight	Weighted standardized difference	Squared weighted standardized difference
Living area	1,800	1,660	140	225.7	0.62	2	1.24	1.54
Age (years)	10	4	6	4.1	1.46	1	1.46	2.14
Quality class	3.5	5	−1.5	0.9	−1.67	1	−1.67	2.78
								6.46

The metric value for this comparable is 6.46 (sum of the squared weighted standardized differences)

Table 17. Automated Sales Comparison Computation of the Euclidean Distance Metric—A Dissimilarity Index

Attribute	Subject property	Sale property	Difference	Standard deviation	Standardized difference	Appraiser-assigned weight	Weighted standardized difference	Squared weighted standardized difference
Living area	1,800	1,700	100	225.7	0.44	2	0.89	0.79
Age (years)	10	4	6	4.1	1.46	1	1.46	2.14
Quality class	3.5	5	−1.5	0.9	−1.67	1	−1.67	2.78
								5.70

The metric value for this comparable is 5.70 (sum of the squared weighted standardized differences)

Table 16 illustrates this algorithm for a single comparable sale. The value of the sale attribute is subtracted from the value of the subject attribute, yielding the difference between subject and comparable. This difference is divided by the standard deviation of that attribute in the sales file, yielding the standardized difference. The standardized difference is weighted to assign the attribute's relative importance. The weight is determined by the appraiser. The weighted standardized difference is squared, eliminating the negative signs. These attribute metrics are summed to produce the metric for the sale property.

Table 17 illustrates metric calculations on the same subject against a different comparable. This comparable differs from the comparable in table 16 only by the number of square feet. Note that the metric for the property in table 17 is lower than the metric in table 16, because the sale in table 17 is more similar to the subject. Because the selection routine is automated, the computer then sorts the sales in ascending order of the metric. The most comparable sales are placed at the top of the list. They are then transferred to the attribute display grid and adjusted to yield a final estimate of value.

Weighting Selecting the appropriate weight is the most difficult aspect of the selection routine. The weight changes the relative contribution of the attribute in the metric. The higher the weight, the greater the importance assigned to the attribute in the selection process. As the weight for an attribute is increased, the routine will substitute less of the difference in that attribute for more of a difference in other attributes. For example, if a high weight has been placed on size, the routine will select properties close in size, with less emphasis on their age, condition, and so on. Therefore, if the difference between the size of comparables selected is too large, the weight to be placed on size should be increased. However, it is not a specific weight on any one attribute that is important, but rather the relative weights on all attributes.

The Minkowski metric differs from the Euclidean in that absolute percentage differences are computed for each attribute, rather than by squaring the differences and dividing by the standard deviation. Table 18 illustrates the method. Note that, even after weighting, little penalty is exerted for living area, which differs from the subject property by only 5.88 percent, versus 150 percent for age, and 30 percent for quality class (see table 18).

Table 18. Illustration of Minkowski Metric

Attribute	Sale property	Subject property	Difference	Absolute percentage difference	Appraiser assigned weight	Weighted absolute percentage difference
Living area	1,800	1,700	100	5.88	2	11.76
Age (years)	10	4	6	150.00	1	150.00
Quality class	3.5	5	− 1.5	30.00	1	30.00
						191.76

These metrics are well suited for automation. They are easily programmed and modified. The appraiser can change weights to simulate market behavior. The final measure of performance is whether the selected sales make sense. An appraiser dissatisfied with the comparables selected can review the process and make corrections.

Summary

This chapter presented the traditional sales comparison approach as it is used in single-property appraisal. The approach starts with observations of market prices for comparable properties and adjusts these prices for differences between each comparable and the subject property. The choice of units of comparison and of attributes to be adjusted is model specification. Developing the adjustment weights is model calibration.

The selection of comparables, attributes, and adjustment weights requires an analysis of the supply and demand factors operating in the subject property's market and may be done by traditional methods or with statistical techniques.

Land Valuation

7

Introduction

Importance of Accurate Land Values

Accurate land values are crucial to an effective assessment system. They contribute to the accuracy of appraisals of improved parcels and ensure that land owners pay their fair share of taxes. Accurate land values promote well-informed land use decisions by both the public and private sectors. Urban economists and planners have long recognized that outdated land values contribute to inefficient land use and undesirable growth patterns.

Nature of Land Valuation

Physically, land may be defined as the surface of the earth together with everything beneath and above. The shape of a parcel of land is like a three-dimensional pyramid, with its apex at the center of the earth, extending upward through the surface into space. Legally, land is the right to enjoy, use, and dispose of this physical space, subject to limitations imposed by government. For example, one cannot put land to an illegal use or interfere with aircraft flying through air space.

The assessor annually identifies, lists, and values all land and improvements thereto. These tasks require, first, a complete and current set of cadastral maps showing the boundaries and other relevant features of all parcels in the jurisdiction and, second, an accurate inventory of land data, including location, ownership, classification and use, size, shape, and physical characteristics. Both maps and records are updated as land is split, assembled, or physically improved. The assessor analyzes the local market for property and annually estimates the assessment value of each parcel. This chapter treats market analysis and valuation as they apply to land.

Market Value and Use Value

Assessment administration often requires the appraiser to distinguish between *market value* and *use value*. In brief, market value is the most probable sale price of a property in an open-market, arm's-length transfer. Use value is the value of a property for a particular use. For many properties, but not for all, market value equals use value. For example, the market value of a farm on the periphery of an expanding city may far exceed its use value. Many jurisdictions require that nonagricultural lands be appraised for tax purposes at market value and agricultural lands at use value. Statutes, rules, and guidelines often prescribe special formulas or procedures for use value assessment of agricultural or other lands, usually by income capitalization. This chapter discusses the appraisal of land on a market value basis only.

Land Valuation Theory

Land holds a unique and pivotal position in social, political, and economic theory. Land supports all life and stands at the center of human cultures and institutions. Wars have been waged over land, and rights to the ownership of land are embedded in the laws of all free nations and defended by their courts.

Land's uniqueness stems from its fixed supply and immobility. Land cannot be manufactured or reproduced. Also, land is a factor of production required directly or indirectly in the production of all other goods. Our most basic resource, land is the source of all other wealth.

Appraisal Principles Important in Land Valuation

Principles discussed in chapter 3 that are important in land valuation are supply and demand, highest and best use, surplus productivity, and change and anticipation.

Supply and Demand   Supply and demand are the cornerstone of valuation theory. The forces of supply and demand interact to determine the market value of property, which is reflected in sales prices.

Supply and demand have special significance in land valuation because the supply of land is essentially fixed. This means that the price of land in a particular area will be determined by demand factors such as population density and rate of growth, local employment and income levels, the capacity of local transportation systems, and mortgage interest rates. Figure 1 illustrates the interaction of supply and demand to determine the price of land. Note that the supply curve, s, is vertical, meaning that the quantity of

land is fixed: regardless of price, additional land cannot be produced. Hence, its price will vary with local demand. When the demand curve rises from d to d', the price rises from P to P'.

Figure 1. Land Supply and Demand Curve—Short Term

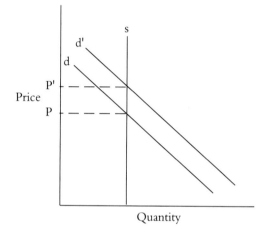

Although the total supply of land is fixed, the supply for a particular use may increase or decrease. For example, forest or farm land on the periphery of a city may be developed for residential use. The increased supply slows price increases. However, the practical limits to such development and continued growth in demand lead inevitably to higher prices and more intensive use, for example, smaller lots and the substitution of apartments for single-family houses (see figure 2).

Local transportation networks strongly influence the pattern of development and prices. Before the automobile, urban land markets were concentrated near central business districts, resulting in sharp price differences between centrally located and peripheral land. Improved roads and transportation increased demand for peripheral land and increased the effective supply of urban land. Price differences between central and peripheral land were reduced.

Zoning and other land use controls have an opposite effect because they limit the available supply of land for a given use. This usually results in higher overall prices but lower prices for land whose use is restricted.

Figure 2. Land Supply and Demand Curve for a Particular Market

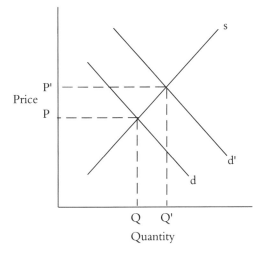

The principles of supply and demand explain the large differences in land values between urban and rural areas, between different urban areas, and even between different neighborhoods in the same urban area. No other commodity exhibits such large variations in price—certainly not consumer nondurables, such as food and clothing; nor consumer durables, such as appliances and automobiles; nor buildings. In general, the more immovable an item, the more its price will vary by area. Land, which is totally immovable, varies more in value than other economic goods, although transportation and accessibility can reduce locational differences.

Highest and Best Use The principle of highest and best use means that the market value of property depends on potential use rather than on current use alone. The principle is most obvious in the case of vacant land, which commands value based on potential use. The more profitable the potential use, the higher the demand and market value. Vacant land in an urban area commands greater value than vacant land in a rural area.

The principle of highest and best use applies to improved land as well. Take, for example, a single-family residence in an expanding urban area zoned for commercial use. The value of the land for commercial use may far exceed its value for residential use, and may even exceed the combined value of the land and building for residential use. The property may then be purchased for commercial use, the residence removed or destroyed, and a commercial structure built in its place. Similarly, small, single-story commercial structures are often destroyed to make way for large, multistory structures.

Surplus Productivity Economists divide factors of production into four groups: land, labor, capital (buildings, machinery, equipment, and supplies), and management. The principle of surplus productivity states that returns attributable to land are what remain after returns to labor, management, and capital are satisfied. Hence, gross income less income paid for labor, management, and capital equals income residual to land.

The principle of surplus productivity underscores the unique position of land in production and helps explain why land values can vary dramatically. If two parcels are used for identical purposes and are similar in their labor, management, and capital requirements, but one, because of its location, produces greater gross income than the other, then the difference in net income will be capitalized entirely into differences in land values.

Consider two similar and adjacent businesses, one with a corner location and the other on an interior lot of the same size (figure 3). The two businesses have the same labor, management, and capital requirements, but the first, because of its corner location, generates 10 percent more in gross income than the second. After returns attributable to the other three agents of production are subtracted, the net income attributable to land on the corner parcel is twice that of the adjacent parcel, resulting in a land value that is also twice as high.

Figure 3.   Illustration of Surplus Productivity

	Corner location	Interior location
Gross income	$1,100,000	$1,000,000
Income paid to labor	−300,000	−300,000
Income paid to management	−100,000	−100,000
Net income attributable to land	−500,000	−500,000
	$200,000	$100,000
Capitalization rate	÷ 0.16	÷ 0.16
Land value	$1,250,000	$625,000

Change and Anticipation   Change and anticipation are closely related principles. The principle of change states that market value is determined by dynamic economic, political, and demographic factors such as zoning, rent controls, interest rates, transportation, and local economic conditions. Because the supply of land is fixed, its value is particularly affected by changes in these market forces.

The principle of anticipation, which underlies the income approach to value, states that market value equals the present value of future benefits. In the case of vacant commercial land, the principle means that land values will reflect the capitalized value of anticipated net incomes from commercial development of the land. Similarly, the value of vacant residential lands will reflect the capitalized value of rents (either actual or imputed) attributable to the land. The principles of anticipation and change underscore the need to estimate market value for assessment purposes as of a given date, the assessment date.

Factors Affecting Land Values

Factors affecting land values can be divided into four categories: economic; social; legal, governmental, and political; and physical, environmental, and locational.

Economic Factors   Economic factors relate to the general state of the international, national, regional, and local economies. Demand variables that affect land values include employment levels, wage rates, income levels and purchasing power, the availability of financing, interest rates, and transaction costs. Supply variables include the quantity of available land; development, construction, and financing costs; and taxes and other holding costs. These factors, particularly those that relate to the supply of land, can vary substantially from one area to another.

Social Factors   Social factors help explain patterns of land use as well as demand and price. Sociologists hold that people have basic desires for territory and companionship. These desires are manifested in the "clustering" of people near urban centers and in variations in the use of land. Prestige also plays a major role in land use, as individuals and groups seek particular locations for social and economic reasons. These motives lead to "invasion" and a "succession" of land uses. Invasion occurs as one population, for example, affluent retirees seeking waterfront homes, seeks to expand its territory and improve its position. Succession occurs as the new population displaces the old, for example, fishermen. This pattern occurs until a new equilibrium is achieved with an obviously different pattern of land use and values. Age distributions, education, crime rates, and pride of ownership are other social factors that affect land use patterns and values.

Legal, Governmental, and Political Factors   Legal, governmental, and political policies can increase or decrease the demand for land. Favorable policies promote efficient land use and development. At the national level, economic, fiscal, and monetary policies can either spur or retard economic growth and the demand for land. State, provincial, and local governments often provide specific incentives or disincentives for land development through such mechanisms as taxation, zoning, land use controls, and rent controls. The quality of local governmental services, such as roads, schools, public transportation, and police and fire protection, also affects demand.

Physical, Environmental, and Locational Factors   These factors largely explain patterns of land values within a city or market area. In analyzing such factors, it is useful to distinguish the concepts of site and situation. Site attributes are the size, topography, and other physical features of a given parcel. Situation, or linkage, attributes focus on the location of the parcel relative to other places, such as the central business district, freeway access, shopping, schools, the oceanfront, or a dump. Site attributes affect land values because owners are able to use the land's inherent resources; situation attributes affect value because of nearness or accessibility to other resources. A successful land valuation model must include site and situation variables.

Land Value Model

Like the value of any other economic good, the market value of land reflects the present worth of future benefits. Vacant land has value because of its potential to produce rental income in the future. For commercial land, future benefits relate to expected rents less development, maintenance, and holding costs. For residential land, net income can be viewed as the annual value of residential use (imputed rent) less annual maintenance expenses. The general model takes the form:

$$LV = \frac{PGI - C}{R} , \qquad (1)$$

where LV is land value, PGI is projected gross income (real or imputed), C is expected costs, and R is a capitalization rate.

The projected income reflects the economic forces influencing supply and demand—population density and growth, income levels, the supply of competitive sites, accessibility, public services, and so on. Expected costs include operating expenses, maintenance, and costs of development. The capitalization rate is a function of interest rates, risk, loss of liquidity, and anticipated gains or losses over the holding period.

The interaction of all these factors determines current market prices. An improvement in local economic conditions, for example, will increase projected revenues and result in higher prices. An increase in interest rates will curtail demand, lower the present worth of the projected income stream, and result in lower prices. As this formulation makes clear, the demand for land is a derived demand. Land earns income only in conjunction with capital and labor, the costs of which must be satisfied first. For example, if residences in an area sell for $100,000, and the costs of site preparation and construction are $75,000, builders and developers will bid the price of land to $25,000. If an increase in demand raises housing prices to $110,000 while costs increase to only $80,000, the market price of the land rises to $30,000. If housing prices remain constant while construction costs increase to $80,000, land prices will fall to $20,000.

Historical trends in land prices underscore the residual nature of land values. Land prices rose sharply during the economic expansion of the 1920s and then plummeted during the Great Depression. Since World War II, land values have increased at an average annual rate of 5–7 percent, usually gaining momentum during business expansions and slowing during recessions. The overall rate of increase has been somewhat higher than the rate of inflation but consistent with returns on other investments.

In general, land values in the suburbs have increased faster than in the central business districts. In terms of the land model in equa-

tion 1, improvements in transportation and accessibility, along with associated population shifts, have increased potential returns to suburban land relative to central business district land. Regional employment and shopping centers have followed, further stimulating demand. Returns to land in the central business districts have also increased, but more slowly. The net results include (1) increased intensity in the use of land, both in the central business districts and suburbs, and (2) smaller price differences between suburban and central business district lands.

Government can affect the components of the land model in a number of ways. Fiscal policy, road construction, public services, and land use controls influence potential gross incomes. Taxes, fiscal policy, and building codes affect construction costs. Capitalization rates are, first and foremost, a function of interest rates, which reflect government monetary policies.

Location Analysis

Geographers and economists have studied the pivotal effect of location on land values since at least the early nineteenth century. The seminal work in this field is *Der Isolierte Staat (The Isolated State)* by Johann Heinrich von Thünen, a German land baron and economist. Using data from his own estates, von Thünen categorized each land use by its location relative to the town center, transportation costs, and the price of each crop or product. von Thünen made the following assumptions: (1) The "isolated state" was dominated by a single urban center. (2) It was cut off from the rest of the world, surrounded by waste on all sides. (3) The city was set in a featureless plain where fertility and transportability were everywhere equal. (4)

Farmers supplied the city with produce in return for industrial products. (5) Transport costs were in exact proportion to distance. (6) All farmers maximized profit by adjusting crops to meet the needs of the central market.

These assumptions stem from an agricultural land use pattern characterized by concentric rings around the city ranging from more intensive to less intensive uses. Although von Thünen's assumptions are unrealistic in today's world, they depict agricultural land use patterns around many relatively isolated towns.

Other geographers and economists interested in location analysis relaxed von Thünen's assumptions and developed modifications to his model. Of primary importance is the Ernest W. Burgess model of urban growth, developed from observations in early twentieth-century Chicago and broadly descriptive of many large cities. Unlike von Thünen, who conceived of land use as static, Burgess, who lived in times of rapid economic growth and technological change, theorized that land use patterns and values were subject to constant change. Burgess suggested that land use rings would endure but be pushed outward with the growth of the city. The business zone would "invade" the transition zone, the working class would be pushed farther out, and white collar workers would have to commute from ever greater distances.

Modern urban economists and sociologists have modified von Thünen's and Burgess' concentric ring models to account for social conditions, modern transportation systems, and other factors. Commercial strips, regional shopping centers, enclaves of nonconforming use, and other developments cannot be explained by the concentric ring concept.

Location still plays the primary role in land value determination, but modeling location's effects has become more complicated. Land values for physically similar sites can vary greatly between several blocks, let alone several miles. Most urban areas contain many value influence centers and their effect on land values is usually not linear. The appraiser must understand these patterns and build them into appraisal models. The rest of this chapter addresses the mechanics of land value analysis and appraisal; chapters 14 and 15 discuss quantitative methods for land valuation appropriate in mass appraisal.

Market Analysis in Land Valuation

The first step in land valuation is market analysis: stratification, determination of units of comparison, and data analysis.

Stratification

Stratification is the sorting of sales and other market data into homogeneous groups. In land valuation, strata should reflect geographic areas subject to different market influences, variations in zoning and other land use controls, and probable use. Stratifying land by area and then by zoning or probable use produces useful groupings. These sorting criteria ensure that land values will reflect market data for parcels with similar or competitive uses in the same area. Systems for coding location and land use, sometimes specified by statute, make stratification easier.

Figure 4 contains a hypothetical example of land stratification. Land is divided into four market areas and then, within market area, into zoned use. There are fifteen strata in all; zoning does not permit every use in every market area. If there are too few parcels for meaningful analysis in the resulting strata, it may be possible to combine certain uses across geographic areas, for example, to combine all industrial zoned land into a single stratum.

Figure 4.   Hypothetical Land Stratification System

Area	Zoning
Market area 01	Residential: Single-family Residential: Two- to four-family Commercial Industrial
Market area 02	Residential: Single-family Residential: Apartment Commercial
Market area 03	Residential: Single-family Residential: Two- to four-family Residential: Apartment Commercial Industrial
Market area 04	Residential: Two- to four-family Residential: Apartment Commercial Mobile home

Units of Comparison

Within strata, land should be analyzed and valued according to common units of comparison. Sales prices are expressed as price per unit. The units chosen should conform to the basis upon which land is analyzed and sold in the market. For residential land, the parcel or lot, the square foot or acre, and, oc-

casionally, the front foot provide appropriate units of comparison. For stores and most other commercial properties, the square foot or front foot is usually appropriate, although the acre can be used for large commercial or industrial sites. For large tracts of vacant land, another good unit of comparison is the number of buildable units, for example, the number of home sites, condominium units, or apartment units allowed under existing zoning. Units of comparisons for agricultural land are often expressed as yields per acre of particular crops.

Land Data Analysis

Once land sales have been stratified and prices expressed per common unit of comparison, the appraiser can determine patterns and trends in land values. Plotting market data on land value maps, calculating descriptive statistics, and graphing land value data are three ways to discover and display trends.

Plotting Land Value Data Maps on which land sales and other market data are plotted provide an excellent picture of land value patterns. Many jurisdictions routinely post sales to land value maps. Before reviewing an area, the appraiser can also request land value maps showing such market data as sale price, sale price per unit, sale date, and sale ratio based on current valuations. If available, time-adjusted sales prices can be plotted in place of nominal sales prices.

At a more sophisticated level, computerized mapping and land information systems can produce land maps displaying selected information in a desired scale and format. Appraisers can request preparation of land maps displaying sales and other selected data before reviewing or reappraising an area. Although costly to set up, computerized mapping systems provide an effective land analysis and appraisal tool, as well as other advantages.

Descriptive Statistics Descriptive statistics useful for analyzing patterns and trends in land values include the number of vacant land parcels; number of sales; measures of central tendency, particularly the median and mean; and measures of dispersion, such as the range, average deviation, and standard deviation (see chapter 20 for a review of these measures). The measures of central tendency and dispersion should be calculated for sales prices (or other available measures of market value) expressed in common units of comparison. In this way, the measures of central tendency will indicate the typical or average sale price *per unit*. Similarly, the measures of dispersion will indicate the degree of variation in terms of standard units. Table 1 shows several of these statistics for hypothetical data in the strata from figure 4.

The statistics are helpful in several respects. First, the number of sales in each category tells the appraiser which categories contain enough sales. In the example in table 1, the apartment and heavy commercial categories do not have enough sales in individual market areas and can be combined in further analyses.

Second, the measures of central tendency (median) and dispersion (average deviation) give the appraiser a good indication not only of the typical sale price per unit, but also of the consistency of the data and, thus, of the confidence that can be placed in the computed measure of central tendency. For example, in market area 04, compare the average deviation in sale price per square foot

between mobile-home lots and land zoned for light commercial use. Clearly, the median sale price per unit will provide a more reliable and consistent indicator of market value for the former than the latter. Appraisers know that they will have little trouble valuing the mobile-home lots but will have to conduct a detailed analysis of the commercial land.

Graphic Analyses

Graphic analyses can help the appraiser discern systematic relationships in land values, which can then be incorporated in valuation schedules and adjustment factors. In general, sale price per unit is the dependent variable and should be depicted on the vertical (y) axis of the graph. Any other variable for which data are available can be selected as the independent variable and represented on the horizontal (x) axis.

One variable of particular interest is the number of units, that is, the number of square feet, front feet, or buildable units. Often there is a systematic negative relationship between the number of units and sale price per unit: the greater the number of units, the lower the sale price per unit, at least up to a point. When graphed, this relationship results in a downward sloping curve, the standard market demand curve, as illustrated in Figure 5. A graph of this sort helps one to visualize the relationship and make appropriate adjustments in land valuation schedules.

Other land data—such as distance to the central business district or other value influence center, lot depth, and neighborhood desirability code—can be analyzed in the same way. Software for personal computers simplifies the graphing of land data. Most

Table 1. Descriptive Statistics for Land Valuation

	Number of parcels	Number of sales	Percent sold	Sale price per square foot	
				Median	Average deviation
Market area 01					
Residential: Single-family	1,210	104	8.6	2.85	0.84
Residential: Two- to four-family	294	36	12.2	4.34	2.50
Light commercial	109	14	15.6	5.67	3.98
Heavy commercial	24	3	12.5	7.35	3.17
Market area 02					
Residential: Single-family	2,203	314	14.3	1.36	0.42
Residential: Apartment	88	10	11.4	6.35	1.65
Light commercial	154	18	11.7	4.88	1.40
Market area 03					
Residential: Single-family	1,810	145	8.0	1.98	0.55
Residential: Two- to four-family	76	12	15.8	3.78	2.42
Residential: Apartment	40	4	10.0	6.14	1.12
Light commercial	318	29	9.8	7.55	3.33
Heavy commercial	49	6	12.2	7.64	2.67
Market area 04					
Residential: Two- to four-family	214	38	17.8	5.01	2.89
Residential: Apartment	48	6	12.5	6.09	1.22
Light commercial	180	13	7.2	5.83	3.14
Mobile home	888	76	8.6	1.67	0.26
Totals					
Residential: Single-family	5,223	563	10.8	1.87	0.75
Residential: Two- to four-family	584	86	14.7	4.69	2.51
Residential: Apartment	176	20	11.4	6.22	1.30
Light commercial	761	74	9.7	6.69	3.89
Heavy commercial	92	9	9.8	7.55	2.99

spreadsheet, statistical, and general-purpose software provides easy-to-use graphic capabilities that require only an ordinary printer.

Land Valuation Methods

The primary methods of land valuation are applications of the sales comparison approach, which is always preferred when enough sales are available. There are two principal applications of the approach in land valuation: the comparative unit method and the base lot method.

Comparative Unit Method

In the comparative unit method, the appraiser determines the average or typical per unit value for each stratum of land. The average value can be found by calculating the median or mean sale price per unit. A typical value can be found by carefully considering

Figure 5. Graph of Sale Price per Front Foot

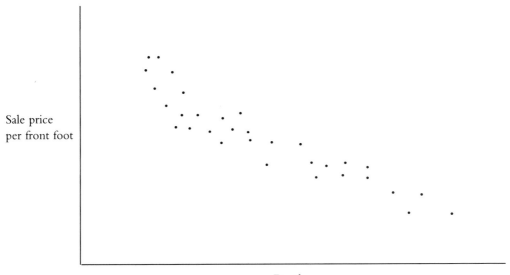

Sale price
per front foot

Depth

the available data, analyzing them with the techniques just described, and making an informed judgment. High average deviations within strata indicate that additional refinements may be necessary. When sales are few or are suspect, the appraiser may select a comparative unit value that is well above or below the mathematical mean or median. In any case, the figures chosen for each stratum should be rooted in market data whenever possible, but should also be reasonable and consistent among strata.

Consider again table 1, which shows the median and average deviation of sale price per square foot for each land stratum in a hypothetical jurisdiction. The appraiser can use computed medians as the comparative unit values. This would work well in those strata with enough sales data, which certainly includes each stratum of single-family residential land, as well as a number of the other strata. Where sales are insufficient, the

appraiser can compare computed medians among strata for reasonableness and consistency. If the medians appear reasonable, they can be used to establish comparative unit values; if not, the appraiser can use other information or judgment to override them.

When there are too few sales within strata but sales prices per unit are similar between strata, the appraiser can combine strata in order to develop per unit values. For example, heavy commercial and apartment strata in table 1 might be combined.

Once comparative unit values have been established for each stratum, they are refined to the individual parcel level. One method of approaching this is to develop unit values for each block face. This will address most variations in land values within the area, leaving only minor adjustments for individual parcels.

The appraiser can estimate appropriate unit values for block faces by evaluating their relative desirability. This is best done by analyzing market data plotted on land maps and driving around the area. In residential neighborhoods, the same unit value can often be reasonably applied to many, perhaps even most, of the blocks in the neighborhood. In other cases, unit values will vary considerably from block to block due to differences in housing styles, among other factors. In general, land commands a premium when surrounding residences are attractively designed, well constructed, and well maintained. Inevitable differences arise because of traffic patterns, noise levels, proximity to parks and schools, and so on. Commercial land values can vary greatly from one block face to another, depending on traffic patterns and other factors.

Base Lot Method

In the base lot method, the appraiser establishes the value of the standard, or "base," parcel in each stratum through a traditional sales comparison analysis, with the base lot serving as the subject parcel. The base lot may be an actual or hypothetical standard parcel. Once the base lot value is established, it is used as a benchmark to establish values for individual parcels.

As a simplified example, consider table 2, which shows the base lot in a stratum and six sales considered to be usable as comparables in determining market value for the base lot. The analysis assumes that the major factors causing variations among land values in the area are view (restricted, standard, or premium), traffic (heavy, moderate, or light), and size (quarter acre or half acre). Appropriate percentage adjustments for these factors have already been developed through paired

sales analysis or other market research. The time-adjusted sale price for each comparable is adjusted to the base lot using the percentage adjustments (in this case, the percentage adjustments are added; multiplicative adjustments would be equally valid). The sale price of the first comparable, for example, is adjusted downward because it has less traffic than the base lot. Note that the comparables are adjusted to the base lot, not vice versa. The resulting sales prices adjusted to the base lot are shown in the last column of table 2, followed by selected measures of central tendency and dispersion. In this case, provided the sales are representative, it appears that the market value of the base lot is approximately $26,500 (the median or mean could also be used).

Confidence in the accuracy of base lot values can be gauged by examining the measure of dispersion. In the example, the average deviation is only $1,478, which is but 5.6 percent of $26,500, indicating high consistency among the comparables. If the measures of dispersion are large, additional analyses are needed. Perhaps the strata should be redefined, or the adjustments applied to the comparables modified, or several base lots defined by substrata. In any case, base lot values will need to be adjusted for site characteristics in the valuation of individual parcels.

Comparison of Methods

If properly applied, the comparative unit value and base lot methods of land valuation are both good and should produce similar results. Each, however, has advantages and disadvantages. The base lot method has the advantage of being rooted in benchmark market comparison appraisals. When adjust-

Table 2. Illustration of Base Lot Method

	Time-adjusted sale price (in dollars)	View	Traffic	Size	Adjusted sale price (in dollars)
Base lot	N/A	Standard	Moderate	¼-acre	N/A
Comparable 1	26,500	Standard	Light (−.05)	¼-acre	25,175 (−.05)
Comparable 2	26,500	Standard	Moderate	¼-acre	26,500
Comparable 3	39,700	Premium (−.25)	Light (−.05)	¼-acre	27,790 (−.30)
Comparable 4	23,500	Restricted (+.15)	Moderate	¼-acre	27,025 (+.15)
Comparable 5	32,000	Standard	Moderate	½-acre (−.30)	22,400 (−.30)
Comparable 6	22,500	Restricted (+.15)	Heavy (+.10)	¼-acre	28,125 (+.25)
				Low	22,400
				High	28,125
				Median	26,763
				Mean	26,189
				Average deviation	1,478

ing the sales to the base lot, the appraiser explicitly considers differences in location, size, traffic flow, accessibility, and other relevant factors. Thus, the method can produce accurate, supportable benchmarks and is conceptually superior to the comparative unit value method when parcels differ significantly in size, view, traffic flow, and other important site factors.

The primary advantage of the comparative unit value method is its relative ease and simplicity. Suppose there are ten to twenty vacant land sales in a residential neighborhood, that each has been adjusted to the assessment date, expressed in terms of a common unit (say square feet), and plotted on a map of the neighborhood. An appraiser knowledgeable about the neighborhood could probably derive a reliable per square foot value for the neighborhood with little difficulty. Of course, this is only a starting point; the comparative unit value must then be refined by block and site adjustments applied at the individual parcel level, just as in the base lot method.

There is no reason to assume that either method must be used exclusively. The comparative unit value method is well suited to strata in which parcels vary substantially in size but are relatively homogeneous in other respects. In such cases, the appraiser might want to take advantage of the efficiency of the method. The base lot method, however, is well suited to strata in which parcels are similar in size but vary substantially in site characteristics. The method helps the appraiser to adjust appropriately for such factors in establishing base lot values.

Site Adjustments

After establishing comparative unit values or base lot values by strata and, perhaps, by substrata or block face, the appraiser can determine individual parcel values by applying any necessary site adjustments. Site adjustments recognize the characteristics of individual parcels, such as size, shape, and topography.

Mechanics of Site Adjustments

Site adjustments can be developed and applied in one of three ways: (1) by adding and subtracting dollar amounts; (2) by adding and subtracting percentages, as illustrated in table 2; or (3) by multiplying factors. To illustrate the difference between the last two techniques, assume that two adjustments are required for a subject parcel: a premium of 10 percent (+0.10) for size and a decrement of 15 percent (−0.15) for restricted access. The base lot value is $25,000.

If these percentages are summed, the net adjustment to the subject parcel is −0.05:

$$0.10 \ + \ (-0.15) \ = \ -0.05.$$

The net percentage adjustment of −0.05 is applied to the subject property by multiplying the base lot value ($25,000) by a factor of 0.95 (1 − 0.05). Hence, the computed value is $23,750:

$$\$25,000 \ \times \ 0.95 \ = \ \$23,750.$$

When factors are multiplied, the size adjustment of 10 percent would be stated as the factor 1.10 (1 + 0.10) and the access adjustment of 15 percent as 0.85 (1 − 0.15). The net adjustment is then

$$1.10 \ \times \ 0.85 \ = \ 0.935.$$

The computed value of the subject parcel is then

$$\$25,000 \ \times \ 0.935 \ = \ \$23,375.$$

In general, the two methods of applying percentage adjustments yield similar results. Choosing one over the other is a matter of individual preference, but may depend on the way the model was specified and calibrated.

Types of Site Adjustments

Site adjustments required in land valuation can be grouped into the following categories: (1) depth adjustments, (2) other size adjustments, (3) irregular shape, (4) corner influence, and (5) location and other.

Depth Adjustments   Size is perhaps the most important site characteristic requiring adjustment, because larger parcels often sell for less per unit than smaller parcels. One kind of size adjustment, depth adjustments, are important when land is appraised on a front-foot basis. Assume, for example, that the comparative unit value of a block face in a commercial area has been established at $425 per front foot and that the standard depth of parcels in the area is 100 feet. The land value of a 100-foot by 100-foot parcel is

$$100 \ \times \ \$425 \ = \ \$42,500;$$

but the value of a lot 100 feet wide and 200 feet deep is probably more than $42,500 but less than twice $42,500.

Depth tables provide a means of adjusting front-foot values for parcels of nonstandard depth. The tables result in front-foot values that increase with depth, but at a slower rate. Depth tables apply the principle of *contribution*, which states that the value of a characteristic is measured by its contribution to the value of the whole.

Depth tables generally have two columns, depth and depth factor. The depth factor is the factor which, when multiplied by the standard front-foot value ($425 in the example above), gives the front-foot value of a property with the indicated depth. Table 3 shows a sample depth table. The standard depth of 100 feet has a corresponding depth factor of 100 percent. As depth increases beyond 100 feet, depth factors increase, but at a slower rate than depth. The depth factors for 150- , 200- , and 250-foot deep lots, for example, are 114 percent, 121 percent, and 123 percent, respectively (beyond this point the factors change little). As depth decreases below 100 feet, depth factors decrease from 100 percent, although more slowly than decreases in depth.

Application of a depth table (table 3) is simple. Assume that a lot is 110 feet wide and 140 feet deep and that the standard front-foot value is $350 per foot. The appropriate depth factor is 112 percent, or 1.12, and the indicated value is

$$110 \times \$350 \times 1.12 = \$43,120.$$

Depth factors should be based on market analysis. They can be developed by plotting sale price per front foot against depth (as in figure 5) and then drawing a smooth line or curve to fit the data. The relationship is not likely to be linear, so use of statistical techniques that assume a straight-line relationship should be avoided. In this case, manually fitting a smooth curve to the data is probably preferred. Sales used in the analysis should either have similar site characteristics or be adjusted for such characteristics.

A rule of thumb sometimes used to help construct depth tables is the "4-3-2-1 rule." As illustrated in table 4, this rule states that the first 25 percent of depth represents 40 percent of the value; the second 25 percent, 30 percent of the value; the third 25 percent, 20 percent of the value; and the final 25 percent, 10 percent of the value. Although this rule of thumb can be helpful, actual depth tables should be supported by available market data.

Depth factors for various zoning classifications and areas often differ greatly. In some cases, land values increase or decrease in proportion to direct depth. This is often so with industrial or farm property and some commercial properties, particularly shopping centers. At the other extreme, the front-foot, or strip, value of commercial property may increase only slightly as depth increases beyond norms. Residential property usually falls somewhere between these two extremes.

Other Size Adjustments When land is appraised on a basis other than the front foot, size adjustments can be derived and applied in a manner analogous to that described for depth adjustments. For example, if the square foot is the unit of comparison, sale price per square foot should be plotted against square feet and an appropriate curve fit to the data. When the parcel or lot is used as the unit of comparison or when the base lot method is used, adjustments may be required for "excess" land or for undersized lots. As with depth tables, consistency in making such adjustments requires that the size (or range in size) of the standard parcel or base lot be specifically defined beforehand.

Irregular Shape All assessment jurisdictions should have a guideline for appraising

Table 3.　Sample Depth Table (standard depth = 100 feet)

1–40		41–80		81–120		121–160		161–400	
Depth	Percent	Depth	Percent	Depth	Percent	Depth	Percent	Depth	Percent
1	7	41	66	81	92	121	106	161	116
2	9	42	67	82	92	122	107	162	117
3	11	43	67	83	93	123	107	163	117
4	13	44	68	84	93	124	107	164	117
5	15	45	69	85	94	125	108	165	117
6	17	46	70	86	94	126	108	166	117
7	19	47	71	87	95	127	108	167	117
8	21	48	71	88	95	128	108	168	118
9	23	49	72	89	96	129	109	169	118
10	25	50	73	90	96	130	109	170	118
11	27	51	74	91	96	131	109	175	118
12	29	52	75	92	97	132	110	180	119
13	31	53	75	93	97	133	110	185	120
14	33	54	76	94	98	134	110	190	120
15	35	55	77	95	98	135	110	195	121
16	37	56	78	96	98	136	111	200	121
17	38	57	78	97	99	137	111	205	121
18	40	58	79	98	99	138	111	210	121
19	41	59	79	99	100	139	112	215	121
20	43	60	80	100	100	140	112	220	122
21	44	61	81	101	100	141	112	225	122
22	46	62	81	102	101	142	112	230	122
23	47	63	82	103	101	143	113	235	122
24	49	64	82	104	101	144	113	240	123
25	50	65	83	105	101	145	113	250	123
26	51	66	84	106	102	146	113	260	124
27	52	67	84	107	102	147	114	270	124
28	53	68	85	108	102	148	114	280	125
29	54	69	85	109	103	149	114	290	125
30	55	70	86	110	103	150	114	300	126
31	56	71	87	111	103	151	114	310	126
32	57	72	87	112	103	152	115	320	127
33	58	73	88	113	104	153	115	330	127
34	59	74	88	114	104	154	115	340	128
35	60	75	89	115	104	155	115	350	128
36	61	76	89	116	105	156	115	360	129
37	62	77	90	117	105	157	116	370	129
38	63	78	90	118	105	158	116	380	130
39	64	79	91	119	106	159	116	390	130
40	65	80	91	120	106	160	116	400	131

Table 4. 4-3-2-1 Rule

Percent of depth	Percent of value
First 25%	40%
Second 25%	30%
Third 25%	20%
Fourth 25%	10%

triangular or other irregular lots. In general, a triangular lot is worth less than a rectangular lot with the same area and frontage because of the lost utility for construction and general use. A rule of thumb sometimes used in appraising triangular commercial lots is the "65-35 rule." As illustrated in figure 6, this rule states that the value of a triangular lot with its base on the facing street will be approximately 65 percent of that of a rectangular lot of the same frontage and depth. Similarly, the value of a triangular lot with its apex on the facing street will be 35 percent of that of a rectangular lot of the same frontage and depth.

As an illustration of the 65-35 rule, assume that a commercial triangular lot is 100 feet wide and 100 feet deep and has its base on the main street. Land in the area is appraised on a front-foot basis, the standard front-foot value is $500, and the standard depth is 100 feet. The indicated land value using the 65-35 rule is

$$100 \times \$500 \times 0.65 = \$32,500.$$

Trapezoids and other irregular lots can be appraised in one of two ways. First, the lot can be divided by a series of lines drawn parallel to the facing street. The portion of the lot within each interval is approximated with a rectangle and valued by a depth table. The total value of the lot is found by adding the values calculated for each of its parts. Second, the lot can be segmented by a series of

Figure 6. 65-35 Rule

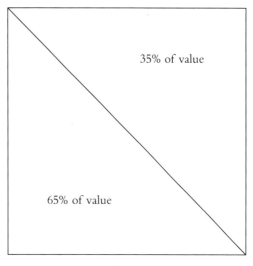

65% of value

35% of value

Street

lines drawn perpendicular to the facing street, the object being to divide the property into a number of rectangles or triangles. Again, the value is found as the sum of the parts. Figure 7 illustrates each method using an assumed front-foot value of $140 and the depth table shown in table 3. Triangular segments are handled using the "65-35 rule" (figure 6). In both cases, accuracy requires a set of carefully drawn parcel maps. The exercise of good appraisal judgment is always important in such cases.

Corner Influence The effect of corner influence on value is largely a function of property type and location. Corner influence is most consistently found in commercial properties, especially retail stores, grocery stores, and gas stations. The advantages of a corner location for these properties include greater ease of entry and exit, accessibility to a higher volume of street traffic, and increased show-window and advertising space.

Figure 7. Valuation of Irregular Lots

(a)   Lines parallel to facing street

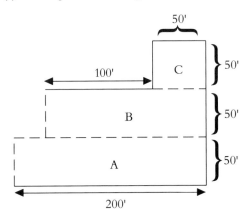

A = \$140 × 200 × .73 =   \$20,440
B = \$140 × 150 × (1.00 − .73) =   5,670
C = \$140 × 50 × (1.14 − 1.00) =   980
                                                        \$27,090

(b) Lines perpendicular to facing street

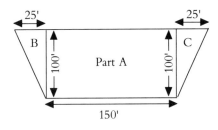

A = \$140 × 100 =   \$14,000
B = \$140 × 25 × .35 =   1,225
C = \$140 × 25 × .35 =   1,225
                                            \$16,450

Corner location can also influence residential land values, although the degree of influence is much smaller and less consistent. On the one hand, property values are raised by easier access and better landscaping op-

portunities. On the other hand, corner lots generally entail increased maintenance responsibilities, exposure to traffic, and added liability to special assessments for street maintenance and improvements. If a regional or local pattern is not evident, a reasonable policy is to ignore corner influence altogether in appraising residential properties. Nevertheless, it is relatively easy to test the effect (if any) of corner influence on residential property values through multiple regression analysis or other applications of the sales comparison approach to value.

Adequately adjusting for corner influence for commercial properties presents one of the most difficult appraisal problems. One theoretical question to resolve at the outset is how far corner influence extends. There are three possibilities. The first is to view corner influence as extending the full length of the corner lot. The second is to view corner influence as extending a certain distance, say 100 feet. The third is to view corner influence as extending a certain distance, perhaps less than, but not beyond, the corner lot.

There are also three basic approaches to computing the value of corner influence. The first is to compute corner influence simply as a percentage of the base land value. Assume, for example, that a parcel is 100 feet square, the standard front-foot value is \$375 per front foot, the standard depth is 100 feet, and corner influence increases values in the area by 50 percent. Then the corner influence factor is 1.50 and the indicated land value is

$$100 \times \$375 \times 1.50 = \$56,250.$$

Second, corner influence may be computed as a function of the ratio of side street to main street front-foot values. Assume, for example, that standard front-foot values are $600 for the main street and $400 for the side street. The estimated corner influence adjustment is 67 percent ($400 divided by $600), an adjustment factor of 1.67. This method recognizes the relative advantage of different side streets, applying a larger adjustment for side streets with higher value than for side streets with lower value.

The third method, known as the Bernard rule, is to appraise the corner lot as the sum of two separate lots, one facing on the main street and one facing on the side street. This method has been criticized as applying too much corner influence. However, it is easy to modify the approach. The value of the corner lot, for example, may be computed as the value of the facing lot plus, say, two-thirds of the value of the lot viewed as facing on the side street. Note, however, that when the zone of corner influence is considered to extend beyond the boundary of the corner lot, the Bernard rule, or a modification of it, can be applied only to the corner parcel.

Such computations may not be practical or necessary in mass appraisal. Nonetheless, the assessor should plot and analyze available market data and reflect market patterns in appraisal policies, guidelines, and tables. The resulting values should be consistent and explainable.

Location and Other Adjustments Land values will often vary significantly within an area due to proximity to schools, shopping centers, public transportation, nuisances, and so on. If comparative unit or base lot values have been refined at the block level, no further adjustments will be required for these factors. Otherwise, appropriate adjustments

should be developed based on paired sales and other market analyses. Plotting sales and other market data on land maps can make such analyses easier.

Other site characteristics often requiring adjustment include view, topography, traffic flow, limited access, flooding susceptibility, noises and other nuisances, golf course or water frontage, and soil conditions and drainage. Such adjustments, however, are required only when some of the parcels in the neighborhood or stratum are affected. If none or all of the parcels are affected, no adjustments are required, because standard or common features are reflected in comparative unit and base lot values.

Land Valuation with Insufficient Sales

When vacant land sales are insufficient for the sales comparison approach, the appraiser must resort to one or more less preferred methods. Successful application of these techniques requires careful research and good judgment.

Abstraction Method

In the abstraction method, also known as the land residual method, improvement values obtained from the cost model are subtracted from sales prices of improved parcels to yield residual land value estimates: Sale price (S) minus improvement value (IV) equals land value LV:

$$S - IV = LV. \qquad (2)$$

These calculated values are then used as a supplement or alternative to vacant land sales in application of the sales comparison approach. The method is particularly useful in highly developed areas where there are few, if any, vacant land sales. Its reliability depends on the accuracy of the sales data and improvement values used in the analysis. In general, the method is more accurate for parcels with relatively new structures, for which replacement cost and depreciation are more easily estimated.

When sales of improved parcels are scarce, appraised values can be used in lieu of sales prices to obtain estimates of total property values. Improvement values are then subtracted from total values to obtain land residuals. Calculated land residuals are completely divorced from direct sales data. In such cases, the land residuals will only be as accurate as both the total and improvement value estimates from which they are derived. Accordingly, appraisers should use the method only as a last resort when sales data for both vacant and improved parcels are inadequate and then only when the total and improvement value estimates have been carefully validated.

The land residual method should never be used to establish land values directly, because inconsistencies in land values from parcel to parcel will result. Instead, land residuals should be analyzed in the same way as vacant land sales in order to establish comparative unit or base lot values. Then estimation of land values for both vacant and improved parcels in the usual way will be uniform and consistent from parcel to parcel.

Allocation Method

The allocation method is also known as the land ratio method. In theory, for a given type of property and area there tends to be a consistent overall relationship between land and improvement values. Hence, when there are insufficient vacant land sales in a given area, the appraiser can seek comparable areas with sufficient land sales, determine the typical ratio of land value to total value, and apply the ratio to sales of improved parcels or other benchmark parcels in the subject area.

Assume, for example, that an older residential neighborhood has too few vacant land sales or sales of newly built houses for the appraiser to apply either the direct sales comparison approach or the abstraction method. However, three other neighborhoods in the jurisdiction have approximately equal desirability and residences are of the same vintage as those in the subject neighborhood. Recent reappraisal of residential property in the three neighborhoods resulted in the values shown in table 5. From these results, it appears reasonable to apply a land ratio of about 0.23, or 23 percent, to the subject neighborhood.

Table 5. Illustration of the Allocation Method

Neighborhood	Average land value	Average total value	Land ratio
1	$18,545	$83,619	.222
2	21,020	90,888	.231
3	20,163	85,950	.235

As with the abstraction method, however, the allocation method should not be used to establish land values directly. Once obtained, the typical land ratio is applied to sales prices to obtain a set of estimated benchmark values. The ratio may be applied to appraised values for selected parcels, but this is less desirable. If a typical property in the subject neighborhood of our example recently sold for $87,900, its land value would be estimated as

$$\$87,900 \times 0.23 = \$20,217.$$

Benchmark values computed in this way are used to establish either comparative unit or base lot values for the neighborhood or area.

An advantage of the allocation method over the abstraction method is that estimated improvement values are not explicitly required in the analysis. This makes the allocation method particularly useful in older neighborhoods with few sales of vacant or newly improved parcels. The method can be reasonably accurate if applied with care and validated to ensure that calculated land and improvement value estimates are consistent with available sale price data.

Capitalization of Ground Rents

Capitalization of ground rents is a feasible method when land is rented or leased independently of improvements. The method is most applicable to farmland and to commercial land leased on a net basis (lessee responsible for property taxes and all other expenses). If the lease has been recently negotiated or is still representative of current market rents, the net rent can be directly capitalized into an indicated land value.

Assume, for example, that a parcel of downtown land was recently leased on a net basis at a rate of $6,000 per year for ten years. If the appropriate capitalization rate is 12 percent, the indicated land value is

$$\$6,000/0.12 = \$50,000.$$

The capitalization rate should, of course, be based on market analysis. Leases that are out-

dated and no longer representative of the current market should be rejected. Also, as with the abstraction and allocation methods, land values computed in this way should not be used directly, but rather as benchmarks in establishing comparative unit or base lot values for the strata under analysis.

Cost of Development Method

The cost of development method can be appropriate for newly subdivided land or land ripe for subdivision. The appraiser projects improvements to the land, estimates the total revenues and development costs, and calculates the value residual to the land after subtraction of all costs, expenses, and profit. The method is based on the principle of surplus productivity. Land value is calculated as a residual after the requirements of labor, capital, and management are satisfied.

For example, assume that the subject property is a 40-acre parcel zoned for residential use with four home sites allowed per acre. Developers are currently selling ¼-acre lots in the area, with street improvements and utilities, for $17,500 to $22,000 ($20,000 is typical). Site preparation, street improvements, and utilities will cost approximately $1,400,000; planning, administrative, sales, and other overhead costs average 25 percent of gross sales in such projects; and a reasonable allowance for interest expenses, other holding costs, and profit is 40 percent of net income. The estimated value is found as shown in figure 8.

The method involves considerable speculation and should be used cautiously. The projected improvements must represent the most probable use of the land. Estimated costs should include the direct costs of site preparation, utility hookups, all indirect

Figure 8.   Cost of Development Method

Projected sale price of lots (160 × $20,000)	$3,200,000
Site development costs	−1,400,000
Total overhead costs (25% of $3,200,000)	−800,000
Net income before holding costs and profit	1,000,000
Holding costs and profit (40% of $1,000,000)	−400,000
Indicated value of undeveloped land	$600,000

costs, and a reasonable allowance for profit. As long as the land is not subdivided, anticipated revenues and expenses should be discounted for time. Once subdivided, however, each parcel becomes an individual entity, and its value should reflect its most probable sale price if exposed to the current market.

Some states and provinces, through either statute or administrative rule, have adopted procedures for applying discounts to parcels in a new subdivision until a specified percentage of the sites have sold. Assessors should review any such requirements carefully. The intent is usually to compensate the developer for time on the market, which may be several years. Where this is the case, holding costs (interest expense) should not be included as an allowable expense in computing the net present value of the subdivision, because this would account twice for such costs.

Using Computers for Land Valuation

Although land valuation relies heavily on field observation and appraisal judgment, computerization of land data makes processing and analysis more efficient. Computerization allows the appraiser to retrieve sales and other selected data for a given area, edit the data, develop comparative unit values, calculate land residuals and ratios of land to total value, and perform other market analyses with speed and efficiency. Personal computers are well suited to most land analyses.

Land Valuation Models

Multiple regression analysis, adaptive estimation procedure (feedback), or other automated versions of the sales comparison approach can be used to develop land valuation models (see chapters 14 and 15 for a detailed discussion of these methods). The dependent variable in such models is sale price or sale price per unit, for example, sale price per square foot when the square foot is the unit of comparison. Independent variables can include parcel size, for example, square feet or front feet; distance to value influence centers, such as the central business district; and site characteristics, such as utilities, traffic flow, view, and topography. Separate models should be developed for different areas and land uses.

An example of a linear multiple regression model is

$$S = b_0 + b_1 SQRTSF + b_2 IRREG \\ + b_3 VIEWPR + b_4 VIEWGD \\ + b_5 NBHD01 + b_6 NBHD03 \\ + b_7 NBHD04, \qquad (3)$$

where
    $SQRTSF$ is square root of land square feet
    $IRREG$ is irregular topography (0 = no, 1 = yes)
    $VIEWPR$ is poor view (0 = no, 1 = yes)

VIEWGD is good view (0 = no, 1 = yes)

NBHD01 is neighborhood 01 (0 = no, 1 = yes)

NBHD03 is neighborhood 03 (0 = no, 1 = yes)

NBHD04 is neighborhood 04 (0 = no, 1 = yes)

b_0 is a constant

$b_1, \ldots, b_7$ are coefficients, or dollar value adjustments, derived from multiple regression analysis

The model assumes that the typical lot is level, has a standard view, and is located in neighborhood 02. For the typical lot, S equals b_0 plus the value per square foot times the square root of the square feet ($b_1 SQRTSF$). All the remaining terms become zero. For other lots, the model adjusts for size and any differences from these assumptions.

Multiple regression analysis may produce the following coefficients:

S = \$5,400 + \$137 (*SQRTSF*) − \$1,600 (*IRREG*) − \$2,300 (*VIEWPR*) + \$3,100 (*VIEWGD*) + \$525 (*NBHD01*) − \$1,750 (*NBHD03*) + \$4,080 (*NBHD04*).

In this case, the value of a 10,000-square-foot lot with irregular topography and a standard view in neighborhood 04 would be computed as:

S = \$5,400 + \$137 *SQRT* (10,000) − \$1,600 + \$4,800 = \$21,580.

If the parcel had 20,000 square feet, the computed value would be:

S = \$5,400 + \$137 *SQRT* (20,000) − \$1,600 + \$4,080 = \$27,255.

This model is a linear model, which means that the adjustments are summed. Feedback and multiplicative multiple regression analysis can be used to specify multiplicative land value models. An example of such a model is:

$$S = b_0 SQFT^{b_1} \times b_2^{IRREG} \times b_3^{VIEWPR} \times b_4^{VIEWGD} \times b_5^{NBHD01} \times b_6^{NBHD03} \times b_7^{NBHD04}, \qquad (4)$$

where *SQFT* is square feet of land area, and all other terms are as defined previously.

Assume that the coefficients are determined as follows:

$$S = \$327 \, (SQFT)^{0.44} \times 0.93^{IRREG} \times 0.84^{VIEWPR} \times 1.12^{VIEWGD} \times 1.04^{NBHD01} \times 0.90^{NBHD03} \times 1.18^{NBHD04}. \qquad (5)$$

The value of a 10,000-square-foot lot with irregular topography and a standard view in neighborhood 04 is computed as:

$$S = \$327(10,000)^{0.44} \times 0.93 \times 1.18 = \$20,650.$$

The computed value of a 20,000-square-foot parcel with the same characteristics is:

$$S = \$327(20,000)^{0.44} \times 0.93 \times 1.18 = \$28,013.$$

Successful development of land valuation models depends on adequate land sales and property characteristics data. Unfortunately, many areas, particularly older, established areas, simply have too few vacant land sales. In some cases, carefully verified land residuals, preferably derived from sales of parcels with relatively new improvements, can be used as a supplement or substitute for vacant land sales.

In addition, multiple regression analysis, adaptive estimation procedure, and similar models developed for *improved* parcels can aid greatly in land analyses if land characteristics are included, or at least tested, in the models. The models will quantify the relationship, if any, between land characteristics and market value. The appraiser can then use this information in developing comparative unit values and site adjustments in preparation for a land reappraisal.

Separation of Land and Improvement Values

The value of an improved parcel is usually separated into a land value and a building value. When the sales comparison or income approach is used, an independent estimate of the land value is subtracted from the total estimated value to obtain a residual improvement value. This method, of course, requires the appraisal of improved land, which can be particularly difficult in older or highly developed areas.

As an alternative, some computer-assisted mass appraisal models, notably adaptive estimation procedure, provide for automatic separation of land and building values. Such models automate the land appraisal process and provide market-based land valuations in the complete absence of vacant land sales.

Administration

A land valuation system must be well planned and controlled. The assessor must develop and carry out effective policies and procedures, continually monitor appraisal accuracy, and regularly update values to reflect the market.

Components of a Land Appraisal System

An effective land appraisal system has five basic components: cadastral maps, land characteristics data, sales and other market data, appraisal procedures, and staff and resources.

Cadastral Maps   Land appraisal requires a complete, current, and accurate set of cadastral maps showing parcel boundary lines, dimensions, pertinent legal and descriptive information, and parcel numbers. The scale should provide the necessary scope of coverage and required detail. Maps should be maintained continuously to reflect new subdivisions, splits, and assemblages, as well as changes in political boundaries, zoning, and physical features (see chapter 17 and the *Standard on Cadastral Maps and Parcel Identifiers* (IAAO 1988) for a complete discussion of cadastral mapping).

Land Characteristics Data   Land data maintained in the assessment system should include all the factors and characteristics that strongly influence land values. The assessor should distinguish between factors that are often important in the jurisdiction and those that are only occasionally important. To conserve resources, the former should be collected routinely and provided for on data collection forms and in computer files. The latter can be collected as needed using specially provided "other" categories.

Sales and Other Market Data   The success of any land appraisal program depends largely on sales and other market data. Useful land sales data include sale price; date of sale; name, address, and relationship (if any) of buyer and seller; type of transfer (for example, warranty deed, quit claim deed, or land contract); type of financing; interest transferred (fee simple or partial interest); and other circumstances surrounding the sale.

Real estate transfer documents providing for the above items are the least expensive source of sales data. Other sources include sales questionnaires; interviews with buyers, sellers, or their agents; and third-party sources, such as real estate agencies, financial institutions, private appraisers, and multiple-listing agencies. Particularly in single-property appraisal, it is good practice to verify sales data with a second source; for example, to confirm sales data obtained from transfer documents with the buyer, seller, or other party knowledgeable about the sale.

Once obtained, sales data are edited to remove non-arm's-length transfers, such as sales between related parties, forced sales, and sales of legal convenience. Land contracts should be rejected unless the date of agreement is recent. Multiple parcel and partial interest sales can be used in market analysis, but extreme care must be exercised if they are used for estimates of single parcel, fee simple estates.

The method of financing sales should also be considered. If possible, sales involving nonmarket financing (generally, assumed mortgages and seller carrybacks) should be rejected or, preferably, adjusted to a cash equivalent price. If financing information is not available on individual transfers, appropriate adjustment factors can be developed and applied based on knowledge of local financing practices.

When land values are appreciating or depreciating, sales prices should be adjusted for time of sale, area by area, because changes in land values can differ substantially from one area to another. See chapter 5 for a more complete discussion of collecting, processing, and adjusting sales data.

In addition to sales, the assessor should gather market data on land rents, ground leases, and other land development costs. This information can be particularly helpful when few vacant land sales exist. Also, land residuals obtained by subtracting improvement values from sales prices of improved parcels can be used to provide indirect estimates of land values. Land residuals, however, are only as valid as the sales prices and building values from which they are derived. They tend to be more accurate for properties with newer improvements, because the problem of estimating accrued depreciation is minimized.

Appraisal Methods Land appraisals must be rooted in the market. Applications of the sales comparison approach are the primary techniques used in land valuation. When sufficient sales data are not available, the appraiser must resort to other methods. In any case, land values must reflect market value in each neighborhood or area; they should also account adequately for differences in size, topography, and so forth among individual parcels within each area. The *Standard on Urban Land Valuation* (IAAO 1987) recommends that land be physically inspected and revalued at least every four years and that land values be reviewed annually to maintain market values and equity among areas. Annual updates between revaluations can be accomplished through the use of market adjustment factors based on ratio studies.

Staff and Resources Accurate land valuation requires a knowledgeable staff and adequate computer support. The appraisal staff should be sufficient to inspect physically and revalue each area at least every fourth year and to review other areas and develop appropriate market adjustments in intervening years. Land appraisers must be skilled in appraisal principles and methods and knowledgeable about the areas for which they are responsible. Accurate land appraisals also require good judgment, which is particularly critical in the selection of proper appraisal techniques and in the development and use of land valuation schedules.

Computers are an important tool in land appraisal, permitting better research and speeding calculations. Among other things, computers can be used to store and retrieve data; analyze market patterns and trends; calculate values by applying land valuation schedules and formulas; and derive land valuation models through multiple regression analysis, adaptive estimation procedure, or other statistical techniques. The flexibility offered by personal computers and general-purpose software, such as spreadsheet and statistics programs, can be particularly helpful in land appraisal.

Monitoring Appraisal Accuracy

Every jurisdiction should monitor the accuracy and equity of land values through ratio studies and other market analyses. Measures of central tendency, such as the median and mean, computed in ratio studies will indicate the general level of appraisal in the jurisdiction, as well as for individual areas. It is important to ensure that the level of appraisal is consistent from area to area. Measures of uniformity, such as the coefficient of dispersion, will indicate the uniformity of appraisals within each area. Ratio

studies, including standards of appraisal performance, are discussed in detail in chapter 20.

Market Adjustment Factors

When land in an area is underappraised, market adjustment or trend factors can be applied based on measures of central tendency calculated in ratio studies. Assume, for example, that the calculated median sales ratio for vacant residential land in an area is 0.72 and it is desired to bring the level of appraisal to 0.95 (1.0 would be better). The appropriate trend factor is 0.95 divided by 0.72, or 1.32.

For a subject parcel with a current land value of $25,000, the indicated land value is

$$\$25,000 \times 1.32 = \$33,000.$$

Market adjustment factors can also be developed separately for land and building values. Assume, for example, that in the present case the calculated median ratio for *improved* residential property is 0.85, that the land-to-building ratio is 1 to 4, and that it is reasonable to assume that vacant and improved land in the area are similarly appraised. Then, the level of appraisal for residential improvements in the area can be calculated as shown in figure 9.

Thus, the required adjustment factor for residential *improvements* in the area is 1.08 (0.95 divided by 0.88). Together, land and improvement adjustment factors developed in this way will yield the target level of appraisal, 0.95, which can be verified as shown in figure 9.

For improved parcels, use of separate adjustment factors for land and building will yield a better, more supportable allocation between land and building values than will a single adjustment factor applied to both land and building values.

Figure 9. Applying Market Adjustment Factors

(a)

$$0.85 = 0.20 \times 0.72 + 0.80X,$$

where X is the level of appraisal.

$$0.85 = 0.144 + 0.80X$$

$$0.80X = 0.85 - 0.144$$

$$0.80X = 0.706$$

$$X = 0.88$$

(b)

	Land	Buildings		
Percent of total value	0.20	0.80		
Appraisal level	× 0.72	× 0.88		
Adjustment factor	× 1.32	× 1.08		
	= 0.19	+ 0.76	= 0.95	

As emphasized in chapter 20, market adjustment factors are best applied when appraisal uniformity within strata is acceptable. Sample sizes must also be adequate. When these conditions are met, market adjustment factors provide an efficient and effective method of maintaining current market values and uniformity among strata.

Physical Reviews and Reappraisals

Every assessment jurisdiction should have a current plan or program providing for the periodic field review and reappraisal of land. Either the jurisdiction can review each area or stratum at regular intervals, such as every three or four years, or areas or strata that are "hot spots" can be reviewed. Hot spots have unusual physical and economic activity as indicated by sales ratio studies or other market analyses. In any case, the assessment jurisdiction should ensure that no more than six years elapse before the complete physical review and reappraisal of a given neighborhood or stratum.

Summary

Land is one of the factors of production and has value because of its role in the production of goods and services. Its value is seen as a residual value after all other factors have earned a return.

Land values are particularly sensitive to location and may be affected by zoning and land use controls. The sales comparison approach is the best method of appraising land, but other methods are available when there is insufficient sales information.

The Cost Approach

8

This chapter describes the theory and principles of the cost approach and its application, especially in single-property appraisal. Applications in mass appraisal are discussed in more detail in chapters 14 and 15.

Introduction

Theory of the Cost Approach

The cost approach, also known as the summation approach, is based on the theory that the market value of an improved parcel can be estimated as the sum of the land value and the depreciated value of the improvements:

$$MV = LV + IV, \qquad (1)$$

where MV is the market value, LV is the land value, and IV is the depreciated value of the improvement. IV is broken down into replacement cost new (RCN), the cost to build a structure of equal utility, and depreciation, (D). The formula then reads,

$$MV = LV + (RCN - D). \qquad (2)$$

The cost approach is justified in part by the principle of substitution: an informed buyer will pay no more for an improved property than the price of acquiring a vacant site and constructing a substitute building of equal utility, assuming no costly delays in construction. Also, as explained in chapter 4, rational, profit-maximizing entities will set prices so as to cover all direct and indirect costs, and competition will limit profit margins to reasonable levels. Thus, when markets are in balance (long-run equilibrium), prices of new buildings will equal construction costs, including reasonable profit equal to the opportunity cost of capital in alternative uses.

The cost approach requires estimates of land value, accrued depreciation, and the current cost of constructing the improvements. Depreciation is subtracted from current construction costs to obtain an estimate of improvement value. A land value that reflects the value of the site as if vacant and available to be developed to its highest and best use (see chapter 7) is added to the value of the improvement.

The cost approach attempts to replicate the workings of the real estate market. The current cost of construction and cost of a site of equal utility represent the supply side of the market. Other components of the cost approach, such as depreciation, the price of substitutes, location, and other noncost market adjustments, represent the demand side of the market. Because these components are derived from the market, the cost approach is often characterized as a hybrid cost-market approach.

If estimates of land value or depreciated improvement value fall below market value, the value estimated by the cost approach will also be too low. The cost approach, therefore, requires accurate, current land values and construction cost data, and depreciation must be derived from the market. Estimated values should be validated against current sales, and market adjustments applied as necessary.

In mass appraisal, the cost approach, if correctly applied, provides stable, consistent estimates of value. The cost approach usually works best for newer buildings, which have less depreciation and more easily estimated construction costs. It is especially useful for appraisal of property types—such as industrial and special-purpose—for which sales and income data are scarce. Even when values from the other approaches are used for assessments, calculation of cost values is recommended as a check and support.

The cost approach model, like other models, must be *specified* and *calibrated*. Specification in the cost approach means deciding on procedures to be used in estimating building costs, applying depreciation, determining land values, and adjusting preliminary values to the market. In mass appraisal, it means land model development, cost model formulation, and provisions for depreciation and other market adjustments. Calibration means estimating cost and depreciation schedules and land value tables.

Specification takes place only occasionally, for example, for a revaluation or new appraisal system, although refinements may be made annually. Calibration is required each year to keep values current and accurate.

In mass appraisal practice, many assessment jurisdictions use hybrid cost-sales com-parison approaches to compensate for the difficulties in keeping land values, construction costs, and depreciation estimates up-to-date. Equation 3 is a common hybrid model.

$$MV = GQ \ [LV + (RCN - D)]. \ (3)$$

GQ is a multiplicative adjustment for qualitative factors not otherwise accounted for in the basic cost model, such as neighborhood influences. Techniques similar to those used to construct depreciation tables (discussed later in this chapter) are used to calibrate GQ.

Data Requirements

Besides construction cost and market data, the cost approach requires descriptive data on the improvements being appraised. These data should be gathered from a physical inspection of the property (see chapter 5). A typical survey would include

- designed use
- dimensions and areas
- number of stories and heights
- foundation
- basements
- framing
- exterior walls
- roofs
- interior finish and amenities
- plumbing and baths
- heating and cooling
- electrical service
- garages and parking
- other improvements
- year built and effective age or condition

From these data, appraisers can judge the overall quality of construction and condition of the property. Appraisers should also judge *functional utility*, the ability of the improvements to satisfy market standards and demand. Functional utility is affected by building design, amenities, and appearance. Poor or inappropriate design, wasteful floor plans, poor natural lighting, inappropriate room sizes, no covered parking, and inadequate heating or cooling are examples of *functional obsolescence* that can have a major effect on value. Such conditions should be noted and accounted for in the application of accrued depreciation, which is discussed in detail later in this chapter.

Types of Cost

In appraisal, costs consist of all expenditures necessary to complete construction of an improvement and place it in the hands of the buyer. Costs are either direct or indirect. *Direct costs* include materials, labor, supervision, equipment rentals, and utilities. *Indirect costs* include architectural and engineering fees, building permits, title and legal fees, insurance, interest and fees on construction loans, taxes incurred during construction, advertising and sales expenses, and reasonable overhead and profit.

Accurate cost estimates will include all direct and indirect costs. Builders, contractors, and publishers of cost manuals sometimes neglect to include certain items in reporting costs. Accordingly, when developing cost schedules, appraisers should be sure that all costs are accounted for.

Costs can be estimated on the basis of either reproduction or replacement cost. *Reproduction cost* is the cost of constructing a replica, or identical structure, using the same materials, construction standards, design, and quality of workmanship. *Replacement cost* is the cost of constructing a substitute structure of equal utility using current materials, design, and standards.

The degree to which a cost estimate approximates reproduction cost as opposed to replacement cost is affected by how costs are estimated. Generalized cost estimation techniques tend to produce replacement costs; detailed methods that recognize unique features of the subject property tend to produce reproduction costs. Replacement costs are usually less than reproduction costs because the latter include the added cost of obsolete design, building techniques, and materials. When reproduction costs are used, the appraiser adjusts explicitly for any such obsolescence.

Replacement costs, which require less detail and fewer adjustments, are commonly used in mass appraisal. Special-purpose properties, however, usually require more detailed, reproduction cost estimates. If the structures are old, building materials and standards may be obsolete, so that reproduction costs are not available. Unless the original (historical) cost can be trended, the appraiser will have to estimate the replacement cost of a modern structure of similar utility.

For either replacement or reproduction costs, costs must be typical. Actual costs for similar properties sometimes vary unpredictably, just as sales prices vary among similar properties. In private as well as public construction, contractors' bids may vary substantially; cost estimation is not an exact science. Selection of a bid requires a judgment as to which contractor will complete the job satisfactorily at the lowest cost and with no undue risk. On occasion, costs are higher than usual, as when a premium is paid to shorten the construction period or the bid process is prejudiced. Assessors should disregard or adjust for atypical costs in developing cost schedules.

Costs should also reflect the local market and be current as of the appraisal date. If nationally published manuals are used, they should be tested on buildings of known cost and local adjustments made as necessary. Profit margins, in particular, can vary with local economic conditions. Most manuals contain indexes for adjusting reported costs for time. If manuals are developed in house, they should be kept current through annual indexing and periodic revisions.

Methods of Estimating Costs

The four methods of specifying and calibrating models that estimate costs are quantity survey, unit-in-place, comparative unit, and trended original cost.

Quantity Survey Method

The quantity survey, or contractor's method, is the most time-consuming and detailed of the four methods. The method requires complete itemization of all construction, labor, and material costs, by components and subcomponents, and of all indirect costs. Table 1 shows an example for exterior wall costs. Costs for other building components would be estimated in the same way and added to overhead, profit, and other indirect costs to arrive at total reproduction costs. One problem in applying the method is the absence of reliable data on the hours of labor required for obsolete construction methods.

Proper application of the quantity survey method requires a detailed knowledge of construction and familiarity with local labor laws and work rules. Costs developed are specific to the subject building and can be very accurate. Contractors, cost estimators, and builders often use the method in estimating costs and preparing bids, but because it is so time-consuming, it has limited use in mass appraisal. Appraisers use the quantity survey method to estimate reproduction costs of large, special-purpose properties, for which other methods may not be sufficiently accurate. It can also be used to estimate the reproduction cost of benchmark structures from which local cost schedules and indexes are developed. Appraisers may also encounter the quantity survey method in valuation appeals.

Unit-in-Place Method

The unit-in-place segregated cost method expresses all the direct and some of the indirect costs of structural components as units. In general, *horizontal costs*, such as those for foundations, floors, roofing, and electrical systems, are expressed as cost per square foot. *Vertical costs*, such as those for exterior walls and interior partitions, are expressed as cost per linear foot. Constant cost components, such as water heaters, may be expressed as lump sums. To estimate total costs for a component, the unit cost of each component is multiplied by the number of units in a building. To obtain a total cost estimate, the component costs are summed with lump sum or percentage adjustments for applicable indirect costs.

Unit-in-place costs include all direct labor and building costs. For example, roof support costs would include all materials needed for trusses, rafters, sheathing, or decking, as well as all labor costs. These costs may vary by roof pitch and other factors. Similarly, roof covering costs would include felt paper,

Table 1. Quantity Survey Method for Exterior Walls

	Material	Labor	Total
Concrete blocks: 98 per tier × 12 tiers = 1,176 × $1.01	$1190.70	. . .	$1190.70
Labor: 1,176 × $.88	. . .	$1034.88	1034.88
Gable: ends: 400 blocks × $1.01	405.00	. . .	405.00
Labor: 400 blocks × $.88	. . .	352.00	352.00
Steel rods: 364 linear feet × $.45	163.80	. . .	163.80
Labor: 364 linear feet × $.11	. . .	40.04	40.04
Concrete lintel: 2.13 cubic yards × $90.00	171.70	. . .	171.70
Labor:	. . .	22.50	22.50
Mortar: 1,576 blocks × $.23	354.60	. . .	354.60
Labor — forms removal	. . .	112.50	112.50

shingles, drip edges, flashing, and any other material, plus all labor. In both cases, costs would be expressed as cost per square foot of roof surface.

Costs for exterior and interior walls and certain other vertical cost components would be expressed as cost per linear foot. The cost of interior walls, for example, might include costs for the following:

- 2″ × 4″ × 8′ studs
- single bottom plate
- double top plate
- ½″ drywall taped and sanded on both sides
- metal corner head on outside corners
- one prime coat of paint
- one finish coat of paint

If the cost were $15 per linear foot, and a subject property had 120 linear feet, total costs for this component would be

$$120 \times \$15 = \$1,800.$$

Table 2 contains a complete example of the unit-in-place method applied to a hypothetical building. This method is detailed and highly accurate, although not as precise as the quantity survey method. Builders and con-

tractors often use the unit-in-place method in developing cost estimates. Many cost manuals contain unit-in-place sections that appraisers can use to adjust for features not included in the base specifications for a given building class. Appraisers can also use the method to estimate costs for unusual or special-purpose structures.

Comparative Unit Method

The comparative unit method is the easiest, fastest, and most widely used method of cost estimation in mass appraisal. Direct and indirect costs, both horizontal and vertical, are summed and divided by an appropriate unit (square feet of ground area or floor area, or cubic feet) to derive a cost per unit. Comparative unit costs may be obtained from cost services or developed locally from an analysis of actual costs of benchmark structures. These costs are arranged in schedules based on type and quality of construction, size, and perhaps shape. Table 3 contains a simplified example. Percentage or lump-sum adjustments for features not included in comparative unit costs may be made with the unit-in-place method.

Table 2.   Unit-in-Place Method

Cost estimate for industrial property
Occupancy: industrial manufacturing

Class: A fireproof steel frame
Effective age: 1 year
Number of stories: 1.0
Floor area: 113,270 square feet

Cost rank: 2.0 Average
Condition: 6.0 Excellent
Average story height: 27.0
Cost as of: 2/90

Component	Units	Cost	Replacement cost new
Excavation and site preparation			
Site preparation	113,270	$0.17	$19,256
Foundation			
Concrete	113,270	1.90	215,213
Frame			
Steel	113,270	5.81	658,099
Floor structure			
Concrete on ground	113,270	3.04	344,341
Floor cover			
Hardener and sealer	113,270	0.52	58,900
Terrazzo	1,560	6.15	9,594
Vinyl composition tile	7,100	1.26	8,946
Subtotal			77,440
Ceiling			
Acoustical, mineral fiber	8,660	1.56	13,510
Suspended ceiling	8,660	1.09	9,439
Subtotal			22,949
Interior construction			
Interior construction, masonry	8,660	2.38	20,611
Plumbing			
Plumbing fixtures	45	2,562	115,290
Fire protection			
Sprinklers	113,270	1.14	129,128
Heating and cooling			
Forced air	104,611	2.50	261,528
Hot water	8,660	5.56	48,150
Refrigerated cooling	8,660	4.73	40,962
Subtotal			350,640
Electrical			
Electrical A	8,660	2.58	22,343
Electrical B	104,611	0.92	96,242
Subtotal			118,585

Table 2. Unit-in-Place Method (cont.)

Component	Units	Cost	Replacement cost new
Exterior wall			
Common brick	8,490	10.76	91,352
Face brick	8,490	1.76	14,942
Standard block	20,606	12.36	254,690
Reinforced concrete	8,490	13.12	111,389
Subtotal			472,373
Roof structure			
Steel joists, steel deck	113,270	4.86	550,492
Roof cover			
Built-up composition	113,270	1.33	150,649
Total			3,245,066
Architect's fees	6.2%		200,112
Replacement cost new		$30.42	$3,445,178

Table 3. Simplified Example of Comparative Unit Costs

Ground area in square feet	Minimal quality		Standard quality		Semi-custom		Custom built	
	One-story	Two-story	One-story	Two-story	One-story	Two-story	One-story	Two-story
1,000	$39.08	$63.18	$51.10	$80.39	$58.11	$87.50	$68.44	$97.42
1,050	38.71	62.79	50.68	79.94	57.60	86.99	67.89	96.90
1,100	38.34	62.43	50.26	79.57	57.22	86.58	67.33	96.24
1,150	37.08	61.06	49.85	79.26	56.78	86.25	66.74	95.71
1,200	36.75	60.69	49.41	78.70	56.30	85.83	66.26	95.40

Example: for a standard quality, two-story residence with 1,150 feet of ground area, replacement cost is estimated as $79.26 × 1,150 = $91,149.

As with the other methods of cost estimation, accuracy depends on the quality of the data used in the analysis. All direct and indirect costs must be included, except perhaps architect's fees, which can be added as a percentage adjustment. The chosen units of comparison should be based on industry standards. Usually, ground or total square footage is used for residential and commercial structures. A volume unit such as cubic feet may be used for warehouse and industrial structures. Although not as precise as the unit-in-place and quantity survey methods, the comparative unit method ensures that costs are typical and produces reliable replacement cost estimates. Costs produced by this method may also be converted to formulas, as shown later in this chapter and in more detail in chapter 15.

Trended Original Cost

The trended original cost method obtains an estimate of the reproduction cost of a structure by trending its original, or historical, cost with a factor from an appropriate construction cost index. The method is used to appraise structures for which comparable cost data are not available, as well as large industrial properties that would take too long to describe accurately enough for the unit-in-place or quantity survey methods. Trended original costs can also be used to validate cost estimates produced by other cost methods and are especially useful for recently constructed properties.

For example, a 200-bed general hospital was built nine years ago for $7,853,000. An appropriate cost index shows that hospital construction costs have since increased 68.3 percent. The trended original cost is

$$\$7,853,000 \ \times \ 1.683 \ = \ \$13,216,600.$$

Accuracy depends on knowledge of the date(s) and original cost of construction. Costs attributable to land, personal property, and site improvements should be subtracted from total costs. Further, reported costs should be adjusted to exclude extraneous or atypical costs and include unreported costs. Such determinations should be made by an appraiser skilled in auditing construction cost records.

Cost Manuals

A cost manual is one way to represent a cost model in a form that is easy to use. The model must be specified and calibrated be-

fore it can be expressed in table form. Physically, a cost manual is a set of cost factors organized in schedules or tables, with instructions for their use. This section discusses desirable features of cost manuals, third-party sources of cost manuals, development of local cost manuals, trending costs contained in manuals, and conversion of cost manuals to formulas.

Desirable Features of Cost Manuals

Cost manuals should

1. *Be applicable to most building types.* A cost manual should provide appropriate base specifications and comparative unit values for most buildings found in the jurisdiction. The need to use several manuals or make large adjustments to base specifications impedes mass appraisal and jeopardizes uniformity.

2. *Be based on actual costs.* Actual costs provide a reliable starting point. The manual should include indexes for updating costs on a regular basis (at least annually). If the manual is not developed locally, it should contain location adjustments based on the local market.

3. *Indicate which indirect costs are included.* Indirect costs, with the possible exception of architect's fees, are usually included in reported costs. The manual should note any exceptions and provide guidelines for their inclusion.

4. *Be easy to update.* Cost manuals should be based on costs in specific locations as of specific dates. Manuals from third-party vendors should provide either time and location modifiers or directions for updating costs.

5. *Be easy to use.* The manual should contain clear and complete instructions on

its use. Clear descriptions and illustrations of building type and construction quality will help appraisers classify structures correctly and consistently. The manual should also explain when and how to make adjustments to base costs for superior and inferior building features. The instructions should contain examples or sample problems. Photographs should be professionally done, and buildings in photographs should represent clearly the type or quality class being described.

6. *Be flexible.* Cost manuals should make it easy to adjust for differences from base specifications. A good manual will be simple, flexible, and accurate. Although easy-to-use manuals require fewer decisions and operations, they may for that very reason be less accurate. On the other hand, manuals that provide for many small adjustments are also time-consuming and may cause users to focus on minor construction features and lose sight of important ones. The best manuals provide appraisers with several options, such as using the comparative unit method alone, modifying comparative unit method cost estimates with unit-in-place costs, or using the unit-in-place method alone.

7. *Contain guidelines for estimating accrued depreciation.* As a minimum, the manual should provide normal depreciation tables, which show the effect of physical wear and tear. The manual should indicate the normal lives of structures and any mathematical functions or formulas used to derive the tables. Such information is essential for understanding the basis for the tables, making adjustments

for abnormal depreciation, and converting the tables to formulas.

8. *Be supported by appropriate forms.* Cost manuals require certain data items for accurate computation of costs. The manual should be accompanied by a form for collecting the necessary information. This form should be clear, well organized, and easy to use. There should also be a form for manual calculation of values. This form should provide a pricing ladder for replacement (reproduction) cost new, accrued depreciation, and the value of added features not covered in the base specifications.

9. *Be supported by a training program.* A training program promotes accurate and consistent cost estimates. Problems with the manual uncovered during training should be corrected and appraisers informed of the changes.

10. *Be suitable for computerization.* Cost manuals should be computerized to speed calculations and ensure accuracy. There are two choices. The manual can be reproduced in computer format or approximated with mathematical equations. The latter option speeds processing and updating. In either case, computerization and updating is easier if the manual provides alphanumeric codes for the listing of *add items* (features not included in base specifications). In this way, costs for these items can be updated by computer; appraisers need not recalculate them manually.

Third-Party Cost Manuals

Several firms supply cost manuals and periodic updates that are national in scope. Perhaps the best known are the *Building Valuation*

Manual and *Boeckh Building Cost Modifier* (E. H. Boeckh and Company), the *Dodge Building Cost Calculator and Valuation Guide* (McGraw-Hill), and the *Marshall Valuation Service* (Marshall and Swift). Each of these services contains comparative unit and unit-in-place costs for a variety of building types. Each contains local cost modifiers and is updated at least quarterly.

Assessors can evaluate these or other cost manuals using the desirable features listed above. Of particular concern will be computerization of the manual. Although commercial vendors usually market software that supports cost calculations for individual properties, batch processing may not be provided. This means that before values are computed, the characteristics of each building must be manually entered. The assessor may have to arrange separately to computerize the required cost tables. In some cases, states have contracted with cost firms specializing in construction costs to develop customized batch cost systems.

Assessors should also understand that cost services assume that buildings have been classified according to the manual and that cost data have been collected in accordance with forms supporting the manual. If data are not in this format, an entire recanvass may be required. In some cases, a computer conversion or partial conversion may be made, depending on the similarities and correspondence between the current and required data formats.

Most mass appraisal firms offer software that supports the cost approach. Some firms will provide and maintain cost data in computerized form, usually for a separate fee. The cost data may be researched by the firm itself or, more often, are developed from one or more commercial cost services. Assessors who are considering such software should evaluate not only the software but also the source of cost data required by the software and provisions for regularly updating such costs. Often the assessor will be responsible for acquiring and maintaining construction cost data.

Regardless of source, assessors should be sure that cost data obtained from commercial services accurately reflect the local market. One method is to compare cost estimates based on the manual or software against new structures of known cost. Another is to compare local costs with costs of labor and materials on which the cost service is based, including any location adjustments. Additional adjustments are often required.

Developing Local Cost Manuals

When third-party manuals are not adequate, national, state, provincial, or local agencies can develop their own manuals. Well-designed local manuals can be customized to the local market and existing data files and can be highly accurate. Although design and maintenance are huge tasks, they foster understanding of construction cost markets and a sense of ownership in the appraisal staff.

Designing a local cost manual has the following steps: (1) determine the building types (models) to be included, (2) determine typical building specifications for each model, (3) determine construction costs for each model at various size increments, (4) determine the relationship between construction costs and size, (5) develop adjustments for variations from base specifications, and (6) test the schedules by applying them to buildings of known costs. These steps are discussed briefly below and illustrated in more detail in chapter 15.

Design of a manual requires a firm grasp of construction materials and techniques, especially of the methods used to classify buildings. For appraisal purposes, buildings are usually classified according to one or more of the following criteria:

1. *Use*. Buildings are usually first classified by the use for which they were designed: residential, commercial, industrial, and rural. Each type may have subtypes (figure 1).

Figure 1.   Examples of Use Subtypes

Residential
    Single-family
    Condominium
    Duplex
    Triplex, fourplex
    Apartment

Commercial
    Retail store
    Convenience mart
    Fast food restaurant
    Restaurant, tavern
    Supermarket, discount store
    Office building
    Medical office building
    Bank, savings and loan, credit union
    Movie theater
    Auto service, garage
    Hotel, motel
    Hospital

Industrial
    Warehouse
    Self-storage, mini-storage
    Light manufacturing
    Heavy manufacturing

Rural
    Barn
    Grain storage
    Feed lot

2. *Construction type*. Construction type refers to the structural characteristics of a building, particularly the materials used in frames and walls and the degree of fireproofing. The letters A, B, C, D, and S are frequently used to designate five recognized structural types (figure 2).

3. *Construction quality*. Construction quality refers to the types of materials used and the quality of workmanship. Buildings of better quality cost more to build per unit of measure and command higher value. Construction quality, however, is the most difficult criterion to apply. Base specifications should clearly identify the characteristics that distinguish each quality class, and appraisers who assign construction quality ratings should be thoroughly familiar with these characteristics.

4. *Floor area*. Smaller buildings usually have higher building costs per square foot than larger buildings because fixed costs are spread over a greater area in larger build-

Figure 2.   Construction Types

Class A—fireproofed steel frames that support all floor and roof loads. Walls, floors, and roofs are built of noncombustible materials.

Class B—fireproofed, reinforced concrete frames that support all floor and roof loads. Walls, floors, and roofs are built of noncombustible materials.

Class C—exterior walls are built of noncombustible materials. Interior partitions and roof structures are built of combustible materials. Floors may be concrete or wood frame.

Class D—exterior walls are wood or wood and steel frame.

Class S—specialized structures that do not fit the above categories.

ings. In particular, larger buildings require fewer linear feet of wall surface per square foot of building area (figure 3). Variations in building costs with size can be treated in one of two ways. Either cost tables can be developed for various square foot increments (table 3), or a base rate can be specified for structures of standard size and size multipliers developed. In table 3, for example, if the base specifications for a minimal-quality one-story home included 1,000 square feet, the base rate for this construction class would be $39.08, and size multipliers could be developed as shown in figure 4.

5. *Building shape.* Among rectangular buildings, a square building is the most economical to construct. The greater the deviation from this shape, the higher the per square foot cost of construction, reflecting the effect of area/perimeter ratios (the higher the ratio, the lower the per square foot cost). The examples in figure 3 show that a square structure, 20 feet by 20 feet, has five square feet of area for every linear foot of wall structure and that another structure, 10 feet by 40 feet, has four square feet of area for every linear foot of wall structure. Any building with a lower ratio of square feet of area to linear feet of wall structure (in this case, the nonsquare structure) will have a higher overall cost per unit. Construction costs also vary with roof shape. The least costly is a flat roof; more expensive is a steep-pitched roof with many ridges, valleys, or dormers.

6. *Story Height.* Building costs often vary with story height. For example, a two-story residence ordinarily costs less per

Figure 3. Area/Perimeter Ratios

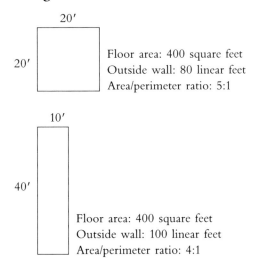

Floor area: 400 square feet
Outside wall: 80 linear feet
Area/perimeter ratio: 5:1

Floor area: 400 square feet
Outside wall: 100 linear feet
Area/perimeter ratio: 4:1

Figure 4. Developing Size Multipliers

Floor area (square feet)	Unit cost		Base cost		Multiplier
1,000	$39.08	÷	$39.08	=	1.000
1,050	38.71	÷	39.08	=	0.990
1,100	38.34	÷	39.08	=	0.981
1,150	38.08	÷	39.08	=	0.974
1,200	37.75	÷	39.08	=	0.966

The cost of constructing a 1,200 square-foot building would then be computed as
1,200 × $39.08 × 0.966 = $45,300.

square foot of living area to construct than a one-story home.

Classifications used in the comparative unit method should be based on some combination of the above criteria. Criteria not used in the classification scheme should be used for adjustments. For example, residential buildings may be classified by design, construction (wall) type, and quality class, with adjustments made for size, shape, and story height. Similarly, commercial structures may be classified by design, wall type, and story height, with adjustments made for construction quality, size, and shape.

A typical, or benchmark, building should be determined for each class and described in a set of base specifications. Construction costs for the benchmark structures should then be determined from local contractors and builders using the unit-in-place or quantity survey methods and divided by square feet to determine base rates. Adjustment factors should be determined for size, area/perimeter ratios, or any of the other classification criteria above not used in defining separate building classes.

Adjustments must also be provided for variations from base specifications. Adjustments should be derived from detailed cost estimates provided by builders and contractors. If, for example, a subject property has a shake roof, although building specifications assume an asphalt shingle roof, then the cost manual should specify the per-unit (square foot) difference in construction costs. Adjustments for horizontal building costs are usually expressed as cost per square foot, and adjustments for vertical costs (for example, walls) as cost per linear foot. Both horizontal and vertical cost adjustments can be expressed as multipliers, as illustrated in figure 4 for floor area.

Finally, the manual should be tested on recently constructed buildings of known cost, and adjustments made as necessary. These buildings should not be the same as those used in development of the manual. The degree of dispersion should be no greater than what is considered acceptable in the appraisal of newly improved properties (chapter 20).

Appraisers should be trained to use the manual and the accompanying property record card. The manual should also be regularly updated to reflect changing building costs.

Cost Trending

Costs vary geographically and over time, yet cost schedules reflect a specific time and location. Most commercially available cost services contain time and location indexes. Cost indexes are also published in a number of trade magazines and government publications. Perhaps the most useful trade magazine is the *Engineering News-Record*, a weekly publication, with "quarterly cost round-up" issues. Relevant United States government publications are the Department of Commerce's *Construction Reports* (quarterly with serial updates), *Construction Review* (monthly), *Survey of Current Business* (monthly), and *Statistical Abstract* (annual).

To develop a cost trend factor from a cost index, divide the index for the current assessment date by the index for the base date, that is, the cost date of the current manual. For example, assume that the index for the assessment date is 184.3 and the index for the base date is 159.4. Then the cost trend factor for time is

$$184.3 \div 159.4 = 1.156.$$

Location trend factors would be derived in the same way, although most cost services report them directly. For example, one area may have a location factor of 0.956, indicating that construction costs are less than in the base area, but another may have an index of 1.042, indicating that costs are higher than in the base area. To combine a time and location factor, simply multiply them together, for example,

$$1.156 \times 1.042 = 1.205.$$

When published cost trend factors do not adequately reflect local conditions, the appraiser can develop local trend factors. To do this, the appraiser determines current construction costs for a benchmark property in each building class. The benchmark properties usually correspond to the base specifications for the class. Cost trend factors are then calculated by dividing current construction costs by previous costs. Assume, for example, that the current cost of constructing a one-story, 1,500 square-foot, single-family house of average construction quality in accordance with base specifications for the class is $109,300; the cost based on the current manual is $103,850. Then the appropriate cost trend factor for the class is

$$\$109,300 \div \$103,850 = 1.0525.$$

This factor could be applied to values based on the current manual or applied against base rates and other costs for the building class. The latter is particularly effective when adjustments to base costs are maintained as percentages or multipliers. (Chapter 15 illustrates the derivation of a local cost trend factor in more detail.)

Cost trend factors may work satisfactorily for several years, but costs used in manuals must be periodically updated, item by item, because labor and material costs change at different rates. Manuals trended over a long time lose accuracy, consistency, and credibility.

Converting Cost Manuals to Cost Models

Cost models can take the form of tables, formulas, or a combination thereof. Most cost models have been expressed in table form, although cost model software uses formulas because they speed processing and are easier to enter, store, and update.

Like cost manuals, formula-driven cost models can be developed from the local market, as illustrated in chapter 15. Procedures are similar to the development of local cost manuals except that adjustments to base rates are expressed as multipliers.

Existing cost manuals can also be converted to formulas by expressing as many adjustments as possible as multipliers. For example, replacement cost new can be expressed as a function of size and price:

$$RCN = Bsize \times P_B, \qquad (4)$$

where $Bsize$ is building size (square feet) and P_B is building price per unit. This basic expression can be expanded further by developing more complete formulas for the land and improvement values (see chapters 14 and 15). Basically, however, building prices are a function of base rates and quality adjustments.

Assume, for example, that the typical single-family residence in a jurisdiction has one story, wood siding, average construction quality, and 1,200 square feet of living area, and that the replacement cost of the house based on the jurisdiction's cost manual is $62,700, or $52.25 per square foot. The replacement cost of other benchmark structures can also be computed from the manual and expressed as a percentage of the base house. For example, assume that the cost of a house with the same characteristics as the base house except for brick veneer walls has a replacement cost of $64,250, or $53.54 per square foot. The added cost of brick versus wood siding can be expressed as the factor 1.025 (53.54 ÷ 52.25).

Adjustment factors for other qualitative features can be developed in the same way. As shown in chapter 15, size differences can be approximated by a smooth curve, eliminating the need for table look-ups and interpolation. Of course, some building components of a constant nature (for example, a fireplace) cannot be converted easily to multipliers and should be added as lump-sum adjustments. Building additions, such as basements, garages, and patios, can be expressed as separate products of size and price, again adjusted for quality factors, and added to the main structure.

The formula to compute replacement cost new (RCN) would then appear as

$$RCN = [\pi BQ \times \Sigma(Bsize \times P_B)] + \Sigma OA, \quad (5)$$

where πBQ is the product of qualitative and size adjustment factors, $\Sigma(Bsize \times P_B)$ is the sum of quantity and price for each of the additive components (main living area, basement area, garage area, and so forth), and ΣOA is the sum of the dollar or lump-sum adjustments.

Extending the example above with hypothetical numbers, RCN for a subject building with 1,400 square feet (adjustment factor = 1.138), a brick exterior (adjustment factor = 1.025), a 350-square-foot built-in garage ($15 per square foot), and a fireplace ($2,500) would be computed as

$$1.025 \times 1.138 \times (\$52.25 \times 1,200 + \$15 \times 350) + \$2,500 = \$81,760.$$

A cost model in the above format could be updated each year by simply adjusting the base rate ($52.25) and applying a cost trend factor to the lump-sum adjustments as necessary. (In the equation above, $52.25 and 1,200 are constants that, when multiplied, give $62,700, the base value of the subject before application of size, quality, garage, fireplace, or depreciation adjustments.)

Estimating Accrued Depreciation

In appraisal, *accrued depreciation* is the loss in value from reproduction or replacement cost new due to all causes except depletion, as of the date of appraisal. This differs from accounting depreciation, which is the difference between the original cost and current book value of an item. Accrued depreciation is measured as of the appraisal date and applies only to improvements.

Accrued depreciation reflects the demand side of the market in conjunction with the principle of contribution. The cost of construction represents the supply side of the market. Cost and value are most similar when improvements are new and represent highest and best use. As improvements age, they suffer physical deterioration and obsolescence and, as a result, lose value relative to newer structures. This loss in value is caused by a perceived diminished utility for the property on the part of potential buyers. The demand curve, therefore, shifts to the left (figure 5) and sales prices are lower than those of properties with new improvements. The true measure of depreciation, then, is the effect on marketability and sales prices. The appraiser estimates depreciation (loss in value) by analyzing the market and subtracts depreciation from replacement cost new to estimate the market value of improvements. Only items included in replacement cost new can be depreciated.

Figure 5. Effect of Depreciation on Demand Curve

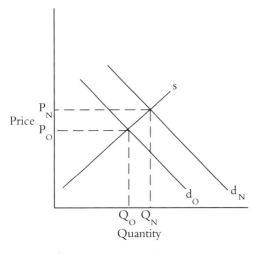

d$_N$ demand curve for newer homes

d$_O$ demand curve for older homes

Causes of Depreciation

There are three general causes of accrued depreciation: physical deterioration, functional obsolescence, and economic obsolescence. Ways of measuring these are discussed later in this chapter.

Physical Deterioration Physical deterioration is loss in value due to wear and tear and the forces of nature. All structures suffer natural physical decay due to tension, friction, compression, and chemical changes in the composition of materials. Some causes of physical deterioration are normal use, breakage, neglect, infestation of insects, dry rot, moisture, and the elements. Maintenance can

slow physical deterioration but not arrest it altogether.

Physical deterioration may be classified as *curable* or *incurable*. Curable physical deterioration occurs when the value added by a repair equals or exceeds the cost of repair. A prudent property owner would make such repairs, which correct conditions caused by deferred maintenance. Examples include a failed heat pump or compressor, leaky plumbing, broken windows, cracked paint or plaster, a worn-out floor covering, a leaking roof, and broken built-in appliances. This classification may include items that are considered 100 percent depreciated as of the sale date.

Incurable physical deterioration is that which, as of the date of the appraisal, is not economical to repair or replace, that is, the cost of repair exceeds the gain in value. Physical components that are not easily seen, such as the structural framework, foundation, subflooring, and ceiling structures, are more likely to suffer from incurable physical deterioration. Partially depreciated items, such as siding that does not yet need replacement, are usually treated in this category.

The classification of depreciation as curable or incurable will vary with the age and location of properties. Extensive renovations may be worth doing in an improving neighborhood but not in a declining one.

Functional Obsolescence Functional obsolescence is loss in value due to inability of the structure to perform adequately the function for which it is used, as of the appraisal date. Functional obsolescence results from changes in demand, design, and technology and can take the form of deficiency (for example, only one bathroom), need for modernization (for example, outmoded kitchen), or superadequacy (for example, overly high ceilings). In any case, buyers perceive a loss in utility; therefore, the price offered is lower due to reduced demand. Sometimes a deficiency in a single building component can affect the utility of the entire improvement. For example, the electrical system installed in an older house may be inadequate for today's energy demands.

Functional obsolescence is also classified as either curable or incurable, depending on whether the cost to cure is economically justified as of the appraisal date. Examples of curable functional obsolescence include inadequate heating or cooling systems, old-fashioned bathroom and kitchen fixtures, a too-small hot water heater, too few electrical outlets per room, low-hanging pipes in commercial or industrial buildings, and the absence of a ventilating system. In these examples, the increase in value from correcting the problem usually exceeds the cost.

For deficiencies, curable functional obsolescence is measured by *excess cost to cure*—the difference in cost between adding the expected item to the existing structure and installing it in a new structure, as of the date of the appraisal. For example, if installing a ventilating system in an existing structure costs $12,000 and installing the same system in new construction costs $9,000, the excess cost to cure is $3,000. In general, the excess cost to cure reflects added labor costs to install the component in an existing structure.

Incurable functional obsolescence occurs when the cost of correcting the condition exceeds the increase in value. Examples include outmoded design, poor room arrangement, no garage (and no space to build one), inadequate column spacing in a warehouse, and inadequate frontage in a commercial structure.

Sometimes an entire structure can be functionally obsolete because of its location, for example, a large, custom-built house in a moderately priced neighborhood or a small, low-quality house in a high-priced neighborhood.

Economic Obsolescence   Economic obsolescence, also called locational or external obsolescence, is loss in value as a result of impairment in utility and desirability caused by factors outside the property's boundaries. Economic obsolescence often arises from changes in the highest and best use of a property due to market shifts or governmental actions. It may be the result of inadequate public services, lack of parking facilities in a retail business district, narrow streets and heavy traffic in a residential neighborhood, or proximity to inharmonious industrial and commercial land use.

Economic obsolescence is seldom, if ever, curable, and the assessor measures its effect from market data. Of course, an undesirable location can affect land as well as improvement values, but the effects should be separated because land value, calculated from the market, already reflects this influence.

Age/Life Concepts

Depreciation is a function of time (figure 6). Every building has a *total economic life*, the period of anticipated profitable use or contribution to the value of the land. Economic life is often shorter than physical life, because many buildings outlive their economic usefulness. In the income approach, economic life is the period over which a property produces income and capital is recovered.

Total economic life may be divided between effective age and remaining economic

Figure 6. Depreciation and Time

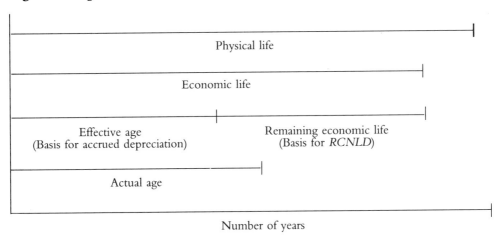

RCNLD – replacement cost new less depreciation

life. *Effective age* is the typical age of structures equivalent to the one in question with respect to condition and utility, as of the appraisal date. Effective age is an indicator of accrued depreciation. *Remaining economic life* is the number of years remaining in the economic life of a building on the appraisal date and provides a basis for estimating replacement cost new less depreciation (*RCNLD*).

Effective age can be either shorter or longer than actual age (the historical or chronological age of a structure), depending on maintenance, remodeling, and renovation. Good maintenance often reduces effective age and thus extends the remaining economic life. Effective age and remaining economic life are also influenced by competition and market conditions.

As of the appraisal date, only actual age, which does *not* determine depreciation, is known. Effective age and remaining economic life, which form the basis for accrued depreciation and market value, must be estimated.

Some methods of estimating depreciation require the appraiser to distinguish short-lived and long-lived items. *Short-lived items* have a shorter life than the basic structure, for example, roofing, interior finish, floor coverings, the heating system, and plumbing fixtures. *Long-lived items* are in the basic structure of the building and are not usually replaced during economic life, for example, the foundation, frame, floor and roof structure, piping, heat ducts, insulation, and electrical wiring.

Methods of Estimating Depreciation

Field inspection is required for the analysis and measurement of accrued depreciation. The appraiser should note all conditions that diminish utility, including economic obsolescence, and estimate their combined effect on market value.

Five methods are used to measure depreciation in single-property appraisal: sales comparison, capitalization of income, overall age-life, engineering breakdown, and observed condition breakdown. The first two are considered *indirect methods* in that depreciation is deduced from an analysis of similar properties. The last three are considered *direct methods* because they are based on direct analysis of the subject property, relying on accurate estimates of effective age and remaining economic life.

Sales Comparison Method The sales comparison method is borrowed from the sales comparison approach. Recent sales of properties similar to the subject property are identified. Building residuals, calculated by subtracting land values from sales prices, are subtracted from replacement cost new to yield accrued depreciation. In equation form,

$$D = RCN - (S - LV), \qquad (6)$$

where D is accrued depreciation, RCN is replacement cost new, S is sale price, and LV is land value. Because no two properties are exactly alike, the estimates of accrued depreciation should be expressed as factors (or percentages).

$$\%D = D/RCN \times 100, \qquad (7)$$

where $\%D$ is a depreciation factor.

From the available data, a typical depreciation factor should then be selected and multiplied against the RCN of the subject building to estimate its total accrued depreciation from all causes.

For example, assume a building has an estimated RCN of $56,800 and is 30 years old. A comparable property in the same neighborhood with a building constructed at approximately the same time as the subject and in similar condition recently sold for $65,000. The comparable's estimated RCN is $55,000 and estimated land value is $30,000. The comparable property is analyzed as follows:

Sale price	$65,000
Land value	−30,000
Building value (BV)	$35,000

$$\begin{aligned} D &= RCN - BV \\ &= \$55{,}000 - \$35{,}000 \\ &= \$20{,}000; \end{aligned}$$

$$\begin{aligned} \%D &= D/RCN \\ &= \$20{,}000/\$55{,}000 \\ &= 0.364 \ (36.4\%). \end{aligned}$$

Thus, for the subject property,

$$\begin{aligned} D &= \%D \times RCN \\ &= 0.364 \times \$56{,}800 \\ &= \$20{,}675. \end{aligned}$$

Replacement cost new less depreciation $(RCNLD)$ for the subject is

$$\$56{,}800 - \$20{,}675 = \$36{,}125.$$

For the subject, $RCNLD$ could also be computed directly as a function of *percent good*, which is the percentage by which a building has *not* depreciated. In this case,

$$\%GOOD = 1.000 - 0.364 = 0.636 \ (63.6\%).$$

$$RCNLD = 0.636 \times \$56{,}800 = \$36{,}125.$$

As in any application of the sales comparison approach, more than one comparable property should be analyzed. The selected depreciation factor should be one that the appraiser determines is most supportable based on the available data.

Note that in this case depreciation has averaged 0.012 (1.2 percent) per year (0.364 divided by 30 years). This does not mean, however, that newer or older residences in the same neighborhood should also be depreciated at this rate, as depreciation may not occur at a constant, or linear, rate. Depreciation for ten-year-old and fifty-year-old structures may be at a different average rate.

The sales comparison method works well with the comparative unit method of cost estimation, which treats the structure as a single unit. When adequate comparable sales exist, the method is reliable because it is based on market analysis.

Capitalization of Income Method This method is the same as the sales comparison method except that values based on the income approach are used instead of comparable sales. Although conceptually inferior to the sales comparison method because appraisals are substituted for actual sales, the capitalization of income method can be useful for income-producing properties for which good comparable sales are usually scarce. Reliability depends on the accuracy of the income data, capitalization methods, and land values used in the analysis.

Overall Age-Life Method The overall age-life method provides a direct estimate of depreciation of the subject property. Borrowed from accounting, the method is based on straight-line depreciation, in which the building is assumed to depreciate by a constant percentage each year over its economic life. For example, if an improvement is esti-

Figure 7. Straight-Line Depreciation at 2 Percent per Year

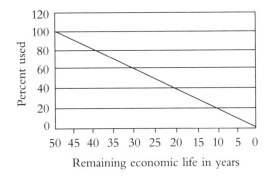

mated to have a total economic life of fifty years, then depreciation can be calculated at 2 percent per year (figure 7).

The method requires the appraiser to estimate accurately the economic life of the subject and either its effective age or remaining economic life. For example, assume a building is estimated to have a total economic life of 50 years, an effective age of 15 years (remaining economic life of 35 years), and a replacement cost new of $85,000. Then the estimated depreciation and value of the structure are computed as follows:

$$\%D = 15/50 = 0.30.$$
$$D = 0.30 \times \$85,000 = \$25,500.$$
$$RCNLD = \$85,000 - \$25,500 = \$59,500.$$

Alternatively,
$$\%GOOD = 35/50 = 0.70.$$
$$RCNLD = 0.70 \times \$85,000 = \$59,500.$$

Although the overall age-life method is simple, it has several shortcomings. For example, it recognizes primarily physical depreciation and does not distinguish between curable and incurable conditions. More serious is the assumption that depreciation occurs in a straight line. Most structures depreciate more rapidly in early life and more slowly later. Actual rates vary with type of property, location, and market conditions. This method may produce satisfactory results for short-lived items, notably personal property, but it is simplistic for real property appraisal, in which depreciation estimates should be derived from the market.

Engineering Breakdown Method To some extent, the methods used to estimate depreciation will depend on the method used to estimate *RCN*. The engineering breakdown method is actually a detailed age-life method that can be used in conjunction with the quantity survey or unit-in-place methods of estimating *RCN*. Each building component is separately depreciated based on its cost, total economic life expectancy, and effective age or remaining economic life. For example, if roofing has an expected economic life of 20 years and an effective age of 10 years, it is calculated to have depreciated 50 percent. The cost is multiplied by the percentage to arrive at depreciation for that item. If the heating system has an expected economic life of 40 years and an effective age of 10 years, it is assumed to have depreciated 25 percent. This process is done for each item, with indirect costs depreciated at a weighted average of the direct costs. Total estimated depreciation is the sum of the estimated depreciation for all items.

The engineering breakdown method eliminates one of the disadvantages of the age-life method by considering the building components separately. Again, however, functional and economic obsolescence are not addressed, and straight-line depreciation

is assumed. Because the method is so detailed and time-consuming, it has little applicability in appraisal for assessment purposes.

Observed Condition Breakdown Method
This method breaks down depreciation into all its various components: curable physical deterioration, incurable short-lived-item physical deterioration, incurable basic structure (long-lived items) physical deterioration, curable functional obsolescence, incurable functional obsolescence, and economic obsolescence.

The observed condition breakdown method is the most complete and detailed way to handle depreciation but is so time-consuming that assessors rarely use it except to defend appeals. The method is worth mastering because it provides a basic understanding of depreciation and its many forms and causes.

The following section illustrates ways to measure each form of depreciation. Appendix 8-1 provides an example of the observed condition breakdown method.

Measuring Forms of Depreciation

The techniques described here for measuring the various forms of depreciation do not allow for interactive effects. Some forms of depreciation may cause others. For example, if owners do not make repairs to a property that has significant incurable functional obsolescence, physical deterioration will occur. Sales and income analyses based on sound market data will capture these interactive effects better than mechanical estimation techniques. The mechanical techniques described here can, however, help bridge gaps in available market data.

Although it may not always be necessary to distinguish and label different forms and causes of depreciation, it is essential to account for *all* depreciation. The depreciation estimate must be supported by current market data. Depreciation, like land value and replacement cost new, must be estimated anew each time a property is reappraised.

Curable Physical Deterioration   Curable physical deterioration is measured by the cost to cure the defect. If, for example, a kitchen floor has been damaged by broken water pipes and will cost $750 to replace or repair, but this repair will increase the property's value by $750 or more, then $750, or the cost to cure, is the amount of curable physical deterioration. To be classified as curable, the defect must be in such poor condition that it should be cured as of the date of appraisal. A roof that is 50 percent deteriorated and a paint job that will last two more years do not have to be cured as of the appraisal date, so are not classified as curable.

Incurable Physical Deterioration   Incurable physical deterioration is physical deterioration that is not economical to repair as of the appraisal date. This usually includes all basic structural or long-lived items, as well as short-lived items that are still functional, such as the 50 percent deteriorated roof just mentioned. Functional items should be partially depreciated as of the appraisal date. For example, assume a hot water heater has an RCN of $650, an economic life of 10 years, and an effective age of 3 years. Using straight-line depreciation, physical depreciation is calculated as follows:

$$\%D = 3/10 = 0.30.$$
$$D = 0.30 \times \$650 = \$195.$$

Physical deterioration for other incurable short-lived items is calculated in the same way.

Depreciation is then calculated separately for the basic structural, or long-lived, items, to avoid double depreciation of the short-lived items. Assume, for example, the RCN of a building is $55,000, its economic life is 50 years, and its effective age is 12 years. Assume further that total RCN of curable short-lived items is $500 and that total RCN of incurable short-lived items is $2,450. Then, the balance attributable to long-lived items is $52,050 ($55,000 − $500 − $2,450). Straight-line depreciation applied to the long-lived items gives,

$$\%D = 12/50 = 0.24.$$
$$D = 0.24 \times \$52,050 = \$12,492.$$

This figure would be added to depreciation for the curable short-lived and incurable short-lived items to obtain total physical deterioration.

Functional Obsolescence   *Curable functional obsolescence* relates to deficiencies or superadequacies within the structure that would be corrected as of the date of appraisal. In analyzing such conditions, it is necessary to determine what is included in replacement or reproduction cost new and whether any physical depreciation has already been applied to the items in question.

As an example of a curable functional deficiency, assume that the current market expects air conditioning and the subject has none. The cost to add air conditioning to the existing structure as of the appraisal date is $1,500. The cost to include air conditioning in the original construction as of the appraisal date is $1,200. In this case, replacement or reproduction cost new has not included air conditioning, and the measure of functional obsolescence is simply the excess cost to cure: $300 ($1,500 − $1,200).

When a deficiency is due to the need for modernization, the loss in value is measured by the *RCNLD* of the items to be replaced plus any excess cost to cure. For example, a kitchen countertop measuring 14 linear feet would be modernized by replacing linoleum with formica:

Linoleum (replaced) @ $19 per linear foot	$266
Less 22 percent physical deterioration	−59
Cost to be replaced	$207
Excess cost to cure (extra labor due to replacement)	+100
Loss in value for curable modernization	$307

The loss in value is thus the undepreciated *RCN* of the discarded countertop plus the extra labor due to replacement. For a given item, modernization will require a larger depreciation adjustment than a deficiency because one must consider the remaining *RCNLD* of the item as well as the excess cost to cure.

As an example of how to handle a superadequacy, assume that a house has a huge, oddly shaped skylight that reduces the value of the property by $5,000 as compared to similar houses in the neighborhood with standard skylights. If replacement cost is used, only the normal cost of a standard skylight would be assumed, say $1,000 at time of construction ($500 materials plus $500 installation). If replacing the superadequate skylight with a standard skylight costs $2,500 ($500 materials plus $2,000 installation), curable functional obsolescence is sim-

ply $2,500, the cost to cure. Looked at another way, it will cost $2,500 to bring the structure to the condition assumed in calculating replacement cost new. The condition is curable because the value added ($5,000) exceeds the *excess* cost to cure, which in this case is $1,500:

Current cost (as of appraisal date) to add	$2,500
Current cost if included when structure was built	−1,000
Excess cost to cure	$1,500

If reproduction costs are used instead, they will include the cost new of the superadequate skylight, say $5,000. Part of this cost, say $3,000, would have been subtracted during the computation of physical deterioration. The cost to cure not already accounted for is $4,500:

Current reproduction cost of existing skylight	$5,000
Depreciation already charged	− 3,000
Depreciated value of existing skylight	$2,000
Installation cost of new, standard skylight	+ 2,500
Functional obsolescence	$4,500

The computed functional obsolescence for reproduction cost new is greater than for replacement cost because the former includes the excess cost of the superadequate skylight. However, the excess cost to cure remains $1,500, the difference between installation costs in the existing structure and in a newly built structure. In effect, part of functional obsolescence in this case is attributable to the write-off of past expenditures.

Incurable functional obsolescence is a condition that decreases the utility of the property and is not economically feasible to cure as of the date of appraisal. Buyers who can live with the deficiency will accept it if compensated by a lower purchase price or lower rent. This condition is best measured by comparable sales analysis. For example, consider a house with an unpopular design. If sales analysis shows that houses with this kind of design sell for $3,000 less than otherwise comparable houses, functional obsolescence is $3,000.

As another example, assume that a twelve-unit apartment building has no covered parking for its tenants and limited space to add parking. Installing covered parking usually costs $1,400 per unit but will cost $2,000 per unit for the subject property because of logistical problems. An analysis of apartment sales shows that covered parking adds $1,750 per unit in market value. The incurable functional obsolescence is computed as follows:

Difference in
   market value   12 × $1,750 = $21,000
Typical cost of
   construction   12 × $1,400 = $16,800
Functional obsolescence $4,200

The obsolescence is not curable because the cost to cure, which is $24,000 (12 × $2,000), would exceed the increase in market value, namely $21,000. Investors who will accept the condition will tend to pay $4,200 less than *RCN* for the property because of the adverse condition.

Incurable functional obsolescence can also be measured by the capitalization of income loss (chapters 9–12). In this method, the loss in value is computed by capitalizing the loss in income associated with the obsolescence.

Consider an aging retail store that has high ceilings, poor placement of electrical fixtures, and inadequate doorway widths. Investigation reveals that these conditions cannot be cured economically at the time of the appraisal. A prudent buyer would realize that potential rents are adversely affected by these deficiencies. A rental study can determine estimated rent loss. The present value of the loss in rent over the remaining economic life of the building provides a measure of the amount of functional obsolescence.

For example, a 25,000-square-foot retail store not suffering from the above functional defects rents for $6.50 per square foot per year. A comparable retail store of approximately the same size, location, and general amenities, but suffering from the defects, rents for less and therefore has a net operating income that is lower by $18,750 per year. Sales and rentals in the same neighborhood indicate a building capitalization rate of 13 percent. Dividing the $18,750 net income loss by the 13 percent rate results in an estimated loss of improvement value (from the developed *RCN*) of $144,230. This amount, functional incurable obsolescence, is deducted from the developed *RCN* of the building.

Economic Obsolescence   *Economic obsolescence* is loss in value from forces external to the property and is almost always considered incurable because the property owner can rarely do anything to overcome the defect. (An owner could move a building to a different location or buy an adjacent property that is causing the obsolescence, but in both cases the cost to cure is likely to exceed any increase in value.) In analysis of economic obsolescence, loss in value attributed to the land should not be applied against the improvements.

Like incurable functional obsolescence, economic obsolescence can be measured either by comparable sales or capitalization of income. As an example of the former, assume that a house is located on a busy street. Analysis of paired sales reveals that this condition reduces market value by $5,000. The land is appraised at $3,000 less than comparable sites not located on a busy street. The additional loss in value of $2,000 is attributable to the improvements.

As an example of the measurement of economic obsolescence using income data, assume that properties located on streets in the subject neighborhood and not affected by heavy traffic rent for $600 per month, and that the subject property, which is affected, rents for $575 per month. The monthly rent loss is thus $25 ($600 − $575). Multiplying the monthly rent loss by a developed gross rent multiplier of 100 results in a $2,500 loss of value.

Because improvement values represent 80 percent of total property values in the subject neighborhood, the loss of value accruing to the building would be $2,500 times 80 percent (0.80), or $2,000. The remaining $500, the loss of value to the land, should have been estimated when the site was valued in the site valuation section of the cost approach.

Depreciation Schedules

The methods discussed above for estimating depreciation in single-property appraisal are usually too time-consuming for mass appraisal (with the exception of the overall age-life method, which is too arbitrary). In mass appraisal, depreciation is usually estimated using depreciation schedules, which show the typical loss in value at various ages or effective ages. By nature, such tables primarily recognize physical deterioration, so additional adjustments are usually required for functional or economic obsolescence. Because different property groups depreciate at different rates, depreciation schedules should be tailored to different types of properties.

Depreciation schedules are prepared by the cost services that specialize in construction cost manuals. Such schedules, however, reflect only a particular location or national averages and have to be adjusted to the local market. Appraisers can also develop their own schedules from market data. The steps are: (1) stratify sales by building type, (2) subtract land and miscellaneous improvement values to obtain residual building values, (3) subtract residual building values from RCN to obtain market-derived depreciation, (4) divide by RCN to obtain depreciation percentages, (5) plot depreciation percentages against effective age, (6) fit a curve to the data, and (7) extract a depreciation table. Figure 8 contains an example of a simple depreciation plot and associated depreciation table.

As a slight variation, percent good figures can be extracted from sales and plotted against effective age to construct percent good tables. Chapter 15 discusses the development of depreciation and percent good tables in more detail. The reliability of such schedules depends on the accuracy of the sales prices, RCN figures, and land values used in the analysis. If ratio studies show that land is not appraised at market value, land values should be adjusted to market value when developing depreciation tables. Otherwise, the calculated building residuals will be too high, and depreciation percentages too low.

Figure 8. Depreciation Plot and Table

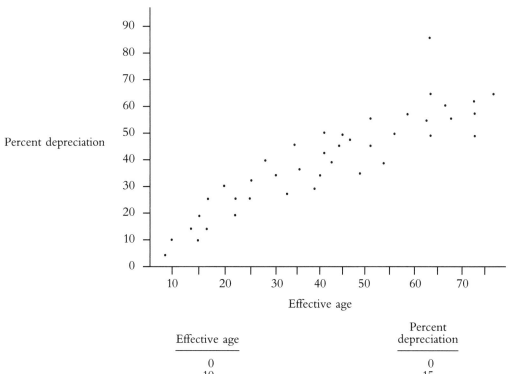

Effective age	Percent depreciation
0	0
10	15
20	25
30	33
40	40
50	45
60	50
70	55

Summary

Cost approach models have had widespread use in mass appraisal. They are typically expressed in table form but increasingly are being expressed in formulas. Formula-driven cost models are easier to use within a computer-assisted mass appraisal system.

Cost models, like other valuation models, should be specified and calibrated using local market information so that they reflect accurately the operation of local real estate markets.

An Introduction to the Income Approach

9

Overview

The income approach is based on the principle that the value of an investment property reflects the quality and quantity of the income it is expected to generate over its life. That is, value is the estimated present value of future benefits (chiefly income and proceeds from the sale of the property).

Estimating the value of an income-producing property is done by *capitalization*. In its simplest form, capitalization is the division of a present income by an appropriate rate of return to estimate the value of the income stream. The model used to estimate the value today of income expected in the future is known as the *IRV* formula.

$$\text{Value} = \text{Income/Rate}$$
$$V = I/R. \tag{1}$$

The formula can also be expressed in other forms to calculate an unknown income or rate when value is known.

$$\text{Income} = \text{Rate} \times \text{Value}$$
$$I = R \times V, \tag{2}$$

or

$$\text{Rate} = \text{Income/Value}$$
$$R = I/V. \tag{3}$$

Figure 1 shows the relationships among income, rate, and value.

The *IRV* formula is the general model used as the basis for all applications of the income approach. To use the model to estimate value, however, income and a rate must be estimated. Income is the annual net operating income expected for the property being valued. The rate is the capitalization rate appropriate for the subject property as of the appraisal date. Finding values for (*calibrating*) income and rate is the hardest part of the income approach. Indeed, the different methods of

Figure 1. The IRV Equation

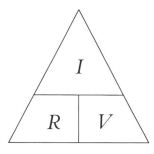

A simple triangle incorporates income, rate, and value into a memory jogger. Think of the short, horizontal line in the triangle as a division sign and the short, vertical line as a multiplication sign, then block out the one unknown for which you are solving. In this way, you will obtain the three basic equations:

$$I = R \times V,$$
$$R = I / V,$$
$$V = I / R,$$

231

capitalization (direct and yield) explained in chapter 12 are mainly different ways to measure and calibrate rates and incomes used in the basic income model.

The following three chapters divide the discussion of the income approach into three areas that appraisers need to master to apply the income model: real estate investment and finance, income and expense analysis, and capitalization. Understanding the income approach begins with understanding real estate investment and finance. Appraisers must be knowledgeable about the varied types of investors and their motives, as well as the many financial devices available to investors to finance either debt or equity. Real estate is a popular investment medium, in which the potential rate of return can be increased through the use of borrowed money. Chapter 10 discusses investment and finance.

Appraisers must also learn how to analyze income and expenses. The income from rental real estate should be examined carefully (as explained in chapter 11). The appraiser first determines the gross amount the property is earning, then compares that amount with earnings of comparable properties to estimate the amount the property should earn (its *potential gross rent*). Comparable properties are properties of the same type and size (apartment buildings with 100–200 units, for example). A standard unit, such as square feet, apartment units, or number of rooms, is used to make comparisons. Income is then stated as income per unit (income per square foot, for example). From potential gross rent the appraiser subtracts a reasonable vacancy and collection loss as well as expenses required to operate the property and adds miscellaneous income. The result is *net operating income*, an estimate of the property's earning capacity free of debt and before income taxes.

Capitalization, conversion of an annual income into a lump-sum value for a property (as of a given date), can be done using either direct capitalization or the more complex yield capitalization. Both can give satisfactory results when appropriate data are available. Chapter 12 discusses direct and yield capitalization methods. Direct capitalization uses only two numbers—annual income and the capitalization rate or factor. However, deriving these numbers requires thorough, systematic analysis of income streams—the series of payments derived from an investment during its life (holding period). Such analysis considers whether the income streams will grow or decline, their duration, and their capital markets. For capital markets, the appraiser determines current discount rates, including the risk premium associated with both equity and debt (mortgage) financing of real estate investments. In direct capitalization, income is divided by an overall capitalization rate or multiplied by a factor, also called an income multiplier. Income multipliers are reciprocals of capitalization rates and are used most often with gross income estimates; rates are used most often with net operating income.

Like direct capitalization, yield capitalization requires analysis of anticipated income and the yield rates observed in capital markets. Yield capitalization also requires the appraiser to make explicit assumptions concerning, for example, the direction and duration of the income stream, the holding period, income estimates over the holding period, and the value of the property at the end of the holding period.

To assign a time value of money to the income stream, yield capitalization applies compound interest functions, which are valuable tools for analyzing the value of estimated future income. Chapter 12 explains each of six functions and its relationship to the other functions.

Value in the Income Approach

Ad valorem appraisals should produce market value, which is based on analysis of local supply and demand. *Investment value*, which is sometimes sought by an appraiser in lieu of market value, is the value to a specific investor. Investment value is based on a specific situation; for example, an investor may be able to use a property's tax losses advantageously and therefore is willing to pay more than other potential investors. The reverse is also true: the value of a specific property may be less to a specific person than the property can command in the market. Market value reflects the most likely sale price, given supply and demand for the type of property under consideration.

Value in use represents the value of a property to a specific user for a specific use. For example, a church property may have high value for its members; however, the demand for church buildings may be minimal, and an offer to sell will bring few buyers, possibly none. The property has a high value in use for its current users but little or no market value.

Application of Economic and Appraisal Principles

The income approach is a means of converting future benefits to present value. Essential to the approach is the idea that income

to be received in the future is less valuable than income received today. Several principles related to this idea—supply and demand, anticipation, substitution, and competition—are discussed briefly in the following paragraphs. (See chapters 3 and 4 for fuller discussions.)

Supply and Demand

Supply is the quantity of goods available at a given price schedule. Demand is the quantity of goods desired at that price schedule. Supply and demand interact to establish prices in the marketplace. An understanding of the supply and demand factors operating in a particular market is essential for understanding which investments are comparable and in particular how the principles of substitution, anticipation, and competition each work in the application of the income approach.

The appraiser determines how reliably observed sales prices reflect market value. In general, markets that are more competitive generate sales prices that reflect true market value. Less competitive markets may produce prices that reflect investment value or value in use.

Anticipation

Future benefits are one determinant of demand. Because future benefits are such an important part of a real estate investment, the principle of anticipation is particularly important in appraising income-earning real estate. In relation to the income approach, anticipation is the idea that present value is determined by future benefits. Because a dollar to be received in the future has less value than a dollar held now, the value of future dollars anticipated from the ownership of real estate should be adjusted to present value according to the time they are expected to be received. *Discounting* is the process of adjusting the value of future dollars to present values.

Substitution

The price of substitutes also determines demand. A property's maximum value is set by the lowest cost or price at which another property of equivalent utility can be acquired. Investors who consider buying an income stream, then, establish a maximum price in terms of the prices of other income streams of similar risk, duration, and quality. This principle also guides the appraiser's selection of discount rates for direct capitalization and underlies the idea that the discount rate for a subject property can be derived by examining equivalent properties.

The principle of substitution is related to the concept of *opportunity cost*. Opportunity cost measures what an investor would lose by investing in a particular venture, thus giving up other opportunities to use the invested funds.

Competition

Competition, the attempt by two or more buyers or sellers to buy or sell similar commodities, influences the rate of return on invested capital. The rate of return, reciprocally, influences both supply and demand in a particular market. For example, additional buyers and suppliers enter markets that appear to have excess rates of profit. Analysis of competition is important in estimation of the value of an income stream generated by above-market rents. Unless the excess profits are locked in (for example, with a long-term lease and a reliable tenant), the future of the income stream is open to question. Competition in the market is likely to cause a return to more appropriate rates.

Steps in Capitalization

Capitalization is the conversion of a single income stream or a series of income streams into a lump-sum value. For real property appraisal, it is helpful to think of capitalization as discounting, that is, converting future worth or benefits into present worth. The simplest method of doing this is to use annual income and annual rates for discounting future benefits.

For example, if annual net operating income is $60,000, it can be capitalized by a rate of 8 percent with the basic income model

$$V = I/R, \qquad (1)$$

where V is value or present worth, I is annualized income or future benefits, and R is capitalization rate or discount rate.

$$\$60,000/.08 = \$750,000.$$

Another way to compute value is to multiply income by a factor, a reciprocal of a rate. In this example, the factor is 12.5 (1 divided by .08):

$$\$60,000 \times 12.5 = \$750,000.$$

Analyzing Income and Expenses

To solve the basic income model, the appraiser must be able to derive an income estimate and build a capitalization rate. To arrive at an annual net operating income, the appraiser follows a specific sequence that accounts for the total potential income of the subject property and the expenses needed to continue to generate this income. When such expenses are subtracted from gross income, the result is net operating income. The following sequence is usually followed.

1. Estimate potential gross rent. This is the amount of annual rent the property is capable of producing at 100 percent occupancy.
2. Estimate vacancy and collection loss. This is loss of income due to unrented space (vacancies) and tenant delinquencies.
3. Add estimated other income, often referred to as miscellaneous income. Some sources of such income are parking, vending machines, and laundry facilities. This income is not subject to vacancy and collection loss.
4. Calculate effective gross income. This is the potential gross rent less the vacancy and collection loss, plus other income.
5. Estimate total operating expenses. These are the expenses necessary to operate the property so that it will continue to generate the estimated income. They should be stabilized so that the net operating income can be stabilized. Categories of allowable operating expense include insurance; administrative costs (for the property, not the owner) such as legal, accounting, advertising, and management fees; repair and maintenance costs such as snow removal, exterminating, janitors' salaries, trash collection, hardware, and supplies; utilities such as fuel, water, and electricity; and replacement expenses prorated to an annual figure. Ad valorem taxes are included as operating expenses except when

the appraisal is done to estimate an assessed value for ad valorem tax purposes. In such cases, the property tax portion of the operating cost is usually expressed as a percentage in the capitalization rate rather than as an operating expense.

6. Calculate net operating income by subtracting total operating expenses from effective gross income. When stabilized annual operating expenses are subtracted from effective gross income, the result is a stabilized net operating income. When this income is divided by an overall rate, a final value estimate is generated for the entire property.

Capitalization Rates

A capitalization rate converts net operating income into an estimate of value. Terms used to describe the capitalization rate and its components are often confusing to beginners. Figure 2 and the following discussion explain the various terms and their relationships.

The capitalization rate is made up of several components: a *discount* rate, a *recapture* rate, and an *effective tax rate*.

Figure 2. Components of the Capitalization Rate

Discount rate (synonym: required rate of return *on* investment)

Interest rate (synonym: required rate of return on borrowed funds)
Yield rate (synonym: required rate of return on equity)

Recapture rate (synonym: rate of return *of* investment)

Effective tax rate (include when appraising for ad valorem tax purposes)

Discount Rate   The discount rate is sometimes called a *required rate of return on investment*, or required rate of return. The discount rate is made up of an *interest* rate (a required rate of return on borrowed funds) and a *yield* rate (a required rate of return on equity).

Recapture Rate   A recapture rate provides for the recovery of capital on an annual basis. The recapture rate is also called the rate of return *of* investment. This rate applies only to the portion of the investment that will waste away during the investment period. Recapture rates are not included in land capitalization rates because land does not waste away.

Effective Tax Rate   The effective tax rate is the property tax rate expressed as a percentage of market value (see chapter 1 for calculation of this rate). When an appraisal is done for ad valorem tax purposes the capitalization rate must include an effective tax rate. Property taxes are not subtracted as an operating expense because they are not yet known. Indeed, the appraisal's purpose is to estimate a property value from which property taxes can be calculated.

Overall Rate   Overall rate is another term used to describe the capitalization rate in direct capitalization. The overall rate blends all requirements of discount, recapture, and effective tax rates. The overall rate is a ratio of net operating income to value.

Estimating Capitalization Rates   Capitalization rates express complex market factors and relationships. Overall rates in the direct capitalization method are derived from market transactions for properties that are similar to the subject—they entail similar risk and have similar land-to-building ratios, remaining economic lives, and operating expense ratios. Yield capitalization also derives rates from market transactions but explicitly takes into account the yield sought by particular investors, changes in the income stream, changes in capitalization rates, and reversionary value (the lump-sum value expected at the end of the holding period).

Small errors in estimating the capitalization rate will have a pronounced effect on the estimate of property value. For example, estimating the capitalization rate at 9 or 11 percent instead of 10 percent will change the estimated value by approximately 10 percent. For this reason, capitalization rates should be derived with care and supported with market data.

Choice of Capitalization Method

The choice of direct or yield capitalization methods depends on the type of property, its economic life, and the quality, quantity, and duration of the income stream. The quality and quantity of data available for similar properties are also important in rate development and in determining the method of estimating the recapture rate. Both direct and yield methods may be used with residual techniques.

Summary

This chapter introduced the income model with a simple presentation of principles and terms relevant to the income approach. The three chapters that follow treat three areas that appraisers need to master to apply the income approach: real estate investment and finance; income, expense, and lease analysis; and income capitalization.

The income approach is more difficult to apply than either the cost or sales comparison approaches. Readers are encouraged to learn basic definitions as they go along. Definitions of the following important terms appear in this and the next chapters and also in the glossary: income, income stream, holding period, capitalization rate, overall rate, discount rate, interest rate, yield rate, recapture rate, effective (tax) rate, nominal (tax) rate, direct capitalization, yield capitalization, residual techniques (building residual, land residual, property residual, equity residual), reversion, and reversionary value.

Real Estate Investment and Finance

This chapter discusses how buyers see the risks and benefits of real estate investment. Because borrowing money is part of the typical purchase of income-producing real estate—indeed, contributes to its attractiveness as an investment—this chapter also provides an overview of debt financing and commercial property mortgages.

Introduction

One key to the income approach is understanding why investors choose income-producing real estate from a wide array of investment opportunities. The prudent investor plans to receive a larger sum in the future than the amount invested now and also tries to choose the highest yield with the lowest risk. Before investing, the investor analyzes the opportunities available and asks, "Should I make this investment?"

The answer may be found by asking a few more questions. First, can the investor afford it? If so, the investor then asks:

"How much will it cost?"
"How much will I get back?"
"When will I get it back?"
"What are the risks?"
"What is the return on investments of similar risk?"

That is, the investor wants to know the expected risks and the amount and timing of potential returns; yet none of this can be known with certainty because it will occur in the future.

Individual investors satisfy different needs with investments. Investments appropriate for a forty-year-old surgeon will be different from those of a seventy-year-old retiree or a twenty-three-year-old recent college graduate. With time to wait for the fruition of an investment, and adequate income provided by a job, the young investor may seek long-term capital appreciation and be willing to accept a high degree of uncertainty about potential rewards. A retired person with modest savings must have security and a regular income. Investors with high incomes will be interested in income tax shelter.

Likewise, the investment strategy of a savings and loan institution will differ markedly from that of a life insurance company. Pension funds and life insurance companies are concerned with safety of principal as well as with yield. Savings and loan institutions face special problems with liquidity: as interest rates change, they may be flooded with either withdrawal requests or new deposits, but their assets will not expand and contract in the same pattern.

Required Rate of Return (Discount Rate)

A rate of return on investment (discount rate) is the percentage of dollars earned each period compared to the investment cost (rate of return is used in this chapter interchangeably with discount rate because rate of return captures the investor's perspective). Rates of return should be on a *present value* basis. For example, growth in asset value is usually realized upon the sale of the property. The anticipated growth in value has to be converted to an annual rate in today's dollars to provide a meaningful comparison with an investment today. Not converting future income to today's value would cause $1.00 received now and $1.00 to be received years from now to appear equal in value.

Components of the Discount Rate

Three factors are considered in determining the adequacy of the rate of return from a proposed investment: degree of risk inherent in the investment, liquidity (ease of resale), and level of investment management skill required. Risk, liquidity, and management skill required, expressed as rates, are components of the rate of return. The proportion of each component is theoretical because direct market evidence for each is not usually available. These three components are added to a safe rate (the interest available on a safe investment) to make up the discount rate.

Build-up Method (Summation Concept)

The build-up method constructs a discount rate using a safe, liquid rate as a foundation and adding rates for risk, liquidity, and investment management to the base rate. This method is helpful for comparing real estate investments with other investments. The base rate is that offered by a government-insured investment that is readily convertible to cash, such as a passbook savings bank account. Table 1 shows how the discount rate could be developed for different investments using the build-up method. Market data are limited on the rate adjustment warranted for risk, liquidity, and management of different investments. Nonetheless, the appraiser must reach informed, but still subjective, judgments about appropriate adjustments. Some of the elements affecting risk, liquidity, and investment management are described next.

Risk   Risk is the likelihood that returns generated by an investment will be poorer than the safe rate. Risk is always related to the rate earned on a safe investment and is the opportunity cost of allocating investment dollars in some investment other than the most reliable investment. In a financial sense, risk means uncertainty. Figure 1 shows expected rates of return from two investments, A and B. The rate from B falls within a narrower range than that from A; B holds less risk. A, however, offers a greater opportu-

Figure 1. Expected Returns from Two Investments

Expected
rate of return

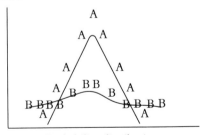

Probability distribution

Table 1.   Required Rate of Return through Build-up Method

	Blue chip stock	Income from triple net lease to major corporate tenant	Income from small apartment project
Risk-free rate	6.0%	6.0%	6.0%
Allowance for risk	4.0%	4.0%	7.0%
Allowance for illiquidity	0.0%	2.0%	3.0%
Allowance for investment management	0.5%	1.0%	2.0%
Rate derived by build-up	10.5%	13.0%	18.0%

nity to earn either higher or lower rates. Investors need to be aware of differences in risk.

Risk is relative and no investment is risk-free. Even the most reliable investments, national government securities, are subject to risk when inflation erodes the real value of principal. For real estate, risk is lower for a commercial or industrial property leased to a reliable tenant, but higher for a property leased to a weak tenant with a marginal business.

Liquidity   The absence of liquidity is of greater concern to real estate investors than to investors in stocks, bonds, and similar commodities that can be sold by a brief phone call to a broker, with cash proceeds available in a few days. In contrast, the time required to secure a contract to sell a parcel of real estate is usually measured in months; many more weeks will pass before the seller transfers title and is paid. A seller who has to sell within a given time usually has to accept a lower price or less attractive terms.

The cost of selling real estate is high. Typical brokerage commissions are 3–10 percent of the sale price; commissions in commodity, stock, and bond markets are usually less than 1 percent. Higher selling costs and a relative lack of liquidity diminish the appeal of real estate as an investment or cause real estate investors to seek rates of return higher than those for other investments. Higher rate-of-return requirements reduce the present value of an investment.

Investment Management   Investment or portfolio management is not to be confused with property management. *Property management* refers to everyday concerns such as rent collection and the physical upkeep of property. All costs of this day-in, day-out management task are operating expenses. *Investment management* is a decision-making process to safeguard the funds invested. Investment managers consider which investments should be bought and sold, and when. They decide whether it is worthwhile to make extensive repairs, capital improvements, or renovations.

Investment management requires careful thought and planning based on factual knowledge and constant review of decisions.

In a changing legal, financial, and physical environment, an owner must decide whether to hold, sell, exchange, or refinance property. The owner must seek out tax, legal, accounting, and real estate counsel and decide in which areas counsel is unnecessary. A prospective real estate owner should be aware of the extra burden of investment management. The higher rate of return required by this burden reduces the value of future income, thereby reducing the present value of real estate as compared to other investments with less of a management burden—bank savings accounts, for example.

Why Invest in Income-Producing Real Estate?

Real estate investors are offered an array of choices far greater than all the stocks and bonds listed on all exchanges: each parcel of land is physically and geographically unique, and improvements can be of various sizes, shapes, styles, and uses. Realty is tangible and has a fixed location, attributes that make real estate excellent loan collateral. The financing of realty can be as unique as its physical form; borrowers and lenders may include in their contracts many variations that are legal.

In addition to physical and financial diversity, division of real estate ownership into several different interests can provide even greater variety for investors. A mortgage is one such interest. Others are leaseholds, air rights, mineral rights, remainder estates, and so on. Furthermore, each ownership interest can be held by groups as well as single owners; so real estate may be owned by a sole proprietorship, tenancy in common, joint tenancy, tenancy by the entirety, in con-

dominium, or as community property; it may be owned by a corporation, subchapter (S) corporation, general partnership, or limited partnership. Each ownership form has advantages and drawbacks and is not always available to every owner or for every type of property, but enough variation is available to allow tailoring to suit the individual needs of the property owner(s). Other potential benefits for real estate investors are diversification and personal satisfaction.

Although expected returns from income-producing real estate are often difficult to forecast, they are received in four distinct forms: cash flow, appreciation, mortgage loan reduction, and income tax savings.

Cash Flow

Cash flow means regular, periodic cash income. It is a kind of "bottom-line" figure, although not identical to *net income*. Cash flow is the amount of money left after subtracting operating expenses and debt service from rents collected. Operating expenses include both fixed and variable expenses generated by the production of the income. Debt service is the interest and principal payments on debt incurred for the property. Figure 2 shows the estimated cash flow of a hypothetical twenty-five–unit apartment complex acquired for $1,000,000.

Unlike wages, cash flow is not always fully subject to income tax. It is, therefore, often described as either *before-tax* or *after-tax* cash flow. Before-tax signifies that income taxes have not been subtracted; after-tax includes income tax savings generated by ownership. The unqualified term *cash flow* usually refers to the before-tax amount and is sometimes called *cash throw-off*.

Figure 2. Estimating Cash Flow

Potential gross income:

25 units × $600 × 12 months	$180,000
Less vacancy and collection allowance (5 percent)	– 9,000
Plus miscellaneous income (from laundry, etc.)	+ 4,000
Effective gross income	$175,000

Less operating expenses

Fixed:

Real property taxes	$15,000
Insurance	5,000

Operating and maintenance:

Management fee	10,000
Utilities	7,000
Supplies	3,000
Painting and decoration	7,000
Salaries and payroll taxes	8,000

Repairs and replacement reserves:

Appliances	5,000
Plumbing, electrical, other components	7,000
Total operating expenses	– $ 67,000
Net operating income	$108,000
Less debt service (interest and principal repayment)	– 75,000
Cash flow	$ 33,000

Property Appreciation

Property appreciation is the increase in value that is realized on sale. It can occur for numerous reasons and may result from economic factors such as supply and demand or simply from inflation.

Inflation is a general increase in price levels, or a decline in the purchasing power of money. Inflation can increase net operating income for the owner, which leads to increased property values. If in the hypothetical twenty-five–unit apartment complex described above, inflation increases the net operating income of the complex by $5,400 per year (and there is no change in the discount rate), the value of the complex could increase by perhaps ten times the income increase, or $54,000. All of the increase will accrue to the equity investor, who put up only one-fourth of the $1,000,000 original cost.

Appreciation can also be *real*. Increased demand for well-located land or local demand for certain types of structures can cause appreciation even when measured against constant dollars. For example, an investor in timberland who patiently waits for trees to mature may get both forms of appreciation: timber prices tend to increase with inflation, as does the land value, and tree growth is a genuine, tangible form of appreciation. Or the land may be in the path of urban growth and may eventually qualify for a more intensive use. Whether increased prices are real or simply a result of inflation, they are called appreciation.

Economics and politics also influence rental income and property values. A freeze on rents could be imposed without similar limits on operating expenses, thereby decreasing the value of real estate. Inflation often brings higher interest rates. Potential purchasers then seek higher rates of return, so will pay less for a given income stream. Property values then decrease.

Mortgage Loan Reduction

Loan repayment cannot be regarded as income. One does not earn income by repaying a debt. Nevertheless, a real estate owner will benefit from reducing a loan, with cash realized at sale or refinancing. Unless the property is depreciating as rapidly as the mortgage is being paid off, the amount of equity increases, and all equity will be realized upon a sale. Refinancing allows part of the equity to be extracted tax-free without a sale. Refinancing is accomplished by taking out a new loan and repaying the entire balance of the previous loan; if cash remains after retiring the old loan and paying transaction costs, part of the equity has been captured.

Equity buildup is another name for mortgage loan reduction. Most real estate loan terms require payments of principal (which amortize the loan) in addition to interest payments. The total loan payment must be paid from the property's net operating income. The amortization portion increases as the loan is retired, becoming substantial late in the mortgage term. The typical equity investor usually wants current cash flow and slow amortization, with the result that investors often pay less for properties that have higher amortization requirements than interest-only or other forms of financing with deferred payments (see figures 3 and 4).

Income Tax Savings

Real property ownership may offer the opportunity for income tax deferral or, in some cases, outright elimination of taxes. Proper planning and knowledge of tax laws provide the key to successful reduction of taxes during ownership and when the property is sold. Owning real estate usually produces two kinds of income or loss: current and deferred. Current income or loss is produced during the period of ownership; deferred income or loss, upon sale. When the property is sold, for income tax purposes a *capital gain* will be realized if the price received is higher than the adjusted tax basis (original cost plus capital improvements less tax depreciation). If the price is lower, a *capital loss* is realized.

Figure 3. Distribution of Interest and Principal Payments on Self-amortizing Mortgage

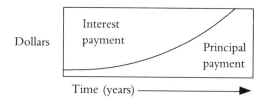

Figure 4. Self-amortizing Mortgage Loan Balance over Time

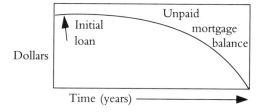

Reducing Taxes during Ownership   Depreciation accounting (tax depreciation) is the principal means of obtaining tax deferral during ownership. United States federal income tax law permits an annual reduction of taxable income for accounting depreciation, one form of loss of value over time. This tax deduction without a cash requirement allows a real estate investment to produce cash flow, offer an artificial tax loss, and appreciate in value all at the same time!

Reducing Taxes at Time of Sale   A real estate owner may reduce or defer taxes on capital gains in at least two ways. First, if the property is held long enough (timing depends on current tax laws), the capital gain may receive automatic preferential tax treatment. Second, sale of real estate on an installment basis spreads the buyer's payments over several years, which can spread the tax over a number of years. However, tax laws are constantly changing. In the United States, the Tax Reform Act of 1986 sharply reduced depreciation deductions for real estate owners and eliminated preferential treatment for capital gains.

Diversification and Personal Satisfaction

Investors sometimes buy a given investment to diversify an investment portfolio. When too much of an investor's wealth is concentrated in one asset, diversification can reduce risk. Indeed, modern portfolio theory demonstrates that investors can improve the rate of return and reduce certain types of risk by diversifying into investments offering returns that are negatively correlated with one another. For example, prices of common stocks and real estate often move in opposite directions. Investing half of a portfolio in each can reduce overall risk.

Pride of ownership, community involvement, prestige, and other psychological benefits may motivate some investors to acquire real estate instead of other, less tangible investments.

Financing Income–Producing Real Estate

Most real estate is purchased with the aid of mortgage financing. The financing package itself may have value, and when it does, its value is certain to affect the price paid. Appraisers seek to estimate market value. When financing influences the price, the amount shown in sale documents will not represent market value.

There are several reasons to finance real estate. For income-producing real estate, various mortgages are available with different repayment plans and from a variety of sources. An overview of mortgage financing follows.

Influence of Financing on Price

The terms of financing, whether good or poor, affect price. For example, a buyer would pay a high price for real estate that carries a low-interest-rate mortgage. To estimate market value, the appraiser adjusts the price paid to eliminate the influence of special financing. The market value of real estate reflects the seller's net cash receipt, whatever the source of money. For example, if the seller received $1 million in a transaction but must pay $50,000 for discount points on the buyer's new loan, then $950,000 is the actual cash received for the property. Appraisals for such a transaction should reflect a market value of $950,000 rather than the $1 million price. Similarly, when the seller finances the property at a low rate or provides some other concession, the stated price is adjusted to reflect the true price paid.

Reasons for Financing

Buyers of income-producing real estate have many reasons for debt financing. Few have enough cash to pay the entire price in cash. Borrowing money allows an investor to gain leverage and to control more property. Even those able to pay all cash want to spread the risk by diversifying their investments. Finally, interest on borrowed money may be tax deductible. Depreciation deductions on income property are generally allowed for the full price, not just the equity. (Of course, nondepreciable components, particularly land, are excluded.)

Inadequate Cash   Unlike stock, which can be sold in units as small as one share, a unit of most income-producing real estate often requires hundreds of thousands of dollars. Most investors do not have the cash to buy property outright, so they must borrow.

Leverage and Control   *Financial* leverage is the use of borrowed money to complete an investment transaction. If the assets bought with borrowed money offer annual financial benefits at a rate above the loan's interest rate, leverage is positive, or favorable. The investor makes money by borrowing. On the other hand, if assets bought with borrowed money fail to increase in value, or if they fail to provide benefits in excess of the interest rate on the borrowed money, the lender earns more than the borrower: leverage is negative. Leverage is neutral when the property earns at the same rate as the interest rate on borrowed money.

Operating leverage is the potential increase in cash flow, especially when debt service is fixed. For example, suppose rental income and operating expenses, a smaller figure, both rise by the same percentage. When debt service is fixed, cash flow rises by a much larger percentage because of the leverage effect. That is, rental income rises from a higher base than operating expenses, causing a substantial percentage increase in cash flow.

Borrowing allows an investor to control more property, which may help satisfy other needs. For example, it may reduce competition, provide more property management fees for a related party, or increase influence. It is difficult to measure the effect on the property's market value of a desire to control property.

Diversification   Borrowing, because it permits more investments, increases the ability to diversify. Spreading risk reduces reliance on a single asset. However, larger assets and increased debts create additional risks.

Income Tax Deductions   Income tax deductions may be allowed for interest paid and for depreciation based on asset cost. An investor who raises both interest and depreciation deductions through leverage may reduce taxable income.

Mortgage Sources for Income-Producing Property
Types of Financial Institutions

Financial organizations that are important in primary real estate lending vary from country to country. In the United States, they are life insurance companies, commercial banks, savings and loan associations and mutual savings banks, mortgage bankers, real estate investment trusts, and pension funds.

Life Insurance Companies   Large life insurance companies are usually interested only in loans that exceed $1 million because they lack the facilities to service many small loans. With billions of dollars in assets, some life insurance companies can achieve adequate diversification even though $10 million or more is placed in a single project. Life insurance companies rarely offer construction loans; they want the long-term yield and safety provided by permanent mortgages on finished products.

Commercial Banks   Commercial banks are active in issuing construction loans on all types of property. Such loans are offered only with a *take-out* commitment from a permanent lender; upon project completion, the permanent loan will repay the construction loan. Banks are also active, long-term investors in a variety of properties.

Savings and Loan Associations and Mutual Savings Banks Savings and loan associations (S&Ls) and mutual savings banks (MSBs) primarily offer residential first mortgages on local property, including one- to four-family houses. Only the largest S&Ls offer loans of more than $1 million on a single property, although many lend on multifamily properties in the $100,000–$1,000,000 range. Many S&Ls and MSBs offer construction loans to builders. For a *commitment fee*, some offer the privilege of permanent financing at a predetermined interest rate.

Mortgage Bankers These companies originate and sell loans, then service the loans for a fee. They will originate any type of loan they can sell. Because they deal with borrowers and lenders in the same transaction, mortgage bankers must know both sides of the market for commercial property loans.

Real Estate Investment Trusts Real estate investment trusts (REITs) invest in construction loans, permanent mortgage loans, equities, and leasing arrangements. Each REIT may specialize in just one or two of these types of investments.

Pension Funds Pension funds often acquire permanent mortgages on income-producing properties. In recent years, many have acquired equity in large income-producing properties or have acquired properties without the aid of mortgage financing.

Types of Loans

Institutional lending to finance income property takes the form of a permanent loan, with or without equity participation, or various shorter-term loans. Each loan may be structured to provide level payments, an adjustable interest rate, or interest payments for a specified period, followed by amortization at a specified rate.

Fixed-Rate Permanent Loans A permanent loan is usually underwritten for fifteen to thirty years. It is often fully amortizing (that is, self-retiring through payments) over the loan term. For borrowers, an adjustable-rate loan is riskier than a fixed-rate loan because large rate-index increases can increase periodic payments significantly. When interest rates fall, however, the borrower's periodic payment is reduced. Typically, interest rates on fixed-rate loans are one to two percentage points higher than the initial rates on adjustable-rate loans.

Adjustable-Rate Permanent Loans Adjustable-rate mortgages (ARMs) provide an opportunity to enter an investment at a lower interest rate (therefore, with lower initial payments), with the rate increasing to a specified limit (cap) over the life of the loan. After the initial rate, the rate is usually indexed to a short-term rate such as the prime rate or the one-year United States Treasury Bill rate. This rate is usually adjusted each year, with a cap on both the annual amount of increase and an overall rate cap over the life of the loan. For example, an ARM might have an initial interest rate of 8 percent, review once a year with the annual rate indexed to the prime rate, and increases limited to two percentage points, not to exceed six percentage points over the life of the loan. If all annual reviews resulted in increases of two percentage points, the interest rates over seven years would look like this:

Year	Interest rate
1	8 percent
2	10 percent
3	12 percent
4	14 percent
5, 6, 7, . . .	14 percent

The advantage of an ARM to the borrower is the lower initial rate and the possibility of rate decreases. For the lender, the ARM provides protection against changes in the economy and interest rates.

Loans Requiring Lump-Sum Payments
Balloon loans, miniperm loans, and bullet loans have shorter terms than permanent loans. Loan payments do not fully amortize the loan; the balance must be paid in a lump sum (balloon payment or bullet) at the end of the loan term. Miniperms and bullet loans offer gap financing to pay off a construction loan and provide time for the borrower to obtain permanent financing. Interest rates are high compared to long-term rates (about two percentage points above the prime rate) and usually are readjusted each time the prime rate changes. Miniperms entail the greatest risk to the borrower compared with other loans available in the market.

Participation Mortgages Participation mortgages, often referred to as equity participations, provide an inflation hedge to the lender as compensation for possible increases in market interest rates. The borrower gives up rights to a portion of annual earnings. The expectation is that inflation will increase the property's income. Payments are based on an annual debt service (ADS) payment plus a percentage of gross income (or net operating income) above a specified level. (Lenders prefer to use gross income because amounts are easier to validate by audit.) For a $750,000 fixed-rate loan at an interest rate of 9 percent for twenty-six years, the ADS payment is approximately $75,000. If gross income is $252,000 and net operating income is $163,000 per year, the participation might require an additional payment of 10 percent of gross income in excess of $200,000 per year ($5,200) or 40 percent of net operating income in excess of $150,000 per year ($5,200).

Financing Terms

Most real estate investors seek the best financing terms. Opinions on how to define "best" differ. The most important factors are interest rate, including points and fees; degree of leverage; and amortization terms.

Interest Rate Interest is a charge for the use of money. The lower the rate, the more attractive the loan. Interest also affects the degree of leverage. Sellers sometimes provide below-market financing to buyers or pay discount points on a buyer's loan, but raise prices to compensate.

Degree of Leverage The larger the loan, the greater the leverage. Many investors will pay a higher interest rate to enjoy a lower cash down payment and therefore be able to exercise more leverage. When interest rates are low, the criterion limiting the loan amount is usually loan-to-value ratio. When rates are high, the debt coverage ratio (ratio of expected cash flow to debt service) is usually the criterion for the maximum loan amount. For conservative lenders, the loan-to-value ratio is usually from 65–70 percent. Other lenders may use a criterion of 75–80 percent.

Amortization Term The longer the amortization term of a mortgage loan, the lower the annual debt service; therefore, the greater the annual cash flow to the equity investor. However, there are diminishing returns from longer amortization terms because the debt service payment change does not have a linear relationship to the amortization term. As loan terms are stretched, the annual mortgage payment requirement declines, but the changes become increasingly smaller, Of course, the annual payment for self-amortizing loans can never become less than the interest rate applied to the principal. Many loans on income property, however, are not self-amortizing and become due years before being fully amortized. Table 2 shows typical loan terms and amortization provisions of various types of loans.

Other Considerations

Other important considerations in arranging mortgage loans include prepayment privileges, exculpation, assumability and escalation, call or acceleration, and subordination.

Prepayment privileges   Prepayment privileges allow the borrower the right to pay off remaining debt ahead of schedule. Some loans include penalties for prepayment, although usually the penalty declines with time. For example, the penalty may be 3 percent if the loan is prepaid during the first five years, 2 percent the next five years, then decline by 0.5 percent for each of the following years until there is no penalty. Some mortgage loans are locked in for the first five to ten years; prepayment without the lender's consent is prohibited.

Exculpation   Exculpation is freedom from blame. When a mortgage loan includes an exculpatory clause, the property is the sole collateral for the loan. Should the property be foreclosed, the lender can look only to the property for full satisfaction of the debt, not to other property owned by the equity investors. In the absence of exculpation, borrowers are usually personally liable for their debts. *Nonrecourse* is another term used to describe mortgages with exculpatory clauses; the lender's only recourse in the event of borrower default is to the property itself, not to the borrower's personal assets.

Assumability and Escalation   Assumability is the borrower's right to transfer the property and obligation to another party. Because the transferee may not be as good a credit risk as the original owner, lenders often reserve the right to approve ownership changes. In recent years, some lenders have been willing to approve changes routinely, provided that they can escalate (increase) the interest rate on the debt. Such provisions in mortgage loans make assumption privileges less attractive. Despite lender approval of changes in ownership, original borrowers remain liable for the mortgage debt. Sellers have recourse to those who assumed their debt, but the sellers remain liable when the new owner acquires the property "subject to" the debt.

Call   Call, or acceleration, provisions are, in effect, balloon payment provisions. Although the loan has a term of twenty-five or thirty years, lenders, at their option, can accelerate payment of the principal after ten or fifteen years, whether or not the loan is in default. This puts the lender in a strong position. Upon reaching the "call" date, the lender can force repayment or escalate the interest rate. "Canadian roll-over" mortgages are those in which the loan is not called, but its interest rate is adjusted to the market rate at fixed intervals, such as every five years.

Table 2. Income-Property Mortgage Loans: Typical Terms of Selected Types of Loans

Loan type	Points and fees	Minimum debt coverage ratio	Amortization term (years)*	Typical loan term (years)
Permanent	0.5-2%	1.05-1.20	less than 30	10-15
Miniperm	0.5-2	1.05-1.20	less than 30	2-7
Bullet**	0-2	1.10-1.20	0-30	3-25
Participation	0-1	1.05-1.15	less than 30	10-15

* Conservative lending practices require amortization.
** Borrower is generally not permitted to prepay, transfer title, place junior financing, or change the loan in any way.

Sources: Fantini, George J., Jr., Real estate finance data-bank, *Real Estate Finance Update,* Boston: Warren, Gorham & Lamont, June 1985 through October 1986; Urban Land Institute, *Dollars and Percent of Development Finance,* second quarter through fourth quarter 1984, Washington, DC, 1985; and a telephone survey of twenty-two large financial institutions (five commercial banks, nine savings and loans, and eight mutual savings banks) conducted by W. L. Born and the Real Estate Center at Texas A&M University in 1986 and 1987.

Subordination Subordination means moving a mortgage loan to a lower priority. Land financed by a seller with a first mortgage and now ready for development is not acceptable collateral for a construction lender. Construction lenders want a first lien. If the holder of an existing mortgage is willing to subordinate, the existing mortgage will be reduced to a second lien position to allow a first lien for the new mortgage. If a subordination clause will be needed, the borrower should include it when the mortgage agreement is drafted; lenders are reluctant to reduce collateral later. Subordination claims are favorable to borrowers because they increase the flexibility of additional financing.

Summary

An appraisal is an estimate of the market value of property. It considers the typical purchaser and the financing available in the market. Consequently, an appraiser must understand the rationale for investor behavior and the operation of the real estate market.

Advantages of investing in real estate include cash flow, appreciation, income tax benefits, mortgage reduction, portfolio diversification, and personal satisfaction. Real estate investment is varied and versatile, offering many different property types and ownership interests. It therefore benefits investors who have different needs, wants, and tastes.

Mortgage financing is available to aid the purchase of investment real estate, supplying cash to the buyer for an average of about 75 percent of appraised value. Major financial institutions that supply capital for real estate purchases include life insurance companies, commercial banks, savings and loan associations, mortgage bankers, real estate investment trusts, and pension funds. There are four major dimensions of mortgage financing: amount of principal, interest rate, amortization term, and monthly payment. Different types of loans vary along one or more of these dimensions. Although the standard mortgage loan has a level payment and is self-amortizing, others may feature income participation, adjustable interest rates, or balloon payments.

Income, Expense, and Lease Analysis

Appraisers analyze income and expenses to calibrate the income model. The values for income are estimated from analysis of market data obtained from questionnaires, published sources, and owners. This chapter defines standard terms used for income and expenses, discusses types of leases, and examines the effects of expected profits from resale on perceptions of value.

Levels of Income

The appraiser uses one or more levels of income in estimating value. Potential gross income (the sum of potential gross rent and miscellaneous income) represents the highest possible level of income. The owner's net return (after-tax cash flow) is what remains after various expenses and allowances are deducted (see figure 1).

Potential Gross Rent

Potential gross rent is the rent that would be collected if the property were fully occupied at market rent. In estimating potential gross income, the appraiser distinguishes between *market rent* (sometimes called economic rent) and *contract rent*. Market rent is the rate prevailing in the market for comparable properties and is used in calculating market value by the income approach. Contract rent is the actual amount agreed to by landlord

and tenant. If the leases are long term, contract rent is important in calculating investment value. For short-term leases, the appraiser should determine whether it is reasonable to assume that contract rent will equal market rent when the leases are renegotiated.

Contract rents should be analyzed to determine (1) if the lease amount is typical for the type of property and (2) if the lease agreement provides for any consideration other than the lease of the subject property. Contract rents are compared with market rents for comparable properties. Contracts are examined just as sales data are in the sales comparison approach. The appraiser verifies that the contract is bona fide, that the parties to the contract are unrelated, and that there were no undue influences on either party. The contract rent may have been established in earlier lease negotiations that no longer reflect current rent levels. The rent may have been set lower than prevailing market rates to allow the lessee to provide site improvements or as part of the financing for a future purchase by the lessee.

Market rents represent what a given property should be renting for, based on analysis of contract rents for comparable space—but only those contract rents considered to represent market rent. The market rent should be the amount that would result from a lease

Figure 1.   Levels of Real Estate Income

Potential gross rent*

less

Vacancy and collection allowance

plus

Miscellaneous income*

equals

Effective gross income

less

Operating expenses (allowable):
Maintenance and operating
Aministrative
Utilities
Insurance
Real estate taxes**
Replacement reserves

equals

Net operating income

less

Debt service:
Mortgage principal
Mortgage interest

equals

Before-tax cash flow
(cash throw-off or equity dividend)

less

Income tax liability
(Taxable income = net operating income less
depreciation and mortgage interest)

Tax liability = taxable income × tax rate
(negative tax = tax savings)

equals

After-tax cash flow (net return)

---

* Potential gross income is the sum of potential gross rent and miscellaneous income.
** Real estate taxes, although an operating expense, are reflected for assessment purposes by an increase in the capitalization rate, instead of a net operating income reduction.

negotiated on the open market between a willing lessor and a willing lessee, both knowledgeable and free of influence from outside sources (compare the definition of market value).

Market rent is capitalized into an estimate of value. Market value estimates, regardless of method, represent the sum of the present worth of each individual year's income over the anticipated productive life of the property (including proceeds from resale). Reliable value estimates depend on accurate estimates of the income stream.

Market rent for mass appraisal purposes is often estimated from operating statements submitted by commercial property owners. Not many assessment jurisdictions have access to detailed lease data on masses of properties. Most operating statements from property owners begin with effective gross income. Operating statements and rent rolls do not usually show potential gross income. If the appraiser confuses effective gross income with potential gross rent or income, vacancy and collection loss may be counted twice. The first priority in analyzing an income statement, then, is to identify correctly the level of income reported.

Excess Rent   Excess rent is the difference between contract and market rents and implies that the tenant is paying more rent than is being paid for comparable properties. If a property has several leases, the appraiser prepares a schedule with the expiration date of each lease to assist in estimating the quality and duration of the income stream.

Rent Concessions   Rent concessions take the form of free rent, usually for a period at the beginning of a lease, or other benefits. Concessions are offered when the supply of rental property exceeds demand. Appraisers should analyze such concessions and take them into account when calibrating a model.

Rental Units of Comparison Rents are stated as rent per unit and compared in terms of a common unit. Typical units of comparison are square foot, room, apartment, space, and percentage of gross business income of the tenant, as shown in table 1.

Some office building and shopping center leases that state rent per square foot are based on *net leasable area* (floor area occupied by the tenant) and others on *gross leasable area* (net leasable area plus common areas such as halls, restrooms, and vestibules). An office building with 100,000 square feet of gross leasable area might have only 80,000 square feet of net leasable area, a difference of 20 percent. An appraiser comparing leases should determine whether rent is based on gross or net leasable area.

Rents may be stated on a monthly or annual basis. Rent per month cannot be compared with rent per year. In the capitalization process, both income and expenses are expressed as annual amounts.

Vacancy and Collection Allowance

The losses expected from vacancies and bad debts are subtracted from potential gross income. These losses are calculated at the rate expected of typical management in a given market. A well- or poorly managed property may have rates different from the average, but that is attributable to management, not the property, and might change under new ownership.

Projects occupied by a single tenant require evaluation of the tenant's creditworthiness and length of lease term, and an estimation of the probability of a vacancy in the future and when it might occur.

Miscellaneous Income

Miscellaneous income is received from concessions, laundry rooms, parking space or storage bin rentals, and other associated services integral to operating the project. Miscellaneous income includes any money reasonably related to the ordinary operation of the project, but not money earned from individual entrepreneurial activities of the owner or property manager.

Effective Gross Income

Effective gross income is the amount remaining after the vacancy rate and bad debt allowances are subtracted from potential gross rent and miscellaneous income is added. Calculating effective gross income is an intermediate step in deriving cash flows.

Operating Expenses

The list of potential operating expenses for real estate leased under a gross lease includes

- Administration
- Repairs and maintenance
- Utilities
- Insurance
- Property taxes (do not include when the purpose of the valuation is a property tax assessment)
- Replacement reserves

Operating expenses may be divided into two categories. *Fixed expenses* do not change as the rate of occupancy changes. *Variable expenses*, however, are directly related to the occupancy rate: as more people occupy and use a building, variable expenses increase.

Fixed expenses include property taxes, license and permit fees, and property insur-

Table 1.   Rental Units of Comparison for Types of Income-Producing Property

Rental unit of comparison	Type of income-producing property
Square foot	Shopping centers, retail stores, office buildings, warehouses, apartments, and leased land
Room	Motels, hotels, and apartment buildings
Apartment	Apartment buildings
Space	Mobile home parks, travel trailer parks, and parking garages
Percentage of gross business income	Retail stores, shopping centers, restaurants, and gas stations

ance. Variable expenses include utilities (such as heat, water, and sewer), management fees, payroll and payroll taxes, security, landscaping, and supplies and fees for services provided by local government or private contractors. There may be a fixed component in expenses usually classified as variable, for example, a basic fixed management cost regardless of occupancy rate.

The appraiser compares expenses reported for the subject property to expense information for comparable properties. This information may be obtained from reports published by trade organizations and from fee appraisers, property managers, assessment jurisdictions, and other professionals (see chapter 5). The appraiser analyzes the external environment and underlying economic conditions to estimate expenses for a property type as of the appraisal date and judges whether any expense items are likely to change substantially in the near future. The historical costs of operation of the subject property are examined to determine if reporting practices have been consistent throughout the period. For example, in one year the owner paid all utilities, but in the next a separate metering system was installed so that tenants began to pay some.

When appraising for ad valorem tax purposes, an appraiser should not include property taxes as an operating expense. Property taxes are calculated from an estimated value; taxes considered as an operating expense would help define that value. The appraiser allows for the effect of property taxes by making an adjustment to the capitalization rate instead.

Replacement Reserve   The replacement of short-lived items (such as roofing, appliances, and some mechanical equipment) that will not last for the remaining economic life usually requires expenditures of large lump sums. A portion of the expected cost can be set aside each year to stabilize expenses. An appraiser provides for the replacement reserve even if an owner has not done so. If the market does not provide for reserves, the appraiser either estimates a figure from some other source or excludes the reserve in all calculations. If reserves are excluded, the net operating income will be overstated or understated, depending on the dollar cost of major replacements during the year being analyzed. To ensure consistency, the treatment of replacement reserves should be kept in mind when expense ratios and overall rates are developed and analyzed.

Net Operating Income

Net operating income is estimated by subtracting operating expenses and the replacement reserve from effective gross income. Any interest or principal payments are not considered in computing net operating income.

Because appraisers use net operating income to support value estimates, it must be accurately determined. Each dollar by which revenues or expenses are misstated is magnified in the final value estimate. Net operating income is useful for comparing one property to another and provides an excellent point from which to estimate property value. Table 2 shows how a net operating income schedule prepared by a property owner, if accepted at face value by an appraiser, would distort net operating income by 70 percent.

Debt service, the interest and principal payments that amortize a mortgage loan, is not included as an operating expense. The payments depend on the interest rate and financing and cannot, therefore, be used to estimate property value.

Table 2.   Reconstructed Owner's Income Statement

Account	Reason for adjustment	Owner's statement	Adjusted statement
Potential gross rent	Owner's statement is based on actual rent, which is below market.	85,000	$100,000
Less vacancy and collection allowance	Owner's statement began with actual rent collected.		− 5,000
Plus miscellaneous income	Owner's figures did not include $3,000 of laundry room income.		+ 3,000
Effective gross income		$85,000	$ 98,000
Less current operating expenses		− 31,000	− 31,000
Property taxes	For tax assessment purposes, property taxes are reflected in the capitalization rate.	− 11,000	N/A
Mortgage payments	Interest and principal payments are financing costs, not operating expenses.	− 24,000	N/A
Replacement reserve	Owner had no replacement reserve account.	none	− 2,000
Net operating income		$19,000	$ 65,000
Difference			$ 46,000
Percentage difference			70.7 percent

Before-Tax Cash Flow

Debt service (and property taxes if they have not already been subtracted) are subtracted from net operating income to derive before-tax cash flow, also known as cash throw-off, equity dividend, or cash flow. It represents the amount an owner receives from the property each year, before any deduction for income taxes.

Taxable Income

Income taxes, an owner expense that does not affect the property's operating expense, are excluded from calculation of property value. However, appraisers should be aware of the changing effects of income taxation on price and value. For example, in the United States in the early 1980s, real estate prices went up sharply as investors took advantage of tax shelter benefits. The Tax Reform Act of 1986 then eliminated most tax benefits of real estate ownership, and the price increase slowed or stopped.

Taxable income from a real estate investment is computed by deducting operating expenses, property taxes, interest, and depreciation from actual rental income. The amount of tax is usually a percentage of that income.

Another method of computing taxable income is to add back reserves to net operating income, then subtract interest and depreciation to derive taxable income, and apply a tax rate to the income or loss to derive the tax payment or saving. Under the 1986 law, a tax loss from rental real estate may not be used to offset active income (such as salary) or portfolio income (such as interest and dividends). However, a loss from rental property can offset the current year's passive income from other rental property; if there is no income, the loss may be carried forward to offset future passive income from the property or gain on its sale.

The Tax Reform Act mandates straight-line depreciation on most buildings bought after 1986. The life used is 31½ years for nonresidential property and 27½ years for apartments and other dwellings. This limited tax depreciation allowance removes most potential tax shelter from real estate.

After-Tax Cash Flow

After-tax cash flow is before-tax cash flow adjusted for current income taxes and is calculated by subtracting income taxes from before-tax cash flow. The Tax Reform Act of 1986 neutralized the effect of taxes on real estate values by eliminating tax shelter from most real estate investments and by limiting depreciation and preventing the offset of rental property losses against other types of income.

Improper Expenses

For appraisal purposes, the income approach relies on an accurate estimate of net operating income and thus on an accurate estimate of expenses to be deducted from effective gross income. Owners' operating statements often show improper expenses, that is, those not to be used in the income approach. ("Improper" does not imply fraud or deceit.) Some such expenses are described below.

Property Taxes Property taxes are sometimes considered proper expenses for the income approach. To avoid circularity, however, property taxes are accounted for in valuations for assessment purposes by adjusting the capitalization rate. Otherwise, the amount of tax affects the estimate of value used to calculate the tax.

Economic and Tax Depreciation   Depreciation, defined as a loss in value from any source, is considered in the income approach as recapture and treated as part of the capitalization rate rather than as an operating expense. Another type of depreciation, that claimed for income tax purposes, is usually shown on the owner's financial records. It is not the same as the recapture provision in the capitalization rate, nor is it an operating expense for appraisal purposes.

Debt Service   Debt service, the interest and principal payments required to amortize a loan, is a financing expense, not an operating expense. Although financing, whether good or poor, affects price, it should not affect the value of real estate. When estimating value, an appraiser assumes typical financing for that kind of property. The influence of atypical financing should be removed. Transactions need not be in cash as long as what the seller receives is measured by its cash value. Any other standard of measurement would create inconsistencies from property to property.

Income Taxes   Income tax is not an operating expense, but a tax on personal income, which may be affected by items other than the subject property.

Capital Improvements   Capital improvements are long-lasting additions to the property that usually increase income, total value, or economic life. They should not be considered operating expenses.

Owner's Business Expenses   Any business expenses not necessary or reasonable for generating income from the property are not operating expenses of the property.

Leasing and Financing
Leases
Rental income from real estate is received in accordance with the lease. A typical lease requires base rent to be paid each month at the beginning of the month. Additional rent may be based on gross sales, net operating income, a consumer price index, or other adjustment. Variations of lease terms and lease features are numerous. Because of these, and the potential influence of a lease on value, an appraiser should read and highlight significant portions of the lease. Some common lease provisions are described below.

Net Versus Gross Leases   Leases are usually referred to as *net* or *gross*, although many are not completely one or the other. A net lease is the most straightforward approach for a single-tenant structure. The tenant pays all taxes, insurance, and operating expenses such as maintenance (repairs, alterations, replacements, improvements, ordinary or extraordinary repairs whether interior or exterior, and so on). The owner is not involved with property operations. The terms *triple-net lease* or *net-net-net lease* are often used for the complete net lease.

In a gross lease, the landlord (lessor) pays all operating expenses. Some leases have clauses that reduce or raise the rent under specific conditions, for example, a clause that limits a landlord's responsibility for certain expenses to a negotiated amount. The tenant pays any excess. When a gross lease is used, the landlord is responsible for controlling operating expenses and ensuring that money spent to comply with the lease is spent prudently.

Operating Expenses The lease should specify whether landlord or tenant pays for each operating expense. It should also specify that the responsible party must present proof of payment, such as a paid property tax bill or insurance policy in conformity with requirements of the lease, to provide assurance of protection from risks covered by the lease. If the lessee in a net lease does not supply the information, the lessor should request it.

Leases often specify that the landlord is responsible for the structural integrity of the building, including the roof and exterior and supporting walls, and that nonstructural repairs and problems caused by tenant negligence are the tenant's responsibility.

Ad Valorem Taxes Although a lease can be negotiated that requires either the landlord or the tenant to pay ad valorem taxes, the tenant usually pays such expenses in a single-tenant building. In a stop (or escalation) clause, the landlord pays a base year amount and the tenant pays the tax increase each year. A net lease or a tax stop clause reduces the need for frequent rent adjustments, cost-of-living indexes, and short-term leases.

Although tenants may pay property taxes, special assessments, and the like, they do not pay other tax obligations of the landlord, such as gift, income, inheritance, franchise, or corporate taxes, or a tax on the rental receipts of the landlord.

Percentage Leases Most percentage leases require a fixed minimum rent plus a percentage rent based on gross sales in excess of a certain amount. The base rent is often set as an anticipated average amount of sales per square foot for that type of business. For ex-

ample, suppose industry norms for a ladies' fashion shop indicate that annual sales of $200 per square foot are typical. Rent for a 10,000-square-foot shop could be $100,000 per year plus 5 percent of sales above $2 million (10,000 square feet times $200 per square foot). Percentage rents would be imposed only when sales exceed the norm of $200 per square foot of floor area.

A percentage lease, commonly used for retail tenants, gives incentive to the landlord to make the property attractive and thus encourage retail sales. The landlord must be prepared to audit the tenant's retail sales records and enforce provisions of the lease that give rights to a percentage of sales.

Different types of businesses have different typical percentage rents (table 3). For example, retail stores selling luxury items are often small and have a high markup and low inventory turnover. These stores, therefore, have a higher percentage rental rate than grocery or discount stores with low markup and high turnover. Publications from the International Council of Shopping Centers and the Urban Land Institute provide information about leasing and operating costs.

To assure fairness to both parties, monthly or annual sales reports may be required, and the landlord may have the right to hire an auditor, whose fee will be paid for by the tenant if it appears that sales are understated; if no discrepancies are found, the lessor pays.

Cost-of-Living Index Leases for multiple years without rent adjustments result in hardships during highly inflationary or deflationary periods. A long-term lease may have a cost-of-living adjustment that calls for changes in rent based on the change in some published index.

Table 3.   Percentage Lease Rates in Neighborhood Shopping Centers for Various Types of Businesses*

Firm type	Percent	Firm type	Percent
Automotive	2.0–5.0	Ladies specialty	4.0–7.0
Bakery	4.0–6.0	Liquor and wine	1.5–5.0
Books and stationery	2.5–6.0	Menswear	3.0–6.0
Cameras	2.0–6.0	Paint, wallpaper	2.0–6.0
Cards and gifts	5.0–8.0	Pet shop	5.0–8.0
Computers, calculator	1.0–5.0	Records, tapes	3.7–7.0
Drug store	2.5–4.0	Restaurant	4.0–7.0
Food specialty	2.0–6.0	Shoes	3.0–6.0
Furniture	2.0–6.0	Sporting goods	3.0–6.0
Hardware	2.5–6.0	Supermarket	1.0–2.0
Health food	1.5–6.0	Variety store	2.5–5.0
Jewelry	4.5–5.0		

* Extracted from *Dollars and Cents of Shopping Centers* Urban Land Institute, 1987.

The index and the frequency and amount of adjustment are negotiable. The Consumer Price Index, published by the Bureau of Labor Statistics of the United States Department of Labor, is often used because it is computed and published frequently. A less known local index tied to rental rates, operating expenses, or real estate values may be satisfactory but introduces elements of instability or potential manipulation and may lead to litigation.

Leases may be adjusted annually or after a period of years. This period should be short for a gross lease but may be longer for a net lease. With a net lease, the landlord has less financial exposure to the risk of inflation because the tenant pays operating expenses.

The degree of adjustment may be only part of the full change in the index selected. For example, if 50 percent of the index were selected as the multiplier and the index rose by 20 percent, rent would increase by 10 percent. This provides some protection to the landlord (who perhaps bought the property with preinflation dollars) but does not inflict the full effect of inflation on the tenant.

Premises   The premises section of a lease describes the property being leased. An appraiser may need to confirm that the description in the lease agrees with the parcel being appraised.

Term   The term of a lease may affect property value. Long leases with fixed rents may increase or decrease the value of property. Leases with creditworthy tenants frequently have an initial term from five to fifty years, with renewal options every one to ten years. Often there are multiple renewal terms, such as four options of five years each, with adequate notice to the landlord required for renewal. Rent need not be level throughout a term.

Specialized Financing and Partial Interests

The value of an investment is often affected by special financing or the dividing of ownership interest. Chapter 3 gives a brief overview of common forms of partial ownership. Specialized procedures, often used in the financing of income-producing property, are explained below. Note, however, that the ad valorem appraiser appraising a fee simple interest of a property ignores financing arrangements. As explained earlier, typical financing is assumed.

Equity Participation   Equity participation, also called mortgage participation, entitles a lender to receive a share of income or appreciation from the property in addition to payments for interest and principal retirement. Each participation agreement is unique. Some agreements require the payment of a stated percentage of effective gross income, net operating income, or cash flow. Others require a share of income in excess of a base amount, such as 5 percent of effective gross income above $500,000, or allow the lender to share in the appreciation or resale proceeds. Definitions of annual income or resale proceeds used to determine participation amounts vary from contract to contract. Consequently, an appraiser should understand the details of each agreement considered, although these financing agreements do not affect market value.

Partial Interests   Ownership of land and of improvements is sometimes separated for tax or financial purposes. By splitting property ownership, each party can receive the particular ownership interest and collateral desired. Fractionating is worthwhile when the sum of the prices paid for each component exceeds the price that would be realized from the sale of the property as a whole.

For example, it is possible to sell the land beneath a shopping center or office build-

ing and simultaneously lease it back for a long term (more than twenty-five years). The seller retains use of the property yet receives substantial cash from the sale. The new landowner receives periodic lease payments and resale rights. Sometimes an improvement is sold to another party who wants the right to depreciate it for tax purposes. Land and improvements may be encumbered by separate mortgages. Management rights, including the privilege of sharing in property income, may be sold separately.

When attempting to value a partial interest, such as a land lease, or the right to income from improvements, the appraiser analyzes the entire agreement to estimate the risks and potential returns from the particular interest being considered. It is preferable to estimate annual income for the entire property, then subtract requirements for prior claims, to derive the income or cash flow available to the interest being appraised. The income to the interest and the forecast residual can be capitalized to estimate its value.

Joint Ventures   A property or an interest in real property can be sold to investors who have pooled their resources for a specific investment called a joint venture. The variety of forms include tenancy in common, in which each participant's share is alike; general partnership, in which each participant is a partner; limited partnership, in which at least one partner (the general partner or partners) is liable beyond the amount invested and at least one partner's liability is limited; or an agreement that gives one participant preferred returns. Preferred returns allow an investor to claim a certain amount of income or cash flow before other participants receive any income. An appraiser attempting to estimate the value of an interest should understand the entire agreement, including whether the interest is subordinated, the degree of risk, and personal liability.

Options and Conditional Sales Contracts
An option is the right, but not the obligation, to buy certain property at a stated price within a period of time. A conditional sales contract imposes the obligation to buy unless the stipulated conditions are not met. Commonly used conditions include financing, rezoning, approval by partners, soil-boring test results, transfer of marketable title, and so forth.

When an option or conditional sales contract encumbers property, the highest price the fee simple owner can realize is the amount specified in the option or contract. Opportunities for further value appreciation for the fee owner are limited to those situations in which the contract is not exercised.

The option or contract can be valuable. With rapid appreciation, the agreed contractual price for the property soon becomes less than the property's market value. The excess of property value over the agreed price accrues to the option or contract holder, who can sell or assign rights without acquiring title to the property. The estimated market value of an option or contract is usually the difference between the market value of the property and the contractual price. During an option's exercise period, some speculators would pay a premium for the extreme leverage if the market is active and rising.

Leases as Partial Interests
The value of a leasehold can be substantial. Long-term leases at rents that are fixed and below market have value that can be estimated from the remaining term and below-market rent. For example, if the lease requires $1,000 as the annual net rent for the next fifty years, and the market rental rate is $5,000 per year, the $4,000 per year difference may be capitalized to estimate the leasehold value. The leased fee is worth the present value of the $1,000 annual payment (discounted at a riskless rate because the tenant is unlikely to default) plus the discounted present value of the property upon the lease expiration date (reversion). Taken together, the two interests should approximate the total market value of the property. The leasehold can be sublet to create another ownership interest that may have value (see figure 2).

Value Change Expectations
Investment results from real estate depend on lease terms and economic conditions. If the tenant's credit is rated triple A and the lease is long term at a fixed net rental rate, income should be assured. Under these circum-

Figure 2. Leasehold and Leased Fee Valuation

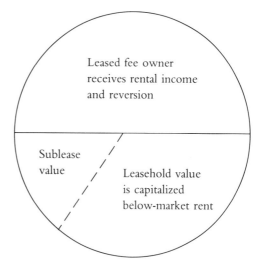

Leased fee owner receives rental income and reversion

Sublease value

Leasehold value is capitalized below-market rent

stances, property values tend to fluctuate like high-grade bonds, falling when interest rates rise and vice versa. If the tenant's credit rating is not high, or the lease is not net, or its term is short, value will depend more on such factors as competition and local economic conditions.

Today's values may also be strongly affected by expectations about future resale prices. An appraiser, therefore, reflects resale expectations when selecting a capitalization rate. This capitalization rate is raised when future value decline is expected, and lowered when appreciation is anticipated by the market.

A resale price is based on expectations for the future. The gain or loss, less selling costs, has a present value that, added to the present value of cash flow, may be used to estimate today's equity value. Tables 4 and 5 show how a $1 million sale price is diminished by transaction costs.

Sales Contract Terms

From the seller's viewpoint, negotiable terms could include an all-cash transaction, an exchange of the property for other real estate, or seller financing using a wraparound mortgage or other financing technique. Seller financing may be the only method of closing a sale when institutional financing is unavailable. A purchase money mortgage can provide first mortgage financing or be used as a wraparound mortgage that preserves intact an existing first mortgage.

If the seller does not require cash immediately, the installment payment method can be used. If the seller wishes to get cash and continued current income from operations, a sale-leaseback agreement can be considered.

Table 4.   Sale Price Diminished by Transaction Costs

Sale price	$1,000,000
Less seller's estimated expenses of sale	
Title insurance policy	$ 4,000
Attorney's fees	3,500
Release of lien	300
Survey of property	500
Escrow fees	500
Recording fees	200
Broker's commission	50,000
Prepayment penalty on loan	6,000
Subtotal	$ 65,000
Estimated receipts to seller	$935,000

Table 5.   Estimated Taxable Gain and Tax on Sale

Sale price		$1,000,000
Less expenses of sale (see table 4)		– 65,000
Less adjusted tax basis:		
Cost	$750,000	
Less depreciation	– 174,570	
		– 575,430
Gain		359,570
Tax at 33 percent		$ 118,658

Income Tax Implications of Sale

A seller can often adjust the date of sale of a major asset to fit a tax plan. On the sale of income property, gain or loss for income tax purposes is measured by the difference between the sale price and the adjusted tax basis. Some of the gain may be taxed as a capital gain and some as ordinary income. The distinction is less important since the Tax Reform Act of 1986, because rates for capitalization and income became equal in

1988. When the seller finances the sale, installment payments may be used to spread the income tax over several years. A tax-free exchange may defer taxation of the gain to future years. If the property is owned in corporate form, choices include selling the stock of the corporation, liquidating the corporation and selling the assets, or selling the assets without a corporate liquidation.

Gain or Loss The amount paid for income property is the original tax basis. That amount is allocated among various assets, based on their relative market values, for purposes of determining depreciation. For example, suppose a $750,000 property comprises $200,000 in land and $550,000 in improvements. The cost is allocated and improvements depreciated. Land is not subject to depreciation.

Capital improvements are added to the tax basis; depreciation claimed for income tax purposes is subtracted. The result is the adjusted tax basis. If there are no capital improvements, and depreciation is $17,457 per year ($550,000 spread over 31.5 years), the adjusted tax basis will be reduced from $750,000 to $575,430 in 10 years. If the property is sold for more, the excess is a taxable gain (see table 5).

Installment Sale Real estate is often sold with seller financing in the form of a first, second, or wraparound mortgage. As the principal of the note is collected, the gain is reported and capital gains tax paid. Interest is taxed as ordinary income.

To determine the taxable amount, a gross profit ratio is computed based on the relationship of the profit to the total amount (not including interest) the seller will collect. That ratio is applied to principal payments received. For example, suppose property with an adjusted basis of $55 is sold for $100, resulting in a $45 gain. The first mortgage assumed by the buyer was $30. Subtracting this $30 from $100 leaves a $70 contract price. The contract price is the amount the seller will receive (not including third-party debt assumed by the buyer). The gross profit ratio is $45 gain divided by $70 contract price, or 64.3 percent. Of each principal payment, 64.3 percent is taxable as gain; the rest of the total payment is a nontaxable return of capital. Sellers who borrow must be mindful of tax rules that treat debts as though cash was received from an installment sale.

Tax-free Exchange A tax-free exchange of real estate under Section 1031 of the Internal Revenue Code may be used to postpone recognizing the gain on a sale. Both the property surrendered and that received must be held for use in a trade on business or held as an investment. To the extent one receives unlike property (called *boot*) to equalize the exchange, the gain will be taxable. Relief from indebtedness is a form of boot, as are receipts of cash and personal property.

Under the 1986 Tax Reform Act, a tax-free exchange need not be simultaneous. The seller of real estate can put proceeds into escrow pending acquisition of replacement real estate. However, there is a 45-day deadline to identify the replacement and a 180-day deadline to close the purchase. The 180-day maximum is shortened by the due date of the taxpayer's return; an extension for filing may be necessary to achieve the full 180-day period.

Summary

Information about expected income and estimated proceeds from resale is necessary for estimating the value of income-producing property. The appraisal profession has standardized terminology and classifications of income and expenses to simplify comparison of properties. The effect of encumbrances such as leases and long-term mortgages must be considered. To calibrate the income model, the appraiser analyzes income, expenses, lease terms, and expectations about resale.

The next chapter discusses direct and yield capitalization. These methods differ in how rate and income stream are calibrated and used within the income approach.

Income Capitalization

I2

Overview

Income capitalization translates a stream of future income into a single present value. It considers the quantity and quality of future income, when the income is to be received, and the duration of the income stream.

A capitalization rate is used to convert the income stream into one lump-sum value by the formula

$$V = \frac{I}{R}, \qquad (1)$$

where V is present value, I is income, and R is capitalization rate.

The capitalization rate used in real estate appraisal includes both a return *on* and a return *of* investment. Return on investment, called the discount rate, is compensation to an investor for the risk, time value of money, and other factors associated with a particular investment. It takes into account interest costs and required yield on equity. Return of investment, called recapture, is recovery of invested capital.

Any investor seeks a return on and a return of invested money. A prudent investor looks to the future income stream, as well as potential resale (reversion of the investment), to provide this return. Some investments, such as amortizing mortgages,

provide only periodic cash flow when held to maturity, whereas other investments, such as undeveloped land, provide only resale proceeds and may have negative cash flow, due to property taxes for example. When deciding how much to pay for an investment, investors consider potential income, resale proceeds, and income tax benefits.

Economic Basis of the Capitalization Rate

The overall capitalization rate has three components, a discount rate (its largest part), a recapture rate, and an effective tax rate (when the appraisal is done for an ad valorem assessment). These components were described fully in chapter 9.

Building up a capitalization rate (as shown in figure 1) is a helpful means of understanding how market behavior enters into estimations of capitalization rates (see also the discussion in chapter 10 on building up a discount rate).

The discount rate, usually the largest part of the overall capitalization rate, is the required rate of return *on* investment. The discount rate takes into account four aspects of investment: safety, risk, liquidity, and management cost. Building up a capitalization rate, therefore, begins by identifying the

Figure 1.   Components of the Capitalization Rate

Discount rate (synonym: required rate of return *on* investment)

   Interest rate (synonym: required rate of return on borrowed funds)

   Yield rate (synonym: required rate of return on equity)

Recapture rate (synonym: rate of return *of* investment)

Effective tax rate (include when appraising for ad valorem tax purposes.)

Safe rate	6%
Risk rate	3
Illiquidity rate	1
Investment management rate	1
Discount rate	11%
Recapture rate	2
Effective tax rate	1
Built-up overall rate	14%

rate for a safe, liquid, risk-free investment that requires little management, such as a bank account insured by a government agency. This rate is the minimum paid as compensation for the time value of money.

To the risk-free rate are added provisions for risk, illiquidity, and the burden of management. These four components compose the discount rate.

A recapture rate is then added. Recapture is a return of the portion of the investment in an asset that will waste away (be used up) during the investment period. Recapture represents the annual amount needed to provide a return *of* the investment over the period the investment is held. The annual recapture rate depends primarily on the expected path of the income stream over time

(rising, level, declining, or fluctuating) and the expected value of the asset at resale. If income from a real estate investment is forecast to be level in perpetuity, or level income is forecast and no change is expected in the capital value of the income-producing asset, then return of the entire investment will take place, recapture is not necessary, and the capitalization rate is the same as the discount rate.

Appraisers must distinguish between a decline in improvement value due to a wasting away of the asset and a decline in value due to changing demand patterns. In the former situation, the overall capitalization rate must include a recapture component. The appraiser should reflect the latter situation in the discount rate (theoretically, the risk component should be increased). If appreciation in value due to changing demand patterns is forecast, the annualized rate of appreciation is subtracted from the risk component of the discount rate.

A final component of the overall capitalization rate, an effective tax rate, is included when the appraisal is for ad valorem purposes.

Capitalization Methods

Direct and yield capitalization are two ways of calibrating the income model. Direct capitalization methods focus on the outcome of investors' decision-making processes. Yield capitalization methods attempt to simulate those processes. In direct capitalization, the appraiser analyzes the relationship between current year income and sale price to develop an overall capitalization rate (see table 1). If expense data are not available, gross income multipliers can be developed.

Table 1. Deriving an Overall Rate from the Market

Comparable	Net operating income	Sale price	Indicated overall rate
#1	$120,000	$1,000,000	0.12
#2	88,000	800,000	0.110
#3	105,000	1,000,000	0.105

In yield capitalization, the appraiser estimates various components of an overall capitalization rate and the weights that should be attached to those components. The characteristics of the income stream can be explicitly modeled in yield capitalization as well.

Direct capitalization is appropriate if two conditions are met. First, the investment opportunities provided by the properties being appraised are similar to those provided by recently purchased income-producing properties. Second, a consistent pattern of overall rates (or multipliers) emerges from the analysis of sales of income-producing properties.

Yield capitalization is not so dependent on sales data. However, the yield capitalization technique chosen must realistically reflect the expectations and behavior of probable purchases of the income-producing properties being appraised. The model can be stated simply in words: value equals the present value of all cash flows plus the present value of the reversionary value.

Direct Capitalization

Direct capitalization describes simple valuation models of two kinds. In the theoretically preferred kind, normal net income from a single year is divided by an overall capitalization rate to produce an estimate of value. The overall capitalization rate is developed from an analysis of actual ratios of income to sale price of properties similar to the ones being appraised. Some examples of this kind of model are:

$$\text{property value} = \frac{\text{net operating income}}{\text{overall rate}}$$

$$\text{equity value} = \frac{\text{cash flow}}{\text{equity yield rate}}$$

$$\text{initial mortgage principal} = \frac{\text{annual debt service}}{\text{mortgage constant}}$$

The other kind of direct capitalization model is used when data on operating expenses are unavailable. By convention in this type, gross income from a single period is multiplied by a factor to produce an estimate of value. Again by convention, the factor is called a *gross rent multiplier (GRM)* if the period is a month and a *gross income multiplier (GIM)* if the period is a year. It is customary to use monthly rent for single-family residences and annual incomes for other income-producing properties. As with the development of overall capitalization rates in direct capitalization, GIMs and GRMs are developed through an analysis of the relationship between income (or rent) and sale price of properties similar to the ones being appraised. It should be noted that factors are simply the reciprocals of rates, and appraisers sometimes develop net income multiplier models.

Direct capitalization is simple, straightforward, and can be applied without an in-depth knowledge of the mathematics of finance. Ease of computation can make direct capitalization deceptively attractive; appraisers should always remember that subject properties and comparables (from which rates or multipliers are derived) must be similar or adjusted for differences. There also must be a consistent pattern in the market-derived overall capitalization rates or multipliers. This section contains a discussion of the factors that determine comparability in the development of rates or multipliers. The calibration of direct capitalization models is illustrated in chapter 15.

Development of an Overall Capitalization Rate

Defining the Overall Rate An overall capitalization rate blends all requirements of discount, recapture, and effective tax rates for both land and improvements. Therefore, development of separate capitalization rates for land and improvements is not necessary, and appraisers do not need to know separate land or improvement values in advance. Because the overall rate is a blend, and recapture rates do not apply to land, the overall rate is higher than the land rate and lower than the improvement rate. The overall rate as a weighted average of land and improvement capitalization rates is illustrated in figure 2. In the example in figure 2, weighted recapture is 3 percent.

Stratifying Properties to Choose Comparables In figure 2, the factors that affect the make-up of an overall capitalization rate were given. That does not happen in reality. Appraisers must analyze the factors that affect overall capitalization rates. The objective of this analysis is to choose the properties whose market-derived overall capitalization rates theoretically should be similar to the rates appropriate for the properties being appraised. Similar considerations apply in the development of multipliers.

As previously mentioned, the following factors affect the composition of an overall capitalization rate: risk, remaining economic life, land-to-improvement ratio, expense ratio, and date and terms of sale. Those factors often are correlated with location, use, and other property characteristics, such as size, condition, and age. Accordingly, appraisers can stratify properties on the basis of such physical characteristics to control for the unobservable factors that affect overall capitalization rates.

Risk If discount rates are to be similar, subject and comparable properties should have similar risk. This can usually be achieved if properties are stratified by type and location.

Expense Ratios If a gross rent multiplier is used, operating expense ratios should be comparable. If they are not (if, for example, the owner pays taxes, utilities, and insurance costs at one property but not at another), the same multiplier will produce substantially different value estimates for sales with comparable net incomes. In figure 3, the two properties generate the same net operating income, thus would be expected to have similar market values. However, when the same gross rent multiplier is applied, the value estimates are different because effective gross income—and therefore the ratios of operating expense to gross income—are so different.

Land-to-Improvement Ratio Land-to-improvement ratios should be consistent. When they are not, the overall rates cannot be expected to provide consistent values (see figure 4). Note that as the ratio of improvement

Figure 2. Weighting Land and Improvement Rates to Give Overall Rate

Deriving an overall rate from the market

$$\frac{\text{Net operating income}}{\text{Total sale price}} = \frac{\$\ 12,000}{\$100,000} = 12\% \text{ overall rate}$$

Assumptions

Land value = $40,000   (40%)
Improvement value = $60,000   (60%)

Improvement rate		Land rate	
Discount rate	7%	Discount rate	7%
Recapture rate	5%	Recapture rate	—
Effective tax rate	2%	Effective tax rate	2%
	14%		9%

Three ways of calculating overall rate

40%	×	9% (Land rate)	= 3.6%
60%	×	14% (Improvement rate)	= 8.4%
		Overall rate	12.0%

Discount rate	7%	Improvement rate	14%
Recapture component weighted by percent of improvement value	3% (60% of 5%)	Less recapture component weighted by percent of land value	−2% (40% of 5%)
Effective tax rate	2%		12% overall rate
	12% overall rate		

value to total property increases, more net income is necessary to satisfy the resulting additional recapture requirement.

Remaining Economic Life The remaining economic life of improvements should be similar for comparable sales and the subject property; this expected remaining life affects the duration of the income stream and, therefore, the recapture component of the overall capitalization rate.

Improvements deteriorate over time and require a recapture provision in the capitalization rate, whereas land is nonwasting. When a nonwasting asset such as land is considered, recapture is unnecessary. The shorter the recapture period, the higher the annual recapture rate. The example in table 2 illustrates that with the land-to-improvement ratio held constant the following hold:

- As the remaining economic life of the improvement increases, the recapture rate, and thus the overall rate, decreases.
- As the remaining economic life of the improvement decreases, the recapture rate, and thus the overall rate, increases.

Figure 3. The Effect of Different Expense Ratios on Value

	Property A	Property B
Effective gross income	$80,000	$60,000
Operating expenses	40,000 (50%)	20,000 (33%)
Net operating income	$40,000	$40,000
Effective gross income	$80,000	$60,000
Gross income multiplier	×6	×6
Indicated value	$480,000	$360,000

Date and Terms of Sale Capitalization rates change over time, especially with changing interest rates and changing supply and demand conditions. An overall rate of return can quickly become obsolete. Consequently, appraisers monitor capitalization rates in times of changing market conditions so that as of the date of appraisal the correct rate will be used. This can be done by adjusting available sales for sale date and terms of sale if sales close to the appraisal date are not available.

Yield Capitalization

In yield capitalization, as in direct capitalization, appraisers analyze market data to develop capitalization rates and apply them to anticipated income streams to estimate the market value of those income streams. In yield capitalization, however, many factors that affect overall capitalization rates, such as degree of risk and the nature of the income stream, are explicitly considered as appraisers attempt to simulate investors' decision-making processes. Yield capitalization models usually are more complex than direct capitalization models because they include more variables. The general structure of the yield model is:

$$V = \frac{I_1}{1+Y} + \frac{I_2}{(1+Y)^2} + \frac{I_3}{(1+Y)^3}$$

$$+ \cdots + \frac{I_n}{(1+Y)^n}, \qquad (2)$$

where V is present value, I is income (or cash flow), Y is the appropriate discount (or yield) rate, and n is number of periods.

The income to be capitalized and the rate applied should be consistent with each other. When net operating income is capitalized, the rate should be applicable to the property as a whole. That is, the discount rate is applied and is arrived at, for example, by blending mortgage and equity rates, or improvement and land rates, or leasehold and leased fee rates. When cash flow to the equity position is capitalized, however, an equity yield rate, which represents the return on investor equity, is appropriate instead.

Compound Interest Functions

An understanding of the six compound interest functions and their interrelationships is necessary to investment analysis and the valuation of income-producing properties. Compound interest functions are based on the concept of the time value of money: an amount of money receivable or anticipated as income in the future is always worth less than an equal amount actually in hand at the

Figure 4. The Effect of Different Land-to-Improvement Ratios on Value

	Sale A	Sale B
Land-to-improvement ratio	(1:1 ratio)	(1:2 ratio)
Sale price	$300,000	$300,000
Land value	$150,000	$100,000
Improvement value	$150,000	$200,000
Discount rate	10 percent	10 percent
Recapture rate		
(20 years remaining economic life)	5 percent	5 percent
Discount on land and improvements	$ 30,000	$ 30,000
Recapture dollars	$ 7,500	$ 10,000
Total net income required	$ 37,500	$ 40,000
Overall rate (net operating income divided by sale price)	12.50 percent	13.33 percent

Table 2. The Effect of Change in Recapture Rate on Overall Rate (Improvement Value, 75%; Land Value, 25%)

	Estimated remaining economic life (years)			
	25	30	40	50
Annual recapture rate	4.0%	3.3%	2.5%	2.0%
Discount rate	10.0%	10.0%	10.0%	10.0%
Improvement capitalization rate	14.0%	13.3%	12.5%	12.0%
Land capitalization rate	10.0%	10.0%	10.0%	10.0%
Improvement component of overall rate (75% × 14%)	10.5%	9.975%	9.375%	9.0%
Land component of overall rate (25% × 10%)	2.5%	2.5%	2.5%	2.5%
Overall rate	13.0%	12.475%	11.875%	11.5%

present time. The degree of time preference can be viewed as a function of risk, anticipated loss in purchasing power (inflation), loss in liquidity, and cost of loan or investment management. Once appropriate rates are derived from the market, they can be applied mechanically from the tables.

Table 3 displays a 10 percent annual compound interest table. The columns contain the names and formulas of the six compound interest functions along with precalculated factors for sixty annual periods. The first three functions use the concept of compounding. Under compounding, interest is paid on accumulated principal and interest payments. Compounding is the principle used to calculate interest earnings or charges, bank account balances, principal payments on a loan, and so on.

The three remaining functions use the concept of discounting, which is the reverse of compounding. Compounding involves accumulation; discounting involves the reduction of a future lump sum income or series

Table 3. Annual Compound Interest Table (Effective Rate = 10 Percent; Base = 1.10)

	1	2	3	4	5	6	
	Future worth of 1 at compound interest	Future worth of 1 per period	Sinking fund factor	Present worth of 1	Present worth of 1 per period	Partial payment	
Years	$S^n = (1+i)^n$	$S_{\overline{n}} = \dfrac{S^n-1}{i}$	$1/S_{\overline{n}} = \dfrac{i}{S^n-1}$	$V^a = \dfrac{1}{S_n}$	$a_{\overline{n}} = \dfrac{1-V^n}{i}$	$1/a_{\overline{n}} = \dfrac{i}{1-V^n}$	n years
1	1.100000	1.000000	1.000000	.909091	.909091	1.100000	1
2	1.210000	2.100000	.476190	.826446	1.735537	.576190	2
3	1.331000	3.310000	.302115	.751315	2.486852	.402115	3
4	1.464100	4.641000	.215471	.683013	3.169865	.315471	4
5	1.610510	6.105100	.163797	.620921	3.790787	.263797	5
6	1.771561	7.715610	.129607	.564474	4.355261	.229607	6
7	1.948717	9.487171	.105405	.513158	4.868419	.205405	7
8	2.143589	11.435888	.087444	.466507	5.334926	.187444	8
9	2.357948	13.579477	.073641	.424098	5.759024	.173641	9
10	2.593742	15.937425	.062745	.385543	6.144567	.162745	10
11	2.853117	18.531167	.053963	.350494	6.495061	.153963	11
12	3.138428	21.384284	.046763	.318631	6.813692	.146763	12
13	3.452271	24.522712	.040779	.289664	7.103356	1.40779	13
14	3.797498	27.974983	.035746	.263331	7.366687	.135746	14
15	4.177248	31.772482	.031474	.239392	7.606080	.131474	15
16	4.594973	35.949730	.027817	.217629	7.823709	.127817	16
17	5.054470	40.544703	.024664	.197845	8.021553	.124664	17
18	5.559917	45.599173	.021930	.179859	8.201412	.121930	18
19	6.115509	51.159090	.019547	.163508	8.364920	.119547	19
20	6.727500	57.274999	.017460	.148644	8.513564	.117460	20
21	7.400250	64.002499	.015624	135131	8.648694	.115624	21
22	8.140275	71.402749	.014005	.122846	8.771540	.114005	22
23	8.954302	79.543024	.012572	.111678	8.883218	.112572	23
24	9.849733	88.497327	.011300	.101526	8.984744	.111300	24
25	10.834706	98.347059	.010168	.092296	9.077040	.110168	25
26	11.918177	109.181765	.009159	.083905	9.160945	.109159	26
27	13.109994	121.099942	.008258	.076278	9.237223	.108258	27
28	14.420994	134.209936	.007451	.069343	9.306567	.107451	28
29	15.863093	148.630930	.006728	.063039	9.369606	.106728	29
30	17.449402	164.494023	.006079	.057309	9.426914	.106079	30
31	19.194342	181.943425	.005496	.052099	9.479013	.105496	31
32	21.113777	201.137767	.004972	.047362	9.526376	.104972	32
33	23.225154	222.251544	.004499	.043057	9.569432	.104499	33
34	25.547670	245.476699	.004074	.039143	9.608575	.104074	34
35	28.102437	271.024368	.003690	.035584	9.644159	.103690	35
36	30.912681	299.126805	.003343	.032349	9.676508	.103343	36
37	34.003949	330.039486	.003030	.029408	9.705917	.103030	37
38	37.404343	364.043434	.002747	.026735	9.732651	.102747	38
39	41.144778	401.447778	.002491	.024304	9.756956	.102491	39
40	45.259256	442.592556	.002259	.022095	9.779051	.102259	40
41	49.785181	487.851811	.002050	.020086	9.799137	.102050	41
42	54.763699	537.636992	.001860	.018260	9.817397	.101860	42
43	60.240069	592.400692	.001688	.016600	9.833998	.101688	43
44	66.264076	652.640761	.001532	.015091	9.849089	.101532	44
45	72.890484	718.904837	.001391	.013719	9.862808	.101391	45
46	80.179532	791.795321	.001263	.012472	9.875280	.101263	46
47	88.197485	871.974853	.001147	.011338	9.886618	.101147	47
48	97.017234	960.172338	.001041	.010307	9.896926	.101041	48
49	106.718957	1057.189572	.000946	.009370	9.906296	.100946	49
50	117.390853	1163.908529	.000859	.008519	9.914814	.100859	50
51	129.129938	1281.299382	.000780	.007744	9.922559	.100780	51
52	142.042932	1410.429320	.000709	.007040	9.929599	.100709	52
53	156.247225	1552.472252	.000644	.006400	9.935999	.100644	53
54	171.871948	1708.719477	.000585	.005818	9.941817	.100585	54
55	189.059142	1880.591425	.000532	.005289	9.947106	.100532	55
56	207.965057	2069.650567	.000483	.004809	9.951915	.100483	56
57	228.761562	2277.615624	.000439	.004371	9.956286	.100439	57
58	251.637719	2506.377186	.000399	.003974	9.960260	.100399	58
59	276.801490	2758.014905	.000363	.003613	9.963873	.100363	59
60	304.481640	3034.816395	.000330	.003284	9.967157	.100330	60

of incomes to its present value. Discounting provides the mechanics of capitalization and accordingly is used by appraisers to calculate the present value of a projected income stream at a specified discount rate.

The last five functions are based on the first, which is the basic compound interest formula. The following paragraphs describe and illustrate each function. The examples use $1,000 as the base amount and the factors for fifteen years.

The factors are used for calculation when appraisers work with discounted cash flow, mortgage-equity capitalization, sinking fund and annuity (Inwood) capitalization methods, and the development of amortization schedules and mortgage constants.

The Future Worth of One   The first compound interest function (column 1 of table 3), the future worth of one (also called the compound amount of one or amount of one at compound interest), provides for the accumulation of annual interest payments on a single deposit or investment over a number of periods. The formula is

$$S^n = (1 + i)^n, \qquad (3)$$

where S_n is the amount after n periods, i is the effective rate of interest, and n is the number of periods.

The factors in column 1 may be applied to the amount invested to calculate its value after 15 years at 10 percent. For example, $1,000 at 10 percent interest compounded annually will grow in 15 years to $4,177.25 ($1,000 × 4.177248—see table 3). Figure 5 shows the growth of $1.00 reinvested with interest, and table 4 illustrates the growth of a $1.00 deposit that earns 10 percent compound interest for five years.

Table 4. $1.00 Deposit at 10 Percent for Five Years

Year		Compound interest
0	Deposit	$1.00
1	Interest earned	0.10
1	Balance, end of year	1.10
2	Interest earned	0.11
2	Balance, end of year	1.21
3	Interest earned	0.121
3	Balance, end of year	1.331
4	Interest earned	0.1331
4	Balance, end of year	1.4641
5	Interest earned	0.1464
5	Balance, end of year	$1.6105

Figure 5.   Compound Amount of $1.00

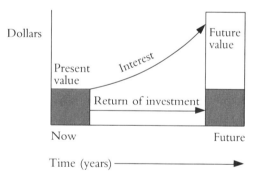

Although these examples use a compounding period of one year, compounding may occur per day, month, quarter, or other agreed-on period. Interest rates are usually stated at a nominal annual rate, but compounding increases the effective rate—the shorter the compounding period, the more the effective rate increases. The general formula is the same. At a 10 percent rate, daily compounding for a 360-day "year" would be determined by equation 3:

$$S^n = (1 + \frac{0.10}{360})^{360}$$

$$S^n = 1.105156$$

The Future Worth of One per Period

The second compound interest function (column 2 of table 3), the future worth of one per period (also called the compound amount or accumulation of one per period), shows the growth of a series of equal amounts deposited at the end of periodic intervals. It is the sum of the deposits plus accrued interest. For example, the factor of 31.772482 applied to $1,000 deposited or invested at the end of each year for 15 years shows that the $1,000 will grow in 15 years, at 10 percent interest compounded annually, to $31,772.48.

The future worth of one per period differs from the future worth of one in two ways. First, the accumulation factor is based on a series of deposits, rather than a single deposit. Second, deposits occur at the end of each period, not the beginning.

The formula for the second function is

$$S_n = \frac{S^n - 1}{i}, \qquad (4)$$

or

$$\frac{(1 + i)^n - 1}{i}, \qquad (5)$$

where S_n is the future worth of one per period and the other terms are as defined for equation 3.

Table 5 shows the annual interest earned and end-of-period balances of an accumulation of one per period at 10 percent interest for four periods. Figure 6 illustrates the accumulation graphically.

Table 5. Accumulation of $1.00 per Period at 10 Percent for Four Periods

End of period 1, initial deposit	$1.00
Interest, period 1	−0−
Balance, end of period 1	1.00
Interest, end of period 2	0.10
Deposit, end of period 2	1.00
Balance, end of period 2	2.10
Interest, end of period 3	0.21
Deposit, end of period 3	1.00
Balance, end of period 3	3.31
Interest, end of period 4	0.331
Deposit, end of period 4	1.00
Balance, end of period 4	$4.641

Figure 6. Accumulation of One per Period

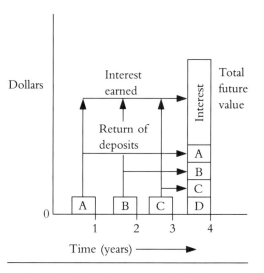

A, B, C, and D each represent $1.00 deposited at the end of a year. Each deposit earns compound interest from the date deposited until the date that a terminal amount is sought. The terminal value is the sum of all deposits plus compound interest.

The Sinking Fund Factor   The third compound interest function (column 3 of table 3), the sinking fund factor, shows the deposit required at the end of each period to accumulate a specific amount after a certain number of periods, assuming interest is earned on the deposits. For example, the factor of 0.031474 applied to a future worth of $1,000 shows that a deposit or investment of $31.47 at the end of each year, at 10 percent interest compounded annually, would grow to $1,000 in 15 years.

The formula for the sinking fund factor is

$$\frac{1}{S_n} = \frac{i}{S^n - 1}, \qquad (6)$$

or

$$\frac{i}{(1 + i)^n - 1}, \qquad (7)$$

where $1/S_n$ is the sinking fund factor and other terms are as defined for equation 3. Table 6 shows how four periodic deposits grow to $1.00 with interest. Figure 7 presents the growth of the deposits graphically.

Table 6.   Sinking Fund Factor to Reach $1.00 in Four Periods at 10 Percent

Deposit, end of period 1	0.215471
Interest for period 1	−0−
Balance, end of period 1	0.215471
Interest for period 2	0.021547
Deposit, end of period 2	0.215471
Balance, end of period 2	0.452489
Interest for period 3	0.045249
Deposit, end of period 3	0.215471
Balance, end of period 3	0.713209
Interest for period 4	0.071321
Deposit, end of period 4	0.215471
Balance, end of period 4	1.000000

Figure 7.   Sinking Fund factor

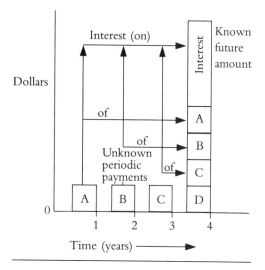

A, B, C, and D are equal amounts deposited at the end of each year. Each deposit earns compound interest for the period of time it remains on deposit. The sinking fund factor is computed such that the terminal value will always equal one (dollar).

The Present Worth of One   The fourth compound interest function (column 4 of table 3), the present worth of one (also called the reversion factor), shows the present worth of a single future amount to be received. Money has a time value; a dollar to be received in the future is worth less than a dollar now. The amount of discount depends on the length of time and the required discount rate. For example, the factor of 0.239392 shows that $1,000 to be received in 15 years has a present worth of $239.39, at 10 percent interest compounded annually.

Because the purpose of investing is to receive returns in the future, applying a present value (reversion) factor to anticipated future income is a crucial step in valuing an investment. When applying a present worth factor, the terms *discounting* and *discount rate* are used, as contrasted with *compounding* and *interest rate*, which are used in calculating the compound amounts of one.

The formula for the present worth of one (reversion) is

$$\frac{1}{S^n}, \tag{8}$$

or

$$V^n = \frac{1}{(1 + i)^n}, \tag{9}$$

where V is the present worth of one factor and other terms are as defined for equation 3.

Table 7 shows the present value of a reversion at 10 percent interest for four years. Figure 8 illustrates the present values graphically.

The Present Worth of One per Period

The fifth compound interest function (column 5 of table 3), present worth of one per period (also called the annuity factor or Inwood coefficient), shows the present worth of an annuity, that is, a series of equal payments (or receipts) beginning one period from the present. For example, the factor of 7.606080 shows that the present worth of such a series (an annuity) of $1,000 per year for 15 years, at 10 percent interest compounded annually, will be $7,606.08.

The formula for an annuity is

$$a_n = \frac{1 - \dfrac{1}{(1 + i)^n}}{i}, \tag{10}$$

or

$$\frac{1 - V^n}{i}, \tag{11}$$

where a_n is the present value of an annuity and other terms are as defined earlier. An annuity is also the summation of the present values of the individual reversions at the end of each period, which is:

$$a_n = \sum_{t=1}^{n} \frac{1}{(1 + i)^t}, \tag{12}$$

where t is the period and other terms are as defined earlier.

Table 8 shows the present value of an annuity each year for four years at 10 percent. Figure 9 provides an illustration.

Table 7.   Present Value of a $1.00 Reversion at 10 Percent for Four Years

Year	Compound amount	Reciprocal		Present value of $1.00 reversion
1	1.1	1/1.1	=	0.909091
2	1.21	1/1.21	=	0.826446
3	1.331	1/1.331	=	0.751315
4	1.4641	1/1.4641	=	0.683013

Figure 8.   Present Value of Reversion

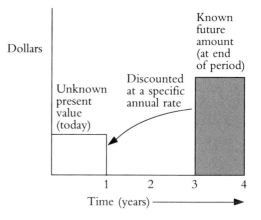

Partial Payment Factor The sixth compound interest function (column 6 of table 3), partial payment (also called the amortization or periodic repayment factor), shows the level periodic payment required to repay a loan at a specified interest rate over a given number of periods. For example, the factor of 0.131474 shows that the loan constant is 13.1474 percent and a loan of $1,000 would be fully amortized after 15 years, at 10 percent interest compounded annually, by annual payments of $131.47.

As interest rates increase or the amortization term shortens, the required periodic payment is increased. Conversely, lower interest rates and longer repayment periods reduce the required periodic payment. Each level payment in the partial payment factor is a blend of interest and a reduction of the original principal. The formula is

$$\frac{1}{a_n} = \frac{i}{1 - V^n}, \tag{13}$$

or

$$\frac{i}{1 - \dfrac{1}{(1 + i)^n}}, \tag{14}$$

where all terms are as defined earlier.

Table 9 shows that the partial payment factor is the reciprocal of the ordinary annuity factor. Figure 10 illustrates the distribution of periodic payments to interest and principal retirement.

Table 8. Present Value of an Annuity for Four Years at 10 Percent

Year	Present value of reversion	Present value of annuity
1	0.9091	0.9091
2	0.8264	1.7355
3	0.7513	2.4868
4	0.6830	3.1698

Figure 9. Present Value of Ordinary Annuity

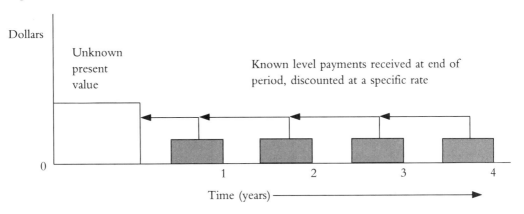

Factors from corresponding columns are reciprocals. In columns 1 and 4, for example, 1 divided by 4.177248 equals 0.239392, and 1 divided by 0.239392 equals 4.177248. In columns 2 and 3, 1 divided by 31.772482 equals 0.031474, and 1 divided by 0.031474 equals 31.772482. In columns 5 and 6, 1 divided by 7.606080 equals 0.131474, and 1 divided by 0.131474 equals 7.606080.

These reciprocal relationships will always hold for these pairs of functions, given the same interest rate and number of periods. In addition, the difference between the sinking

fund and partial payment factors will always be the interest rate, in this example 10 percent (0.031474 plus 0.100000 equals 0.131474).

Appraisers may need to use more than one compound interest function, even all six, for a single appraisal. The functions are programmed into financial calculators which are used for complex calculations. Printed tables are also available.

Development of Discount, Recapture, and Tax Rates

Discount Rate When yield methods are used, capitalization rates are usually developed by estimating discount, recapture, and effective property tax rates separately and then combining them. This combined rate, like the overall rate developed in direct capitalization, is valid to the extent that it reflects market activity.

The return *on* portion of the combined rate is called the discount rate. Although sometimes confused with the interest rate, which

Table 9.   Installment to Amortize One as Reciprocal of Present Value of Annuity for Four Years at 10 Percent

Year	Present value of annuity	Installment to amortize one
1	0.9091	1.10
2	1.7355	0.5762
3	2.4868	0.4021
4	3.1698	0.3155

Figure 10.   Installment to Amortize One

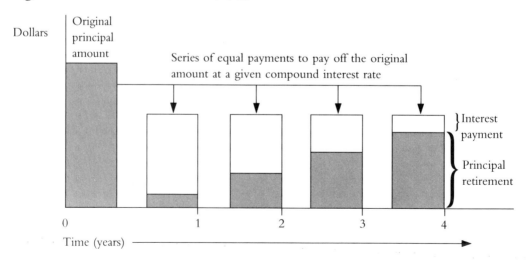

is the cost of borrowing money to finance an investment, the discount rate includes a yield rate (required rate of return on equity) as well. The interest rate is usually known, but the discount rate, because it includes yield, is an estimate, an anticipated return on investment. Build-up, band-of-investment, and market comparison methods are used to develop discount rates.

Build-up Method In the build-up (summation) method (described more fully in chapter 10), the discount rate has four components. It begins with a risk-free safe rate, the opportunity cost of capital if invested in a safe investment vehicle such as a government-insured passbook savings account. To the safe rate are added provisions for risk, lack of liquidity, and the cost of management.

Band-of-Investment Method In the band-of-investment method, interest and yield rates are weighted by the proportion each would contribute in typical financing and summed to form a discount rate. This rate is then used to estimate property value by capitalizing all net operating income.

For example, suppose that lenders usually lend 75 percent of the required purchase capital and seek a 10 percent rate of return on investment. Equity investors want a 12 percent return. The discount rate for the entire property would be 10.5 percent, as shown in table 10.

Market Comparison Method The market comparison method is the most accurate and acceptable method of developing a discount rate because it relies on the behavior of typical purchasers and sellers of income-producing properties, taking into account factors such as investment risk, location of

Table 10. Discount Rate for a Mortgaged Property

Source of funds	Portion of purchase capital		Discount rate on investment		Weighted rate
Mortgage	0.75	×	0.10	=	0.075
Equity	0.25	×	0.12	=	0.03
Discount rate (rate of return on investment) for entire property					0.105

Figure 11. Discount Rate Developed by the Market Comparison Method

Net operating income (NOI)	$15,000
Less income attributable to recapture	− 3,200 ($80,000 × 0.04)
Less income attributable to property taxes	− 2,000 ($100,000 × 0.02)
Equals discount income	$ 9,800

$9,800/$100,000 = 0.098, or 9.8 percent.

the property, and the quality and quantity of the estimated future income stream. Use of this method may be limited by lack of data, for example, sales prices and incomes of comparable properties, estimates of remaining economic life, and relevant improvement-to-land ratios. An example of the method is shown in figure 11.

In this example, the comparable property being analyzed for rate development sold for $100,000 with an estimated 4:1 improvement-to-land ratio, indicating an $80,000 value for the improvement. The estimated remaining economic life of the improvement was 25 years, indicating a recapture rate of 4 percent (assuming straight-line recapture—

discussed below). The effective tax rate was 2 percent. The annual net operating income was $15,000.

If income attributable to recapture and real estate taxes is subtracted from the stated net operating income, the income attributed solely to return on investment (discount) is $9,800. Dividing this income by the value of the property (sale price) results in a 9.8 percent discount rate.

Recapture Rate   A recapture rate is a measure of the annual amount needed to provide a return *of* the investment over the holding period. Income streams may increase faster than improvement value declines due to deterioration. However, the effects of inflation or deflation are reflected in the risk rate as a part of the discount rate and should not be included in the recapture rate except to the extent that the resale price is affected by the deterioration of improvements.

The three traditional methods of providing for recapture are straight-line, sinking-fund at a safe rate, and sinking-fund at the property's earnings rate (Inwood, level annuity, or graduated annuity method). Selection of a method depends on the shape and behavior of the estimated future income stream.

Some standard shapes and durations of income streams are

1. *Level perpetual series.* The owner expects equal periodic receipts, assumed to be perpetual.
2. *Level terminal series.* The owner expects equal periodic receipts that will stop at the end of a lease, at which time the owner plans to sell the property.
3. *Declining terminal series.* The owner of improved property expects declining periodic receipts, terminating at the end of the lease or when the improvement has no remaining economic life.
4. *Increasing series.* The owner expects increasing periodic receipts, at least for the short term.
5. *Single future-income payment (reversion).* An investor may buy property to hold, hoping for appreciation and profit from a single future-income payment upon resale.

The expectation of a level or declining income stream is influenced by economic conditions, the type of property, the financial strength of the tenant, and the terms and length of the lease. Combinations of income streams and reversions may be expected. For example, a property under a fixed lease to a good tenant would be expected to produce a level terminal series of receipts (2 above) and a single future-income payment at the end of the lease period (5). This kind of income would probably call for the annuity capitalization method and the land, building, or property residual techniques. Other examples would be the combination of (3) and (5) or (4) and (5). Figure 12 shows the shape and duration of level and declining income streams with the corresponding appropriate capitalization methods.

The straight-line, sinking fund, and annuity capitalization methods give different values for the property. The straight-line method gives the lowest value, the sinking-fund method gives a middle value, and the annuity method gives the highest value. Figure 13 summarizes the behavior of the income stream with respect to income, discounting, and recapture, together with assumptions made in the straight-line, sinking-fund, and annuity methods.

Figure 12. Shape and Duration of the Income Stream

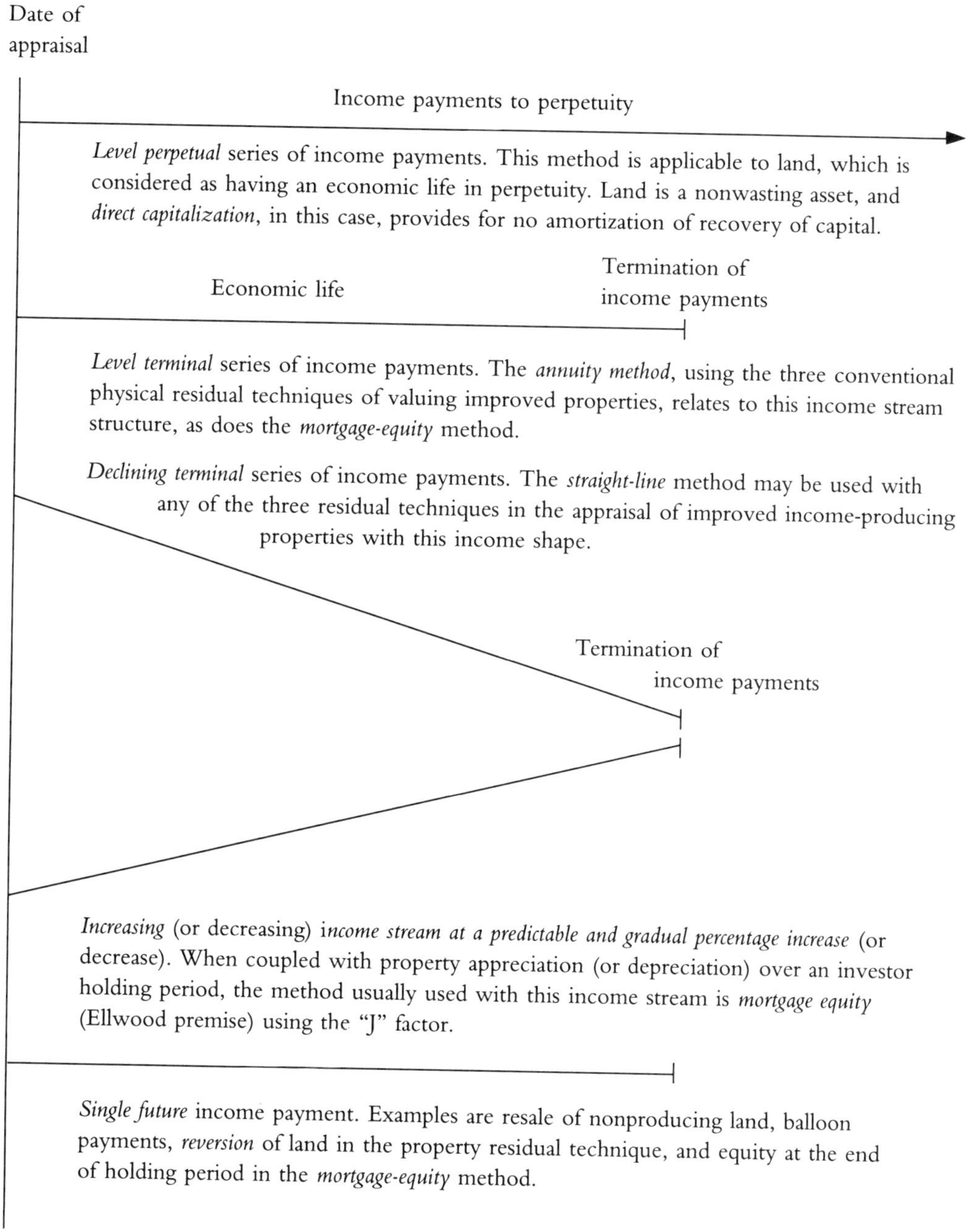

Date of
appraisal

Income payments to perpetuity

Level perpetual series of income payments. This method is applicable to land, which is considered as having an economic life in perpetuity. Land is a nonwasting asset, and *direct capitalization*, in this case, provides for no amortization of recovery of capital.

Economic life

Termination of
income payments

Level terminal series of income payments. The *annuity method,* using the three conventional physical residual techniques of valuing improved properties, relates to this income stream structure, as does the *mortgage-equity* method.

Declining terminal series of income payments. The *straight-line* method may be used with any of the three residual techniques in the appraisal of improved income-producing properties with this income shape.

Termination of
income payments

Increasing (or decreasing) *income stream at a predictable and gradual percentage increase* (or decrease). When coupled with property appreciation (or depreciation) over an investor holding period, the method usually used with this income stream is *mortgage equity* (Ellwood premise) using the "J" factor.

Single future income payment. Examples are resale of nonproducing land, balloon payments, *reversion* of land in the property residual technique, and equity at the end of holding period in the *mortgage-equity* method.

Figure 13. Income Stream Behavior and the Selection of Capitalization Methods

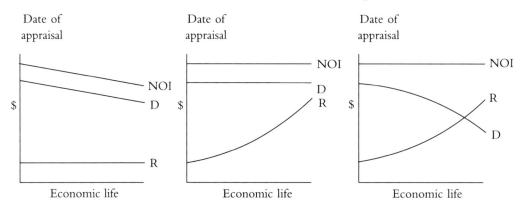

Straight-Line	Sinking-Fund	Annuity
1. Net operating income (NOI) decreases as property age increases.	1. Net operating income remains constant over time.	1. Net operating ncome remains constant over time.
2. Recapture (R) is received in equal amounts during the economic life of the improvement.	2. Recapture is invested at a safe rate in a sinking fund.	2. Discount is based on remaining life of improvement and decreases over time.
3. Discount (D) is received on the balance of the investment.	3. Discount is received in equal amounts each year on the total original investment in the depreciating asset.	3. Recapture increases by the amount that discount decreases.

Straight-line Method   Straight-line recapture assumes a declining income stream that provides an equal amount of recapture for each year of the property's economic life. Straight-line recapture is simply computed as the reciprocal of the remaining economic life. For example, if the property has an estimated remaining economic life of twenty years, the recapture rate is 5 percent per year (100 percent divided by twenty years). That is, a part of the net operating income received each year should be considered as a return of asset cost, not as earnings from the property, in this example 5 percent of the asset value.

If net operating income is expected to decline steadily, capitalization using straight-line recapture can be appropriate.

Straight-line recapture is appropriate if the following conditions are met: financially, the tenant is ranked average or weak; the lease is month-to-month or short-term; and the income is likely to decline steadily over the remaining economic life of the improvement.

Sinking Fund Method   Sinking fund recapture at a safe rate is used principally in accounting and is not usually appropriate in appraisal for ad valorem tax purposes, except when mineral rights and regulated industries are being valued. Sinking-fund recapture should be used when the income is constant and level, the recapture is invested at a safe rate in an interest-bearing account, and discount (return on) is received each year on the total original investment in the depreciating asset.

In sinking fund recapture, the portion of net operating income that is considered recovery of capital is, in theory, invested to replace the asset at the end of its economic life. The amount saved each year is placed in a hypothetical account to earn interest at a low, safe rate—say, 5 percent. These earnings reduce the annual recapture provision as compared with straight-line recapture. For an asset with a twenty-year economic useful life, the annual recapture rate is 2.18 percent at an 8 percent interest rate, compared with 5 percent at straight-line recapture. The 2.18 percent figure is the sinking fund factor at 8 percent for twenty years.

Annuity Method   Recapture at the investment earnings (discount) rate is called the annuity or Inwood method. The recapture rate component of the capitalization rate is the sinking-fund factor at the same discount rate as the investment. A portion of the income stream represents earnings, a return *on* investment. The balance of the income stream represents recapture, a return *of* investment. In the case of 100 percent capital depreciation, the recapture portion of income will grow to exactly the same amount as the initial principal; thus, the entire original capital is recovered.

For example, a property with a twenty-year economic life is sold for $200,000, with the expectation of a 10 percent net rate of re-

turn on the investment, after recapture. Using the annuity, or Inwood, method, the sinking-fund factor for twenty years at 10 percent is 0.017460 (approximately 1.75 percent), and the combined discount and recapture rates therefore equal 11.75 percent. The annual income stream is expected to be $23,500 ($200,000 × 0.1175) throughout the life of the investment. The discount portion of this $23,500 will decrease every year in proportion to the decreasing value of the improvements. The recapture portion is expected to increase accordingly (see figure 13) because of the consistent $23,500 income stream (see table 11).

Annuity recapture assumes that the investor discounts or values all income equally rather than arbitrarily distinguishing between income attributable to return *on* and return *of* investment and discounting them at different rates. The annuity recapture method is appropriate if the following conditions are met: the property is in a stable or prime location; the improvements are modern and appropriate; the property is leased at market rent; and the tenant is financially sound. If increasing income is expected, the income stream can be converted to a stabilized level equivalent. See *Improving Real Property Assessment* (IAAO 1978, section 8.8).

Partial Recapture   When an investment is partially wasting, but less than a 100 percent decline in value is expected, the recapture rate should be a fraction of the 100 percent rate. This allows a fraction of the capital to be recovered from resale instead of from current income.

For example, when straight-line recapture is used, an asset that is expected to be resold after ten years for 50 percent of its current

Table 11.   Inwood Method for First Five Years of Investment

Year	Income at 11.75 percent	Discount (return on) at 10 percent	Recapture (return of) at 1.75 percent	Remaining building investment
0	—	—	—	$200,000
1	$23,500	$20,000	$3,500	196,500
2	23,500	19,650	3,850	192,650
3	23,500	19,265	4,235	188,415
4	23,500	18,842	4,658	183,757
5	23,500	18,376	5,124	178,633

value would have 5 percent of its annual income as a recapture rate. The 5 percent for recapture plus a 10 percent earnings rate equals an income capitalization rate of 15 percent.

Annuity recapture with a 50 percent forecast decline in value at a 10 percent discount rate would give a capitalization rate as follows (the sinking fund factor is 0.0627): The recapture rate is 0.0314 (50 percent × 0.0627). The discount rate plus the recapture rate gives a capitalization rate of 0.1314 (0.1000 + 0.0314). The asset would be valued by dividing net operating income by 0.1314 and adding the present value of the reversion.

Component Separation   Another approach to partial recapture is available through the separation of the components that represent different investments. For example, suppose an investor pays $2,000 for land and improvements combined, expecting a 10 percent rate of return. The appraisal report estimates the market value of the land alone to be $1,000; the improvements alone are worth $1,000, with a twenty-year life, after which they will be worthless. Income attributable to the improvements will gradually decline, but the land value and income

to the land will remain level in perpetuity. Therefore, the recapture component for the improvements is 50 percent of the total investment. Considering a 5 percent recapture rate (twenty-year straight-line), this amounts to a 2.5 percent rate of recapture for the total investment. The capitalization rate for the property is, therefore, 12.5 percent.

The composition of this rate, with separate weighted rates for land and improvements, is shown in figure 14.

Forecast Appreciation in Capital Value
Some investments are expected to appreciate in value. The purchaser anticipates future growth in income and value. So does the seller, who may negotiate a price that reflects a premium over the property's value based on its current income.

Given the expectation of appreciation, it is defensible to subtract a provision for future capital gain from the discount rate to derive a rate to capitalize current income. For example, assume a 12 percent rate of return is desired. Current income is level at $100 per year. The investment is expected to increase in value by 30 percent over the next four years. The capitalization rate is computed as shown in figure 15.

Figure 14. Developing a Capitalization Rate by Separation of Components

Building

Return on investment: 50 percent of total investment at 10 percent discount rate		0.05
Return of investment: 50 percent of total investment (over 20 years)	+	0.025

Land:

Return on investment: 50 percent of total investment at 10 percent discount rate	+	0.05
Return of investment (not applicable)	+	0.00
Capitalization rate		0.125 = 12.5 percent

Figure 15. Computing a Capitalization Rate from Deferred Returns

Discount rate desired (12 percent)	0.1200
Less deferred return (appreciation) of 0.30 × 0.2090 (0.2090 is the sinking fund factor for four years at 12 percent):	− 0.0627
Capitalization rate	0.0573

Therefore, the current value of the asset is $100 divided by 0.0573:

$$\text{Value} = \$100/0.0573 = \$1,745$$

Effective Tax Rate Because any deduction from gross income affects value in the income approach, only typical and reasonable expenses can be deducted in calculating net operating income. When property is valued for ad valorem tax purposes, therefore, property taxes cannot be shown as an operating expense because the actual taxes are not known as of the assessment date. Indeed, the appraisal is often done to estimate the amount of tax. The problem can be resolved by developing an effective tax rate and including it in the capitalization rate for the subject property.

Assessors should know the effective tax rates of their jurisdictions. This effective tax rate, when developed, becomes part of the capitalization rate applied to income produced by the entire property because both land and improvements are subject to property taxes.

Tax rates may be expressed as dollars per hundred or dollars per thousand of assessed valuation. Many jurisdictions express the rate in mills, that is, one-thousandth part of one dollar. A tax rate of $20 per $1,000 of value is 20 mills per dollar, or 2 percent.

Where fractional assessments are used, often mandated by law, the actual and effective rates will differ. If the assessment ratio (level) is 60 percent, and the actual tax rate is $3 per $100 ($30 per $1,000, or 30 mills per $1), the effective tax rate is calculated as 0.60 times 0.030 equals $0.018, or 1.8 percent of value.

Discounted Cash Flow Analysis

Discounted cash flow analysis is the method of estimating present values of income streams by applying a present-value factor to the individual dollar amounts of cash flow expected for each period. An example for a level net operating income stream of $10,000 per year for five years, followed by a sale of the property for $150,000 at the end of the fifth year, is shown in table 12. A 12 percent discount rate is used.

Table 12. Discounted Cash Flow Techniques

Year	Net operating income		Present-value factor at 12 percent		Amount at present value
1	$10,000	×	0.8929	=	$ 8,929
2	10,000	×	0.7972	=	7,972
3	10,000	×	0.7118	=	7,118
4	10,000	×	0.6355	=	6,355
5	10,000	×	0.5674	=	5,674
	Subtotal				$ 36,048
	Resale				
5	$150,000	×	0.5674	=	85,114
	Total				$121,162

Although a level income stream was used for simplicity, the reader should observe that any amount of net operating income could have been included for any year. When expected net operating income is level each year at $10,000, one year's income can be multiplied by the annuity, or present worth of one, factor, 3.6048, to provide exactly the same result, $36,048. An alternative is to divide the annual net income by the partial payment factor, 0.2774, which gives precisely the same result.

Annuity Capitalization An annuity is a series of equal amounts of income, paid or received at equal intervals over a period of time. For example, the five-year income stream shown in table 12 is an annuity of $10,000 per year (the $150,000 resale proceeds in table 12 are a reversionary value, not part of the annuity income).

Dividing the annuity factor of 3.6048 into 1 provides an annuity capitalization rate of 0.2774. That rate, when divided into the

$10,000 of periodic income, results in the lump-sum value of $36,048.

The 0.2774 annuity capitalization rate has two components: a discount rate of 0.12 and a recapture rate of 0.1574. The 12 percent discount rate provides spendable income on the asset balance, and the 15.74 percent for recapture allows the investment cost to be recouped in five years. Recapturing 15.74 percent for five years would result in 78.7 percent of the asset being recovered (5 × 15.74 percent = 78.7 percent), but, with compound interest on the amount recovered, the total is 100 percent. Note that the 0.1574 is the sinking fund factor at 12 percent interest at year five.

Split Rates for Uncertainty of Income In single-property appraisal, adjustments may be made in the discount rate to accommodate the riskiness of the income stream. For example, suppose that the net operating income is provided by two sources, base rent and percentage overages. The base rent, amounting to $7,000 per year, can be counted as safe, reliable income and only a 10 percent discount rate may be appropriate. Percentage overages, estimated at $3,000 per year, depend on tenant sales, which are uncertain. The greater uncertainty may justify a 15 percent rate. Table 13 offers detail. Although the present value of $36,592 in this table is little different from the $36,048 in table 11 (where 12 percent is applied to the entire net operating income), the example demonstrates the use of split rates to adjust for different levels of risk from income generated by one property.

Split Rates for Timing Differences of Income Discount rates may also be modified for timing differentials. Income expected

Table 13.   Different Yield Rates Applied to Base Rent and Percentage Rent

Year	Net operating income		Present-value factor		Amount at present value
	Base rent		at 10 percent		
1	$7,000	×	0.9091	=	$ 6,364
2	7,000	×	0.8264	=	5,785
3	7,000	×	0.7513	=	5,259
4	7,000	×	0.6830	=	4,781
5	7,000	×	0.6209	=	4,346
	Percentage rent		at 15 percent		
1	3,000	×	0.8696	=	$ 2,609
2	3,000	×	0.7561	=	2,268
3	3,000	×	0.6575	=	1,973
4	3,000	×	0.5718	=	1,715
5	3,000	×	0.4972	=	1,492
	Total				$36,592

Table 14.   Different Yield Rates Applied to Different Years of Holding Period

Year	Net operating income		Present-value factor		Amount at present value
			at 10 percent		
1	$ 10,000	×	0.9091	=	$ 9,091
2	10,000	×	0.8264	=	8,264
3	10,000	×	0.7513	=	7,513
			at 15 percent		
4	10,000	×	0.5718	=	$ 5,718
5	10,000	×	0.4972	=	4,972
	Subtotal				$ 35,558
	Resale				
5	150,000	×	0.4972	=	74,577
	Total				$110,134

in the next year could be discounted at a lower rate than income in the distant future, even if the credit risk is impeccable. This is consistent with the yield curve for government securities, in which rates on near-term securities are sometimes 2 percentage points below long-term rates.

In addition, the credit risk may be different; for example, if an improvement is leased for three years to a creditworthy tenant, a low discount rate may be applied to that term. However, a higher rate might be applied to income for the balance of the projection period and to the resale proceeds. This is shown in table 14.

Net Present Value and Internal Rates of Return

Net Present Value   Net present value (NPV) is a method of determining the feasibility of investments. In the NPV technique, the analyst discounts all of the forecast cash inflows and outflows to a present value at a specified rate. If the net result is negative, then the specified rate is not forecast to be achieved and the proposed investment is not considered. If the NPV is positive, the proposed investment can be considered.

For example, in table 11 a 12 percent rate was selected, and the present value of all income, including proceeds from resale, was $121,162. From that, the present value of the investment is subtracted. If the investment cost were $125,000, payable at the beginning of the investment, the NPV would be −$3,838. Thus, the price is higher than one that would offer a 12 percent rate of return.

Selection of the rate for discounting forecast inflows and outflows is crucial to the analysis. In the example, 12 percent was somewhat arbitrarily selected. Had a lower rate been selected, the NPV would have been positive. Therefore, the rate must be chosen carefully. It should approximate rates offered on alternative investments that are perceived to bear equal risk and allow for differences in liquidity and investment management in the subject investment.

Internal Rate of Return The internal rate of return (IRR) technique seeks the required rate of return (discount rate) on the subject property. It is the rate at which the cash inflows and outflows are exactly equal. The IRR is thus used as a measuring device to compare various investment proposals.

Solving for the IRR is a trial-and-error process, one that computers and financial calculators have made much easier. In the net present value example above, the 12 percent rate that was specified resulted in a present value of outflows that exceeded inflows at a $125,000 investment cost. The greater the rate used, the lower the present value of inflows. (The present value of outflows in the example is unaffected by the rate selected because all outflows occurred at the inception of the investment and, therefore, were not discounted.) The IRR for the subject property is, therefore, below 12 percent and can be determined through trial and error.

Table 15 tests 11 percent as the internal rate of return. The net present value is $977, indicating that the IRR is above 11 percent.

Table 16 offers a trial at 11.2 percent. The net present value is a mere −$6, indicating it is very close to the IRR. A solution resulting in zero would be the exact IRR; for this purpose, 11.2 percent is an adequate approximation.

Net Present Value vs. Internal Rate of Return The NPV technique seeks the difference between the present value of cash

Table 15.   Internal Rate of Return Trial at 11.0 Percent Yield Rate

Year	Cash flow		Present-value factor at 11 percent		Amount at present value
0	($125,000)	×	1.000	=	($125,000)
1	10,000	×	0.9009	=	$9,009
2	10,000	×	0.8116	=	8,116
3	10,000	×	0.7312	=	7,312
4	10,000	×	0.6587	=	6,587
5	10,000	×	0.5935	=	5,935
	Resale				
5	$150,000	×	0.5935	=	$89,018
	Net present value				$977

Table 16.   Internal Rate of Return Trial at 11.2 Percent Yield Rate

Year	Cash flow		Present-value factor at 11.2 percent		Amount at present value
0	($125,000)	×	1.000	=	($125,000)
1	10,000	×	0.8993	=	$8,993
2	10,000	×	0.8087	=	8,087
3	10,000	×	0.7273	=	7,273
4	10,000	×	0.6540	=	6,540
5	10,000	×	0.5881	=	5,881
	Resale				
5	$150,000	×	0.5881	=	$88,220
	Net present value				($6)

inflows and outflows at a specified rate, whereas the IRR is the rate at which inflows and outflows are equal. From a theoretical standpoint, the NPV is preferable because it includes an inherent assumption that the earnings rate on capital recovery occurs at the selected rate, whereas the IRR implicitly assumes reinvestment at its rate. Because an appraiser cannot determine that the IRR's reinvestment rate will be achieved, the bias is a drawback. Further, the IRR technique will produce more than one mathematically correct rate for each year in which inflows alternate with outflows. In the NPV technique, the appraiser introduces bias by specifying a rate, whereas the IRR technique has inherent biases.

Modified Internal Rate   A modified internal rate of return (MIR) is sometimes used to avoid the assumption of reinvestment at the IRR. The MIR technique is most frequently used when the investment outflow is to occur over multiple periods.

For example, in a purchase in which equity must be contributed in two installments, the IRR technique assumes that the second installment, while waiting to be invested, can earn interest at the same rate as the IRR. This assumption is erroneous because the investor must keep the money adequately liquid in a relatively risk-free investment medium. The MIR allows the assumption that the second installment will earn at a lower rate while waiting to be invested. If the appropriate rate of earnings is 5 percent after taxes, then the outflows would be discounted at that rate.

Financial Management Rate of Return   The financial management rate of return (FMRR) is an attempt to improve further on the IRR. Applying the FMRR requires the analyst to specify two rates: a safe, liquid, after-tax rate, and a "run-of-the-mill" after-tax rate. The safe, liquid rate is one that can be earned on short-term investments such as tax-free obligations that mature within one year. It is applied to investment outflows that are forecast to be incurred after the initial investment. Those outflows are generally discounted to a lump sum at the start of year 1 (or end of year 0). In this respect, it is similar to the MIR. Under some conditions, cash outflows that are expected to occur during the holding period may be discounted using the safe, liquid rate.

Generally, cash inflows are compounded forward at a run-of-the-mill rate to a terminal value at the forecast resale point. The run-of-the-mill rate is an after-tax rate of return that could be earned on other investments available during the holding period.

The effective lump-sum investment at the start of year 1 is then compared to the lump-sum terminal value to derive a rate of return, using the IRR method for two lump sums (from column 1 of the compound interest tables). The result is the FMRR.

Mortgage-Equity Techniques

Real estate bought for its income-producing capability is usually acquired by an investor with the aid of mortgage financing. Thus, two investments are involved: equity and mortgage. The two assume different risks and expect different returns. The mortgage-equity technique, therefore, separates mortgage and equity components on the basis of typical loan-to-value ratios.

To simplify the presentation, this analysis considers a conventional fixed-rate, fixed-payment, self-amortizing mortgage loan. The lender receives level monthly payments until full amortization or early retirement (prepayment). The property is collateral for the loan, allowing the lender to foreclose upon default. In contrast, the equity investor's return is variable, depending on rent, occupancy, and operating expense levels. In addition to cash flow, the investor may receive proceeds from resale.

Conventional Mortgage-Equity Technique This technique assumes current market finance rates for the mortgage and typically requires the appraiser to know all the mortgage terms available for the property (interest rate, amortization term) with either a loan-to-value ratio or a mortgage principal amount selected. From the interest rate and amortization term, a constant payment can be computed. An equity yield rate appropriate for the subject property, so financed, is carefully selected by the appraiser. The estimated cash flow expected to be received by the equity investor (net operating income less debt service) and proceeds from resale (net selling price less unpaid mortgage) are valued at that equity yield rate, given a certain holding period. The result is the present value of equity (V_E), which, when added to the mortgage balance, (V_M), is the estimated property value or overall value (V_O).

$$V_O = V_M + V_E. \qquad (15)$$

EXAMPLE The property generates level net operating income of $10,000 per year. An equity investor can arrange an $80,000 loan at 10 percent interest that requires payments of $727 per month over twenty-five years for full amortization. Mortgage payments total $8,724 in a year.

Prospects for property appreciation are excellent. The appraiser expects that the property can be resold in five years for $150,000. Amortization will have reduced the mortgage balance to $75,331 by that time. Equity investors seek a 15 percent yield rate.

Table 17 offers year-by-year detail of net operating income, debt service, cash flow, present-value factors, and the amount at present value. Annual cash flow is $1,276, which is worth $4,277 when discounted to a present value at the 15 percent equity yield rate. Proceeds from expected resale in five years are $74,669, which has a present value of $37,124. Therefore, an equity investment of $41,401 ($4,277 + $37,124) provides a 15 percent equity yield rate if these assumptions are proven. An investor is justified in paying that equity amount above the $80,000 mortgage considered, or a value of $121,401. The amount may be rounded to $121,000 or $121,500 to avoid a false impression of exactness.

The mortgage equity technique is flexible and can be applied with various mortgage amounts and resale price expectations, as shown in equations 16 and 17. The V_E term in equation 15 can be replaced by:

$$V_E = \text{present worth of cash flow} + \text{present worth of reversion}, \quad (16)$$

or

$$
\begin{aligned}
V_E = (NOI - DS) &\times \text{annuity factor} \\
&+ \text{present worth of reversion factor} \\
&\times (\text{value realized at resale} \\
&- \text{mortgage at resale}), \qquad (17)
\end{aligned}
$$

where NOI is net operating income and DS is debt service.

Ellwood Technique The Ellwood technique, when properly applied, offers results that are precisely identical to those of the conventional technique. The late L. W. ("Pete") Ellwood created tables that offer an overall

Table 17. Conventional Mortgage-Equity Technique

Year	Net operating income	Debt service	Cash flow to equity	Present-value factor at 15 percent	Amount at present value
0					
1	$ 10,000	$ 8,724	$ 1,276	0.8696	1,110
2	10,000	8,724	1,276	0.7561	965
3	10,000	8,724	1,276	0.6575	839
4	10,000	8,724	1,276	0.5718	729
5	10,000	8.724	1,276	0.4972	634
					$ 4,277
	Sale				
5	150,000	75,331	74,669	0.4972	37,124

Present value of equity at 15 percent yield rate	$ 41,401
Add present mortgage balance	80,000
Property value estimate	$121,401

capitalization rate (R_O) figure, thus making the math required by conventional cash flow analysis unnecessary. Ellwood's overall rate can be adjusted for expected value change by adding to the basic capitalization rate the sinking fund factor at the equity yield rate multiplied by the expected value decline (or subtracting an expected value increase).

Ellwood's C table is general, usable for any loan-to-value ratio. The formula is

$$R = Y - mC + dep\,(SFF) - app\,(SFF), \quad (18)$$

where R is the overall capitalization rate, Y is the equity yield rate, m is the loan-to-value ratio, C is the factor from the C table (mortgage coefficient), dep is the fractional decline in value of property over the holding period, app is the fractional increase in value of property over the holding period, and SFF is the sinking fund factor at the equity yield rate.

In the example in figure 16, which substitutes data from table 15 in equation 18, the result is within $50 of the conventional technique, an insignificant difference attributable mainly to rounding.

Figure 16. Application of Ellwood Technique

$C = 0.049610$ from C table
$dep = (150{,}000 - 121{,}400)/121{,}400 = 0.2355$
$R = 0.15 - 0.66\,(0.049610)$
$\quad - 0.2355\,(0.148315)$
$R = 0.15 - 0.0327 - 0.0349$
$R = 0.0824$
$V = \dfrac{I}{R}$
$V = \dfrac{\$10{,}000}{0.0824}$
$V = \$121{,}359$

dep is the fractional decline in value of the property over the holding period.

Ellwood's formula can allow for either the loan-to-value ratio or the actual mortgage balance and value of property. When the mortgage balance and property value are known, Ellwood's *m* becomes the mortgage principal amount divided by *V*.

Similarly, when the resale price is known, the fractional change in value can be expressed as a fraction, or

$$dep/app = \frac{RP - V}{V}, \qquad (19)$$

where *RP* is the resale price. Although not usable for ad valorem appraisal (because the value of the property is presumed known), this alternative formulation can be useful in investment analysis.

Residual Capitalization Techniques

Residual capitalization techniques separate the property into two components, the value of one of which is presumed known. Net operating income attributable to the known component is estimated and subtracted from total net operating income to obtain the residual income attributable to the other component. The three primary residual techniques used in ad valorem appraisal are the land, building, and property residual techniques.

Land Residual Technique

The land residual technique is useful when improvements are appropriate to the highest and best use of the property, are relatively new, and have no observed depreciation of any type, so that their value can be closely estimated. For example, suppose recently

constructed real estate improvements cost $1 million and have a fifty-year useful economic life. The appropriate discount rate is 10 percent because that rate is competitive with other investment opportunities perceived to have equal risk. The effective tax rate is 2 percent. For simplicity, assume that straight-line recapture is considered appropriate for the improvements; thus the annual recapture rate is 2 percent (100 percent divided by fifty years). The capitalization rate for the improvements is, therefore, 14 percent. Annual net operating income for the first year is estimated to be $150,000. The improvements require a 14 percent return on $1 million of cost, or $140,000 in income. Subtracting this amount from the $150,000 net operating income leaves $10,000 residual income for the land. That amount, capitalized in perpetuity at 12 percent, gives a land value of $83,300. Capitalization of land income in perpetuity is appropriate because land does not wear out. This example is summarized in figure 17.

Figure 17. Land Residual Technique— Straight-Line Recapture for Buildings

Net operating income (first year)		$150,000
Less income attributable to improvements (0.14 × $1,000,000)		140,000
Discount	10%	
Recapture	2%	
Real estate taxes	2%	
	14%	
Residual income to land		$ 10,000
Capitalized at 12% (10% discount + 2% taxes) = (rounded)		83,300
Plus value of the building		$1,000,000
Total property value		$1,083,300

Straight-line recapture (figure 17) assumes that income attributable to the improvement systematically declines with time. If, instead, the income to the improvement was projected to be level for fifty years, an annuity recapture rate would be appropriate. The capitalization method should match the income forecast. Unless income stream assumptions and capitalization rates are matched, values will be invalid. Diagrams of income to improvements and to land under two different recapture assumptions are shown in figures 18 and 19, demonstrating how such assumptions influence residual income and value.

Another use of the land residual technique is in estimating the highest and best use of land. Costs of different proposed improve-

ments, and the net operating income for each, can be estimated. A capitalization rate is multiplied by the estimated improvement cost and the result subtracted from forecast net operating income. The result is forecast land income. Whichever type or level of improvement offers the highest residual income to land is the highest and best use of the land, subject to legal and physical constraints.

Building Residual Technique

The building residual technique assumes that the value of the land is known, so that income attributable to it can be estimated and subtracted from total net operating income to obtain residual income to the building, which is then capitalized at the appropriate building capitalization rate. Total property value is obtained by adding the estimated land and building values. The technique is appropriate when land value can be estimated reliably.

Figure 18. Land Residual with Straight-Line Building Capital Recovery

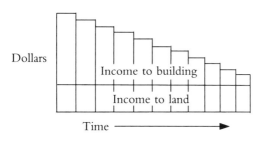

Figure 19. Land Residual with Annuity Building Capital Recovery

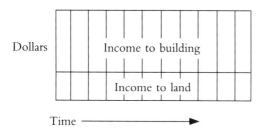

As an example of the building residual technique, suppose that the land value is estimated at $250,000 through a careful analysis of several recent sales of comparable vacant tracts in the area (figure 20). Annual net operating income is $150,000 and is projected to remain constant. The appropriate discount rate is 10 percent, and the improvements are estimated to have a remaining economic life of fifty years. The effective tax rate is 2 percent. Thus the land capitalization rate is 0.12 (discount rate plus effective tax rate). Income attributable to the land is thus $30,000 ($250,000 × 0.12), and residual income attributable to the building is $120,000. The appropriate building capitalization rate is 0.120859 (partial payment factor at 10 percent for 50 years of 0.100859 plus the effective tax rate of 2 percent). The building value is therefore estimated at $992,893 ($120,000 divided by 0.120859), giving an estimated total value of $1,242,893, as shown in figure 20 (sinking fund recapture is used).

Figure 20.   Residual Capitalization Technique

Net operating income	$150,000
Less income attributable to land	
(0.12 × $250,000)	− 30,000
(10% discount + 2% taxes)	
Residual income to	
improvements	$120,000
Building capitalization rate	
0.120859 (0.100859 + 0.02)	
Capitalized building value	$992,893
Land value	+250,000
Total property value by	
residual technique	$1,242,893

Property Residual Technique

In the property residual technique, the value of the property at the end of its remaining economic life or investment holding period is projected and discounted to present value. The income stream is capitalized over this period and added to the present value of the reversion to estimate total property value. This avoids the difficult step of separating the income stream between land and buildings. The technique is appropriate when the income stream can be projected with reasonable certainty. Misjudging the resale value usually will not seriously affect the result when it is many years away (and, thus, has little present value).

As an example, assume that a property has an annual net operating income of $350,000 expected to continue for twenty years. It is projected that the building will have no value at that time but that the land will be worth $2,000,000. The required rate of return (discount rate) is 11.25 percent, and the effective tax rate is 2 percent. The indicated value of the income stream is $350,000 divided by 0.147634 (partial payment factor at 0.1125 for twenty years plus 2 percent effective tax rate), or $2,370,728. The present value of the reversion is $2,000,000 times 0.118577 (present worth of one at 0.1125 in twenty years) or $237,154. Adding the two components together gives a total value of $2,607,882 ($2,370,727 plus $237,154).

The value of the reversion can also be estimated as a percentage of present value. Assume, for example, that net operating income is estimated to remain stable at $500,000 over a remaining economic life of fifteen years. It is estimated that the land is 25 percent of the total present value and will increase in value by 50 percent over the remaining economic life of the improvement. The discount rate is 10 percent and the effective tax rate is 1.5 percent, giving a capitalization rate of 0.131474 (partial payment factor at 10 percent for fifteen years) plus the effective tax rate, or 0.146474. Therefore the income stream has a present value of $3,413,575 ($500,000 divided by 0.146474). The value (V) of the property, including the reversion, can now be found as follows:

$$V = \$3,413,575 + 0.25V \times 1.50 \times 0.2394,$$

where 0.2394 is the present worth of one in fifteen years at 10 percent.

$$V = \$3,413,575 + 0.0898V$$
$$0.9102V = \$3,413,575$$
$$V = \$3,413,575/0.9102 = \$3,750,357.$$

The present value of the reversion is $336,782 ($3,750,357 less $3,413,575), or 9 percent of the total present value.

Income Tax Considerations

Mortgage-equity analysis and the other techniques noted above consider cash flow, resale price, and mortgage amortization. They do not, however, reflect any income tax effects of real estate ownership. Most investors look to after-tax income to evaluate their rate of return, their main concern being how much they get to spend from their investment. However, the income tax is subject to political and economic shifts in policy that affect real estate investors.

The United States Internal Revenue Code allows a deduction from rental income for ordinary and necessary business expenses. Interest on a business loan is deductible, but retirement of principal is not. A reserve for replacements is not deductible, but depreciation is. These are the major items that distinguish taxable income from cash flow for real estate.

Depreciation accounting for income tax purposes does not involve a cash expense. Rapid depreciation allowances generate high tax deductions. The depreciable basis is one's cost, excluding land, which does not wear out. The depreciable amount is allocated over a period of time at a rate allowed by the Internal Revenue Code. At one time, the life and rate allowed were an approximation of the estimated useful life of the property. Since 1981, however, Congress has manipulated the life and rate without regard to actual or estimated property lives. For example, in the first year of purchase, an investor could deduct 12 percent of the cost of depreciable commercial property bought in 1981–84 as allowed by the 1981 tax act. By contrast, the 1986 Tax Reform Act limits first-year depreciation to 3.17 percent for commercial property bought in 1987 or later.

The depreciable basis of real estate, which is used to measure gain or loss on a sale, is reduced by depreciation expenses claimed each year. The faster the depreciation, the lower the basis, resulting in a greater taxable gain on the sale. Therefore, rapid depreciation results in less taxable income or even tax losses during the holding period, albeit greater taxable gain upon resale.

Tables 18 and 19 illustrate the effect of income taxes on after-tax returns to the investor. The investor is presumed to have purchased the property for $125,000 and resold it five years later for $150,000. The top half of table 18 shows net operating income ($10,000 per year), interest expenses, principal amortization, and before-tax cash flow.

The bottom half of table 18 shows after-tax calculations. The improvement is presumed to be 80 percent of the purchase price, or $100,000, and is depreciated at the rate of 3.17 percent per year. Taxable income is net operating income less interest and depreciation expenses (for example, $10,000 − $7,966 − $3,040, or − $1,006 in year 1). Because the losses are all usable in the current tax year, there is no passive loss comparison. Income taxes are then computed at 28 percent (for example, 0.28 × (− $1,006) = − $282 in year 1). Finally, after-tax cash flow is before-tax cash flow plus tax savings.

Table 19 shows treatment of the capital gain. The mortgage balance at resale is $75,331 ($80,010 less principal amortization) and the adjusted tax basis is $109,280 ($125,000 less annual depreciation expenses). The taxable gain is then $150,000 less $109,280, or $40,720, and the tax is $11,402 (28 percent). After-tax resale proceeds are $63,267 ($150,000 − $75,331 − $11,402).

Table 18.   After-Tax Cash Flow, Resale Proceeds, and Internal Rate of Return

Year	Net operating income	Interest expense	Principal amortization	Before-tax cash flow
1	$10,000	$7,966	$ 758	$1,276
2	10,000	7,887	837	$1,276
3	10,000	7,799	925	$1,276
4	10,000	7,702	1,021	$1,276
5	10,000	7,595	1,128	$1,276

Year	Depreciation expense	Taxable income	Passive loss used	Passive loss carryover	Tax paid (−savings)	After-tax cash flow
1	$3,040*	−$1,006	$1,006	0	−$282	$1,558
2	3,170	−1,057	1,057	0	−296	1,572
3	3,170	−969	969	0	−271	1,548
4	3,170	−872	872	0	−244	1,521
5	3,170	−765	765	0	−214	1,491

* Midmonth convention applied to January 1 purchase.

Table 19.   Values for a Sale in Year Five

Resale price before expenses	$150,000
Selling expenses	0
Resale price after expenses	150,000
Mortgage balance at resale	75,331
Adjusted tax basis at resale	109,280
Passive loss released	0
Taxable gain on sale	40,720
Tax on gain (−savings)	11,402
After-tax resale proceeds	63,267
Internal rate of return on initial equity	10.07 percent

Net present value of equity at:

5 percent	10 percent	15 percent
$11,238	$127	−$8,373

20 percent	25 percent	30 percent
−$14,956	−$20,112	−$24,193

The bottom of table 19 shows the after-tax net percent value of the investment at equity yield rates ranging from 5 to 30 percent. At a rate of 10 percent, the net present value is $127. The internal rate of return is 10.07 percent, that is, the investment yields an *after-tax* rate of return of 10.07 percent.

Investment value and market value are different. When income tax considerations are included in an appraisal, a specific investor is involved and the result is investment value. Appraisals done for assessment estimate market value; income tax is not considered. However, during appeals assessors encounter appraisals done from the investor's point of view and should be able to understand them.

Summary

Direct and yield capitalization are both methods of estimating the present value of an income-producing property from its anticipated future benefits. Both start from the basic income approach formula for value,

$$V = \frac{I}{R}. \qquad (1)$$

In both, rates and factors—and thus values—are derived from the market using the principles of anticipation and substitution.

It is up to appraisers to choose capitalization methods appropriate to particular circumstances. Because each method has its own strengths and weaknesses, the choice will depend on many factors. Availability of accurate market data and the quality, quantity, and duration of property income as required by the market are especially important.

In direct capitalization, appraisers must derive rates and factors from the market using only properties that are similar to the subject property *as investments*, that is, have similar expense ratios, land-to-building ratios, investment risk potential, physical and locational characteristics, and so on. In mass appraisal, adjustments can be applied to compensate for differences in these respects.

Yield capitalization, unlike direct capitalization, is an estimation of value that takes into account specific, typical investor goals, assumptions, and expectations. These are simulated in a complex process that may apply several formulas and special calculations in a single appraisal. Appraisers analyze the property in greater detail than they do when using direct capitalization.

Yield capitalization focuses on profit to the investor, that is, "yield." Appraisers make assumptions as to special profit (yield) requirements for a particular property. The return *on* and return *of* investment may be analyzed separately. In this analysis, "rate" reflects the yield rate expected by typical investors, any anticipated change in value (and resulting reversionary value), and the shape and duration of the income stream. These may be taken into account in a single overall rate; on the other hand, various future benefits (incomes) may each be calculated at a different rate, depending on such variables as lease terms, changes in financing, and so forth.

The appraiser estimates the anticipated period of the investment, the amount and nature of the cash flow to investors, a reversion value, and the appropriate rate or rates. Capitalization formulas are then applied to convert anticipated benefits to a current value estimate.

Mass Appraisal

Mass appraisal has become an important tool in assessment. A good mass appraisal system produces equitable values for many properties at a fraction of the cost of one-at-a-time appraisals. Chapter 13 reviews the history of mass appraisal, describes the components of a mass appraisal system, and explains the steps in the mass appraisal process.

Chapters 14 and 15 deal with the specification and calibration of mass appraisal models. Chapter 14, on model specification, discusses basic economic concepts, the explanation and expansion of a general real estate valuation model, principles of data analysis, and the application of the general model in the sales comparison, cost, and income approaches to value. Chapter 15, on model calibration, describes how to use quantitative methods to calibrate the general model in the sales comparison, cost, and income approaches.

Mass Appraisal

13

Mass appraisal is the systematic appraisal of groups of properties as of a given date using standardized procedures and statistical testing. Single-property appraisal, or "fee" appraisal, in contrast, is the valuation of a particular property as of a given date. As noted in chapter 4, the steps in both approaches are similar, but market analysis, valuation, and quality control are handled differently.

This chapter outlines the history, uses, and principles of mass appraisal and shows how mass appraisal is incorporated in the assessment process. The purpose of mass appraisal is the equitable and efficient appraisal of all property in a jurisdiction for ad valorem tax purposes. Effective mass appraisal requires an adequate budget, staff, and resources.

Mass appraisal, unlike single-property appraisal, requires the development of a valuation model capable of replicating the forces of supply and demand over a large area. Appraisal judgments relate to groups of properties rather than to single properties. The assessor must be able to develop, support, and explain standardized adjustments in a valuation model among use classes, construction types, neighborhoods, and other property groups.

In contrast, single-property appraisers conduct a market analysis and develop one or more valuation models capable of estimating the value of the subject parcel only. They provide the client with an appraisal report stating a conclusion of value.

Quality control is handled in a fundamentally different way in the two methods. In single-property appraisal, with the focus on the individual parcel, the reliability of valuations can usually be judged by the depth of the research and analysis or by a comparison with sales of comparable properties. In mass appraisal, statistical methods are used to gauge the accuracy and consistency of valuations (chapter 20). The single-property appraiser usually has just one client to satisfy, although regulatory agencies might have an interest in the appraisal. Assessors, however, must satisfy all taxpayers that assessments are fair and all taxing bodies that assessments are at the legal level.

The assessor needs skills in both mass appraisal and single-property appraisal, mass appraisal skills for producing initial values in a reappraisal and single-property appraisal skills to defend those values and to appraise special-purpose properties that do not lend themselves to mass appraisal techniques.

Managing a mass appraisal system is both a challenge and an opportunity. To meet the challenge, assessors use modern technology in the form of computer-*assisted* mass appraisal (CAMA) systems. These systems provide an opportunity to increase the efficiency and technical capabilities of the assessor's office and produce more accurate and equitable valuations.

Evolution of Mass Appraisal

Mass appraisal evolved out of the need for uniformity and consistency in ad valorem appraisals. According to Joseph Silverherz (1936), William A. Somers' reappraisal of St. Paul, Minnesota, marked the beginning of scientific mass appraisal. Writing in the 1920s, John A. Zangerle, county assessor of Cuyahuga County (Cleveland), Ohio, observed:

The first important question confronting every public appraiser is whether to appraise on a uniform or on a particular basis. The appraiser may seek the many conflicting evidences of value of land or building, and adopt some safe, sane, conservative, intermediate value; or he may, as heretofore has usually been done, appraise each site or building on the sale price, irrespective of general values. . . .

From any viewpoint, it is therefore highly desirable that some uniform values be adopted and that particularity of appraisement be, as far as possible, eliminated. No greater asset accrues to the appraiser than uniformity in appraisal. Nothing so discourages complaint. On the other hand, from the standpoint of the public, nothing so stimulates resentment, revolution, and rebellion as a feeling of discrimination or favoritism in taxation. The greatest asset of merchant, manufacturer or real estate owner is his sense of security in the enjoyment of equality of appraisement with his neighbor. His greatest burden is the suspicion that others are getting special consideration. Of what avail is it to the merchant, e.g., to be appraised at 90% or to get an abatement of 10% when his competitor is appraised at 80% or gets 20% depreciation? (Zangerle n.d, 3).

Zangerle also describes the development of land valuation schedules, cost and depreciation tables, and other valuation tools that assessors can use to achieve valuation uniformity. He emphasizes that appraisal schedules should be kept current and be based on local market studies.

The National Association of Tax Assessing Officers (now the International Association of Assessing Officers [IAAO]) was formed in 1934 for the purpose of improving mass appraisal through education, research, and the promotion of uniform appraisal practices. An early, landmark accomplishment of the association was the publication in 1938 of *Assessment Principles*, which was reprinted nine times, most recently in 1948. This report contains a classic description of the assessment process and sets forth eighty specific recommendations for achieving accuracy and uniformity. One important recommendation was that all real and personal property be subject to annual revaluation. The report explains that the advantages of annual revaluation, aside from legal requirements, include greater uniformity, better use of resources, and the avoidance of large assessment shifts during revaluations.

Improvements in mass appraisal accelerated with the introduction of computers in the 1950s. The rapid evolution of computer-assisted mass appraisal (CAMA) since then can be divided into four phases paralleling improvements in computers: (1) the early years of the 1950s, (2) the growth years of the 1960s, (3) the maturation years of the 1970s, and (4) the current era beginning in the early 1980s.

Computers were first used in assessment administration in the 1950s, primarily in large jurisdictions that could afford the expense. Initial applications took the form of assessment and tax calculations, preparation of assessment notices and tax bills, and the processing of tax collections. By today's standards, the first-generation computers of the time were very big, slow, unreliable, and expensive. Nevertheless, they provided welcome improvements in processing efficiencies over manual operations.

Second-generation computers, introduced in the 1960s, were responsible for the continued growth of the computer industry. These computers were many times faster, more powerful, and more reliable, yet less expensive, than their predecessors and permitted a growing number of assessment jurisdictions to take advantage of computer technology. During this time, many jurisdictions began using computers to store property record data and to automate the cost approach. California began to use multiple regression analysis in 1966.

The mid-1970s saw the advent of third-generation computers, which were again many times faster, more powerful, more reliable, and less expensive than second-generation computers. During this time, the range of commercially available statistical and mass appraisal software also increased greatly. Many jurisdictions began using multiple regression analysis or other automated applications of the sales comparison and income approaches to value. During these years, CAMA systems matured in the sense that technological advances and reduced costs made it cost effective for most assessment jurisdictions with the inclination and necessary expertise to set up highly sophisticated systems.

Hardware improvements, software advances, and cost reductions continued into the 1980s. Most notable was the introduction of microcomputers, desktop computers that provide at low cost all the necessary storage, speed, and power required by a small

assessment jurisdiction. At the same time, the commercial marketplace was quick to develop statistical and mass appraisal software for the microcomputer at only a fraction of the cost of comparable software on large computers. By the late 1980s, jurisdictions with 10,000 parcels could afford a system (including several workstations, a printer, and general-purpose software) capable of supporting their needs.

Components of a Mass Appraisal System

Mass appraisal builds on the same principles as single-property appraisal. Mass appraisal techniques, however, emphasize valuation models (expressed as equations, tables, and schedules), standardized practices, and statistical quality control. A mass appraisal system, whether computerized or manual, has four subsystems (shown in figure 1): (1) a data management system, (2) a sales analysis system, (3) a valuation system, and (4) an administrative system. The four subsystems are interdependent. The valuation system, for example, uses information maintained in the sales analysis and data management systems and produces output (valuations) required by the administrative system in the production of tax bills.

Data Management System

The data management system has components for collection, entry, editing, organization, conversion, and storage and security of property and ownership data. This data management system is the heart of the mass appraisal system and should be carefully planned and designed. Quality control is vital, because the accuracy of values depends

Figure 1. Components of a Mass Appraisal System

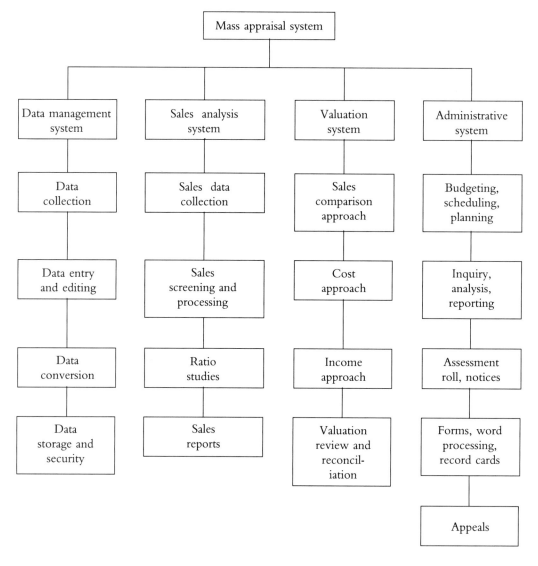

on the reliability of the data from which they are generated. Moreover, data collection, conversion, and maintenance are the most expensive aspect of most mass appraisal systems. Design decisions made in this area will, more than anything else, determine the operating costs of the system.

Property characteristics data are used in the valuation system to conduct research and to generate values, and in the sales analysis system to stratify properties for ratio studies and to identify and list comparable sales. Property characteristics data are also used in the administrative system.

System designers decide what data elements to collect and maintain. Because data are expensive to collect and process, a jurisdiction should capture those property characteristics important in the estimation of values and minimize those that are redundant or insignificant. Pilot studies help determine which data items are needed. Some property characteristics (for example, number of bedrooms) not vital to valuation may have to be retained because they are useful for explaining values to taxpayers.

Sales Analysis System

The sales analysis system has components for sales data collection, sales screening and processing, ratio studies, and sales reporting. Ratio studies, the primary product of this system, generally provide the best available measures of appraisal performance and are a valuable tool for monitoring appraisal results, identifying reappraisal priorities, adjusting valuations to the market, and assisting management in planning and scheduling.

For ratio studies and sales reports, the sales analysis system draws on values produced by the valuation system and on property characteristics maintained in the data management system. The results of ratio studies are used by the valuation system for evaluating the accuracy of different valuation approaches and techniques and by the administrative system for budgeting, planning, and scheduling.

Valuation System

The valuation system consists of mass appraisal applications of the sales comparison, cost, and income approaches to value. Sales comparison applications include multiple regression analysis, adaptive estimation procedure (AEP, or feedback), and automated comparable sales analysis. The cost approach requires maintenance of computerized cost schedules and equations, derivation of depreciation schedules from market data, and reconciliation of cost-generated values with the market. Mass appraisal applications of the income approach include the development and use of income multipliers and overall rates. Values produced by these three approaches should be reviewed and reconciled to select a final value for assessment purposes.

The valuation system uses property characteristics maintained in the data management system, along with sales data and ratio study results from the sales analysis system. Ratio study results can help refine valuation models and determine which valuation methods produce the best results. Values produced by the valuation system are used in both the sales analysis and administrative systems. The valuation system indicates which data items are required to support effective valuation methods.

Administrative System

The administrative system is composed of a variety of functions and activities subject to varying degrees of automation. One of the first functions to be automated was the preparation of assessment notices and tax bills. Many jurisdictions have also computerized other administrative functions.

Each activity in the administrative system requires information from the sales analysis, valuation, or data management systems and produces products used by one or more of these other systems. For example, the appeals process requires valuation and property characteristics data and can also make good use of ratio studies and sales reports produced by the sales analysis system. The results of the appeals process, in turn, are used by these other systems in the form of revised values, data changes, and recalculated ratio statistics. The appeals process also affects other parts of the administrative system, such as the preparation of the assessment roll, tax billing, planning, budgeting, and scheduling.

Functions of Mass Appraisal

There are three basic functions of a mass appraisal system: reappraisal, data maintenance, and value updates. A reappraisal provides an excellent opportunity to develop a mass appraisal system and introduce new appraisal procedures. Once the reappraisal is done, the new system simplifies data maintenance and annual value updates.

Steps in a Reappraisal

Every assessment jurisdiction must prepare for periodic reappraisals and the upgrading of its mass appraisal system. Required activities are presented below in the order they occur.

Performance Analysis A performance analysis determines whether values are equitable and consistent with the market. In mass appraisal, the primary tool for analysis is the ratio study (see chapter 20), which should be conducted at least annually. If performance is poor, a reappraisal is needed, particularly if one has not been done for a long time.

Reappraisal Decision Statutes or administrative rules sometimes impose reappraisal requirements. Some jurisdictions use a cyclical schedule, in which a portion of the jurisdiction is physically reviewed and revalued each year. Other jurisdictions revalue all properties in mass at periodic intervals, for example, every three or four years, or in response to ratio study results or external factors. Whatever the timing, a reappraisal requires careful planning and a major commitment of resources. Nevertheless, the resulting improvements in valuation uniformity and related benefits should justify the time and expense.

Analysis of Available Resources Before defining goals and objectives for the reappraisal, the jurisdiction must take stock of its available resources: staff, budget, existing systems and practices, data processing support, and existing data and maps. An adequate budget is crucial because it can overcome deficiencies in the other areas. The resources available determine the kind of system that can be supported and the time required to make it work.

Planning and Organization This is the most important aspect of a reappraisal. The jurisdiction identifies its target completion date and performance objective, then develops a specific action plan and schedule to achieve its objective on time. The plan defines critical activities and their completion dates, assigns responsibilities, and sets production standards for data collection and field work.

A current organization chart should reflect the division of responsibilities. Often work groups, teams, or committees are the best way to staff parts of the project. New employees may have to be hired, particularly if a major data collection effort is involved or specialized expertise is required.

System Development System development produces the procedures, methods, manuals, and software for each of the subsystems of a mass appraisal system. The first products should include forms, manuals, and procedures for collecting and processing property characteristics, sales, and income data.

Pilot Study A pilot study tests new procedures in one or two areas of the jurisdiction and should be considered whenever major changes are made. A pilot study, which should include a ratio study, will show if the new system produces accurate and reliable values and also suggest modifications in procedures.

Data Collection Once the required forms and procedures have been developed, tested, and approved, data collection can begin. Quality control is critical; the data are thoroughly edited and tested before being used for valuation. The quality of the available data will, more than anything else, determine valuation accuracy.

Production of Values Production of values begins with market analysis, model development, model calibration, and calculation of preliminary values. A ratio study then evaluates the accuracy and consistency of the values between property types and areas. When the models produce acceptable results, they can be used to produce values, which are then subjected to office and field reviews.

Preparation of the Assessment Roll Final values are listed on the assessment roll in a form satisfying legal requirements, and the assessor certifies the roll. Valuation notices are mailed. Assessors should have prepared for informal and formal appeals. Although processing appeals consumes much staff time, it provides an opportunity to review individual values in detail and make necessary corrections. After the appeals process is completed, tax billing can begin. This billing, although occasionally done by the assessor's office, is not an assessment function.

Final Performance Analysis The assessor conducts a final ratio study to measure and evaluate the accuracy and uniformity of the new values. This study plays a key role in summarizing the achievements of the new system or reappraisal and in preparing for the next reappraisal.

Data Maintenance

Data maintenance is the process of capturing and valuing new construction and other changes to the property base. A good maintenance program will have two components. The first centers on building permits and subdivision plats. As the assessor's office receives copies of building permits, property records are pulled or flagged and inspections scheduled. Construction in progress toward the end of the assessment year should be inspected as near to the assessment date as practical.

Recorded subdivision plats alert the assessor to the creation of new parcels. These must be mapped, assigned parcel numbers, and listed. Subdivision activity can create substantial value and should be inspected and appraised as close to the assessment date as possible.

The second component of a good maintenance program is periodic reinspection of all properties in the jurisdiction. No matter how good a building permit reporting and monitoring system is, undetected changes will always occur. Therefore, all properties should be routinely reinspected (at least once every six years). Because the chief function of these inspections is to verify existing information, a drive-by inspection, during which the property and property record are compared, is usually sufficient. Two-person teams, in which one drives and the other handles the records, can review and verify a few hundred records per day.

Routine field visits can be supplemented with information obtained from aerial photographs and taxpayer returns. Information supplied by taxpayers during assessment reviews and appeals can also alert assessors to inaccurate or out-of-date information. Changes indicated by these sources should be verified in the field. (See chapter 5 for a discussion of data collection strategies and techniques.)

Value Updates

Updates are annual adjustments applied to properties between reappraisals. A mass appraisal system can use ratio studies or other market analyses to derive trending factors based on property type, location, size, age, and the like.

Principles of Mass Appraisal

Mass appraisal builds on the same basic principles as single-property appraisal. Because it involves the appraisal of many properties as of a common date, however, mass appraisal techniques emphasize equations, tables, and schedules, collectively called models. Constructing such models can be viewed as a two-step process: (1) specification of the basic model structure and (2) model calibration.

Specifying the General Model

A general mass appraisal model is one that permits the appraiser to determine its specific format or content. A general model provides a framework to simulate supply and demand forces operating in a real estate market and is adaptable to many uses. The model builder specifies the *variables*, or property characteristics, to be used in the model and their relationships. A simple general model can be expanded to reflect the complexities of the market by expansion of each variable (see chapters 2, 4, 6, 8, 9, and 14 for general models and their expansion for the three approaches to value).

For example, the simplest general model for the cost approach,

$$MV = IV + LV, \tag{1}$$

where MV is market value, IV is improvement value, and LV is land value, can be expanded, as shown in chapter 4, to

$$MV = P_I \times ISIZE + P_L \times LSIZE. \tag{2}$$

Improvements can be divided into a primary improvement (or building), B, and other additions, O. The value of the building, BV, can then be expressed as the sum of prices of specific size-related features and represents replacement (or reproduction) cost new (RCN):

$$\begin{aligned} BV = {} & (PB_1 \times BSIZE_1) \\ & + (PB_2 \times BSIZE_2) \\ & + \ldots + (PB_n \times BSIZE_n), \end{aligned} \tag{3}$$

where $BSIZE_1$, $BSIZE_2$, ..., $BSIZE_n$ are number of units (for example, square feet of main living area, basement area, and number of bedrooms), and PB_1, PB_2, ..., PB_n, their corresponding unit prices.

Real estate values also vary because of features related to utility and quality. These values are incorporated into the model as percentage adjustments that affect the entire value of the building:

$$BV = BQ_1 \times BQ_2 \times \ldots \times BQ_n \times (PB_1 \times BSIZE_1 + PB_2 BSIZE_2 + \ldots + PB_n BSIZE_n), \qquad (4)$$

where BQ_1, BQ_2, ..., BQ_n are building qualitative factors for such features as construction quality, condition, design, and effective age. In general, factors above 1.00 increase value, and factors below 1.00 reduce value. Chapter 14 shows further expansion of the cost model.

Model specification is the first step in the development of any mass appraisal model. Mass appraisers must understand the models they use and be sure they reflect the way property is valued in the local market. When the model structure is imposed, as it often is in commercial mass appraisal software, the user may not be able to select the property characteristics and their relationships in the model. In contrast, other software, particularly general-purpose statistical software, affords the user complete freedom in determining model structures.

Model Calibration

Model calibration is the process of adjusting mass appraisal formulas, tables, and schedules to the current market. In the cost approach, for example, calibration involves setting or updating base rates and cost adjustments. Although the structure of a mass appraisal model may be valid for many years, the model is usually calibrated or updated every year. To update for short periods, trend factors may suffice. Over longer periods, complete market analyses are required. The

goal is for mass appraisal equations and schedules to reflect current local market conditions. The most common mass appraisal models and schedules are listed below. Each is discussed in detail elsewhere in this book.

Cost Approach

Cost Tables Cost tables include base rates, per square foot adjustments, and lump sum adjustments used to determine replacement cost new. Options include manuals provided by oversight agencies, appraisal firms, or commercial cost services, as well as locally developed cost tables. When costs are adapted from a commercial cost service, copyrights should be respected. Local cost tables should be complete, accurate, consistent, and able to support values during appeals.

Depreciation Schedules Depreciation schedules are developed for each major class of property in the jurisdiction, then tested to ensure that they reflect the local market. In a reappraisal, there should be a guide setting condition ratings and estimating effective age.

Time and Location Modifiers Time and location modifiers are used to adjust cost data for local variations and changes in costs over time. If a national, state, or provincial cost manual is used, location modifiers will be required for individual counties, cities, or market areas. The modifiers can be developed from commercial cost services or through local studies.

Market Adjustment Factors Market adjustment factors are often required to adjust values obtained from the cost approach to the market. These adjustments should be applied by type of property and area based on sales ratio studies or other market analyses. Accurate cost schedules, condition ratings, and depreciation schedules will minimize the need for market adjustment factors.

Income Approach

Market Rents The income approach begins with the development of typical current market rents, expressed on a per unit basis. Market rents can be developed from income data obtained from property owners or, in some cases, local third-party sources.

Vacancy and Expense Ratios Vacancy and expense ratios are required to adjust potential gross income (market rent multiplied by number of units) to typical net income. These ratios should be based on a study of the local market and reflect typical management. Separate ratios are developed for different types of commercial properties (apartments, hotels and motels, office buildings, retail stores, warehouses, and so forth) and perhaps for age groups.

Rates and Multipliers Income rates and multipliers are used to convert income to market value. They include the gross income multiplier, overall rate, and discount rate. Each is used in specific applications. Rates and multipliers usually vary by type of property and must be based on a thorough analysis of the local market.

Sales Comparison Approach

Land Valuation Tables These tables contain land values per unit, along with standard adjustments for topography, depth, water frontage, and other locational features. They should be based on an analysis of local sales and updated annually.

Sales Comparison Adjustments As traditionally applied, the sales comparison approach estimates the value of a subject property from the sales prices of comparable properties; sales prices of the comparables are adjusted for physical and locational differences from the subject property. In mass appraisal, the adjustments should be stored in tables for consistency and ease of application. The adjustments are derived from local sales analysis and, in mass appraisal, can be based on such statistical techniques as multiple regression analysis and feedback (see below).

Multiple Regression Analysis Equations Multiple regression analysis has emerged as the preeminent mass appraisal application of the sales comparison approach. Provided that sales are adequate and property characteristics data coded consistently, the technique can produce highly accurate and consistent values for most residential properties. Separate equations should be developed for each market area in a jurisdiction, or a "global" model should be adjusted for locational variations.

Feedback Equations Adaptive estimation procedure (AEP, or feedback) is another automated version of the sales comparison approach. The structure of the technique is similar to that of the cost approach but the "prices" assigned to each property characteristic are based on sales analysis. The technique can also be used to adjust cost data to the market.

Base Home Tables Base home tables repackage a statistical equation, derived through multiple regression analysis or feedback, into a table. Although the base home approach is not a separate method of calibration, it helps users and taxpayers understand and accept mass appraisal models.

Summary

This chapter outlined the history, uses, and principles of mass appraisal. A mass appraisal system designed according to the principles described here should enable a jurisdiction to produce accurate, equitable values cost-effectively. Two essential parts of mass appraisal, model specification and model calibration, are treated in more detail in the next two chapters.

Mass Appraisal Model Building

14

General Model Types

A model is a representation of how something works. Models are designed by researchers, scientists, and analysts to test theories and predict the outcome of events.

Models may be physical, conceptual, or mathematical. An example of a physical model is a model airplane, which can be tested in a wind tunnel to evaluate its stability and aerodynamic characteristics. An example of a conceptual model is a persuasion theory, based on psychological and sociological concepts and used in marketing to develop sales strategies. An example of a mathematical model is the fixed relationship of electrical circuits, which states that the power used in a circuit can be determined by multiplying the current by the voltage (watts equal amperage times voltage).

Property valuation models seek to explain or predict the market value of properties from real estate data. Models are constructed to represent the operation of forces of supply and demand in a particular market and have evolved from three broad theories of value: the cost approach, the sales comparison approach, and the income approach.

Model building requires good theory, data analysis, and research methods. Appraisers who learn to build models that reflect the market will find it easier to defend values.

The best valuation models will be accurate, rational, and explainable.

Appraisers are often too quick to use an already defined model without examining its assumptions and structure. Examples of questionable models include cost manuals not tuned to the local market, statistically generated but untested sales comparison equations, and simplistic income models.

Model specification and calibration are distinct steps in modeling. Model specification is the designing of models based on economic and appraisal theory and market analysis. It includes selecting the supply and demand variables to be considered and defining their relationship to both value and one another. Model calibration is the process of solving for unknown quantities in a model, for example, construction costs and depreciation in the cost approach, the adjustment amounts in the sales comparison approach, and the capitalization rate in the income approach. This chapter focuses on specification, chapter 15 on calibration.

Economic Basis of Model Building

As explained in chapters 3 and 4, appraisal models represent both the supply and the demand sides of the market. The supply of housing within an area (Q_s) can be represented as a function (f) of housing prices (P)

and a set of n supply factors, $s_1, s_2, \ldots, s_n$. Similarly, the demand for housing (Q_d) can be represented as a function (f) of housing prices and a set of n demand factors, $d_1, d_2, \ldots, d_n$. Thus,

$$Q_s = f(P, s_1, s_2, \ldots, s_n); \quad (1)$$

$$Q_d = f(P, d_1, d_2, \ldots, d_n). \quad (2)$$

When the housing market is in equilibrium, supply equals demand $(Q_s = Q_d)$, and price can be viewed as a function of supply and demand factors:

$$P = f(s_1, s_2, \ldots, s_n, d_1, d_2, \ldots, d_n). \quad (3)$$

Real estate prices are a function of supply and demand factors operating simultaneously within a market (see figure 1). Demand factors for residential properties include characteristics important to buyers: living area, location, condition, construction quality, parking, and so forth. Supply factors relate to availability and therefore reflect building costs, interest rates, and economic conditions. For income properties, demand factors include market location and condition; supply factors include operating expenses and required rates of return on capital. Rents are equilibrium prices that represent both supply and demand factors in the rental market. The model builder analyzes the local market to determine the importance of these factors.

The cost, sales comparison, and income approaches are all traditional methods of developing valuation models that replicate the workings of the market. All three approaches should reflect the supply and demand factors relevant to value determination. How-

Figure 1. Real Estate Prices as a Function of Supply and Demand

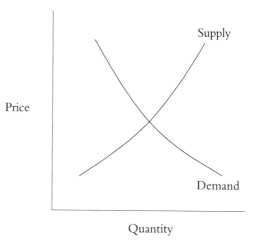

ever, each approach calibrates models differently. In the cost approach, supply factors are based on the principle of substitution and calibrated from the construction market; demand factors in the form of locational influences, depreciation schedules, and market adjustments are calibrated from the real estate market. In the sales comparison approach, all factors are calibrated from sales information in the local real estate market according to the principles of supply and demand, contribution, and substitution. In the income approach, direct capitalization methods typically require that capitalization rates be developed from the local real estate market. Yield capitalization methods use information from other markets as well to develop capitalization rates. Yield methods require that income estimates be prepared for the expected holding period; direct methods require estimates of only the current year's income.

All three approaches to value reflect supply and demand. Although this statement is easy to understand in the context of the direct sales comparison[1] and cost approach, where the factors in both models directly represent supply and demand factors, it is also true in the case of the income approach. Typically the income approach is shown as being only one equation:

$$V = \frac{I - EXP}{R}$$

where V is value, I is income, EXP is expense, and R is a capitalization rate.

The full model, however, contains additional equations that relate building gross income to supply and demand factors in the rental market for the building use.

$$Rents = f \int_{x=1}^{n} s_F \, , \, \int_{y=1}^{n} d_F$$

where s_F is a vector of supply factors and d_F is a vector of demand factors. Likewise,

rates and expenses can each be modeled and depend on supply and demand factors in the construction markets.

Consequently, value in the income approach can be seen to depend on supply and demand factors in the rental market, on the capitalization rate, and on the building expense factors that are supply factors in construction markets.

Researchers have recently developed direct market models for rental, commercial, and industrial properties that use this insight. These valuation models are based on models that observe supply and demand factors directly and don't use rents, rates, or expenses as proxies for them.

---

1. In the indirect sales comparison approach, sales prices are adjusted for differences between the subject properties and its comparables. The sales prices are market equilibrium prices representing both supply and demand factors operating in the market. Consequently, the indirect approach is just another form of the direct sales comparison approach, which observes supply and demand factors directly.

General Model Structures

A model is composed of one dependent variable and one or more independent variables. The *dependent* variable is what is being estimated, for example, property value. An *independent* variable is an item used to predict or explain the dependent variable, for example, square feet of living area or gross income. During model specification, the appraiser decides which variables to use and how they are related. During model calibration, the

relationship is quantified, that is, the *coefficient* (a price or percentage adjustment) for each independent variable is determined, for example, dollars per square foot of living area (see chapter 15).

A basic valuation model is

$$MV = IV + LV, \qquad (4)$$

where MV is the estimated market value, IV is the estimated improvement value, and LV is the estimated land value.

The above model can be expanded to a fuller presentation of the components of improvements and land that contribute to value. The principle of contribution says that value is related to effective demand for housing services and utility (as opposed to cost). The principle of substitution says that such amenities are worth no more than the cost to acquire reasonable substitutes. We can quantify these notions by letting improvement and land size be proxies for services. Unit prices are the values established by studying substitutes. The model in equation 4 can then be expanded to describe improvement and land values as depending on size and price:

$$IV = P_I \times ISIZE; \qquad (5)$$

$$LV = P_L \times LSIZE, \qquad (6)$$

where P_I is the price of the improvement (per unit), $ISIZE$ is the improvement size, P_L is the price of land (per unit), and $LSIZE$ is the land size.

The components of this model can be combined:

$$MV = (P_I \times ISIZE) + (P_L \times LSIZE). \qquad (7)$$

This *additive linear* model assumes that land and improvement values can be determined separately and that the value of each increases proportionately with size. Figure 2 shows the linear relationships graphically.

Improvements can be divided into a primary improvement (or building), B, and other additions, O. The value of the building, BV, can then be expressed as the sum of the prices of specific size-related features as follows:

$$BV = (PB_1 \times BSIZE_1) + (PB_2 \times BSIZE_2) + \ldots + (PB_n \times BSIZE_n), \qquad (8)$$

Figure 2. Linear Relationship between Size and Value

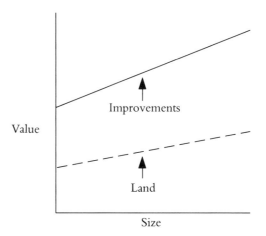

where $BSIZE_1$, $BSIZE_2$, . . . , $BSIZE_n$ are number of units (for example, square feet of main living area, basement area, and number of bedrooms), and PB_1, PB_2, . . . , PB_n, their corresponding per unit prices. This part of the model represents the supply side of the market and in cost models represents replacement (or reproduction) cost new.

In addition, the demand side of the market must be represented in the model. The economic and appraisal concept of utility, defined as the ability to satisfy human needs, dictates that real estate values will vary with features related to utility and quality. The values of these features can be incorporated into the general model as percentage adjustments. In the case of building value,

$$BV = BQ_1 \times BQ_2 \times \ldots \times BQ_n \times (PB_1 \times BSIZE_1 + \ldots + PB_n \times BSIZE_n), \qquad (9)$$

where BQ_1, BQ_2, . . . , BQ_n are building qualitative factors for such features as construction quality, condition, design, and effective age. In the cost approach, the market adjustments for physical, functional, and economic obsolescence should be included here. In general, factors above 1.00 increase value, and factors below 1.00 reduce value. Note that in this model building qualitative factors affect the entire structure.

The land value can be expanded in the same way, although models usually have only one size-related component, either square feet or front feet of land area. Thus,

$$LV = LQ_1 \times LQ_2 \times \ldots \times LQ_n \\ \times (PL_1 \times LSIZE_1), \quad (10)$$

where $LQ_1, LQ_2, \ldots, LQ_n$ are land qualitative factors for such features as topography, shape, traffic, and view.

In addition to the land and building, a property's utility and market value can reflect such additional improvements as pools, guest houses, storage sheds, and unattached garages. These other additions (O) can be expanded in terms of size and price:

$$OV = (PO_1 \times OSIZE_1) + (PO_2 \times \\ OSIZE_2) + \ldots + (PO_n \times OSIZE_n), \quad (11)$$

where OV is the value of other additions, $OSIZE_1, OSIZE_2, \ldots, OSIZE_n$ are the number of units (for example, square feet of pool area), and $PO_1, PO_2, \ldots, PO_n$, their corresponding prices. Quality adjustments for these features will have to be developed as well to represent the utility of these features to consumers of housing.

Finally, there are some general qualitative factors ($GQ_1, GQ_2, \ldots, GQ_n$) such as location and time that affect the entire parcel. The complete general model can now be written as:

$$MV = \pi GQ[(\pi BQ \times \Sigma BA) \\ + (\pi LQ \times \Sigma LA) + \Sigma OA], \quad (12)$$

where
   πGQ is the product of general qualitative components
   πBQ is the product of building qualitative components (including depreciation)
   πLQ is the product of land qualitative components
   ΣBA is the sum of building additive components
   ΣLA is the sum of land additive components
   ΣOA is the sum of other additions additive components

The model contains both additive and multiplicative components. Size-related features are additive (added to each other) and quality-related features are multiplicative (multiplied by each other). Once determined, the values of the building, land, and other additions components are added together and multiplied by the product of the general qualitative factors.

This model is general in the sense that it can incorporate virtually any set of property descriptors. The model builder determines what variables to use in the model, how they are related, and how to calibrate the model.

Model Specification

This section considers the wide choice of data, variables, and model structures available in specifying mass appraisal models.

Types of Data

Data may be categorized as either *qualitative* or *quantitative* (see chapter 5). Qualitative data are based on discrete, predefined categories.

Examples include neighborhoods, cooling systems, and roof types. The appraiser describes the attribute from a list of predefined codes. A special case of qualitative data is an item that is either present or absent, for example, corner location or a jacuzzi. Such data items are termed *binary*, or "dummy," variables and coded "1" if present and "0" if not. Figure 3 shows examples of qualitative data.

Figure 3.   Examples of Qualitative Data

Interior finish	Cooling system	Jacuzzi
1 = poor	A = central air	1 = yes
2 = average	B = evaporative	0 = no
3 = good	cooling	
4 = very good	C = no cooling	

Quantitative data, on the other hand, are based on measuring or counting, for example, square feet or number of rooms. Quantitative data can be used to construct qualitative variables. For example, data on building age could be used to construct a qualitative variable as follows:

1 = 0–10 years
2 = 11–25 years
3 = 26–50 years
4 = More than 50 years

Data Transformations

The variables used in model building are constructed from property data. A *simple,* or *untransformed,* variable is one that directly describes a data element, for example, age, square feet, or number of bedrooms.

Binary Variables   Often, however, mass appraisal models can be improved by applying a mathematical transformation to the data. One such transformation is the conversion of qualitative data to binary variables. For example, type of cooling coded as shown in figure 3 could be converted to three binary variables: Central Air (0 or 1), Evaporative Cooling (0 or 1), and No Cooling (0 or 1). This allows the model builder to determine the contribution of each to market value without assuming any predetermined relationships.

In such cases, one of the categories (usually the most typical) should be designated the reference category and *not* used as a variable in modeling. For example, if No Cooling is most typical, it is excluded, and variables for Central Air and Evaporative Cooling are used in modeling. The coefficients for the included variables are then interpreted by reference to the excluded category, for example, a coefficient of $4,350 for Central Air would indicate that houses with central air conditioning tend to sell for $4,350 more than comparable houses with no cooling. Coefficients developed in this manner reflect the principle of contribution, indicating how much the market adds or subtracts for a feature.

Scalar Variables   Alternatively, qualitative data can be converted to numbers, or values, that express their relative value or desirability. For example, cooling might be recoded as follows:

Central Air	= 1.00
Evaporative Cooling	= 0.50
No Cooling	= 0

This approach has the important advantage of minimizing the number of independent variables and sales needed for model calibration.

To the extent possible, the relative values should be derived through market analysis. The preferred technique is to analyze binary variables. Assume, for example, that condition is coded as either poor, fair, average, or good. Binary variables could be created for poor, fair, and good condition. Assume that their coefficients are −$6,000, −$2,400, and +$4,000, respectively. Then a scalar variable could be created as follows:

poor	= −1.50	fair	= −0.60
average	= 0	good	= +1.00

Note that the relationship between these values is proportionate to their coefficients. In general, scalar variables should be centered on 0 in additive models and on 1.00 in multiplicative models.

Another method of deriving scalar variables is based on sale price per square foot. Assume the following average sales prices per square foot by condition category:

poor	= $18.23	fair	= $26.65
average	= $34.10	good	= $39.88

Each of these values can be divided by the value for average condition ($34.10) to obtain the following relative values:

poor	= 0.53	fair	= 0.78
average	= 1.00	good	= 1.17

In an additive model, these values would be centered on zero (by subtracting 1.00) as follows:

poor	= −0.47	fair	= −0.22
average	= 0	good	= +0.17

Although simple, this approach should be used with caution because average sales prices, even when expressed as dollars per square foot, reflect other influences as well. In this case, for example, the low value for poor condition may partly reflect poor construction quality or location.

Scalar variables can also be based on cost data. Although cost values do not equal market values, cost data can often provide a stable starting point. Relative values can then be refined during model calibration. Finally, results from previous models and the appraiser's judgment can be helpful in developing relative values.

Mathematical Transformations   The usefulness of quantitative data can also be increased by mathematical transformations. For example, the appraisal principle of increasing and decreasing returns usually implies that as the quantity of land is increased, value per unit will decrease. Hence, land values are often more closely related to the square root or natural logarithm of land area than to land area itself. Common mathematical transformations used in mass appraisal modeling include reciprocal, exponential, logarithmic, multiplicative, and quotient transformations.

Reciprocal Transformation   A reciprocal is the result of dividing a number into 1.00. For example, the reciprocal of 4 is

$$1/4 = 0.25.$$

If the original number is greater than 1.00, the result will be less than 1.00 (as above). If the original number is less than 1.00, the result will be greater than 1.00; for example, the reciprocal of 0.20 is

$$1/0.20 = 5.$$

Figure 4. Reciprocal Transformations

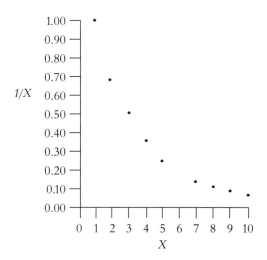

Figure 4 shows the result of reciprocal transformations on the numbers 1, 1.5, and 2 through 10. An example of a reciprocal transformation useful in mass appraisal is the reciprocal of distance in miles to the central business district. For example, the reciprocals of 2, 5, and 10 miles are, respectively,

$$1/2 = 0.50, 1/5 = 0.20, 1/10 = 0.10.$$

As the distance increases, the value of the variable decreases.

The reciprocal transformation (and the exponential and logarithmic transformations that follow) is based on the principle of increasing and decreasing returns. In this case, the marginal contribution associated with additional increments of a variable fall rapidly at first and then level off, as illustrated in figure 4.

Exponential Transformation This is a transformation in which a number is raised to a power or exponent. If the exponent is greater than 1.00, the effect will be to increase the numbers and the values between them, for example,

$$2^2 = 4 \quad 4^2 = 16 \quad 6^2 = 36 \quad 8^2 = 64.$$

If the exponent is between 0 and 1.00, the effect is to reduce and compress the values, for example,

$$2^{0.5} = 1.4142 \quad 4^{0.5} = 2 \quad 6^{0.5} = 2.4495$$
$$8^{0.5} = 2.8284.$$

Negative exponents are equivalent to reciprocals of the same number with a positive exponent; for example,

$$2^{-0.5} = 1/1.4142 = 0.7071;$$
$$2^{-2} = 1/2^2 = 0.25.$$

A number raised to the exponent zero is always 1.00; also, zero raised to any power is zero; any number raised to the power 1.00 is itself. Negative numbers cannot have exponents less than 1.00.

Figure 5. Positive Exponential Functions

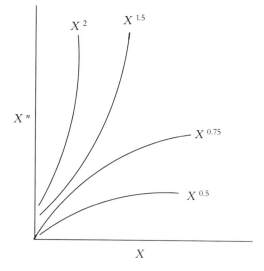

Figure 6. Negative Exponential Functions

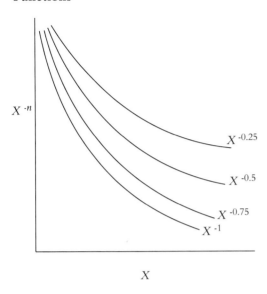

X^{-n}

$X^{-0.25}$

$X^{-0.5}$

$X^{-0.75}$

X^{-1}

X

Table 1 shows the results of some common exponential transformations on a range of values. Compare the results for the number 100. Figures 5 and 6 show the results of exponential transformations graphically. The result of an exponential transformation is always a positive number, whether the exponent is positive or negative.

Logarithmic Transformation　A logarithm is the exponent to which a given base must be raised to obtain a specified number. Logarithms to the base 10 are called *common* logarithms and abbreviated "log." They are used to represent very large or very small numbers. Another useful base is the number 2.71828, or base *e*. Numbers to base *e* are *natural* logarithms and abbreviated "ln." For example, the natural logarithm of 25 is 3.2189, because

$$e^{3.2189} = 25.$$

Logarithms are readily found with a calculator or computer.

Natural logarithms have the mathematical property that each doubling of the underlying data is associated with an equal increase in the logarithm, for example,

$$\ln(2) = 0.693, \ln(4) = 1.386, \ln(8) = 2.079.$$

In this example, each doubling of the data value increases the natural logarithm by 0.693.

Figure 7 graphs the natural logarithm of the numbers 1, 1.5, and 2 through 10. Note that as X increases, the log of X also increases, but by decreasing amounts. With each doubling of X from 2 to 4, from 4 to 8, and so on, the logarithm increases by 0.693.

Reciprocal, exponential, and logarithmic transformations provide means of handling *nonlinear* relationships in linear models and allow the model builder to address the issue of the principle of increasing and decreasing returns. A *linear* relationship is one in which constant increments in the independent variable result in equal changes in the dependent variable, for example, depreciation is the same every year, or a fourth bedroom adds as much to value as a third bedroom.

Multiplicative Transformation　Property characteristics affect value interactively. For example, air conditioning may contribute greater value in a large, well-built house than in a small house of minimal construction. Such interactions can be captured in linear models by using a multiplicative, or product, transformation, in which one variable is multiplied by another. One particularly useful transformation of this type is the mul-

Table 1. Exponential Transformations

X	X^{-2}	$X^{-1.5}$	$X^{-0.5}$	$X^{0.5}$	$X^{1.5}$	X^2
0.25	16	8.0000	2.0000	0.5000	0.1250	0.0625
0.50	4	2.8284	1.4142	0.7071	0.3536	0.2500
0.75	1.7778	1.5396	1.1547	0.8660	0.6495	0.5625
1	1.0000	1.0000	1.0000	1.0000	1.0000	1.0000
2	0.2500	0.3536	0.7071	1.4142	2.8284	4
3	0.1111	0.1925	0.5773	1.7321	5.1962	9
4	0.0625	0.1250	0.5000	2.0000	8.0000	16
5	0.0400	0.0894	0.4472	2.2361	11.1803	25
6	0.0278	0.0680	0.4082	2.4495	14.6969	36
7	0.0204	0.0540	0.3780	2.6457	18.5203	49
8	0.0156	0.0442	0.3535	2.8284	22.6274	64
9	0.0123	0.0370	0.3333	3.0000	27.0000	81
10	0.0100	0.0316	0.3162	3.1623	31.6228	100
20	0.0025	0.0112	0.3015	3.3167	89.4428	400
30	0.0011	0.0061	0.1826	5.4773	164	900
40	0.0006	0.0040	0.1581	6.3246	253	1,600
50	0.0004	0.0028	0.1414	7.0711	354	2,500
60	0.0003	0.0023	0.1291	7.7460	465	3,600
100	0.0001	0.0010	0.1000	10.0000	1,000	10,000
1,000			0.0316	31.6228		
5,000			0.0141	70.7107		
10,000			0.0100	100		
20,000			0.0071	141		
40,000			0.0050	200		
80,000			0.0035	283		

tiplication of a size-related variable by a quality-related variable, for example, square feet of living area by construction quality. Assume, for example, that $SQFT$ is square feet of living area and $QUAL$ is a scalar variable for construction quality coded as follows:

poor	=	0.50
fair	=	0.75
average	=	1.00
good	=	1.25
excellent	=	1.40

If one were to calibrate the model,

$$MV = b_1 \times SQFT + b_2 \times QUAL, \quad (13)$$

the coefficient, b_1, would add a given dollar value per square foot regardless of quality, and b_2 would add a lump sum amount regardless of size. This may prove satisfactory for typical houses but is likely to overstate the value of small, good-quality houses and understate the value of large good-quality houses, because each receives the same quality adjustment.

Figure 7. Logarithmic Transformations

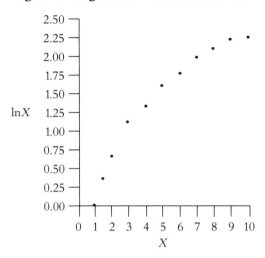

To avoid this problem, create the variable, *QUALSQFT*, as follows:

$$QUALSQFT = QUAL \times SQFT. \quad (14)$$

The coefficient for *QUALSQFT* will express the effect of square footage as a function of construction quality class. For example, if the coefficient for *QUALSQFT* is $40.00, each square foot of living area will add $20.00 to value in poor-quality houses (0.50 × 40.00), $30.00 in fair-quality houses (0.75 × $40.00), $40.00 in average-quality houses (1.00 × $40.00), $50.00 in good quality houses (1.25 × $40.00), and $56.00 in excellent-quality houses (1.40 × $40.00). Thus, the better the quality class, the greater the per-square-foot value.

Quotient Transformation A quotient transformation is the division of one variable by another, for example, square feet by number of rooms to obtain average room size. When real estate is purchased on a per-unit basis or when sales prices vary widely, it is help-ful to compute the dependent variable as sale price per unit, for example, sale price divided by square feet or by number of apartment units. A sale price per unit reflects market relationships more accurately and prevents the model from being dominated by properties with very large sales prices.

Multiplicative and quotient transformations make it unnecessary to assume that the effect of the independent variables on the dependent variable is independent, or *additive*. For example, the variable *QUALSQFT* states that the effect of square footage on value varies by construction quality and, by the same token, that good construction quality adds more to value in a large house than in a small one.

Finally, transformations can be combined. Consider, for example, the variable,

$$QUAL \times SQFT^{0.90}. \quad (15)$$

This transformation states that *SQFT* adds to value at a decreasing rate and, further, that the effect is interactive with construction quality (*QUAL*).

Types of Models
The general model structure developed earlier is usually preferred in mass appraisal. It is open, flexible, and reflects the market. However, software that will calibrate the general model structure is just beginning to be widely used. For this reason, model builders often use two simpler structures, additive and multiplicative, that have produced satisfactory results.

Additive Models Additive models are of the form:

$$S = b_0 + b_1 X_1 + b_2 X_2 + \ldots + b_p X_p, \quad (16)$$

where

   S is the dependent variable

   $X_1, X_2, \ldots, X_p$ are the independent variables (p is the number of independent variables)

   b_0 is a constant

   $b_1, b_2, \ldots, b_p$ are the coefficients for the independent variables

The dependent and independent variables are specified by the appraiser during model specification and $b_0, \ldots, b_p$ are determined during model calibration.

An example of a simple additive model is:

$$S = \$23,940 + \$34.20 \times SQFT + \$5,880 \times QUAL - 0.34 \times AGESQFT - \$3,100 \times NBHD1 + \$6,550 \times NBHD2 - \$2,480 \times NBHD4, \quad (17)$$

where

   S is sale price

   $SQFT$ is square feet of living area

   $QUAL$ is construction quality (scalar variable: poor = 0.70, average = 1.00, good = 1.25, very good = 1.50)

   $AGESQFT$ is the product of AGE and $SQFT$

   $NBHD1$, $NBHD2$, and $NBHD4$ are binary variables for neighborhood ($NBHD3$ is the excluded reference neighborhood)

In an additive model, the dependent variable is estimated by multiplying each independent variable by its coefficient and *adding* the results to the constant. In the present example, the estimated value of an 1,800-square-foot, 20-year-old house of average construction quality in neighborhood 4 is:

$$S = \$23,940 + (\$34.20 \times 1,800) + (\$5,880 \times 1.00) - (\$0.34 \times 20 \times 1,800) - (\$2,480 \times 1.00);$$

$$S = \$23,940 + \$61,560 + \$5,880 - \$12,240 - \$2,480 = \$76,660.$$

Multiplicative Models   In a multiplicative model, the variables are not multiplied by their coefficients. Instead, they are either raised to powers or themselves serve as powers; the results are then *multiplied*. An example of a simple multiplicative model is

$$S = b_0 \times SQFT^{b_1} \times QUAL^{b_2} \times PERGOOD^{b_3} \times b_4^{NBHD1} \times b_5^{NBHD2} \times b_6^{NBHD4}, \quad (18)$$

where $PERGOOD$ is $(100 - AGE)/100$ and the other variables are as described above. In this model, the variables $SQFT$, $QUAL$, and $PERGOOD$ are raised to powers; the variables $NBHD1$, $NBHD2$, and $NBHD4$ are exponents with values of either 0 or 1 depending on neighborhood. (Recall that any number raised to the power 0 is 1 and that any number raised to the power 1 is itself.)

A multiplicative model is solved by first converting it to an additive model. This is done by taking the natural logarithm of both sides:

$$\ln S = \ln (b_0 \times SQFT^{b_1} \times QUAL^{b_2} \times PERGOOD^{b_3} \times b_4^{NBHD1} \times b_5^{NBHD2} \times b_6^{NBHD4}). \quad (19)$$

Once calibrated and converted back to its original units, the model might appear as follows:

$$S = \$58.28 \times SQFT^{0.988} \times QUAL^{1.09} \times PERGOOD^{0.873} \times 1.133^{NBHD1} \times 0.968^{NBHD2} \times 0.952^{NBHD4}. \quad (20)$$

For the house described above,

$$S = \$58.28 \times 1{,}800^{0.988} \times 1.00^{1.09}$$
$$\times\ 0.80^{0.873} \times 0.952;$$

$$S = \$58.28 \times 1{,}645 \times 0.823$$
$$\times\ 0.952 = \$75{,}114.$$

Multiplicative models directly capture economies of scale and interactions present in real estate markets. However, they cannot incorporate additive relationships or permit separation of land and building components.

Hybrid Models A hybrid model is one that incorporates both additive and multiplicative components, for example,

$$S = [\$23{,}940 + (\$34.20 \times SQFT)$$
$$+ (\$5{,}880 \times QUAL) - (0.34$$
$$\times\ AGESQFT)] \times [1.133^{NBHD1}$$
$$\times\ 0.968^{NBHD2} \times 0.952^{NBHD4}]. \quad (21)$$

This model is similar to the additive model in equation 17 but incorporates multiplicative neighborhood variables. This allows the model builder to hypothesize, for example, that location in a desirable neighborhood (neighborhood 1 above) will increase the value of a large, well-built house more than that of a smaller and less-well-built one.

The model builder has more freedom in specifying hybrid models and, indeed, more descriptive and higher-quality models should result. However, hybrid models cannot be calibrated directly and have no unique solution. Instead, they are calibrated through a trial-and-error process. (Statistical methods available for hybrid model development include multistage multiple regression analysis [MRA], nonlinear MRA, and adaptive estimation procedure [feedback].)

Determining Model Structures from Data Analysis

Mass appraisal models must reflect appraisal theory and market behavior. Successful modeling begins with market analysis, including a profile of the properties being modeled. During this phase, the appraiser identifies appropriate units of comparison, considers stratification of the data, and decides which data elements and variables to use in model specification. Principal tools used in data analysis are data profiles and two- and three-way analyses.

Data Profiles

Data profiles, discussed in chapter 20, consist of arrays and associated statistics such as the median, minimum, maximum, range, and quartile. Table 2 shows arrayed sale price data and associated statistics for sixteen parcels. Such profiles are useful in describing small data sets but cumbersome and less meaningful for large samples.

Measures of central tendency and dispersion should be calculated for quantitative data, such as square feet and year built. Appropriate measures of central tendency are the median and mean. Appropriate measures of dispersion include the average absolute deviation, coefficient of dispersion, standard deviation, and coefficient of variation (see chapter 20 for a review of these statistics). Together, these measures will indicate typical or average values for each variable and the degree of spread about the average. It is also useful to summarize measures of central tendency and dispersion by stratum. Table 3, for example, shows average sales prices of single-family houses by neighborhood.

Qualitative data should be analyzed using frequency distributions, histograms, and

Table 2.   Array and Associated Statistics

Case number	Sale price
1	$ 8,960
2	15,250
3	18,400
4	24,900
5	25,500
6	30,340
7	35,000
8	42,000
9	46,750
10	49,310
11	55,200
12	60,000
13	64,500
14	72,830
15	86,890
16	95,000

Minimum = $8,960   First quartile = $25,200
Maximum = $95,000   Third quartile = $62,250
Median   = $44,375   Range   = $86,040

Table 3.   Average Sale Price by Neighborhood

Neighborhood	Number of sales	Average sale price	Standard deviation
100	26	$ 78,459	$ 35,823
101	94	67,819	33,912
102	39	124,110	50,348
104	19	98,834	65,876
105	32	76,968	34,982
106	48	53,902	18,424
107	8	165,319	102,412
108	36	102,887	54,335

polygons. Figure 8 shows a frequency distribution and histogram of quality-class data.

Two-Way Analyses

The statistical tools just discussed usually relate to a single independent variable. There

Figure 8.   Frequency Distribution and Histogram

Frequency distribution

Quality class	Parcel count
1	670
2	3,489
3	5,517
4	2,020
5	532
6	176

Histogram

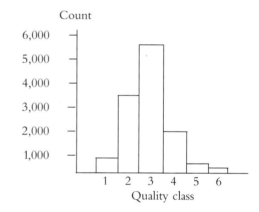

are, however, other tools for evaluating the relationship between two variables. *Cross-tabulations* are used for comparing two qualitative variables or grouped quantitative variables. Table 4, for example, tabulates number of parcels by building class and age group. It shows that newer properties tend to be in higher building classes than older properties.

Scatter diagrams provide a graphic analysis of the relationship between two quantitative variables. The independent variable should be represented on the horizontal (x)

Table 4. Cross-tabulation of Number of Parcels by Age Group and Building Class

Building Class

Age group in years		1	2	3	4	5	6	Total
0–10		0 (0)	420 (.027)	1,246 (.082)	760 (.050)	208 (.014)	109 (.007)	2,743 (.180)
11–25		128 (.008)	1,045 (.069)	2,547 (.167)	845 (.055)	503 (.033)	245 (.016)	5,313 (.348)
26–50		762 (.050)	1,235 (.081)	988 (.065)	381 (.025)	90 (.006)	58 (.004)	3,514 (.231)
Over 50		905 (.060)	1,623 (.106)	750 (.049)	302 (.020)	76 (.005)	10 (.001)	3,666 (.241)
Total		1,795	4,323	5,531	2,288	877	422	15,236

axis and the dependent variable on the vertical (y) axis. Figure 9 shows a scatter diagram of sale price per square foot plotted against building age (numbers in the diagram are number of sales).

Correlation analysis can be used to quantify the degree of linearity between two variables. The *correlation coefficient*, abbreviated r, ranges from −1 to +1. If two variables are perfectly linearly related, plotting one against the other will produce a straight line and r will be either −1 or +1, depending on the direction of the relationship. If the variables bear no linear relationship to each other, r will be zero.

The correlation coefficient of the data in figure 10 is approximately −0.60. In figure 10, correlation coefficients are +1 in panel (a), −1 in panel (b), +0.6 in panel (c), −0.8 in panel (d), and 0 in panels (e) and (f). Note in panel (f) that the correlation coefficient is 0, even though the two variables are highly related. This occurs because the relationship is nonlinear. A *correlation matrix* shows the correlation coefficients between each pair of variables in a data set. Figure 11 contains an example.

Another effective tool for analyzing relationships between variables are breakdowns by strata, for example, sale price by age range, construction class, or neighborhood, as in table 3. Analyses of this kind are useful in revealing potential stratification criteria, data interactions, and outliers.

Three-Way Analyses
Several techniques compare the relationships among three variables. Contingency tables

Figure 9. Scatter Diagram

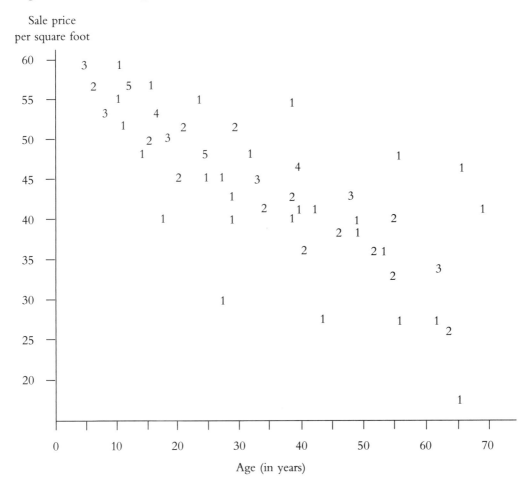

Limits of Statistical Analysis

show how a response variable varies with changes in two control variables. For example, table 5 shows average sales prices by neighborhood and construction class (number of cases is in parentheses). The response variable in such analyses should be a quantitative variable, and the control variables should be qualitative or grouped quantitative variables. Software that will produce three-dimensional graphs is widely available. Figure 12 contains an example of the output.

Limits of Statistical Analysis

Data profiles and graphic analyses are limited to three dimensions or variables. The real world, of course, is more complex. The calibration of mass appraisal models, therefore, requires multivariate statistical tools, such as MRA and feedback, that can handle many variables simultaneously. Nevertheless, successful model building begins with the careful analysis of each variable and its interrelationships, as discussed above. Even so,

Figure 10. Correlation Coefficients

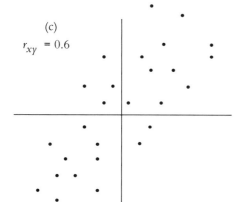

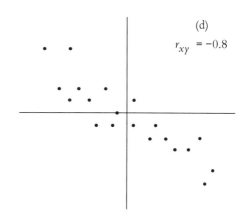

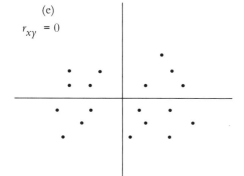

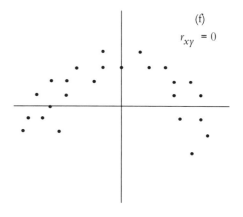

Figure 11.   Correlation Matrix

	Y	X_1	X_2	X_3	X_4	X_5
Y	1.000	.790	− .560	.655	.690	− .300
X_1	.790	1.000	.065	.493	.855	− .423
X_2	− .560	.065	1.000	− .465	.777	.200
X_3	.655	.493	− .465	1.000	− .799	− .132
X_4	.690	.855	.777	− .799	1.000	− .558
X_5	− .300	− .423	.200	− .132	− .558	1.000

Table 5.   Contingency Table of Average Sale Price in Dollars by Neighborhood and Construction Class

Neighborhood	Construction Class					Total
	1	2	3	4	5	
1001	34,065	32,673	39,843	52,456	73,897	40,947
	(10)	(24)	(35)	(18)	(3)	(90)
1002	43,447	50,908	67,810	85,413	105,678	66,872
	(7)	(40)	(25)	(19)	(11)	(102)
1003	47,325	55,657	78,112	95,673	123,510	93,069
	(2)	(8)	(38)	(41)	(28)	(117)
1004	39,008	47,423	82,442	88,980	110,517	71,540
	(14)	(22)	(53)	(10)	(6)	(105)
Total	38,956	45,841	69,056	83,857	114,699	68,824
	(33)	(94)	(151)	(88)	(48)	(414)

different model builders will draw different conclusions and specify different models from similar analyses of the same data. Many different models may prove equally accurate and supportable for a given data base; good judgment is always essential.

Specifying the Cost Approach

General Considerations

The cost approach is based on the principle of substitution: a purchaser will pay no more for a property than the cost of acquiring land and constructing a substitute building of

equal utility. The cost approach follows the structure of the general model developed earlier in equation 4:

$$MV = IV + LV, \qquad (4)$$

which can be expanded, as shown earlier, to a market-adjusted hybrid cost model:

$$MV = \pi GQ[(\pi BQ \times \Sigma BA) + (\pi LQ \times \Sigma LA) + \Sigma OA], \quad (12)$$

where the variables are as defined above for equation 12.

Figure 12. Three-Dimensional Graph

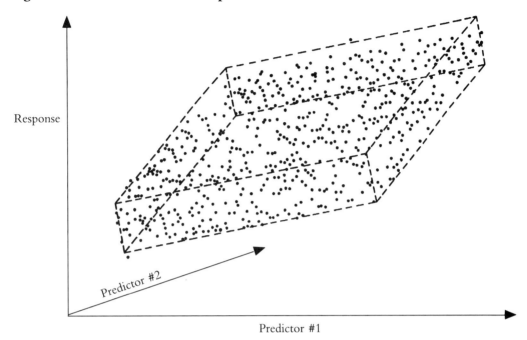

The building and additions components (*BQ*, *BA*, and *OA*), except for depreciation, represent the supply side of the market and are calibrated from construction cost data. Depreciation and the other components represent the demand side and are calibrated from market data. The result, if done properly, is an accurate estimate of market value. Chapter 7 discussed the determination of land values used in the cost approach and chapter 8 discussed the theory and mechanics of the cost approach. This section discusses specification of residential and nonresidential market-adjusted cost models used in mass appraisal. Chapter 15 discusses calibration of such models.

Residential Improvements

The first step in specifying cost models is to stratify improvements into homogeneous groups. There is usually a different market for each group. Potential purchasers of properties in one group are unlikely to consider a purchase from another group as an alternative. For residential properties, properties are usually stratified by occupancy, story height, and construction grade or wall type. A typical inventory is:

Occupancy
  One-family residential
  Two-family residential
  Three-family residential
  Four-family residential
Story height
  One story
  One-and-one-half stories
  Two stories
  Two-and-one-half stories
  Three stories
  Three-and-one-half stories

Wall type
  Wood frame or metal siding
  Brick or stone veneer
  Concrete block

This classification structure implies seventy-two model types (4 × 6 × 3). One model would consist of single-family, one-story houses of wood or metal siding; a second model would consist of single-family, one-story houses with wood or brick veneer; and so forth.

Next, the typical characteristics, or *base specifications*, of each model are specified. Using the unit-in-place or quantity survey method (chapter 8), reproduction or replacement cost new is then estimated. In mass appraisal, however, these costs are converted to comparative unit costs. For residential structures, costs can usually be divided into horizontal, vertical, building addition, constant building component, qualitative, and other addition costs.

Horizontal Costs Horizontal cost components are those related to area. Examples are floors and roofs. Total costs for such components are estimated by applying a price per square foot to the applicable area. For example, if a building has 600 square feet of hardwood floors, the cost of which is $4.50 per square foot, the total cost is

$$\$4.50 \times 600 = \$2,700.$$

Most costs in residential buildings are horizontal. The sum of such costs for a house meeting the base specifications is the *base rate* for that model.

Vertical Costs Vertical cost components relate to items that are physically vertical and tend to increase in direct proportion to linear feet or perimeter. Exterior walls and interior partitions are examples. These costs should be expressed per linear foot, with adjustments for atypical story heights. Total costs for such components are estimated by multiplying the linear foot cost rate against the linear feet of the component and applying any required height adjustments. For example, if the cost of constructing a 9-foot, average quality brick veneer wall on wood frame is $55.00 per linear foot, the cost for a home with a 200-foot perimeter having this type of wall would be

$$\$55.00 \times 200 = \$11,000.$$

Vertical costs can be converted to horizontal by dividing total costs by square footage. In the above example, assuming a 2,100-square-foot building, the cost per square foot is

$$\$11,000/2,100 = \$5.24.$$

This method is often used to build exterior wall costs into base rates, with adjustments provided for atypical area-to-perimeter ratios.

Building Addition Costs Building additions are structures attached to the main living area, such as basements, garages, and porches. Their costs are usually expressed per square foot.

Constant Building Component Costs For items whose costs are usually not related to size, such as bathrooms, fireplaces, and kitchen appliances, costs are expressed as lump sums, such as $3,000 for a bathroom or $600 for a water heater. The cost of such items varies with quality, for example, a flagstone fireplace costs more than a prefabricated one. Constant cost items are one major reason that horizontal building costs per square foot tend to decrease as size increases, because the costs of such components are spread over a larger area.

Qualitative Cost Components These are percentage adjustments made to the primary structure (including attached additions) to reflect variations in quality and workmanship. They are usually referred to as *grade* adjustments in cost manuals.

Other Additions Some structures or miscellaneous items are not attached to the primary residence. Examples include fencing, swimming pools, and outbuildings. Their cost may be calculated on a square foot, linear foot, or lump-sum basis. However, unlike attached additions, they are treated independently from the primary structure, meaning that they do not receive the same qualitative adjustments.

The combination of horizontal, vertical, attached, constant, qualitative, and other addition cost components yields replacement cost new (*RCN*). Mathematically,

$$RCN = [\pi BQ \times (\Sigma BA_H + \Sigma BA_V + \Sigma BA_A + \Sigma BA_C)] + \Sigma OA, \quad (22)$$

where

πBQ is the product of building qualitative factors

ΣBA_H is the sum of horizontal building component costs

ΣBA_V is the sum of vertical building component costs

ΣBA_A is the sum of building addition (attached) costs

ΣBA_C is the sum of constant building component costs

ΣOA is the sum of other addition (for example, outbuilding) costs

This formulation is the same as that of the general market-adjusted cost model in equation 12, except that the additive building components have been broken down into horizontal, vertical, attached, and constant market-adjusted cost components.

Once determined, *RCN* must be adjusted for depreciation and general qualitative factors. With these final adjustments, the market-adjusted cost model appears as follows:

$$MV = \pi GQ \times [(1 - BQ_D) \times RCN + LV], \quad (23)$$

where BQ_D is a building qualitative factor for depreciation (several factors may apply to different improvements), and all other terms are as defined previously.

Nonresidential Improvements

Nonresidential cost models operate on the same basic principles as residential ones, although stratification and cost components are somewhat different. Stratification is usually based on structure type and number of floors. Structure types, similar to fire code classifications, reflect major differences in structural quality. Story groupings capture cost variations inherent in building heights. The following represents a typical stratification scheme:

Structure type
  Fireproofed steel frame (Class A)
  Fireproofed reinforced concrete frame (Class B)
  Masonry/steel frame (Class C)
  Wood/masonry/steel frame (Class D)

Stories
   0–4
   5–10
  11–15
  16–20

This scheme implies sixteen models (4 × 4) and accommodates most structures found in a typical assessment jurisdiction.

Nonresidential cost models contain the same six basic cost components found in residential properties, but there are some important differences in the format of the horizontal and vertical components. First, horizontal components are divided between structural and interior finish costs. This is necessary because many nonresidential buildings accommodate multiple tenants, each requiring a different interior finish. For example, a five-story Class B structure with brick on block curtain walls might well have ground-level retail stores and upper-level offices and apartment units. Such a building would have one structural rate and many interior finish rates. Each such rate would include costs for floor finish, ceiling finish, plumbing, and other features that depend on occupancy and would be applied against the number of square feet in each particular use. For example, interior finish costs applicable to a light warehouse may be as shown in table 6.

Typical interior cost rates for other occupancy groups can be computed in the same way and included in cost manuals. Figure 13 lists interior finish types (occupancy groups) found in many jurisdictions. To compute total horizontal interior costs, multiply the square feet of each occupancy group by the appropriate rate, make any required adjustments for atypical features, and sum the results.

Table 6. Interior Finish Costs for a Light Warehouse

Floor finish	10% vinyl tile 90% concrete with sealer	$0.8511
Ceiling finish	Gypsum board, taped & paneled	1.2383
Interior partitions	8″ concrete block, typical wall/floor ratio	1.4895
Heating	Suspended space heaters	0.8976
Electrical/lighting	Typical for occupancy	2.0148
Plumbing	Typical for occupancy	1.7468
Total rate per square foot		$8.2381

Vertical costs for nonresidential properties are also divided between structural and interior costs. Vertical structural costs are a function of type of wall and materials. Typical costs should be determined for each wall type, for example, wood, masonry, and steel. The base wall cost for a building can then be computed as follows:

Linear feet × average floor height × number of floors × wall rate.

Assume, for example, that a building has a perimeter of 400 feet, a ground floor area of 10,000 square feet, 5 floors, and an average wall height of 10 feet per floor, implying a total floor area of 50,000 square feet (10,000 × 5). If structural building costs are $12.89 per square foot of wall area, total structural exterior wall costs are

400 × 10 × 5 × $12.89 = $257,800,

Figure 13. Interior Finish Types (Occupancy Groups)

Store — one story	Hotel
Department store	Motel
Discount store	Light manufacturing
Supermarket	Heavy industrial
Shopping center — mall	Food processing
Shopping center — finished	Warehousing
retail shell	Cold storage warehouse
Shopping center — Community	Dairy building
Office building — one-story,	Church
non-fireproof	Covenant
Office building — multistory,	Rectory
fireproof	Private, elementary,
Commercial airport terminal	secondary school
Private airport hanger	Private college
Restaurant/cafeteria	Private dormitory
Drive-in/fast food	Private fraternity house
Financial — main office	Private hospital
Financial — branch office	Homes for the aged
Appliance service/repair	Mortuary, cemetery
Service, paint, electrical	building, crematorium
repair, laundry	Club, lodge, union hall
Service station	Yacht club
Automotive showroom	Country club
Bus terminal	Library
Truck terminal	Public school
Parking garage	Government-owned college
Wholesale outlet, produce	Government-owned hospital
outlet, manufacturing outlet	Municipal building
Florist, greenhouse	Movie theater
Theater, auditorium, arena	Stage theater
Bowling alley, skating rink	

or $5.156 per square foot of floor area ($257,800/50,000). The latter could be added to the structural rate applicable to the building and multiplied against the total square footage to compute a combined structural cost.

Interior partitions are handled in the same way:

Linear feet × average partition height
× number of floors × partition rate.

If a building is occupied by more than one group, the calculations should be repeated for each and totaled. As with structural costs, vertical interior costs can be combined with horizontal interior costs and expressed as square-foot rates in a cost manual. However, adjustments must be provided for nonstandard features and floor heights.

In summary, *RCN* of nonresidential improvements can be calculated as follows:

$$RCN = [\pi BQ \times (\Sigma BA_S + \Sigma BA_I$$
$$+ \Sigma BA_A + \Sigma BA_C)] + \Sigma OA. \tag{24}$$

where

πBQ is the product of building qualitative factors

ΣBA_S is the sum of structural components costs (including exterior walls converted to cost per square foot)

ΣBA_I is the sum of interior finish components costs (including partitions converted to cost per square foot)

ΣBA_A is the sum of building addition (attached) costs

ΣBA_C is the sum of constant building component costs

ΣOA is the sum of other addition costs

As with residential properties, RCN is depreciated, adjusted for qualitative factors, and added to the value of land and other (unattached) additions:

$$MV = \pi GQ \times [(1 - BQ_D) \times RCN + LV], \tag{25}$$

where BQ_D is a building qualitative factor for depreciation.

Specifying Sales Comparison Models

Overview

The sales comparison approach reflects the principles of supply and demand, contribution, and substitution. Directly rooted in market data, the sales comparison approach is preferred when adequate sales exist. As discussed in chapter 6, in single-property appraisal the approach takes the form,

$$MV_s = S_c + ADJ_c \tag{26}$$

where MV_s is the estimated market value of the subject property, S_c is the sale price of a comparable property or properties, and ADJ_c are adjustments made for quantitative and qualitative differences between the comparable and subject properties. In this approach, the value for the subject property is derived through a comparison with other parcels rather than directly from a common valuation model. The technique suffers in that it is tedious, prone to inconsistency, and unstable over time.

In mass appraisal, the sales comparison approach is based on the general model structure introduced earlier:

$$MV = IV + LV. \tag{4}$$

As explained above, this model can be expanded to incorporate both additive and qualitative building and land components, additional structures, and general qualitative adjustments:

$$MV = \pi GQ[(\pi BQ \times \Sigma BA) + (\pi LQ \times \Sigma LA) + \Sigma OA], \tag{12}$$

where the variables are as defined above for equation 12.

This hybrid model is adaptable to most types of improved properties and most data bases. It can be calibrated using multistage MRA, nonlinear MRA, or feedback (see chapter 15). It cannot, however, be calibrated by the most common type of MRA, linear MRA, or by multiplicative MRA, because the model components are neither totally additive nor totally multiplicative.

In many situations, however, a strictly additive or multiplicative substitute will suffice. The additive form of the sales comparison approach is

$$MV = b_0 + b_1X_1 + b_2X_2 + \ldots + b_pX_p, \qquad (27)$$

where

MV is estimated market value

$X_1, X_2, \ldots, X_p$ are the independent variables (p is the number of variables)

b_0 is a constant dollar amount

$b_1, b_2, \ldots, b_p$ are the coefficients for the independent variables (compare equation 16)

In this model, market value is estimated as a total amount without separation between land and buildings. Although strictly additive in structure, the model can include multiplicative and nonlinear variables. For example, a variable may represent the product of square feet and building quality, so that living area in good-quality houses is assumed to command greater value per square foot than in average-quality homes. An example of a nonlinear variable would be the square root of land area. Through the wise use of such transformations, model builders can often obtain highly satisfactory results with additive models, particularly in relatively homogeneous markets.

The multiplicative form of the sales comparison approach is

$$MV = b_0 \times \pi b_i^{X_i} \times \pi X_j^{b_j}, \qquad (28)$$

where b_0 is a constant dollar value per square foot (base rate), X_i are binary qualitative variables (coded 0 or 1), b_i are factors or multipliers associated with the presence of given characteristics, X_j are either quantitative or scalar qualitative variables, and b_j are their corresponding exponents (compare equation 18). In effect, the constant is adjusted for various qualitative features to obtain a modified value per unit (usually per square foot) and multiplied against the number of units (square feet) raised to an appropriate power to reflect economies of scale. The earlier discussion of multiplicative models contains a simple example. Such models easily incorporate multiplicative relationships but have difficulty in recognizing additive components and in separating land and building factors. The latter problem can sometimes be addressed by incorporating a proxy for land and building relationships, such as the ratio of land area to building area. Such models are calibrated by taking logarithms, which reduces them to additive models, and then using linear MRA. As with additive models, thoughtful specification can often produce good results.

Stratification and Location Analysis

Perhaps the most important aspect of market analysis is location. Property values for otherwise similar parcels can vary substantially due to location. During market analysis, one should include location as an independent variable in cross-tabulations, breakdowns, and the like. This will reveal patterns in values due to location and aid in model specification.

Three basic ways to analyze location in mass appraisal model building are: multiple models based on geographic stratification, multiple models based on cluster analysis, and a single model with location adjustments.

Geographic Stratification   In geographic stratification, boundaries are drawn along rivers and other natural barriers, major streets, and subdivision lines to reflect major differences in location. Separate models are then specified for *each* such area.

Geographic stratification is appropriate whenever the value of various property attributes varies significantly among areas and is particularly effective when housing types and styles are relatively uniform within areas. In general, boundaries should be drawn between two areas when buyers would consider purchasing in one area but not the other. At the same time, drawing too many boundaries should be avoided. Successful modeling requires adequate sales and a reasonable mix of property characteristics. If areas are too homogeneous, calibration techniques cannot reliably estimate the effect on value of each characteristic, particularly those that occur infrequently.

Geographic stratification has the strong advantage of being tailored to local supply and demand factors that may vary substantially across a jurisdiction. Thus, the sales used to calibrate a given model will reflect the market influences and conditions only of that area, so more accurate and supportable models are produced. Nevertheless, there are also potential shortcomings. First, the use of multiple models might create inconsistencies when adjacent properties are assigned to different neighborhoods. Careful selection of boundaries can reduce this problem. Second, assigning and maintaining neighborhoods and developing many models can be an administrative burden. A good neighborhood maintenance system permits neighborhood codes based on geographic coordinates, book

and map numbers, and so on to be assigned without having to access individual parcels.

Stratification Using Cluster Analysis
Cluster analysis is a statistical technique for combining items based on analysis of their similarities and differences. In mass appraisal, cluster analysis can be used to combine properties into relatively homogeneous strata based on location and physical characteristics such as age, size, style, and construction quality. The appraiser can choose which characteristics to use in the analysis, what weight to give to each, the number of clusters (strata) desired, and the algorithm for determining similarity. With respect to the last, several procedures are available. One common algorithm, the Euclidean distance metric, is based on squared differences between properties. Another, the city block metric, is based on absolute differences. (See the discussion of dissimilarity functions in chapter 7).

Once strata are determined, a single, or "global," model is developed for each, just as in geographic stratification. Neighborhood binary variables may be used (see below). Although the properties in each strata will be physically similar, adjacent parcels that are not physically similar may well fall in different strata. Inconsistencies between adjacent parcels are thus potentially more serious than in neighborhood stratification.

Proponents of cluster analysis usually concede that it is appropriate only when neighborhood boundaries cannot be clearly defined. The technique works best when properties differ more within neighborhoods than between neighborhoods. In such conditions, buyers will conduct a broad search and give greater weight to physical attributes than to geographic area.

Single Model with Location Adjustments In this method, a single model with locational variables is used for the entire jurisdiction. Advantages include reducing model-building efforts and locational inconsistencies. On the negative side, one model may not adequately fit a heterogeneous jurisdiction.

There are two ways to address locational variations in the context of a single model. One is simply to employ neighborhood, or "subarea," binary variables. In the additive model shown in equation 27, several of the independent variables (X_1, X_2, ..., X_p) would be binary variables for neighborhood (1 if the property is located in the neighborhood and 0 if not). A typical neighborhood should be selected as the reference and *not* included in the model, so that the coefficients for the other neighborhoods reflect their differences in value relative to the reference neighborhood. In a multiplicative or hybrid model structure, neighborhood variables would appear as general qualitative variables. Again, one equation is developed for each market area.

A more sophisticated technique (location value response surface analysis) is to identify *value influence centers* (VICs) and compute the distance of each parcel from these centers. The distances are then employed as independent variables in the valuation model. This technique has the advantage of adjusting smoothly for location, virtually eliminating boundary problems (see chapter 15).

Considerations by Property Type

Residential Property Mass appraisal applications of the sales comparison approach usually work well for residential properties. However, success depends on adequate data. As a general rule, there should be fifty or more contemporary sales per model (see appendix 5.3 for adjusting sales prices for time). Property data should be accurate and include those attributes important in explaining value in the jurisdiction. Model specification varies by property type.

Single-Family Residential Additive, multiplicative, and hybrid models can all be used effectively for single-family residential property. Additive models are the simplest and most common. Their results can usually be improved through interactive and nonlinear terms. A simple example is

$$
\begin{aligned}
MV = {} & b_0 + (b_1 \times SQFT \times QUAL) + \\
& (b_2 \times FINBASE \times QUAL) + (b_3 \times \\
& UNFBASE) + (b_4 \times GARSQFT) + \\
& (b_5 \times PATSQFT) + (b_6 \times BATHS \\
& \times QUAL) + (b_7 \times LNAGE) \\
& + (b_8 \times SQRTLAND) + (b_9 \\
& \times NBHD2) + (b_{10} \times NBHD3) \\
& + (b_{11} \times NBHD4),
\end{aligned}
\tag{29}
$$

where
  SQFT is square feet of main living area
  QUAL is construction quality (scalar variable centered on 1.00)
  FINBASE is finished basement area
  UNFBASE is unfinished basement area
  GARSQFT is garage area
  PATSQFT is patio area
  BATHS is number of baths (1, 1½, 2, and so on)
  LNAGE is the natural log of effective age
  SQRTLAND is the square root of land area
  NBHD2 is a binary variable for neighborhood 2 (0 or 1)

NBHD3 is a binary variable for neighborhood 3 (0 or 1)

NBHD4 is a binary variable for neighborhood 4 (0 or 1)

This model has eleven variables, including three interactive and two nonlinear terms. Note that *SQFT*, *FINBASE*, and *BATHS* are multiplied by *QUAL*, implying that their relationship to market value interacts with construction quality. The variable *LNAGE* is a nonlinear term, which assumes that depreciation advances at a slower rate as buildings become older. Similarly, the variable *SQRTLAND* means that land value does not increase proportionately with lot size. Neighborhood is represented by three binary variables (neighborhood 1 is the reference neighborhood). This simple model captures essential market relationships and is easily explained.

Although the model uses several interactive variables, all the terms are additive, and the result cannot be separated into land and building values. A model incorporating both additive and multiplicative terms would require the hybrid model structure, for example,

$$MV = [PERGOOD^{b_1} \times QUAL^{b_2}] \times$$
$$[(b_3 \times SQFT) + (b_4 \times FINBASE) +$$
$$(b_5 \times BATHS) + (b_6 \times UNFBASE)$$
$$+ (b_7 \times GARSQFT) + (b_8 \times$$
$$PATSQFT)] + [b_8^{NBHD2} \times b_9^{NBHD3}$$
$$\times b_{10}^{NBHD4} \times LAND^{b_{11}}], \quad (30)$$

where *PERGOOD* is a scalar variable for "percent good" ranging from some minimum value, say 0.30, for very old buildings to 1.00 for new construction. In this model, *PER-*

GOOD and *QUAL* are building qualitative variables and *NBHD2*, *NBHD3*, and *NBHD4* are land qualitative variables. If location is felt to affect both land and improvements, then the latter could be used as general qualitative variables. The variables *PERGOOD* and *QUAL* will be rescaled appropriately, depending on the value of their computed exponents. The resulting values are easily divided between land and buildings.

For simplicity, the above models use few variables. Characteristics often important in single-family residential models are listed in figure 14.

Figure 14. Important Characteristics for Single-Family Residential Models

Important characteristics	Land characteristics
Main living area	Neighborhood
Finished basement area	Lot size
Unfinished basement area	Lot shape
Usable attic area	Topography
Construction quality	Traffic
Design	Distance to central
Wall type	business district
Roof type	Schools, shopping
Garage type and area	Lake or golf frontage
Patio type and area	View
Actual age	Utilities
Effective age or condition	Other
Bathrooms	Outbuildings
Fireplaces	Swimming pool
Heating	Hot tub/jacuzzi
Cooling	Fencing
Interior finish	

Although adding variables tends to improve accuracy, models should also be simple and explainable. In addition, increasing the number of variables increases proportionately the number of sales required to calibrate the regression coefficients. As a general rule, the number of sales should be at least four times the number of independent variables. A model with twenty independent variables, for example, requires at least eighty sales. With respect to location, any of the three procedures described can be appropriate for single-family models.

Condominiums/Townhouses The sales comparison approach is particularly well suited to condominiums and townhouses. Because of their relative homogeneity, a simple additive or multiplicative model will usually suffice. One difference from single-family properties is that complexes or groups of similar complexes can be used in lieu of neighborhood variables. Such variables usually capture the unique locational, common area, and other features of each complex. A simple additive model is:

$$MV = b_0 + (b_1 \times SQFT \times QUAL) + (b_2 \times GARSQFT) + (b_3 \times PATSQFT) + (b_4 \times AGE) + (b_5 \times COMPLEX1) + (b_6 \times COMPLEX2) + \ldots + (b_p \times COMPLEXn), \qquad (31)$$

where *COMPLEX1*, ..., *COMPLEXn* are binary variables for each complex or group of similar complexes. The coefficients for these variables will reflect their relative locational desirability, construction quality, and common-area attributes. A typical complex should be selected as the reference and *not* included as a binary variable in the model.

Alternatively, separate, highly simplified models can be developed for each large complex or group of smaller complexes. Such a

model requires very few variables (and therefore sales), because all the units will share the same building, common area, and locational features. A simple model of this type is

$$MV = b_0 + (b_1 \times SQFT) + (b_2 \times GARAGE) + (b_3 \times ENDUNIT) + (b_4 \times GOLF), \qquad (32)$$

where *GARAGE* is number of garage stalls (0, 1, or 2), *ENDUNIT* is end unit (0 or 1), and *GOLF* is golf view (0 or 1). In many situations, such a model could be adequately calibrated with only fifteen or twenty sales.

Duplexes, Triplexes, and Fourplexes These properties can often be modeled in the same way as single-family houses. Smaller sales volume, however, may dictate fewer variables and the use of a global model with neighborhood adjustments rather than separate models by area. In addition, a variable (or binary variables) for number of units can be used to adjust for any investor preferences between two-, three-, and four-unit properties. A simple multiplicative model of this type is

$$MV = b_0 \times b_1{}^{3PLEX} \times b_2{}^{4PLEX} \times QUAL^{b_3} \times GAR/UNIT^{b_4} \times SQFT^{b_5} \times PERGOOD^{b_6} \times L/B^{b_7} \times b_8{}^{NBHD1} \times \ldots \times b_p{}^{NBHDn}, \qquad (33)$$

where *3PLEX* is a binary variable for triplex, *4PLEX* is a binary variable for fourplex, *QUAL* is a scalar variable for construction quality (average = 1.00), *GAR/UNIT* is garages per living unit (0–2), *SQFT* is total living area (all units), *PERGOOD* is a scalar variable for percent good (maximum 100 percent), *L/B* is the ratio of land area to building area, and *NBHD1*, ..., *NBHDn* are binary variables for neighborhood. In this case, the constant, b_0, represents the per square foot value of a new duplex of average quality.

Alternatively, the dependent variable can be expressed on a per unit basis, for example,

$$
\begin{aligned}
MV/UNIT = {} & b_0 + (b_1 \times SQFT/UNIT) \\
& + (b_2 \times QUAL) + (b_3 \times \\
& GAR/UNIT) + (b_4 \times AGE) \\
& + (b_5 \times 3PLEX) + (b_6 \times \\
& 4PLEX) + (b_7 \times NBHD1) \\
& + \ldots + (b_p \times NBHDn).
\end{aligned}
$$

$$(34)$$

Values would be computed by multiplying the estimated value per unit by the number of units.

Mobile Homes Sale price data for mobile homes can often be obtained from dealers or other sources. In such cases, additive or multiplicative mobile home models are possible. The value of the mobile home can be computed separately and combined with the value of the land and any additions (hookups, cabanas, and so on). Land and site improvement variables are, therefore, not required in modeling. An example of a simple multiplicative model is

$$
\begin{aligned}
MV = {} & b_0 \times SQFT^{b_1} \times QUAL^{b_2} \\
& \times PERGOOD^{b_3}.
\end{aligned}
$$

$$(35)$$

Income Properties Larger jurisdictions may be able to develop effective sales comparison models for certain income properties. Because income properties are so varied, however, separate models are usually required for different property types.

Apartments Of all income properties, apartments are easiest to model. Because of large variations in sales prices, the dependent variable is usually best expressed on a per-unit basis. An example of a hybrid model is

$$
\begin{aligned}
MV/UNIT = {} & (b_1{}^{NBHD1} \times b_2{}^{NBHD2} \times b_3{}^{NBHD3}) \\
& \times \{(PERGOOD^{b_4} \times \\
& QUAL^{b_5}) \times [(b_6 \times SQFT/ \\
& UNIT) + (b_7 \times BED/UNIT)] \\
& + VIEW^{b_8} \times [(b_9 \times \\
& DISTCBD) + (b_{10} \times \\
& LNLAND)] + (b_{11} \times \\
& POOL)\},
\end{aligned}
$$

$$(36)$$

where
   NBHD1, . . . , NBHD3 are general qualitative binary variables for neighborhood (*NBHD4* is assumed to be the reference neighborhood)
   PERGOOD and *QUAL* are as previously described (building qualitative)
   SQFT/UNIT and *BED/UNIT* are square feet and bedrooms per unit, respectively (building additive)
   VIEW is a land qualitative variable for view (average = 1.00)
   DISTCBD and *LNLAND* are land additive variables for distance to the central business district and the natural log of land area, respectively
   POOL is pool area (other additive)

With eleven variables, approximately forty-four sales (11 × 4) would be required to calibrate this model reliably.

If available, income data can be used in apartment models. However, such data will be highly correlated with property characteristics data, so that the coefficients for the latter may be insignificant or difficult to interpret. For this reason, some appraisers prefer to use only property characteristics data in sales comparison models.

Commercial Property   Because of their heterogeneity, commercial properties present greater difficulties than apartments. Binary variables are needed to distinguish different types of property. Also, because of wide variations in sales prices, multiplicative and hybrid models are preferred to additive models. In additive models, the dependent variable should be expressed as value per square foot. The following is an example of a simple multiplicative model:

$$MV = b_0 \times b_1{}^{STORE} \times b_2{}^{REST} \times b_3{}^{AUTO}$$
$$\times b_4{}^{CONV} \times SQFT^{b_5} \times QUAL^{b_6}$$
$$\times PERGOOD^{b_7} \times L/B^{b_8}, \quad (37)$$

where *STORE* is retail store (0 or 1), *REST* is restaurant or tavern (0 or 1), *AUTO* is auto sales and service (0 or 1), *CONV* is convenience mart or fast food (0 or 1), and the other variables are as previously defined.

In this model, office buildings are assumed to be the reference property type (other property types are excluded because of insufficient sales). Hence, b_0 will represent the value per square foot of a new office building of average construction quality. The coefficients $b_1, \ldots, b_4$ are percentage multipliers for other property types. For example, if b_0 is \$50.00 and b_1 is 0.86, then the value per square foot of a new retail store of average construction quality is \$43.00 (\$50.00 × 0.86). The variables *QUAL* and *PERGOOD* provide adjustments for variations in construction quality and effective age. Approximately thirty-two sales (8 variables × 4 required sales per variable) would be required to calibrate the model.

Several methods are available for expanding the usable number of commercial sales: (1) use older, time-adjusted sales (see appendix 5-3); (2) adjust rather than discard sales with nonmarket financing, personal property, and the like (appendix 5-1); (3) use sales from similar jurisdictions. In any case, the number of sales will largely dictate the number of variables that can be used. Often the model builder will have to combine property types for analysis, such as convenience marts and fast food stores in the example above. If sales permit, separate models can be developed for certain property types, such as office buildings and retail stores.

As with apartments, income data can be used in models, although this can confuse interpretation and compromise the independence of the sales comparison and income approaches. Perhaps more important, this will limit direct application of the models to subject properties for which income data have been obtained and audited.

Industrial Property   In general, modeling considerations applicable to commercial properties also apply to industrial properties. Except for warehouses, however, there are rarely enough sales of industrial properties for modeling. In some cases, it may be possible to model warehouses separately. Because they tend to be relatively homogeneous, a simple model with several variables can give satisfactory results. Alternatively, if there are too few warehouse sales for a separate model, they can be combined with commercial properties.

Land Value Models

Urban Land   Urban land models are discussed separately in chapter 7.

Agricultural Land   Agricultural land models are possible where adequate sales permit. Independent variables should relate to soil productivity, location, and other significant attributes. Because of wide variations in parcel size and sale price, the dependent variable should be expressed as value per acre. The value of any improvements included in the sale price should be subtracted. Additive and multiplicative models will usually suffice. A simple additive model is

$$MV/ACRE = b_0 + (b_1 \times SQRTDIST) \\ + (b_2 \times IRRIG) + (b_3 \times \\ CLASS1) + (b_4 \times CLASS2) \\ + \ldots + (b_p \times CLASSn), \tag{38}$$

where *SQRTDIST* is the square root of distance (miles) to the county seat or other major city (b_1 will usually be negative), *IRRIG* is a binary variable for irrigation (0 or 1), and *CLASS1, CLASS2, ..., CLASSn* are the percentages of land in various soil classifications.

By law, most jurisdictions must assess qualifying farmland on the basis of its value for farm use. In such cases, models should either be developed from sales not subject to urban influences or such influences should be ignored in application of the models. In the above model, for example, it might be determined that urban influences become insignificant after twenty-five miles. One could thus estimate the use-value of farmland closer than twenty-five miles from the city by assuming a distance of twenty-five miles. If, for example, b_1 were −$210, the use-value of farmland within twenty-five miles of the city would be estimated as

$$MV/ACRE = b_0 - \$1,050 + b_2 \times IRRIG \\ + b_3 \times CLASS1 + b_4 \times \\ CLASS2 + \ldots + \\ b_p \times CLASSn, \tag{39}$$

because

$$-\$210 \times SQRT(25) = -\$1,050.$$

Similar farmland more than twenty-five miles from the city would have only a slightly lower value, reflecting additional transportation costs.

As with commercial and industrial properties, there are often not enough sales of farmland for accurate model calibration. Again, however, several methods are available to increase the number of sales, including multi-jurisdictional models and adjustment of sales for time, cash equivalency, and personal property.

In summary, models used to specify the sales comparison approach can be additive, multiplicative, or hybrid. Additive models are the simplest and will usually suffice for residential properties. Multiplicative models are well suited to commercial properties and vacant land. Hybrid models are the most generally useful but require less-common statistical procedures. Calibration techniques for all these model structures are addressed in chapter 15.

Specifying the Income Approach

The income approach is based on the principle of anticipation: present value is a function of anticipated future benefits. In the case of income properties, anticipated future benefits take the form of income, which is discounted to present value. Using direct capitalization,

$$MV = NOI/OAR, \qquad (40)$$

where MV is the estimated market value, NOI is the net operating income, and OAR is the overall capitalization rate. If gross income (GI) is used in lieu of NOI, then the relationship is usually stated as

$$MV = GI \times GIM, \qquad (41)$$

where GIM is the gross income multiplier.

Gross incomes, allowable expenses, net incomes, gross income multipliers, and overall rates can all be estimated in one of two basic ways: stratification and typical units of comparison, often using spreadsheet software, as explained in chapter 15; or statistical models using MRA or alternative techniques, as explained below.

Modeling Gross Income

A common problem in the income approach is the scarcity of income and expense data. Models can be developed from available data and used to estimate typical figures for other parcels. In the case of gross income, the dependent variable should be gross income per unit (for example, apartment unit or square foot). A per-unit variable prevents the largest properties from dominating the model and helps focus attention on other than size-related variables. Independent variables should be those that affect gross income per unit, such as type of property, quality, condition, location, and amenities.

An example of a simple additive gross income model for apartments is

$$\begin{aligned} GI/UNIT = {} & b_0 + (b_1 \times QUAL) + (b_2 \times \\ & BED2) + (b_3 \times BED3) + \\ & (b_4 \times EFFAGE) + (b_5 \times \\ & AMENITY) + (b_6 \times NBHD1) \\ & + (b_7 \times NBHD2) + \ldots + \\ & (b_p \times NBHDn), \qquad (42) \end{aligned}$$

where

QUAL is a scalar variable for construction quality (average = 1.00)

BED2 is the percentage of units with two bedrooms and BED3 is the percentage of units with three bedrooms

EFFAGE is effective age (years)

AMENITY is the dollar value from the cost model (replacement cost new less depreciation ($RCNLD$) of pools, common areas, and other unattached amenities

NBHD1, NBHD2, ..., NBHDn are binary variables for neighborhood (0 or 1).

Thus, the constant represents typical gross income of one-bedroom units in new buildings of average construction quality with no unattached amenities.

Once calibrated, the model can be used to estimate GI per unit for parcels with unreported data. Total GI is then estimated by simply multiplying by number of units. For properties with reported figures, the appraiser has several options. First, actual figures can be used as long as they have been verified or are reasonably close to typical figures, for example, within 1.65 standard deviations, which, in a normal distribution, contain 90 percent of the data. Otherwise, estimated figures can be consistently used.

Gross income models can produce accurate results. Such models have the advantage that gross income data are usually easier to obtain and more reliable than net income data. Either potential gross income (*PGI*) or effective gross income (*EGI*) can be used, as long as use is consistent. The parcels need not have sold and expense data need not be obtained.

Modeling Net Income

Like *GI*, net operating income (*NOI*) can be modeled on a per-unit basis using independent variables related to the income-generating capacity of properties. Alternatively, expense ratios can be modeled and the results applied to *GI* to obtain *NOI*. An example of a multiplicative model for commercial properties is

$$EXP/GI = b_0 \times b_1^{REST} \times b_2^{CONV} \times b_3^{AUTO} \times QUAL^{b_4} \times COND^{b_5} \times SQFTZ^{b_6} \times b_7^{CBD}, \qquad (43)$$

where
  EXP/GI is the ratio of allowable expenses to *GI*
  REST, *CONV*, and *AUTO* are binary variables for restaurant/tavern, convenience, and auto sales/service properties, respectively (stores constitute the reference group)
  QUAL and *COND* are scalar variables for construction quality and condition;
  SQFTZ is total square feet in thousands
  CBD is a binary variable for location in the central business district

The constant b_0 represents the typical expense ratio for store properties of average quality and condition not located in the central business district. The variable *SQFTZ*

captures any variations in expense ratios related to building size; if b_6 is approximately 0, expense ratios tend not to vary with size.

The model can be used to estimate expense ratios for properties not reporting expense data and to gauge the reasonableness of reported figures. In effect, a unique expense ratio is estimated for each property based on type of property, quality, condition, size, location, and other variables included in the model.

Gross Income Multiplier Models

A gross income multiplier (*GIM*) is the ratio of value to gross income. Theoretically, *GIM*s are a function of those factors that determine how much investors will pay per dollar of current income. These factors include the required rate of return or discount rate, which varies with degree of risk; the projected path of the income stream (stable, increasing, or decreasing); the expected longevity of the income stream; and the percentage of income needed to pay operating expenses. From a practical viewpoint, these factors are related to the type, location, condition, and other attributes of property. Thus, *GIM*s can be modeled from such characteristics. An additive or multiplicative model will usually suffice.

An example of a simple multiplicative *GIM* model for apartments is

$$GIM = b_0 \times QUAL^{b_1} \times COND^{b_2} \times STDSQFT^{b_3} \times b_4^{NBHD1} \times b_5^{NBHD2} \times \ldots \times b_p^{NBHDn}, \quad (44)$$

where all terms are as described previously except *STDSQFT*, which is standardized square footage, that is, actual square feet divided by average square feet. The constant in this model is the estimated *GIM* for a typical apartment of average size in the base neighborhood. The other terms in the model adjust for variations from this standard.

GIM models have several advantages over manual procedures. In the latter, properties are grouped by type, age, and so on, and an average or typical *GIM* is computed for each group. To obtain adequate samples in each group, many sales are needed. In contrast, *GIM* models make more efficient use of sales data. It may be possible, for example, to calibrate the above model on as few as twenty sales (5 variables × 4 sales per variable), assuming only two neighborhoods. More important, *GIM* models adjust smoothly for differences between properties. In stratification, the number of *GIM*s is limited to the number of strata. This can imply significant differences between borderline properties assigned to different groups. In contrast, *GIM* models estimate a unique multiplier for each property, thus smoothing out such differences.

Overall Rate Models

An overall rate (*OAR*) expresses the relationship between net operating income (*NOI*) and property value. Models for *OAR*s are similar to those for *GIM*s, except that one need not be concerned about capturing differences in expense ratios, because the *NOI* is net after expenses.

A simple additive *OAR* model for commercial properties is:

$$OAR = b_0 + (b_1 \times OFFICE) + (b_2 \times REST) + (b_3 \times CONV) + (b_4 \times QUAL) + (b_5 \times AGE) + (b_6 \times CBD) + (b_7 \times FF/GF) + (b_8 \times STDSQFT), \qquad (45)$$

where

   OFFICE, *REST*, and *CONV* are binary variables for offices, restaurants/taverns, and convenience/fast food stores, respectively (retail stores are the reference group)

   QUAL, *AGE* and *STDSQFT* are as defined previously

   CBD is a binary variable for location in the central business district

   FF/GF is the ratio of front feet of land area to ground floor building area

In this case, the constant b_0 is the *OAR* for retail stores that are new, of average quality, and not located in the central business district. The variable *FF/GF* recognizes that investors may pay more for a given income stream if lot frontage is large relative to building area. The variable *STDSQFT* captures any differences in *OAR*s related to building size.

Models for *OAR*s have an advantage relative to *GIM* models in that *NOI*, being net of expenses, more accurately reflects investor concerns and may require fewer variables to model. On the other hand, *OAR* models require accurate expense data, both for development of the models and their application to unsold parcels.

Summary

Model specification, the first task in building models, is the designing of models based on economic and appraisal theory and market analysis. Models are constructed to represent the operation of forces of supply and demand in a particular market. Accurate, rational, and explainable models not only produce defensible values but make it easier to defend values when it is necessary to do so.

Model calibration, the second task in building models, is the estimating of values for the coefficients in a model. The next chapter treats calibration of cost, income, and sales comparison models, important tools for calibration, evaluation of model results, and administrative issues.

Mass Appraisal Model Calibration

Calibration is the process of estimating the coefficients in a mass appraisal model. The coefficients can be costs, market adjustments, capitalization rates, and the like. The first three sections of this chapter discuss calibration of cost, income, and sales comparison models. Discussion then focuses on important tools for model calibration: multiple regression analysis (MRA), adaptive estimation procedure (AEP, or feedback), and location value response surface analysis (LVRSA), a tool for incorporating location adjustments in mass appraisal models. The final two sections of this chapter discuss evaluation of model results and updating strategies and related administrative issues.

Calibrating Cost Models

In mass appraisal, the cost approach often has the structure of the general hybrid model presented in chapter 14 (equation 4):

$$MV = IV + LV, \qquad (1)$$

which can be expanded to

$$MV = \pi GQ \times [(\pi BQ \times \Sigma BA) + (\pi LQ \times \Sigma LA) + \Sigma OA], \quad (2)$$

where

MV is the estimated market value

πGQ is the product of general qualitative variables

πBQ is the product of building qualitative variables

ΣBA is the sum of building additive variables

πLQ is the product of land qualitative variables

ΣLA is the sum of land additive variables

ΣOA is the sum of other additive variables

As shown in chapter 14 (see equation 12), the components of this model can be separated into replacement cost new (RCN), depreciation, land value, and general qualitative adjustments:

$$MV = \pi GQ \times [(1 - BQ_D) \times RCN + LV], \qquad (3)$$

where BQ_D is a building qualitative factor for depreciation (D), and LV is land value before application of general qualitative adjustments (see equation 25 in chapter 14).

The cost approach is applied in four steps: estimate RCN, estimate and apply depreciation, estimate and add land value, and apply any general qualitative adjustments (trend factors). Chapter 8 discussed important concepts in the cost approach and chapter 7 discussed land valuation. This section addresses calibration of RCN for mass appraisal and the development of formula-driven cost models, cost-trend factors, depreciation schedules, and market adjustment factors.

Calibration of Replacement Cost New

Costs used in mass appraisal are usually replacement costs, which represent the cost of constructing a substitute structure of equal utility based on current construction standards and materials. Replacement costs should include all direct and indirect costs, including materials, labor, supervision, architect and legal fees, administrative expenses, overhead, and reasonable profit.

Costs can be estimated by one of four methods: comparative unit, unit-in-place, quantity survey, and trended original cost (see chapter 8 for a review of these). Mass appraisal uses the comparative unit method to find the "base" cost of a structure. Adjustments are then made for differences from base specifications using either the comparative unit or unit-in-place methods. Nevertheless, all costs should be derived from the quantity survey method. Commercially prepared cost manuals reflect such costs and many assessors use them, making local adjustments as necessary.

Assessors can also develop their own manuals from local quantity survey costs obtained from contractors and cost estimators. Labor and material costs should be separated from land and local demand-side factors, which are properly considered elsewhere in the cost approach. Derivation of cost tables from local cost data involves the following steps.

1. *Determine the building types (models) to be included in the manual.* These should include all building types commonly found in the jurisdiction. For residential property, building types can vary with occupancy (one-, two-, three-, or four-family), construction grade, story height, and wall type. Commercial property types usually vary with structure type (fire code classification) and number of stories.

2. *Determine typical building specifications for each model.* These are referred to as *base specifications.* Figure 1 contains an example for a single-family, one-story house of average construction.

3. *Determine RCN for each model at various size levels.* These costs should be quantity survey costs and can be obtained either from commercial cost services or from local builders, developers, and contractors. If the former, costs should be validated against local costs and adjusted as necessary. Remember to include all direct and indirect costs.

4. *Plot cost per square foot against building size and determine their relationship.* This can be done using a scatter diagram, as in figure 2. From the relationship, which is likely to be nonlinear, construct a cost table relating cost per square foot (base rate) to number of square feet. Fifty-foot increments will give a good approximation. Table 1 shows a cost table based on figure 2.

5. *Develop adjustments for variations from base specifications.* Adjustments can take the form of multipliers per square foot, other per unit costs, or lump sum dollar costs. Multipliers are computed by dividing costs per unit with a feature by the base rate. Assume, for example, that the base rate is $44.18 and does not include air conditioning. If the comparable cost per

Figure 1. Sample Building Specifications

Building type	One-story frame, single-family, average quality.
Foundation	Continuous concrete perimeter footing and concrete or concrete block foundation under load bearing walls.
Floors	Hardwood or carpeting, vinyl asbestos tile and ceramic tile; substantial subfloor and wood structure.
Exterior wall	Vinyl, wood, aluminum, partial medium-priced brick, or masonry. Average studs $2'' \times 4''$ on $16''$ center. Rafters $2'' \times 6''$ on $24''$ center or $2'' \times 4''$ truss and joist $2'' \times 8''$ on $16''$ center.
Roof	Exterior-grade plywood or wood sheeting with medium-weight composition shingle or built-up with small rock roof cover.
Interior	Sheetrock taped and painted or inexpensive wood paneling; production-grade millwork and trim. Stock-type cabinets, hardware, and average-grade built-in features. Partitions $\frac{1}{2}''$ taped sheetrock on $2'' \times 4''$ studs on $6''$ center; $8'$ height.
Heating/Cooling	Average-grade forced air heating and cooling.
Electrical	Romex or BX 110/220 volt circuits, adequate outlets, average-quality fixtures with some luminous fixtures in kitchen and baths.
Plumbing	Eight average-quality white or color fixtures, 50-gallon hot water heater, laundry facilities, floor drain, and outside fixture.

Figure 2. Scatter Diagram of Cost per Square Foot

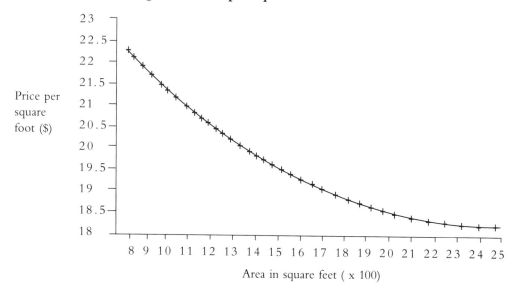

Price per square foot ($)

Area in square feet (x 100)

Table 1.   Relationship between Cost per Square Foot and Number of Square Feet

Square feet	Cost per square foot
800	$22.40
850	22.10
900	21.90
950	21.70
—	—
2,450	18.45

square foot with air conditioning is $47.11, the appropriate multiplier is 1.066 ($47.11/$44.18). Conversely, if the base specifications include air conditioning, then the appropriate multiplier for a building without air conditioning would be $44.18 divided by $47.11, or 0.938. Multipliers are more efficient in cost algorithms than additive adjustments and easier to maintain. However, some adjustments, for example, for a fireplace or hot tub, are constant and must be handled as dollar amounts that often depend on the quality of the feature.

6. *Test the schedules by applying them to buildings of known cost.* If estimated costs are inconsistent with actual costs, review cost data used in the analysis and make necessary adjustments. Estimated costs must reflect actual local costs.

Formula-Driven Cost Models

Formula-driven cost models speed computer processing and cost updating. As indicated above, existing cost manuals can be converted to equation form by expressing additive adjustments as multipliers. To derive a formula-driven cost model from the local market, proceed as outlined above, determine base cost for benchmark properties, and express cost relationships as multipliers.

As a simple example, consider table 2, which shows base construction costs for twelve benchmark properties based on grade, square feet, story height, and wall type. The base property (designated by an asterisk) is a 1,500-square-foot, grade C, one-story house with wood siding. The other benchmarks have been selected so as to isolate differences attributable to each construction feature: five differ only in construction class, three differ only in size, two differ only in story height, and one differs only in wall type. Base rates for each benchmark are obtained by simply dividing base construction costs by square feet. For the base home, this yields $60,400/1,500 = $40.27. Cost multipliers are then obtained by dividing base rates for the other benchmark properties by that of the base property.

Note that although there are 144 possible combinations of construction features (6 × 4 × 3 × 2), the base value of any property can be found by using only its base rates and multipliers. One can multiply the square feet of the subject property by the base rate for its grade, followed by adjustment factors for size, story height, and wall type (see first example at bottom of table 2). Or, one can multiply the square feet of the subject property by the base rate of the base property, $40.27, and adjustment factors for grade, size, story height, and wall type (second example at bottom of table 2). In the second case, no table look-ups are required, and the entire formula can be updated by simply updating the base rate of the base property, as long as no major changes occur in construction practices or in the relative cost of building components.

The example is simplified in that there are no other quality adjustments, no additions

Table 2. Derivation of Cost Formula

Grade	Story	Wall	Square feet (SQFT)	Base cost	Base rate (cost ÷ SQFT)	Multiplier (base rate ÷ 40.27)	
A	1	Wood	1,500	47,540	31.69	.787	GRADE
B	1	Wood	1,500	53,900	35.93	.892	
*C	1	Wood	1,500	60,400	40.27	1.000	
D	1	Wood	1,500	66,570	44.38	1.102	
E	1	Wood	1,500	75,830	50.55	1.255	
F	1	Wood	1,500	90,250	60.17	1.494	
C	1	Wood	1,000	43,200	44.38	1.102	SQFT
*C	1	Wood	1,500	60,400	40.27	1.000	
C	1	Wood	2,000	73,350	36.68	.911	
C	1	Wood	2,500	84,930	33.97	.844	
*C	1	Wood	1,500	60,400	40.27	1.000	STORY
C	1½	Wood	1,500	59,100	39.40	.978	
C	2	Wood	1,500	58,650	39.10	.971	
*C	1	Wood	1,500	60,400	40.27	1.000	WALL
C	1	Brick	1,500	62,390	41.59	1.033	

Cost = SQFT × base rate × size adjustment × story adjustment × wall adjustment
  or = SQFT × 40.27 × grade adjustment × size adjustment × story adjustment × wall adjustment

Example for 2,000 square foot, grade D, 1½-story, brick home:
  (1) Cost = 2,000 × 44.38 × 0.911 × 0.978 × 1.033 = $81,690
  (2) Cost = 2,000 × 40.27 × 1.102 × 0.911 × 0.978 × 1.033 = $81,690

*Base property

(basements, garages, and so forth), and only four size categories. As mentioned above, other quality adjustments (for example, air conditioning) can also be expressed as multipliers and added to the formula. Additions should be expressed as separate products of size and quality factors and their results added to base costs, as explained in chapter 14. Constant costs (for example, a water heater) require table look-up and should also be added to base costs.

Although at first glance it may appear that many benchmark properties of different sizes must be identified, say at fifty-square-foot intervals, this is not so. Instead, size adjustments (SIZEADJ) can be derived by fitting the equation

$$SIZEADJ = b_0 \times SQFT^{b_1}, \quad (4)$$

where b_0 is a constant, and b_1 is the result of a loglinear regression of all size multipliers.

Values for b_1 of less than 1.00 indicate that as building sizes increase, costs per square foot decrease. For example, loglinear regression of the four size multipliers from table 2 (1.102, 1.000, 0.911, and 0.844) on size yields the equation

$$SIZEADJ = 8.284 \times SQFT^{-.29086}, \quad (5)$$

which produces the adjustment factors shown in table 3.

Table 3.   Size Adjustment Factors Derived by Loglinear Regression

Size multiplier	Square feet	Size adjustment factors
1.102	1,000	1.110
1.000	1,500	0.987
0.911	2,000	0.908
0.844	2,500	0.851

Equation 5 can be used to find the appropriate size adjustment for any subject property. For example, for a 1,733-square-foot house,

$$SIZEADJ = 8.284 \times 1,733^{-.29086} = 0.947.$$

Expressing size adjustments in this way speeds calculations and produces smooth, continuous adjustments without interpolation.

Size adjustments can be extracted from existing cost manuals by a similar method. Assume, for example, that the most typical, or base, property for a particular construction class has 1,500 square feet, and construction costs vary as shown in columns 1 and 2 of table 4. The base rate is $31.90 with size adjustments computed as shown.

Table 4.   Derivation of Size Adjustment

Square feet	Cost per square foot	Base rate	Size adjustment
800	$37.30 ÷	$31.90	= 1.169
850	36.80 ÷	31.90	= 1.154
900	36.40 ÷	31.90	= 1.141
—	—		
1,450	32.20 ÷	31.90	= 1.009
= >1,500	31.90 ÷	31.90	= 1.000
1,550	31.60 ÷	31.90	= 0.991
—	—		
2,400	29.30 ÷	31.90	= 0.918
2,450	29.10 ÷	31.90	= 0.912
2,500	28.90 ÷	31.90	= 0.906

Again, the size adjustments could be approximated with a formula. In any case, cost models in the form of multipliers or equations can be updated annually by simply adjusting the base rate of the benchmark property to reflect current costs (see below). Size and other percentage adjustments need only be reviewed periodically, say every three or four years.

Cost-Trend Factors

Once determined, construction costs are periodically updated. One way to do this is to repeat the six steps above; another is to develop cost-trend factors. The latter is easier, and acceptable as long as no major changes occur in construction practices or the relative costs of building components.

Several major publishers of construction cost data report cost indexes for various building types. To apply such an index, simply divide the index corresponding to the assessment date by the index corresponding to the period in which construction costs were obtained:

$$F = I_c/I_b, \qquad (6)$$

where F is the appropriate cost-trend factor, I_c is the current cost index (as of the assessment date), and I_b is the base index. Base costs are updated by simply multiplying them by the appropriate cost-trend factor.

When published cost indexes prove incapable of adequately reflecting local costs, appraisers must develop their own cost-trend factors. The steps are as follows: First, define a benchmark property for each building class. This property will be of typical size and correspond to the base specifications.

Second, identify the required materials and labor to construct the benchmark property (table 5, columns 1 and 2). Third, using the quantity survey method, estimate base and current unit costs (columns 3 and 4). Fourth, for each component, multiply number of units by base unit costs and current unit costs to obtain total costs (columns 5 and 6). Fifth, sum the results to obtain total direct building costs. Indirect costs can be analyzed the same way. Often it is reasonable to assume that indirect costs will increase in the same proportion. Finally, divide total current costs by total base costs to obtain the appropriate cost-trend factors (1.153 in table 5) to use in updating base rates.

Table 5. Derivation of Construction Cost Index

(1)	(2)	(3)	(4)	(5)	(6)
		Base	Current	Base	Current
Item	Quantity	unit cost	unit cost	total cost	total cost
Materials					
Concrete block/hundred	15	$ 57	$ 75	$ 855	$ 1,125
Lumber/1,000 board feet	18	226	300	4,068	5,400
Cement/cubic yard	30	17.40	22.00	522	660
Gravel/cubic yard	20	8.00	11.00	160	220
Plumbing	1	5,560	6,200	5,560	6,200
Iron and steel	1	4,500	5,040	4,500	5,040
Electrical wiring	1	2,875	2,990	2,875	2,990
Labor					
Common laborer/hour	300	10.40	11.00	3,120	3,300
Carpenter/hour	300	11.73	14.00	3,519	4,200
Mason/hour	75	12.20	15.40	915	1,155
Plasterer/hour	100	11.91	13.00	1,191	1,300
Plumber/hour	150	12.00	13.80	1,800	2,070
Painter/hour	125	11.48	12.25	1,435	1,531
				$30,520	$35,191

Cost adjustment factor = $35,191/$30,520 = 1.153

If adjustments to base rates are expressed as multipliers, they will usually require no adjustment. If they are expressed in lump sums or dollars per unit, they should be updated by comparing current and base costs for the items.

Construction costs can usually be trended in this way for several years. Periodically, however, base specifications and construction costs should be updated to conform to current technology.

Depreciation Analysis

Depreciation schedules represent the demand side of the market and should, therefore, be derived from the market. Many published cost manuals have tables indicating depreciation or "percent good" based on the type and age of improvements. Such tables may be unrealistic for the local market and should be used with caution. Because demand varies by location, so too should depreciation schedules. In general, depreciation schedules should reflect typical physical deterioration and include separate adjustments for functional and economic obsolescence. However, it is also important that appraisers have the ability to override depreciation schedules or assign additional depreciation for individual parcels.

Depreciation schedules can be extracted from the market by correlating sales prices, less the value of land and other additions, with effective age. Success, however, depends on the reliability of the data used in the analysis. The steps are as follows:

1. Stratify sales by building type. The sales should include only arm's-length sales adjusted as necessary for financing, personal property, and time. Sales involving mixed-use parcels should be excluded.

2. Subtract the value of land and other additions to obtain residual building values. Properties with extreme land-to-building ratios should be excluded.

3. Divide by RCN to obtain percent good (%GOOD). Mathematically,

$$\%GOOD = \frac{S - (LV + OV)}{RCN}, \quad (7)$$

where S is the sale price, LV is land value, and OV is the value of other improvements.

4. Plot percent good against effective age or plot accrued depreciation (1 − percent good) against effective age (see figure 3). If effective ages are not available, use actual ages and exclude improvements in very good or poor condition relative to actual age.

5. Fit a curve to the data by hand, with graphics software, or by multiplicative or nonlinear MRA.

6. From the curve, construct a percent good or accrued depreciation table. Tables constructed from the data in figure 3 might include the ten-year increments shown in table 6.

Mechanics aside, the success of these procedures rests on the accuracy of the data used in the analysis, including land values and effective age estimates. The accuracy of land values should be verified from ratio studies and adjusted to the market as necessary. For individual parcels, when effective age estimates are too high (too low), too much (too little) depreciation will be applied.

Depreciation tables, like cost tables, can be stored as equations. In the present example, a simple multiplicative regression of depreciation (D) on effective age (EFFAGE) yields the following:

$$D = 0.0335 \times EFFAGE^{0.6646}. \quad (8)$$

Figure 3. Percent Good and Depreciation Plots

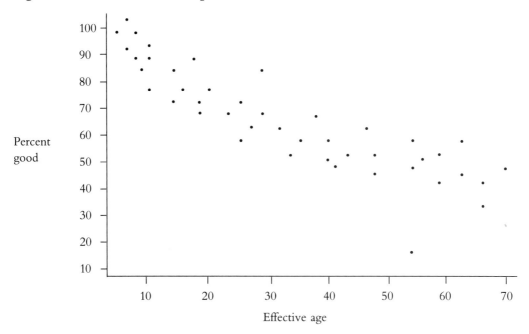

Percent good

Effective age

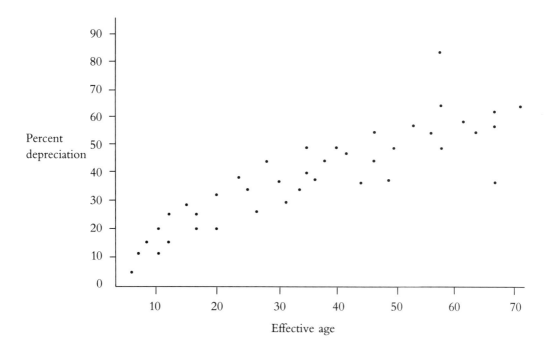

Percent depreciation

Effective age

Table 6.   Percent Good and Depreciation Tables

Percent good table		Depreciation table		
Effective age	Percent good	Effective age	Percent depreciation	Percent depreciation derived by multiplicative regression
0	100	0	0	0
10	85	10	15	15.5
20	75	20	25	24.5
30	67	30	33	32.1
40	60	40	40	38.9
50	55	50	45	45.1
60	50	60	50	50.9
70	45	70	55	56.4

Equation 8 gives the ten-year increments shown in table 6. These results are similar to the table values from which they were derived, and the table values could be adjusted to achieve an exact match.

Market Adjustments

The final step in the cost approach is ensuring that estimated values are consistent with the market. This is particularly important because the cost approach separately estimates land and building values and uses replacement costs, which reflect only the supply side of the market.

Market adjustments take several forms. Ratio studies can be used to evaluate appraisal accuracy by selected property strata (chapter 20). Within the cost approach, stratification by construction class helps evaluate the accuracy of base rates, stratification by size groups indicates whether cost models appropriately reflect economies of scale, and stratification by age groups helps monitor the accuracy of depreciation schedules. Ratio studies for vacant land indicate whether land values are accurate.

In addition, MRA and feedback can help to calibrate the cost approach to the market.

Again consider the simple general cost model:

$$MV = IV + LV. \tag{1}$$

This model can be calibrated using linear MRA (with the constant constrained to zero):

$$S = b_1 LV + b_2 IV, \tag{9}$$

where S is sale price, and b_1 and b_2 are coefficients.

If land and improvement values reflect the current market, the coefficients b_1 and b_2 will be close to 1.00. Values significantly above 1.00 indicate underappraisal, and vice versa. For example, a value of 1.40 for b_1 and 0.90 for b_2 indicates that land values need to be increased by 40 percent and building values decreased by 10 percent.

This basic model can be refined as follows:

$$S = b_1 RCN - b_2 D + b_3 LV_1 + b_4 LV_2, \tag{10}$$

where $LV_1, LV_2, \ldots, LV_n$ equal land value if the parcel is in the specified neighborhood, and zero otherwise. Again, all coefficients should be close to 1.00. Where they are not, procedures should be reviewed and adjustments considered.

A hybrid model that could be used to similar effect is:

$$S = (LV^{b_1} + BV^{b_2}) \times b_3{}^{NBHD1} \times b_4{}^{NBHD2} \times b_n{}^{NBHDn}. \tag{11}$$

The neighborhood variables are general qualitative binary variables coded 1 if the property is in the neighborhood and 0 if it is not. Nonlinear MRA or feedback can be used to calibrate the model. Again, all coefficients should be close to 1.00.

Calibrating Income Models
Income and Expense Analysis

Successful income models require accurate income and expense data. Although data are not required for each individual property, the appraiser must obtain sufficient data to estimate typical income and expense figures for various types of income-producing property. Chapter 11 discussed collection of income and expense data, lease analysis, and identification of allowable expenses.

In mass appraisal, income and expense analysis is made easier by microcomputer spreadsheet software. The appraiser enters available data, establishes typical income figures and expense ratios by property type, and estimates unreported figures. Tables 7 and 8 contain a hypothetical example for ten 8 to 24-unit apartment buildings built since 1980. Although shown separately, the two tables are from the same spreadsheet.

Table 7 relates to gross income estimation. From reported data, the appraiser enters the address, number of one-bedroom and two-bedroom units, rent per unit, vacancy and collection loss ratio, and other income. Note that these data are not available for all the properties. The appraiser has also highlighted the reported rents and vacancy and collection loss ratio at 924 E. Park and reported other income at 214 W. Kamp as being atypical. The atypical figures are ignored in calculating median rent per unit, vacancy and collection loss ratio, and other income per unit.

The spreadsheet calculates potential gross rent (PGR) from reported figures. However, the appraiser overrides the figures at 924 E. Park and instead calculates PGR based on median figures:

$14 \times \$400 + 10 \times \$445 = \$10,050$ per month; $12 \times \$10,050 = \$120,600.$

The PGR for 471 Cougar, for which no data were reported, is calculated the same way. The program calculates effective gross rent (EGR) by multiplying PGR by the complement of the median vacancy and collection loss ratio $(1 - 0.07 = 0.93)$. Effective gross income (EGI) is then calculated by adding other income to EGR, where other income is based on median figures. For example, EGI at 825 Linwood is

$\$89,280 + (20 \times \$475) = \$98,800$ (rounded).

Note that the appraiser has used reported rents as long as they appear reasonable. This recognizes the uniqueness of each property. However, to compensate for differences in management, the appraiser uses the median vacancy and collection loss ratio and the median other income per unit. These choices, however, are a matter of appraisal judgment.

Table 7. Income Analysis: 8- to 24-Unit Apartment Buildings Built Since 1980

Address	One-bedroom units Units	One-bedroom units Rent	Two-bedroom units Units	Two-bedroom units Rent	Potential gross rent (yearly)	Vacancy and collection loss ratio	Effective gross rent	Other income Total	Other income Per unit	Effective gross income
418 Clark	16	$400	0	$ 0	$ 76,800	0.06	$ 71,424	$7,600	$475	$ 79,000
825 Linwood	10	370	10	430	96,000		89,280	9,100	455	98,800
115 State	8	420	12	450	105,120	0.10	97,762			107,300
516 Touhy	10	380	8	440	87,840	0.04	81,691			90,200
308 Mentor	0	0	8	470	45,120	0.02	41,962	4,550	569	45,800
903 E. Park	10	350	6	420	72,240	0.09	67,183	6,000	375	74,800
924 E. Park	14	(450)	10	(520)	120,600	(0.13)	112,158			123,600
811 S. Gray	12	410	0	0	59,040	0.08	54,907	7,000	583	60,600
214 W. Kamp	10	420	6	450	82,800		77,004	(2,000	125)	84,600
471 Cougar	8		8		81,120		75,442			83,000
Median		$400		$445		0.07			$475	
Number		6		6		6			5	

In general, reported figures can be used as long as they appear reasonable, or typical figures based on the median, for example, can be used.

Table 8 shows the expense analysis. Below reported expenses are listed the percentage of EGI that expenses constitute. This helps in evaluating the reasonableness of reported figures. The appraiser has circled atypical reported expenses for replacements and management at 115 State. Median expense ratios are then computed with atypical expenses excluded.

In this case, the appraiser has accepted reported expenses as long as they appear reasonable. Where figures are not reported or do not appear reasonable, median expense ratios are used. At 825 Linwood, for example, replacements are computed at 3.4 percent of EGI

$$0.034 \times \$98,800 = \$3,360,$$

so that total expenses are $31,400 (rounded):

$$\$4,100 + \$7,400 + \$5,900 + \$3,400 + \$10,600 = \$31,400.$$

When no expenses are reported, the appraiser has multiplied the median expense ratio of 0.377 against EGI. Normal expenses at 516 Touhy, for example, are estimated as

$$0.377 \times \$90,200 = \$34,000 \text{ (rounded)}.$$

Net operating income is then estimated as EGI less normal operating expenses.

Note that, as with rents, the appraiser has decided to accept reported expenses as long as they appear reasonable. This recognizes differences in construction quality, physical condition, on-site amenities, and other factors. An equally valid approach, provided that properties are comparable, is to use typical expense ratios throughout.

Multiple regression analysis (MRA) provides another method of determining nor-

Table 8. Expense Analysis: 8- to 24-Unit Apartment Buildings Built Since 1980

Address	Effective gross income	Reported expenses						Normal expenses	Net income
		Insurance	Heat/ Utilities	Maintenance	Replacements	Management and other	Total		
418 Clark	$ 79,000	$3,600 4.6%	$8,300 10.5%	$ 6,150 7.8%	$ 2,650 3.4%	$ 9,900 12.5%	$30,600 38.7%	$30,600	$48,400
825 Linwood	98,800	4,100 4.1%	7,400 7.5%	5,900 6.0%		10,600 10.7%		31,400	67,400
115 State	107,300	5,760 5.4%	9,250 8.6%	13,600 12.7%	10,000 9.3%	28,400 26.5%	67,010 62.5%	44,700	62,600
516 Touhy	90,200							34,000	56,200
308 Mentor	45,800	2,300 5.0%	5,200 11.4%	2,620 5.7%	1,500 3.3%	5,300 11.6%	16,920 36.9%	16,900	28,900
903 E. Park	74,800	3,456 4.6%	5,800 7.8%	9,200 12.3%	2,420 3.2%	7,320 9.8%	28,196 37.7%	28,200	46,600
924 E. Park	123,600							46,600	77,000
811 S. Gray	60,600	3,250 5.4%	5,900 9.7%	4,000 6.6%	3,050 5.0%	8,200 13.5%	24,400 40.3%	24,400	36,200
214 W. Kamp	84,600	2,980 3.5%	9,000 10.6%	5,450 6.5%	4,000 4.7%	10,000 11.8%	31,440 37.2%	31,400	53,200
471 Cougar	83,000							31,300	51,700
Median		4.6%	9.7%	6.6%	3.4%	11.6%	37.7%		
Number		7	7	7	5	5	5		

mal expense ratios and income figures. As explained in chapter 14, models can be constructed to estimate gross income, normal expense ratios, and net income as a function of construction type, effective age, location, and other relevant characteristics. This has the advantage that unique figures are estimated for each parcel based on its particular characteristics without the need to accept reported figures. In effect, "normalized" figures are computed for each parcel. In general, data from spreadsheet programs can easily be transported to statistical programs for such analyses.

Gross Income Multipliers and Overall Rates

In mass appraisal, the appraiser typically uses direct capitalization models, in the form of gross income multipliers (*GIMs*) and overall rates (*OARs*) (see chapter 12 for an introduction to such techniques). These models are developed in two ways. In the first, stratification, sales are grouped by factors that tend to affect the relationship between income and value. From a theoretical viewpoint, four major factors affect the relationship between current net income and market value: the discount rate or required rate of return on investment, which tends to vary with risk; remaining economic life; the expected rate of change in net income; and the percentage of income attributable to land, because land requires no depreciation allowance. If *GIMs* are being developed, then expense ratios should also be considered, because properties with lower expense ratios will usually command higher *GIMs*.

Differences in the above theoretical factors vary primarily with type of property, location, and condition. In some cases, land-to-building ratios and size may also be important. The first step, then, is to stratify sales based on these criteria. *GIMs* and *OARs* can then be computed and analyzed by strata.

Table 9 contains an example of the development of overall rates for store properties in a midsized jurisdiction. Available sales have first been stratified by location: downtown (more desirable) and other location (less desirable). Within location, sales are stratified by effective year built into three groups: 1900–1945, 1946–1970, and 1971 or later. Finally, the older properties are further stratified by the ratio of land area to building area. This factor becomes more important as commercial improvements approach the end of their economic life; an old building on a half-acre can command a considerably higher income multiplier than an old building on a quarter-acre. Note that eight strata have now been created.

Net incomes are divided by sales prices to obtain individual overall rates. Medians, means, coefficients of dispersion (CODs), and coefficients of variation (COVs) are then computed for each stratum. In practice, the median would be a good choice for the measure of central tendency because it is not overly influenced by extremes.

The appraiser can evaluate the reliability of the results by noting the number of sales in each stratum; the consistency within strata based, for example, on the COD; and the consistency among strata. In this case, the results appear generally good. With the exception of properties built outside of the downtown area after 1970, measures of dispersion are good. With respect to consistency among strata, note first that sales in each age group command a lower *OAR* in the downtown (more desirable) area than in the other

Table 9. Overall Rate Analysis—Store Properties

Downtown location (more desirable)

	Year built: 1900-1945		Year built: 1946-1970	Year built: after 1970
	Land/building area ≤ 2.00	Land/building area > 2.00		
Median	0.152	0.144	0.130	0.114
Mean	0.150	0.145	0.133	0.113
Coefficient of dispersion	10.1	9.6	12.7	7.8
Coefficient of variation	13.3	12.5	18.2	10.3
Number	9	8	3	11

Other location (less desirable)

	Year built: 1900-1945		Year built: 1946-1970	Year built: after 1970
	Land/building area ≤ 2.00	Land/building area > 2.00		
Median	0.189	0.185	0.157	0.182
Mean	0.193	0.180	0.156	0.184
Coefficient of dispersion	8.4	7.5	9.6	17.3
Coefficient of variation	15.5	10.2	12.0	31.9
Number	2	9	8	3

(less desirable) area, as we would expect. Also, again with the single exception of sales in the "other" area built after 1970, OARs decline with age, again as we would expect. Finally, for properties with the oldest improvements, OARs are lower when land-to-building ratios are greater than 2.00.

The appraiser can, therefore, apply the results with reasonable confidence, despite the rather small sample sizes within strata. The results for properties built after 1970 outside of the downtown area, however, are not acceptable. The appraiser reviews these sales and may have to override the results, using an OAR more consistent with the other strata, or rely on other appraisal techniques.

The success of this technique depends on the availability of adequate sales data. Older sales can be used in the analysis by adjusting both income and sales prices to the appraisal date as necessary. In fact, sales prices need not be adjusted for time if income data reflect the same period as the sale. Sales from one period, however, should not be matched against income data from another period.

In addition to stratification, MRA provides a second way to develop GIMs and OARs from market data. As explained in chapter 14, models can be developed that use the same variables used in stratification: type of property, location, effective age or condition, size, and so forth. Once developed, the models can be used to estimate income multipliers or OARs for unsold properties, so that a unique figure is developed for each property based on its specific characteristics. Where properties are heterogeneous, this can produce a more supportable result than use of a single figure for an entire stratum of properties.

In addition, MRA makes more efficient use of sales data than stratification. This permits the appraiser to test more variables in the models, which is particularly helpful when *GIM*s are being developed. In this case, the appraiser can include variables in the model that may be associated with differences in expense ratios, for example, air conditioning, elevators, swimming pools, and other recreational services.

The models can be calibrated using additive or multiplicative MRA. Stepwise MRA is particularly effective because it automatically eliminates redundant and unnecessary variables. Such models should usually be developed for broad strata of income-producing properties, for example, apartments, office buildings, retail space, and warehouse and industrial properties. Location can be included in the models as a series of binary variables or as distance variables — for example, distance to the central business district or a key transportation center.

Whether stratification or multiple regression is used, *OAR*s have both advantages and disadvantages relative to *GIM*s. From a theoretical standpoint, *OAR*s are preferred because all allowable operating expenses are explicitly recognized in calculated net income. If *GIM*s are used, additional stratification or regression variables may be required to ensure similarity in expense ratios. On the other hand, *GIM*s have the practical advantage of not requiring expense data, which are difficult to collect and analyze. Because expense ratios tend to vary with the same property characteristics that affect *OAR*s (type of property, location, condition, and so on), reliable gross income models may require little, if any, additional stratification and no more variables than overall rate models.

Treatment of Property Taxes

In general, income models should include data *before* property taxes are subtracted as an expense, with an effective property tax rate added to *OAR*s and *GIM*s after calibration. Thus, a model of expense ratios should not include property taxes as an expense; an *OAR* model should use net income before property taxes are subtracted as an expense, and add an appropriate allowance to the result. Assume, for example, that the indicated *OAR* is 0.106 and the effective tax rate is 0.014. The adjusted *OAR* is 0.120 (0.106 + 0.014). Handling property taxes in this manner accommodates properties subject to different tax rates and relieves the appraiser of the problem of estimating real estate taxes before the appraisal is completed.

*GIM*s can be adjusted for effective tax rates as follows:

$$GIM' = \frac{GIM}{1 + (GIM \times ETR)}, \quad (12)$$

where GIM' is the adjusted GIM, and ETR is the effective tax rate. For example, if GIM before taxes is 6.5 and ETR is 0.02, then:

$$\text{GIM}' = \frac{6.5}{1 + (6.5 \times 0.02)} = 5.75.$$

If *GIM*s are not adjusted for *ETR*s, the appraiser should apply them only to properties with tax rates similar to those used in developing the *GIM*s.

Calibrating Sales Comparison Models

Chapter 14 discussed the specification of "direct" sales comparison models. Such models develop an equation that relates estimated market values to property characteristics directly from market data. Sales are analyzed statistically "in mass" rather than individually, as in the traditional sales comparison approach. Sales comparison models can be additive, multiplicative, or hybrid. They must be rooted in appraisal theory and reflect the local market.

The success of sales comparison models also depends on accurate sales and property characteristics data. Appraisers must verify reported sales prices, eliminate non-arm's-length transfers, and, as necessary, adjust sales prices for financing, personal property, and time (chapter 5). They must also collect and edit property characteristics data important in estimating property values in the jurisdiction. These data include improvement characteristics such as square feet of living area, type of construction, and effective age; land characteristics such as lot size, view, and utilities; and locational factors such as neighborhood and zoning.

When adequate data are available, sales comparison models have proven their ability to produce accurate results. CODs typically range from 5 to 15 percent, with results at the low end of this range easier to achieve in comparatively homogeneous jurisdictions. Heterogeneous jurisdictions may initially obtain CODs up to 20 but should strive to reduce them to 15 or less.

In general, assessment jurisdictions with a good data base and one hundred or more arm's-length residential sales per year can de-velop effective sales comparison models. In addition, larger jurisdictions are increasingly using such models in the appraisal of non-residential properties, including income properties and vacant land.

Sales comparison models permit annual reappraisal at comparatively little incremental cost. If an accurate data base and ongoing maintenance procedures are in place, property inspections can be spread over a longer period, such as three or four years, based on budgetary considerations. The reduction in time required for residential properties frees staff for other appraisals.

Two techniques available for calibrating sales comparison models are MRA and feedback. MRA is older and more common. Feedback was first used in property appraisal in the late 1970s. Each has technical advantages and disadvantages; if properly used, either produces satisfactory results.

Multiple Regression Analysis

MRA is a statistical technique for estimating unknown data on the basis of known and available data. In mass appraisal, the unknown data are market values. The known and available data are sales prices and property characteristics.

MRA models can be additive, multiplicative, or hybrid. Additive models are the least flexible, but are the simplest and most common. This section illustrates MRA using additive model structures and then introduces multiplicative and hybrid models.

The general structure of an additive MRA model is:

$$S = b_0 + b_1 X_1 + b_2 X_2 + \ldots + b_p X_p,$$
$$(13)$$

where S is estimated sale price (dependent variable); $X_1, X_2, \ldots, X_p$ are the independent variables; $b_1, b_2, \ldots, b_p$ are coefficients or prices assigned by the algorithm to the independent variables; and b_0 is a constant determined by the algorithm. (This general model can be used for any dependent variable Y. S is used throughout this discussion because it is the dependent variable of interest to property appraisers.)

As a simplified illustration, consider the equation,

$$S = \$7{,}800 + \$32.10\ X_1 - \$746\ X_2, \tag{14}$$

where X_1 is square feet of living area and X_2 is effective age. In this case, b_0 is \$7,800, b_1 is \$32.10, and b_2 is −\$746. For a house with 2,000 square feet and an effective age of 5 years, the predicted value is:

$$
\begin{aligned}
S &= \$7{,}800 + \$32.10(2{,}000) - \$746(5) \\
  &= \$7{,}800 + \$64{,}200 - \$3{,}730 \\
  &= \$68{,}270.
\end{aligned}
$$

A more realistic example would contain additional independent variables. In any case, the coefficients calculated for the variables are derived from sales analysis and reflect their contribution to the estimation of values.

MRA tends to work well when sales are plentiful enough and property characteristics are accurate. Predicted values are particularly accurate for parcels with typical characteristics. However, predicted values for parcels with atypical characteristics usually have a high margin of error and should be field reviewed.

Theory and Method

The objective of MRA, as applied to mass appraisal, is to model the relationship be-

tween property characteristics and value, so that the latter can be estimated from the former. For example, the relationship between housing size and value can be investigated from data on square feet of living area and sale price. Table 10 shows such data for twenty-five recently sold single-family residences. These data are graphed and a straight line fitted to the points with a ruler, as was done to generate line AA′ in figure 4. (For ease of illustration, the horizontal line is truncated at 1,000 square feet, because all twenty-five properties sold were larger than 1,000 square feet; most software performs this scal-

Table 10. Regression Data

Sale number	Square feet	Sale price
1	1,050	\$ 59,000
2	1,090	66,900
3	1,150	68,000
4	1,220	75,000
5	1,250	59,800
6	1,275	74,500
7	1,300	79,000
8	1,300	75,900
9	1,340	67,000
10	1,360	80,000
11	1,400	86,000
12	1,425	87,000
13	1,480	73,900
14	1,520	84,000
15	1,590	74,000
16	1,610	79,600
17	1,650	93,500
18	1,680	102,000
19	1,700	94,900
20	1,750	98,200
21	1,790	100,500
22	1,830	118,000
23	1,880	82,000
24	1,980	93,000
25	2,140	124,500

Figure 4. Plot of Regression Data

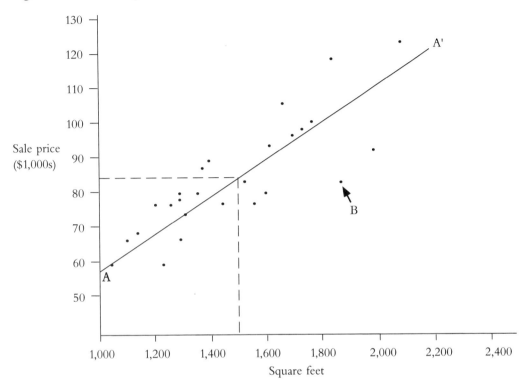

ing automatically.) The sale price of an unsold property can be estimated by noting its square footage and reading the corresponding estimated sale price from the line. For example, to estimate the value of an unsold house with 1,500 square feet, draw a vertical line upward from 1,500 square feet to line AA'. Then draw a second line horizontally from line AA' to the vertical axis. This process is illustrated by the dashed lines in figure 4. The estimated value of the house is approximately $84,000.

Regression analysis, a more scientific and efficient method of fitting the line, uses the principle that a straight line can be determined by one point and the slope. In fact,

the regression equation for one independent variable,

$$S = b_0 + b_1 X_1, \qquad (15)$$

is simply the equation of a straight line, where b_1 is the slope and b_0 the point at which the line intersects the vertical axis. The slope of line AA' in figure 4 thus corresponds to b_1. The major difference is that the slope of AA' was "eyeballed," whereas b_1 is calculated.

Consider point B in figure 4, which corresponds to sale 23 in table 10. The property has 1,880 square feet and sold for $82,000. Based on line AA', the estimated sale price is approximately $100,000. The difference is the amount of *error* (e_i) in the estimate. Regression analysis calculates b_0 and b_1 in a manner that minimizes the sum of squared errors between actual and predicted prices, that is, MRA minimizes

$$\Sigma e_i^2 = \Sigma (S_i - \hat{S}_i)^2, \qquad (16)$$

where S_i is the actual sale price of property i and $\hat{S}_i$ is the estimated price.

In the present example, regression of sales prices on square feet produces the equation

$$S_i = \$11,493 + \$47.90\ X_i, \qquad (17)$$

where X_i is square feet of living area. On average, that is, sales prices increase at a rate of $47.90 per square foot of living area. The "constant," $11,493, is the value at which the regression line intersects the vertical axis when $X = 0$ (not shown in figure 4). This equation minimizes the sum of the squared differences between S_i and $\hat{S}_i$; any other equation would produce a larger sum of squared errors. In the example of an unsold house of 1,500 square feet, the regression estimated value is

$$\hat{S}_i = \$11,493 + \$47.90(1,500) = \$83,343,$$

which agrees closely with the previous "eyeballed" estimate.

How well does this equation estimate property values? Consider figure 5, which illustrates a regression of sales prices on square feet of living area for three different neighborhoods (in each case, models are developed from sales in only that neighborhood). In plots for Neighborhoods A and B, the regression line has the same slope and inter-sects the vertical axis at the same point. However, this equation does not estimate property values with equal precision in all three. In Neighborhood A, actual sales prices lie very close to the values predicted by the regression line. In other words, the sum of squared errors, Σe_i^2, is small, and it appears that we can be confident of the regression-estimated values. In Neighborhood B, actual sales prices are loosely fitted by the regression line. In Neighborhood C, there is virtually no relationship between living area and value, making it impossible to draw the line of best fit. Σe_i^2 is very large, and the average sale price would produce almost equally good value estimates. We conclude that regression analysis is a useful predictor of property values when Σe_i^2 is small, but not when it is large.

One means of minimizing Σe_i^2 is to use additional variables. In figure 4, many points probably lie below AA' because they represent properties with some negative features, such as poor physical condition. Other points probably lie above AA' because they represent properties with generally positive features, such as good physical condition.

The model might be respecified, then, as

$$S = b_0 + b_1 X_1 + b_2 X_2, \qquad (18)$$

where X_2 represents physical condition. Again, MRA would calculate the regression coefficients b_0, b_1, and b_2 in such a way as to minimize Σe_i^2, where, in this case, the predicted values are a function of both living area and physical condition. Note that the importance of any one variable in the regression equation is directly related to its contribution in reducing Σe_i^2.

Figure 5. Comparison of Regression Results

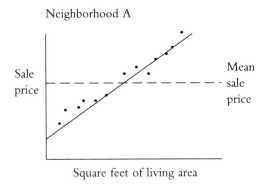

Neighborhood A

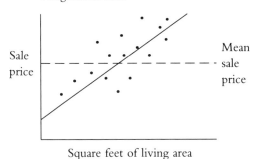

Neighborhood B

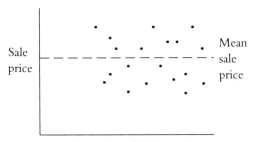

Neighborhood C

Evaluating Regression Results

Users of MRA should be familiar with eight statistics. Four are measures of *goodness of fit* and relate to evaluation of the predictive ac-

curacy of the equation. They are the coefficient of determination (R^2), the standard error of the estimate (SEE), the coefficient of variation (COV), and the average percent error. In different ways, each indicates how well the equation succeeds in minimizing Σe_i^2 and predicting sales prices. The other four statistics relate to the importance of individual variables in the model. They are the coefficient of correlation (r), the t-statistic, the F-statistic, and the beta coefficient.

Coefficient of Determination   The coefficient of determination, R^2, is the percentage of the variance in sales prices explained by the regression model. Assuming that no records are kept of the physical description, location, and other characteristics of residential parcels in an assessment jurisdiction, other than sales prices, how would the market value of any given residential parcel be estimated from sales prices alone? The answer, of course, is the average sale price. For those properties that have sold, the sum of the squared errors (SSE) associated with this estimate is

$$SSE = \Sigma (S_i - \overline{S}), \qquad (19)$$

where
  S_i is the sale price of property i
  $\overline{S}$ is the average sale price
  $i = 1, \ldots, n$ (where n is the number of sales)

One of the errors, or "residuals," associated with this estimate is depicted in figure 6 as the distance AB.

Now assume one additional data item, the number of rooms in each house. We hypothesize that we should be able to im-

Figure 6.   Illustration of R^2

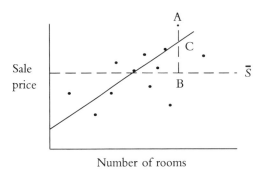

Number of rooms

prove our estimates and fit the regression line depicted in figure 6. Inspection of the graph reveals that the vertical deviations from the regression line are less than those from $\bar{S}$. Consider, for example, the distance AB. Part of this distance, BC, is explained by the regression line. The same could be said for most of the other points on the graph; that is, they differ from the regression line less than they do from $\bar{S}$. The sum of the squared deviations explained by the model (SSE_{EX}) can be written as

$$SSE_{EX} = \Sigma\,(\hat{S}_i - \bar{S})^2. \qquad (20)$$

Nevertheless, it is clear that the regression line cannot explain all the differences between S_i and $\bar{S}$. For example, point A in the graph varies from the regression line by the distance AC. The sum of such remaining or unexplained squared errors (SSE_{UN}) is the statistic,

$$SSE_{UN} = \Sigma e_i^2 = \Sigma\,(S_i - \hat{S}_i)^2. \quad (21)$$

The following important relationship always holds:

$$SSE = SSE_{EX} + SSE_{UN}. \qquad (22)$$

That is,

$$\Sigma\,(S_i - \bar{S})^2 = \Sigma\,(\hat{S}_i - \bar{S})^2 + \Sigma\,(S_i - \hat{S}_i)^2. \qquad (23)$$

In other words, the total variation in sales prices can be decomposed into those portions explained by and not explained by the regression model. This relationship is analogous to division of the distance AB in figure 6 into segments BC and AC. The coefficient of determination, R^2, based on this relationship, is computed as

$$R^2 \;=\; \frac{SSE_{EX}}{SSE} \;=\; \frac{\Sigma\,(\hat{S}_i - \bar{S})^2}{\Sigma\,(S_i - \bar{S})^2}. \quad (24)$$

Thus, R^2 equals the percentage of the variance in sales prices explained by the regression model. Possible values of R^2 range from 0 to 1. When R^2 equals 0, none of the variation in sales prices is explained by the model. In this case, $\bar{S}$ provides overall estimates of individual sales prices just as good as those from the regression model (see Neighborhood C in figure 5). On the other hand, when R^2 equals 1, all deviations from $\bar{S}$ are explained by the regression equation and Σe_i^2 equals 0. In a one-variable model, this implies that all sales prices lie on a straight line (Neighborhood A in figure 5 best approximates this condition). For the twenty-five observations in table 10 and figure 4, R^2 is 0.704.

Note that R^2 can also be written as

$$R^2 \;=\; 1 \;-\; \frac{SSE_{UN}}{SSE}. \qquad (25)$$

This makes clear that R^2 is a function of

$$SSE_{UN} = \Sigma e_i^2. \qquad (26)$$

The smaller SSE_{UN} is as a percentage of SSE, the larger is R^2.

The use of R^2 has two shortcomings. First, as we add more regression variables, R^2 can only increase or stay the same, which can overstate goodness of fit when insignificant variables are included or the number of variables is large relative to the number of sales. Assume that we have regressed sales prices on eighteen independent variables and obtained an R^2 of 0.920. Now suppose we re-run the model with a nineteenth variable, number of windows. As long as number of windows has any correlation whatsoever with sale price, R^2 will increase from 0.920.

Fortunately, R^2 can be adjusted to account for the number of independent variables. Its sister statistic, adjusted R^2 or $\overline{R}^2$, is calculated as

$$\overline{R}^2 = 1 - \frac{(n - 1)\ SSE_{UN}}{(n - p - 1)\ SSE}, \quad (27)$$

where n is sample size and p is the number of regression variables. In the present example, the addition of number of windows as a nineteenth variable will cause R^2 to fall unless the variable makes some minimum contribution to the predictive power of the equation.

The second shortcoming of R^2 (shared also by $\overline{R}^2$) is more a matter of care in interpretation. Recall that R^2 measures the percentage of the variation in sales prices explained by the regression model. In mass appraisal, we often divide properties into homogeneous strata and develop separate equations for each. Because this reduces the variance among sales prices within each stratum, we should not expect MRA to explain as large a percentage as when one equation is fit to the entire jurisdiction. For example, values of R^2 of 0.82, 0.91, and 0.87 for three individual neighborhoods may well be associated with better predictive regression models (as indicated by Σe_i^2) than an R^2 of, say, 0.94 for the three neighborhoods combined.

Standard Error of the Estimate The standard error of the estimate (SEE) measures the *amount* of deviation between actual and predicted sales prices. It is computed as:

$$SEE = \left[\frac{\Sigma (S_i - \hat{S}_i)^2}{n - p - 1} \right]^{1/2}, \quad (28)$$

where n is the number of observations (sales) and p is the number of independent variables. Note that the SEE is the sum of squared errors (see equation 16) divided by its degrees of freedom $(n - p - 1)$. This yields a measure of the average squared error or *variance* of the regression model. The square root is then taken to extract the standard error. The SEE is calculated in a manner analogous to the standard deviation (chapter 20), and indeed can be viewed as the standard deviation of the regression errors. Thus, if the errors are normally distributed, two-thirds of actual sales prices will fall within 1 SEE of their predicted values, 95 percent within 2 SEEs, and so on. Note that whereas R^2 is a percentage figure, the SEE is a dollar figure. For the twenty-five observations in table 10, the SEE is \$9,107. The SEE is free from the second interpretive shortcoming of R^2 mentioned above. In other words, whereas R^2 evaluates the seriousness of the errors indirectly by comparing them with the variation of the sales prices, the SEE evaluates them directly in dollar terms.

In addition, regression software often provides an option to calculate standard errors and corresponding confidence intervals for individual predicted values. These values are a function of the overall *SEE* and the individual characteristics of a parcel. In general, the more typical the characteristics, that is, the closer they are to the average, the lower the standard error and the confidence interval about the predicted value.

Coefficient of Variation   In regression analysis, the coefficient of variation (*COV*) is the *SEE* expressed as a percentage of the average sale price and multiplied by 100:

$$COV = \frac{(100)\ (SEE)}{\overline{S}}. \qquad (29)$$

The statistic is analogous to the *COV* in sales ratio analysis, which expresses the standard deviation of the sales ratios as a percentage of the mean ratio.

Most MRA software reports the *SEE* but not the *COV*. Nevertheless, the *COV* is preferred for assessment purposes, because its interpretation is independent of the average sale price. Consider the present example in which the *SEE* equals $9,107. This would indicate a good predictive model when average property values are high, but not when they are low. Expressing the *SEE* as a percentage of the mean sale price removes this source of confusion. In the present example, the mean sale price is $83,848 (not shown), so that

$$COV = \frac{(100)(\$9,107)}{\$83,848} = 10.86.$$

This implies that, given a normal distribution, roughly two-thirds of sales prices lie within 10.86 percent of their MRA-predicted values.

Average Percent Error   The average percent error is analogous to the *COD* in ratio studies. It is calculated as the average absolute percent error between actual and predicted sales prices multiplied by 100:

$$\text{Average percent error} = \frac{100 \times \Sigma |S_i - \hat{S}_i|/S_i)}{n}. \qquad (30)$$

Although this statistic is not standard output with most computer software, the necessary programming is simple.

Coefficient of Correlation   The coefficient of correlation, abbreviated *r*, is the first of four statistics that relate to individual regression variables. The statistic, discussed in chapter 14, measures the degree of linear relation between two variables. Its range is from −1 to +1. When r_{XS}, the coefficient of correlation between variables *X* and *S*, is +1 or −1, differences between *X* and $\overline{X}$ are proportional to differences between *S* and $\overline{S}$. In other words, in a plot of *S* on *X* (or of *X* on *S*) all points will lie on a straight line, as illustrated in panels (a) and (b) of figure 10 in chapter 14.

However, r_{XS} says nothing about the causality or slope of the line relating variables *X* and *S*. When all points lie on a straight line with positive slope, r_{XS} equals +1, regardless of the degree of the slope; when all points lie on a straight line with negative slope, r_{XS} equals −1. Thus, r_{XS} measures the direction and consistency of linear correlation between *X* and *S* but says nothing about the causality or slope of the relationship.

Also, r_{XS} measures only the *linear* relation between two variables. In figure 10(f) of chapter 14, variables *X* and *S* are strongly related but not linearly related. Any straight line through the origin would fit the distribution equally well and, accordingly, r_{XS} equals 0. A zero or very low value of r_{XS}, therefore, does not necessarily imply "no relation." Rather, it means "no linear relation."

MRA software usually includes an optional correlation matrix showing the correlation coefficient between each pair of variables, as illustrated in figure 11 of chapter 14. In analyzing correlations with the dependent variable, remember that the correlation coefficient is a dimensionless figure or percentage, indicating only whether two variables are linearly related. Regression coefficients, on the other hand, indicate *how* variables are related, that is, how many units (dollars) the dependent variable changes when the independent variable changes by one unit (for example, one square foot) with other variables in the equation held constant. For the data in table 10, the coefficient of correlation between square feet and sale price is 0.839; b_1, the regression coefficient, is $47.90.

t-**Statistic**   The *t*-statistic is a measure of the significance or importance of a regression variable in explaining differences in the dependent variable (sale price). It is calculated as the ratio of the regression coefficient, b_j, to its standard error, s_j (not to be confused with the *SEE*):

$$t_j = b_j / s_j . \qquad (31)$$

The standard error of b_j, s_j, is akin to a standard deviation; it measures the error associated with using b_j as an estimator of the true, but unknown, relationship between X_j and S.

When t_j is large, one can be confident that X_j is significant in the prediction of S. Conversely, when t_j is small, one cannot reject the hypothesis that b_j equals 0 and that X_j is unimportant in explaining S. It should be emphasized, however, that this does not mean that X_j is not correlated with S. The *t*-value measures the *marginal contribution* of a variable in predicting S when all other variables included in the equation are held constant. Because some variables duplicate information provided by others, they may be highly correlated with sale price, but insignificant predictors as indicated by their *t*-values. Conversely, other variables possess the peculiarity of predicting sales prices in combination, although individually none may be highly correlated with sales prices.

The significance of *t*-statistics can be evaluated by reference to the *t*-table in appendix 20-6, where

$$\text{degrees of freedom} = n - p - 1.$$

In general, provided that sample size is large (at least fifty), a *t*-statistic in excess of ± 2.00 indicates that one can be 95 percent confident that $b_j \neq 0$ and therefore that X_j is significant in predicting S. Similarly, a *t*-statistic in excess of ± 2.58 indicates that one can be 99 percent confident that X_j is significant in the prediction of S. For the data in table 10, the *t*-statistic for square footage, the sole regression variable, is 7.40. For twenty-five sales, degrees of freedom equals 23 (25 − 1 − 1). Referring to the *t*-table, when degrees of freedom equal 23 and $t_j \pm 3.77$, one can be 99.9 percent confident that $b_j \neq 0$. Therefore, in this case we can conclude with confidence that square feet of living area is significant in estimating residential values.

F-Statistic   The F-statistic is related to the t-statistic and is also used to test whether or not individual regression variables are significant in predicting the dependent variable, S. The F-statistic is calculated by forming the ratio

$$\frac{\text{additional variance explained by } X_j}{\text{unexplained variance}}. \qquad (32)$$

"Additional" variance refers to variance without X_j included in the model less variance with X_j included. Obviously, the larger this ratio, the more important is X_j in reducing Σe_i^2 and the more confident one can be of the variable's significance in predicting S. As with the t-statistic, however, it should be understood that the F-statistic provides a measure of the *marginal* importance of an individual variable in explaining the dependent variable when all other variables are also taken into account (by including them in the regression equation).

In MRA, the F- and t-statistics are mathematically related:

$$F = t^2. \qquad (33)$$

That is, the F-statistic is the square of the t-statistic. Tables to evaluate the significance of F-statistics can be found in most textbooks on statistics. In general, an F-statistic of 4.0 or larger indicates that a variable is significant in predicting S at the 95 percent confidence level, provided that sample size is large. Some regression programs report t-statistics and others report F-statistics. Both measure the same thing, and one may easily be derived from the other.

Beta Coefficients   Beta coefficients are "standardized" regression coefficients that measure the *relative* importance of individual variables, b_j, in explaining differences in the dependent variable. Beta coefficients are obtained by transforming the dependent and independent variables so that they have means of zero and standard deviations of one. For each variable, this is accomplished by subtracting its mean and dividing by its standard deviation. A beta coefficient, β_j, thus measures the percentage change in S associated with a percentage change in X_j with all other variables held constant. Beta coefficients are related to regression coefficients by the formula

$$\beta_j = b_j (s_j/s_S), \qquad (34)$$

where s_j is the standard deviation of X_j and s_S is the standard deviation of S. (In a one-variable linear regression,

$$\beta_j = r_{jS},$$

the correlation coefficient between X_j and S.)

Beta coefficients are useful if one wishes to compare the relative importance of independent variables. Assume, for example, that an appraiser is interested in determining whether living area or effective age is more important in explaining property values. Because living area is measured in square feet and effective age in years, the regression coefficients cannot be compared directly. If, however, both variables are standardized, a meaningful comparison can be made. Assume, for example, that the beta coefficient for living area is 0.25 and that the beta coefficient for effective age is -0.38. This means that, with all other variables held constant, an increase in living area of, say, 10 percent will increase sale price by 2.5 percent. Similarly, an increase in effective age of 10 percent will decrease sale price by 3.8 percent. In this case, effective age does more to explain differences in sales prices than does living area.

Stepwise Regression Analysis

Model builders have several options in applying MRA. One of the most effective for mass appraisal is stepwise MRA, of which there are two versions—forward and backward. In forward stepwise MRA, variables are entered iteratively until all significant predictors have been included. In backward stepwise MRA, the algorithm begins with all variables and iteratively eliminates those that are insignificant. This section illustrates the former.

In forward stepwise MRA, the first variable entered, say X_1, is that variable most highly correlated with S. A least-squares regression of S on X_1 is performed. A search is then made to determine the remaining variable most highly correlated with the remaining errors. Suppose that this variable is X_4. A second regression is performed with X_1 and X_4 as independent variables. The remaining variables are searched to determine which has the highest correlation with residual errors from the second regression. This variable, say X_6, is then included in a third regression. The process continues until all variables have been included or the remaining variables fail to meet some predetermined significance level as measured by their t- or F-values. At each step the algorithm may either add a new variable or delete a variable that falls below the minimum significance level. The algorithm prevents redundant and insignificant variables from making the model more complex than necessary.

For illustrative purposes, consider a hypothetical case of 180 edited, time-adjusted sales and eight independent variables (table 11). Note that some of the variables are quantitative (*SIZE*, *ROOMS*, *EFFAGE*, and *LOT*) and others are qualitative binary variables coded either 0 or 1 (*FRPL*, *VIEWAV*, and *VIEWGD*). *QUAL* is a qualitative scalar variable.

Table 12 shows descriptive statistics for the variables. The first step in reviewing MRA output should be verification of the reasonableness of such statistics. One should verify that each variable occurs the expected number of times (180) and check the means and standard deviations for each variable. A mean number of rooms of 19.24, for example, would indicate that a major recording or processing error has occurred. The mean of a binary variable indicates the percentage of properties possessing that characteristic. For example, 32 percent of the 180 properties have a fireplace, 69 percent have an average view, and 17 percent have a good view.

Figure 7 shows the correlation matrix for the nine variables and 180 cases. The first row indicates the correlation coefficients between the independent variables and sale price. The rest of the matrix indicates the extent to which the independent variables are linearly correlated with each other. An inspection of the matrix reveals potential information overlaps or interrelationships. For example, the coefficient of correlation between *SIZE* and *ROOMS* is 0.888. This indicates that the two variables essentially measure the same thing (living area) and that one or both may behave unpredictably if

Table 11.   Stepwise Regression Variables

Variable	Coding	Definition
S	Dollars	Time-adjusted sale price
SIZE	Square feet	Square feet of living area
ROOMS	Number	Number of rooms
EFFAGE	Numeric (0–50)	Effective age of structure in years
QUAL	Scalar (0.50–1.50)	Quality class of structure
FRPL	Binary (0,1)	Fireplace: 0 = no, 1 = yes
LOT	Square feet	Square feet of lot area
VIEWAV	Binary (0, 1)	Average view: 0 = no, 1 = yes
VIEWGD	Binary (0, 1)	Good view: 0 = no, 1 = yes

Table 12.   Descriptive Statistics

Variable	Mean	Standard deviation	Number of cases
S	47,121.97	20,585.23	180
SIZE	1,823.55	1,017.18	180
ROOMS	7.24	3.44	180
EFFAGE	20.17	16.39	180
QUAL	1.09	0.26	180
FRPL	0.32	0.64	180
LOT	16,986.78	13,443.92	180
VIEWAV	0.69	0.48	180
VIEWGD	0.17	0.84	180

simultaneously included in the regression model. Another relatively high correlation occurs between QUAL and FRPL (0.540), indicating that homes with fireplaces are well constructed.

The stepwise regression output is presented in figure 8. At the first step, the variable SIZE enters the equation. As the correlation matrix shows, this variable possesses the highest correlation with sale price, 0.744. Several measures of goodness of fit are presented: "multiple R," R^2, adjusted R^2, and the standard error of the estimate (SEE). The first of these is the correlation coefficient between S and $\overline{S}$ and mathematically equals the square root of R^2. The other measures were discussed previously.

An analysis of variance (ANOVA) table is presented in the upper right-hand portion of the output. This information is used to compute R^2, the SEE, and other regression statistics. The regression sum of squares is

$$\Sigma \ (S_i \ - \ \overline{S})^2,$$

and the residual sum of squares is

$$\Sigma \ e_i^2 \ = \ \Sigma \ (S_i \ - \ \hat{S}_i)^2.$$

The ratio of SEE_{EX} to $(SEE_{EX} \ + \ SSE_{UN})$ is R^2. The regression mean-square error is the regression sum of squares divided by its degrees of freedom:

$$\frac{\Sigma \ (\hat{S}_i \ - \ \overline{S})^2}{p}$$

Similarly, the residual mean-square error is the residual sum of squares divided by its degrees of freedom:

$$\frac{\Sigma \ (S_i \ - \ \hat{S})^2}{n \ - \ p \ - \ 1}$$

Figure 7. MRA Correlation Matrix

	SIZE	ROOMS	EFFAGE	QUAL	FRPL	LOT	VIEWAV	VIEWGD
S	.744	.689	−.510	.590	.195	.348	.156	.202
SIZE	1.000	.888	−.143	−.032	−.066	−.112	.080	−.095
ROOMS		1.000	−.129	−.075	−.033	−.055	.069	−.080
EFFAGE			1.000	−.290	.090	.235	.148	.296
QUAL				1.000	.540	−.118	−.006	−0.29
FRPL					1.000	.091	−0.52	.160
LOT						1.000	.004	−.092
VIEWAV							1.000	−.699
VIEWGD								1.000

Recall that the *SEE* is the square root of this expression. The *F*-value presented in the ANOVA table is the ratio of the regression mean-square error to the residual mean-square error. This ratio can be used to test the hypothesis that multiple *R* equals 0, that is, that $\hat{S}_i$ is not correlated with S_i. Rejection of this hypothesis means that the regression equation is a significant improvement over $\overline{S}$ in predicting values of S_i. In the present example, the *F*-value of 220.689 indicates that, without doubt, the regression equation,

$$S = b_0 + b_1 (SIZE), \qquad (35)$$

is a significant predictor of S_i.

Variables in the equation are summarized in the lower left-hand portion of the output. With only one variable in the equation, its *F*-statistic is equal to the overall *F*-value in the ANOVA table. Variables not included in the equation are listed, with their respective "*F*-to-enter" values in the lower right-hand portion of the output. The *F*-statistics indicate the significance of the variables if they were included in the equation. For example, the *F*-to-enter value for *ROOMS* is its *F*-statistic in the equation,

$$S = b_0 + b_1 (SIZE) + b_2 (ROOMS). \qquad (36)$$

At the second step, the algorithm selects that variable most highly correlated with the unexplained residuals, Σe_i^2. This is also the variable with the highest *F*-to-enter value, in this case *EFFAGE*. A second regression is run with the variables *SIZE* and *EFFAGE*. As a result, R^2 increases to 0.7183, and *SEE* falls to \$10,987. Beginning at step 2, adjusted R^2 departs slightly from R^2 because the former statistic exerts a small penalty as additional variables are brought into the equation. Note that the variable *ROOMS* does not enter the model second, although it possesses the second highest correlation with sale price (0.689 versus −0.510 for *EFFAGE*). This is because, with *SIZE* already in the equation, *ROOMS* has little additional information to contribute.

At the third step, *QUAL* enters the equation. Adjusted R^2 increases to 0.7823, *SEE* falls to \$9,606, and all three variables, as indicated by their *F*-values, are extremely significant predictors.

LOT enters the equation at the fourth step, with an *F*-value of 9.463. This is much less than that of the other included variables but still easily significant at the 99 percent confidence level. Adjusted R^2 makes another good gain to 0.8347 and *SEE* falls to \$8,369.

Figure 8. Stepwise Regression Output

STEP NUMBER 1
VARIABLE ENTERED SIZE

		ANALYSIS OF VARIANCE	DF	SUM OF SQUARES	MEAN SQUARE	F
MULTIPLE R	.7440					
R SQUARE	.5535					
ADJUSTED R SQUARE	.5535	REGRESSION	1	41986565380	41986565380	220.689
STD ERROR OF EST	13793.2136	RESIDUAL	178	33864987870	190252741	

----------VARIABLES IN EQUATION---------- | ---VARIABLES NOT IN EQUATION---

VARIABLE	B	BETA	STD ERROR B	F		VARIABLE	F TO ENTER
SIZE	24.815	.744	1.670	220.689		ROOMS	2.059
						EFFAGE	36.487
						QUAL	15.296
						FRPL	12.465
						LOT	7.498
						VIEW—AV	0.724
						VIEW—GD	2.526

STEP NUMBER 2
VARIABLE ENTERED EFFAGE

		ANALYSIS OF VARIANCE	DF	SUM OF SQUARES	MEAN SQUARE	F
MULTIPLE R	.8475					
R SQUARE	.7183					
ADJUSTED R SQUARE	.7151	REGRESSION	3	54484170700	27242085350	225.664
STD ERROR OF EST	10987.2506	RESIDUAL	177	21367382550	120719675	

----------VARIABLES IN EQUATION---------- | ---VARIABLES NOT IN EQUATION---

VARIABLE	B	BETA	STD ERROR B	F		VARIABLE	F TO ENTER
SIZE	30.533	.662	1.543	391.568		ROOMS	2.164
EFFAGE	−643.281	−.489	46.863	188.424		QUAL	23.499
						FRPL	18.565
						LOT	7.003
						VIEW—AV	.711
						VIEW—GD	1.646

STEP NUMBER 3
VARIABLE ENTERED QUAL

		ANALYSIS OF VARIANCE	DF	SUM OF SQUARES	MEAN SQUARE	F
MULTIPLE R	.8865					
R SQUARE	.7859					
ADJUSTED R SQUARE	.7823	REGRESSION	3	59611735700	19870578560	215.349
STD ERROR OF EST	9605.8155	RESIDUAL	176	16239817550	92271691	

----------VARIABLES IN EQUATION---------- | ---VARIABLES NOT IN EQUATION---

VARIABLE	B	BETA	STD ERROR B	F		VARIABLE	F TO ENTER
SIZE	28.695	.623	1.598	322.447		ROOMS	2.094
EFFAGE	−562.341	−.492	40.694	190.958		FRPL	5.389
QUAL	3477.828	.379	339.707	104.811		LOT	9.463
						VIEW—AV	.698
						VIEW—GD	3.041

STEP NUMBER 4
VARIABLE ENTERED LOT

		ANALYSIS OF VARIANCE	DF	SUM OF SQUARES	MEAN SQUARE	F
MULTIPLE R	.9156					
R SQUARE	.8384					
ADJUSTED R SQUARE	.8347	REGRESSION	4	63593942240	15898485560	226.980
STD ERROR OF EST	8369.1990	RESIDUAL	175	12257611000	70043491	

----------VARIABLES IN EQUATION---------- | ---VARIABLES NOT IN EQUATION---

VARIABLE	B	BETA	STD ERROR B	F		VARIABLE	F TO ENTER
SIZE	27.443	.610	1.587	299.026		ROOMS	3.194
EFFAGE	−549.341	−.469	45.816	143.764		FRPL	5.242
QUAL	3522.149	.402	295.554	142.017		VIEW—AV	1.708
LOT	.969	.242	.315	9.463		VIEW—GD	3.247

Figure 8.   Stepwise Regression Output (cont.)

STEP NUMBER 5
    VARIABLE ENTERED   FRPL

		ANALYSIS OF VARIANCE	DF	SUM OF SQUARES	MEAN SQUARE	F
MULTIPLE R	.9257					
R SQUARE	.8569					
ADJUSTED R SQUARE	.8528	REGRESSION	5	64997195980	12999439190	208.387
STD ERROR OF EST	7898.1874	RESIDUAL	174	10854357270	62381364	

-----------VARIABLES IN EQUATION----------- ---VARIABLES NOT IN EQUATION---

VARIABLE	B	BETA	STD ERROR B	F	VARIABLE	F TO ENTER
SIZE	29.655	.643	1.587	349.174	ROOMS	3.343
EFFAGE	−659.281	−.501	42.969	235.413	VIEW—AV	1.719
QUAL	3066.494	.296	502.156	37.291	VIEW—GD	2.844
LOT	.964	.235	.316	9.306		
FRPL	2497.117	.115	1090.663	5.242		

STEP NUMBER 6
    VARIABLE ENTERED   ROOMS

		ANALYSIS OF VARIANCE	DF	SUM OF SQUARES	MEAN SQUARE	F
MULTIPLE R	.9305					
R SQUARE	.8658					
ADJUSTED R SQUARE	.8611	REGRESSION	6	65672274800	10945379130	186.020
STD ERROR OF EST	7670.7079	RESIDUAL	173	10179278440	58839760	

-----------VARIABLES IN EQUATION----------- ---VARIABLES NOT IN EQUATION---

VARIABLE	B	BETA	STD ERROR B	F	VARIABLE	F TO ENTER
SIZE	34.142	.450	4.393	60.403	VIEW—AV	1.720
EFFAGE	−704.819	−.533	45.980	234.973	VIEW—GD	2.679
QUAL	2885.336	.299	488.553	34.879		
LOT	.966	.236	.313	9.525		
FRPL	2349.060	.118	1072.817	4.794		
ROOMS	−105.007	−.069	57.431	3.343		

STEP NUMBER 7
    VARIABLE ENTERED VIEW—GD

		ANALYSIS OF VARIANCE	DF	SUM OF SQUARES	MEAN SQUARE	F
MULTIPLE R	.9330					
R SQUARE	.8705					
ADJUSTED R SQUARE	.8652	REGRESSION	7	65778466980	9396723854	160.454
STD ERROR OF EST	7652.7417	RESIDUAL	172	10073086270	58564455	

-----------VARIABLES IN EQUATION----------- ---VARIABLES NOT IN EQUATION---

VARIABLE	B	BETA	STD ERROR B	F	VARIABLE	F TO ENTER
SIZE	33.273	.451	4.310	59.598	VIEW—AV	6.499
EFFAGE	−710.161	−.529	47.953	219.549		
QUAL	2879.443	.299	487.663	34.864		
LOT	.963	.241	.307	9.840		
FRPL	2340.615	.117	1066.118	4.820		
ROOMS	−109.128	−.070	58.312	3.502		
VIEW—GD	842.677	.032	489.053	2.679		

STEP NUMBER 8
    VARIABLE ENTERED VIEW—AV

		ANALYSIS OF VARIANCE	DF	SUM OF SQUARES	MEAN SQUARE	F
MULTIPLE R	.9570					
R SQUARE	.9129					
ADJUSTED R SQUARE	.9088	REGRESSION	8	69244882960	8655610370	224.033
STD ERROR OF EST	6215.7460	RESIDUAL	171	6606670288	38635499	

-----------VARIABLES IN EQUATION----------- ---VARIABLES NOT IN EQUATION---

VARIABLE	B	BETA	STD ERROR B	F	VARIABLE	F TO ENTER
SIZE	33.004	.459	4.296	57.021		
EFFAGE	−739.642	−.550	48.866	229.102		
QUAL	2854.894	.301	461.119	38.331		
LOT	.960	.245	.305	9.907		
FRPL	2234.511	.113	1048.222	4.544		
ROOMS	−108.228	−.068	60.037	3.250		
VIEW—GD	3105.695	.183	701.738	9.587		
VIEW—AV	2019.447	.152	792.153	6.499		

At the fifth step, *FRPL* enters the model with an *F*-value significant at the 95 percent confidence level. Adjusted R^2 increases to 0.8528, and *SEE* falls to $7,898. Note the large decrease in the *F*-value of *QUAL*. As pointed out earlier, *FRPL* and *QUAL* are highly correlated, so the significance of each is reduced when both are considered simultaneously.

At this point, had the minimum *F*-to-enter value been set at 4.00 (*t*-value of 2.00), which corresponds to the 95 percent confidence level, the routine would terminate, because the three excluded variables all have *F*-to-enter values less than 4.00. Instead, the *F*-to-enter and *F*-to-delete values have been set at zero in order to "force" all variables into the model. Thus, the variable *ROOMS* enters at step 6 with a coefficient of −$105, indicating that the model subtracts $105 per room. Although this seems counterintuitive, recall that *ROOMS* is highly correlated with *SIZE* and that regression coefficients measure the *marginal* effect of the independent variables. Thus, although the market places a high value on living area, it subtracts value for a large number of rooms relative to living area (that is, when rooms are "too small").

It now appears that there is little point to continuing the routine, because the *F*-to-enter values for both of the view-related variables are small. Nevertheless, with the *F*-to-enter value set at zero, the variable *VIEWGD* enters at step 7. Adjusted R^2 increases trivially from 0.8611 to 0.8652 and the *SEE* falls only $18. Note, however, what happens to the excluded variable, *VIEWAV*: its *F*-to-enter value suddenly becomes significant at the 95 percent confidence level. Why is this? When *VIEWGD* was not in-

cluded in the equation, *VIEWAV* measured the marginal effect on value of an average view as opposed to either a poor or good view. Thus, *VIEWAV* had little opportunity to assert its superiority over a "poor" view. However, when *VIEWGD* is forced to enter, *VIEWAV* measures the marginal effect on value of an average view relative to a poor view. In this context, the variable emerges as a significant predictor.

Finally, note that at step 8, with *VIEWAV* in the equation, *VIEWGD* also takes on new significance. More important, adjusted R^2 increases from 0.8652 to 0.9088 and the *SEE* falls from $7,653 to $6,216. The reason for the new-found importance of *VIEWGD* is analogous to that of *VIEWAV*. With *VIEWAV* not in the equation, *VIEWGD* represented only the marginal effect of a good view as opposed to either a poor view or an average view. However, with *VIEWAV* included, *VIEWGD* represents the effect on value of a good view versus a poor view.

This demonstrates a point of caution. When two or more binary variables work in combination, none is rejected until they have been tested simultaneously. One of the advantages of stepwise MRA is that it enables the analyst to compare results at each step. If "forcing in" variables beyond a desired cutoff level yields no additional significant predictors, one can select the equation at an earlier step of the output.

Table 13 summarizes the stepwise results. Note that the first two variables (*SIZE* and *EFFAGE*) succeed in explaining 71.83 percent of the variation in sales prices. This is not uncommon. With all eight variables in the equation, $R^2 = 0.9129$. In the present example, no variables were removed from the equation, so that the number of steps equals the number of independent variables included in the equation.

Table 14 contains an abbreviated residuals printout. Sales prices are printed in column 2, predicted values in column 3, and differences (residuals) in column 4. The total of the residuals is zero. Column 5 expresses the residuals as a percent of sales prices. The total of the absolute percent errors is 17.2578. Dividing this figure by 180 and multiplying by 100 yields the average percent error: 9.59. In conclusion, the final measures of goodness of fit are $R^2 = 0.9129$, adjusted $R^2 = 0.9088$, $SEE = \$6,216$, $COV = 13.19$ ($\$6,216 \div \$47,122 \times 100$), and average percent error = 9.59.

Finally, note in table 14 that the sum of the actual sales prices equals the sum of the predicted sales prices. This means that the predicted values average 100 percent of actual values. Thus, in addition to reducing the variability of assessments, MRA provides value estimates that, on average, automatically reflect the current market.

Regression Outliers

Outliers in MRA are properties whose estimated values differ from sales prices by unusually large amounts. When regression residuals are normally distributed, two-thirds of sales prices can be expected to fall within one SEE of their estimated values, 95 percent within two SEE, and 99 percent within three SEE.

It is good practice to examine critically all residuals that exceed a specified amount or percentage of sale price, for example, those that exceed more than two standard errors. A residuals printout, such as that illustrated in table 14, will reveal properties exceeding the desired bounds. For example, property 178 has a predicted value of $49,623 but a sale price of only $34,500. The difference of $15,123 is more than twice the SEE of $6,216. Alternatively, a printout can be prepared only of properties for which residuals exceed a specified bound.

Outliers can have at least three causes. First, data may be incorrectly coded. If this occurs frequently, it will not only cause large errors for individual properties but bias the entire model. Thus, once data errors have been corrected, the model should be rerun. Second, outliers may be due to a failure to screen sales adequately or to adjust them for personal property, financing, and the like. Such sales should be excluded or adjusted as

Table 13.   Stepwise Summary Table

Step	Variable entered	Variable deleted	R	R^2	Increase in R^2	F to enter or remove	Number of variables
1	SIZE		.7440	.5535	.5535	220.689	1
2	EFFAGE		.8475	.7183	.1648	188.424	2
3	QUAL		.8865	.7859	.0676	104.811	3
4	LOT		.9156	.8384	.0525	9.463	4
5	FRPL		.9257	.8569	.0185	5.242	5
6	ROOMS		.9305	.8658	.0089	3.343	6
7	VIEWGD		.9330	.8705	.0047	2.679	7
8	VIEWAV		.9555	.9129	.0424	6.499	8

Table 14.   Residuals Printout

Case number	Actual	Predicted	Residual	Residual-to-actual
1	$ 55,200	$ 53,186	$ 2,014	.0365
2	39,500	38,488	1,012	.0256
3	44,600	49,322	− 4,722	− .1059
4	43,900	43,625	275	.0063
5	34,000	38,211	− 4,211	− .1239
6	77,900	78,454	− 1,544	− .0198
7	65,000	58,183	6,817	.1049
8	41,500	40,187	1,313	.0316
9	48,000	48,115	− 115	.0024
10	33,800	34,989	− 1,189	− .0352
—	—	—	—	—
176	43,900	39,315	4,585	.1044
177	40,100	38,827	1,273	.0317
178	34,500	49,623	− 15,123	− .4383
179	51,000	52,323	− 1,323	− .0259
180	37,900	39,010	− 1,110	− .0293
Totals	$8,481,955	$8,481,955	0	17.2578

appropriate and the models rerun, although it is far better to address such problems during routine sales processing *before* models are developed. Third, outliers can result from unusual property characteristics or an unusual combination of characteristics. Such properties should not be indiscriminately purged from the model. In any model, outliers are always expected. In many cases, they provide clues as to additional variables or other refinements that might improve the model. One should always strive to fit the model to the property base, not manipulate the data to improve the model artificially.

Constrained Variables

Often it is desirable to preset the coefficient for a variable, constrain a coefficient to a predefined range, or create aggregated or synthetic variables. This applies particularly to seldom occurring variables (SOVs) for which there are inadequate sales for calibration. Examples might include guest houses, tennis courts, or hot tubs. These variables can be constrained to their depreciated cost values or other reasonable amounts. One method of accomplishing this is to subtract the predetermined amount from the sale price, so that the dependent variable reflects sale price net of value for the SOVs. Such variables are not included in model calibration, but are added back during model application.

For example, the value of a hot tub might be estimated to be $1,000. For properties with hot tubs, $1,000 is subtracted from the sale price, so that the properties are modeled as if they had sold for $1,000 less without a hot tub. Then $1,000 is added back when applying the model.

Some software will allow the user to impose direct constraints on the regression coefficients. For example, the coefficient for hot tubs may be preset to $1,000 or the coefficient for garage stalls might be constrained to $2,000–$5,000. In this case, the sale price need not be adjusted, and the variables need to be excluded.

Sometimes several SOVs can be aggregated into a single variable, which can be included in model calibration. In an apartment model, for example, variables for interior amenities might be aggregated into a variable, *INSIDE*, computed as follows:

$$INSIDE = BATHS + FIREPLACES + HEATING + COOLING, \quad (37)$$

where

BATHS is number of baths/(total units − 1)

FIREPLACES is number of fireplaces/total units

HEATING is −1 if none, −0.5 if inferior, 0 if forced air

COOLING is 0 if none, 0.5 if wall unit, 1 if central air conditioning

The variable *INSIDE* will have a value of zero if the apartment building has one bath per unit, no fireplaces, forced air heating, and no cooling. A more desirable set of amenities will result in values above zero, and less desirable amenities in values below zero. Recreational facilities could be aggregated in a similar manner.

When aggregated in this manner, the resulting variable provides a quality index. In an additive model, it is good practice to center the index near zero, as above; in a multiplicative or hybrid model it should ordi-narily be centered near one. Such variables can often be calibrated satisfactorily, whereas individual variables could not, because of limited sales, high collinearity, or other data problems.

MRA Assumptions

The validity and interpretation of an MRA model depend on the extent to which certain assumptions are met. The most important in the context of mass appraisal are complete and accurate data, linearity, additivity, normally distributed errors, constant variance of the errors, uncorrelated independent variables, and sample representativeness.

Complete and Accurate Data MRA models are data-dependent; that is, estimated values can be no better than the data on which they are based. The best means of guaranteeing complete and accurate data is a well-designed data collection and maintenance program. Computerized edits can help identify missing, inconsistent, or unusual data. Sales prices should be verified, screened for non-arm's-length transfers, and adjusted for financing, personal property, and time as necessary.

Linearity Linearity means that the marginal contribution to value of an independent variable is constant over the entire range of the variable. For example, for the variable square feet of living area, linearity requires each square foot of living area to add equally to value. Because the linearity assumption often cannot be supported, it may be necessary to transform the data used in additive MRA models through various mathematical manipulations (chapter 14). For example, taking the logarithm of square feet of living area may produce an approximately linear relationship. In addition, stratifying properties into neighborhoods or other homogeneous clusters can help achieve linearity. In contrast, multiplicative MRA does not require linearity.

Additivity Additivity means that the marginal contribution of any one independent variable is unaffected by the other variables in the model. The additivity assumption would be violated, for example, if additional living area added more to value in a new house than in an old house. When variables have an interactive effect on sale price, additivity can often be approximated through a multiplicative or quotient transformation. Stratification also helps achieve additivity. Highly interactive models, however, cannot be adequately approximated through data transformations. In such cases, one must turn to a multiplicative or hybrid model structure.

Normally Distributed Errors MRA assumes that the regression residuals are normally distributed as in figure 9(a). Violation of this condition affects interpretation of the *SSE* and *COV*. If the residuals are abnormally skewed, as in figure 9(b), more than 68 percent will lie within one *SEE* and more than 95 percent within two *SEE*. On the other hand, if the residuals are dome-shaped, as in figure 9(c), fewer than 68 percent will lie within one *SEE* of their predicted values. In addition, nonnormal error terms can affect *t*- and *F*-values and, thus, the reliability of individual regression coefficients. Nonnormal error terms can result from poorly edited data or improper model specification.

Constant Variance of the Error Term Constant variance of the error term implies that the residuals are uncorrelated with the dependent variable, sale price. Violation of this assumption, known as heteroscedastic-

Figure 9. Residual Plots

Panel (a)

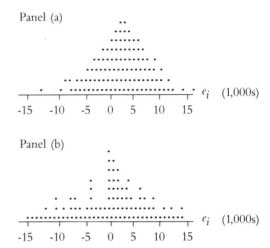

Panel (b)

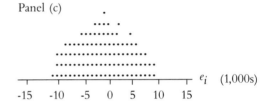

Panel (c)

Panel (d)

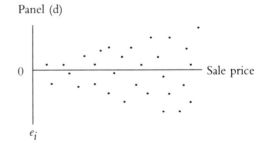

ity, is depicted in figure 9(d), which suggests that higher-priced properties tend to sell over a broader range than lower-priced properties. This situation causes concern because the regression model will be unduly influenced by the high-value properties and, thus, be less reliable when applied to low-value properties.

Heteroscedasticity is not usually significant when separate models are developed for neighborhoods or other homogeneous property strata. When the condition does occur, constant variance can usually be obtained by dividing sale price by a variable with which it is highly correlated, for example, square feet of living area. Alternatively, weighted least squares MRA, a technique of assigning equal weight to each observation, can be used. Multiplicative MRA avoids the problem by taking the natural logarithm of the dependent variable, which usually produces a sufficiently normal distribution.

Uncorrelated Independent Variables
MRA assumes that the independent variables are uncorrelated. Violation of this assumption, known as multicollinearity, is common in mass appraisal. It is crucial, however, to distinguish two types of multicollinearity: perfect and imperfect. Perfect multicollinearity exists when there is a linear relationship between two or more variables. This means that one of the variables can always be expressed as a constant multiple of the other or others. Two variables, X_1 and X_2, would be perfectly collinear if, for example, X_2 equals $1.5X_1$ for all values of X_1 and X_2. If X_1 were number of bathrooms and X_2 were number of bedrooms, this would imply that one could always compute the number of bedrooms from the number of bathrooms and vice versa. MRA is unable to find a unique solution in the face of perfect multicollinearity and may produce an error message or exclude one or both of the problem variables.

Imperfect multicollinearity occurs when certain of the independent variables are correlated but there are no exact linear relationships. The problem with this more general form of multicollinearity is that, as emphasized in the stepwise demonstration problem, interpretation of the regression coefficients is confused. In such cases, remember that the regression coefficients measure the *marginal* contribution of a variable with all other variables in the equation held constant. This makes it possible to explain coefficients with unexpected signs or amounts, for example, a negative coefficient for room count.

One simple procedure to reduce multicollinearity is to eliminate redundant variables. When two variables are highly correlated, one can often be excluded from the model with little loss in predictive accuracy. The other variable should have a reasonable coefficient, its standard error should fall, and its t- or F-value should increase. To a large extent, stepwise regression performs this process automatically by excluding variables that fail to meet a specified significance level.

Representativeness MRA requires sold properties on which models are constructed to be representative of properties to which they are applied. If, for example, most sales in a neighborhood occur for newer houses, yet there are an equal number of older houses, the model will lose reliability when applied to the older houses. Comparing descriptive statistics (such as means and standard deviations), frequency distributions, or histograms between sold and unsold properties is one means of monitoring representativeness. In addition, in pilot testing MRA models it is good practice to divide available sales into two groups: a *test sample* and a *control sample*. The test sample is used to develop the model, which is then tested on the control sample. A model custom-designed to the unique features of the test sample may not perform well when applied to the control sample.

Of the above assumptions, the most important relate to complete, accurate, and representative data. MRA is "robust" in that it tends to work well even when the other assumptions are violated. Of course, serious violations can cause unreliable models and require the model builder to take corrective measures.

Multiplicative MRA

A multiplicative model takes the form:

$$S = b_0 \times X_1^{b_1} \times X_2^{b_2}. \quad (38)$$

In addition, binary variables can appear as exponents in the model. Thus, as illustrated in chapter 14 (see equation 18), a simple model might be

$$S = b_0 \times SQFT^{b_1} \times QUAL^{b_2} \times PERGOOD^{b_3} \times b_4^{NBHD1} \times b_5^{NBHD2} \times b_6^{NBHD4}, \quad (39)$$

where

QUAL is quality class (scalar variable centered on 1.00)
PERGOOD is $(100 - AGE)/100$
NBHD1, ..., NBHD4 are binary variables (NBHD3 is the reference neighborhood).

Note that the neighborhood variables serve as exponents in the model.

This model can be calibrated by taking natural logarithms of both sides:

$$\ln (S) = \ln [b_0 \times SQFT^{b_1} \times QUAL^{b_2} \times PERGOOD^{b_3} \times b_4^{NBHD1} \times b_5^{NBHD2} \times b_6^{NBHD4}]; \quad (40)$$

$$\ln (S) = \ln (b_0) + b_1 \times \ln (SQFT) + b_2 \times \ln (QUAL) + b_3 \times \ln (PERGOOD) + NBHD1 \times \ln (b_4) + NBHD2 \times \ln (b_5) + NBHD4 \times \ln (b_6). \quad (41)$$

In this form, the model is additive and can be calibrated with additive MRA. Assume that the following model results:

$$\ln (S) = 4.065 + 0.988 \times \ln (SQFT) + 1.09 \times \ln (QUAL) + 0.873 \times \ln(PERGOOD) + 0.125 NBHD1 - 0.033 NBHD2 - 0.049 NBHD4. \quad (42)$$

The model can be converted back to its original units by taking the antilog (exponential) of both sides:

$$S = \$58.265 \times SQFT^{0.988} \times QUAL^{1.09} \times PERGOOD^{0.873} \times 1.133^{NBHD1} \times 0.968^{NBHD2} \times 0.952^{NBHD4}. \quad (43)$$

Thus, the predicted value for an 1,800-square-foot, 20-year-old house of average quality in Neighborhood 4 is

$$S = 58.265 \times 1,800^{0.988} \times 1.00^{1.09} \times .80^{0.873} \times 0.952$$

$$S = \$58.265 \times 1,645 \times 1.00 \times 0.823 \times 0.952 = \$75,095.$$

Alternatively, the logarithmic model can be applied directly and the antilog taken of the result:

$$\ln(S) = \ln(58.265) + 0.988 \times \ln(1,800) + 1.09 \times \ln(1.00) + 0.873 \times \ln(0.80) + \ln(0.952)$$

$$\ln(S) = 4.065 + 0.988 \times 7.4955$$
$$+ 1.09 \times 0 + 0.873 \times (-.2232)$$
$$- 0.049 = 11.2266$$

$$S = \text{antilog}(11.2266) = \$75{,}101.$$

Although the latter may be more direct for computing estimated values, models should always be converted back to their original units for evaluation and review.

Multiplicative models free the model builder from the additivity assumption. Also, when sales prices vary widely, logarithms can help normalize the distribution, thus equalizing the weights assigned to each parcel. On the other hand, multiplicative models make it impossible to incorporate additive relationships. For example, one cannot treat main living area, basements, garages, and patios independently. Nor can land and improvements components be separated.

Hybrid MRA

Hybrid models combine both additive and multiplicative components. As explained in chapter 14, the general hybrid model takes the form:

$$MV = \pi GQ \times [(\pi BQ \times \Sigma BA) + (\pi LQ \times \Sigma LA) + \Sigma OA], \quad (2)$$

where the variables are as defined for equation 2.

This model cannot be transformed to an additive model and solved with linear MRA. However, two solutions using MRA are available. First, some statistical software includes "nonlinear MRA," which by a trial-and-error process seeks to minimize the sum of squared errors (equation 16). From judgment and experience, the user specifies initial coefficients, which the algorithm modifies until converging on a solution. Goodness-of-fit statistics obtained with this method are approximations, and stepwise MRA is not available.

Second, a multistage process using both additive and multiplicative MRA can be used. Appendix 15-1 demonstrates one such process.

Adaptive Estimation Procedure

Overview

Adaptive estimation procedure (AEP, or feedback) was introduced to assessors in the early 1980s by Robert Carbone and Richard Longini, who used it to estimate property values for Allegheny County, Pennsylvania, which includes Pittsburgh. They and others developed versions of the technique, which was used for both research and revaluations. The Lincoln Institute of Land Policy (LILP) developed the first mass appraisal package for personal computers, *SOLIR*, which incorporated feedback. Today, feedback is available from various sources, including several mass appraisal vendors.

Carbone and Longini adapted feedback from the engineering sciences, in which the principle is used to make continual corrections to a process from information on its current course or movement, thus the term "feedback." An example is the series of corrections made to the direction of a space vehicle from information on its current location, speed, and direction. In mass appraisal, a valuation equation is specified and adjusted as data on individual sales are sequentially processed and analyzed. The process continues, with each sale processed many times, until the model converges on a satisfactory solution.

Feedback Algorithm

Feedback calibrates the general hybrid model, (equation 2) and incorporates the influence of time trends, although time variables can also be included in the model as general qualitative variables.

In addition to the distinctions between model structures and types of variables discussed in chapter 14, the following terms and concepts are important to understanding feedback: reference descriptors, starting coefficients, damping factors, exponential smoothing average, iteration sequence, number of iterations, and convergence.

Reference Descriptors Reference descriptors are the benchmark, or starting, values of qualitative or scalar variables. Usually these values are 1.00, with more desirable features having higher values and less desirable features lower values. Cooling, for example, may be coded as none = 0.88, window units = 1.00, and central air = 1.10. The values assigned should reflect the appraiser's best estimate of relative value. Often MRA can be used to help determine proper starting values. As with MRA, the coefficients for such variables are exponents, which are calibrated during the feedback process.

Starting Coefficients Starting coefficients are the values initially assigned by the user to each variable's coefficient, for example, $50.00 per square foot of living area or a location multiplier of 1.07 for a given neighborhood. Proper selection of the starting coefficients will speed convergence and possibly give a more satisfactory result. Starting coefficients for qualitative variables are usually set at 1.00. Ending coefficients greater than 1.00 have the effect of expanding initial differences between the values of a scalar variable; coefficients of less than 1.00 reduce the differences. For example, if the coefficient for cooling, as coded above, were 0.65, the adjusted multipliers for cooling would be:

$$0.88^{0.65} = 0.920; \ 1.00^{0.65} = 1.00;$$
$$1.10^{0.65} = 1.064.$$

Damping Factors Damping factors are system- or user-specified control parameters that prevent the coefficients from oscillating widely from sale to sale. Setting a factor at 0.10, for example, would limit changes in the coefficients to 10 percent of the amount statistically computed at each step of the operation. If, for example, the model estimated a value of $110,000 for a $100,000 sale, the coefficients would be adjusted downward so as to eliminate only 10 percent, or $1,000, of the prediction error. If the next sale had the same characteristics as the previous sale, the model would compute an estimated value of $109,000 and the coefficients would be adjusted downward so as to eliminate another 10 percent, or $900, of the $9,000 difference. Thus damping factors stabilize the model so that it does not forget or "unlearn" all knowledge gained to that point. The actual operation and effect of damping factors may differ from one version of feedback to another. Also, setting these values at different levels can give different results.

Exponential Smoothing Average The exponential smoothing average is the moving average of a variable as additional sales are processed. It is used in computing the amount of adjustment made to quantitative coefficients. The more a variable differs from its exponential smoothing average, the more its coefficient is adjusted upward or downward to help explain the difference between the estimated and actual sale price. The magnitude of adjustment, however, is also controlled by the damping factor and, again, algorithms may differ from one version of feedback to another.

Iteration Sequence The iteration sequence is the backward and forward pattern in which sales are processed. It is usually desirable to have the initial pass begin at the latest (most recent) sale and cycle backward to the earliest sale, and to have the final pass set at a forward pass so that the final model coefficients will reflect the most recent market level.

Number of Iterations The number of iterations is the number of times the file is processed backward and forward. It is selected by the user and, in part, should reflect the number of cases available and heterogeneity of the data. If the initial coefficients are set close to market levels, the number of iterations required for convergence will be fewer. More than two or three iterations are usually required for convergence; ten to fifty iterations are common.

Convergence Convergence refers to stabilization of the coefficients from one iteration to another. There is no single solution to a feedback run. Usually, the process is terminated when the *mean absolute percent error* reaches a predefined value or the maximum number of iterations is reached. Because it is based on a tracking principle rather than a unique mathematical solution, feedback does not ordinarily contain R^2, t- and F-values, or other goodness-of-fit statistics available with MRA. However, the reliability of the overall results can be evaluated

through the absolute percent error, akin to the coefficient of dispersion, and other sales ratio statistics (chapter 20).

The Correction Algorithm

The correction is the core of the feedback system. Mathematically, the corrections to the coefficients are each determined with the introduction of each new sale into the model.

The corrections to *multiplicative (qualitative) coefficients* are made as follows. The corrected coefficient is equal to the previous coefficient times $(1 + C)$, where C is the correction.

The correction is

$$\frac{S - \hat{S}}{\hat{S}} \times \frac{DF}{n}, \qquad (44)$$

where S is the sale price, $\hat{S}$ is the estimated sale price, DF is the damping factor, and n is the number of qualitative characteristics in the model.

The corrections to *additive* (quantitative) coefficients are made as follows. The corrected coefficient is the previous coefficient plus the product of the previous coefficient and the correction. The correction is

$$\frac{S - \hat{S}}{\hat{S}} \times DF \times \frac{datum}{\substack{exponential \\ smoothing\ average}}, \qquad (45)$$

where the datum is the actual value for a variable, and the exponential smoothing average is

$$(SIGNIFICANT\% \times X) + (1 - SIGNIFICANT\% \times \overline{X}). \qquad (46)$$

The *SIGNIFICANT*% is a user-defined quantity from 0 to 1 that regulates the amount of X to use. X is the actual value of the variable entering the model, and $\overline{X}$ is the mean value of all the variables that have already entered the model. If the *SIGNIFICANT*% is 1, X will strongly influence the exponential smoothing average. If *SIGNIFICANT*% is 0, X will not influence the exponential smoothing average.

Note that the average will continually change as each parcel is introduced, and both the damping factor and *SIGNIFICANT*% can be determined by the user in most software packages. Both control the rate of "learning" within the feedback system.

Illustration

Table 15 illustrates a simple feedback model containing one general qualitative variable (neighborhood), three building additive variables (living area, bathrooms, and garages), two building qualitative variables (construction type and condition), one land additive variable (land area), and two land qualitative variables (traffic and view). The right-hand column of the table contains data for a hypothetical parcel. As shown in the lower portion of the table, the estimated value, $81,154, can be readily decomposed into a building value of $68,785 and a land value of $12,369.

Comparison with MRA

Whereas MRA minimizes the sum of the squared errors, feedback seeks to minimize the average *absolute* error. Thus, feedback is less influenced by outliers than MRA and may produce a more stable result.

Because stepwise procedures are not available with feedback, the model must be carefully specified before calibration. Stepwise MRA can be used to help select the significant variables. As noted, feedback does not ordinarily contain goodness-of-fit statistics such as R^2, *SEE*, and *t*- or *F*-values. Nevertheless, it does compute the average percent error, and estimated values can be analyzed in ratio studies. As in MRA, outliers should be identified, analyzed, and possibly excluded from final models.

Because of its ability to calibrate the general hybrid model structure, feedback, when used properly, should produce results that are comparable to or better than those obtained with additive or multiplicative MRA. Success will depend, in part, on the model builder's choice of variables, initial weights, and damping factors, and on the number of iterations. If well chosen, models will converge quicker and give more satisfying results.

Location Value Response Surface Analysis

Location value response surface analysis (LVRSA) provides a means of adjusting smoothly for location in MRA, feedback, or other valuation models. Although it could be applied by geographic area, a primary purpose of LVRSA is to eliminate the need for multiple models and the associated boundary problems. Thus, usually the technique uses only one model. The "response surface" is a geographic grid based on *x-y* (north/-south and east/west) coordinates, such as the United States State Plane Coordinate System.

Analysis begins with development of a single MRA or other valuation model that includes building and situs but not location variables. Values estimated by the model are divided by sales prices and displayed on the geographic grid or response surface. Ratios of different magnitudes can be differentiated in several ways: by different colors, by different symbols, or by the same symbol in different sizes. Figure 10 illustrates the latter method, with ratios plotted as squares of five sizes:

$$
\begin{aligned}
1 &= 0\text{--}0.749 \\
2 &= .750\text{--}0.899 \\
3 &= .900\text{--}1.099 \\
4 &= 1.100\text{--}1.249 \\
5 &= 1.250 \text{ or greater}
\end{aligned}
$$

The north-central and, to a lesser extent, southeast portions of the grid are pockmarked with smaller squares. The northeast

Table 15. Feedback Illustration

Variable	Type	Coding	Coefficient	Subject property
Living area	Building additive	Square feet	35.24	1,500
Bathrooms	Building additive	Fixtures	510	6
Garages	Building additive	Stalls	3400	2
Construction type	Building qualitative	1 = frame	.92	2
		2 = block	.96	
		3 = brick	1.08	
Building condition	Building qualitative	1 = poor	.76	3
		2 = average	.95	
		3 = good	1.12	
Land area	Land additive	Square feet	1.43	8,000
Traffic	Land qualitative	1 = heavy	.93	2
		2 = moderate	1.06	
		3 = light	1.15	
View	Land qualitative	1 = average	1.00	1
		2 = premium	1.28	
Neighborhood	General qualitative	1 = Glenwood	1.02	1
		2 = Roosevelt	.95	
		3 = Bellair	1.07	
		4 = Grover	.86	

General qualitative = πGQ = 1.02
Building qualitative = πBQ = .96 × 1.12 = 1.0752
Building additive = ΣBA = 35.24 × 1,500 + 510 × 6 + 3400 × 2 = 62,720
Land qualitative = πLQ = 1.06 × 1.00 = 1.06
Land additive = ΣLA = 1.43 × 8000 = 11,440

Market value = πGQ × (πBQ × ΣBA + πLQ × ΣLA)
Market value = 1.02 × (1.0752 × 62,720 + 1.06 × 11,440) = \$81,154
Building value = 1.02 × 1.0752 × 62,720 = \$68,785
Land value = 1.02 × 1.06 × 11,440 = \$12,369

Figure 10. Global Response Surface after First Run

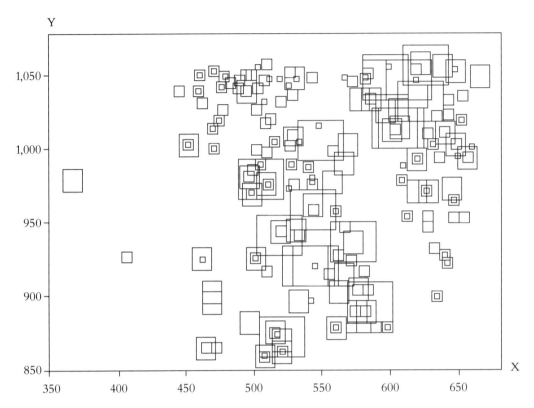

and, to a lesser extent, south–central areas contain larger squares. This suggests that the former areas are usually undervalued and the latter overvalued.

The location of "value influence centers" (VICs), geographic points or areas that influence values either positively or negatively, can also be plotted on the grid. VICs can include the central business district, major shopping centers, scenic areas, or heavily industrial areas. Once VICs are identified, variables are created to measure their distance from individual parcels. If, for example, five VICs are identified, five variables are created. The distances can be squared or otherwise weighted to form nonlinear measures. After

distances are calculated and assigned to each parcel, the model is rerun with the distance variables included. Sales ratios are recomputed and again plotted on the response surface. The process continues until no additional VICs or geographic patterns are apparent. Figure 11 shows the response surface after incorporation of all VICs.

LVRSA need not be limited to use with MRA or feedback. It could, for example, be used to calibrate location influences in cost models as well.

The technique has several advantages. Geographic influences are market-derived and smooth, as opposed to the sharp breaks that can occur with submodels. Also, a sin-

Figure 11. Global Response Surface after Final Run

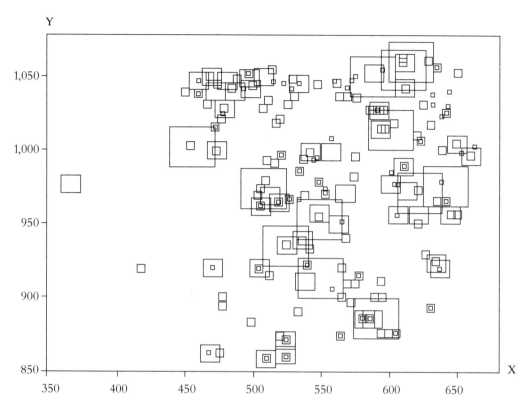

gle equation maximizes sample size and increases model stability. On the negative side, a single model may not adequately capture differences in market relationships that may exist across a jurisdiction.

Evaluating Models

Models must be evaluated for accuracy, stability over time, and explainability.

Accuracy

The accuracy of values produced by a model can be measured by goodness-of-fit statistics, ratio studies, pilot studies, and field and office reviews.

Goodness-of-Fit Statistics As discussed above, MRA produces a battery of goodness-of-fit statistics for evaluating the confidence that can be placed in models. Feedback lacks many of these but does include one of the most important, the average percent error. These statistics allow the model builder to judge the accuracy of models *before* values are estimated. Attention to such statistics not only improves accuracy but also saves time and expense in the review and support of values.

Ratio Studies Ratio studies provide the most widely used measure of appraisal performance. As discussed in chapter 20, these studies allow the assessor to evaluate the level and equity of appraisals both between and within property strata. They reveal where performance is good and where it should be improved, thus helping to allocate resources effectively. It is good practice to perform ratio studies both before and after a reappraisal. Ratio studies should also be conducted on *preliminary* values, so that adjustments can be made before value notices are mailed.

Pilot Studies   A pilot study is a test of new procedures on a sample of properties. When a jurisdiction is implementing a new appraisal system or new valuation procedures, it should conduct a pilot study on a neighborhood or other group of properties before attempting to apply the new techniques to all properties. This will reveal problem areas and save time. One particularly effective technique is to separate sales into a *test* group and a *control* group. Models are developed from the test group and then applied to the control group. Models that are inherently unstable will not perform well on the control group. Such models should be discarded in favor of more stable alternatives.

Office and Field Reviews   Values should be reviewed before being used for assessment purposes. If goodness-of-fit and ratio statistics show that results are good overall, the review process will largely involve the identification and review of outliers, that is, parcels with unusual characteristics or parcels for which estimated values fall outside of typical norms. Criteria for identifying outliers include extreme values per square foot, large differences between the current and previous year's value, and large differences between values generated by the different approaches or techniques (for example, MRA versus cost).

Another procedure for identifying outliers involves the use of a control model, a simple MRA or other automated model based on as few as four or five key characteristics, such as size, quality, effective age, and location. In general, values generated from the full model and control model should be similar. If they differ by a large amount, either the model is in error or the property has unusual characteristics or has been incorrectly coded.

Stability over Time

Except for major reappraisals, it is desirable that values for individual parcels remain consistent from year to year. Several measures of interyear stability are available. One, similar to the coefficient of dispersion, is the average absolute percentage change

$$APC = \frac{\Sigma \mid (V_c - V_p)/V_p \mid}{n}, \quad (47)$$

where APC is the average absolute percent change, V_c is the current value, and V_p is the previous value. A second measure, similar to the coefficient of variation, is the standard deviation of percent changes:

$$SPC = \left[\frac{\Sigma \, [(V_c - V_p)/V_p]^2}{n - 1} \right]^{1/2}, \quad (48)$$

where SPC is the standard deviation of the percent changes. In a normal distribution, approximately 68 percent of the changes will lie within one SPC and 95 percent within two SPCs.

Although frequent reappraisals promote accuracy, they can also cause inconsistent year-to-year value changes for individual parcels. This is due to recalibration of the appraisal models and associated changes in cost factors, MRA coefficients, and other valuation parameters. Techniques for minimizing year-to-year instability are discussed in the section in updating techniques.

Explainability

Values should be understandable and explainable. Models should be no more complex than necessary. Appraisers should understand the components of the model and how it works. Coefficients should be generally consistent with appraisal theory, for example, coefficients for size-related variables should be positive and for age-related variables, negative. As discussed, stepwise MRA helps to eliminate unnecessary, highly correlated variables that may have unreasonable coefficients. Also, as discussed below, constrained MRA can be used to ensure that coefficients are reasonable.

In addition to care in model building, explainability can be achieved by converting valuation equations to the Base Home Approach (chapter 21) or to a similar format. The Base Home Approach finds the value of the typical parcel and constructs a table of adjustments for physical and locational differences. Although it gives the same result as the equation from which it is derived, the Base Home Approach helps appraisers to review and evaluate the model and to explain the results to others.

Updating Techniques

Appraisers can adopt various strategies for achieving accurate and stable valuation models. Some major alternatives are discussed below.

Full Recalibration

Full recalibration involves a fresh determination of valuation models each year. If done properly, this strategy can maximize valuation accuracy, but it also has substantial costs. First, it is likely to increase year-to-year instability for individual parcels. Second, it entails additional work, particularly in the review and defense of values.

Fortunately, there are several measures that help minimize instability during full recalibration. First, avoid respecifying models each year. Using new variables and procedures introduces instability, whereas simple recalibration promotes consistency in results. Second, constrain coefficients so they do not differ greatly from the previous year's coefficients. Some MRA software will permit the user to specify such limits directly. In feedback and nonlinear MRA, coefficients can be set initially to the previous year's values.

Third, use sales from several years in model calibration. A relatively long sales period not only increases sample size but also ensures stability in the data base. In a three-year period, for example, some two-thirds of the sales used to generate the previous year's model will be used to calibrate the current year's model as well. Of course, the older sales may have to be adjusted for time. Not more than five years of sales should be used—three years, when markets are changing rapidly.

Cyclical Recalibration

Models are calibrated every two or more years, with market adjustments applied in the interim. There are two variations. First, all parcels can be periodically recalibrated in mass. Second, a schedule for recalibrating only part of the jurisdiction each year can be established. The latter more evenly distributes workloads from year to year. This can be particularly effective when combined with ratio studies to monitor the level of appraisal by key property strata and provide market adjustments as necessary.

Partial Recalibration

Partial recalibration involves combining the previous year's model with the recalibrated current year's model. In MRA this is accomplished through a technique known as Bayesian regression, which, in effect, gives partial weight to both years' models in determining the regression coefficients, thus sacrificing some accuracy for better stability. If feedback is used for calibration, parts of the model, for example, the land and building qualitative components, can be frozen so that all changes are allocated to the remaining components. This tends to improve year-to-year consistency in the models and their estimated values.

Use of Previous Year's Values

Stability can also be ensured by using the prior year's values in estimating current values. One procedure is simply to calculate current value as a weighted average of the prior year's value and the recalibrated value:

$$V_c = (w_p)(V_p) + (1 - w_p)(V_r), \quad (49)$$

where V_c is the current year's value, V_p is the prior year's value, V_r is the recalibrated value, and w_p is the weight (0 to 1) assigned to the previous year's value. If w_p were 0.50, equal weight would be given to the prior year's and recalibrated values.

Alternatively, the previous year's value can be included as a major variable in the current year's model. In effect, current values are estimated as previous values adjusted for other terms included in the model.

Although these procedures clearly increase stability, they may decrease accuracy. Also, they are not applicable to new or physically changed parcels, which introduces an additional source of inconsistency. In addition, the rationale of the chosen weighting scheme may be difficult to explain to taxpayers and appeal boards.

Administrative Issues

Selection of reappraisal strategies and updating techniques will also turn on various administrative and practical issues. One is the available budget and resources. Another is the quality of the existing data and current appraisal performance. Of course, a full revaluation is required when current performance is poor. The timing and nature of the reappraisal, however, are limited by the available budget and resources. On the other hand, when current performance is good, cyclical or partial recalibration is a practical course of action.

Mass appraisal requires careful planning and analysis. Assessors can choose from many effective valuation tools, but they must understand how these tools perform and which are most useful in constructing and maintaining a successful valuation system in the local environment.

Administration

This section of the text deals with administration of an assessment system. Chapter 16 traces the history of management theory and shows how current systems theory should be applied to assessment administration. The chapter also discusses planning and budgeting, organizational structure, leadership, and hiring and firing. The remaining chapters treat development and management of a mapping system, the planning and management of a revaluation, the role of computers in assessment administration, sales ratio studies, quality assurance, notification, appeals, and public relations.

Elements of Administration

16

This chapter presents fundamental principles of good management and applies them to assessment administration, taking into account differences in scale and structure from office to office. Managers who wish to improve their skills and those preparing to be managers will find this chapter useful.

Assessors — whether in a national, state, or provincial agency, a small township with part-time staff, or a large local jurisdiction with hundreds of thousands of parcels — are expected to provide leadership, make decisions, and get results. In doing so, they begin with awareness of goals and of the tasks to be accomplished in reaching those goals. Assessors plan, budget, organize, lead, and control, within social, economic, and governmental limits.

To fulfill their managerial responsibilities, assessors gather information, create strategic plans and budgets, make decisions under conditions of uncertainty, and communicate effectively both within and beyond the assessing office. They are expected to be effective (do the right things), efficient (do things right), and economical (consume minimal resources).

Statutes, court decisions, the state of the economy, local land use patterns, and — sometimes — politics limit what assessors can do and accomplish. Within these limits, they are required, by law and professional obli-

gation, to create the best assessment system possible and to produce accurate assessments.

Perspectives on Management

Management and decision-making have been studied, analyzed, and theorized about for many decades. Each new theory or technique has its advantages and disadvantages. What works in one situation may not work in another. The real world does not change easily or quickly just because a theory is applied.

However, managers who know something about management theory can more readily convert theory into practices that work well in their own offices. A good grasp of theory enables managers to add to their knowledge of management, make prudent judgments about what they read and hear, and — best of all — recognize what they are already doing right.

The Assessor and Public Policy

Statutes and regulations assign to assessors limited roles in setting policy on tax, economic, and social issues. Assessment is viewed as a straightforward administrative activity. However, policy, once written into law, must be carried out, and assessors can have a substantial effect on public policy by how they carry it out — faithfully, slowly, or not at all.

Because assessors have specialized knowledge and experience in tax administration, they also have a professional responsibility to make a contribution to policy. Through their professional association, the International Association of Assessing Officers (IAAO), assessors have taken policy positions and have adopted standards covering important areas of assessment practice. The IAAO also has worked with other professional appraisal organizations to develop the *Uniform Standards of Professional Appraisal Practice* and to establish The Appraisal Foundation to maintain and expand the standards, which are incorporated by reference in the *IAAO Code of Ethics and Standards of Professional Conduct*. A complete list of standards published by the IAAO and The Appraisal Foundation appears in the bibliography, and the standards are referenced throughout the text. Assessors can use these standards as benchmarks to evaluate their systems and to ask, "Are the right things being done? In the right way?"

Ways to Look at Management

In the last century, many theories have developed on how to manage organizations. These theories can be organized into traditional theories (the classical school), the behavioral revolution (the neoclassical school), and systems approaches (the modern school).

The Classical School   Traditional management theories began with Max Weber, a German academic who taught that organizational forms from feudal and agricultural societies were not relevant to industrial society. As old forms died out, a new form, which he called bureaucracy, developed in their place. Bureaucracy had new characteristics: division of labor, centralization of authority, rational personnel administration, written rules and regulations, and written records. Believing bureaucracy to be the fairest and most logical form of organization, Weber advocated competitive examinations for jobs, clear job descriptions, and rules and procedures governing every organizational process.

Another contributor to classical theories, Henry Fayol, was especially interested in the functions of a manager. He was a mining engineer who spent much of his life working as an executive in a huge mining organization. Developing elements of organization similar to those of Weber, Fayol emphasized the rational selection of employees and discussed topics such as the division of work, authority and responsibility, discipline, unity of command, and unity of direction. He identified five key functions of a successful manager: planning, organizing, directing, coordinating, and controlling.

In the 1930s, a student of public administration, Luther Gulick, expanded this list to planning, organizing, staffing, directing, coordinating, reporting, and budgeting. Most basic management books today still address themselves to these functions, although management can be analyzed in other ways, as this chapter shows.

A fourth contributor to classical theory was F. W. Taylor, father of "the scientific management movement," which began in the United States at about the turn of the nineteenth century. Taylor was an engineer who believed that there was a best way of doing any job. He addressed the problems of how a society goes about increasing productivity and what methods management can use to increase the level of worker effort. He originated time and motion studies, the aim of which was to identify optimum production levels and associated levels of pay for workers.

In 1931, two Americans, J. D. Mooney and A. C. Reiley, published *Onward Industry*, thought to be the first complete statement of classical organization theory to appear in the United States. Although their theory of organization was similar to Weber's theory of bureaucracy, they identified coordination, rather than division of labor, as the prime force in organization.

Principles of Organizational Growth   Classical theory gave rise to four key principles about the growth of organizations (functional, scalar, line/staff, and span of control). These four principles are a good place to begin a study of organizational structure, although neoclassical and modern theorists challenge them.

Organizations grow horizontally, spreading as tasks are divided among specialized departments, and vertically, deepening as authority is delegated downward.

The *functional* principle describes how the division of labor, or departmentalizing, occurs as an organization grows. As an organization expands, work must be broken up in a way that provides clear areas of specialization. The functional principle explains the horizontal growth of organizations, via the division of labor, as well as the tendency of organizations to aggregate related activities into a single department.

The *scalar* principle deals with the vertical growth of organizations: the delegating of authority as an organization grows to extend the chain of command when additional areas are added to the organization. The classical theorists believed that as an organization grows, the competence of those chosen to fill new positions should equal the authority of the new positions. The scalar principle includes two important subprinciples: *unity of command* — a subordinate should be accountable to only one superior; and *determinate hierarchy* — gaps or overlaps in areas of authority within the chain of command should be avoided.

Figure 1 illustrates the vertical and horizontal growth of the organizational structure. To classical theorists, delegation of authority and the amount of autonomy of action allowed subordinates should both be limited. In their view, coordination was best achieved by centralization of authority along the chain of command, such that supervisors could monitor the work of subordinates closely. In figure 1, the supervisor of commercial/industrial appraisals remains accountable for the performance of those tasks that were delegated as the organization expanded from step 2 to step 3, and the assessor remains ultimately accountable for all tasks.

The *line/staff* principle provides guidelines for the relationship between production (command) and auxiliary (advisory) functions. Command (line) functions flow in a vertical line down the organization; advisory (staff) functions are supported by personnel who advise those in command positions. Classical theorists, addressing the issue of ultimate authority, believed that staff could only advise, never command, the line. In figure 2, the dotted line shows the advisory role of a quality assurance specialist for the various appraisal departments.

The *span of control* principle defines the optimum number of employees a manager can supervise. Classical theorists favored close supervision (usually no more than four to six subordinates under one manager) — that is, a short span of control and a tall structure. In

Figure 1. Functional and Scalar Principles of Organizational Growth

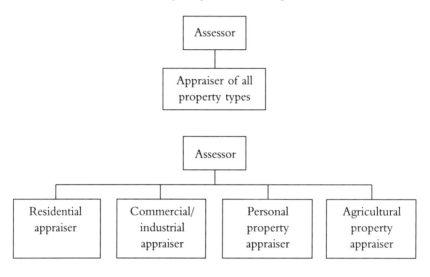

Functional principle: Horizontal growth

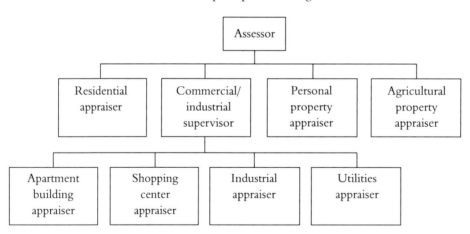

Scalar principle: Vertical growth

a tall organization, a manager supervises few subordinates. In a flat organization, a manager supervises many subordinates (figure 3).

The classical theories of organization view human beings as an input into the production process and management as an impersonal process. Human beings are seen as rational and as motivated only by economic motives.

The Neoclassical School   The neoclassical school emphasized the study of behavior. This shift in focus, often called the behavioral revolution, began with the research of Elton Mayo, F. J. Roethlisberger, and E. N. White-

Figure 2. Relationship between Line and Staff Functions

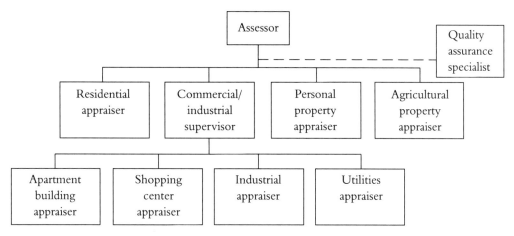

Figure 3. Span of Control

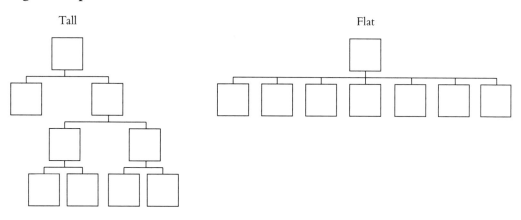

head at the Hawthorne plant of the Western Electric Company between 1927 and 1932. This team extended the research of industrial engineers who were studying the effects of lighting on worker productivity. The industrial engineers found little relationship between increased lighting and productivity. Indeed, when the experiment was reversed and lighting was decreased, productivity unexpectedly went up. Mayo and his associates were called in to establish better experimen-

tal methods and isolate intervening variables that could explain the unexpected results. Their work covered five years and included three phases: the relay assembly test room experiment, the interview program, and the bank wiring observation room.

The relay assembly test room experiment involved extensive observation of six workers whose working conditions were varied systematically over time. Whatever the experimenters did to change working conditions, productivity went up. The researchers concluded that social and psychological factors, not changes in working conditions, caused productivity to rise. By asking the help of the workers, the experimenters had made them feel important. Workers no longer felt like parts in a machine but like important members of a group trying to solve a company problem.

In the interview program, interviews of more than 21,000 employees were analyzed. The conclusions were:

- Complaints may not truly represent the real cause of dissatisfaction. They tend to be symptomatic of personal issues that workers bring with them to the workplace.
- Workers give all actions of management a subjective meaning that may be significantly different from the intended meaning of the action.
- The behavior of workers is based on how their personal values and attitudes interact with those of coworkers.
- The relative status of workers determines how they assign meaning to features of their workplace.
- An informal organization exists within the formal organization and acts as a powerful controlling force over the behavior of its members.

The third phase of the research clarified the power of the informal organization. The bank wiring study concluded that the informal work group set performance standards that were often in conflict with those set by management. The researchers discovered that the workers limited their output to a certain level decided on by the work group and that the company's financial incentive program had no effect on performance.

Another contribution to neoclassical thinking in the 1930s was Chester Barnard's *The Functions of the Executive* (1938). Its central idea is that all organizations are cooperative systems. Management's responsibility is to create and sustain a system that will satisfy both human and organizational objectives. Barnard believed that psychological as well as material inducements are needed to sustain worker motivation within the system. He stressed the role of communication in maintaining the organization and the need to understand the informal organization and its relationship to the formal structure.

The neoclassical school as a whole was critical of many of the classical principles. For example, it believed that the division of labor, although theoretically improving work efforts, also caused worker inattention and lack of commitment because employees could not see the big picture. Later neoclassicists such as Likut, McGregor, Argyris, Maslow, and Bennis emphasized the need for a more democratic, less authoritarian and hierarchical organization than proposed by the classical school. Neoclassical writers offered various models of participatory decision-making to increase workers' productivity by increasing their dedication to their work.

Neoclassical writers also believed that some aspects of the scalar principle did not work and that an ideal match between worker capacity and job requirements is almost never achieved. Not only is human capacity hard to measure, but because individuals develop and grow over time, mismatches are bound to develop between abilities and job requirements. The informal structure of peer influence is also capable of creating or maintaining inconsistencies between abilities and job requirements.

The neoclassical writers also had problems with the line/staff principle of delegation of authority as seen by the classical school. In some cases it seemed necessary and even desirable for line authority within a limited area of jurisdiction to be delegated to staff. For example, for quality assurance it is sometimes desirable to have staff exercise line authority over a department head so that the department meets standards set by staff. Arrangements like this, however, violate the classical principle of unity of command.

The neoclassical school questioned the classical span of control principle, believing that no set supervisor-subordinate ratio could be ideal for every case and that an effective span of control depends on the management abilities of supervisors, the effectiveness of organizational communication, the effectiveness of control over operations, the organization's philosophy about centralized versus decentralized decision-making, and the product of the work.

Furthermore, this school had a bias for loose, rather than tight, supervision. From research on effective leadership styles, the neoclassicists concluded that a more democratic leadership climate, permitting more individual discretion on the job, leads to greater job satisfaction and a more efficient organization.

A final development in the neoclassical school extended the classical notions of scientific management. A field called management science, operations research, or qualification analysis (related to industrial engineering and managerial economics) studied ways to optimize the operation of the total work environment.

Operations research divided problem solving into the following steps:

1. Formulate a problem.
2. Construct a mathematical model to represent the system to be studied.
3. Develop a solution to the problem from the model.
4. Test the solution using the model.
5. Carry out the solution.

Neoclassical theorists tried to find ways to make the general classical principles of hierarchy work within organizations that did not share the characteristics of those studied by the classical writers. These efforts were not completely successful because the behavioral sciences had not developed ways of dealing with emerging socioeconomic changes, particularly within large, technologically advanced organizations. A new formulation of organization theory, the systems approach, was needed to account for behavior within this new kind of organization.

The Systems School Modern management theory has its basis in the biological and physical sciences. All biological systems receive inputs, transform them in some way, and export the results. Similarly, the business or governmental organization receives inputs in the form of labor, capital, materials, and information; it transforms these into products and services, profits for owners, and rewards for the workers in the system. Modern organizational systems theory asks questions about this process that were considered by classical and neoclassical theorists but not effectively addressed, such as:

1. What are the important parts of the system?
2. How do they interrelate?
3. What are the system's goals?
4. What should managers do to maintain organizational health?

5. How does the system interact with its environment?

Components of Modern Business and Governmental Systems Modern organization theory views the business or governmental organization as a system composed of several subsystems that convert inputs into outputs. The major subsystems within the organization are the psychosocial subsystem, the technical subsystem, the structural subsystem, and the planning subsystem.

The psychosocial subsystem includes what individuals bring to the system—personal motives and expectations; how individuals work within small groups and small groups within the larger organization (group dynamics); and what formal and informal status and role arrangements operate.

The technical subsystem refers to the technical information and processes required to transform inputs into outputs, as well as specialized management techniques related to the production of a product or provision of a service.

The structural subsystem includes the organization's formal structure as expressed in the organization chart, position and job descriptions, and written rules and procedures. The structural subsystem is also concerned with both formal and informal patterns of authority and communication, as well as how labor, capital, information, and materials are used.

The planning subsystem includes development of comprehensive strategic and operational plans, feedback structures, and budget control processes. Its principal functions are to keep the system healthy by relating the organization to its environment and to ensure that the organization is meeting its goals.

Each of the historical schools emphasized a particular set of subsystems with little recognition of the value and importance of the others. Classical management theory emphasized the structural and planning subsystems and tried to define the principles of their development. The behaviorally oriented neoclassical theorists studied the psychosocial subsystem and focused on individual motivation and group dynamics. Meanwhile, the management science segment of the neoclassical school emphasized the technical subsystem and methods for quantifying decision-making and control processes.

The modern approach integrates and extends classical and neoclassical theories by looking at the organization as an organic system. It considers all primary subsystems and how they interact. In addition, the modern school sees organizational success as a more complex process than did the earlier schools.

Classical and neoclassical thinkers regarded efficiency as the indicator of success. The modern school takes a broader view. If an organization is an organic unit then, like living organisms, it must exhibit certain characteristics to be considered healthy. First, it should be stable, its subsystems harmoniously interrelated. Second, it should be able to grow and adapt; as part of a larger system, the organization survives by adjusting to outside changes. The modern view of organizational effectiveness adds stability, growth, and adaptability to the older idea of efficiency.

Characteristics of Systems All systems are made up of interdependent parts. Identifying the parts is one way to understand organizational structures. However, no matter how the parts are labeled, their interaction can be explained by eight principles:

1. Changes introduced into any part of a system will cause changes elsewhere.
2. All systems tend to seek a new equilibrium after a change is introduced, whether from inside or outside the system.
3. Systems maintain equilibrium by developing formal and informal feedback mechanisms.
4. An entire system and each of its parts have boundaries that range from being fully opened to being fully closed to outside influences.
5. Systems or subsystems with open boundaries are called open systems. They are more responsive to outside changes and, as a result, exhibit the characteristics of a healthy organization. Systems with closed boundaries are called closed systems. Self-contained, they are shut off from outside influences and tend to self-destruct in the long run.
6. Human systems have both formal and informal power structures that interact in complicated ways.
7. A person's behavior within the system depends on the interaction of individual psychological factors with the system's values. As a consequence, mutual modification of expectations occurs between the individual and the organization.
8. Systems are hierarchical; a system is composed of subsystems of a lower order and is itself part of a larger system.

The Manager from a Systems Perspective The principal function of the manager from the systems perspective is to create an open organizational system and appropriate informal and formal feedback mechanisms within it, such that the major subsystems work well together and the organization can exhibit growth, stability, and equilibrium in the face of environmental changes. In contrast, the classical school emphasized technical rationality—how best to use people, material, and capital to produce a product that maximizes profits. This view, which saw the organization as a closed system, was appropriate for the technical and structural subsystem only.

The systems view defines a complicated role for the manager. The manager has to be aware that managerial problems are constantly changing and frequently ambiguous. The manager is not always in full control, as the classical school had suggested, but is constrained by external and internal (technical, structural, and psychosocial) forces.

Unlike classical theories, the systems view emphasizes flexibility in organizational structure. For example, span of control is evaluated by analyzing job complexity, physical proximity of workers, and leadership styles of management. It is not enough to say that the span of control should not exceed four to six employees. In fact, the systems view proposes that highly technical organizations requiring a great deal of managerial specialization may best be organized in project, or matrix, form. That is, some functions are accomplished using the traditional line/staff hierarchy, but others require the use of employees from other units to accomplish special projects.

The most important difference between matrix structures and the traditional line/staff structure is behavioral. A matrix structure requires lateral interactions between line and staff or management and workers; the line/staff structure discourages such interaction. A significant implication of the matrix structure is that some goals are best achieved with a minimum of hierarchy.

A systems view supports the following propositions about behavior:

- No behavior takes place in isolation.
- No behavior can be traced to a single cause.
- Every act sets off a chain of reactions.

Within the systems perspective, the single-cause assumption for explaining human behavior is swiftly disposed of. Such explanations are inadequate and deceptive. All parts of the system are related, and changes in one part bring about changes in all of the others. Managers must understand all subsystems and how they function within the organization.

The remainder of this chapter deals with elements of the planning and structural subsystems in assessment administration—planning, budgeting, organizing resources, and managing personnel.

The balance of the book deals with the assessment office's technical subsystem. This book does not deal explicitly with the psychosocial subsystem. Although a study of psychological theory and group dynamics is essential for managers, the material has been well presented elsewhere and is outside the scope of this book. The bibliography lists references for further study.

Planning

From any perspective, planning is an essential task of managers. Planning prepares organizations for the future and is crucial in an era of rapid technological and social change. Such changes affect the demands placed on government and the means of satisfying them. Citizens increasingly expect governments to perform satisfactorily and hold government officials accountable for their performance. Plans provide a blueprint for improving performance, a justification for budget requests, and standards for evaluating performance.

Overview

A plan is simply a method for accomplishing something. Planning is the process of devising a plan. The "something" to be accomplished and the timing of the accomplishment distinguish one type of plan from another.

Broad-scale plans for accomplishing several objectives affecting events several years in the future are called either *long-range* or *strategic* plans. The distinction between a long-range plan and a strategic plan is not always clear, but a strategic plan usually embodies the notion of entrepreneurship, of *creating* the future; a long-range plan merely anticipates the effects of trends without attempting to change them. A strategic plan for an assessment office might have as its goal improving assessment equity by performing a total reappraisal using a new computer-assisted mass appraisal (CAMA) system, while improving performance in other operations as well. This plan would not spell out specific operational details but would provide a general framework.

Broad-scale plans for accomplishing several objectives in the immediate future, usually a budget cycle, are called *operational plans*. An operational plan supports the strategic plan and serves as the basis of a budget request. It contains detailed information about objectives, work loads, measures of performance, and resources required.

Project plans and *action plans* are plans for accomplishing a single objective, such as creating a sales file, or a set of closely related objectives, such as those associated with a reappraisal. The duration of an action plan is usually no longer than that of the operational plan it is designed to carry out. The duration of a project plan might be longer than that of an operational plan. Project planning and action planning involve programming and scheduling, as well as developing the information needed for an operational plan.

Strategic planning begins with an attempt to answer the questions "What is the purpose of our organization?" and "What should it be?" From the answers to those questions will come statements of goals and objectives, the development of strategies, the commitment of resources, work assignments, and so on. Answering the questions is not as straightforward as it might seem. Is the purpose of an assessment office to provide a plentiful source of tax revenue, to assure property owners that their assessments are correct and fair, to minimize property taxes, to foster economic development, to spend its budget, or merely to satisfy a legislative mandate without much concern for either taxpayers or the governments that depend on property tax revenues? Answering the questions will require research and open discussion.

Such research is called situation analysis or environmental scanning. A situation analysis not only studies factual matters such as legislation, existing work loads, economic and social trends, and current capabilities, but also examines the values of individuals and institutions (the psychosocial system), because those values can profoundly affect the level of performance that can be achieved or politically accepted. The purpose of the analysis is to identify problems and opportunities and to assess strengths and weaknesses and answer the questions "What is the purpose of our organization?" and "What should it be?"

The answers are contained in a *mission statement* and in statements of goals and objectives. The mission statement succinctly describes what the organization wants to accomplish, for whom, and how. Statements of goals and objectives provide more detail. An objective should be realistically attainable and, most important, measurable.

Accomplishing objectives requires such additional planning activities as programming and scheduling. Budgeting can be viewed as a bridge between planning and doing—assigning and performing work. But planning also embraces performance evaluation and feedback as part of situation analysis. Thus, planning is cyclical and should be an ongoing activity of management.

An important function of planning is to coordinate operational and financial aspects of management. Planning documents the assumptions on which the budget is based. Before each budget cycle, plans are prepared that lay the groundwork for the next budget.

Planning also meshes with performance evaluation. Operational plans state, in measurable terms, objectives to be accomplished. Performance evaluation measures the degree to which such objectives are accomplished. For individuals, for different levels in the organization, and for specific activities, the operational plan provides a formal statement of objectives against which performance can be evaluated. Managers and their subordinates can then be held accountable.

Guidelines for Strategic and Operational Planning

Strategic planning is practical and realistic. It starts with a review of the current situation, including mission, legal requirements, organization, methods, work outputs, levels of effort, budget constraints, strengths and weaknesses, and so forth. Using this review as a base, goals, and even the mission statement, may be revised and new resource requirements formulated (see figure 4).

An existing mission—and the goals, objectives, and budgets that flow from them—is always subject to change. For example, if laws are changed to require shorter assessment cycles and 100 percent assessment levels, the assessment office will evaluate its mission statement, goals, objectives, budget, and so forth in light of these new requirements.

To evaluate a mission statement, managers first compare it and the associated goals and objectives with budget allocations and current operations to see if the stated purposes are being carried out. Then the purposes, and current practices if different, are analyzed in terms of legal, social, economic, and technological realities to determine what is worth continuing and what needs changing. A reformulated mission statement leads to a reformulated strategic plan and budget projections.

A strategic plan provides a consistent framework for operational and project planning, in which departments set objectives, determine resource requirements, and pre-

Figure 4. The Planning Process

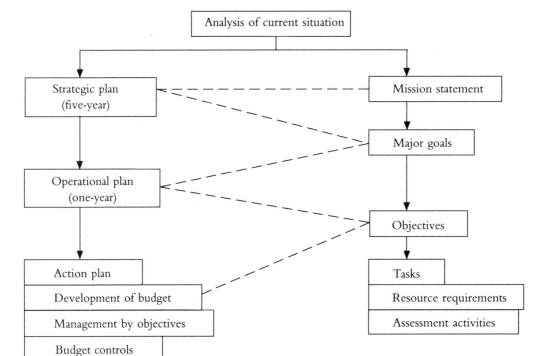

pare an action plan setting out the sequence of tasks required to accomplish the objective. Planning moves in a simple, logical sequence: systematic review of the strategic planning mission and goal statements, then determination of short-run objectives, resource requirements, and intended applications for the coming budget cycle. This process usually becomes more effective with each repetition.

The elements of the strategic plan are revised as necessary. An operational plan, however, is developed anew for each planning cycle (usually annually), to reflect past progress and current work loads. A checklist can be prepared of the documents and types of analyses that should be assembled or performed to assist in the progression from strategic to operational planning. The checklist might cover the following subjects:

1. Status of existing plan
   a. Legal and administrative mandates
   b. Mission statement
   c. Goals
2. Organizational background
   a. Organization chart
   b. Description of organizational unit functions
   c. Personnel assignments
3. Operational background
   a. System descriptions and work flow charts
   b. Operational strengths and weaknesses
4. Performance history
   a. Work loads
   b. Past performance vs. objectives
5. Planning assumptions and forecasts, noting trends and cyclical aspects of key activities
6. Plan objectives
   a. Production work objectives
   b. Recurring project objectives
   c. Special project objectives
7. Resource requirements
   a. Employees
   b. Services, supplies, and equipment

Status of Existing Plan The following paragraphs explain the items in the above checklist.

Legal and Administrative Mandates Legal and administrative mandates strongly influence the organization's mission, goals, and objectives. The assessment function is governed by laws and administrative regulations, which should be monitored at regular intervals.

Mission Statement Missions are expressed in broad, comprehensive statements that describe fundamental purpose: what the office or unit is trying to do. An example of a complete mission statement is, "The mission of the assessment office is to discover, list, and value all properties in the jurisdiction at a legally correct level of value, achieving as much equity and as little variation as is possible with the staff and resources available."

Goals Goals state the major operational objectives that support the mission statement. For example, a goal statement that supports the above mission statement is, "develop within three years a computer-assisted mass appraisal (CAMA) system able to be modified quickly as circumstances warrant."

The following are other examples of goals in a strategic plan:

The assessment office will list promptly all properties in the jurisdiction by processing deeds received from the recorder's office within one week of receipt.

The assessment office will appraise all properties at a level between 95 percent and 105 percent of their current market value as of the appraisal date as shown by a ratio study. This level will be achieved by the coming year. Within two years, the level of appraisal will be maintained between 97 and 103 percent of current value.

The assessment office will appraise all assessable properties uniformly, so that the coefficient of dispersion will be 20 or less by January of the coming year, 15 or less by January of the year following, and 10 or less by January of the third year.

The assessment office will have the ownership listing function automated by January of the coming year and the appraisal function automated by January of the year following.

Organizational Background

Organization Chart An organization chart shows the assignment of responsibilities within each assessment office by identifying subunits, key management positions, lines of authority, and reporting relationships. If a significant reorganization is to take place during the planning period, the chart should show the new structure and the dates that changes are to be made. (Organization charts are covered in more detail later in this chapter.)

Description of Organizational Unit Functions Descriptions of organizational unit functions are a natural adjunct to the organization chart. Descriptions should be specific enough to cover significant areas of activity and responsibility. Where a process involves units other than the one being described, the description should identify work relationships and how involvement begins and ends.

Personnel Assignments Summaries of personnel assignments within each organizational unit should specify the positions in each job classification that are allocated for each unit and the number occupied or vacant.

Operational Background

System Descriptions and Work Flow Charts System descriptions and work flow charts

outline the purposes and processes of the systems (manual and computer) used by organizational units and identify processing methods: how work moves through the various steps and is distributed, and any interactions with other units. Because of the importance of standard forms in many assessment operations, copies of forms should be referenced or included.

System descriptions and work flow charts should be developed for

- ratio studies
- roll and map maintenance
- gathering and verification of sales and creation of sales files
- reappraisal programs, including property data collection and recording, valuation, and appraisal review
- gathering income and expense data and developing valuation standards for commercial and industrial properties
- processing building permits and appraising new construction and building improvements
- processing exemption applications, including verification of eligibility

Operational Strengths and Weaknesses By identifying operational strengths and weaknesses, management can establish objectives and projects to improve the office and pinpoint overall problem areas, determine the relative importance and prevalence of different kinds of problems, and establish priorities in addressing such problems. Common operational weaknesses include bottlenecks in work flow that indicate problems with schedules and assignments, and poor work.

Performance History

Work Loads Development of work load measures, such as numbers of parcels of assessable property, personal property accounts, and annual transactions such as sales, building permits, exemption applications, and appeals, is essential to planning and to performance evaluation.

Past Performance vs. Objectives   Records of the quantity and quality of work indicate how well the previous year's objectives were accomplished. A review of the current year's objectives will determine whether they can be accomplished on time. The coming year's objectives can then be based on accomplishments, to ensure realistic schedules.

Planning Assumptions and Forecasts
Analysis of background information sets the stage for the development of an operational plan. The first step in developing this plan is to compile information on cyclical features and key activities in the assessment process and on forecasts that may affect the volume of work for the planning year, for example:

- A total reappraisal is due in two years, and field review and collection of property characteristics must be completed in the planning (next) year.
- Real estate market activity will increase (or decrease) by some estimated percentage.
- Major construction, such as office buildings or shopping centers, will be completed in the planning year and must be appraised.

For planning purposes, work may be categorized as

- Production work—activities related to keeping abreast of events and transactions that affect the assessment process. Such work is appropriately measured in terms of volume, such as the number of parcels reappraised, sales transactions processed, building permits processed, and so forth.

- Recurring projects—activities that are repeated from year to year and are measured by completion within a deadline, for example, updating a cost manual, completing valuation modeling and formulas, and doing ratio studies.
- Special projects—one-time tasks such as automating the property data base and valuation procedures and conversion of maps to a computerized geographic information system.

For each kind of work, both objectives and performance need to be expressed in terms of the quantity, quality, and timeliness of the final product.

Plan Objectives
Production Work Objectives   Production work objectives may be expressed by output in work units; productivity per employee; timeliness of work performed; and accuracy, quality, and reliability. Some examples of production work objectives in assessment are

- to reappraise all or a specified number of parcels in each use class of property
- in a reappraisal, to check and update property characteristics data for all or a designated number of parcels in each class, or independently to collect new data for such parcels—and complete such work at a designated level of accuracy
- to process all sales within one month of recording
- to process all building permits and appraise parcels with new construction or building improvements within one month of the assessment date

Recurring Project Objectives   Recurring projects are best measured in terms of completion of the work according to an established schedule. Some examples of recurring project objectives in assessment are:

- to update a cost manual by a designated date as required by a reappraisal schedule
- to establish current land values by a required date
- to analyze income and expense statements by a required date
- to conduct sales ratio studies to assist in planning a reappraisal or to test the quality of a reappraisal

Special Project Objectives   Special project objectives, because they relate to one-time projects that have a definable end product and scheduled starting and completion dates, should clearly indicate the purpose, timetable, milestones, project approach, and required resources.

Special projects are designed to improve procedures, capabilities, work quality, and so forth. Examples include projects to streamline procedures, automate all or part of the property data base and valuation processes, develop quality control standards, and upgrade training.

Resource Requirements
Employees   Staffing requirements for each operation and for the office as a whole should state the number and type of position for each organizational unit and for each production activity, recurring project (including general administration), and special project. In this way, staffing requirements will be correlated with specific activities and objectives. An adequate number of employees is essential to a realistic operations plan.

Services, Supplies, and Equipment   Allocations for services, supplies, and equipment document the need for such items as data and word processing equipment, microfilming

services, office equipment and supplies, and contractual services. Contractual services may be a major resource in the case of reappraisal by contract, or a smaller resource in the case of individual property appraisals. Requirements are identified for each organizational unit and for each of the production activities, recurring projects, and special projects. The resources needed to support each objective are described in terms of cost, quantity, and level of service. A resource such as word processing equipment may support a wide range of activities and be separately identified. However, if a service is primarily tied to a particular production activity, recurring project, or special project, then it is so allocated.

Budgeting

Budgeting, a crucial link between planning and doing, makes the plan a reality. Budgeting expresses resources required in monetary terms and is a tool for setting rational priorities. An assessor might use budget data to help decide whether to conduct a field canvass to improve property records or to convert legal descriptions into a digital form to install a geographic information system. A jurisdiction's governing body might use budget data to help decide whether to fund the assessor's request or the hospital administrator's. Once the decisions are made, the budget becomes an expression of public policy in terms of the resources a government is willing to allocate to equitable property taxation.

Budgeting may not achieve rational allocation of resources if allocations are based on the previous allocation or the size of staff rather than on needs and results. Government finance officers have recognized this problem and have developed budgetary approaches to aid rational decision-making. In the absence of separate planning processes, some of them incorporate elements of planning. The following discussion of approaches to budgeting relies heavily on *The Effective Local Government Manager*, a publication of the International City Management Association (Anderson, Nowland & Stillman 1983).

Three theoretical criteria help evaluate whether a spending proposal increases net public benefits (that is, provides greater benefits than any other spending proposal and provides benefits greater than incremental costs): (1) *intersector efficiency*: the incremental spending provides greater net benefits than could be obtained if the resources were left with individuals and organizations in the private sector; (2) *interprogram efficiency*: the allocation of resources to a given governmental program provides greater net benefits than allocating those resources to any other program; and (3) *intraprogram efficiency*: for any given program, resources are used to maximize net benefits. Assessors are chiefly concerned with intraprogram efficiency — decisions such as whether a reappraisal should be contracted out or done in house.

Assessors' roles in budgeting range from negligible participation to almost complete control. However, assessors who understand approaches to budgeting, their relationships to planning, and budget development can demonstrate the importance of their operational plans and their budget requests to decision makers.

Approaches to Budgeting

Most governmental budgeting is a variant of one of four basic approaches: line-item

budgeting, performance budgeting, program budgeting, and zero-base budgeting.

Line-item Budgeting Line-item, or object-classification, budgeting is designed to achieve financial control and minimize opportunities for corruption by controlling spending. Managers are not authorized to spend more than the amount contained on a particular budget line. Estimates of spending by object class (current operating costs, capital outlays, and debt service) are prepared and submitted to the executive budget officer and governing body for approval. After the budget is approved, periodic (usually monthly) allotments of budget appropriations are established. Proposed expenditures may be preaudited to ensure they are appropriate and within the allotment. Periodic financial reporting helps track spending.

Major object classifications are usually broken down into subclassifications, such as services and supplies, which can be further broken down into full-time salaries, fringe benefits, and stationery, for example, which can be still further broken down to detail the compensation of a particular individual or the amount that can be spent on pencils and erasers.

The more detailed the appropriation, the less discretion a manager has, which can have undesirable consequences. The manager may be forced to waste resources. Suppose, for example, that after an assessor's line-item budget for long-distance telephone calls has been exhausted the office receives an income and expense report on a major office building from an out-of-town property owner. The appraiser has several questions about the report that could be answered with a ten-minute telephone call. The manager has these choices: make an illegal budget expenditure and allow the telephone call, not allow the call and direct the appraiser to do the best job possible with available information (risking a substantial underassessment and loss of tax base or a substantial overassessment and the costs of an appeal), or direct the appraiser to write the property owner, which will take more time than a phone call and delay resolution of the problems.

In strict line-item budgeting, there is an incentive to exaggerate needs in hopes of receiving a budget appropriation that provides for maneuvering room. There is little incentive or means to analyze spending requests in terms of public benefits or program efficiencies because data on what the spending can accomplish are not used for drawing up the budget.

Performance Budgeting Performance budgeting, first used in the late 1940s, attempts to overcome some of the shortcomings of line-item budgeting by using cost-efficiency to make spending decisions and evaluate management. Cost-efficiency is achieved when the unit costs of performing a given function are minimized. This approach requires the multitude of activities to be sorted into major functions such as "government management and supporting services." A function can encompass a number of programs, such as "the assessment and collection of taxes." Programs, in turn, are made up of activities, such as "property assessment," "appeals," and "property tax billing and collection," which are done by performance units, such as the assessment office, the board of appeals, and the treasurer's office. Each activity has associated with it a specific product, such as the assessment of 100,000 properties. Each activity also has as-

sociated with it a mix of object-class expenditures.

In other words, performance budgeting prepares a line-item budget for each activity. In theory, the manager proposes the mix of objects of expenditure that will produce the maximum output for the least cost. Budget estimates and decisions are based on total costs, rather than line-item detail. The manager justifies the budget request by documenting a unit's responsibilities and goals, the tasks necessary to achieve the goals, how the proposed funding will make it possible to perform the tasks, and the schedule for accomplishing the work. Financial oversight focuses on total expenditures rather than line-item detail. A performance reporting system and performance audits can increase managerial accountability.

A shortcoming of performance budgeting is that unit cost measures for a unit may not reflect costs borne by other units and so provide a misleading measure of cost efficiency. Because benefits are not measured, intersector efficiency cannot be estimated, and interprogram efficiency cannot be established because unit costs do not measure the net benefits yielded by competing programs. Finally, if reductions in budget requests are required, officials have no basis for cutting the requests submitted for each activity, because only one level of funding is presented.

Program Budgeting Program budgeting centralizes budgeting to examine net public benefits. The planning-programming-budgeting (PPB) systems that became popular in the 1960s are examples of this approach. A program structure shows how a community's goals will be achieved organizationally. Systematic examination of alternative programs for achieving of goals determines which will produce the greatest net benefits in the long run, so long-range planning is needed. If benefits cannot be calculated, funding is awarded to the programs that afford the greatest gains in objectives. Program managers are held accountable for spending by comparisons of performance with targets and audits of performance that evaluate efficiency. Managers have authority to mix objects of expenditure as long as expenditures are consistent with long-range planning goals and are within lump-sum program appropriations.

Program budgeting can be difficult. It may be hard to articulate missions and goals, to develop meaningful measures of benefits, and to articulate measurable objectives. Goals are subject to change. When they change, the program structure must be changed to correspond, which is not a trivial task. Most important, it may be impossible to evaluate systematically all possible ways to achieve a goal. As with performance budgeting, having only a single budget request for each program makes it difficult to bring individual program budgets into line with the total budget.

Zero-based budgeting   Zero-based budgeting, which became popular in the 1970s, addresses the fact that a government's fiscal resources are limited and may even be declining in the face of inflation, population growth, and increasing service demands. "Decision packages" submitted by managers of units responsible for certain services identify the unit's mission and goals and outline different ways to achieve goals at different levels of performance corresponding to minimum, current, and improved levels of funding (stated in percentages of current year funding). The manager identifies the benefits

of each alternative and selects the one producing the greatest gain in benefits. In successive stages, higher-level managers rank decision packages in order of priority. Packages with the highest priority are funded first. Packages whose priority places them below available funding levels are not funded.

More sophisticated budgeting systems are more expensive to administer, and the increased complexity and expense may be unnecessary in small governments. However, most governments will benefit from a program structure, from attention to the benefits that can be realized from any given program, and from a consideration of funding levels.

Development of a Budget

Funding for the assessment office is determined through the budget process of the jurisdiction and authorized by an annual budget document and appropriation decision. Budgeting follows the annual governmental budget cycle of preparation, adoption, implementation, and evaluation. The process by which a budget is developed and approved—the form of the budget request, documentation, timing for submission, administrative reviews, public hearings, adoption, and control—is prescribed by law, rule, or custom.

Budget development is a series of analytical steps. First, service needs and specified goals and objectives are defined. Alternative ways of meeting goals and objectives are identified along with work load analyses, facilities and equipment requirements, and so forth for each alternative. Expenditures for different funding levels and intervals are estimated. Finally, management and work load plans are prepared for each budget unit. A budget in the program format is best for internal purposes because it complements the formal planning document. If it is the custom of the jurisdiction to present a line-item budget for the approval of various political bodies, then the expenditures for staff and equipment for each program can be easily brought together in a line-item format.

Funding Patterns in Assessment Administration

Assessors may find comparative data helpful in developing and defending budget requests. Survey data on funding patterns in assessment administration reveal considerable variation, although patterns and trends are reasonably consistent and logical.

The International Association of Assessing Officers (IAAO) conducted large-scale surveys of assessment budgets and expenditures in 1974 and 1986. In 1974, the mean and median expenditures were $6.85 and $6.11 per parcel, with a range from $1 and $26. Comparable figures for 1986 are displayed in table 1, which also contains data for different types of jurisdictions.

Figure 5 presents data on percentage allocations by major object classification by type of jurisdiction. These data may be compared with similar allocations for all types of jurisdictions from the 1974 survey: personnel services, 84 percent; contractual services, 12 percent; materials and supplies, 2 percent; and other expenses, 2 percent.

Staffing Patterns and the Effect of Computerization

Size of jurisdiction affects size of staff, of course. One full-time employee for each 2,500 parcels is typical, although this proportion varies greatly among jurisdictions. In smaller jurisdictions, the work load averages about 1,500 to 1,700 parcels per employee; in larger jurisdictions, about 3,000 to 3,500. Work loads vary depending on the quality of the staff, the complexity of the properties, and so on.

IAAO's 1986 survey also tabulated number of parcels and parcels per employee for several hundred county, township, and municipality jurisdictions (table 2). The same survey also tabulated the effect of computers on parcel per employee ratios. Table 3 shows the average number of parcels per employee in assessment agencies with and without computer assistance. Such assistance increases the mean number of parcels per employee.

Organizational Structure

Assessors organize resources around key activities that accomplish the major assessment functions, such as appraisal of residential

Table 1.   Expenditures per Real Property Parcel

Type of local government	Sample size	Mean	Standard deviation	Median	Minimum	Maximum
County	341	$11.40	$23.50	$ 8.90	$0.89	$429.16
Municipality/city	162	12.00	6.50	11.60	1.49	45.51
Town/township	323	8.70	6.20	7.50	0.40	63.79
Joint or combined	9	7.30	4.60	6.00	1.92	18.37
Total (summary)	835	(10.40)	(15.80)	(8.60)	(0.40)	(429.16)

Figure 5. Budget by Expense

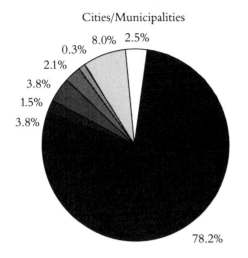

Cities/Municipalities

8.0% 2.5%
0.3%
2.1%
3.8%
1.5%
3.8%
78.2%

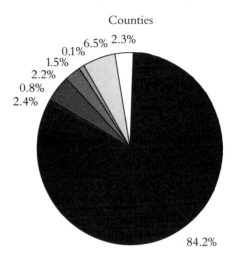

Counties

0.1% 6.5% 2.3%
1.5%
2.2%
0.8%
2.4%
84.2%

Towns/Townships

0.1% 8.3% 1.6%
0.8%
3.1%
1.1%
3.7%
81.2%

■ Salaries and benefits
☐ Travel and training
■ Rent and utilities
■ Equipment and supplies
■ Data processing
☐ Public information
■ Outside services
☐ Other

Table 2. Parcels per Employee

Type of local government	Sample size	Parcels per employee (rounded)	
		Mean	Median
County	358	3,100	2,600
Municipality	172	2,200	2,100
Township	364	1,800	1,600
Total	894	2,400	2,100

property, maintenance of ownership records and cadastral maps, and preparation of assessment abstracts, certifications, and reports.

Developing an Organizational Structure

The organizational structure should complement the strategic (long-range) and operational plans. Its elements should be written

Table 3.　Average Number of Parcels per Employee

	Agencies having computer assistance		Agencies without computer assistance	
Type of local government	Sample size	Mean	Sample size	Mean
County	308	3,200	49	2,900
Municipality	127	2,500	42	1,500
Township	185	2,000	152	1,500
Total	620	2,700	243	1,800

into an organization chart and into statements of duties and responsibilities for each of the key positions on the chart (figure 6).

The development of an organizational structure starts with the concept that greatest efficiency is obtained by dividing work into specialized tasks. Grouping of tasks into jobs and departments and establishing relationships among them creates an organizational structure. The administrator should aim for divisions and groupings of tasks that are efficient and can be easily coordinated.

A job is a group of tasks assigned to one person and is the smallest component of the organizational structure. At a minimum, a job has three elements:

- *Tasks* (job duties) to be performed, for example, appraising residential properties or receiving and processing applications for an exemption
- *Performance standards*, for example, appraising a given number of properties per week with an error rate of less than 5 percent
- *Access to resources* needed to perform tasks and fulfill responsibilities, for example, forms, vehicles, computers, and office machines

Deciding on an organizational pattern is not easy. Decisions must be made about degree of specialization, assignment of tasks, and the number of employees to be supervised by each manager (span of control). Size of jurisdiction, employees' skills, management style, computer facilities, types of properties assessed, and statutory responsibilities must be taken into account.

Specialization Specializations for appraisers in an assessor's office are often defined along *functional* or *geographic* lines (see figures 7 and 8). If functional, the division might be between operations and appraisal, with operations responsible for all support, records, and reporting, and appraisal responsible for appraisals. These departments can be further subdivided.

A functional division into departments for land and improvements grows naturally from the assessment office's historical reliance on the cost approach. However, although the cost approach continues to be useful, a land/improvements division creates problems. Because estimates of land value and improvement value must be combined for a final property value, one person or department cannot be held accountable for an appraisal. Application of the income and sales comparison approaches becomes more difficult because these approaches usually apply to the property as a whole. A land/improvements division violates the principle of determinate hierarchy, which states that gaps or overlaps

Figure 6.   Statement of Responsibilities of Departmental Divisions and Sections

1. Purpose of this memorandum is to detail the responsibilities of departmental divisions and sections.
2. *Organization:* The department consists of the following divisions and sections.
   a) Standards Division
   b) Business Division
   c) Real Property Division
   d) Map Section
   e) Exemption Section
   f) Record Section
3. *Responsibilities and functions:*
   a) *Standards Division:* Under direction of the assessor and in coordination with other divisions of the department, the Standards Division is responsible for the establishment and maintenance of standards and procedures for the appraisal of real and personal property, for the coordination of electronic data processing and design of EDP systems, for staff supervision of training, and for forms control. Specific functions are
      (1) Preparation and maintenance of appraisal procedures in the form of manuals, handbooks, and memorandums.
      (2) Preparation and maintenance of the administrative procedures necessary to support the operation of the department.
      (3) The necessary staff supervision of training and operations to ensure that approved procedures and standards are understood and being complied with.
      (4) The exercise of forms control. All requests for forms approval and supply will be submitted through the Standards Division.
      (5) The development, maintenance, and coordination of EDP systems. All requests for EDP service will be submitted through the Standards Division.

· · ·

Statement of Responsibilities for Standards Division

1. The Standards Division consists of the following personnel:
   1 chief appraiser, chief of Standards Division
   1 property analyst
   2 senior real property appraisers
   1 senior auditor-appraiser
   1 real property appraiser II
   1 steno-clerk II
2. Functions:
   a) In coordination with the Real Property and Business Divisions, establishes and maintains uniform standards for appraising real and personal property by
      (1) Preparation and maintenance of appraisal procedures.
      (2) Providing staff supervision of training.
      (3) Maintain training and certification records.
      (4) The exercise of forms control.
      (5) Supervising the development and maintenance of EDP systems.

Figure 6.   **Statement of Responsibilities of Departmental Divisions and Sections (cont.)**

    (6) Internal audit.

    (7) Preparing sales-ratio studies.

    (8) Monitoring the computer-assisted appraisal programs for single-family residential properties, multifamily properties and commercial/industrial properties.

    (9) Monitoring the computer-assisted system of unsecured property.

  b) In coordination with the assessment-roll supervisor, provides for:

    (1) Preparation and maintenance of the assessor's secured and unsecured assessment roll.

    (2) Supervision and development of EDP systems for the assessor's secured and unsecured roll.

  c) In coordination with the supervising exemption clerk, provides for:

    (1) Preparation and maintenance of the homeowner's exemption claim processing.

    (2) Supervision and development of EDP systems for the homeowner's exemption.

3. The chief appraiser is responsible for the overall supervision and operation of the division. In order to carry out this responsibility, it is necessary that the following procedures be followed:

  a) All procedures, forms, and formal written documents will have his or her approval before final printing and/or dissemination.

  b) All documents or communications originating in the division requiring a signature will be signed by the chief appraiser and, as necessary, the individual initiating the correspondence.

  c) All requests for EDP service will be approved and signed by the chief appraiser or, in his or her absence, the property analyst.

  d) It is not intended that the above controls preclude daily informal contact by members of this division with other divisions in the carrying out of their responsibilities. On the contrary, it is expected that they will work directly with the operating divisions in carrying out their responsibilities. However, the chief appraiser must be kept informed of their activities and must approve any final decisions.

  e) In the absence of the chief appraiser, the senior person present will sign for him or her.

4. Work assignments for systems and standards:

  a) Property analyst

    (1) Is responsible for the development and updating of the single-family appraisal system, the multifamily appraisal system, and the commercial/industrial appraisal system, and the coordination of these systems with the secured master file.

    (2) Is responsible for the coordination of programmers and EDP service associated with system developments.

    (3) Participates with the Real Property Division in the development of user requirements for the appraisal systems.

    (4) Supervises the development of sales data and the maintenance of statistics for computing sales ratios, and computes trend factors when necessary.

    (5) Develops and/or assists regression formula and other statistical inferences.

    (6) Assists in department training as necessary.

    (7) Conducts special research projects whenever necessary and produces statistical reports.

  b) Senior real property appraiser for multifamily properties (MFP):

    (1) Writes and maintains the multifamily appraisal manual.

    (2) Prepares and maintains real property forms for MFP.

    (3) Assists the chief appraiser and property analyst in the development and maintenance of EDP systems for MFP.

Figure 6. Statement of Responsibilities of Departmental Divisions and Sections (cont.)

(4) Establishes procedures and maintains internal auditing of appraisals and conformance to appraisal procedures as established in the manual for MFP systems.

(5) Edits and processes all returned sales confirmation letters for MFP systems.

(6) Edits and processes all income and expense questionnaires for MFP systems.

(7) Annually develops the necessary percentage for cost-updating the MFP system.

(8) Maintains the daily operations of the MFP appraisal system with EDP, including but not limited to completing input documents for EDP services, scheduling EDP services, developing EDP outputs to Real Property Division, and maintaining file controls.

(9) Prepares as required sales-ratio and coefficient-of-dispersion studies for MFP.

(10) Confers with the property analyst in developing regression formula or other statistical inferences.

(11) Assists in department staff training as necessary.

(12) Makes field checks and property reviews as required.

(13) Maintains a high degree of cooperation and rapport with the Real Property Division in carrying out work assignments.

• • •

f) Steno-clerk II

(1) Takes and transcribes dictation as required.

(2) Maintains individual time production report files and prepares summary reports as required.

(3) Maintains individual educational and training records.

(4) Maintains general files as directed.

(5) Maintains forms control register and file and prepares all requests for reprographics.

(6) Does general typing as required.

(7) Takes telephone messages and routes calls.

---

in authority should be avoided. (If allocation of values between land and improvements is a statutory or administrative requirement, it can be provided separately by the appraisal department or a valuation standards unit.)

A structure in which one department is responsible for the appraisal of one property type or use class helps avoid overlapping authority and has an additional advantage: it may be easier to match appraiser skills to appraisal difficulty. Residential appraisal usually requires different skills from appraisal of industrial properties, complex income-producing properties, or other unusual property types.

Geographic specialization, in which appraisers are assigned to specific districts, al-

lows appraisers to broaden their skills and understand locational factors better, and reduces travel time.

If the jurisdiction is a large one, departments may be organized along geographic lines with subdivisions organized by function, or vice versa. If carried further, functional and geographic division can give each staff member a specific responsibility; for example, one appraiser, or a team of appraisers, may be assigned to all apartment appraisals or to all properties in certain neighborhoods or small towns. In this way, lines of responsibility are clear for an identifiable portion of the overall assessment product. Geographic specialization in which appraisers are given broad responsibility for all the ap-

Figure 7. Chesterfield County, Virginia, Functional Organization Chart, 1986

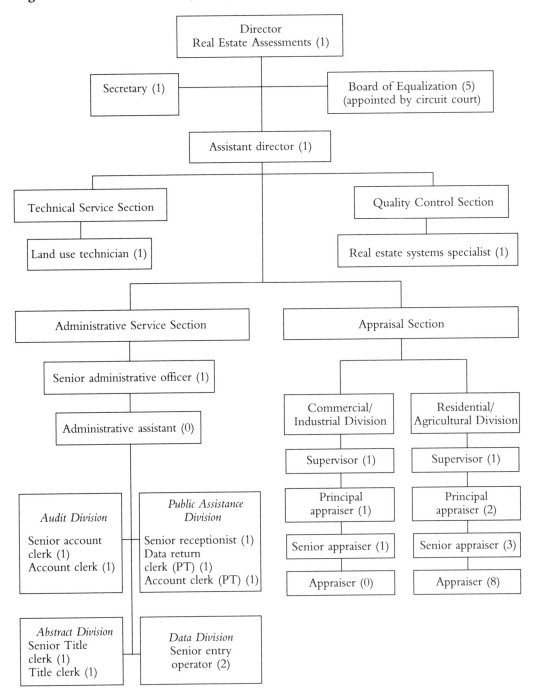

Figure 8. Geographic Organization Chart: Montreal Urban Community, Valuation Department, 1990

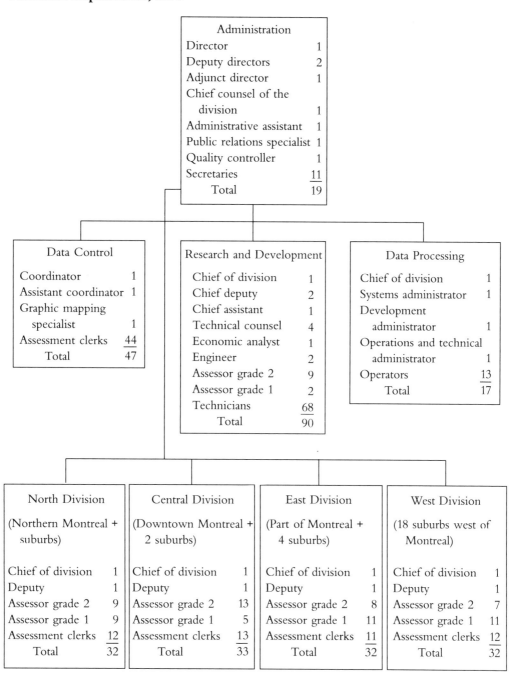

Administration	
Director	1
Deputy directors	2
Adjunct director	1
Chief counsel of the division	1
Administrative assistant	1
Public relations specialist	1
Quality controller	1
Secretaries	11
Total	19

Data Control	
Coordinator	1
Assistant coordinator	1
Graphic mapping specialist	1
Assessment clerks	44
Total	47

Research and Development	
Chief of division	1
Chief deputy	2
Chief assistant	1
Technical counsel	4
Economic analyst	1
Engineer	2
Assessor grade 2	9
Assessor grade 1	2
Technicians	68
Total	90

Data Processing	
Chief of division	1
Systems administrator	1
Development administrator	1
Operations and technical administrator	1
Operators	13
Total	17

North Division	
(Northern Montreal + suburbs)	
Chief of division	1
Deputy	1
Assessor grade 2	9
Assessor grade 1	9
Assessment clerks	12
Total	32

Central Division	
(Downtown Montreal + 2 suburbs)	
Chief of division	1
Deputy	1
Assessor grade 2	13
Assessor grade 1	5
Assessment clerks	13
Total	33

East Division	
(Part of Montreal + 4 suburbs)	
Chief of division	1
Deputy	1
Assessor grade 2	8
Assessor grade 1	11
Assessment clerks	11
Total	32

West Division	
(18 suburbs west of Montreal)	
Chief of division	1
Deputy	1
Assessor grade 2	7
Assessor grade 1	11
Assessment clerks	12
Total	32

praisal tasks in an area is consistent with the principles of determinate hierarchy.

Task forces or teams, which are matrix organizational forms, are temporary arrangements of staff organized to accomplish a specific task. They violate both the classical line/staff principle and the scalar principle of unity of command, but are useful when functional and geographic specialization produce temporary mismatches between labor needs and staff assignments. A jurisdiction may need to use employees where the needs are greatest, for example, to complete a revaluation project. If used too frequently or for too long a time, however, task forces may prevent employees from attending to their regular duties and may also undermine traditional authority relationships.

Employees that do not do appraisals are also organized by specialized skill or responsibility; for example, designated units will handle mapping, exemptions, data processing, and administrative services.

Span of Control   Decisions about span of control depend on the tasks to be accomplished and the skills required to accomplish them. For example, employees doing high-level appraisal tasks such as mass appraisal valuation model building, valuation of complex properties, and valuation defense should have a great deal of autonomy. For these tasks, the span of control can be wide (one supervisor for many employees). Employees doing data collection and entry, on the other hand, benefit from close supervision; a tighter span of control is appropriate.

In the assessment office, *line* (command) positions, produce the assessment product. *Staff* functions such as personnel administration and quality assurance support line func-

tions. Staff functions in general should be strictly advisory to line functions. However, staff responsible for developing and monitoring appraisal standards should have the authority to insist that employees doing appraisal work meet standards. This violates the classical line/staff principle – necessarily in this case.

Delegation

The organization chart and related job descriptions formalize the manager's delegation of work. They also provide uniform information about assignments, help avoid duplication of tasks, and are the basis for mutual agreement about personnel policies and procedures.

The chart is a graphic representation of supervisory positions and lines of authority for all employees. In a large office, the number of employees in a classification is listed by department. The chart should be prepared so that the chain of command is clear to someone unfamiliar with the office.

Lines of Communication

The lines of communication may be as formal as a standard monthly report or as informal as a casual telephone call. From a systems perspective, formal and informal communication links are the feedback mechanisms that keep an organization healthy; they need to be developed and maintained. Managers must understand and plan for communication within the office, with other departments of government, and with the public in general.

Communication networks should be established within the unit of government of which the assessment office is a part. The assessor should have well-developed means of communicating with the local appeal board, recorder of deeds, and planning department, and with mapping and computer support departments if they are separate units. Local jurisdictions also maintain formal and informal ties with the agency that supervises ad valorem taxation.

The "public" of importance to assessors is really a variety of publics: taxpayers, policy makers, the news media, real estate professionals, and so forth. Many employees meet these publics, but administrators have the ultimate responsibility for maintaining good relationships with these groups. They discharge this responsibility by creating an organized public relations program that establishes contacts with key individuals, trains all employees to communicate effectively with the public, and monitors communications (see IAAO's *Standard on Public Relations* (1988) and chapter 21.

Personnel Management

Personnel management begins with the budget allocation and the listing of numbers and classes of positions on the organization chart, which shows the classification and sometimes the compensation level or range for each position. Even if job classifications and salary levels are usually determined for the jurisdiction as a whole, at a higher level than the assessment office, the assessor should help write job descriptions, determine classifications, and set salary levels.

Selection of Employees

Salaries and benefits are typically 80 to 90 percent of the assessment office's budget. Careful selection of employees is the first part of an effective program to use this money

wisely. The planning document determines staff needs, and managers should consult it before authorizing new positions or filling vacancies.

An effective hiring process, outlined in the following steps, will help avoid hiring mistakes and legal difficulties.

1. If a personnel system does not exist, prepare application forms, review current legislation, and prepare hiring and employment policies and procedures (have these reviewed by the jurisdiction's attorney to be sure they comply with the law).
2. Analyze the tasks required and prepare a job description. This analysis may be in the existing plan or may require plan revisions and a new analysis.
3. Prepare an accurate summary of the job and qualifications.
4. Announce the job by posting the summary and qualifications in house and advertising in appropriate ways.
5. Review the applications and determine specifications for screening (when possible, preference should be given to in-house applicants). Screen applications to select candidates for interviewing. Plan an interview strategy that will identify the best candidates and ensure equitable treatment of all candidates.
6. Schedule and hold interviews.
7. Select finalist(s).
8. Offer the position to the best candidate; negotiate as necessary; send letter of appointment when decision is final.
9. Notify other applicants that the position is filled.

In some jurisdictions, personnel functions such as testing, recruiting, and job classification are not carried out within the assessment office. Yet the assessor, like other department heads, is the appointing authority responsible for recommending or approving personnel actions and should, therefore, take the initiative in communicating departmental needs to the personnel officer and setting appropriate standards for pay, training, evaluation, and job classification.

Employee Development

Although employees may improve their skills by their own efforts and the help of their peers, managers have organizational responsibility for employee development. They use training, education, counseling, and performance reviews to identify talents and help employees grow.

The new employee will be productive only if adequately trained for a position. The job description (figure 9) defines the job for both employee and supervisor. Procedural manuals clarify tasks. A training program, formal or informal, builds necessary skills and monitors progress. The organization chart enables the employee to know *who* is responsible for *what* within the organization and defines the chain of command for reporting and resolving conflicts.

Courses, seminars, and other opportunities help employees grow beyond the requirements of the immediate position. For example, periodic training sessions conducted by senior staff can improve skills and train employees to do other jobs. As opportunities arise, employees are then ready to advance. Opportunities for promotion keep morale and interest high.

Certification or professional designation programs give individuals pride of accomplishment, and give taxpayers an impartial measure of staff competence. These programs verify externally that staff knowledge has been tested and found acceptable. The assessor should be familiar with certifying agencies, certification requirements and procedures, and opportunities for education.

Compensation

Employees feel better about their work if wage and salary schedules are adequate and individual wage and salary decisions are sound. Salary schedules should be competitive with the market, if budget permits, and equitable among classes of positions.

Wages and salaries should reflect each position's responsibilities. Often, wages and salaries in a public office are established by the rules of the governing body of the jurisdiction. But some jobs in the assessment office, clerical jobs, for example, may be more difficult than those performed in other public offices. Handling property record cards and sales data requires more judgment than routine filing or typing. The assessor should prepare job descriptions that show how clerical jobs in the assessment office compare to other positions and present an effective case for more compensation to the personnel department.

Violations of established personnel policy by overclassification or an inappropriate salary increase will reduce the administrator's effectiveness in the long run by lowering employee confidence and creating internal disharmony. If a position is underpaid for the skills required, the position should be upgraded. Employees who have developed skills that would qualify them for higher salaries should be offered promotions or more suitable positions, if possible.

Figure 9. Job Descriptions

Class title
Appraiser Trainee

Definition
Under immediate supervision; performs work of routine difficulty in collecting property information and appraising real estate for assessment purposes; performs related work as required.

Examples of duties
Makes field and office appraisals of less complex residential and commercial property after undergoing sufficient training under close supervision; collects and analyzes data relative to the valuation of real property; researches cost, income, and sales data; measures buildings; collects data on number and type of rooms, type of construction, age, and other conditions affecting values; makes calculations and applies results to appraisals of specific buildings; attends appraisal courses as prescribed by the appointing authority.

Desirable knowledge and skills
Some knowledge of social and economic factors affecting real property values; some knowledge of trends in urban development; some knowledge of basic mathematics and statistics.

Suggested training and experience
Completion of the core curriculum for a baccalaureate level major in business, marketing, economics, or a related field; or an equivalent combination of training and experience.

Class title
Supervising Appraiser

Definition
Under general direction; performs work of considerable difficulty in supervising a unit responsible for the appraisal of all real estate located within an assigned geographical area of the city; and performs related work as required.

Examples of duties
Supervises a unit engaged in the appraisal of residential, commercial, industrial, special-purpose, and vacant properties within an assigned geographic area; assigns work to appraisers and trains and assists them in the performance of appraisal activities; supports appraisals in hearings before the Board of Review and courts of record; makes appropriate disposition of complaints by the public concerning assessments; keeps quantitative and qualitative records of appraisal activities; makes reports and performs administrative activities as required; assists the public with questions about state assessment laws and local policies and procedures.

Desirable knowledge and skills
Considerable knowledge of the principles and practices of real estate appraisal; considerable knowledge of laws and ordinances pertaining to the assessment of real property; considerable knowledge of local, social, and economic factors affecting property values; considerable knowledge of mathematical and statistical tools used in appraisal work; good knowledge of office management and supervisory principles and practices.

Figure 9. Job Descriptions (cont.)

Considerable skill in dealing tactfully and courteously with the public; considerable skill in determining complex property values; working skill in planning and supervising the work of subordinates.

Suggested training and experience
Completion of the core curriculum for a baccalaureate level major in business, marketing, economics, or a related field and five years' experience in real estate field appraisals of large commercial and industrial properties; or an equivalent combination of training and experience.

Necessary special requirements
Possession of professional designation by the International Association of Assessing Officers (CAE) or membership in the American Institute of Real Estate Appraisers (MAI).

Class title
Appraiser

Definition
Under general supervision; performs work of considerable difficulty in appraising real estate for tax assessment purposes; and performs related work as required.

Examples of duties
Makes field and office appraisals of residential, commercial, industrial, special-purpose, and vacant properties; gathers, records, analyzes, and maintains a variety of data such as zoning, selling and asking prices, income, and building cost in order to make appraisals; receives and investigates complaints about property assessments, makes reappraisals, and submits recommendations for consideration at hearings; assists in training lower-level appraisers; prepares and supports technical cases to defend contested assessments in court proceedings or Board of Review appeal hearings; corrects and updates file property information.

Desirable knowledge and skills
Good knowledge of the principles and practices of real estate appraisal; good knowledge of laws and ordinances pertaining to the assessment of real property; good knowledge of local social and economic factors affecting property values; good knowledge of mathematical and statistical tools used in real property appraisal.

Considerable skill in dealing tactfully and courteously with property owners and the public; considerable skill in determining real property values.

Suggested training and experience
Completion of the core curriculum for a baccalaureate level major in business, marketing, economics, or a related field and two years' experience in real estate field appraisal work; or an equivalent combination of training and experience.

Necessary special requirements
Candidacy for or possession of the professional designation of the International Association of Assessing Officers (CAE or RES) or membership in the American Institute of Real Estate Appraisers (MAI) or the Society of Real Estate Appraisers (SRPA), to be acquired within six months from the initial date of employment.

Figure 9. Job Descriptions (cont.)

Class title
Senior Appraiser

Definition
Under direction; performs work of considerable difficulty in appraising real estate for tax assessment purposes; and performs related work as required.

Examples of duties
Makes field and office appraisals of more difficult and complex residential, commercial, industrial, special-purpose, and vacant properties; gathers, records, analyzes, and maintains a variety of data such as zoning, asking and selling prices, income, and building costs to determine appraised values; receives and investigates complaints about property assessments, makes reappraisals, and submits recommendations for consideration at hearings; assists in the training of lower level appraisers; prepares and supports technical cases to defend contested assessments in court proceedings or Board of Review appeal hearings; updates and corrects file property information.

Desirable knowledge and skills
Considerable knowledge of the principles and practices of real estate appraisal; considerable knowledge of laws and ordinances pertaining to the assessment of real property; considerable knowledge of local, social and economic factors affecting real property values; considerable knowledge of mathematical and statistical tools used in real property appraisal.

Considerable skill in dealing tactfully and courteously with property owners and the public; considerable skill in determining complex real property values.

Suggested training and experience
Completion of the core curriculum for a baccalaureate level major in business, marketing, economics, or a related field and three years' experience in real estate field appraisal work; or an equivalent combination of training and experience.

Necessary special requirements
Possession or active candidacy for either the professional designation of the International Association of Assessing Officers (CAE or RES) or membership in the American Institute of Real Estate Appraisers (MAI) or the Society of Real Estate Appraisers (SRPA), to be acquired within six months of the initial date of employment.

Internal Communication

Internal communication affects the climate of the workplace. Managers are responsible for creating healthy systems for communicating, both formally and informally.

Internal communication begins with a statement of goals, objectives, and values. General rules and policies should be in writing, except in unusual circumstances, and should be administered firmly but fairly. All supervisors should be responsible for enforcement of policies.

Productivity may be considerably reduced by lax compliance with established rules. For example, employees allowed to be habitually late coming to work or returning from lunch can undermine morale in an entire office. Rules about hours, absences, vacations, attire and conduct, and lunch or coffee breaks must be adhered to.

The policy manual given to each employee should include instructions on office organization, procedures and filing systems, specific dates of required completion for various portions of the assessment process, and a code of ethics. Members of the IAAO subscribe to a *Code of Ethics and Standards of Professional Conduct*, as well as The Appraisal Foundation's *Uniform Standards of Professional Appraisal Practice*. These are good models for a jurisdiction's code of ethics.

The program of internal communication should be continuous, with meetings, performance reports, progress reports on projects, and possibly a staff newsletter. If major policy changes are made, employees should be informed of the need and reason for change.

Employees also need frequent evaluations of job performance. To be fair and effective, a formal evaluation should be related to specific duties and performance standards, the job description, and the operational plan; for example, if the plan calls for an average of ten appraisals per day, then the performance standard for appraisers should state this requirement, and individual evaluations should measure the quantity of appraisals completed. The manager may use standard review forms or develop forms that fit specific needs.

In addition to a formal written evaluation, employees should have frequent informal feedback to help them achieve expectations. The supervisor should praise good performance and identify problems for prompt remedial action. In some cases, it may be necessary to discipline or even dismiss an employee.

The purpose of discipline is to promote behavior that achieves goals. Discipline should be progressive, beginning with the least severe method for changing behavior. The steps in discipline should be fair, yet serve the needs of the office. These procedures should be in the *written* information given to every employee.

Discipline usually leads either to improvement or dismissal. When a problem is first noted, a meeting with the person or persons directly involved provides an opportunity for counseling. If this results in improvement, the supervisor rewards the improved behavior in some appropriate way, perhaps by simply telling the employee that the change has been observed. If adequate improvement does not take place, the supervisor gives an oral warning. Again, improvement is rewarded, but if it does not occur, the supervisor gives a second oral warning to be followed up in writing. If a problem persists, the groundwork has been laid for a formal written reprimand, after which the only further steps are suspension or dismissal.

The following principles are helpful for dealing with employee problems.

1. Use the procedures specified in writing for the office. Take action only if further training and counseling will not be effective.

2. Act promptly. Begin with a fair, objective, thorough investigation.

3. Seek out the facts, impartially. Let all persons involved tell their stories. Listen! And remember that most problems have more than one cause.

4. Keep in mind that the purpose is to change behavior and improve the office, not to punish.

5. Apply standards that are fair, uniform, and reasonably related to office operations. Be sure the employee has been in-

formed of these standards and has had adequate time to meet them.

6. Follow the sequence of steps outlined above, documenting as you go. Be sure appropriate oral and written warnings are given. Give the employee a specific timetable for improvement.

7. Discipline only after there is substantial evidence of fault.

8. Be sure the penalty applied is appropriate to the fault.

9. Consider asking a third party to review a decision before final action.

10. Follow up to a satisfactory conclusion, including a written report. Remember that an employee usually has a right to appeal. A written record and good procedures provide the best basis for defense.

Motivation and Leadership

Using interpersonal skills, administrators release and direct talent and energy within an organization by motivating and leading their employees. To motivate, managers must help employees feel a sense of responsibility and achievement. They can do this by knowing their employees, delegating authority, expecting and rewarding excellence, encouraging teamwork and participation, and recognizing the strength of self-motivation in the workplace.

Managing is the art of accomplishing institutional goals through people. The development of a leadership style appropriate for managing the people in an organization with complex functions is not simple.

Research about leadership styles has been done since at least the 1940s. Douglass McGregor, in *The Human Side of Enterprise*, compared classical with motivation theories

about management style. He listed the following assumptions about human behavior as the basis for the classical belief that a directive, autocratic style of management (which he called theory X) is the most effective:

- The average human being dislikes work and will avoid it if possible.
- Most people must be coerced to get them to achieve the organization's objectives.
- The average human being prefers to be directed, has little ambition, and wants security above all.

Building on the motivation theory of Abraham Maslow, McGregor argued that these traditional assumptions were inadequate to explain most human behavior. He proposed the following assumptions as reflecting more accurately the findings of modern motivational theory:

- The average human being does not inherently dislike work; it is as natural as play or rest.
- External control and the threat of punishment are not the only ways to get employees to work for an organization's objectives. People will exercise self-direction in the service of objectives to which they are committed.
- The motivation to work results from such high-level needs as self actualization, achievement, and self-esteem, not only the need for security.
- Under proper conditions, the average human being both accepts and seeks responsibilities.

This view supports a leadership style that is more democratic and less directive and autocratic than the classical model. McGregor called this style theory Y.

Studies conducted by the University of Michigan in a wide variety of organizations, including automotive, electronics, food, insurance, paper, and railroad companies, looked at the efficiency of leadership styles in various situations from a viewpoint similar to McGregor's. These studies identified two basic orientations of managers and supervisors: job-centered or employee-centered. The job-centered manager analyzes the job, finds the best way to do it, hires the right person, supervises closely, and rewards with money. The employee-centered manager focuses on the human aspects of the job: team building, democratic goal setting, and developing personal relationships with subordinates. The general conclusion drawn from these studies was that employee-centered managers were more effective.

The Michigan model has undergone some changes over the years, and the two orientations are not seen as mutually exclusive. For instance, an Ohio State University study found that leadership could be described in terms of two general factors, degree of structure provided and degree of consideration for employees. The original Michigan model, from the Ohio State point of view, had two poles; the job-centered manager exhibited low consideration and high structure, and the employee-centered manager exhibited high consideration and low structure. The Ohio study suggested that at least two other types were also possible. A manager could also exhibit high consideration and high structure, or low consideration and low structure.

The major problem with the basic Michigan model, in its original form and as modified by the Ohio State study and other researchers, is that it fails to predict effectiveness in all cases. For instance, a study conducted by W. S. Reddin on productivity in sectors of one company reported that six out of seven high-producing sectors were managed by an employee-centered manager and one by a job-centered manager; in the less productive sectors, seven out of ten were managed by job-centered managers and three by employee-centered managers. These data, typical of many studies on the efficiency of leadership styles, are supportive of employee-centered management—but also of the notion that no one management style is always best.

Reddin, building on the Ohio State findings, argued that the four basic styles of leadership that result from combinations of high and low degrees of consideration and structure are *all* effective, depending on the situation. The question is how to identify which situation requires what management style. In *Introduction to Organization Behavior*, Robin Stuart-Kotze has labeled the four basic styles identified in the Ohio study as facilitative (low structure, high consideration), systematic (low structure, low consideration), directive (high structure, low consideration), and interactive (high structure, high consideration).

The *facilitative* manager exhibits a low degree of task orientation and a high degree of relationship-centered behavior, delegating and playing an advisory role. Subordinates are seen as equals and friends. This style is appropriate where creativity is required, group members are experts, and commitment to decisions is important. In assessment administration, the appraisal staff usually benefits from this style of management.

The *systematic* manager exhibits low degrees of both task-oriented behavior and relationship-oriented behavior. The manager directs energy to the administration of a system of rules and procedures. This is useful when group operations are bound by a large number of rules and the major task is administering routine duties prescribed by a formal set of procedures. Within assessment administration, the exemptions department might benefit from this management style.

The *directive* manager, who exhibits a high degree of task orientation and a low degree of relationship-oriented behavior, directs energy to planning, controlling, and the direction of subordinates. In assessment administration, large data collection or field review projects might benefit from this management style.

The *interactive* manager exhibits a high degree of both task-oriented behavior and relationship-oriented behavior and directs energy to guiding and coordinating the activities of others. Planning and controlling are important but are done by making the manager a part of the group, involving all of the members in decisions about these issues. This style is appropriate when group members have diverse backgrounds and the decisions to be made are complex and not guided by past precedent. In assessment administration, the assessor's relationship with the top administrative staff could benefit from this style.

An appropriate management style, then, depends on the situation. Managers often use different styles in different situations and should experiment until the right fit is achieved.

Systems Issues in Management

Three systems insights about human behavior are especially important in personnel management:

1. *No behavior takes place in isolation.* The behavior of any person or group takes place within some context. Everything is done for a reason. Even strange actions are rational to the actor. When we see an act as irrational, it only means that we have failed to see what the individual or group sees.

2. *Behavior can rarely be attributed to a single cause.* Problems cannot be explained and solved in simple terms. For instance, employees complain that their work space is inadequate. One might conclude that the problem would be solved by providing a better arrangement. If the real cause of the problem is a feeling that they have no chance to be promoted or that their tasks are unpleasant, then rearranging the workspace may not solve the problem.

3. *Every action sets off a chain of reactions.* For example, an employee who receives a smaller merit increase than other employees feels he has been treated unfairly. Rather than discussing the problem with his supervisor, he persuades other employees that merit increases are awarded unfairly, causing them to become dissatisfied with their raises. Many employees slow production, complain to each other about other problems, until a widespread morale problem exists. Attempts to deal with the problem of productivity may simply intensify the morale problem, which may lead to resignations or firings.

Other examples of systems problems where simple answers are not appropriate are those that might occur if the classical principles of unity of command, determinate hierarchy, and line/staff are violated. For instance, if employees or groups report to more than one superior, the principle of unity of command is violated; conflicts within the group may erupt because the relative authority of the superiors has not been clearly defined or because they have different leadership styles. Employee reactions to the implicit lack of definition may hurt productivity. In this case, violation of unity of command, not interpersonal conflicts, is the real issue.

If one manager gives overlapping responsibility to two or more subordinates, conflicts may occur between the subordinates that at first appear entirely interpersonal in origin. However, the principle of determinate hierarchy has been violated. The manager might solve the apparent personality conflict by simply clarifying the relative areas of responsibility. If this is not done, the interpersonal conflict might eventually generate broader unrest as the subordinates involve others in their struggles.

Intentional differences in management style might also cause systems problems. If the organization has work groups that require different management styles to maximize organizational productivity, then systems problems in the form of worker claims of unfairness or unequal treatment might arise if the style differences are too extreme. As noted above, in an assessment office a facilitative manager might manage the appraisal staff, and a directive manager, the data collection and record-keeping process. A unified management style for all operations might lower productivity. Making clear to all the need for different management structures for different kinds of work is the appropriate way to handle this situation, as well as giving employees opportunities to advance to a kind of work that requires a different management style.

Finally, systems problems can occur if the formal and informal feedback mechanisms that develop in all organizations are not managed properly. Localized system problems that arise from the way the organization is structured can become organizationwide problems because of informal feedback. A good manager monitors the informal feedback network and knows about problems before they begin to affect productivity. "No surprises, please," and "tell *me* first" are good ground rules for supervisors to convey to employees.

Events outside a department can also have unexpected effects on its internal system. Two examples from the IAAO's technical consulting files illustrate this. In one case the IAAO was called in to determine why equity, which had initially increased after the introduction of a CAMA system, had now decreased. In addition, there was a serious conflict between staff responsible for appraisals and staff responsible for field review. The IAAO research team determined that installation of the CAMA system had increased equity but had also increased appeals, which increased the work load of the appeals staff. Informal feedback from this staff to the field review staff resulted in the field review staff changing their standards from ones that emphasized equity to ones that emphasized valuation stability between the old and new values. This reduced appeals—but also decreased equity. These changes were made without the knowledge of senior management. Clarifying the formal policy on field review practices and upgrading the budget of the appeals department solved the original problem of reduced equity, as well as the interpersonal problems between the appraisal and field review staffs.

In a second example, a jurisdiction introduced improved procedures that resulted in values being kept more current. The IAAO was brought in because of proposed state legislation that would have undermined the reforms. The IAAO research team discovered that the increase in equity and valuations had resulted in drastic cuts in state aid to communities with certain profiles. The politicians in these communities were influential in getting legislation introduced that, if it had passed, would have undermined good assessment practice. In this case, solving the system problem lay not in changing the law governing assessment but in revising the state's equalization formula.

The above examples remind us that individual and general system problems within the organization involve looking at issues of structure, feedback, and leadership styles, and that the problem as it is presented may well be only a symptom of other problems in one or all of these three areas.

Summary

This chapter has discussed fundamental principles of good management, touching upon major theories of management. Planning, budgeting, and personnel management within the assessment office were discussed in detail. The following chapters look more closely at management of specific areas and tasks: mapping, revaluation, computers, ratio studies, quality control, notifications, appeals, and public relations.

Mapping System Management

17

Overview of Cadastral Mapping

Complete and accurate maps and ownership records are essential to the assessment office. A well-maintained mapping system provides both a graphic representation of the real property tax roll and an inventory of the ownership documents pertaining to the legal subdivision of land. A good mapping system is essential for the location, identification, and inventory of all parcels within a jurisdiction. The maps are used by appraisers in their everyday work and by the public in its quest for land information. Computerized maps and ownership records can be shared with other government and public-service agencies to improve public service.

Cadastral maps show the boundaries of parcels of land and display the size and location of each parcel relative to other properties, streams, roads, and other major physical and cultural features. Maps are drawn to appropriate scales and show dimensions or areas, together with parcel identification. Maps may exist in hard copies (pencil or ink on paper or plastic film) or as computer data bases, ready to be manipulated and produced in a variety of forms. Cadastral maps are also called assessment, appraisal, ownership, property, real estate, and tax maps.

Mapped information includes lines, measurements, and identifiers. In addition to property boundaries, lines delimit easements, road and railroad rights-of-way, subdivision lots, soil types, zoning, political jurisdictions, floodplains, and taxing districts. Measurements include property line dimensions, parcel acreage, and right-of-way widths. Identifiers include parcel numbers; subdivision block and lot designations; and the names of streets, railroads, subdivisions, and administrative jurisdictions.

The ownership and land information records that are part of the mapping system identify legal owners and ownership interests as well as separate or partial ownership rights such as minerals and timber. Administrative information such as property address, zoning, taxing jurisdiction, taxpayer account number, deed and survey references, and owners' mailing addresses may also be included.

As a tool of the assessment office, maps should be readily reproducible for field use, public information, and planning. The mapping system information should be easily retrievable and subject to cross-referencing and manipulation for specific purposes. Systematic and continual updating is necessary as parcel ownership changes—including complete transfers, partial sales, and combinations of adjacent properties—occur. The proper creation, use, and maintenance of a cadastral mapping system will ensure that all parcels of property are identified and listed for property tax purposes, no parcel is taxed more than once, and necessary information for the fair and equitable assessment of property is available to the assessment office. See the IAAO *Standard on Cadastral Maps and Parcel Identifiers* (1988) for a description of the elements of a cadastral mapping system.

A mapping program requires skills in research, appraisal, surveying, mathematics, engineering, public relations, and title and boundary law. Whether the mapper works with pencil on paper, ink on drafting film, or numbers in a computer, all new mapping programs have the same requirements.

First, accurate research and thorough documentation are needed. If an important survey, deed, right-of-way alteration, or street abandonment is missed, ripple effects may be felt on many adjoining parcels. A manual map that is poorly drafted but painstakingly researched and documented is preferable to one beautifully drafted yet poorly researched. This problem is made worse by computers, whose plotters make poorly researched maps look just as good as well-researched ones.

Second, effective graphic presentation is needed. Both manual and computer maps should emphasize the most important element to the assessor: the parcel. In depicting detail, cadastral maps should usually strike a delicate balance between the needs of two types of users: members of the public, who may have poor map reading skills; and surveyors and deed processors, who want complex details shown.

Third, standard research procedures and consistent symbols must be used. Adopting standard procedures assures more consistent

maps, better user acceptance, and easier staff turnover transitions.

Finally, considerable space and time are needed to create a new mapping system. Additional employees and space for them to work without interruption are usually necessary. Creating new mapping systems is so demanding that municipalities often contract with a private company or another government agency to do the job.

Land Description Systems

The legal description of land is based on surveys. These may be purely visual and highly subjective or precise mathematical delineations of the limits of the land. The land description systems commonly in use are metes and bounds, public land survey, lot and block, and state plane coordinate systems.

Metes and Bounds

The earliest form of land description was the "bounded" description, which described the property by reference to physical features or adjacent property owners. Typical physical features included trees, ridge lines, streams, and roads. For example, property might be described as "bounded on the north by French Creek, bounded on the east by the land of Ezra Jones, bounded on the south by a wooden fence, and bounded on the west by a line of trees and the county road." Little thought was given to the fact that a fence line or tree might someday cease to exist.

As land became more valuable and disputes over unclear "bounds" became more numerous, better methods of description evolved. It became a common surveying practice to measure the direction of property lines with compass bearings and the distance with measuring chains or tapes. Property described in this manner became known as "metes and bounds." The term "metes" refers to measurement and the term "bounds" refers to the boundaries, including features of the terrain described in conjunction with compass bearings and distances.

The bearing of a line is the angle between a north-south meridian and the line measured from north or south toward the east or west. As illustrated in figure 1, property lines are described in terms of direction within one of the four quadrants of the compass—

northeast, southeast, southwest, northwest (NE, SE, SW, NW).

In a metes and bounds description, each property line is described, with the beginning of each line being the end of the preceding line. A proper metes and bounds description should "close," that is, the last line should come back to the point of beginning. A metes and bounds survey is described below and illustrated in figure 2.

Beginning at an iron pin located in the South Right of Way of Main Street. Said iron pin is located N 88 degrees 15 minutes E at a distance

Figure 1. Quadrants of a Surveyor's Compass

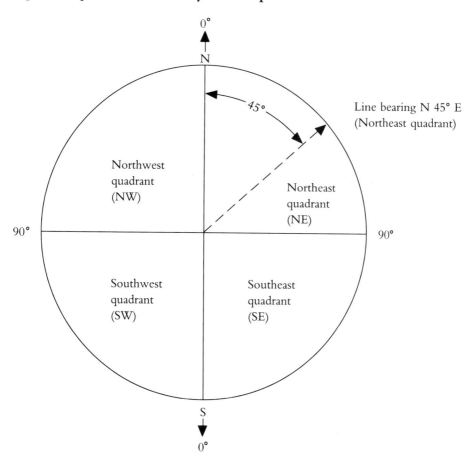

Figure 2.   Plot of Metes and Bounds Description

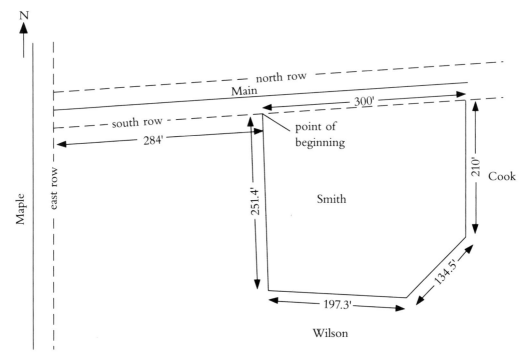

of 284 feet from the intersection of the South ROW of Main Street and the East ROW of Maple Street. Said point is also located at the Northwest corner of a lot now owned by John Smith, thence leaving said ROW and running with Smith's line S 5 degrees 34 minutes E a distance of 251.4 feet to an iron pin at the corner of Wilson; thence along Wilson's North line S 82 degrees 41 minutes E a distance of 197.3 feet to a point in Cook's West line, thence N 46 degrees 10 minutes E a distance of 134.5 feet, thence N 5 degrees W a distance of 210 feet to an iron pin in the South ROW of Main Street, thence along the South ROW of Main Street S 84 degrees 50 minutes W a distance of 300 feet to the point of beginning, consisting of 1.65 acres, more or less.

Rectangular Land Surveys

The United States Public Land Survey System, a rectangular land survey system also called the section-township-range system, was established in 1785 for the purpose of surveying, marking, and disposing of the public domain of the United States. A similar system was established in Canada. Because the legal subdivision of land was made before its sale or grant, one of the primary purposes of the survey was to mark the land "corners" on the ground. All of the United States has been included in the system except the original thirteen colonies, Kentucky, Tennessee, Texas, West Virginia, parts of Ohio, Alaska, and Hawaii. These states were excluded because property was already in the hands of private owners before the system was established or the territory acquired. The Canadian rectangular survey system covers Alberta, British Columbia, Manitoba, Saskatchewan, and northwest Ontario.

The systems have a number of independent points of origin through which pass true meridians of longitude and parallels of latitude, called, respectively, principal meridians and base lines. A principal meridian is a true north-south line that passes through the geographic poles of the earth. A base line is a line that runs east and west parallel to the equator. In the United States, a single principal meridian may serve a portion of a state, an entire state, or a group of states.

Units of land approximately six miles square are established north and south of the base line (only north in Canada) and east and west of the principal meridian (only west in Canada). Each six-mile division north or south is called a township, and each six-mile division east and west is called a range. Each six-mile-square unit is also called a township (figure 3). A township contains approxi-

Figure 3. Rectangular Survey System: Township Illustration

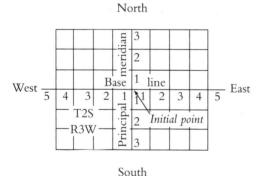

mately thirty-six square miles and is divided into thirty-six sections, each approximately one mile square.

In the United States Public Land Survey System, the sections are numbered consecu-

tively, beginning in the northeast corner of the township and continuing west to the northwest corner, then east, then west, and so on until each of the thirty-six sections is numbered, with section thirty-six in the southeast corner (figure 4). In Canada, the numbering system begins at the southeast corner of the township and ends in the northeast corner.

Figure 4. Section Numbers

6	5	4	3	2	1
7	8	9	10	11	12
18	17	16	15	14	13
19	20	21	22	23	24
30	29	28	27	26	25
31	32	33	34	35	36

Canadian numbering begins here

An ideal section would be one mile square (640 acres). It may be subdivided into quarter sections (160 acres) or quarter–quarter sections (40 acres). However, because the meridians converge toward the poles, it is impossible for townships to be perfectly regular. In addition, surveyors often made mistakes in laying out township and section lines. The discrepancies from either cause are concentrated along the west and north sides

Figure 5. Fractional Lots

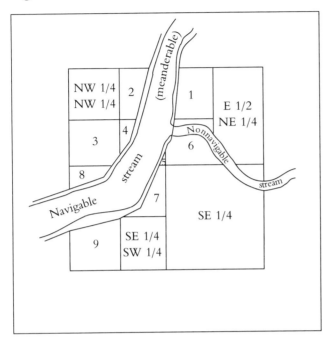

of each township. Quarter–quarter sections that do not have the standard 40 acres are called "fractional lots" or "government lots," whether the irregularity is caused by survey or error, rivers and lakes, Indian reservation boundaries, state lines, or any other reason (figure 5).

The regular subdivision of sections is done by reference to halves and quarters. Although sections may be subdivided into units of 2.5 acres (1/256th of a section), 10-acre units — quarter-quarter-quarter sections — are usually the smallest. In describing land, the smallest unit is given first and the largest last (for example, "the S ½ of the NE ¼ of the NW ¼ of the NW ¼ of Section 14, Township 2 South, Range 3 West"). In locating property, the description is read backwards, from the largest to the smallest unit.

Lot and Block Survey

Small units of land, particularly in urban areas, are commonly described by lot and block survey. This is a map or plat in which a larger parcel of land is subdivided into small units for the purposes of sale. This map is recorded in the office of the recorder of deeds. Although each lot is actually surveyed with a metes and bounds description, conveyances need refer only to the lot, block, and plat book designation. It is not necessary to include the survey bearings and distances in the deed. For example, the deed reference could simply state: "Lot 7, Block 2, Map Book 35, Page 52," or "Lot 10, Cameron's Subdivision" (and then typically the recorder's office and county in which recorded). Figure 6 shows a page from a map book.

Figure 6.   Example of Lot-and-Block Description

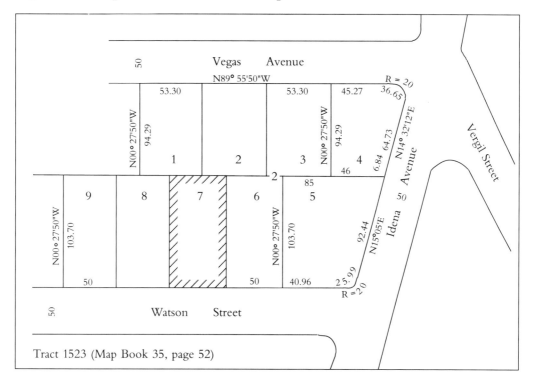

Tract 1523 (Map Book 35, page 52)

Rectangular Coordinates

Most maps are drawn on flat paper, but the earth has a curved surface. When small areas are mapped, the earth is projected on a flat plane. For large areas, however, it is necessary to take the earth's curvature into account. The state plane coordinate system was developed to create a plane grid system of rectangular coordinates expressed in feet. This system was developed during the 1930s by the United States Coast and Geodetic Survey for each of the states. The purpose of this coordinate system is to describe points by the use of perpendicular x and y axes.

As shown in figure 7, a point of origin is located south and west of the area to be covered by the system. Any point can be described by reference to its distance east of the point of origin along the x axis and north of the point of origin along the y axis. The actual location of the point is the intersection of lines drawn perpendicular to the x and y axes.

In the state plane coordinate system, the terms "eastings" and "northings" are used instead of x and y. A parcel of property can be described by giving the coordinates of each corner. It is also possible to convert coordinates to a description with bearings and distances.

Other coordinate systems exist. A familiar one is latitude and longitude. With its reliance on degrees, minutes, and seconds, it can be awkward to use. Another is the Univer-

Figure 7. Description of Land Using State Plane Coordinate System

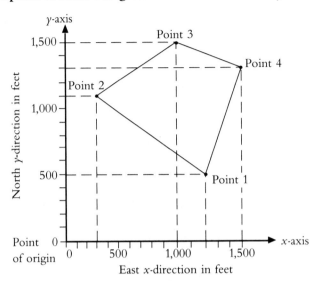

Description by coordinates	Coordinates converted to bearings and distances
Point 1: x = 1,200, y = 500	Point 1 to Point 2: bearing N56° 18'36"W, distance 1,081.66 feet
Point 2: x = 300, y = 1,100	Point 2 to Point 3: bearing N60° 15'18"E, distance 806.22 feet
Point 3: x = 1,000, y = 1,500	Point 3 to Point 4: bearing S68° 11'55"E, distance 538.52 feet
Point 4: x = 1,500, y = 1,300	Point 4 to Point 1: bearing S20° 33'22"W, distance 854.40 feet
Point 1: x = 1,200, y = 500	

sal Transverse Mercator (UTM) grid system. This system has worldwide applicability and relies on the meter for distance measurement. Its usefulness is limited by a grid system that often varies greatly from the four cardinal directions.

Base Maps

Cadastral maps can be compiled without an independently controlled base by matching and assembling field surveys and official records such as Public Land Survey notes and maps, town plan layouts, and subdivision plats. Deed descriptions, if accurate, can be plotted on these maps. However, most cadastral mapping is done either on an aerial photography base or a map base with symbols created from aerial photography. The base provides a physical framework of roads, streams, fences, buildings, and other natural and cultural features on which nonphysical information can be plotted and displayed.

Types of Base Maps

The five general types of mapping bases are aerial photograph enlargement, rectified aerial photograph, orthophotograph, planimetric map, and topographic map.

Aerial Photography A perfectly vertical aerial photograph taken over perfectly level ground with a perfect camera would not have distortions. It would match a map of the area. However, unadjusted aerial photographs are inaccurate due to camera and lens flaws, tilt displacement, and relief displacement. Aerial mapping cameras are periodically checked and calibrated in an effort to minimize mechanical inaccuracies and optical distortion.

Tilt displacement occurs when the aircraft is not flying on a perfectly level path, and the lens is not aiming straight downward at the time of the exposure. As shown in figure 8, the image received on the photo negative is distorted in shape and, therefore, inaccurate in scale. Tilt displacement can be removed through rectification.

Figure 8. Tilt Displacement

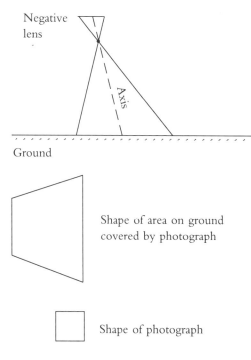

Negative lens

Axis

Ground

Shape of area on ground covered by photograph

Shape of photograph

Relief displacement causes images on aerial photographs to appear at the wrong size and in the wrong place because not all of the land area covered by a photograph is at the same elevation. Features at higher elevations are closer to the aircraft and appear larger. Features at lower elevation appear smaller. Images are also displaced with respect to the point directly below the camera axis at the moment of exposure — objects or topography above the elevation of this point are displaced radially outward, and objects or topography below this point are displaced radially inward, as illustrated in figure 9. The displacement is greater toward the edges of the negative. Relief displacement cannot be removed from a single aerial photograph.

Aerial Photograph Enlargement A simple aerial photograph enlargement is made by projection printing from the negative to a positive at a desired scale. Neither tilt nor relief displacement is removed. The greater the displacement, the more inaccurate the base. Property lines have to be adjusted (either lengthened or shortened) to match the physical features, and area calculations are not correct. Although this base can be obtained relatively quickly and inexpensively (often from existing sources), the lack of accuracy limits its use to the basic need of parcel inventory and on-the-ground location by field appraisers.

Rectified Aerial Photograph A rectified aerial photograph is one in which the tilt displacement in the negative is removed by projecting the photo image onto a plane that adjusts the image to its correct shape. Distortions due to relief displacement, however, cannot be eliminated by the rectification process.

Figure 9. Relief Displacement

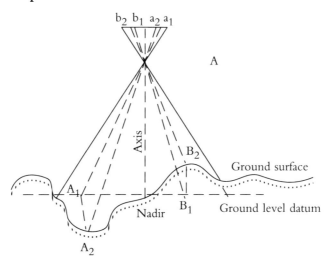

Rectified photography can usually be acquired quickly at moderate cost. Although dimension and area measurements are unreliable, rectified photographs are accurate enough for cadastral mapping in most areas of low to moderate relief. Because relief displacement decreases toward the center of the photograph, mapping-base coverage can be planned so that only the center portion of each photograph is used. The resulting enlargements can also be made to match a geographic grid system (such as the state plane coordinate system or the subdivisions of the United States Public Land Survey System).

Orthophotograph An orthophotograph is a composite product made from overlapping aerial photographs. Thousands of tiny photographs, each of a very small area and each differentially enlarged and rectified, become one image. The orthophotograph appears similar to a standard enlarged or rectified aerial photograph, but because both tilt and relief displacement are eliminated, an orthophotograph is a photograph that comes close to being a map. Property lines plotted on an orthophotograph should match the physical features, because the distance measured by the land surveyor on the ground should "fit" when measured on the photograph. Furthermore, areas calculated from an orthophotograph should be accurate.

The orthophotograph base is particularly useful for cadastral mapping because direct aerial photo interpretation can be used to compile ownership parcels. Orthophotographs are suitable for the creation of a highly accurate mapping system. Although orthophotography is expensive and time-consuming to acquire, it is used in many multiagency base mapping programs. And once the needed computer models have been built, subsequent orthophotographs are less expensive to make.

Planimetric Map A planimetric map is similar to an orthophoto in that it is made from a three-dimensional stereoscopic (stereo) model of overlapping aerial photographs, but it differs in that stereo plotting is used to draw selected lines and symbols on a map. It is thus a "true" map, with no photographic imagery. Standard symbols are used in the creation of the planimetric base. Roads, fences, buildings, tree lines, sidewalks, streams, ditches, utility poles, and any other observable physical features can be transferred from the stereo model to the drawn map. A high level of accuracy can be obtained through this process, and modern analytical plotters can enter digital map information into a computer as they draw lines.

Like the orthophotograph base, the planimetric map is highly accurate, based on a geographic grid system, and suitable for sophisticated multipurpose uses. However, the same disadvantages also exist. The planimetric map base is not usually available from other sources at a proper scale, requires a long time to acquire, and is expensive. Because the planimetric base is a map rather than a photograph, the relative cost is determined primarily by the detail required.

For cadastral mapping, if reliable deed descriptions, plats, and other property line data are available, the planimetric base is suitable. However, if the creation of the maps requires much field work and compilation, in which property lines must be matched to physical features, the orthophotograph base is more useful.

Topographic Map   The topographic map is the most sophisticated base map in general use in the production of cadastral maps. It is essentially a planimetric or orthophoto base with contour lines. Stereo plotting is used to draw lines through points of equal elevation to show relief. In most cadastral mapping systems, contour lines are of little value in determining ownership boundaries (an exception is in mountainous areas with metes and bounds ownership, where ridge crests and streams are often property lines).

Topographic base maps are expensive. They are used primarily for multiagency programs, in which contours are essential for engineering and zoning purposes, such as water and sewer line planning, street and highway development, and land use management.

Map Scale

Map scale is the relationship of linear distance on the map to linear distance on the ground. Scale can be given as a comparison of units on the map to units on the ground (such as $1'' = 400'$). A common international method of presenting map scale is to use a dimensionless ratio or representative fraction in which one unit of any type of measurement system on the map represents so many of the same units on the ground. For example, 1:24,000 or 1/24,000 means that one inch on the map equals 24,000 inches on the ground (this would be the same scale as $1'' = 2,000'$). A graphic scale, also called a bar or line scale, is an illustration drawn on a map showing graduated units of length. The graphic scale is visually effective and has the advantage that if the map is reduced or enlarged photographically, the scale will not be lost. Most maps have a graphic scale and one of the other scales.

The appropriate scale for a base map depends on parcel density (which in turn depends on typical parcel size) and the amount of information to be shown in each mapped parcel. The usual scales for cadastral mapping are the following:

1″ = 400′, which is used for rural areas in which most parcels are greater than one acre and may be several hundred acres. Small lots that are isolated or in small clusters can be shown on this scale.

1″ = 200′, which is used in suburban areas, small towns with few small lots, and subdivisions with frontages of 100 feet or more.

1″ = 100′, which is used in urban areas where the usual lot frontage is at least 50 feet and detailed information is not required.

1″ = 50′, which is used in congested urban areas with small lots.

Other scales are also used. In areas with very large parcels (such as ranches and government land), scales of 1″ = 800′, 1″ = 1,000′, or 1″ = 2,000′ are appropriate. Standard aerial photography scales available from the United States Department of Agriculture for aerial photograph enlargements and rectified aerial photographs are 1″ = 1,320′, 1″ = 660′, and 1″ = 330′.

Coverage

The coverage of individual map sheets in the mapping base is usually planned to match the subdivisions of the United States Public Land Survey System or the coordinates of the state plane coordinate system. The dimensions of the map sheet depend on the area covered by each sheet and the scale of the map. For example, a one-mile-square standard section of the Public Land Survey System is 5,280 feet on each side. At a map scale of 1″ = 400′, each side of the section measures 13.2 inches. Because this would be a very small map

sheet, four sections are usually mapped on one sheet. The actual "mapped" area is 26.4 inches on each side. Depending on the amount of marginal information, the sheet size is 30 inches by 30 inches or 30 inches by 36 inches. At a scale of 1″ = 200′, one section fits on the same sheet size, and at a scale of 1″ = 100′ a quarter section fits.

Similar procedures are followed to plan the coverage format for jurisdictions not in the Public Land Survey, by using arbitrarily defined units of the state plane coordinate grid system.

The areas covered by each map scale can be mutually exclusive. However, it is common to use larger scale insert, detail, or enlargement maps to cover small towns or rural subdivisions located within the basic small-scale coverage areas.

Parcel Identification Systems

Modern mapping systems identify each separate parcel of property by a numeric or alphanumeric code. In addition to locating the parcels on the maps, parcel identifiers are used in ownership and assessment records (both manually and electronically maintained) in lieu of often lengthy and confusing legal descriptions.

There is no single correct definition of a parcel. Every unit of land having a separate legal description, whether one subdivision lot or a single metes and bounds tract in a deed with many tracts, may be considered a parcel. The other extreme is to consider all contiguous land under the same ownership as a parcel. Most jurisdictions take a position in between. For cadastral mapping, a parcel need only be defined as a describable and mappable unit of land that is capable of being separately assessed.

Parcel Identification Standards

Parcel identifiers are evaluated in terms of four standards: uniqueness, permanency, simplicity, and uniformity. These are sometimes incompatible and must be balanced against one another.

Uniqueness An identifier must identify one specific parcel, and each parcel should have no more than one identifier. This, the most important standard, must be followed if the parcel identification system is to work properly.

Permanency An identifier should change only when the boundaries of the parcel change, that is, when the parcel is either split (divided and a part sold) or combined with an adjacent parcel or parcels. The identifier should never change when a simple transfer of ownership (complete sale with no modification of property boundary lines) occurs. The identifier refers to the land, not the owner.

Simplicity The identifier should not contain an excessive number of digits, segments, or elements. It should be relatively easy to generate and easy to understand without special knowledge.

Uniformity The identification system should be applicable throughout a state, province, or country. Patterns of land ownership, methods of property conveyance, and legal provisions relating to land ownership and property assessment should be considered. Electronic data processing should be anticipated, even if some jurisdictions are using manual methods.

Types of Parcel Identification Systems

The parcel identification systems currently used in cadastral mapping are map-base, government survey, and geographic coordinate code.

In metes and bounds areas where parcels tend to be irregular in shape and are individually described and bounded, map-based parcel identification is usually used. Identifiers have no reference to their parcels' legal descriptions. The first component of a map-based parcel identifier is the map sheet designation. Then, depending primarily on the scale of the map and the number of parcels, there may also be a block or group identifier (used on most urban maps). The last unit is the basic parcel identifier, to which a change suffix is added if needed. This system is illustrated in figure 10. In some jurisdictions, the maps are bound in a book, with individual maps as the pages. This variation is called the map book–page system.

Identification systems based on a government survey (such as the United States Public Land Survey System) either use the existing legal identifiers or assign arbitrary numerical identifiers to each unit such as township, section, quarter section, and sometimes quarter–quarter section. Additional numbers are assigned as needed to define further the division of this system into blocks and parcels. Parcel identifiers are at least partially consistent with the legal descriptions because the method of land conveyance and ownership is also the basis for the identification system. This system is illustrated in figure 11.

Geographic coordinate, or geocode, parcel identification systems have been developed for computerized land information

Figure 10. Examples of Map-Based Parcel Identification System

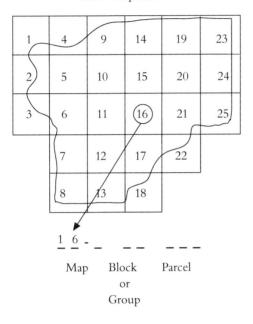

Basic Component

The map sheet is the basic component. In this example, the sheets (scale of 1" = 400') are arbitrarily numbered consecutively north to south beginning in the northwest corner of the jurisdiction.

| 1 6 _   _ _   _ _   _ _ _ |
| Map   Block   Parcel |
| or |
| Group |

Rural System

M2P.16

In rural areas, the second component used is the parcel identifier. Note that the map suffix and the block identifier are not used. Parcels are assigned consecutive numbers throughout the entire map sheet.

1 6 _ 0   0 0   0 1 4

Figure 10. Examples of Map-Based Parcel Identification System (cont.)

Urban System

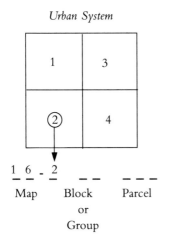

In urban or congested areas, the second component is an enlargement map. In this example, the enlargement maps (scale of 1" = 200') are designated as suffixes of the basic (rural) map sheet.

Map 16-2

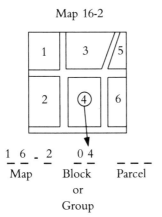

In urban areas, the third component is the block number. A block or group is one or more contiguous parcels completely surrounded by roads, streams, railroads, or the margin of the map.

Block 4

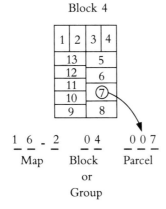

In urban areas, the fourth component is the parcel identifier, assigned consecutively within each block.

Figure 11. Example of Government Survey Parcel Identification System

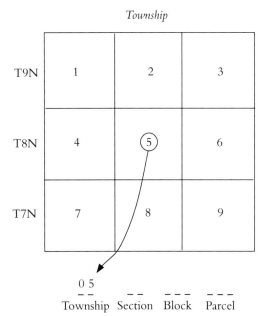

Township

The township is the basic component. In this example, all townships within the jurisdiction are assigned arbitrary consecutive numbers from west to east. An alternative approach would be to use tier and range directly, such as:

$$\underline{0\ 8} \qquad \underline{1\ 4}$$
$$\text{Tier} \qquad \text{Range}$$

Section
Township 5

6	5	4	3	2	1
7	8	9	10	11	12
18	17	16	15	14	13
19	20	21	22	23	24
30	29	28	27	26	25
31	32	33	34	35	36

The section number is the second component.

0 5   2 7
-- --   -- --   --- ---   --- ---
Township Section   Block   Parcel

Figure 11. Example of Government Survey Parcel Identification System (cont.)

Block

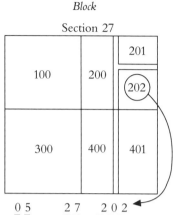

Section 27

The block designation is the third component. In this example, the NW 1/4 is assigned 100–199, the NE 1/4, 200–299, the SW 1/4, 300–399, and the SE 1/4, 400–499.

0 5   2 7   2 0 2 _ _ _
Township Section Block Parcel

Parcel

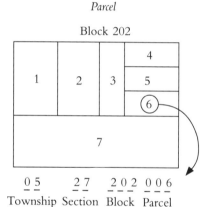

Block 202

The fourth component is the parcel designation. In rural areas, it is common for an entire 1/4 section to be under one ownership. If so, the parcel number is always 001. For example, if the SW 1/4 of Section 27 above is one parcel, the designation would be <u>05</u> <u>27</u> <u>300</u> <u>001</u>.

0 5   2 7   2 0 2   0 0 6
Township Section Block Parcel

systems. Each identifier is referenced to a coordinate system and can therefore be automatically located and retrieved. Geocode parcel identification systems are usually based on state plane coordinates.

The coordinate of a geocode parcel identifier is composed of an x, or east-west, designation and a y, or north-south, designation. The location of each single point is thus defined. Although the exact center of a parcel can be determined by computer, the identification point for each parcel is usually the approximate center, or *paracentroid*, of the parcel. Any other consistently selected point (such as the front center) may be used. This system is illustrated in figure 12.

Uses for Parcel Identifiers

The parcel identification system should be convenient for both office and field work. For the office, identifiers should be logically arranged for manual and automated process-

Figure 12.   Example of Geographic Coordinate Code Parcel Identification System

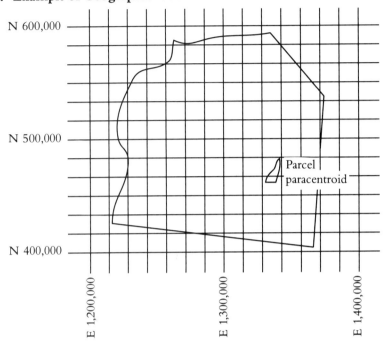

The entire jurisdiction is covered by a continuous grid system. The geocode of the paracentroid (visual center) of the example parcel above is 1,340,000 feet east and 482,416 feet north. This may be written as:

$$\underline{1\ 3\ 4\ 0\ 0\ 0\ 0} \ - \ \underline{0\ 4\ 8\ 2\ 4\ 1\ 6}$$
$$\text{Easting} \qquad\qquad \text{Northing}$$

ing. Data collected at different times and for different purposes should be linked to the correct parcels. The parcel identifier is the link among records of ownership, appraisal, assessment, and tax billing and collection. Identifiers should also be suitable for statistical sampling in studies of assessment quality.

In the field, the system should provide a means of finding parcels readily and efficiently. The system may be a routing-based system (best for door-to-door appraisal purposes) or a purely locational system in which

Alternatively, it may be written as:

$$\frac{10}{\text{EN}} \quad \frac{34}{\text{EN}} \quad \frac{48}{\text{EN}} \quad \frac{02}{\text{EN}} \quad \frac{04}{\text{EN}} \quad \frac{01}{\text{EN}} \quad \frac{06}{\text{EN}}$$

Note: The number of digits could be shortened by identifying the paracentroid to the nearest ten feet.

adjacent parcels are logically, but not consecutively, numbered. The geocode system is least practical for some field applications.

The system should provide for the identification, and possible selection, of all parcels within a certain area (such as the units of the Public Land Survey) or on a specific map or block. The exact location of each parcel is contained in the identifier alone only in the geocode system and, for certain large parcels in the government survey system, where a standard unit area coincides with the parcel identifier. In other systems, the map must be examined to determine the exact location of each parcel.

More than one parcel identifier can be used. Computerized mapping systems can keep track of several identifiers for a parcel; the only cost is in time spent assigning and maintaining more than one number for the same parcel.

Special-Interest Identification

Special-interest identification can be added by using prefixes and suffixes. For example, a county number prefix is often used in state-mandated identification systems, which means that every parcel identifier in the entire state is unique. Prefixes and suffixes are also used to identify taxing district, property classification, land use, city codes, taxable status, partial interests (such as mineral and timber), and leasehold improvements (such as condominiums and mobile homes). These codes add length and complexity to the identifier.

Parcel Identifier Maintenance

A good identification system allows for routine changes. The need to change an identifier arises when a portion of a parcel is conveyed, a parcel is combined with one or more adjacent parcels, or map revision is necessary. Maintenance is easier when the identifiers are simple. In areas experiencing rapid growth, parcels need not be renumbered unless their boundaries change.

One critical issue is how to assign numbers when parcels are divided (split). In the geocode system, split parcels are identified by their coordinates, like all other parcels; consequently, splits are not recognizable from their identifiers. In the other systems,

numeric or alphabetic suffixes (usually following a decimal or hyphen) are assigned to splits. The original identifier may be retired or retained. The reason for retiring is that the boundaries have changed, and the original parcel no longer exists (this supports the uniqueness standard). If retained, the identifier is usually assigned to the grantor if part of the parcel is not sold, to the portion containing the major improvements, or to the largest portion. An alternative method is to assign the next highest unused whole parcel number to the new parcel. This method soon results in scattering nonconsecutive parcel identifiers throughout the map. When large parcels are split into regular subdivisions, preassigned (but unused) identifiers in the government survey system can be used for each of the split parcels. For example, if a section is split into one half-section and two quarter-sections, the three new parcels can be assigned standard locational identifiers. These identifiers would have been used if the three parcels had been in existence at the time of the original mapping project.

Combinations in the geocode system are handled in the same manner as splits: the coordinates of the newly combined parcel are determined and the old parcel identifiers retired. However, unless deliberately avoided, the geocode of the new parcel may be the same as the geocode of one of the old parcels (if their center points are the same). In the other systems, the identifier of one parcel (usually the largest or the one previously owned by the grantee) is often retained and the others retired. Alternatively, the identifiers of all combined parcels may be retired and a new identifier assigned, as for a split.

The development of subdivisions or map congestion resulting from splitting of parcels may require the creation of an enlargement map. The parcels removed from the smaller scale original map and placed on the enlargement are identified as if they had been in existence during the initial mapping of the jurisdiction. Reassignment of parcel identifiers is also usually done if a major remapping program is undertaken in which map coverage and scales are changed.

The Use of Computers in Mapping

The computerization of maps and mapping records increases their value in the assessment process. In addition to meeting the basic functions of real property location, identification, and inventory, a computerized mapping system can be an analytical tool in property appraisal and an efficient means of organizing, displaying, and using spatially oriented data in assessment administration. Productivity can be improved. Instead of being restricted to a series of individual map sheets, often at a variety of scales, with a limited amount of display information (thus requiring the manual retrieval and correlation of pertinent data stored in filing cabinets), the mapping system can be a continuous spatial data base covering the entire jurisdiction and virtually unlimited in its ability to display spatial information and retrieve vast amounts of nonspatial attribute data relating to the parcels. Maps can be printed or plotted in various formats at any desired scale and can display only selected information.

Computerizing a mapping system provides an opportunity to improve quality by eliminating inconsistent symbols and standards. Also, errors due to mismatches between adjacent map sheets or different scale coverages can be corrected. Maps at different scales can be computerized and then overlaid and analyzed in direct relationship with one another. With a continuous data base linked to attribute data for each parcel, property omitted from the tax roll can be identified and double assessments eliminated.

Computerized Mapping Systems

Most computerized mapping systems can be categorized as computer-assisted drafting systems, automated mapping/facilities management systems, or geographic information systems. All three require a base grid with x-y coordinates (such as the state plane coordinate system) and permit the mapping of cartographic features as points, lines, and polygons. Overlapping map layers, each containing a specific kind of information, are used in all three. All offer the ability to change scale, update maps readily, print or plot maps as needed, and display and store text (such as names, labels, dimensions, and other labelling data).

Computer-assisted drafting (CAD) systems are suitable for traditional mapping functions. They provide the same kind of map as a manually produced and manually drafted map but are made and maintained electronically. They are usually created by digitizing or scanning a manually prepared map or entering metes and bounds legal descriptions.

Automated mapping/facilities management (AM/FM) systems differ from CAD systems in that they feature sophisticated data bases capable of storing and manipulating related attribute information; however, because they were developed primarily for utilities, they best serve networking functions and are limited in their ability to analyze relationships between different layers other than through visual inspection (overlapping of layers).

Geographic information systems (GISs) were developed for spatial analysis needs such as planning, natural resources, and land records management. GISs can completely integrate spatial data and attribute data among different layers. The GIS approach is ideal for multipurpose users. Many such systems are used by, but not managed by, the assessment office. Instead, a county or regional office may be responsible for management of the mapping system. A wide range of GIS options is available, from microcomputer to mainframe.

Each layer in the GIS can be compared to a single map overlay, as illustrated in figure 13. The geodetic survey control is usually the first layer, and a grid reference system, such as the state plane coordinate system, is usually the second. Additional base map information, such as the transportation network and other planimetric features, could be next. Further layers could be sewers, zoning, utilities, land use, soil types, topography, property lines, geologic structure, political boundaries, communication networks, streams and bodies of water, and so on. Attribute information relating to each of these layers is also stored and available for manipulation and analysis.

Different layers can be compared, and additional layers and related new data can be generated. For example, the assessment office could create a new map layer by combining the property line, political boundary, and zoning layers. Then the system could select all parcels between one and five acres zoned single-family residential that are in a certain school district but outside the city limits. Accessing the attribute data files could further refine this by asking, for example, for those nonvacant parcels meeting the above criteria in which the houses are less than twenty years old, have more than 2,000 square feet, and are assessed at less than $100,000. An output map could be printed or plotted with the selected parcels shown by color code or symbols. Specific information on each parcel could also be printed out.

Mapping Data Input

Data for a computerized mapping program have traditionally been entered by *digitizing*, moving a cursor across a sensitized surface that generates x-y coordinates either as the cursor is activated or continuously. This produces a data base composed of points, lines, and polygons.

Keyboard data entry is used to enter attribute information and to create names, labels, dimensions, and other mapping data. The keyboard can also be used to enter mapping data such as bearings and distances through coordinate geometry (COGO).

Image scanning can be used to "read" both text and line work into the data base. Image scanning requires a very clean input document, or the time and effort required to edit the maps can outweigh the advantages. Other kinds of data entry include photogrammetric or satellite imagery interfacing and the loading of digital data obtained on magnetic tape from other sources.

Assessment Applications

The computerized linkage of assessment records and parcel maps makes it easier to

Figure 13.   Multiple Layers in a Geographic Information System

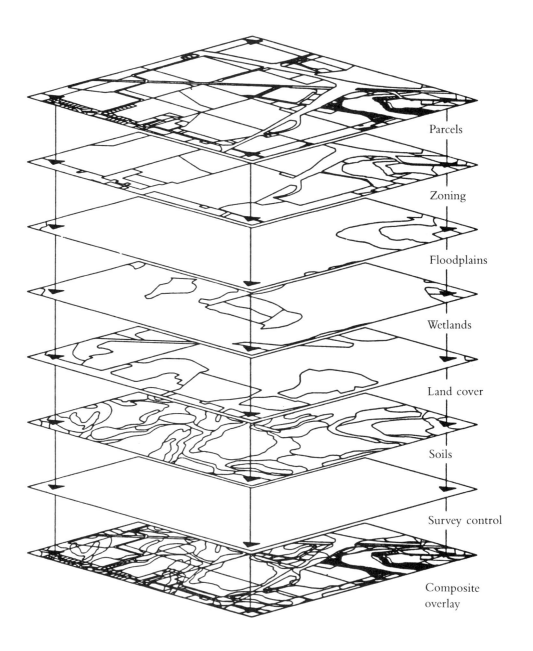

Parcels

Zoning

Floodplains

Wetlands

Land cover

Soils

Survey control

Composite
overlay

keep records of assessment activity. For example, staff can develop a routing plan for field inspection, identify improvements lacking information on characteristics such as square footage, or create a map that shows which parcels have not been physically inspected within a specified time.

The system can be used for administrative purposes such as analyzing property characteristics and assessed values to pinpoint underassessed parcels. It can be used to sort by various characteristics for appraisal purposes. Neighborhoods can be defined and neighborhood analysis conducted. Sophisticated spatial research can be used in sales ratio studies. By using information from other data bases (such as zoning; soils; flood plains; airport "nuisance" zones; school districts; political jurisdictions; and other physical, social, governmental, and economic divisions) with a GIS, it is possible to develop highly sophisticated CAMA models (see the discussion of value influence centers and location value response surface analysis in chapter 15). It is also possible to add distance analysis to the models by including such variables as distance to work, schools, shopping, churches, recreation, and other attractive and unattractive features.

Many assessors prefer a photo-based map to a planimetric map. Computerized mapping systems produce planimetric maps; however, they can be plotted on a polyester base which can then be run through a diazo machine with an aerial photograph to produce a combination photomap for field use. This technique offers the advantages of obtaining new photography of growth areas as needed and using available photography at various scales, because the scale and coverage area of the maps can be easily changed.

Multiuser Systems

In a computerized mapping system, the base map layers link all users. The assessment office may be responsible for maintenance of the parcel map, or property line, layers, but shares parcel data with the recorder's office. The computerized system makes it possible to ensure that all parcel splits and deed descriptions filed are accurate and mappable before the recorder accepts them; no erroneous descriptions would then be received by the assessor. Attribute and ownership information may also be shared between assessor and recorder.

The parcel records can also be used by the collector's office. Analysis of the attribute data on property tax delinquency makes it possible to produce a map for the collector's use in locating parcels with delinquent taxes. This map might then be used for routing purposes to serve notices on delinquent owners.

The assessment office can also be linked to other governmental agencies and offices to further mutual interests. For example, the assessment of farmland requires detailed information on soil type, drainage, land cover, and land use. The assessment of mineral resources or coal seams can be done through linkage with the agencies maintaining geologic and natural resource information. Cooperation between assessors and planning and zoning offices can facilitate acquisition of information on new structures, the demolition of old structures, and changes in land use and zoning.

In a multiuser system, duplication of effort in updating records is reduced. For example, if the highway engineer's office changes road right-of-way widths in one layer, the system can adjust parcel boundaries, areas, and the accompanying property assessment records.

A multiuser system requires careful coordination and management. For example, limits may be put on the right to modify data, by restricting users to inquiry access only for certain information. Modifications to the base map layers affect all users.

Mapping System Maintenance

Because real property is constantly changing ownership, mapping system management needs an organized maintenance program. Ownership records are updated to identify the current legal owner, and boundary changes are made to show the current parcel configuration and size. A mapping system should become more accurate and complete as surveys correct errors made in the original mapping. If maps are not properly maintained, the original investment in the mapping program is lost, and an expensive and time-consuming remapping program will eventually be necessary. An organized maintenance program includes two types of maintenance, systematic and general.

Systematic Maintenance

Systematic maintenance is the making of ownership and property line changes as a result of official documents such as deeds, wills, plats, and surveys. All official documents affecting the ownership of real property are obtained by the assessment office from the office of the recorder and other sources. In a complete transfer, a transfer of an entire parcel from one owner to another, the information found on the transfer document is reviewed to ensure that the parcel is correctly identified. The document is also reviewed to ensure that the parcel, as described, was correctly mapped in the original mapping program or a previous update. A current survey, or resurvey, may be used to correct property lines and improve the accuracy and quality of the original maps. A comparison is also made between the deeded acreage and the mapped, or calculated, acreage. In case of a discrepancy, the assessor should value the property according to the mapped, or calculated, acreage unless local statutes require deeded acreage to be used instead. The property owner should be informed of any significant discrepancy. The accompanying ownership records are also updated to reflect changes in owners' names and addresses, recording information, and other data.

In splits, sales of property resulting in the creation of one or more "new" parcels, the split parcel is plotted, the acreage or dimensions are determined, and a parcel identification number is assigned to the new parcel. The original parcel is changed to reflect property line and size changes. Improvements must be assigned to the correct parcels. Then new ownership records are created for the new parcel and the records for the original parcel are adjusted to reflect the changes.

Cooperation between the assessment office and the recorder's office is necessary to ensure that all transfer documents are received. This is a statutory requirement in some jurisdictions; in others, an arrangement should be made between the offices. Figure 14 shows a maintenance log used to account for the documents received by the assessment office and to show the action taken.

Figure 14. Maintenance Logs

Metes and Bounds

Book	Page	Grantor	Grantee	District	Size	Map—Group Parcel	Date worked	By	Comments

Rectangular Survey System

Volume	Page	Grantor	Grantee	Legal description	Identification number	Date worked	By	Comments

General Maintenance

Mapping systems are corrected and updated for reasons other than ownership changes. New streets and highways are constructed, and the names and right-of-way widths may be changed. Occasionally, roads are vacated. City limit lines are often changed due to annexation. If multiple taxing jurisdictions are the responsibility of the assessment office, boundary changes must be monitored. Natural features, such as wooded areas, lakes, and streams, are subject to physical change. Many mapping systems maintain the location of buildings, which requires updating to reflect the construction of new buildings and the destruction of old ones. If the map updating through general maintenance affects parcel boundaries, acreage should be recalculated and new dimensions determined. As in systematic maintenance, ownership records are updated and corrected to reflect all changes.

Field Checks

Occasionally, maintenance changes cannot be completed in the office due to inadequate information. One solution is field research — visiting the property and interviewing the grantee or grantor (or some other knowledgeable informant). Field research is particularly helpful in areas with old metes and bounds surveys.

In talking with an owner about property lines, the mapper should start by asking for information and discussing the problem rather than by stating a position. Showing a map to a property owner at an interview may be confusing. Notes from an interview can help resolve boundary line problems in the office. Maps can then be produced, and any changes explained to the owner.

The field researcher should study all available data before going to the field but should not develop preconceived ideas. Not all ownership discrepancies can be resolved. In the case of overlapping claims, the property owners should be informed, as it is their right to take appropriate legal action. If parcels are found that lack identifiable owners, the procedures prescribed by statute should be followed. Cadastral maps are intended for property identification and inventory, not to resolve legal disputes over ownership.

Summary

A complete and accurate set of maps is essential for the location, identification, and inventory of all parcels in a jurisdiction. Assessment offices with good mapping systems are an important public resource. Offices that have taken advantage of computer technology for managing maps and assessment information can be an especially important resource for other public agencies. Cooperation among these agencies to create geographic information systems or land information systems can lead to efficient use of mapping information for a variety of purposes.

Revaluation Planning 18

Statutory and Other Considerations

If most property has not been reappraised recently, a revaluation should substantially improve tax equity and appraisal performance. This chapter examines revaluation planning issues, including motives, objectives, timing and frequency, and management strategies.

Revaluation is the process of estimating new values based on specific rules and current data. The rules may be laws, court decisions, or standards of practice; data include sales, replacement costs, neighborhood trends, and current use. If the rules or data change, values may become obsolete or inaccurate.

Revaluation can take more than one form. In jurisdictions that keep values current, revaluation is a routine part of an annual cycle. Where a full value-update is not performed annually or is simply a matter of applying local trend indexes to classes of property, a full revaluation becomes more significant, because it involves the collection and verification of property characteristics and the estimation of a new value for each property in the jurisdiction.

A computer-assisted mass appraisal (CAMA) system installed for a revaluation will provide a foundation for more regular and economical value updates in the future.

The CAMA system may require conversion of the entire data base to a new format or, if the current data are inadequate, may require a full field data collection effort (see chapter 5) and adoption of a new valuation method.

Local jurisdictions are sometimes reluctant to do a revaluation because the resulting tax shifts will have political repercussions. At times, a revaluation program is begun but not completed because of poor planning and lack of broad-based support. The success of a revaluation depends on the assessor's ability to educate other public officials and the public concerning the revaluation and to appraise properties equitably and in accordance with statutes.

Statutory Considerations

Assessors' responsibilities are defined by law. Statutes usually prescribe the level and frequency of reappraisal, property classifications and exemptions, and the mechanics of the assessment and taxation process. The process includes hearing taxpayer appeals and the role of a tax commission or other oversight agency to equalize values across jurisdictions.

Many statutes require that equity or uniformity in appraisal be established annually. In some cases, this requirement is closely followed. In other cases, it is ignored.

Recently in the United States, statewide uniformity of appraisals has become crucial to the states' ability to distribute school aid fairly. Many states now mandate uniform assessments not only within a jurisdiction but also throughout the state. A number of states have mandated either annual reappraisal or cyclical reappraisal programs that include both up-to-date values and periodic visits to every property. Chapter 13 discusses alternative mass appraisal cycles that are consistent with the IAAO's standards.

In a few states, revaluations are mandated if the appraisal level falls below minimum requirements (for example, 80 or 90 percent of current value). The state oversight agency has the authority to order a reappraisal; if the jurisdiction fails to comply, the state can withhold some or all of the state aid to local education.

Other Motivations

The basic motivation for revaluation is equity. Appraisal inequities can hurt a community, and a well-conducted revaluation can correct them.

When a property is overappraised, its owners will be paying more than their fair share of taxes. Where there is a significant overappraisal, taxpayers are likely to complain. If the assessor fails to grant a value reduction, taxpayers may appeal to the board of review and, if still not satisfied, to court. Appeals are time-consuming and expensive for both taxpayers and the community and can burden the assessment office, the board of review, and even the courts. Larger commercial properties are usually well represented and can afford to take their grievances as far as necessary to get a reduction. Dissatisfied taxpayers may seek to put someone in office who will tackle the task of equalization.

Underappraisals contribute to a lower tax base, causing the community to set higher tax rates and reducing its ability to issue bonds. Underappraisals also weaken an assessor's defense of overall values, permitting taxpayers to cite properties similar to theirs that are assessed at substantially lower ratios. Recognition by assessors of their responsibilities to the public and of the problems associated with poor appraisals are strong motivating factors for conducting a revaluation. Modern CAMA systems installed at the time of a revaluation provide an opportunity to improve appraisal accuracy and control long-term costs.

Technical Requirements
Scope of the Project

The nature of a revaluation project will depend on the present state of the assessor's records and values, the time available to conduct the revaluation, budget, long-range goals and plans, availability and capabilities of permanent staff, recruitment and hiring requirements, and statutory requirements.

The budget should not keep the assessor from putting forth a good technical plan. The assessor may need to educate the jurisdiction about its needs. Revaluation projects are often undertaken without well-defined goals. Goal setting may be difficult, but it focuses the jurisdiction's leadership on the real needs of the community and provides a framework for technical and managerial decisions.

If values are to be updated regularly and frequently, a CAMA system is essential. Installing a CAMA system at the time of a revaluation may make the most sense because the cost can often be included in the program, and the jurisdiction will begin to realize benefits immediately. If future updates are a long way off, a CAMA system may be hard to justify. The current need may merely be to bring the assessment records up-to-date. The jurisdiction also needs to determine whether future updates will be done in house or contracted out. One goal of a revaluation program may be to become self-sufficient.

The technical and managerial abilities of permanent staff influence the course of a revaluation project. Can staff be added in time for the project? Does the addition of new permanent staff fit with the long-term goals of the office? Can existing staff manage the work of temporary staff hired to do revaluation work? In many jurisdictions there are hiring restrictions and difficult administrative hurdles to overcome before positions can be approved and competent people hired to meet the technical requirements of a revaluation. The jurisdiction should begin work on filling key positions well before the revaluation.

A court order or a mandate to have the revaluation done by a particular date leaves very little flexibility. The court order may even require completion by a specific date regardless of cost. Reappraisals are sometimes monitored by an oversight agency. Those that do not meet requirements are ordered redone at the jurisdiction's expense. Mailing of tax bills may be delayed until the new values are completed, and borrowing money for several months can be expensive. Delays also hurt other taxing authorities that receive funds from the property tax. Some statutes require that the property be physically reviewed in the field periodically, for example, every third, fourth, or fifth year.

All of these issues determine the assessor's approach to the revaluation program. Beyond these, the technical requirements to be considered are data verification or collection and valuation.

Data Verification or Collection

In designing the data collection effort, the requirements of the CAMA system and the availability of existing information should be considered. If the data are not adequate for valuation, additional data elements should be collected. If the data are inaccurate, coding procedures should be modified to ensure more consistent collection and maintenance of the data in the future.

Time and money affect decisions about data collection. A large jurisdiction with a statutory completion date to be met in fifteen to eighteen months will probably not be able to conduct a full-fledged, in-house data collection and reappraisal effort. Nor will outside reappraisal services be an option unless the groundwork has been laid. The jurisdiction will have to make the best use of existing data through *review by exception*, the process of checking data for reasonableness and consistency. Only properties that fail these data checks are field reviewed. This has worked well in several jurisdictions when combined with a property data inventory mailer program. Data mailers combined with phone and field checks to verify information on the returns can significantly improve the quality of the data base.

Public tolerance of the use of existing data may be low if the level of taxes demands a high level of accuracy. That is, if the effective tax rate is 5 percent, an error that has a 10 percent effect on value would translate into an error of $500 on a $100,000 property; in a jurisdiction for which the effective tax rate is 1 percent, on the other hand, the error would be $100.

Sometimes taxpayers may not be receptive to site inspections, for example, in depressed or crime-ridden areas. Good public information programs can help, but the assessor should recognize people's fears and have alternatives for dealing with them. Laws sometimes allow a recourse to the assessor who has been refused entry or access. For example, the assessor may send the owner a certified letter requesting permission to inspect the property. If permission is refused, the assessor can estimate the property characteristics and the value, and the taxpayer loses any legal right to appeal the valuation and the assessment based on the valuation.

Some jurisdictions rely on self-reporting of property changes. One county monitors building permits obtained from the municipalities within its borders. After the final building inspection, the county mails a letter to the property owner requesting a sketch and description of improvements if they were under $40,000. If they are more than $40,000, an appraiser is sent to obtain the data in the field.

Chapter 5 discusses data collection in more detail.

Valuation Options

In undertaking revaluations, assessors must first know how they plan to value property. This decision is implicit in further decisions such as what information will be collected and what features will be required in a CAMA system.

The three approaches to value are not all applicable to every property. The cost and sales comparison approaches are usually applied to residential property. For commercial properties—stores, apartments, office buildings, and so forth—the income approach is usually the most appropriate (the sales comparison approach is preferred for defending appeals).

Most jurisdictions of even a moderate size can afford to computerize valuation. Smaller jurisdictions may elect to computerize only the valuation of residential property, which often represents 90–95 per cent of improvements. Larger jurisdictions should computerize valuation on all properties, particularly if they will update values annually or biennially.

Sales Comparison Approach   Residential improved property, including single-family detached dwellings, condominiums, and possibly apartment properties, usually changes ownership often enough to provide a good statistical base for the sales comparison approach. Some jurisdictions with good sales data develop sales comparison models manually. Appraisers analyze the sales from a subdivision or neighborhood, extracting typical per-square-foot values for living area, garages, and various additions and other features.

Usually, however, the sales comparison approach takes the form of developing a valuation model using multiple regression analysis (MRA) or other techniques such as the adaptive estimation procedure (AEP, or feedback) to calibrate (estimate the coefficients for) the model. Often the model is combined with a comparable sales program which identifies comparable sales for a subject property and adjusts the sales for differences in property characteristics.

The sales comparison approach may not be applicable where there is little market activity (for example, in smaller jurisdictions, in depressed areas with few sales, or for property classes with sparse sales data). A lack of confirmed sales information, because property owners are not required to disclose it, may also restrict use of the sales comparison approach.

The Cost Approach The cost approach can be applied to all improved properties by developing a replacement cost new (RCN) for the structures; applying adjustments for age, condition, desirability, and utility; and adding a market-derived land value. Vacant land sales can provide a direct estimate of the land value for improved parcels. In areas where there are few or no vacant land parcels, however, the appraiser depends on extraction of land values from the sales prices of similarly improved parcels. In such areas, however, the sales comparison approach is often best because it does not rely on separate estimates of land and improvement values.

In some places, a cost manual provided by an oversight agency must be used to determine value; in other places, the manuals serve as guides to assessors.

Good appraisal manuals are also available from sources such as Marshall and Swift, Boeckh, and R. S. Means and from several mass appraisal firms. Most residential cost manuals are developed using a basic cost model representative of the particular region of the country in which the publisher is based. Components and adjustments reflect the relative costs of construction for that region. Indexes are usually provided for adjusting overall construction costs to other regions.

In practice, however, the cost components themselves are not adjusted. As a result, there are differences between the detailed costs in each manual, although the manuals usually give similar values for the complete building. Proper application of cost manuals requires that data be collected in a prescribed format and that classifications of property as to building class, construction type, and so forth conform to the specifications of the particular manual. As a result, the proper manual should be carefully selected before data requirements, data collection forms, and CAMA system specifications are completed. A poor choice cannot easily be corrected after the project is under way.

Values are often computed manually in small jurisdictions. Inexpensive personal computers, however, make computerization cost effective, even for very small jurisdictions. Manual computation involves using a cost manual to look up rates or costs and a calculator to apply the rates to structure areas and sum component costs into a value. Some or all of the computations may be recorded on a property record to be available for explaining to the taxpayer how the value was determined.

Computerized cost manuals are an essential feature of a CAMA system. The computerized cost manual usually determines what information will be collected and the format for collection. The two basic types of computerized cost procedures are table-driven and formula-driven. In the table-driven approach, all tables and other pricing schedules in the appraisal manual are loaded into the computer exactly as they appear in the manual. The logic for calculating values is programmed into the computer, including the methods for looking up values in tables, interpolating if necessary, rounding the results, and totaling various component

Figure 1. Dwelling Pricing Schedule and Sample Valuation

This dwelling pricing schedule contains square-foot rates that are a function of size. The rates are listed for the nearest 100 square feet.

Square feet	Rates
1,200	$32.90
1,300	31.80
1,400	30.90
1,500	30.00
1,600	29.30
1,700	28.50
1,800	27.80

If the standard procedure is to look up the rate for the area nearest to the area of the subject property, the value for a 1,540-square-foot dwelling is calculated as $46,200; the value for a 1,560-square-foot dwelling (20 square feet larger) is calculated as $45,708, almost $500 (and more than one percent) less.

values. This approach is necessarily designed around a particular manual. It can be expensive, may require more computer resources than a formula-driven procedure, and often carries forward inconsistencies that are part of a manual designed for ease of manual computations. Figure 1, for example, illustrates the value inconsistencies that can result from rounding and failure to interpolate in applying cost factors.

In a formula-driven procedure, cost tables are replaced by formulas that reflect the underlying cost equation used to generate the tables or, if the tables were manually developed, an equation extracted from the tables. Often the estimates of value are better because the irregularities that might be found in a manual cost approach are reduced.

The Income Approach　The income approach is best suited to commercial properties, which are bought and sold for their income-producing capabilities. The income approach considers the income of the property and required rates of return on investment. Often income and expense information is not available or not reliable. When possible, however, this information should be analyzed to develop typical rents, expenses, and returns on investment for various types of property.

In a CAMA system, the income approach can be automated at two levels. At the simplest level, the computer can automate the computations involved in applying the various income techniques and capitalization methods. At this level, the income approach is not applicable for a revaluation because of the detailed analysis required for each parcel, but can help analyze income and expense information for individual properties, as might be required during appeals.

At a higher level, income models are developed and selected on the basis of the property's location and use. MRA and other modeling techniques can be used to develop income models if sufficient data are available. Considerable appraisal and analytical skill is needed to structure a generalized model to deal with the wide range of property types, sizes, ages, and market values.

The assessor developing the revaluation plan must decide what approaches to value to apply to each property class and how the several estimates of value will be reconciled in arriving at a final estimate. Algorithms can be written to check for large inconsistencies between values based on the various approaches or large changes from previous values. These exceptions can then be reviewed by an appraiser in the office or field. If time and money permit, field review is the best way to ensure that the data in the computer or on the property record card and the resulting value are correct before notification of the property owner.

Getting Started
Sources of Information and Assistance

Revaluation and installing a CAMA system are not easy to accomplish. They are highly visible programs in local government, and the assessor should understand the tasks and risks involved.

Help is available from a number of sources. Oversight agencies often provide training and assistance to local jurisdictions. Assessors' organizations sponsor seminars and workshops on aspects of revaluation and CAMA. These organizations can also provide names of assessors who have conducted a similar revaluation. If the revaluation or CAMA installation is a new program with which the assessor and staff have little experience, they should seek some help to reduce the risk of failure or delay.

Consultants can help define requirements, develop project specifications, and monitor the revaluation. The consultant can also help identify needs and assess in-house capabilities to meet those needs. If work is to be contracted out, the consultant can also help draft specifications for the revaluation and the CAMA software.

Forms of Consulting Help

Some jurisdictions may prefer a turn-key operation in which a contractor is hired to do everything. Depending on the long-range goals of the assessor or jurisdiction, the contractor may then leave the assessor and staff in a position to maintain the program through the years following the revaluation. Another alternative is partial assistance, in which some work is done in house and the balance by a contractor. The contractor may provide overall project management and technical expertise; however, the assessment office staff does essential tasks within the revaluation program, which gives on-the-job training and leaves the staff in a better position to conduct the next revaluation.

There are benefits and disadvantages to each of these. Indeed, what may be a benefit in one jurisdiction may be a disadvantage in another. The short-term requirements of the revaluation timetable should be balanced against long-range goals for the CAMA system and the jurisdiction's ability to perform full value-updates with limited outside assistance.

Contracting the Work
Developing the Specifications

Even before the bid process begins, the jurisdiction needs to define clearly goals, objectives, and the motivation for the revaluation. The technical plan should be developed. As part of the planning process, the jurisdiction should also develop an idea of its options for conducting the revaluation.

A jurisdiction planning to issue contracts for outside services should write a request for proposal (RFP) outlining the specifications. Proposals from vendors should explain how they would meet needs and outline timetables and budgets for performing the revaluation.

Similar proposals can be solicited for CAMA systems. The development of CAMA system specifications should start as early as possible. One approach is to set up a team to perform the following tasks: (1) review and document the current assessment operation; (2) interview staff; (3) design the system (walk through current procedures to see how they would work when computerized); (4) analyze the costs and benefits of computerization; and (5) prepare a plan for developing, installing, and maintaining the system and for training users. The analysis of costs and benefits should provide preliminary estimates on system costs and an evaluation of alternatives, for example, modifying the old system, writing new software in house, or acquiring a customized package. Involvement of future users of the CAMA system early in system development not only reduces user dissatisfaction with the system acquired but also begins educating the staff well before the system is in place.

The Bid Process

The bid process begins when the RFP is issued. The RFP solicits proposals from qualified vendors for the work required. Before preparing a requirements document, the assessor should talk to other assessors who are using CAMA systems and to CAMA vendors at conferences and see demonstrations of their systems, find out what the systems can and cannot do, and talk to other departments that are working with systems or have an interest in the assessor's system. Vendors should furnish proposals explaining how they will perform the work and how, while the work is in progress, they will demonstrate that standards are being met.

Someone from the assessor's staff with experience in writing and reviewing bids should be assigned to the bid process. This person becomes fully informed about the work that needs to be done, develops bid specifications, determines vendor qualifications, reviews proposals, and keeps the assessor and key staff informed.

If such a person is not available on the assessor's staff and cannot be recruited from another department, the assessor can hire a consultant. The consultant should understand the current system and CAMA technology in general and, to avoid a conflict of interest, should not be a prospective revaluation contractor.

Often the bid process is handled by a purchasing department within the jurisdiction so that standard bid procedures are followed and bids and proposals are less likely to be mishandled. Purchasing departments often require a bid bond or other guarantee of the bidding firm's sincere interest in providing the services, so the jurisdiction is protected against frivolous responses.

Figure 2 outlines revaluation specifications and contract terms that may help jurisdictions develop their requirements. Jurisdictions can label items "mandatory," "desirable," or optional.

Selecting a Vendor

In selecting the contractor, primary emphasis should be placed on qualifications rather than bid cost. It is important to obtain good rough estimates for the project before the bid process so that funding limitations in the budget do not become a reason for picking the lowest, and often not entirely responsive or qualified, bidder.

Figure 2. Revaluation Specifications and Contract Considerations

I. Outline for revaluation specifications
  A. Instructions to bidders, including forms and format on which bid prices are to be submitted
    1. Receipt and opening of proposals and bids
    2. Submission of bids
    3. Right to reject bids
    4. Performance bond requirement
    5. Examination of facilities; responsibility of vendor to judge the condition of existing records
    6. Proposal outline and format to be followed in submitting proposal
    7. Requirements for identifying exceptions and clarifications
  B. Schedule of key dates, including
    1. Issue date of request for bid (RFB) or request for proposal (RFP)
    2. Bidders' conference dates, requirements for questions to be submitted in writing, dates by which responses will be issued
    3. Dates during which vendor may schedule a site visit
    4. Proposal and bid due dates
    5. Dates during which the jurisdiction will schedule site visits, demonstrations, or vendor presentations
    6. Vendor selection date and contract award
    7. Statutory dates that must be met by the vendor for completing the revaluation
  C. Background information for bidders
    1. Jurisdiction's computer configuration and specific needs
    2. Parcel counts
    3. Unique properties
    4. Availability of assessor's records
    5. Statutory requirements
  D. Contract considerations
    1. Include standard contract terms (many of these are mandated by local ordinance)
    2. Specific contractual requirements, including
      a. Deliverables
      b. Acceptance of deliverables by jurisdiction
      c. Payment terms
      d. Penalties for late delivery, for example, liquidated damages
      e. Retainage and provisions for release
      f. Parcel overages and underages

II. Contract (work) specifications—summary of work to be done
  A. Scope
  B. Public relations
  C. Personnel, behavior of employees
    1. Certification requirements
    2. Behavior of employees
  D. Ownership of records
  E. Responsibilities of parties (jurisdiction and contractor)
  F. Cooperation
  G. Specifics (technical work plan)
    1. Property record cards (PRC)
    2. Unit costs
    3. Appraisal manuals to be used
    4. Valuation schedules to be developed
    5. Inspection requirements
      a. Time of day
      b. Number of callbacks (additional visits to property to contact property owner and conduct interior inspection)
      c. Interior inspection requirements
    6. Land values
    7. Field review requirements
    8. Certification of values
    9. Property owner notification
    10. Informal reviews
    11. Defense of values
    12. Training of the assessor's staff
    13. Information to be provided by the jurisdiction
    14. CAMA considerations

Many jurisdictions break the bid process into three steps, requesting first attendance at a prebid conference during which technical requirements are explained, then a technical proposal without prices, and finally the cost or price proposal. The technical proposal is reviewed first. Any vendor that does not provide an adequate technical proposal is automatically excluded at that point, before price has been considered. Thus, only prices from qualified proposals are reviewed in the final evaluation.

Besides considering the technical approach presented in the vendor's proposal, the assessor should look at the qualifications of the company and its principals. Has the company performed similar projects? Have they performed work of acceptable quality and completed projects on time? Next the assessor should look at the depth and qualifications of the vendor's staff. What would happen if one of the proposed project staff were unavailable because of illness or separation from the company? Would the company be able to assign another qualified person to fill the vacant position? Does the company have a development and training program to prepare staff to fill such positions? Is the vendor financially stable?

A financially unstable vendor may not be able to meet its payrolls on a large project, especially if problems develop and the assessor has to withhold part of the payment until problems are corrected. A financially stable company will be able to commit the resources, even if it means going outside the company, to complete a project on time or to correct problems.

The assessor should investigate references provided by the vendor. A conference call to references, with several individuals listening and contributing to the discussion, can be helpful. A predetermined set of questions helps standardize the analysis. Each person in the group records answers to the questions, and the group consolidates answers after each call. During the call, the group should find out about the vendor's approach to the work; the rapport that developed between vendor and client; the degree of satisfaction with the vendor and the work, services, and products; and problems during the project.

On large projects, site visits to evaluate the past performance of the top two or three vendors will provide insight into the vendor's work performance and verification of the vendor's claims. Using a team provides diversity in expertise and functional responsibility and allows more ground to be covered in the short time available for site visits. The vendor's presence might stifle candid conversation between the evaluation team and the agencies visited. The team should meet with all departments that worked with the vendor to evaluate the vendor's ability to work with different departments.

Writing a Contract

The final contract should clearly identify the responsibilities of all parties. The IAAO *Standard on Contracting for Assessment Services* (1986) deals with many of the issues involved in specifying, bidding, negotiating, and administering contracts for assessment services.

The contract can often be constructed from the bid specifications and the vendor's proposal. As a result of contract negotiations, there may be revisions to the original bid specifications or the vendor's proposal that should be incorporated into the contract. The jurisdiction must be represented in the contract negotiations by someone knowledgeable about project requirements as well as contractual issues. Several key items should be considered to protect the jurisdiction. It is important to identify clearly the responsibilities of both parties to the contract. The assessor, as primary representative of the jurisdiction, will need to see that the jurisdiction meets its obligations.

Requiring a 100 percent performance bond is one way to be sure the contractor fulfills the contract terms. Financially unstable companies will have difficulty procuring a performance bond because surety companies look at a company's assets and ability to perform before underwriting a bond. If the contractor defaults, that is, does not complete the work as specified, the bonding company must provide the funding to complete the work or repay the jurisdiction for its loss up to the amount of the bond. The bond does not necessarily protect the jurisdiction from the full financial impact of default or delayed completion, but it does ensure that the project will be completed, for the contractual amount, and provides an incentive for the contractor to deliver the products and services in accordance with the contract.

Smaller companies may find the cost of bonds excessive. Making payments contingent upon delivery to the jurisdiction's satisfaction or placing part of progress payments in escrow are acceptable alternatives.

Payment schedules and amount to be held in escrow for protection against substandard work should be part of the contract. Most service companies cannot support a project with their own funds until all of the work is completed; they expect and need to be paid as the work is performed. Their employees are paid out of the fees charged to the juris-

diction. Therefore, companies usually prefer to invoice the jurisdiction monthly for services rendered in the previous month. Most contractors expect to be paid within thirty days of billing. Substantial delays in payment may force the contractor to borrow money to meet payrolls or, if the company's financial situation is weak, may result in payrolls not being met.

Nevertheless, the jurisdiction needs ways to guarantee that it gets the services and products paid for. One means is a contract payment schedule that ties payments to fixed deliverables or progress against a mutually agreed on work plan. To reduce the risk of early work later being found substandard, jurisdictions may require that a portion of each vendor's progress payment (usually 5–20 percent, depending on length of contract and the extent to which work is completed) be retained until the vendor fulfills all contractual obligations.

As an incentive to the vendor to provide services and complete work on time, penalty clauses can be negotiated. These penalties may be based on the expected costs to be incurred as a result of late delivery, for example, having to borrow money if tax bills are late. Contractors may be doing several projects simultaneously. Good economics may dictate that key staff be assigned in turn to each project, but problems on one project may affect the others. Penalty clauses encourage contractors to look hard at the alternatives for completing the project on time and avoid costly delays.

The contract may be terminated either for cause or for convenience. The conditions under which a contract can be terminated for cause should be spelled out in the agreement. The termination for cause usually results from the failure of the contractor to deliver the services on time or according to specifications. The company should be offered reasonable time to address the problems but, if it is unable to do so, the contract should be terminated. Often the contractor will lose the portion of the fee held in escrow and not collect payment for work that does not meet specifications.

Termination for convenience occurs when one or both parties to the contract decide that continuation of the contract is not in their best interest. Usually this right is limited to the jurisdiction, which may find, for example, that as a result of legislative changes, it is no longer essential that a revaluation be completed. Contracts may also be cancelled if key deliverables (from the jurisdiction) on which the contractor's performance depends will not be available when needed. If a contract is cancelled, the jurisdiction usually pays the vendor for reasonable closedown costs.

Closedown costs include the costs of closing the project offices, cancelling leases, transporting or storing records, relocating temporary staff moved in for the project, and liquidating computer and other office equipment. These costs often represent a large part of the total project cost.

The project work plan is often incorporated into contracts for which time is of the essence. Payment schedules, penalty clauses, the release of contract retentions, and so forth are often tied to dates in the project work plan.

Monitoring the Work

As part of the RFP, the jurisdiction should state clearly that it will tie payments to performance and delivery. To monitor progress, the jurisdiction must negotiate a timetable and an identifiable set of deliverables. Deliverables are tangible work products such as completed property records, appraised values based on specified techniques and meeting accuracy requirements, and a specified number of hours of value defense.

In a contract for computer software, the vendor should document beforehand the functional and design specifications of the proposed system. The jurisdiction can then follow the progress of the computer system's development by comparing the reported progress against the specifications. As software is installed, it can be tested against the functions identified in the specifications. A checklist can be produced verifying that the installed software produces the screens and reports and performs the functions specified.

Delivery

The assessor should not wait until the last days of the contract to review and accept the vendor's work. The work should be delivered in batches as the project progresses. If this is not feasible, preliminary results should be reviewed. Batches of property records can be periodically pulled during data collection and field checked to determine if the data are accurate. This check should score the vendor on each property using a standard process so that meaningful statistics can be developed. Some mistakes are to be expected, particularly during the early phases of data collection, but the overall results should meet standards specified in the contract. Chapters 5 and 21 provide guidelines on data collection and quality assurance.

The assessor's staff will ultimately be responsible for using the work produced by the project as a basis for maintaining and updating future assessments. The staff should use the project as an opportunity to learn procedures for collecting property information, calculating and reviewing values, and explaining and defending these values before taxpayers. The best way to do so is to work alongside the vendor's staff, possibly even performing some of the vendor's work under supervision. Some assessors may be reluctant to help the vendor in this way, but they are missing an opportunity to learn the system and apply it in the future.

In-house Revaluation

In-house revaluation is a major effort requiring careful preparation, the support of key officials, and adequate time and funds. To obtain these, the assessor should develop a detailed work plan scheduling tasks and activities. The schedule takes into account the relationships among activities. It includes adequate slack time to cover probable delays and contingencies to deal with unforeseen problems.

Unlike the daily operations of the assessor's office, the revaluation project usually is a major one-time effort that can span several years and require many temporary employees. It therefore needs to be viewed as separate and distinct from daily operations and may require a separate staff. If the revaluation involves much of the existing staff, duties, responsibilities, and priorities will need to be modified substantially until the project is completed. If the objectives for the project include installing a CAMA system, the specific requirements of the new valuation techniques must be incorporated into the plan.

Constraints and Political Considerations

Specific statutory requirements and dates constrain the scheduling of some tasks. These dates dictate when information will be available or when tasks must be completed. For example, the assessment date usually dictates the earliest possible completion date for updating property characteristics; the characteristics and estimates of value cannot usually be completed until one to two months after the assessment date. There are also specific dates by which taxpayers need to be informed of any changes in their assessments and dates by which the taxpayer may file an appeal.

The success of a project depends in large part on its leadership. Often a full-time project coordinator should be assigned to organize and manage the project. This is especially true where existing staff will be assigned to the revaluation while still performing regular duties.

Key staff, those who because of their expertise, experience, and responsibility are essential to getting the project done, may include systems support staff. Many computer departments have a support team assigned to the assessor's office. When an error or unexpected result occurs, the team can locate and correct a problem the same day. The team must be continually available to the project, particularly when critical, high-volume processing is scheduled. The effect of changes to one part of the system, say the CAMA system, on other parts of the system should be monitored and tested.

Although key employees from the assessor's staff may be reassigned to manage the project or certain phases of it, and some of the appraisal staff may be reassigned to do some data collection and supervision as well as the value review, additional outside staff will usually be needed. Adequate time should be included in the project work plan for hiring and training these people. Several months may be needed to fill positions.

A new CAMA system will affect all aspects of the revaluation effort, including data collection, field review procedures, and defense of values. The new procedures should be recognized in the planning process.

Sequence of Activities

Tasks should be scheduled in a logical sequence. Figure 3 outlines the steps required for a revaluation that includes installation of a CAMA system.

Several tasks require substantial efforts and are likely to last a long time. Hiring 1,000 data collectors to list 50,000 houses in one week does not make economic sense. On the other hand, one data collector might take 750 weeks to collect data on 50,000 houses. For this situation, a data collection period of 30

Figure 3.   Sequence of Activities for CAMA Revaluation

A. Preparatory activities
   1. Design property record cards.
   2. Order property record card forms.
   3. Computer print name, address, and legal description on the forms.
B. Data inventory activities (per batch of forms).
   1. Route property record cards (or prepare data mailers).
   2. Transfer information to property record cards, if applicable. This might include sketches and characteristics from the existing property record cards or information such as lot sizes and neighborhood codes from cadastral maps.
   3. Collect field data (or mail data mailers).
   4. Conduct callbacks and appointments.
   5. Perform supervisor quality check.
   6. Perform office check of forms (or data mailers).
   7. Enter data into CAMA system.
   8. Edit data.
   9. Make field checks and phone calls.
C. Valuation activities
   1. Collect data.
      a. Sales data
      b. Cost data
      c. Income/expense data

   2. Analyze sales, cost, and income information.
   3. Develop cost index, depreciation tables, and capitalization rates.
   4. Develop market models (using MRA, etc). Requires that the inventory data for sale properties be available in the computer.
   5. Generate computer estimates of value.
D. Review activities
   1. Review estimated values by the appraiser in the office or in the field.
   2. Finalize values. This may include running a final sales ratio analysis and making adjustments to those classes that are out of line.
E. New construction update activities
   1. Complete listing and processing of new construction.
   2. Produce final estimates of value.
F. Taxpayer notification activities
   1. Print notices.
   2. Mail notices.
   3. Schedule hearings.
   4. Conduct hearings.
   5. Make field checks.
   6. Issue change notices.
   7. Finalize roll.

to 60 weeks, with 15 to 25 data collectors (three to five groups of 5 data collectors each) is reasonable.

Project Work Plan

A narrative should be written that lists project objectives with their activities and controls. Then a work plan can be prepared. It should identify each activity, the work units to be completed for the activity (for example, number of houses to be listed), the required production rate (for example, number of houses listed per week), intended staffing (category and number of people to be assigned), and the period in which the activity is to be performed (figure 4). There are a number of microcomputer-based planning packages that can be used for developing this part of the work plan.

Reasonable estimates of production rates for major activities and of the time required for technical activities such as valuation modeling also need to be included. The planner should have a good feel for computer processing time. Schedules are seldom realistic when built on best-case times. Data processing staff will need extra time to learn the operation of a CAMA system.

Figure 4. Sample Revaluation Work Plan

Data inventory phase

Activity	Number units	SW	EW	Nbr wks	Wkly prod rate	Avg staff	Staff classification	Start date	End date
Route PRC's	30000	6	10	4	2000	3.8	1 Clerical	03/18/88	04/15/88
Transfer data from exist. cds	30000	8	24	16	200	9.4	1 Clerical	04/01/88	07/22/88
Field data collection houses	21000	12	40	28	100	7.5	3 Res DC	04/29/88	11/11/88
Callbacks	8400	12	40	28	80	3.8	3 Res DC	04/29/88	11/11/88
Supervision - residential	21000	12	40	28	400	1.9	4 Res GL	04/29/88	11/11/88
Field data collection - C/I	3600	20	44	24	50	3.0	5 Comm DC	06/24/88	12/09/88
Supervision - commercial	3600	20	44	24	300	0.5	6 Comm GL	06/24/88	12/09/88
Office checks	30000	15	44	29	1000	1.0	1 Clerical	05/20/88	12/09/88
Data entry	30000	17	46	29	500	2.1	1 Clerical	06/03/88	12/23/88
Editing of data	30000	17	48	31	5000	0.2	1 Clerical	06/03/88	01/06/89
Print and mail data mailers	21000	24	48	24	3000	0.3	1 Clerical	07/22/88	01/06/89
Data mailer response	6300	26	52	26	800	0.3	1 Clerical	08/05/88	02/03/89
Field checks	1260	30	52	22	80	0.7	4 Res GL	09/02/88	02/03/89
Valuation phase									
Collect/validate sales data	3000	24	48	24	150	0.8	7 Res rev	07/22/88	01/06/89
Collect cost information	8	24	40	16	1	0.5	7 Res rev	07/22/88	11/11/88
Collect income/expense data	3600	24	48	24	120	1.3	8 Comm rev	07/22/88	01/06/89
Analyze sales, cost, income	8	32	52	20	1	0.4	7 Res rev	09/16/88	02/03/89
Develop cost index, depr tbl	8	40	48	8	1	1.0	7 Res rev	11/11/88	01/06/89
Develop land price tables	30000	32	48	16	3000	0.6	7 Res rev	09/16/88	01/06/89
Input rates into CAMA	4	44	48	4	1	1.0	10 Analyst	12/09/88	01/06/89
Develop market models	21000	48	56	8	5000	0.5	10 Analyst	01/06/89	03/03/89
Valuation testing	21000	52	56	4	5000	1.1	7 Res rev	02/03/89	03/03/89
Generate computer estimates	4	54	57	3	1	1.3	10 Analyst	02/17/89	03/10/89
Prepare sheets for field	30000	56	60	4	2500	3.0	1 Clerical	03/03/89	03/31/89

Figure 4.   Sample Revaluation Work Plan (cont.)

Data inventory phase

Activity	Number units	SW	EW	Nbr wks	Wkly prod rate	Avg staff	Staff classification	Start date	End date
Review phase									
Review residential values	25500	58	70	12	550	3.9	7 Res rev	03/17/89	06/09/89
Review commercial values	4500	60	72	12	175	2.1	8 Comm rev	03/31/89	06/23/89
Process review maintenance	30000	64	74	10	2500	1.2	1 Clerical	04/28/89	07/07/89
Produce preliminary values	30000	74	76	2	10000	1.5	10 Analyst	07/07/89	07/21/89
Office review of exceptions	30000	74	80	6	5000	1.0	7 Res rev	07/07/89	08/18/89
New construction update phase									
Process new construction	3000	76	81	1	3000	1.2	1 Clerical	07/21/89	08/25/89
Produce final values	30000	81	82	1	30000	1.5	10 Analyst	08/25/89	09/01/89
Notification phase									
Print and mail notices	30000	82	83	1	3000	10.0	1 Clerical	09/01/89	09/08/89
Schedule hearings (phoning)	7500	83	85	2	750	5.0	1 Clerical	09/08/89	09/22/89
Conduct hearings	3000	84	87	3	150	6.7	7 Res rev	09/15/89	10/06/89
Make field checks	600	86	88	2	50	6.0	8 Comm rev	09/29/89	10/13/89
Issue change notices	1500	88	90	2	500	1.5	1 Clerical	10/13/89	10/27/89
Finalize roll	4	89	92	3	1	1.3	9 Proj mgr	10/20/89	11/10/89

Some of the major tasks will overlap. For example, if data collection is done by geographic area, it is reasonable to start the valuation modeling and analysis phase and even value production and review in some areas before the data collection effort is completed in other areas.

Many tasks require public relations or information programs to inform taxpayers and neighborhood groups of upcoming data collection work. It is also important to keep other local government officials informed as the project progresses and key milestones are accomplished.

In planning the project, contingencies, slack time, and lead times for hiring and training should be built in. Allowances should be made for hardware malfunctions and unexpected employee absences. If the project gets into a pinch, things may need to be scheduled more tightly, but that cannot be the plan from the beginning. Include project milestones at which you can evaluate the progress to date and make adjustments in the staffing or schedule.

Developing the Budget

The plan can be translated into a budget by using the applicable labor rates for each employee and estimating other expenses. The cost of hiring and training, and the probable turnover rates for a project of given size, should also be considered. If the salaries that can be paid are too low, less-qualified people may have to be hired and the better-qualified employees are unlikely to stay.

Hiring and Training Staff

Revaluation requires special skills. Sometimes experience and expertise are available in house, but often not. Staff assigned to the project will need to be trained. Among the available training resources are courses, workshops, and audiovisual materials offered by the IAAO and, in some locations, by local assessors' organizations or an oversight agency.

If existing staff is already heavily committed, a full-time, experienced revaluation manager should be hired to oversee the revaluation. Depending on the scope of the project, other key staff or consultants should also be hired so lack of direction and expertise will not impede progress.

Managing the Revaluation

The following basic management principles should be applied to a revaluation program: (1) Don't lose sight of the program's objectives. Evaluate events in light of the objectives. If circumstances may delay completion of the project without jeopardizing the objectives of achieving an acceptable data base and assessment roll, revise the project schedule. (2) Plan for the unexpected. React to situations as they develop and be flexible. Enough slack time in the original plan leaves room to choose among options when unforeseen circumstances arise. Similarly, be ready to take advantage of favorable developments. For example, if the original plan called for transferring data to an intermediate document before going to the field, but tests show that the transfer is unnecessary, adjust the plan to eliminate the activity. (3) Keep everyone informed. Informed people will be more supportive and willing to accept adjustments

to the plan. An informed public may still want assessments reduced, but it will be more receptive to information supporting new values. Inform key government officials of progress at regular intervals. Elected officials like to be able to give constituents informed responses. An informed administration will also be more likely to provide additional funding if it is needed.

The project work plan should be used to monitor progress. When progress deviates substantially from the plan, the plan should be reviewed and modified to get the project back on track. The work plan can provide weekly or monthly production totals. Actual totals should be compared with scheduled amounts (see figure 5) so the project manager can see where each activity stands and note recent trends.

Managing the project requires attention to quality as well as quantity. It also requires providing resources as needed. Short, but regular, staff meetings help coordinate activities and focus thinking on the sequence of tasks that must occur to keep the project on schedule.

Managing is not a trivial process. Consider, for example, the activities that must come together just for printing and mailing assessment notices to property owners (see figure 6). These activities involve many people. Some of the activities must take place three or four months before the notices are to be printed; others can wait until the last week or two.

Developing a CAMA System
Requirements

The primary purpose of the CAMA system is to help assessors carry out their responsi-

Figure 5. Biweekly Planning Calendar and Production Units for Data Inventory Phase

Activity	Number units	Wkly prod rate	Avg staff		8	10	12	14	16	18	20	22	24	26	28	30	32	34	36	38	40
Route PRCs	30000	2000	3.8 Clerical	Planned	15000	15000	0	0	0	0	0	0	0	0	0	0	0	0	0	0	0
				Cum	11800	25000	29124	29650	29650	29650	29650	29650	29650	29650	29650	29650	29650	29650	29650	29650	29650
				Variance	-3200	-5000	-876	-350	-350	-350	-350	-350	-350	-350	-350	-350	-350	-350	-350	-350	-350
Transfer data from exist. cds	30000	200	9.4 Clerical	Planned	0	3750	3750	3750	3750	3750	3750	3750	3750	0	0	0	0	0	0	0	0
				Cum	0	3750	7500	11250	15000	18750	22500	26250	30000	30000	30000	30000	30000	30000	30000	30000	30000
				Actual	0	2100	3200	3600	3900	4100	4200	4200	4200	150	0	0	0	0	0	0	0
				Cum	0	2100	5300	8900	12800	16900	21100	25300	29500	29650	29650	29650	29650	29650	29650	29650	29650
				Variance	0	-1650	-2200	-2350	-2200	-1850	-1400	-950	-500	-350	-350	-350	-350	-350	-350	-350	-350
Field data collection houses	21000	100	7.5 Res DC	Planned	0	0	0	1500	1500	1500	1500	1500	1500	1500	1500	1500	1500	1500	1500	1500	1500
				Cum	0	0	0	1500	3000	4500	6000	7500	9000	10500	12000	13500	15000	16500	18000	19500	21000
				Actual	0	0	0	923	1284	1486	1568	1653	1637	1500	1492	1612	1920	1673	1417	1215	1260
				Cum	0	0	0	923	2207	3693	5261	6914	8551	10051	11543	13155	15075	16748	18165	19380	20640
				Variance	0	0	0	-577	-793	-807	-739	-586	-449	-449	-457	-345	75	248	165	-120	-360
Callbacks	8400	80	3.8 Res DC	Planned	0	0	0	600	600	600	600	600	600	600	600	600	600	600	600	600	600
				Cum	0	0	0	600	1200	1800	2400	3000	3600	4200	4800	5400	6000	6600	7200	7800	8400
				Actual	0	0	0	364	455	516	624	541	596	600	668	542	420	502	625	500	342
				Cum	0	0	0	364	819	1335	1959	2500	3096	3696	4364	4906	5326	5828	6453	6953	7295
				Variance	0	0	0	-236	-381	-465	-441	-500	-504	-504	-436	-494	-674	-772	-747	-847	-1105
Supervision -residential	21000	400	1.9 Res GL	Planned	0	0	0	1500	1500	1500	1500	1500	1500	1500	1500	1500	1500	1500	1500	1500	1500
				Cum	0	0	0	1500	3000	4500	6000	7500	9000	10500	12000	13500	15000	16500	18000	19500	21000
				Actual																	
				Cum																	
				Variance																	
Field data collection -C/I	3600	50	3.0 Comm DC	Planned	0	0	0	0	0	0	0	300	300	300	300	300	300	300	300	300	300
				Cum	0	0	0	0	0	0	0	300	600	900	1200	1500	1800	2100	2400	2700	3000
				Actual	0	0	0	0	0	0	0	192	256	306	347	296	329	360	321	235	298
				Cum	0	0	0	0	0	0	0	192	448	754	1101	1397	1726	2086	2407	2642	2940
				Variance	0	0	0	0	0	0	0	-108	-152	-146	-99	-103	-74	-14	7	-58	-60
Supervision -commercial	3600	300	0.5 Comm DC	Planned	0	0	0	0	0	0	0	300	300	300	300	300	300	300	300	300	300
				Cum	0	0	0	0	0	0	0	300	600	900	1200	1500	1800	2100	2400	2700	3000
				Actual																	
				Cum																	
				Variance																	

Figure 5. Biweekly Planning Calendar and Production Units for Data Inventory Phase (cont.)

Activity	Number units	Wkly prod rate	Avg staff		8	10	12	14	16	18	20	22	24	26	28	30	32	34	36	38	40
Office checks	30000	1000	1.0 Clerical	Planned	0	0	0	0	2069	2069	2069	2069	2069	2069	2069	2069	2069	2069	2069	2069	2069
				Cum	0	0	0	0	2069	4138	6207	8276	10345	12414	14483	16552	18621	20690	22759	24828	26897
				Actual	0	0	0	0	1428	1740	1863	1924	1905	1986	2011	1920	1832	1945	1960	2040	2002
				Cum	0	0	0	0	1428	3168	5031	6955	8860	10846	12857	14777	16609	18554	20514	22554	24556
				Variance	0	0	0	0	−641	−970	−1176	−1321	−1485	−1568	−1626	−1775	−2012	−2136	−2245	−2274	−2341
Data entry	30000	500	2.1 Clerical	Planned	0	0	0	0	0	2069	2069	2069	2069	2069	2069	2069	2069	2069	2069	2069	2069
				Cum	0	0	0	0	0	2069	4138	6207	8276	10345	12414	14483	16552	18621	20690	22759	24628
				Actual	0	0	0	0	0	1428	1740	1863	1924	1905	1986	2011	1920	1832	1945	1960	2040
				Cum	0	0	0	0	0	1428	3168	5031	6955	8860	10846	12857	14777	16609	18554	20514	22554
				Variance	0	0	0	0	0	−641	−970	−1176	−1321	−1485	−1568	−1626	−1775	−2012	−2136	−2245	−2274
Editing of data	30000	5000	0.2 Clerical	Planned	0	0	0	0	0	1935	1935	1935	1935	1935	1935	1935	1935	1935	1935	1935	1935
				Cum	0	0	0	0	0	1935	3871	5806	7742	9677	11613	13548	15484	17419	19355	21290	23226
				Actual	0	0	0	0	0	320	1428	1740	1863	1924	1905	1986	2011	1920	1832	1945	1960
				Cum	0	0	0	0	0	320	1748	3488	5351	7275	9180	11166	13177	15097	16929	18874	20834
				Variance	0	0	0	0	0	−1615	−2123	−2318	−2391	−2402	−2433	−2382	−2307	−2322	−2426	−2416	−2392
Print and mail mailers	21000	3000	0.3 Clerical	Planned	0	0	0	0	0	0	0	0	0	1750	1750	1750	1750	1750	1750	1750	1750
				Cum	0	0	0	0	0	0	0	0	0	1750	3500	5250	7000	8750	10500	12250	14000
				Actual	0	0	0	0	0	0	0	0	0	0	2231	1938	4169	3622	1452	2304	0
				Cum	0	0	0	0	0	0	0	0	0	0	2231	4169	4169	7791	9243	11547	11547
				Variance	0	0	0	0	0	0	0	0	0	−1750	−1269	−1081	−2831	−959	−1257	−703	−2453
Data mailer response	6300	800	0.3 Clerical	Planned	0	0	0	0	0	0	0	0	0	0	485	485	485	485	485	485	485
				Cum	0	0	0	0	0	0	0	0	0	0	485	970	1455	1940	2425	2910	3395
				Actual	0	0	0	0	0	0	0	0	0	0	0	317	524	802	615	204	413
				Cum	0	0	0	0	0	0	0	0	0	0	0	317	841	1643	2258	2462	2875
				Variance	0	0	0	0	0	0	0	0	0	0	−485	−653	−614	−297	−167	−448	−520
Field checks	1260	80	0.7 Res GL	Planned	0	0	0	0	0	0	0	0	0	0	0	0	115	115	115	115	115
				Cum	0	0	0	0	0	0	0	0	0	0	0	0	115	230	345	460	575
				Actual	0	0	0	0	0	0	0	0	0	0	0	0	0	0	156	123	152
				Cum	0	0	0	0	0	0	0	0	0	0	0	0	0	0	156	279	431
				Variance	0	0	0	0	0	0	0	0	0	0	0	0	−115	−230	−189	−181	−144

bilities to produce and update the appraisals on which assessments are based. System requirements vary. A simple cost- or market-based CAMA system may meet basic requirements and produce acceptable and readily updatable values. Greater sophistication is appropriate only where there is a sufficient base of commercial property, market activity, and so forth, to allow mass application of several valuation approaches or use of several modeling and calibration techniques.

Figure 6. Activities for Taxpayer Notification

1. Notice form to be designed.
2. Notice form to be approved by data processing staff who will have to write the program to print it.
3. Notice form ordered. (In some jurisdictions, if this is contracted out, it may have to be bid.)
4. Notices delivered to data center.
5. Notice print program specification written by programmer.
6. Notice program specification approved by assessor's staff.
7. Notice program written and tested by programmer.
8. Notice test results reviewed and approved by assessor's staff.
9. Appraised values completed on CAMA file and posted to assessment file for the area for which notices are to be printed.
10. Notice production job scheduled.
11. Notices generated. Before actually printing these on the forms, control totals and a short batch may be printed for review.
12. Notices folded and stuffed if they are not in a mailer form (manual or automated process).
13. Permits acquired if the notices are to be bulk mailed. An appropriate permit number must be printed on the notice form. (See step 1.)
14. Notices delivered to post office for mailing.

In some jurisdictions, the CAMA system design may be complicated by additional reporting requirements and use of the assessor's data by other departments. In designing a system, these requirements should be separated from the basic CAMA function as much as possible. They include:

- Value change tracking—required for determining the statutory cap on tax revenue
- Preferential assessments—required for tracking use value, in addition to market value
- Classified assessments—required to break out the parcel's value by use on a property with multiple classes
- Concurrent multiyear processing—required if multiple statuses for a given property are to coexist within the system
- Multijurisdictional processing—allows several local assessors to share a common data base and system at a central location
- Computer links to other departments interested in the assessor's property record information

Chapter 19 discusses the parts of a modern CAMA system and the relationship's among them in more detail.

System Development

System development is the translation of system requirements into operational software programs and user procedures. Figure 7 outlines the steps in the development of a CAMA system. The first phase is defining requirements for software and hardware.

Software

Software packages may be hard-coded, customized, or general purpose. In choosing the type suitable for a jurisdiction, consider how information will be shared with other departments, how independent the assessor's

Figure 7. System Development Phases

1. Functional specifications or definition of requirements
2. Detailed systems design
3. Coding and unit testing—This usually results in completion of the system by testable module (allowing for phased implementation).
4. System testing—This is a comprehensive testing of the system, taking test data through all phases of system operation.
5. Installation—If the system is developed at another site, this is the process whereby the system is installed on the computer to be used by the assessor.
6. User acceptance testing—This is testing of the system by the assessor and staff to verify that the system meets the functional requirements before the system is accepted and put into production.
7. Putting the system into production
   a. Conversion—Existing assessment and characteristic data are converted to the new system and the ongoing interfaces with the other systems with which CAMA must exchange data are established.
   b. Training the staff—Classroom and hands-on training is conducted for the staff in their respective phases of system operation.
   c. Carrying out the production activities
8. System maintenance—This is sometimes a forgotten aspect of system development. The system should not be viewed as static and unchanging. Requirements will change over time. Experience will indicate aspects of the system that can be improved. The life expectancy of a system is increased through a planned, ongoing maintenance process.

computer operations will be, the necessity for meeting deadlines, and the amount of CAMA expertise in the department.

A hard-coded package purchased from a third party has limited flexibility. Usually, the system is designed to run on a particular type of hardware. Most packages will not completely meet the jurisdiction's needs without some modifications. If the jurisdiction is tied to a particular property record format or cost manual, the package solution will not work unless it is based on that format and manual. Customized software can be acquired in a package from a software developer that specializes in local government and, more important, assessors' applications. Customized software can also be acquired from another jurisdiction that developed the software in house, with the acquiring jurisdiction modifying the software to meet its needs. More frequently, customization is provided by a software vendor and should follow the same steps as software development.

General-purpose CAMA software usually runs on microcomputers. Minicomputer and mainframe packages that have general-purpose CAMA features are often limited by the restrictions of the programming languages, file and data base structures, and communication protocols.

Hardware

On what computer should the system run? The main options are mainframes, distributed systems, stand-alone systems, networked systems, and time-share systems.

Mainframe Systems The central mainframe computer houses the software and data files used by the assessor as well as those used by other departments within the jurisdiction. A data processing staff operates the computer and usually handles printing and distribution of reports that cannot be printed in the assessor's office.

Distributed Systems   These systems operate on a mainframe or minicomputer in the assessor's office. There may be an on-line interface between this system and the jurisdiction's central computer. The assessor's staff usually operates the computer, but large print jobs and other batch processes are often handled on the central computer.

Stand-alone Systems   These include minicomputer or microcomputer systems operating independently of other computer systems in the jurisdiction. It is easy to get software for these systems. However, files maintained on a central computer may have to be transferred periodically to the stand-alone system.

Networked Systems   This option includes multiple microcomputer workstations for appraisers that may be networked with each other, a minicomputer, or a mainframe system.

Time-share Systems   Rather than buying computer hardware, the assessor may elect to buy computer time from a service bureau. Service bureaus charge for the computer resources used; these include central processing unit time, on-line disk storage, input-output activity, lines printed, and so forth. There is a premium charge for daytime processing and discounts for off-peak processing (overnight and weekends). Additional costs involved include terminals and printers in the assessor's office, phone lines, and modems.

CAMA System Timetables

It takes time to develop and install a CAMA system. The system should be working before the revaluation starts. An "off-the-shelf"

CAMA package is unlikely to be operational in much less than six months. An unmodified off-the-shelf package will be inadequate. One sufficiently flexible to meet the jurisdiction's needs will require several months' work to define the data base and screens, build the edit and valuation tables, and test them.

In-house CAMA system development will take longer, at least two years. A system developed in-house is unlikely to have as much capability as some package systems and will probably undergo its first test during the revaluation. The revaluation schedule should allow extra time for substantial modification of procedures and reports.

Multiagency Systems

In practice, it is difficult to design a fully integrated data base that ties together the many offices that have responsibility for real property. These offices usually include recorder of deeds, engineer's office (subdivision maps), building inspector, assessor, auditor, treasurer, land use planning and zoning, and police and fire departments.

The ownership of the data (who is responsible for deciding its content, entering it, and maintaining it in the system) must be established. The system must be modular so the duties of each office can be carried out independently.

Developing a CAMA system in conjunction with a revaluation program does not afford the time or flexibility needed to establish a comprehensive multidepartmental system. However, the module created during the revaluation can eventually be integrated into an interdepartmental property information system.

Shared Systems

Recognizing the cost of developing CAMA systems, some governments have designed shared systems. In some cases, software procured at the national, state, or provincial level is provided to county or municipal governments. The local governments are responsible for providing the computer hardware and, if necessary, for converting the software to run on different hardware. In other cases, the CAMA software is provided to jurisdictions as part of a central system operating on a central computer. Terminals and printers are installed at the local assessors' offices to provide on-line access for viewing and updating files.

Summary

Effective revaluations require careful planning. A realistic analysis of the present state of the assessment office's records and values and of the resources available to conduct the revaluation will help the assessor define the scope of the project. Developing project specifications may require technical help, particularly if a CAMA system is to be installed for the revaluation. At the very least, the assessor should gather information from other assessment offices and examine their systems carefully. A revaluation is a costly, highly visible, and politically sensitive undertaking. The assessment office that understands its own resources and the technical requirements of the task is more likely to conduct a successful revaluation.

Computers in Mass Appraisal 19

Introduction

Computers have transformed how we work and live. It is not surprising, then, that they are essential to modern mass appraisal, increasing both analytical capabilities and productivity in the assessment office. This chapter discusses fundamental computer concepts; requirements of an effective computer-assisted appraisal system; and selection, design, and implementation of a computer system.

Fundamental Operations

A computer is a machine of electrical components that can perform certain operations rapidly and efficiently, for example,

1. Arithmetic: addition, subtraction, multiplication, and division. Larger computers can perform millions of computations per second with unfailing accuracy.
2. Logical comparisons: whether one value is less than, greater than, or equal to another. The computer is consistent and accurate in such comparisons, no matter how small the difference.
3. Input/output: retrieval, storage, and writing of data. Many computers can retrieve more than a million characters of data per second. The information contained in a 100-foot stack of printed material can be stored on a single mass storage device. Output can be written on tape or disk,

displayed on a terminal screen, or directed to a printer or plotter.

Types of Computers

Computers can be classified in several ways. One distinction is that between *digital* and *analog* computers. Analog computers process data on a continuous scale, meaning that there are no intervals between the possible values within a given range. These computers measure changes in temperature, current, sound waves, and the like. A thermostat, which measures temperature and translates it into electrical current to control the operation of a furnace, is an example of an analog computer. Digital computers, on the other hand, process discrete data: numbers, letters, and special characters.

Computers are also classified as *special-purpose* or *general-purpose*. Special-purpose computers are programmed for a single application, such as air traffic control or automobile cruise control. General-purpose computers are designed for many applications, such as word processing, payroll processing, or statistical analysis. Computers used in assessment administration are digital, general-purpose computers.

Finally, computers are categorized by size and capacity as *mainframes, minicomputers*, and *microcomputers*. Mainframe, or macrocomputers, are the largest and most expensive computer systems, having the greatest processing speed and storage capacity. They are used when it is necessary to process large volumes of data at the most rapid processing speeds. Mainframes can support thousands of terminals and other devices and run hundreds of programs simultaneously. They require a special physical environment: raised floors and wiring, precise temperature controls, and freedom from dust and other impurities. They also require a technical support team and programming staff.

Minicomputers were originally developed as special-purpose computers, often to perform specific tasks, such as data editing, in a larger computer system. They possessed comparatively limited capabilities but did not require special wiring or a controlled environment. Their ease of use and low cost relative to mainframes made them popular, and they were soon adapted to function as general-purpose computers. Today minicomputers can handle many input/output devices and run many programs simultaneously. Indeed, the overlap in the performance of mini- and mainframe computers has blurred the distinction between the two.

Microcomputers are the smallest computers, able to sit comfortably on a desk. They were introduced in the 1970s, made possible by integrated circuit technology in which hundreds (today thousands) of circuits can be etched onto a single "chip" the size of a dime. Modern microcomputers possess enormous capacity at very low cost. Their main limitation is that they can support relatively few input/output devices.

History of Computers

Computers have had a brief but dramatic history of rapid innovation. Developments can be roughly divided into four phases, or generations.

Computers were introduced for commercial use in the early 1950s. First-generation machines were characterized by vacuum tubes and were very large. Large air conditioners were needed to dissipate the enormous amounts of heat they generated. By modern standards, first-generation computers were very slow, with the time to perform arithmetic operations measured in *milliseconds* (thousandths of a second). Moreover, they failed frequently, typically "going down" after only two hours of use. By today's standards they were also expensive. Several thousand of these machines were produced.

The second generation, in the early 1960s, used transistor technology. Transistors were much smaller, produced less heat, and were more reliable than vacuum tubes. Processing speed was measured in *microseconds* (millionths of a second), meaning that these machines were a thousand times faster than first-generation computers. Cost/performance ratios also improved.

The third generation, begun in the mid-1960s, used solid-state integrated circuits. This new technology again dramatically improved storage capacity, processing speed, and reliability. Processing speeds were measured in *nanoseconds* (billionths of a second). Multiprocessing, which allows several programs to operate simultaneously, was introduced. Unlike their predecessors, third-generation computers enjoyed an abundance of software and support services.

The fourth generation emerged in the mid-1970s and is characterized by very large-scale integrated circuits and yet another quantum leap in operating speeds and cost/performance ratio. The speed of modern mainframe computers is measured in *picoseconds* (trillionths of a second). Minicomputers were introduced in the mid-1970s and microcomputers in the early 1980s, accompanied by a new generation of low cost, high-performance software.

Potential of Computers in Mass Appraisal

Computers are being used more and more in assessment administration, in applications such as data storage and management; market research and analysis; cost, market, and income approach calculations; ratio studies; generation of assessment rolls and value notices; processing of tax payments; and such everyday functions as management planning and word processing. Today, virtually every assessment jurisdiction can make cost-effective use of computers.

Computer technology does not lessen the need for good data and the proper application of appraisal theory. Nevertheless, the capabilities offered by fourth-generation computers increase the assessor's ability to deliver a superior product efficiently. Specifically, computers can assist in updating values annually and achieving good measures of appraisal performance at low per-parcel costs, which improves the image and professionalism of the assessor's office.

Computer Hardware

Computer systems have two basic components: hardware and software. Hardware is the machine itself, or *central processing unit* (CPU), and various input/output devices, or *peripherals*. Software is the programs and procedures that interact with the user, perform operations, and produce output. Figure 1 shows the relationships among the hardware components of a computer system.

Central Processing Unit

The CPU is the brain of the computer. It contains the electronic circuits that control the system and execute programs and instructions. The CPU has three specialized units: memory, arithmetic/logic, and control.

The memory, or storage, unit, also called registers, houses the specific instructions and data being processed by the computer. The memory unit receives instructions and data sequentially from the main memory unit and holds them during execution.

The arithmetic/logic unit performs all arithmetical and logical operations. Arithmetical operations include addition, subtraction, multiplication, and division. Logical operations involve a series of comparisons between values, with the program often "branching" one way or another depending on whether one value is equal to, greater than, or less than another.

The control unit directs the activity of the CPU, much like a traffic cop at a busy intersection. It controls the sequence of operations and moves data between the memory and arithmetic/logic units. It also communicates with the main memory unit and various input/output devices, transferring instructions and data into and out of the CPU and activating the printers and other peripherals as needed.

Main Memory

Main, or primary, memory resides on the system board or expansion boards (not in the CPU) of the computer and houses instruc-

Figure 1. Computer Hardware

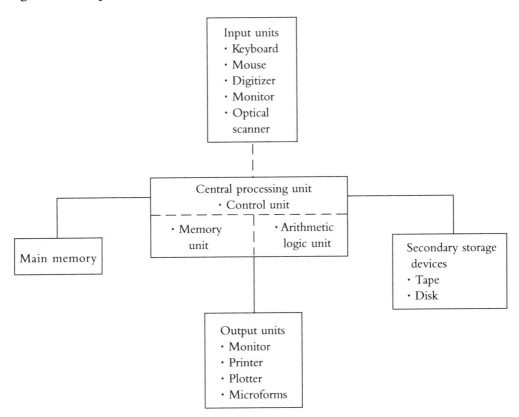

tions (programs) and data awaiting execution by the CPU. Because the computer can only process instructions and data stored in main memory, its size is important. Main memory varies from computer to computer and can usually be expanded to various sizes depending on computer architecture.

The smallest unit of computer memory, a *bit*, is represented as either "0" or "1" (off or on). Bits are collected into groups of eight, called *bytes*. Bytes are used to represent numbers, letters, or special characters according to a coding scheme of on/off bits. Storage capacity can be measured in bytes, with one kilobyte (K) equivalent to 1,024 bytes. Thus,

a 640-K machine has 655,360 bytes (640 × 1,024). Although 640 K may be typical for a microcomputer, larger computers typically have millions or billions of bytes of memory. This much memory is organized not only by bytes but also by "words." Word size is not standardized among all computers, but 64 bits is common; larger word sizes make it easier to address any particular portion of memory when the amount of memory is large.

The size of main memory limits the programs that can be executed by a computer and affects processing speed and efficiency. Most fourth-generation machines use a concept known as *virtual memory*, which creates an illusion of virtually unlimited memory. Through a process called paging or swapping, programs are divided into pages or subfiles and brought into main memory as needed with minimal effect on processing time. Although the shuttling of programs or data into and out of main memory in this manner tends to increase execution time slightly, it enables the computer to work on many programs simultaneously and to process larger and more complicated individual programs and data sets than would otherwise be possible.

Also important is the distinction between *random-access memory* and *read-only memory*. Random-access memory (RAM) is the largest portion of main memory and can be expanded by the addition of microchips. RAM allows data to be written to and read from main memory. The contents of RAM, however, are volatile, meaning that data are lost whenever the flow of electricity is interrupted.

In contrast, read-only memory (ROM) allows data to be read from, but not written to, main memory. The contents of ROM are stored permanently in memory during manufacturing and its size is not expandable. ROM is nonvolatile, that is, not affected by interruptions in electric current. ROM is often used to store programs that control operation of the computer and that should not be altered. The address space occupied by ROM, unlike that of RAM, is not available to the user for programming, processing, or temporary data storage, although most computers that use ROM do it in a way intended to make more RAM available to the user, say for data, by putting some programs normally found in RAM into ROM.

Computer Peripherals

Computer peripherals are devices that supplement main memory and provide communication with the outside world. They can be grouped into secondary storage, input, and output devices.

Secondary Storage The RAM of main memory serves as a temporary storage area for programs and data during processing but is too small and valuable to store data permanently. Also, because RAM is volatile, it is unsuited for permanent storage as its contents are lost when the flow of electric current is interrupted.

Secondary, or auxiliary, storage media, such as magnetic tape and disk, are used for the long-term storage of programs and data. Figure 2 summarizes the primary characteristics and relative advantages and disadvantages of each.

Magnetic tape provides a compact, efficient, and reliable storage medium. Magnetic tape is composed of a magnetic oxide coating (dull side) on a plastic Mylar base (shiny side). Data are recorded on the surface of the tape in a series of magnetic spots, each spot representing one bit. Mainframe and minicomputers use reel-to-reel tape; microcomputers often use cassettes or cartridges.

The speed of data retrieval from tape is largely a function of tape speed and recording density. Tape speed refers to the rate at which the tape travels past the read/write head. Density refers to the number of bytes that can be stored in a given length. Some typical storage densities are 1,600 and 6,250 bytes per inch (bpi). A reel-to-reel tape, used in a mainframe computer system, that is 6,250 bpi and 2,400 feet in length would have a theoretical storage capacity of

Figure 2.   Secondary Storage Media

I. Magnetic tape (for example, reel-to-reel, cassette, cartridge)

Advantages	Disadvantages
1. Large storage capacity at low cost.	1. No random access
2. High transfer rates to and from CPU	2. Data not in human-readable form
3. No limits on record length or format	3. Sensitive to dust, moisture, static electricity, and temperature

II. Magnetic and laser disk (for example, hard disk, floppy disk, laser disk)

Advantages	Disadvantages
1. Files can be organized and accessed randomly or sequentially	1. Relatively expensive (except for floppy disk)
2. Accommodates large volumes of data	2. Data not in human-readable form
3. Rapid data retrieval and response time (interactive processing)	3. Floppy disks sensitive to dust, moisture, static electricity, and temperature

180,000,000 bytes (2,400 × 12 × 6,250). In practice, part of the storage surface is required for labeling and interrecord gaps. Storage efficiency is improved through the "blocking" of records, which reduces the amount of interrecord gaps and unused space on the tape.

The primary disadvantage of magnetic tape is that the data must be processed *sequentially*, that is, the entire tape must be passed to access the last record. Thus, it is relatively inefficient when records must be accessed randomly. On the other hand, magnetic tape makes an excellent backup medium and is efficient for processing data sequentially.

Magnetic disk is the most popular secondary storage medium. Magnetic disks are metal platters coated with magnetic materials on both sides. In a hard disk system the platters are mounted above each other on a disk drive to form a disk pack.

Disks are usually faster and can store larger volumes of data than magnetic tape. The primary advantage of disks, however, is that

they provide direct, or *random*, access to records. Depending on the file size and disk drive, any parcel may be found in a fraction of a second. Disk files may also be read sequentially, which is most efficient when the entire file or a large part of it is required.

Microcomputer systems use both hard (built-in) and floppy disks. Floppy disks are single platters that can be quickly inserted and remove. They come in several sizes and storage capacities. Hard disks offer more storage capacity than floppy disks.

Laser disks offer extremely compact data storage and can support images, such as property records, sales documents, and property photos. The images can be retrieved quickly but cannot usually be modified directly.

Input Devices   The primary devices for entering data into computer-readable form are the keyboard, mouse, digitizing board, and optical character reader. A computer keyboard is a device, similar in appearance to a typewriter keyboard, connected to a cathode ray tube (CRT) or monitor. As numbers and letters are typed, they are converted to binary code (bits) and displayed on the monitor or screen. Users may erase, correct, or otherwise modify the input until they are fully satisfied, at which time it can be saved to disk. A mouse enables users to point to an image, or icon, on the monitor and issue a corresponding command by pressing a button. Digitizing boards are similar except that users place the pointer on a map or other hard copy document. A magnetic grid and cable translate the selected points to digital format.

Optical character readers (OCRs) are light-sensitive devices that are able to read numbers, letters, and codes directly into binary format. Optical character technology comes in several types. The most common is optical mark recognition (OMR), in which data are represented as circles, boxes, or other marks. One familiar application of OMR is the scoring of true/false and multiple choice exams. The use of bar codes on retail products is another common application.

Magnetic ink character recognition (MICR) is widely used in the banking industry. Special machines are able to read, sort, and process checks prepared with the magnetic ink and transmit the data on demand to a computer or storage device.

Of special interest to assessors are optical scanners, which record an image onto disk for later retrieval or processing. Optical scanners preserve a clearer image than the traditional alternative, microfilming. Unfortunately, most optical scanning may involve simple reproduction of the image (black, white, shades of gray, and colors at specific positions relative to one another) without conversion to one of the standard codes (AS-CII or EBCDIC) used to represent numbers, the letters of the alphabet, and so on digitally. However, technology is available for converting numbers and letters that are accurately represented on a form to digital format. Typewritten characters as well as carefully handwritten numbers and letters can be read. This technology can reduce the time spent in data entry.

The videodisc recorder is another interesting input device. Like the images from most optical scanners, images obtained through recording cannot be converted to binary format for further manipulation. Nevertheless, the images can be stored on a laser disk and indexed for quick retrieval (random access). For example, if pictures of all properties in the jurisdiction have been recorded, the office can quickly retrieve an image of one for which an appeal has been filed.

Terminals need not sit on a desk top. Hand-held terminals offer assessors a means of capturing data directly into machine-readable format in the field. Once recorded, the data are electronically transferred to the central computer. Some such terminals are "intelligent," in that they can be programmed to edit data during entry. Small hand-held or "lap-top" computers can also be used in the field. The data are captured on floppy disk and later read into a larger computer.

Output Devices Computer output can be directed to several sources, including monitors, printers, and plotters. Monitors come in various resolutions, measured by the number of dots or pixels (picture elements) on the screen. They also come in monochrome or color, with higher resolutions required for sharp color images. Some monitors support graphic images; other do not.

Printers come in two basic types: *impact* and *nonimpact*. Impact printers form a print image by striking the paper with an impression of the character through an ink ribbon. Some common impact printers are *daisy wheel, dot matrix, drum*, and *chain and belt*. Most microcomputers use dot matrix printers. Drum and chain and belt printers are found in mainframe and minicomputer systems.

Nonimpact printers do not use a print ribbon or make contact with the print surface. *Ink jet* printers use a matrix of ink nozzles that spray tiny drops of ink to form characters. The print matrix on an ink jet printer is denser (more dots) than that of a dot matrix printer, thereby giving a higher print resolution, similar to that of a typewriter. Because the character format is electronically controlled, the size and style of type can be controlled by a software program. Because they are nonimpact, ink jet printers are also very quiet. The technology is used by many mainframe and minicomputers and is available for microcomputers as well. *Laser* printers copy character images onto the print surface in much the same manner as a photocopy machine, except that a line scanner is used. Laser printers produce an image of excellent quality and are extremely fast. Microcomputer laser printers typically produce eight pages per minute; mainframe laser printers can produce up to thirty thousand lines per minute. Laser printers also offer great flexibility in the printing of forms and graphic output.

Plotters make possible high-quality graphic output. Plotters use pens, usually multicolor, to draw lines on a paper surface. Curves, arcs, and circles are formed as a series of very short lines, giving the appearance of a smooth curve. Plotters are excellent for producing maps, charts, and graphs and are used primarily with minicomputer and microcomputer systems.

Microforms—microfilm and microfiche—are another form of computer output. Microfilm comes on a 16-millimeter roll film, not unlike the negative used by a camera. Each frame holds one record, usually a printed page or other document. Microfiche are small film "cards" containing many pages of output. Microfiche can be computer-generated in multiple copies at very high speeds (much faster than a printer) and low cost. Although not generally computer-readable, microfilm and microfiche constitute an excellent alternative to paper for storing large volumes of data. Microforms are an inexpensive, compact way to store data in a form that can be read directly. Copies can be produced quickly. However, images are relatively poor and cannot be updated, and the initial cost of equipment is high.

Computer Software

Software is the programs and procedures that govern the computer's operation, manipulate data, and produce output. Software can perform an unlimited variety of functions, including many related to mass appraisal and assessment administration.

Computer Processing Cycle

The computer processing cycle has three steps: input, processing, and output. During input, the CPU reads instructions and data from a secondary storage medium into main memory. During processing, the computer executes the program instructions, for example, calculating a property value. During output, the results are transmitted to disk, printer, or other output device. The cycle continues until all data have been processed, the program reaches a logical termination point, or the user aborts the program.

Programs can be processed either in *batch* mode or interactively. In batch processing, the data are run in mass in a single "run stream." In *interactive*, or on-line, processing records are processed one at a time, for example, parcel by parcel. For any single record, interactive processing is much quicker, sometimes instantaneous. Batch processing is more efficient for large groups (batches) of records. Also, interactive processing requires disk, so that records can be accessed randomly; batch processing can use either tape or disk. Interactive processing is better suited for retrieval of data in response to taxpayer inquiries. Mass appraisal value calculations and ratio study programs are usually run in batch mode.

Levels of Computer Languages

Programming languages may be at machine level, assembly level, or a higher level. *Machine language*, or machine code, is the language understood by computers. It consists of 0 (off) and 1 (on) bits. Programming in machine language is complicated by the extreme level of detail required in machine code instructions, down to specifying the actual storage addresses to be referenced.

Machine language commands are the only form of instruction that can be executed directly by a computer. Thus, computer instructions in any language other than machine code must be translated into machine language for execution. This translation process is called compiling. Each class or family of computer CPUs has its own in-struction set that reflects its internal architecture (construction). The machine code of one class of CPUs is not necessarily compatible with another CPU class. Thus, for a program written for one class of CPU to be transferred to another, the machine code for that program may need to be regenerated (recompiled).

Assembly language is a symbolic representation of machine code. Assembly languages were the earliest programming languages and were created to provide an alternative to working in machine code. An assembly language statement has three parts: a label by which the statement is referenced, an operation code specifying the operation to be executed, and one or more operands pointing to relevant storage locations (registers). Assembly language statements translate one for one with machine code statements and thus require as much detail in specification.

Together, machine and assembly level programs are called lower level languages because of their close relationship to the computer's internal design. The complexities of programming in these languages greatly hampered first- and second-generation computer software development. Efforts were made to simplify the programming process by making languages more efficient and reflective of human thought and logical processes. The result was the development of higher level languages that more closely resemble mathematical functions and the English language. Examples of widely used higher level languages are COBOL (Common Business Oriented Language), FORTRAN (Formula Translator), and BASIC (Beginner's All-Purpose Symbolic Instruction Code).

Before a higher level language can be executed, it must be translated into machine code. The program as coded by the programmer is referred to as the source code. Its translation to machine code is accomplished by either an interpreter or a compiler.

An interpreter translates and executes source code statements one at a time, each time the program is run. Each statement is processed and the results directed to an output device before the next statement is read. Interpreters are inefficient: each statement must be translated, checked for errors, and then executed for each record. Branching, or "go to," statements necessitate a line-by-line search of the program each time they are encountered. Nevertheless, because programs written in interpreted languages feature "late binding," they are particularly suitable for exploratory data analysis. Late binding means that the characteristics and location of certain objects (such as the dimensions of an array of data) are not finally resolved into machine-executable code until the program is run by the user. With early binding many such things must be resolved before the program is turned over to the user. Once an instruction is interpreted and resolved, it executes immediately. The delays inherent in interpreted programs are less noticeable when the program is one that does retrieval and updating of selected records, rather than consecutively processing each record in a file. Furthermore, interpreted programs use little RAM, an important consideration with microcomputers.

In contrast, a *compiler* translates the entire source program into machine code. It does this once; thereafter the program can be run as many times as desired without further translation or involvement with the compiler.

Compilers are also able to optimize programs for specific machines, so that, for example, the source code is rearranged in a logically equivalent way that results in the machine having to process the minimum number of machine instructions. Compiled programs execute more efficiently and faster than interpreted programs.

Categories of Software

Software is functionally categorized as operating, utility, or application. Operating software, also known as the operating system, manages the overall operation of the computer system, including file management, program execution, and communication with the peripheral devices. Operating software provides the environment in which utility and application programs operate and is a major determinant of overall computer performance.

Operating software may be specific to one manufacturer or model of computer, or "compatible" among several models or even across brands. Microcomputer software is usually more compatible than mainframe or minicomputer software. Because application software must be compatible with the operating system, care must be taken to choose operating software that will support the desired application programs.

Utility software is preprogrammed software that efficiently performs such routine functions as copying files, sorting data, and compiling application programs. Utility software is often supplied as subroutines of the operating system, although other functions may be added later.

Application software is written by or for the user and, in mass appraisal, performs such functions as data maintenance, value calculations, and performance analysis. Application software falls into two general categories: prepackaged (*hard-coded*) and general-purpose.

Hard-coded software is characterized by rigidity: it requires the data to be in a specific format, performs predefined procedures, and produces standard output. Hard-coded software has usually been pretested and can be placed in operation quickly, but can be difficult to modify and maintain. Many vendors market hard-coded mass appraisal and assessment administration software. Potential users should evaluate the extent to which such systems meet specific needs. Some systems allow considerable flexibility; others do not. Issues to consider are compatibility with existing hardware and software, documentation and support, ease of use, maintenance, whether source code is provided, and whether the vendor provides software modifications and customizing. Changes to the standard system are usually difficult and costly and may void the vendor's obligation to support the system.

Assessment agencies can also develop their own hard-coded systems, which will permit customizing to reflect local statutes, administrative requirements, and other options. Involving the user in system design builds understanding and commitment to the system. In-house development of a hard-coded system is difficult and costly. Developing a complete system can take several years, and future improvements and modifications will require additional programming.

General-purpose software has been programmed to accommodate a wide variety of users. This is accomplished by isolating the various program functions and providing the user with the means to customize them without modifying the program itself. Only the basic system and data management functions are hard-coded; application-specific processes are left to be defined by the user and stored in tables or files where they can be modified as needed. In essence, general-purpose software is a program, usually compiled, that lets a user write application code that will be interpreted each time the program is run. Such programs present less complexity, and less flexibility, than other interpreters.

General-purpose software can be either *horizontal* or *vertical*. Horizontal software is written for a general function such as word processing, data management, spreadsheets, and statistics. Excellent general-purpose software is widely available for all types of hardware and at low cost for microcomputers. Assessors can adapt such software to accomplish a variety of functions including file maintenance, data editing, market research, valuation, and ratio studies (see appendix 19-1 for a discussion of the use of computers in ratio studies).

Vertical general-purpose software is written for a particular industry, business, or application, such as accounting, hospital management, or assessment administration. An assessment administration and mass appraisal system would combine in one package all the modules and functions required to accomplish the inventory, valuation, and assessment of property.

Design and Documentation

Software design directly affects system capabilities, processing efficiency, and ease of maintenance. Design should be *modular*, that is, divided into logical parts. Modular design reduces development time and costs because programmers can work concurrently on the various parts. Such programs are more logi-

Figure 3. Flowchart

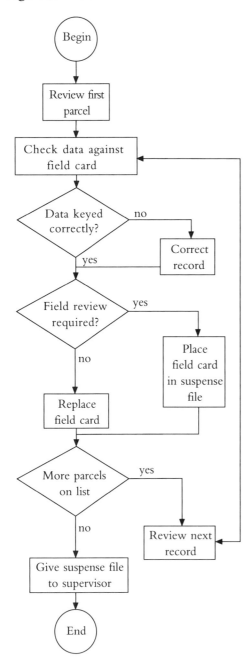

cal and understandable and therefore easier to test, modify, and maintain, particularly for programmers not involved in the original design.

It is equally important that software be well documented. Absence of documentation makes it difficult to modify and maintain programs. There are two kinds of documentation: user and programmer. The user should have a procedural, or user's, guide that explains the system, available options and reports, and proper operation and use.

Programmer documentation includes flowcharts, narrative descriptions of program logic, and explanatory comments inserted into the program code. Flowcharts are schematic outlines of processing logic that show the flow of data between files as well as key decision points, branches, and calculations. Figure 3 shows a simplified flowchart for data review. Flowcharts can also be helpful to users.

Design should also accommodate multiyear processing. Traditionally, assessment systems have been designed to correspond to the tax year cycle, with one year having to be "closed out" before processing for the next year can begin. Multiyear processing allows data maintenance for both years at the same time. Field work for the upcoming tax year can be entered while corrections, appeals, and the like are still being done for the current year. Multiyear processing requires additional programming and storage but reduces processing bottlenecks and improves data accuracy.

Data Base Software

Data have traditionally been stored in a series of "flat" files, as illustrated in figure 4. The files are independent and, in fact, often

Figure 4. Flat File Structure

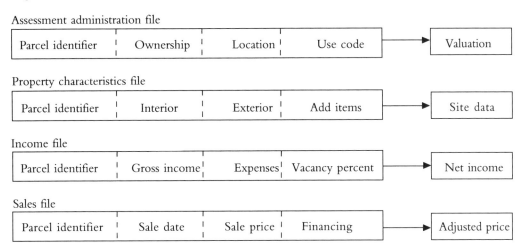

Assessment administration file

| Parcel identifier | Ownership | Location | Use code | → | Valuation |

Property characteristics file

| Parcel identifier | Interior | Exterior | Add items | → | Site data |

Income file

| Parcel identifier | Gross income | Expenses | Vacancy percent | → | Net income |

Sales file

| Parcel identifier | Sale date | Sale price | Financing | → | Adjusted price |

reside on different physical storage devices. This makes it easier to process an individual file but makes it difficult to analyze relationships among data on different files. In figure 4, for example, a sales ratio analysis would require the merging of valuation data from the assessment administration file, sales data from the sales file, and physical characteristics data (for stratification and sales listing reports) from the property characteristics file. This complicates both programming and processing. Also, modifications in file definitions, such as the addition of a new data field, are troublesome, as each application program that references the file must be rewritten to correspond. Many large assessing offices maintain scores of such independent files and hundreds of application programs, which hampers analytical flexibility and data maintenance.

These and related problems led to the development of the concept of a data base management system (DBMS), under which all data of interest reside in a logically related pool. Neither programmers nor users need to know or care about the way the data are physically stored nor about the many possible alternative logical views or files that can be built over the data. A DBMS offers these advantages:

1. *Improved user response.* Storing data in a single logical file makes research and analysis easier. Application programs can usually be written and executed more quickly. DBMS packages usually provide direct query capabilities, so users can perform such operations as listing all properties that sold in a given neighborhood in the last six months or computing the average assessed value per square foot of office buildings of more than 10,000 square feet built since 1980.

2. *Reduced redundancy.* In a data base, with certain exceptions, each data item is entered and stored but once. This can decrease data entry and storage costs and ensures consistency among reports.

3. *Data independence.* A data base creates independence between the data and the application programs. Data definitions can be modified (for example, new fields added) without rewriting application programs. This frees the user to update the data base in response to changing requirements, for example, a revaluation project involving the collection of data items that were not captured previously. Also, from the programmer's viewpoint, it is no longer necessary to merge files and specify file definitions in the writing of application programs.

4. *Centralized security.* Standards for data entry and maintenance can more easily be developed and enforced. Users can be assigned passwords that restrict their access to some parts of the data base and limit the functions they can perform.

5. *Shared data.* Data bases make the sharing of data among departments and agencies easier. For example, the planning and zoning department might be given inquiry/read access to property characteristics data in the assessor's data base. Query functions would permit that department to perform its own analyses without programming assistance.

The following are disadvantages of a data base system:

1. *Expense.* Data base software for mainframe and minicomputers is expensive, and requires a large amount of memory, which may require purchase of more disk storage or upgrading to more powerful hardware. (For microcomputers, however, data base software is inexpensive.)

2. *Complexity.* Mainframe and minicomputer data base processing is complex, requiring a sophisticated support staff. In larger systems, a "data base administrator" is often employed to coordinate operation and maintenance of the system. Furthermore, the complexity of the file structure may make batch programming less efficient.

3. *Vulnerability.* Although the data base improves data security and integrity, it also creates vulnerability in that all the data are in one place. A key software or hardware failure will affect all users. Increased processing complexity makes file backup and recovery more difficult.

Data base systems are not for everyone, but their advantages make them cost-effective for many assessment offices. Conversion to a data base system should be carefully planned. It is important to define requirements in advance, research the available software, and acquire the necessary staff expertise. Conversion of a large office to a data base can take several years; it is good practice to run the existing and new systems in parallel for at least one year.

Smaller jurisdictions may be able to use microcomputer data base software. Even at the microcomputer level, however, careful thought must be given to system design. Adapting microcomputer data base software to the needs and requirements of an assessment office requires a person skilled in both the software and in assessment systems design. Once in place, written documentation and procedures should be maintained on proper use of the system.

Data base structures take several basic forms: *tree, network,* and *relational.* Older mainframe and minicomputer data bases use the tree or network structure; most microcomputer applications and newer mainframe and minicomputer applications are relational.

Figure 5. Tree Data Base Structure

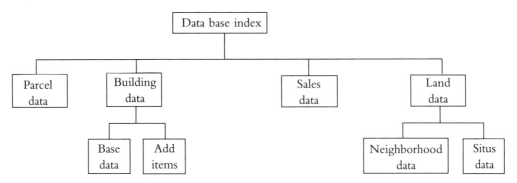

In the tree structure, the data are organized into a logical hierarchy (figure 5). The relationship between data segments is described in terms of parent and child. Except for the root segment, every child has a parent; also, except for the lowest level of data, every parent has children. The data are logically linked, either by the way they are organized on the file or by a data base index and pointers.

A network structure is similar to a tree structure except that each child can have more than one parent. Each series of relationships is akin to a separate file. The relationships are created according to a detailed plan, or "schema," and maintained through indexes and pointers (figure 6). Networks allow the data to be readily processed and analyzed in more ways than a tree structure does. Such flexibility comes at the expense of efficient processing of some routine batch-oriented jobs, however.

A relational data base logically organizes data into sets of related tables. Each row of a table represents a record; each column, a field or data element. Logical relationships

Figure 6. Network Data Base Structure

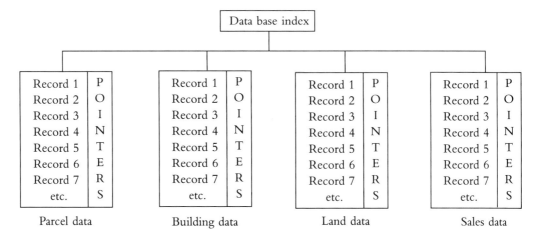

Figure 7. Relational Data Base Structure

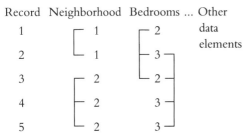

Figure 8. Software Components of a CAMA System

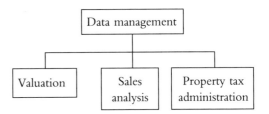

can be established between tables with at least one field in common, for example, neighborhood or number of bedrooms (figure 7). One can readily select, combine, and process records on the data base in a variety of ways based on these relationships. Relational data bases appear to be a series of flat files to designers and programmers, making them less complex to establish and maintain. Relational data bases usually also offer greater processing flexibility and the best combination of flexibility and efficiency, both at the time the application programs are built and each time they are run.

Selecting a CAMA System

Selection of a CAMA system is a major decision with long-term implications for cost and performance. The user must match current requirements against available hardware and software options, as well as consider costs and a host of issues related to technical design, maintenance, and expandability.

System Capabilities and Requirements

A CAMA and assessment administration system should be capable of several broad functions: data management, sales analysis, valuation, and administration (figure 8).

Data Management The system should provide for maintenance of the property data files used for appraisal. This should include the following capabilities:

Selection of Data Items The user should be able to specify the data items (fields) used by the system, with validity checks. The user should be able to add, delete, and redefine data fields.

Logical Ordering of Data The user should be able to establish logical record orders independent of the physical order of the data. This includes the ability to sort and select data according to multiple criteria. The user should be able to modify these logical relationships at will.

Security It should be possible to restrict access to authorized personnel only, to limit certain users to certain functions (for example, inquiry only), and to monitor system use.

Data Editing and Manipulation The user should be able to define logical edit checks between data fields to ensure, for example, that finished basement area is not greater than total basement area. The user should also be able to create new fields by recoding, adding, multiplying, or otherwise manipulating existing fields.

Maintenance Ease of maintenance is crucial to long-term cost-effectiveness. The user should be able to add, delete, and modify records either individually or in mass. An example of the latter would be application of an economic obsolescence factor to all vacant land parcels in a given area.

Sales Analysis The CAMA and assessment administration system should provide for the maintenance and analysis of sales data. This should include the following capabilities:

Maintenance of a Sales File The system should provide for a logical sales file, which need not be a physically distinct file. This file should preserve a physical description or "picture" of each parcel as of the date of sale.

Data Display and Tabulations The system should contain features for arraying, tabulating, graphing, and plotting sales data and sales ratios. The user should be able to specify the records, variables, and type of analysis desired.

Ratio Studies The system should provide the ability to conduct ratio analyses, including calculation of the usual measures of central tendency and uniformity. The user should be able to define the reporting categories (for example, neighborhood or construction class) and specify the sales to be used in the analysis.

Statistical Testing The system should support the calculation of confidence intervals and statistical tests of the level and uniformity of appraisals (see appendices 20-1 through 20-8).

Sales Reports The system should have a report-generator feature for producing sales listings and related reports. The user should be able to specify the data and organization of the reports.

Valuation The valuation system should support automated applications of the three approaches to value.

Cost Approach Whether table- or formula-driven, the cost model should allow the user to enter cost factors and components obtained from a variety of sources and adjusted to the local market. "Add items" should be identified by code to facilitate automated cost recalculations. The user should be able to construct or modify depreciation tables to fit the local market.

A land valuation module should provide for the calculation of land values based on standard units of comparison with adjustments for depth, shape, topography, and the like. The user should be able to specify the units of comparison, strata, and adjustments.

Sales Comparison Approach As a minimum, the system should provide for the selection and adjustment of comparable sales. Advanced systems will feature multiple regression analysis or the adaptive estimation procedure (AEP or feedback). The user should be able to specify the variables to be used in these procedures.

Income Approach The system should provide for income and expense analysis and the calculation of income multipliers and overall rates. The user should be able to define the strata to be used in these calculations. The usual indirect capitalization techniques, particularly annuity capitalization, should also be supported.

Administration The assessment administration system must provide for the calculation and processing of assessments, exemptions, and tax bills. Other useful features include the following:

Appeals Processing　The system may provide for the automated logging and scheduling of appeals.

Building Permit Processing　The system may be used to record and process building permits.

Tax Delinquencies　The system may be used to track and process tax delinquencies.

Use-Value Assessments　The system may provide for the use-valuation of agricultural lands and open space through the application of valuation tables based on soil type.

Forms Generation　The system may be used to develop and generate property record cards and forms.

Project Management　The system may provide various management reports useful in quality control, planning, and scheduling.

Software Sources

Assessors have four basic options for acquiring CAMA software: in-house design, purchase of a commercially available system, acquisition of a public domain system, and adaptation of general-purpose software. Figure 9 summarizes the advantages and disadvantages of each.

The primary advantage of in-house design is the opportunity to tailor the CAMA system to the user's specific requirements. Another advantage is user involvement, which builds understanding and commitment to the system. The jurisdiction should, of course, have the necessary systems design and programming expertise. In-house design is time-consuming and expensive, usually taking at least two years in larger jurisdictions. Once in use, the system must be routinely updated to reflect changing requirements. In-house design should be considered only if there is a reasonable assurance that programming staff will be available to support maintenance and modifications. Unless a highly customized system is required, this option may not be cost-effective.

One of the most common and reliable methods of acquiring a CAMA system is purchase from a commercial firm specializing in CAMA software. If the existing data are compatible with the system, it can usually be ready to use in a short time. Such systems are often pretested and are reliable, having been used in a number of other jurisdictions. On the other hand, because they are hard-coded, commercially available systems may allow little flexibility in specifying desired data items, edit procedures, valuation procedures, and reports. Once the system is in use, in-house modifications may be difficult.

Besides talking with vendors, the assessor should talk to other jurisdictions that are using the systems and observe firsthand any systems being seriously considered. Special attention should be given to maintenance provisions. The assessor should identify who will provide periodic maintenance and modification and what they will cost. Unauthorized changes to the software may void the warranty or the vendor's obligation to support the system.

Before purchasing a system from a commercial mass appraisal firm, it is good practice to develop a request for proposal (RFP). The RFP should clearly define the user's requirements and invite interested vendors to submit proposals and costs by a specified

Figure 9.   Software Options

	Advantages	Disadvantages
In-house development	Fully customized Heavy user involvement	Long period of development Costly
Purchase of commercial system	Quickly implemented Pretested and reliable	Hard-coded (may be custo- mized at additional cost) Difficult to modify
Use of public domain software	Free or only nominal cost Quickly implemented Pretested	Hard-coded Difficult to modify May not be well documented

Adaptation of
general-purpose software
	Highly customized
	Basic system pretested and
	    well documented
	Easily modified
	Heavy user involvement
	Inexpensive
		Requires knowledgeable users
		Need to develop supplemental
		    documentation

date. Guidelines for developing an RFP appear later in this chapter.

Public domain software is software available from another jurisdiction or other source either free or at nominal cost (often the cost of reproduction). Such systems can be good but should be carefully evaluated. The fact that they are virtually free does not necessarily make them cost-effective. There are usually hidden costs in tailoring such systems to fit the user's specific needs. In fact, many such systems will run on only one type of hardware and require a particular data structure. Also, much public domain software performs only a single function. Although it may do so very well, it must be integrated with the rest of the CAMA and assessment administration system. Finally, the available documentation and how the system will be maintained and modified should be considered. The acquiring juris-

diction usually has to rely on its own resources for this.

For jurisdictions using microcomputers, the adaptation of general-purpose software offers an interesting option in developing a CAMA system. The basic system will be pretested, reliable, and usually well documented. A user who is well versed in the software can tailor it to the agency's specific requirements. Ongoing maintenance and modifications can usually be made quickly and easily. Because of a wide user base and high competition, general-purpose software is inexpensive, varying from several hundred to one thousand dollars or more depending on available functions.

Adapting a general-purpose software package to mass appraisal or assessment administration requires considerable time and a knowledgeable user, that is, someone who understands both the software and the re-

Figure 10. Hardware Options

	Advantages	Disadvantages
Purchase	Known total cost Modest annual cost	Large initial cost Obsolescence
Leasing	No fixed cost Upward flexibility	High annual cost High vendor dependence
Service bureau	Efficient for low-volume use No long-term commitments	Actual costs unknown Discourages research Minimal software support
Shared facilities	Shared costs Possibilities of shared software	Requires high coordination Possible difficulties in maintenance and modifications

quirements of a good CAMA system. Also, the assessor should not rely on only one employee; documentation on operation of the system should be prepared, and several of the staff should be trained in its use. Ease of use is essential; except for nonroutine functions and new applications, users should be able to operate the system without recourse to the base software manuals.

Hardware Sources

Once a jurisdiction has selected its software, it can shop for hardware. There are four basic hardware options: outright purchase, leasing, service bureaus, and sharing of facilities. Figure 10 summarizes their advantages and disadvantages.

Outright purchase has the advantages of a known fixed cost and low annual (maintenance) costs. For larger systems, however, the initial outlay can be substantial. Given the rapid change in technology, a purchased system can suffer rapid obsolescence. The purchaser should pay special attention to upgradability. Some systems are more easily upgraded than others, and some vendors will offer discounts on upgraded equipment. Due to their low costs, microcomputers are usually purchased outright, as are most minicomputer systems and some mainframes.

Mainframe systems are usually leased. Terms range from one to five years, with monthly costs usually decreasing with the term of the lease. Leasing is attractive in that it requires no large initial outlay and offers great flexibility in upgrading. On the other hand, annual costs will be greater than with a purchased system. In addition, the lessee must depend on the vendor for service.

Service bureaus are companies that specialize in renting computer time as needed. In addition to batch processing, most service bureaus now offer on-line access via communication lines to terminals placed in the user's office. Service bureaus can be economical for small jurisdictions and usually involve little or no long-term commitment. However, the pay-for-time approach discourages research and exacts penalties for correcting errors or rerunning a program. Also, the jurisdiction will have to supply its own application programs and can expect little soft ware maintenance support from the service bureau.

Many local government agencies share a common mainframe or minicomputer, thus reducing costs per user. Certain software costs, particularly data base software, can also be shared. A system of multiple users, however, requires coordination and system management. Assessors may not be able to get adequate access, maintenance, and systems development support.

Assessing jurisdictions can also band together to share computer hardware and software, including application programs, on a regional basis. This offers potential cost savings but, again, requires careful planning, coordination, and commitment.

Request for Proposal

When considering a major hardware or software acquisition, a jurisdiction should usually develop an request for proposal (RFP). (See the IAAO *Standard on Contracting for Assessment Services* [1986]. Chapter 18 discusses RFPs for revaluation projects.) The RFP should describe the required products, performance standards, completion dates, and maintenance provisions. Figure 11 is a checklist of items that should be covered in the RFP. A clear, complete, and detailed RFP is the key to achieving a desired product.

It is good practice to appoint an advisory committee to coordinate development of the RFP, review proposals, select a vendor, and coordinate contract fulfillment. Proposals should be evaluated on the basis of the bidders' qualifications, responsiveness, and costs. Contracts should never be awarded on the basis of cost alone. The jurisdiction must be confident that the chosen bidder is capable of delivering the specified product on time

and can meet any required training, maintenance, or other obligations. It is helpful to prepare a checklist of requirements for rating proposals. The bidders' experience in providing similar products to other assessment offices should be evaluated.

Once a contract is awarded, the advisory committee should monitor delivery and installation. The hardware or software should be tested to ensure that it meets required performance standards and contains no unanticipated problems or "bugs." Documentation should be reviewed for completeness, and questions about proper operation and use should be resolved as soon as possible.

Sometimes software contracts will call for a customized product, which requires more time for development and installation. In such cases, the agency and contractor should develop a mutually agreeable work plan at the beginning of the project and continually monitor progress against the work plan. The agency should insist on periodic written progress reports and not sign off on project tasks or products until they have been reviewed and tested.

Issues in System Selection

In addition to reviewing the functions required in a good CAMA and assessment administration system, the agency should consider a number of technical hardware and software issues. Many of the following have special importance for microcomputers.

Memory and Processing Speed Of the two types of computer memory, main memory (RAM) and secondary storage, the former should be sufficient to support efficiently such mathematically intensive operations as ratio studies, multiple regression

Figure 11.   Request for Proposal (RFP) Checklist

	Hardware	Software

1. Vendor's qualifications
  a. Experience
  b. Financial position
	x	x

2. Employees' qualifications
  a. Primary contractor
  b. Subcontractors
		x

3. Agency's operating environment
  a. Existing hardware and software
  b. Other relevant considerations
	x	x

4. Performance requirements	x	x

5. Output
  a. Valuations, assessments, tax bills
  b. Reports
		x

6. Training and education	x	x

7. Documentation and maintenance
  a. Manuals
  b. Maintenance, modifications, troubleshooting
	x	x

8. Delivery dates	x	x
9. Method of evaluating bids	x	x
10. Obtaining clarifications to RFP	x	x

analysis, and comparable sales analysis. The current state of the art in computer chip technology and local requirements will determine the cost-effectiveness of various processing alternatives.

Secondary storage should be sufficient to support data and program files, provide adequate work areas, and allow for future expansion. Assuming 1,000–1,500 bytes per parcel, a jurisdiction of 10,000 parcels will require 10–15 million bytes for storage alone. This assumes no duplication of data items; in practice, data are often repeated on several files. For example, the sales and property characteristics files usually duplicate data. Also, required work areas often exceed the size of the data files being analyzed. Given these considerations, and the low cost of the storage media, even very small jurisdictions should purchase no less than 40 megabytes of disk capacity.

Expandability   Expandability is a function of hardware and software design and refers to the ease with which the system can be upgraded to support increased use and new technology. A system should be able to upgrade memory (both internal and secondary), add additional peripherals, convert software without major disruptions, and take advantage of expected technical breakthroughs. For mainframe and minicomputer systems, leasing provides maximum flexibility.

Multitasking and Multiuser Processing
Multitasking is the simultaneous processing of more than one application program; multiuser processing is the ability of the system to support more than one user at the same time. Mainframe and minicomputer systems provide such support in the form of timesharing, in which the system allocates CPU time to the various users and programs based on predetermined priorities. Although such systems usually have large memory and processing capabilities, the assessment office needs to choose a system that will allow priorities to be set fairly and ensure adequate response times.

At the microcomputer level, multitasking and multiuser processing require particular operating systems and additional main memory. The operating system must be more sophisticated than that required for a single user and single program, capable of resolving such questions as: If user A is updating a file, should user B also be able to do so? What if they both want to update the same record? If program A is producing a report from a given file, and program B performs maintenance on the file, should program B be allowed to run simultaneously? Will the results of program A reflect the changes? Although multitasking and multiuser processing are complex (and often unnecessary), they offer gains in productivity to many microcomputer-based assessment offices.

Compatibility Compatibility refers to the ability of the computer system to run a variety of software and accommodate various peripherals. Some operating systems, for example, will not run certain application programs. Some computers will not support certain monitors, printers, and plotters. When acquiring a new system, the best way to approach this problem is first to select the application software and then to select hardware that will run the software. However, software that restricts the hardware selection to a single manufacturer will limit purchase options and future expansion.

Transferability The computer system should be able to exchange data with other computer systems with minimal difficulty. Jurisdictions should also be able to upload and download data between their mainframes or minicomputers and microcomputers.

File Structure and Program Design
Modular, user-friendly software is easier to use, maintain, and modify. A data base structure will make research and analysis easier, because the user can select, sort, and merge data without writing application programs. Data bases are usually accompanied by query programs, which allow the user to prepare ad hoc analyses and reports with minimal instructions. Good data base software is available for microcomputers at low cost.

Security and Backup Data security and backup are important. Some software will, either by default or as an option, make a backup copy of files accessed by the user; if errors are made, the original file can be recovered. In mainframe and minicomputer systems, file backups can be scheduled routinely (for example, every night). In a microcomputer system, backup is made easier by compact tape drives and high-capacity floppy disk drives. The data management system should also provide password protection, so that users can be restricted to certain files or functions (for example, inquiry only access).

System Documentation and Support
Documentation and support are critical to the long-term success of any computer system. The purchaser of hardware and software should expect complete documentation and RFPs should specifically require it. User training, system maintenance, and program modifications necessitated by changes in user requirements should also be provided for. Well-written documentation is particularly important. Even though most microcomputer software documentation is reasonably good, potential users should seek information on its completeness and quality. Product reviews published in trade publications are helpful, and many vendors provide a telephone help line for users.

Summary

Computers have been used for mass appraisal since the 1950s. Improved hardware and software now make it possible for virtually any jurisdiction to develop a CAMA system at reasonable cost. Selection of hardware for a CAMA system depends on the size of the jurisdiction and the complexity of the tasks to be done. Software systems should modular, flexible, and capable of handling data management, sales analysis, valuation, and administration.

Sales Analysis and Mass Appraisal Performance Evaluation

20

Introduction

If the property tax is to be fair and provide adequate revenue for local government, mass appraisal must produce accurate appraisals and equitable assessments. The primary tool used to measure mass appraisal performance is the ratio study.

Definition and Purpose

A ratio study compares appraised values to market values. Market value is the most probable price in cash that a property would bring in a competitive and open market, assuming that the buyer and seller are acting knowledgeably, sufficient time is allowed for the sale, and price is not affected by special influences. In a ratio study, market values are usually represented by sales prices; actual prices may be adjusted for time of sale, financing, personal property, or other considerations. Sales that do not represent open-market, arm's-length transfers should not be used in ratio studies.

Independent, expert appraisals may also be used to represent market values in a ratio study, particularly when valid sales data are insufficient or when the accuracy of appraisals of property not subject to the market value standard is evaluated. In many jurisdictions, for example, statutes require agricultural lands to be appraised on the basis of productivity, or use value, rather than

market value. A ratio study designed to measure appraisal performance for such properties should be based on independent appraisals that reflect the use-value requirement.

Computation of Ratios

The ratios used in a ratio study are formed by dividing appraised values made for tax purposes by other estimates of market value, such as sales prices or independent appraisals. For example, a property appraised for tax purposes at $40,000 and sold for $50,000 has a ratio of 0.80, or 80 percent:

$$A/S = \$40,000/\$50,000 = 0.80,$$

where A is the appraised value and S is the sale price.

Gross assessed values (values before subtraction of partial exemptions) may be substituted for appraised values where the statutory level of assessment is 100 percent of market value. Using gross, rather than net, assessed values avoids complications caused by exemptions.

If the property in the above example were required by statute to be assessed at 50 percent of market value, the *assessed* value of the property would be $20,000 (50 percent of $40,000), and the assessment ratio would be 0.40 or 40 percent ($20,000 divided by $50,000). In this chapter, unless otherwise specified, ratios are based on *appraised* rather than *assessed* values. Also, market values are represented by sales prices, unless independent appraisals are specifically indicated.

Aspects of Mass Appraisal Performance

Ratio studies measure two primary aspects of mass appraisal accuracy: level and uniformity. *Appraisal level* refers to the overall, or typical, ratio at which properties are appraised. In mass appraisal, appraised values do not always equal their indicators of market value (sales prices or independent appraisals), but overappraisals should balance underappraisals, so that the typical ratio is near 100 percent. Measures of appraisal level are treated later in this chapter.

Appraisal uniformity relates to the fair and equitable treatment of individual properties. Uniformity requires, first, that properties be appraised equitably within groups or categories (use classes, neighborhoods, and so forth) and, second, that each of these groups be appraised at the same level, or ratio, of market value. That is, appraisal uniformity requires equity *within* groups and *between* groups.

Uniformity within Groups   Uniformity within a group is determined by measuring the magnitude of the differences between each ratio and the average ratio. Figure 1 illustrates why this measurement is important. In group 1, the largest difference between ratios is 0.20 (1.10 − 0.90), but in group 2 it is 1.20 (1.60 − 0.40). Although the average ratio is the same in both groups, uniformity is better in group 1 than in group 2. Tax burdens will be more uniformly distributed in group 1 than in group 2. Measures of ap-

praisal uniformity within property groups are discussed later in this chapter.

Figure 1.   Examples of Appraisal Uniformity

	Group 1	Group 2
	0.90	0.40
	0.95	0.80
	1.00	1.00
	1.05	1.20
	1.10	1.60
Average	1.00	1.00

Uniformity between Groups   Uniformity between groups of properties is determined by comparing their average ratios (appraisal levels). Large differences indicate inequitable appraisals and thus unequal taxation between groups. For example, if the appraisal level is 90 percent for single-family residential property and 60 percent for multifamily property, multifamily property is underappraised relative to single-family property, and owners would pay one-third less in taxes per dollar of market value.

Systematic differences in appraisal level can be analyzed in terms of *horizontal inequities* and *vertical inequities*. Horizontal inequities are differences in appraisal levels between groups of properties defined by property type, location, age, size, or some other attribute. The above comparison between single-family and multifamily properties illustrates horizontal inequity.

Vertical inequities are differences in appraisal levels for groups of properties defined by value. Assume that appraisal levels are similar among neighborhoods, but that more expensive houses are generally appraised at a lower percentage of market value than less expensive houses. Although there is no horizontal inequity among neighborhoods, vertical inequities exist. In practice, horizontal and vertical inequities are often related. A simple measure of vertical inequity, the price-related differential, is discussed later in this chapter. Appendix 18-1 discusses statistical tests for vertical inequities.

Design of Ratio Studies

The ratio study is a flexible tool that can provide valuable information for a variety of purposes. The design of a ratio study should reflect its purposes, including any legal requirements, and the budget and staff available. Computer software options should also be considered (appendix 19-1). A ratio study usually has six parts: (1) delineation of objectives, (2) collection and preparation of data, (3) matching of appraisal and sales data, (4) stratification, (5) statistical analysis, and (6) evaluation and use of results.

Delineation of Objectives   The objectives of the study determine its scope, content, depth, and flexibility.

Collection and Preparation of Data   The precision and reliability of any ratio study depend on the quantity and quality of the sales and independent appraisals available. Sales data must be collected, screened, and edited, and sales prices adjusted as necessary for financing, personal property, and time of sale.

Matching Appraisal and Sales Data   The appraised value and the sale price (or independent appraisal) must be for the same property in the same physical condition. Par-

cel identifiers and legal descriptions should be reviewed. Parcels that have been split or combined should have new identifiers assigned; otherwise they may be matched against the previous sale of a physically different parcel.

A property may change in some physical way between time of appraisal and time of sale, for example, through a new improvement or room addition. Such sales should be deleted from the study unless they can be used in such a manner that the property appraised corresponds to the property sold. For example, assume that a property sold for $20,000 and is currently appraised for assessment purposes at $80,000, giving an apparent ratio of 4.00, or 400 percent. Review of the sale, however, reveals that the property was vacant when sold and was subsequently improved. The $80,000 appraised value consists of a land value of $25,000 and an improvement value of $55,000. A sale ratio can be computed using the appraised value of the land only, yielding a ratio of 1.25, or 125 percent ($25,000/$20,000).

Stratification   In ratio studies, stratification is the sorting of parcels into relatively homogeneous groups based on use, physical characteristics, or location. Stratification permits analysis of mass appraisal performance within and between property groups.

The objectives of the ratio study determine the strata to be used. Equalization agencies usually stratify properties by jurisdiction and classification. Local assessors should further stratify by such criteria as the valuation model (cost, income, or sales comparison), construction class, neighborhood, size, and age. The chosen strata should reflect statutory classifications of property. The design of the study should be flexible enough to allow the analyst to modify strata for changing needs and special situations.

Statistical Analysis Ratio data can be arrayed, tabulated, and graphed, and various measures of appraisal level and uniformity can be calculated. Assessment officials may also need to develop confidence intervals or test hypotheses (see appendix 20-1) about appraisal performance in order to determine compliance with legal or administrative standards. Such analyses are especially important for equalization decisions.

Evaluation of Results A properly designed and executed ratio study provides valuable information about the quality of mass appraisal work. Areas with good results should need less time and attention, which can then be redirected to areas with poor results. These areas can be targeted for reappraisal or other corrective action.

However, ratio studies have limitations. Perfection is not possible in mass appraisal, nor can a ratio study provide perfect information about appraisal performance. Insufficient sales or overrepresentation of one locale with an active market can distort results. In general, the reliability of a ratio study increases with the number and representativeness of the sales or independent appraisals used in the study. In addition, reliability requires that unsold parcels be appraised in the same manner as sold parcels (appendix 20-2).

Uses of Ratio Studies

Ratio studies serve many purposes. The primary use is evaluation of mass appraisal performance. Local assessors, supervisory agencies, and others can use the studies to determine where appraisal performance meets

acceptable standards and where it does not. Market-based trending factors developed from information provided by ratio studies can be used to adjust appraisal levels to acceptable standards. Ratio studies, then, provide not only a measure of performance, but also a means of improving performance. By providing information on current operations, ratio studies also help in planning, scheduling, and budgeting future activities.

The primary users of ratio studies are equalization agencies, supervisory agencies, assessors, independent appraisers, taxpayers, and appeal boards.

Equalization Agencies Agencies concerned with interjurisdictional equalization can use ratio studies to measure appraisal levels and to make comparisons between types and areas of property. To achieve equalization, they may apply trending or equalization factors or order reappraisals. Often, taxing authorities or districts overlap more than one assessing jurisdiction. In such cases, equalizing values across jurisdiction lines produces uniformity in effective tax rates within taxing districts. Similar considerations apply to state property taxes and exemption programs in the United States. In the case of exemptions, equalization results in the exemptions having equal tax savings. In addition, state agencies often use ratio studies to estimate the full market value of property for purposes of distributing school aid and making intergovernmental transfer payments.

Supervisory Agencies Supervisory agencies that develop appraisal standards, guidelines, and manuals can use ratio studies to monitor the effectiveness of their programs, as well as local appraisal performance. These agencies need relatively detailed studies that reveal both level and uniformity by property class, geographic or economic areas, and major property characteristics. Ratio studies can help them modify appraisal manuals, depreciation schedules, and valuation formulas.

Assessors Local assessors can use ratio studies for a variety of purposes—testing compliance with legal or administrative standards, identifying groups of properties requiring reappraisal or adjustment, evaluating the effectiveness of various appraisal procedures, monitoring the work of individual appraisers, and gauging the merit of taxpayer appeals. In addition to regularly planned studies, assessors often conduct ratio studies in response to specific ad hoc needs. In general, ratio studies conducted by local assessors require more detail and flexibility than studies conducted by others.

Independent Appraisers Independent appraisal firms hired by local jurisdictions can prepare ratio studies to document the results of their efforts and provide assessors with evidence for defending the valuations. Assessors themselves can monitor revaluation results in house by conducting ratio studies before and after revaluations.

Taxpayers and Appeal Boards These parties can use ratio studies to compare appraisal levels between groups of properties and to evaluate whether a given class of properties is appraised at market value.

Data Displays

Ratio study statistics can be confusing to those with little mathematical background. Graphs and diagrams help clarify ratio study statistics and often provide a more complete picture of appraisal performance than statistics alone.

Data displays are used in mass appraisal performance analysis to (1) depict the level of appraisal for the jurisdiction or for categories of property within the jurisdiction; (2) compare the level of appraisal between categories; (3) depict the uniformity of appraisals; (4) depict the relationship between level of appraisal and selected property characteristics, such as size, construction grade, or sale price; (5) determine the pattern or distribution of ratios, including whether or not the ratios are normally distributed; and (6) reveal outlier ratios.

Six useful data displays are arrays, frequency distributions, histograms, polygons, scatter diagrams, and contingency tables. Other techniques can be used for analyzing relationships among multiple variables.

Arrays

In ratio studies, an array is a listing of ratios from lowest to highest. Table 1 is an example. Arrays are used to compute the range, median, and quartiles of ratio data. The *range* is the difference between the highest and lowest ratio. In table 1, the range is 2.200 minus 0.600, or 1.600. The *median* (to be discussed more fully later) is the midpoint of the ratios. In table 1, this is 0.943 (the average of the two middle ratios, 0.926 and 0.960). *Quartiles* divide the data into four equal parts. The first quartile is the upper bound of the first one-fourth of the ratios, the second quartile (median) divides the ratios in half, and so forth. Arrays also help in identifying outlier ratios (unusually large or small ratios), which may be associated with invalid sales that distort ratio study results. Arrays are best suited to small samples in which direct visual analysis is feasible.

Table 1.   Example of Outlier Ratio

Sale number	Appraised value (A)	Sale price (S)	Ratio (A/S)
1	$15,000	$25,000	0.600
2	15,000	22,000	0.682
3	17,000	20,000	0.850
4	19,000	22,000	0.864
5	25,000	27,000	0.926
6	24,000	25,000	0.960
7	25,000	25,000	1.000
8	20,000	16,000	1.250
9	35,000	25,000	1.400
10	55,000	25,000	2.200

Frequency Distributions

A frequency distribution shows the number of ratios falling within specified intervals. A frequency distribution that shows the *percentage* of ratios in each class is termed a *relative frequency distribution*. Frequency distributions reveal trends or patterns that might be missed in viewing a large array but are of little use for very small samples. To construct a frequency distribution, array the ratios, select classes (or intervals) in which to group the ratios, and then count the number of ratios in each interval.

Some general rules for constructing a frequency distribution are:

1. Choose at least five and not more than fifteen intervals. Larger samples require more intervals than smaller ones.
2. Choose intervals that will accommodate all the data.
3. Choose intervals that do not overlap. This requires that interval boundaries have as many decimal places as the individual ratios and that the starting boundary of an interval not be the same as the ending boundary of the previous interval. For example, if ratios are rounded to three decimal places, the following interval scheme would meet these criteria: 0–0.099, 0.100–0.199, 0.200–0.299, and so on.
4. Generally, choose intervals of equal length so results will be easier to interpret. In large samples, more detail can be achieved by choosing smaller intervals near the center and wider intervals toward the ends of the distribution, although the distribution becomes more difficult to interpret. In any case, the first and last intervals can be open-ended to accommodate outliers (for example, ratios less than 0.500 or greater than 2.000).
5. Choose intervals that are easy to work with and understand, for example, multiples of 0.05 and 0.10.

Figure 2 and table 2 illustrate the creation of a frequency distribution. Figure 2 shows forty ratios arrayed from smallest to largest. In table 2, these ratios are grouped into a relative frequency distribution that meets the above criteria. It contains twelve intervals that accommodate all the ratios, do not overlap, and are of equal length, except for open-ended intervals at the low and high ends of the distribution. The same number of intervals (six) was chosen above and below 1.000 (a useful point of reference in ad valorem appraisal).

Frequency distributions provide much information about appraisal performance. The interval containing the greatest number of ratios represents the most common level of appraisal (0.900 to 0.999 in table 2). The distribution of the ratios provides an excel-

Figure 2. Array of Data for Frequency Distribution

0.500	0.820	0.900	0.979	1.099
0.602	0.820	0.912	0.985	1.111
0.611	0.830	0.947	1.000	1.140
0.705	0.847	0.950	1.006	1.175
0.710	0.877	0.955	1.032	1.195
0.744	0.890	0.960	1.045	1.250
0.750	0.895	0.966	1.060	1.550
0.799	0.898	0.973	1.085	1.600

Table 2. Frequency Distribution

Interval	Number of ratios	Relative frequency (percent of ratios)
Less than 0.500	0	0.0%
0.500–0.599	1	2.5%
0.600–0.699	2	5.0%
0.700–0.799	5	12.5%
0.800–0.899	8	20.0%
0.900–0.999	10	25.0%
1.000–1.099	7	17.5%
1.100–1.199	4	10.0%
1.200–1.299	1	2.5%
1.300–1.399	0	0.0%
1.400–1.499	0	0.0%
More than 1.500	2	5.0%
Total	40	100.0%

lent indication of appraisal uniformity. For example, table 2 shows that 72.5 percent of the ratios fall from 0.800 to 1.199, a relatively tight distribution. If uniformity were poor, fewer ratios would fall in this range.

The pattern of the frequency distribution is also meaningful. A symmetrical distribution indicates an even balance between high and low ratios. In practice, most frequency distributions are skewed to the right, which can simply reflect the mathematical properties of ratio data. An appraisal 20 percent above the sale price, for example, results in a ratio that differs from 1.000 more than does an appraisal 20 percent below the sale price: 1.200 versus 0.833. A severely nonsymmetrical distribution, however, indicates an undesirable imbalance between over- and underappraisals.

Histograms

A histogram is a bar chart, or graph, of a frequency distribution. The heights or areas of the bars indicate the number or percentage of the ratios that fall in each interval. In large samples, a histogram using percentages (rather than numbers) is easier to interpret.

To construct a histogram:

1. Choose intervals that match those used in the frequency distribution. Place them along the horizontal axis.
2. Do not delete intervals that contain no ratios; instead leave gaps between the bars.
3. Use the vertical axis to represent the number or percentage of ratios in each interval. Percentages are usually more meaningful than numbers.
4. Draw the histogram as a series of continuous bars rather than as points connected by lines. (The latter is a polygon, better suited to the display of multiple data sets.)

Figure 3 is a histogram developed from the frequency distribution shown in table 2. The scale used for the vertical axis was chosen to allow the tallest bar to fill most of the allotted space.

Like a frequency distribution, from which it is derived, a histogram reveals much about the distribution of ratios and appraisal accuracy. The highest bar represents the most common level of appraisal, and the tightness of the distribution depicts uniformity. In addition, a histogram illustrates the extent to

Figure 3. Histogram

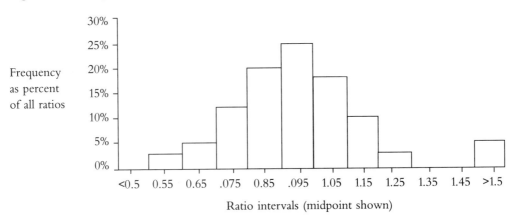

Frequency as percent of all ratios

Ratio intervals (midpoint shown)

which the ratios are in a normal (bell-shaped) distribution, which is important in the interpretation of ratio study statistics. A bimodal (two peaks) or multimodal (multiple peaks) distribution may indicate that distinct property groups are being appraised at different percentages of market value. Finally, the tails of the histogram show the outliers, which are expected in every ratio study. If they are absent, sales screening may be too severe; if excessive, sales screening may be inadequate.

Polygons

Although frequency distributions and histograms can display only a single group of data, a polygon (line chart) can accommodate multiple data sets on the same graph and is also well suited to the display of time series data. For example, in figure 4, a polygon shows trends in appraisal levels for residential, industrial, commercial, and farmland properties from 1975 through 1990. Different symbols are used for each property type. When color plotters are available, different colors can be used.

Polygons are also useful for analyzing changes in price levels over time. Sales ratios can be plotted against quarter or month of sale, as in figure 5. The graph reveals both direction and magnitude of changes. An upward trend indicates deflation, because sales prices tend to fall relative to appraised values. Similarly, a downward trend in the ratios, which implies higher sales prices relative to appraised values, suggests inflation. Analysis of time trends is discussed more fully in appendix 5-3.

Scatter Diagrams

A scatter diagram is a graph of the relationship between an independent variable and a dependent variable. The independent variable is on the horizontal (*x*) axis and the dependent variable on the vertical (*y*) axis. In ratio study analysis, the dependent variable is the ratio and the independent variable is a property characteristic such as square feet, sale price, or age.

The scatter diagram shows the correlation between the independent and dependent variables. If there is no correlation, the points

Figure 4. Sample of Line Chart

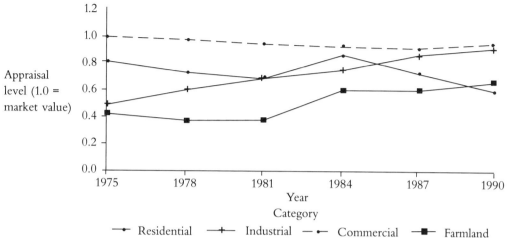

Appraisal
level (1.0 =
market value)

Year

Category

— • — Residential — + — Industrial — • — Commercial — ■ — Farmland

Figure 5. Effect of Market Value Changes over Time on Appraisal Level

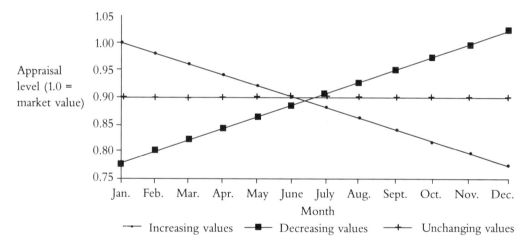

Appraisal
level (1.0 =
market value)

Month

— • — Increasing values — ■ — Decreasing values — + — Unchanging values

in the graph will form a random pattern about a horizontal line. An upward sloping trend implies a *positive* relationship between the variables, that is, the dependent variable increases as the independent variable increases. Conversely, a downward sloping trend indicates a *negative* relationship between the variables, meaning that the dependent variable tends to decrease as the independent variable increases.

Figure 6 is a scatter diagram of the relationship between the square footage and sales ratio data shown in table 3. Each point represents one ratio. The relationship is negative—as square footage increases, the ratios tend to decrease—which implies that larger houses are underappraised relative to smaller houses.

Regardless of the property characteristic represented on the *x* axis, appraisal equity is

Table 3.   Data for Scatter Diagram

A/S	Square feet
0.500	3,000
0.611	1,950
0.710	2,700
0.750	2,650
0.820	2,000
0.830	1,870
0.877	1,500
0.895	2,100
0.900	2,200
0.947	1,600
0.950	1,800
0.960	1,400
0.973	1,500
0.985	1,200
1.006	1,600
1.045	1,100
1.085	1,400
1.111	1,000
1.175	800
1.250	1,200

A/S is the ratio of appraised value to sale price.

indicated by a horizontal pattern, which implies uniformity in the appraisal of properties on the lower and higher ends of the range.

Contingency Tables

Another useful method of displaying ratio data is with contingency tables, which show how a dependent variable, such as sale ratio, varies with respect to *two* independent variables. Table 4 shows median sales ratios by neighborhood and effective age (number of sales is shown in parentheses). A scatter diagram of sales ratios plotted against effective age would show a negative correlation, suggesting inaccurate depreciation schedules. In fact, however, the primary problem is systematic underappraisal in Neighborhood C. Within neighborhoods, age categories are appraised similarly.

Contingency tables can also reveal interactive effects between the dependent variable and two independent variables. For example, if each "cell," or group, were appraised close

Figure 6.   Scatter Diagram of Ratio to Area

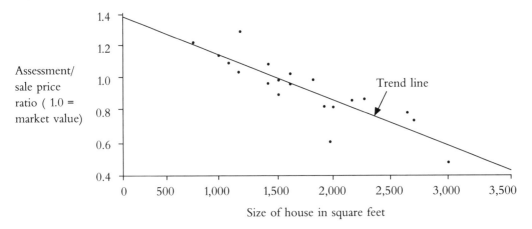

Table 4. Contingency Table

	0–15 yrs	16–30 yrs	More than 30 yrs	Total
Neighborhood A	0.962	0.980	0.955	0.964
	(44)	(19)	(12)	(75)
Neighborhood B	0.933	0.950	0.946	0.940
	(78)	(20)	(4)	(102)
Neighborhood C	0.752	0.803	0.773	0.775
	(16)	(27)	(49)	(92)
Total	0.942	0.891	0.790	0.886
	(138)	(66)	(65)	(269)

to market value, except for one age group in one neighborhood, there would be an interactive effect between age group, neighborhood, and sale ratio.

Multivariate Analyses

In addition to one- and two-variable analyses, techniques are available for investigating systematic appraisal biases with respect to three or more variables. The general procedure is to determine whether ratios are significantly correlated with one or more independent variables. The most commonly used statistical procedure of this type is multiple regression analysis, although other techniques are also available. Such analyses are particularly informative in that they sort out the underlying causes of appraisal biases. In the example in table 4, a multiple regression analysis would show that appraisal errors were due in large part to underappraisal in Neighborhood C and not to biases based on year of construction, as might first appear. Because multivariate statistical techniques can do the same kind of analysis with many independent variables, they offer more precision and efficiency than the analysis of a large number of scatter diagrams and contingency tables.

Also, rather than analyzing ratios directly, multivariate techniques can be applied to appraisal errors, preferably expressed as ratios:

$$Percent \ error \ = \ \frac{S \ - \ A}{S} \ \times \ 100. \quad (1)$$

A multivariate analysis will quantify the relationship between such errors and any independent variables selected for analysis.

Ratio Study Statistics

Ratio study statistics provide concise, formal measures of appraisal performance and often constitute the primary basis for reappraisal or equalization decisions. It is crucial, therefore, that these statistics be properly calculated and interpreted. This section discusses sampling concepts and measures of appraisal level and uniformity.

Sampling

Sampling is the foundation on which the ratio study is built. Statistics calculated in the ratio study are used to draw conclusions (or *inferences*), based on information contained in a sample, about a *population* of properties. The population consists of all parcels in the jurisdiction, class, neighborhood, or other stratum under analysis. The sample consists of those parcels for which sales or expert independent appraisals are available. The characteristics of the population are known as *parameters* and the corresponding characteristics of the sample as *statistics*. Statistics calculated from the sample are used to *estimate* population parameters; for example, the average sale price of the sample can be used as an estimate of the average value of the population. In ratio studies, this means that statistics based on a sample of sales (or independent appraisals) will be used to make decisions that affect all properties in the population.

Most statistical procedures rely on sampling because of the time and expense of attempting to obtain data on all items in the population. Properly done, sampling can be an effective tool and the reliability of the computed statistics can be quantified.

The accuracy of statistics as estimators of population parameters depends on the *representativeness* of the sample. Types of property should appear with approximately the same relative frequency in both the sample and the population. (Ideally, the sample would be a miniature replica of the population.) Representativeness is, in turn, primarily a function of sample size and the method of selection.

The method of selection should be *random* or approximately so. A random sample is one in which each item in the population has an equal chance of being included in the sample. Sales do not meet this strict definition, because some types of property tend to sell more frequently than others. Nevertheless, stratification and other control procedures usually produce samples that are random

enough for a ratio study. Because the objective of ratio studies is to measure appraisal performance, violations of the randomness assumption only become serious when properties overrepresented in the sample tend to be appraised more (or less) accurately than those that are underrepresented.

The other major factor affecting representativeness is sample size. For any given population, the representativeness of a sample will increase with its size. As size increases, the characteristics of the sample converge with those of the population, so that statistics computed from the sample are more likely to be valid measures of corresponding population parameters.

A question frequently asked in ratio studies is, How large must a sample be before it is reliable? There is no single answer. Much depends on the precision required of a particular ratio study. For greater precision, a larger sample size is needed. Also, for any given level of precision, a larger sample is required when ratios are widely scattered. These concepts are depicted in table 5 and, with formulas for computing required sample size, in appendix 20-3.

Table 5. Required Sample Size under Various Assumptions

Dispersion of data	Required degree of precision	
	Low	High
Low	Small sample	Midsized sample
High	Midsized sample	Large sample

In a ratio study using sales data only, there is limited control over sample size, so the interpretation of results is limited by the sample available. In an *appraisal* ratio study, on the other hand, the required sample size can be computed for a desired level of precision and the estimated dispersion of the data.

Measures of Appraisal Level

Measures of appraisal level are calculated statistically by measures of central tendency, which describe the typical level of appraisal by a single number or statistic. The four such measures applicable to ratio studies are the *median*; the *mean* (also known as the average, arithmetic average, or unweighted average); the *weighted mean* (also known as the aggregate mean, dollar-weighted mean, or ratio of the aggregates); and the *geometric mean*.

Because each measure has relative advantages and disadvantages, it is good practice to compute several or even all of them in a ratio study. Comparing them provides useful information about the distribution of ratios. Wide differences among the measures indicate undesirable patterns of appraisal performance.

Besides computing measures of central tendency, it is often important to know their reliability. Confidence intervals, which indicate the range in which one can conclude with a reasonable degree of confidence (usually 95 percent) that the true measure of central tendency lies, can be calculated for the median, mean, and weighted mean (see appendix 20-4). In addition, it is sometimes necessary to combine measures of central tendency for strata into a composite measure for the jurisdiction or major class of property. Appendix 20-5 discusses methods for doing so.

Median The median is the midpoint, or middle ratio, when the ratios are arrayed in order of magnitude. It divides the ratios into two equal groups and is therefore little affected by extreme ratios.

The median is expressed symbolically as $\widetilde{A/S}$.

Once the ratios are computed and arrayed, the rank corresponding to the median ratio can be calculated by the formula

$$median\ rank\ =\ 0.5\ (n)\ +\ 0.5, \quad (2)$$

where n is the number of ratios in the sample. (When the number of ratios is even, the median is computed as the average of the two middle ratios.)

Figure 7 shows the application of this formula for three data sets. In Example A, the computed rank is 3, which corresponds to a ratio of 0.900. In Example B, with an even number of ratios, the two middle ratios, 0.900 and 0.950, are averaged to produce a median of 0.925. Example C illustrates the negligible effect of outliers on the median. Although the sixth ratio (2.000) is much greater than in Example B (1.050), the median is unchanged.

The median has several advantages in ratio studies. It is easy to compute and interpret. Because it discounts the effects of extreme ratios, the median is little affected by data errors, unlike other measures of central tendency. The median is also the base from which the coefficient of dispersion, the primary measure of appraisal uniformity, is calculated. Finally, the sample median provides an unbiased estimate of the population median. Accordingly, the median is the preferred measure of central tendency in many ratio study applications.

A possible disadvantage of the median is that it gives no added weight to legitimate outliers. Some outliers *are* valid and may need to be given extra weight in a ratio study. Also, the median does not lend itself to cer-

Figure 7.   Computing the Median and Mean

Example A			Example B			Example C		
Sale number		(A/S)	Sale number		(A/S)	Sale number		(A/S)
1		0.800	1		0.800	1		0.800
2		0.850	2		0.850	2		0.850
3		0.900	3		0.900	3		0.900
4		0.950	4		0.950	4		0.950
5		1.000	5		1.000	5		1.000
		4.500	6		1.050	6		2.000
					5.550			6.500

Median rank
0.5(5) + 0.5	= 3		0.5(6) + 0.5	= 3.5		0.5(6) + 0.5	= 3.5	
Median	0.900		(0.9 + 0.95)/2	= 0.925		(0.9 + 0.95)/2	= 0.925	
Mean 4.500/5	= 0.900		5.500/6	= 0.925		6.500/6	= 1.083	

A/S is the ratio of appraised value to sale price.

tain statistical calculations as readily as the mean.

Mean   The mean is the average ratio. It is found by summing the ratios and then dividing by the number of ratios. The mean, abbreviated $\overline{A/S}$, is calculated by the formula

$$\overline{A/S} = \frac{\Sigma(A_i/S_i)}{n}, \qquad (3)$$

where A_i/S_i represents each ratio, n is the number of ratios in the sample, and Σ is the mathematical symbol for summation.

Figure 7 illustrates calculation of the mean. A comparison of Examples B and C demonstrates the pronounced effect of outliers on the mean. The medians in the two examples are equal, but the mean is 1.083 in Example C and 0.925 in Example B. The mean accurately reflects the full magnitude of every ratio, which is desirable only if outliers are based on valid data and occur with the same frequency in both the sample and the population. Outliers particularly affect the mean in small samples.

In addition, the sample mean tends to be a biased estimator of the population mean, a bias common to all ratio data in which the denominator is subject to measurement error. The data in table 6 illustrate this bias. Three identical houses with theoretically equal market values ($100,000 each) are assumed to sell for $90,000, $100,000, and $110,000. Although the houses are all appraised and, on average, sold at market value, the mean sale ratio is slightly above 1.000. This measurement bias is due to the random component of the sale price data; it is not a function of sample size.

Like the median, the mean is easy to compute and explain. It is widely used in statistics and is the basis for many other mathematical calculations. Although, as

Table 6. Data Illustrating Bias in Sample Mean

Appraised value (A)	Market value	True ratio	Sale price (S)	A/S ratio
$100,000	$100,000	1.000	$ 90,000	1.111
100,000	100,000	1.000	100,000	1.000
100,000	100,000	1.000	110,000	0.909
		3.000		3.020

True mean = 3.000/3 = 1.000;
Sample mean = 3.020/3 = 1.007

noted above, the sample mean is a biased estimator of the population mean, this bias is slight and unimportant compared to sampling error. When the sample has been properly obtained and the data carefully screened and processed, the mean provides a valid measure of appraisal level.

Weighted Mean The weighted mean is an aggregate ratio determined by the following steps:

1. Sum the appraised values for the entire sample.
2. Sum the sales prices for the entire sample.
3. Divide the total of the appraised values by the total of the sales prices.

Mathematically, the weighted mean is found by the formula

$$\overline{A/S} = \Sigma A / \Sigma S, \qquad (4)$$

where $\overline{A/S}$ is the symbol for the weighted mean, ΣA is the sum of the appraised values for the entire sample, and ΣS is the sum of the sales prices.

The weighted mean weights each ratio in proportion to its sale price, whereas the mean and median give equal weight to each sale price. Table 7 demonstrates calculation of the

weighted mean and illustrates this weighting feature. In Example A, the mean is 0.720 and the weighted mean, 0.600. In effect, the *single* $100,000 sale has as much weight in calculation of the weighted mean as the *four* $25,000 sales. By contrast, the unweighted mean assigns equal weight to each ratio.

In Example B, the mean again is 0.720, but the weighted mean is 0.750, somewhat higher than the mean and very different from the weighted mean in Example A.

Table 7. Calculating the Weighted Mean

Example A

Sale number	Appraised value (A)	Sale price (S)	Ratio (A/S)
1	$ 20,000	$ 25,000	0.800
2	20,000	25,000	0.800
3	20,000	25,000	0.800
4	20,000	25,000	0.800
5	40,000	100,000	0.400
	$120,000	$200,000	3.600

Mean = 3.600/5 = 0.720
Weighted mean = $120,000 ÷ $200,000 = 0.600

Example B

Sale number	Appraised value (A)	Sale price (S)	Ratio (A/S)
1	$ 10,000	$ 25,000	0.400
2	20,000	25,000	0.800
3	20,000	25,000	0.800
4	20,000	25,000	0.800
5	80,000	100,000	0.800
	$150,000	$200,000	3.600

Mean = 3.600/5 = 0.720
Weighted mean = $150,000 ÷ $200,000 = 0.750

Because of this weighting feature, the weighted mean is the appropriate measure of central tendency for estimating the total dollar value of a population of parcels. If, for example, the total appraised value of a class of property is $100 million, and the weighted mean is 0.800, then the best estimate of the total market value of the class is $125 million ($100 million divided by 0.800). The weighted mean is also required in calculation of the price-related differential.

The major disadvantage of the weighted mean is its susceptibility to sampling error, for example, when a sample contains several properties of high value appraised at a different level from other properties in the sample. The weighted mean can also mask problems in the appraisal of properties of low value, which have minimal effect on this statistic.

Geometric Mean The geometric mean offers a measure of appraisal level that, like the median, is not as susceptible to distortion as the mean and weighted mean. It is calculated by multiplying all the ratios in the sample together and finding the nth root of the result. Mathematically,

$$(\overline{A/S})_g = [A_1/S_1)(A_2/S_2), \ldots, (A_n/S_n)]^{1/n}$$
$$(5)$$

where $(\overline{A/S})_g$ symbolizes the geometric mean; A_1/S_1, A_2/S_2, and A_n/S_n represent the first, second, and nth ratios, respectively; and n is the number of ratios in the sample.

The data in Example C of figure 7 illustrate the tendency of the geometric mean to be less influenced by extreme ratios than the arithmetic mean. The arithmetic mean in this example is 1.083, well above the midpoint of

the ratios because of the one high ratio, 2.000. The geometric mean is

$$(\overline{A/S})_g = [(0.80)(0.85)(0.90)(0.95)(1.00)$$
$$(2.00)]^{1/6} = 1.025.$$

Unless every ratio in the sample is identical, the geometric mean will always be less than the arithmetic mean. This tends to offset, more or less, the upward bias in the arithmetic mean.

On the negative side, the geometric mean is relatively complex and does not have an accepted corresponding measure of uniformity. In addition, if the ratios vary widely, the geometric mean can lie considerably below the other measures of central tendency and not be representative of the true center of the distribution.

Measures of Appraisal Uniformity

Determining the quality of mass appraisal also requires measuring uniformity: uniformity *between* groups of properties and uniformity *within* groups. Uniformity between groups can be evaluated by comparing measures of appraisal level calculated for each group. Measuring uniformity within groups is more complex.

The need for measuring intragroup uniformity, not just the level of appraisal, is shown in table 8. In both Examples A and B the overall level of appraisal is perfect, with all three measures of central tendency equal to 1.000. If uniformity were also perfect, each ratio would be 1.000. In Example A, the ratios all lie within 16 percent of 1.000—from 0.840 to 1.160. In Example B, however, the range is much wider—from 0.400 to 1.600. Uniformity, and therefore tax equity, although not perfect in either case, is clearly better in Example A.

Table 8.   Appraisal Level vs. Uniformity

Example A: Good Uniformity

Sale number	Appraised value (A)	Sale price (S)	Ratio (A/S)
1	$ 21,000	$ 25,000	0.840
2	44,000	50,000	0.880
3	28,000	30,000	0.933
4	60,000	60,000	1.000
5	32,000	30,000	1.067
6	56,000	50,000	1.120
7	29,000	25,000	1.160
	$270,000	$270,000	7.000

Median = 1.000
Mean = 7.000 ÷ 7 = 1.000
Weighted mean = $270,000 ÷ $270,000 = 1.000

Example B: Poor Uniformity

Sale number	Appraised value (A)	Sale price (S)	Ratio (A/S)
1	$ 10,000	$ 25,000	0.400
2	30,000	50,000	0.600
3	22,500	30,000	0.750
4	60,000	60,000	1.000
5	37,000	30,000	1.250
6	70,000	50,000	1.400
7	40,000	25,000	1.600
	$270,000	$270,000	7.000

Median = 1.000
Mean = 7.000 ÷ 7 = 1.000
Weighted mean = $270,000 ÷ $270,000 = 1.000

In small samples, such as those in table 8, the degree of uniformity can be seen by direct observation of the array. In larger samples, this is not possible, and one must quantify the degree of uniformity to evaluate the seriousness of any problems. Six measures of appraisal uniformity can be used:
• range, quartiles, and percentiles
• average absolute deviation
• coefficient of dispersion
• standard deviation
• coefficient of variation
• price-related differential

Range, Quartiles, and Percentiles The range, quartiles, and percentiles offer simple measures of data uniformity based on an array of the data. The range is simply the difference between the highest and lowest ratios in the sample. In Example A (table 8), the range is 0.320 (1.160 − 0.840); in Example B, 1.200 (1.600 − 0.400). Larger ranges may indicate poorer uniformity, but because the extreme outliers completely con-

trol the range, it can be a misleading indicator of overall uniformity.

Figure 9 demonstrates the insensitivity of the range to all but the most extreme ratios. Although the ranges in samples A and B are identical, uniformity is better in sample B than in sample A. Because the two most extreme ratios control the range, the statistic is inadequate for larger samples.

Percentiles and quartiles are dividing points between specific percentages of the data. The median, for example, is the 50th percentile and second quartile. It exceeds 50 percent, or two quarters, of the ratios. The first quartile corresponds to the 25th percentile and exceeds one quarter, or 25 percent, of the ratios. Similarly, the third quartile corresponds to the 75th percentile and exceeds three quarters, or 75 percent, of the ratios.

The rank of the ratio corresponding to a specific quartile or percentile can be found by the formula

$$k = (p)(n) + p, \tag{6}$$

Table 9.   Influences of Outliers on the Range

Sale number	Sample A	Sample B
1	0.100	0.100
2	0.100	1.000
3	0.100	1.000
4	0.100	1.000
5	0.100	1.000
6	2.000	1.000
7	2.000	1.000
8	2.000	1.000
9	2.000	1.000
10	2.000	2.000

Range = 2.000 − 0.1000 = 1.900

where k is the rank, p is the chosen percentile or quartile in decimal form, and n is the sample size. For example, the rank of the 75th percentile in an array of 99 ratios is

$$(0.75)\ (99)\ +\ 0.75\ =\ 75.$$

In most cases, the rank will not be a whole number and one must interpolate between ratios. For example, for 100 ratios, the computed rank of the 75th percentile is:

$$(0.75)\ (100)\ +\ 0.75\ =\ 75.75.$$

If the 75th and 76th highest ratios are 0.980 and 1.000, respectively, the 75th percentile is

$$0.980\ +\ (0.75)\ (1.000\ -\ 0.980)\ =\ 0.995.$$

Several measures of data uniformity based on quartiles and percentiles have been developed. The *interquartile range* is the difference between the third and first quartiles. For example, if the first quartile is 0.660 and the third quartile is 0.988, the interquartile range, the range within which 50 percent of the ra-

tios lie, is 0.328 (0.988 − 0.660). Dividing the interquartile range by the median permits it to be interpreted as a percentage. Hence, if the median in the present example were 0.800, then 50 percent of the ratios would lie within 41.0 percent of the median (0.328/0.800).

Other interpercentile ranges can be developed in the same way. For example, to develop the 90/10 interpercentile range, find the ratios corresponding to the 90th and 10th percentiles and subtract the latter from the former. Again, interpretation is improved by dividing the result by the median ratio.

Another measure of uniformity, the *coefficient of concentration*, is found by determining the percentage of ratios falling within a given percentage of the median. The allowable percentage should correspond to an acceptable degree of appraisal error, for example, 15 percent. If 76.5 percent of the ratios fall within 15 percent (plus or minus) of the median, then the coefficient of concentration is 76.5. In table 9, the coefficient of concentration computed in this manner for sample B is 80.0, because eight of the ten ratios lie within 15 percent of the median (between 0.850 and 1.150). The higher the coefficient of concentration, the better (unlike other measures of appraisal uniformity).

Quartiles, percentiles, and related statistics can be useful, but they convey no information about the degree of uniformity outside the chosen range. Unlike other measures, they do not measure overall uniformity using every ratio in the sample.

Average Absolute Deviation   The average absolute deviation, often referred to simply as the average deviation, measures the average spread, or difference, between each ratio and the median ratio. The term *absolute* indicates absolute value: that is, the direction of spread—whether above or below a measure of central tendency—is unimportant. The degree, or magnitude, of the differences is the significant aspect. The mathematical symbol for the absolute value of any number x is $|x|$ ($||$ instructs the analyst to ignore the sign of the number).

The average absolute deviation is calculated by subtracting the median from each ratio, summing the absolute values of the computed differences, and dividing this sum by the number of ratios.

Mathematically, the average deviation about the median is calculated by the formula

$$AAD = \frac{\Sigma|A_i/S_i - \widetilde{A/S}|}{n}, \qquad (7)$$

where AAD is the average absolute deviation $\widetilde{A/S}$ is the median ratio, A_i/S_i is the ratio of parcel i, and n is the number of ratios in the sample.

Table 10 shows how to calculate the average absolute deviation for the two data sets presented in table 8. Although the medians are the same in the two examples, the average deviation is much larger in Example B (0.357) than in Example A (0.099). In fact, the results indicate that appraisal uniformity is more than three times worse in Example B than in Example A:

Calculating the average deviation manually can be time-consuming. A shortcut procedure yielding identical results is: (1) sum the ratios that lie below the median (do not include the median), (2) sum the ratios that exceed the median (do not include the median), (3) subtract the first result from the second, and (4) divide by the number of ratios.

A major drawback to the average absolute deviation is that it measures appraisal uniformity in raw percentage points rather than in relative terms. This limits the usefulness of the statistic because, for example, an average

Table 10. Calculating the Average Absolute Deviation

Example A (from Table 8) Sale number	Ratio (A/S)	Absolute difference from median	Example B (from Table 8) Sale number	Ratio (A/S)	Absolute difference from median
1	0.840	0.160	1	0.400	0.600
2	0.880	0.120	2	0.600	0.400
3	0.933	0.067	3	0.750	0.250
4	1.000	0.000	4	1.000	0.000
5	1.067	0.067	5	1.250	0.250
6	1.120	0.120	6	1.400	0.400
7	1.160	0.160	7	1.600	0.600
		0.694			2.500

Median = 1.000
Average absolute deviation = 0.694 ÷ 7
= 0.099
A/S is the ratio of appraised value to sale price.

Median = 1.000
Average absolute deviation = 2.500 ÷ 7
= 0.357

deviation of 0.10 is good if the median is near 1.000, but not if the median is, say, 0.300. Similarly, average absolute deviations cannot be compared between property groups unless the measures of central tendency are similar.

Coefficient of Dispersion   The coefficient of dispersion (*COD*) is the most used measure of uniformity in ratio studies. The *COD* is based on the average absolute deviation, but expresses it as a percentage. Thus, the *COD* provides a measure of appraisal uniformity that is independent of the level of appraisal and permits direct comparisons between property groups.

The *COD* is calculated by dividing the average absolute deviation by the median and multiplying by 100 to convert the ratio to a percentage:

$$COD = \frac{100\ (AAD)}{\widetilde{A/S}}, \qquad (8)$$

where AAD is the average absolute deviation, and $\widetilde{A/S}$ is the median.

Table 11 shows how to calculate the *COD*. Note that the average absolute deviation is the same as in Example A of table 10, but that the *COD* is twice as large. The median in Example A of table 10 is 1.000, so the *COD* equals the average absolute deviation. By contrast, in table 11 the median is only 0.500, so that the *COD* is twice as large. In general, the lower the level of appraisal (median *A/S* ratio), the greater will be the *COD* relative to the average absolute deviation.

Although the *COD* measures the average percentage deviation from the median, it does not measure the typical or median deviation. In a normal distribution, 57 percent of the ratios will fall within one COD of the median.

Low *COD*s (15.0 or less) tend to be associated with good appraisal uniformity. (Specific mass appraisal performance standards based on the *COD* are discussed later in this chapter.) *COD*s of less than 5.0 are very rare except in (1) subdivisions in which lot prices are strictly controlled by the developer; (2) extremely homogeneous prop-

Table 11.   Calculating the Coefficient of Dispersion

Sale number	Appraised value (A)	Sale price (S)	Ratio (A/S)	Absolute difference from median
1	$ 8,500	$25,000	0.340	0.160
2	19,000	50,000	0.380	0.120
3	13,000	30,000	0.433	0.067
4	30,000	60,000	0.500	0.000
5	17,000	30,000	0.567	0.067
6	31,000	50,000	0.620	0.120
7	16,500	25,000	0.660	0.160
				0.694

Median = 0.500
Average absolute deviation = 0.694 ÷ 7 = 0.099
COD = (0.099/0.500)(100) = 19.8

erty groups, such as condominium units all located in the same complex; (3) appraisal ratio studies in which the assessor's values and the independent appraisals reflect the same appraisal manuals and procedures; or (4) appraisals that have been adjusted to match sales prices.

One drawback to the *COD* is that it does not provide a basis for probability statements concerning appraisal uniformity. We cannot use the statistic, for example, to evaluate the chance, or probability, that a given property will be appraised above a given level (say, 1.000) or within a given range (say, 0.900 to 1.100).

Standard Deviation The standard deviation is the primary measure of dispersion in scientific research and, under certain assumptions, can be a powerful measure of appraisal uniformity. The statistic is computed as follows:

1. Subtract the mean from each ratio.
2. Square the resulting differences (note: squared numbers always have positive signs).
3. Sum the squared differences.
4. Divide by the number of ratios less one to obtain the *variance* of the ratios.
5. Compute the square root of the variance to obtain the standard deviation.

The mathematical formula is

$$s = \sqrt{\frac{\Sigma(A_i/S_i - \overline{A/S})^2}{n - 1}}, \qquad (9)$$

where s is the standard deviation, A_i/S_i is the ratio of the ith property, $\overline{A/S}$ is the mean ratio, and n is the number of ratios in the sample.

It is instructive to compare calculation of the standard deviation with that of the average absolute deviation. Note that the standard deviation is calculated about the mean rather than the median and operates upon squared differences rather than absolute differences. Division by $n - 1$ rather than n makes the calculated standard deviation of the sample an unbiased estimator of the standard deviation of the population, although the magnitude of the adjustment is negligible for large samples.

Table 12 shows how to calculate the standard deviation. The standard deviation is almost four times larger in Example B than in Example A, reflecting the much greater dispersion of the ratios.

When computing the standard deviation by hand using the above formula, carry the squared deviations to at least four decimal places to ensure the accuracy of the final result, which may then be rounded to three decimal places. A mathematically equivalent shortcut formula is

$$s = \sqrt{\frac{\Sigma(A_i/S_i)^2 - \frac{[\Sigma(A_i/S_i)]^2}{n}}{n - 1}} . (10)$$

In this formula, $\Sigma(A_i/S_i)^2$ is the sum of the squared ratios and $[\Sigma(A_i/S_i)]^2$ is the sum of the ratios squared. The steps are:

1. Find the sum of the squared ratios.
2. Square the sum of the ratios and divide by the sample size (n).
3. Subtract the results of step 2 from the result of step 1.
4. Divide by $n - 1$.
5. Extract the square root.

Table 12.   Calculating the Standard Deviation

Example A (from Table 8)

Sale number	Ratio (A/S)	Difference from mean	Difference squared
1	0.840	− 0.160	0.0256
2	0.880	− 0.120	0.0144
3	0.933	− 0.067	0.0044
4	1.000	0.000	0.0000
5	1.067	0.067	0.0044
6	1.120	0.120	0.0144
7	1.160	0.160	0.0256
	7.000		0.0889

Mean = 7.000 ÷ 7 = 1.000
Variance = 0.0889 ÷ 6 = 0.0148
Standard deviation = $\sqrt{0.0148}$ = 0.122
A/S is the ratio of appraised value to sale price.

Example B (from Table 8)

Sale number	Ratio (A/S)	Difference from mean	Difference squared
1	0.400	− 0.600	0.3600
2	0.600	− 0.400	0.1600
3	0.750	− 0.250	0.0625
4	1.000	0.000	0.0000
5	1.250	0.250	0.0625
6	1.400	0.400	0.1600
7	1.600	0.600	0.3600
	7.000		1.1650

Mean = 7.000 ÷ 7 = 1.000
Variance = 1.1650 ÷ 6 = 0.1942
Standard deviation = $\sqrt{0.1942}$ = 0.441

This formula avoids the need to compute and square individual deviations from the mean. Steps 4 and 5 are the same as in equation 9.

Interpretation of the standard deviation depends on an unbiased, representative sample in which the data are normally distributed. A normal distribution is characterized by a symmetrical, bell-shaped curve, in which the mean and median are identical; they should at least be similar for normality to be assumed. Nonnormal distributions are skewed either to the left or right of the median.

Figure 8 shows examples of normal distributions (upper half) and nonnormal distributions (lower half). In the upper half of the illustration, distribution (a) is characterized by a small standard deviation relative to the mean; distribution (b) has a much larger standard deviation; and distribution (c) is an intermediate case. Nevertheless, in terms of standard deviations from the mean, these, and all normal distributions, are variations of the symmetrical, bell-shaped curve of distribution (d).

In the lower half of the illustration, distribution (e) is positively skewed, that is the tail extends toward higher values of the variable, a common occurrence in ratio data; distribution (f) is negatively skewed, that is the tail extends toward lower values of the variable; distribution (g) is attenuated in both directions; and distribution (h) is more clustered than a normal distribution.

When data are normally distributed, the rules shown in table 13 hold. The percentage of the data falling within any other number of standard deviations from the mean in a normal distribution can be found by using a z-table (see table 1 in appendix 20-6), where z represents the number of standard deviations on one side of the mean. To find the percentage of the data on both sides of the mean, simply double the percentages shown in the table.

In ratio studies, the larger the standard deviation, the wider the range within which a given portion of properties are appraised

Figure 8. Data Distributions

Normal distributions:

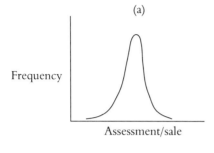
(a)

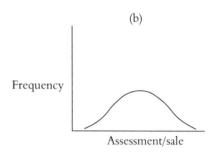
(b)

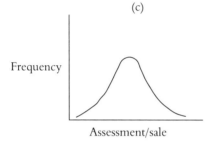
(c)

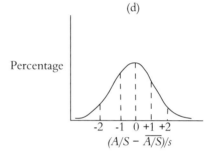
(d)

Non-normal distributions:

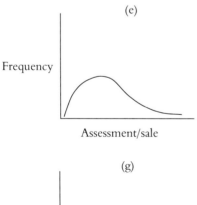
(e)

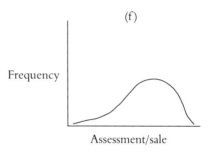
(f)

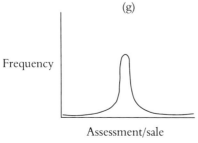
(g)

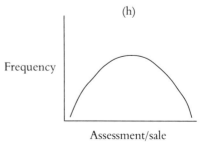
(h)

Table 13. Percent of Data within One, Two, or Three Standard Deviations from the Mean

Normal distribution

Number of standard deviations from mean	Percent of data
± 1	68%
± 2	95%
± 3	99%

Non-normal distribution

Number of standard deviations from mean	Percent of data
± 1	unknown
± 2	75%
± 3	89%

relative to market value. The example in table 14 clearly illustrates this principle. Assume that the ratios in all three property groups are normally distributed about a mean ratio of 0.950. In Group 1, with a standard deviation of 0.100, 95 percent of parcels can be assumed to be appraised between 75 and 115 percent of market value. In Group 2, with a standard deviation of 0.200, 95 percent of ratios will fall between 55 and 135 percent of market value. In Group 3, with a standard deviation of 0.300, the corresponding range is 35–155 percent of market value.

Note also that estimates of this kind apply to the entire population of properties in the group, not just those in the sample. That is, results obtained for the sample apply to the population as well, provided, of course, that the sample is representative of the population.

If the data do not approximate a normal distribution, the standard deviation is less useful. Without a more detailed analysis, only the "worst case" rules in the lower half of table 13 may be assumed.

These rules assume a distribution with aborted tails, somewhat like distribution (h) in the lower half of figure 8. When the data are skewed, as in distributions (e) and (f), or attenuated, as in (g) of figure 8, the percentage of the data falling within a given number of standard deviations of the mean will be *greater* than in a normal distribution. That is, more than 68 percent of the data will lie within one standard deviation of the mean, and more than 95 percent within two standard deviations. This applies to both the sample and the population, if they are similarly distributed.

Depending on the representativeness of the sample and distribution of the data, the standard deviation can be either a powerful or a misleading measure of appraisal uniformity. Accordingly, the analyst must verify that the

Table 14. Range of Appraisal Levels for Parcels within Specified Standard Deviations

Property group	Standard deviation	Appraisal level for indicated percent of parcels		
		68 percent of parcels	95 percent of parcels	99 percent of parcels
1	0.100	0.85–1.05	0.75–1.15	0.65–1.25
2	0.200	0.75–1.15	0.55–1.35	0.35–1.55
3	0.300	0.65–1.25	0.35–1.55	0.05–1.85

data approximate a normal distribution before placing credence in the statistic. Frequency distributions and histograms are good tools for this. More precise techniques for determining normality are discussed in appendix 20-7.

Coefficient of Variation The coefficient of variation (*COV*) expresses the standard deviation as a percentage, just as the *COD* does with the average absolute deviation. Expression as a percentage makes comparisons of appraisal levels between groups easier. The *COV* of ratios is computed by dividing the standard deviation (*s*) by the mean $\overline{A/S}$ ratio and multiplying the result by 100:

$$COV = \frac{(100)\ (s)}{\overline{A/S}}. \qquad (11)$$

Table 15 illustrates calculation of the *COV*. It is instructive to compare table 15 with table 12, Example A. In both cases the standard deviation is 0.122 (rounded to three decimal places), but the *COV* in table 15 is twice as high, because the mean is only 0.500, versus 1.000 in table 12.

The *COV* is interpreted in the same manner as the standard deviation except that it is a percentage of the mean rather than a raw decimal or ratio. The rules in table 13 will hold in a normal distribution.

For example, if the mean is 0.800 and the *COV* is 25.0, then 68 percent of the ratios will lie between 0.600 (0.80 − [0.25 × 0.80]) and 1.000 (0.80 + [0.25 × 0.80]).

Like the standard deviation, the predictive power of the *COV* depends on the extent to which the data are normally distributed. When the normality assumption is met, however, the *COV* is a powerful measure of uniformity.

Table 15. Calculating the Coefficient of Variation (*COV*)

Sale number	Ratio (*A/S*)	Difference from mean	Difference squared
1	0.340	− 0.160	0.0256
2	0.380	− 0.120	0.0144
3	0.433	− 0.067	0.0044
4	0.500	0.000	0.0000
5	0.567	0.067	0.0044
6	0.620	0.120	0.0144
7	0.660	0.160	0.0256
	3.500		0.0889

Mean = 3.500 ÷ 7 = 0.500
Variance = 0.0889 ÷ 6 = 0.0148
Standard deviation = $\sqrt{(0.0148)}$ = 0.1217
COV = (0.1217/0.500)(100) = 24.3

Note: Data are from Table 11.

Price-related Differential Property appraisals sometimes result in unequal tax burdens between high- and low-value properties in the same property group. Appraisals are considered *regressive* if high-value properties are underappraised relative to low-value properties and *progressive* if high-value properties are relatively overappraised.

The price-related differential (*PRD*) is a statistic for measuring assessment regressivity or progressivity. It is calculated by dividing the mean by the weighted mean:

$$PRD = \frac{\overline{A/S}}{\overline{A/S}}. \qquad (12)$$

Recall that the unweighted mean weights the ratios equally, whereas the weighted mean weights them in proportion to their sales prices. A *PRD* greater than 1.00 suggests that the high-value parcels are under-appraised, thus pulling the weighted mean below the mean. On the other hand, if the *PRD* is less than 1.00, high-value parcels are relatively overappraised, pulling the weighted mean above the mean.

In practice, *PRD*s have an upward bias. Recall that, as an estimator of the population mean, the sample mean has a slight upward bias, but the weighted mean does not (except for very small samples). Therefore, the *PRD* has a slight upward bias. Assessment time lags can also contribute to regressivity. In addition to measurement bias, one must leave a reasonable margin for sampling error in interpreting the *PRD*. As a general rule, except for small samples, *PRD*s should range between 0.98 and 1.03. Lower *PRD*s suggest significant assessment progressivity; higher ones suggest significant regressivity.

Table 16 illustrates three conditions. In Example A, the *PRD* is exactly 1.00 and indicates no bias between low- and high-value properties, in Example B the *PRD* of 1.13 indicates assessment regressivity, and in Example C the *PRD* of 0.85 suggests assessment progressivity. Figure 9 is a scatter diagram of the three cases.

Both regressive and progressive *PRD*s can result from misclassifications or systematic problems in appraisal schedules or techniques. The *PRD* provides only an indication, not proof, of appraisal bias. When sample sizes are small, *PRD*s outside the acceptable range may occur simply because of random sampling error. Appendix 18-1 presents tests for determining if different property groups, such as low- and high-value neighborhoods, are appraised equally. These tests consider available sample size.

Ratio Study Standards

Assessment agencies should maintain standards for evaluating ratio study results. Such standards promote improvement in the appraisal process and ensure consistency in reappraisal or equalization actions. They can also be used to set goals for individual appraisers or field crews.

The IAAO *Standard on Ratio Studies* (1990) recommends the following standards for jurisdictions in which *current* market value is the legal basis of assessment.

Appraisal Level

The overall level of appraisal for all parcels in a jurisdiction should be within 10 percent of the legal level that is, between 0.90 and 1.10.

Appraisal Uniformity

1. *Uniformity among strata.* Each major stratum should be appraised within 5 percent of the overall level of appraisal for the jurisdiction. Thus, if the overall level is 0.90, each property class and area should be appraised between 0.855 (0.90 − [0.05 × 0.90]) and 0.945 (0.90 + [0.05 × 0.90]).
2. *Single-family residences.* CODs should generally be 15.0 or less and for newer and fairly homogeneous areas, 10.0 or less.
3. *Income-producing property.* CODs should be 20.0 or less, and in larger, urban jurisdictions, 15.0 or less.
4. *Vacant land and other property.* CODs should be 20 or less.
5. *Other real property and personal property.* Target CODs. should reflect the nature of the properties, market conditions, and the availability of reliable market indicators.

Table 16. Calculating the Price-related Differential (*PRD*)

Example A—No Bias:

Sale number	Appraised value (A)	Sale price (S)	Ratio (A/S)
1	$ 25,000	$ 20,000	1.250
2	24,000	30,000	0.800
3	31,000	40,000	0.775
4	40,000	50,000	0.800
5	60,000	60,000	1.000
6	79,000	70,000	1.129
	$259,000	$270,000	5.754

Mean = 5.754 ÷ 6 = 0.959
Weighted mean = $259,000 ÷ $270,000 = 0.959
PRD = 0.959 ÷ 0.959 = 1.00

Example B—Regressivity:

Sale number	Appraised value (A)	Sale price (S)	Ratio (A/S)
1	$ 30,000	$ 20,000	1.500
2	40,000	30,000	1.333
3	45,000	40,000	1.125
4	50,000	50,000	1.000
5	40,000	60,000	0.667
6	45,000	70,000	0.643
	$250,000	$270,000	6.268

Mean = 6.268 ÷ 6 = 1.045
Weighted mean = $250,000 ÷ $270,000 = 0.926
PRD = 1.045 ÷ 0.926 = 1.13

Example C—Progressivity:

Sale number	Appraised value (A)	Sale price (S)	Ratio (A/S)
1	$ 6,000	$ 20,000	0.300
2	12,000	30,000	0.400
3	30,000	40,000	0.750
4	60,000	50,000	1.200
5	75,000	60,000	1.250
6	90,000	70,000	1.286
	$273,000	$270,000	6.268

Mean = 6.268 ÷ 6 = 0.864
Weighted mean = $273,000 ÷ $270,000 = 1.011
PRD = 0.864 ÷ 1.011 = 0.85

PRD	Interpretation	Favors	Type of bias
0.98 –1.03	Low- and high- value properties appraised equally	Neither	None
Less than 0.98	High-value properties overappraised	Low- value properties	Progressive
More than 1.03	High-value properties underappraised	High- value properties	Regressive

In addition, *PRD*s should be between 0.98 and 1.03. This range is centered slightly above 1.00 to allow for the measurement bias inherent in the *PRD*.

It can be difficult to conclude with confidence that these or other mandated standards have been met for all parcels, not just for those in the sample. When sample sizes are small, calculated statistics may fall outside the requirements because of sampling error. Appendices 20-4 and 20-8 discuss procedures for testing with a required degree of precision whether the above standards have *not* been met. In addition, jurisdictions may develop special standards of appraisal performance where sample sizes are small (less than thirty).

Appraised values made for assessment purposes should not be selectively adjusted so as to match sales prices. Doing so will in-

Figure 9. Price-related Differential (*PRD*)

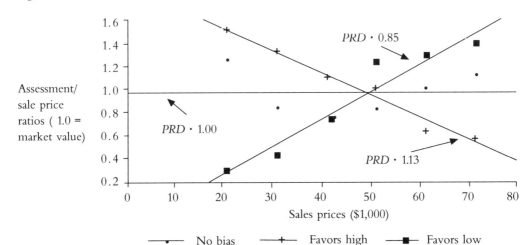

Points represent individual sales from the examples in table 17.

validate the ratio study by making the sample results unrepresentative of true performance. Appendix 20-2 discusses this situation and the evaluation of appraisal performance for unsold parcels.

Performance Evaluation with Limited Sales

Perhaps the most frequent and serious obstacle to effective mass appraisal performance evaluation is the scarcity of sales data for certain types of property, particularly commercial properties. In small jurisdictions, even residential sales data may be in limited supply. Special procedures must be used to resolve problems of insufficient sales data.

Augmenting Sales Data

Sales data provide objective, inexpensive indicators of market value and, as such, are the preferred yardstick for measuring appraisal

accuracy. There are several techniques for expanding the number of sales available for a ratio study.

Obtain Data on Most or All Transfers

All jurisdictions should have laws requiring the disclosure of sales prices on real estate transfer documents. Ideally, these documents should provide good data on almost all property transfers. If not, assessors should strive to improve the completeness and quality of the sales data on transfer documents, perhaps by seeking new legislation; improving the format of transfer documents; working with recording officials, title companies, and real estate brokers; and educating the public on the need for full disclosure of sales information.

Assessors can also obtain sales data from other sources: contacting the buyer or seller through a mail questionnaire, phone call, or personal interview; using multiple listing services; and contacting third-party sources, such as real estate agents, private appraisers, and lending institutions.

Adjust Rather than Reject Sales Many sales are not cash equivalent transfers; they involve nonmarket financing, substantial amounts of personal property, or other special circumstances that make the nominal sale price unrepresentative of the market value of the real estate transferred. Such sales can be either rejected or adjusted to reflect the cash equivalent value of the real property only. When there are enough open-market, arm's-length sales requiring no adjustment, rejecting all other sales is the easier and probably the better method. At other times, the number of usable sales can be expanded by adjusting the sales prices. As noted in chapter 5, even when complete information is not available, standard adjustments based on type of property or type of transfer can be applied. Although such adjustments may not be precise for a given property, they tend to balance for the purpose of measuring the level of appraisal. Commercial properties, in particular, often require sale price adjustments because sales are relatively scarce and complex.

Extend the Sales Period Extending the period from which sales are selected can be a simple and effective way of increasing sample size, particularly when real estate markets are stable. Even when prices are changing, the technique can be effective if sales prices are adjusted for time (see appendix 5-3).

The period need not be the same for all classes of property. One could, for example, use one year of sales for residential property, two years for vacant land, and three years for commercial property. As a rule, however, not more than five years of sales can be used in a ratio study, and not more than three in rapidly changing markets.

Appraisal Ratio Studies

Appraisal ratio studies offer an alternative to sales-based ratio studies for mass appraisal performance evaluation. However, using independent, expert appraisals in place of sales as representatives of market values has both advantages and disadvantages. The major advantage is that a high degree of control in sample selection is possible. One can specify both size and manner of selection. Indeed, *stratified random sampling* helps ensure representativeness. Properties are stratified by class or other criteria and then a random sample is selected from each stratum. Appendix 20-3 gives formulas for determining the required sample size of a stratum based on specified levels of precision in study results.

Appraisal ratio studies are costly and take time. The appraisals used must be accurate, employ valid, objective, and professionally accepted methods and techniques, and be well documented, which usually requires a narrative appraisal and a physical inspection. The appraisals should be based on, or tested against, available sales to ensure that the appraisals reflect the market. The method becomes difficult to apply effectively when sales data are scarce or nonexistent. Despite the care with which they are made, appraisals still involve subjectivity and judgment. In an appraisal ratio study, essentially one set of appraisals is being used to judge another. Appraisal ratio studies are generally best suited to commercial and industrial properties, for which sales tend to be scarce and complex, making sales ratio studies difficult. Many jurisdictions use sales-based ratio studies for residential properties and vacant land and appraisal ratio studies for commercial and industrial properties.

Appraisal ratio studies can also be used to determine whether agricultural or other properties subject to a use-value appraisal requirement are being correctly assessed. In this case, the independent appraisals should reflect the statutory basis upon which such properties are assessed for tax purposes. Finally, appraisal ratio studies can be conducted for personal property (see appendix 1-1).

Can sales and appraisals be mixed as indicators of market value? Yes, if the appraisals accurately reflect the market. For example, if a sample size of thirty is needed, and eighteen valid sales are available, only twelve appraisals are required. A comparison of measures of central tendency for the sales with those for the appraisals indicates whether the sales and appraisals both reflect the market and can be combined into an aggregate sample. If the measures of central tendency do not agree, and the sales are valid, the appraisals may incorporate a systematic bias and should be reexamined (see appendices 18-1 and 20-5).

Unit Value Comparisons

A conceptually different approach to ratio studies is to compare the assessor's appraised value per unit with values obtained from an independent source, either sales prices or independent appraisals. First, stratify properties into appropriate groups for analysis, as for a ratio study. In the case of vacant rural lands, stratification based on the size of parcels should also be considered. Second, determine appropriate units of comparison as in the sales comparison approach, usually

square feet for improved parcels and square feet or acres for vacant land. Third, using sales or appraisals, determine the average value per unit of each group, using any measure of central tendency. Fourth, for the same parcels, compute the assessor's corresponding value per unit. Any significant differences indicate systematic under- or overappraisal.

Unit value comparisons should produce results similar to those of ratio studies based on the same data. However, those unfamiliar with ratio study methods may understand unit value comparisons better.

Procedure Audits

The success of a mass appraisal program is reflected both in its results and how it is performed. Results are measured by ratio studies or analyses of average per unit values, both of which are objective and quantifiable but nevertheless dependent on the availability of sales data. Even appraisal ratio studies require sales data to develop accurate, market-based appraisals.

Procedure audits focus instead on how appraisals are performed. If appraisal procedures and techniques comply with current professional standards, manuals, and guidelines, it can be argued that the resulting values should be presumed to be accurate or at least acceptable. However, procedure audits are time-consuming and expensive. Because they involve a high degree of personal interaction, they can be subjective, and they are difficult to quantify.

Nevertheless, if properly done, such audits can be effective. One key to success is a checklist of specific items to cover and instructions as to how each is to be evaluated or measured. Several IAAO standards, such as the *Standard on Mass Appraisal of Real Prop-*

erty (1984) and the *Standard on the Application of the Three Approaches to Value in Mass Appraisal* (1985), can be helpful starting points.

Mass appraisal performance is best evaluated by measurement of results, as in ratio studies or a comparison of average values per unit, but procedure audits are an excellent supplement, and the only practical means of evaluating performance when market data do not exist. These audits also suggest where and how appraisal techniques can be improved.

Public Relations in Ratio Studies

Ratio studies provide vital information about appraisal performance. Actions based on this information have important consequences for many parties — consequences so important that in the United States, equalization actions based on ratio studies are subject to constitutional and statutory provisions (see appendix 20-9). In addition to supervisory agencies and local assessors, ratio studies can affect the following:

1. *Local government officials*. Ratio studies used as the basis for equalization actions to raise or lower assessed values affect the local tax base. School aid formulas and transfer payments are often tied to assessment levels or estimated full market values computed from ratio studies. In some cases, local governments may have to pay for reappraisals ordered on the basis of ratio studies or repay transfer payments received in the previous year as the result of underappraisal.

2. *Taxpayers*. Equalization actions or reappraisals based on ratio studies will affect the distribution of tax burdens. Some tax-

payers will see their assessments and taxes increase. Where values are increased substantially, a large number of appeals can be expected.

3. *Corporations*. Perceived stability or instability in the property tax system influences corporate decisions about location. Although corporations favor low taxes, they also prefer an equitable and predictable tax structure.

Property tax officials at all levels can improve the use of ratio study results through education and good communications. Ratio studies are a powerful tool for improving appraisal performance and the operations of local government but, like any sophisticated tool, require training and proper use to be effective.

It is the responsibility of those who conduct the studies to take the lead in explaining methods and results. Oversight agencies that perform ratio studies should promulgate administrative rules, guidelines, and manuals that set forth and explain the procedures followed in the studies. Seminars and workshops are particularly helpful. Without adequate guidance, local assessors may not realize that they are in potential conflict with valuation standards and sales ratio requirements. More important, education in the method of ratio studies will promote understanding and technical improvements in the studies. This will, in turn, lead to mutual acceptance and a sense of professional accomplishment as improved results are achieved.

Summary

Ratio studies are the principal tool used by appraisers to assure the quality of mass appraisals. The accuracy of a ratio study depends on proper design. The design should reflect legal requirements, budget constraints, and staff availability. Most important, the design of the study should reflect the purpose for which it is to be used.

After the objectives of a study are delineated, data are collected and prepared, sales and appraisal data are matched, properties are stratified, statistical analysis is performed, and the results evaluated and used.

Quality Assurance, Notifications, Appeals, and Public Relations 21

Previous chapters have taken the reader through the processes of collecting and analyzing data to develop estimates of value. Quality assurance has been treated throughout. This chapter reviews major quality assurance measures, describing the review of values in detail. Notification of property owners, support of values during appeals, and public relations, an important aspect of all stages of assessment work, are also discussed.

Quality is the degree of excellence of a product or service, the extent to which it measures up to certain standards. Quality assurance is any system used to maintain a level of excellence by planning, continuous review, and correction as needed. Quality is designed into a process, not added after the fact, and should be measured throughout.

The chief measure of assessment quality is the ratio study, in which appraised values are matched against validated sales or other independent indicators of market value (see chapter 20). Ratio studies measure the level and uniformity of appraisals. In general, the level of appraisal should be at or near market value, and measures of dispersion should be low, indicating acceptable uniformity. The chief measure of uniformity is the coefficient of dispersion (COD), which, depending on the nature of the properties involved, should not exceed 10.0–15.0 for residential properties, 15.0–20.0 for commercial properties, and 20.0 for vacant land.

The COD directly measures the uniformity of appraised values and indirectly measures the quality of the processes by which these values are developed. The COD can be significantly affected by the objectivity and thoroughness of sales screening and the underlying volatility of the market. When these effects are removed from the analysis, the COD measures the quality of data, valuation models, and model calibration.

Ratio studies should be used to analyze values by neighborhood and property groups (and also by value range, age range, or other pertinent strata if desired). These studies highlight properties that should be field reviewed and identify systematic inequities that should be corrected before final estimates are produced.

Data quality is often the most important factor in the accuracy of values. Valuation accuracy depends on accurate and consistent data and the appropriate use of subjective factors to identify and adjust values on exceptional properties. Data quality has a major influence on field review, as will be seen in the next section.

Appraisal Review

The appraisal review process evaluates data quality, the appropriateness of valuation models, the calibration of those models, and the application of the models. Appraisal review includes prereviews, field testing valuation models, office reviews, and final field reviews. The emphasis that should be given to any particular review depends on the nature of the properties being appraised and the quality of the mass appraisal program.

Prereview

Prereview combines elements of data collection, data review, and valuation model review. During prereview, appraisers establish which factors require judgments, for example, quality grade, condition rating, and land influence. Valuation techniques depend on the accuracy and consistency of subjective data items; these are often beyond the ability of ordinary data collectors to recognize and rate on an exceptional property. They may, however, be able to rate 75–80 percent of the houses in a neighborhood consistently and identify the 20–25 percent that fall outside the norm. Rating of these exceptions can then be done by senior appraisers. Group leaders, if experienced and adequately trained, can do the prereview during data collection.

At the same time, in a computer-assisted mass appraisal (CAMA) program, an appraiser may make an estimate of value to be used as an edit against the computer-generated estimate. If the two estimates differ by some prescribed amount, such as 10 percent, then a property should be flagged for additional field or office review.

Field Testing the Valuation Model

Chapters 14 and 15 discussed the development and calibration of valuation models. Before new models are applied, they should be tested in the field on a representative cross section of sold and unsold properties. Valuation documents listing property characteristics and values should be produced for use in field review.

Appraisers should start by reviewing data and values on properties that have sold recently. This will help establish that the data on which the models are based are accurate and consistent. It will also help the appraiser establish the value range for each area. Sales data should be checked for validity; in particular, new construction and other recent changes may have been made to the property after the sale.

Appraisers should then view properties that have not sold recently, first reviewing data and then testing value estimates produced by the model against their own judgments of value—judgments based on sales prices of recently sold properties. If the data are correct, differences between initial appraiser judgments and the value estimates may be attributable to specific characteristics that the appraiser has missed or underrated. If these are insufficient to explain differences, appraisers should review the valuation model and the subjective factors affecting value (construction quality, deterioration and obsolescence, and so forth).

In analyzing a valuation model, appraisers should look first for completeness. Has the model taken into account everything that affects value? For example, if values are being produced using multiple regression analysis, and factors have been included for full bathrooms, but not half-bathrooms, the model may not adequately address value differences between properties with and without half-bathrooms.

Appraisers should also look at the value relationships built into a model. In the above example, bathrooms could have been combined into one term by adding together the number of bathrooms, allowing one-half for each half-bathroom. Each half-bathroom is assumed to have one-half the effect of a full bathroom. Perhaps, however, the half-bathroom increases value by almost as much as the full bathroom.

Although detailed analysis may not be feasible for every factor, appraisers should be able to take a quick inventory of the factors in the model and their coefficients and compare them against the basic list of factors the model needs to address. (The cost approach often provides a good basis for formulating this list.) The appraiser's analysis can then focus on those factors that do not match the list.

As appraisers review a number of properties, certain patterns may point to systematic errors in the valuation model. Notes on these patterns and other specific problems should be given to modelers. These notes can also be used in reviewing the results of subsequent modeling in the office, which saves a return to the field to check results.

The field test also alerts appraisers of the extent to which data and values will need to be field reviewed for the entire area. If many data errors appear, a field review to correct them is needed.

Model Application and Value Review

Once appraisal models have been refined to reflect the results of field review, the models should be rerun and the value estimates reviewed in more detail. An efficient and effective appraisal review program requires several management decisions. These involve the selection of properties for more intensive review, the information to be made available to reviewers, documentation requirements, training, and, most important, resource requirements.

Office vs. Field Review   Whether to conduct a field review or an office review of the values generated is a critical decision. The field review may be avoided if appraisers have previously reviewed property characteristics data. In some projects, appraisers review the subjective factors, such as condition, desirability, construction quality, and usefulness of the property, before valuation. If this is not done, field review of the values is important.

Often there is not enough time to field review all properties. Procedures are then established to identify properties for which field review is essential. Exception properties and geographic areas or other property groups with a high variance in sales ratios should receive the highest priority.

Value stability is a concern when values are being updated frequently (annually or biennially). Value changes among similar properties should be consistent, that is, change by about the same percentage or dollar amount, assuming confidence in the previous year's values. Problem areas can be spotted using reports that compare current against previous values and produce statistics by neighborhood and class. Chapter 14 discusses value stability in more detail.

Review Manual and Training   Review of data and values, vital to revaluation, requires planning, definition and documentation of procedures, and staff training. A review manual explains standard review procedures and documents. It also explains the steps to follow in becoming familiar with each review area and in establishing final estimates of value for each parcel.

The manual also states the purposes of the appraisal, especially the achievement of a common uniform level of value. It identifies the effective valuation and taxable status dates. (The latter are important in treatment of new construction.) For partially completed structures, an accurate estimate of the degree of completion is made and noted on the property record card. Guidelines (figure 1) are established to assist appraisers in the uniform treatment of partial construction.

The review training program is an opportunity to ensure consistency in review and to emphasize the importance of getting data and values right. A typical training program will include appraisal theory as well as specific procedures.

Field Review   The field review begins with office preparation. Preparation of documents for review appraisers can greatly increase consistency and productivity. Manual valuation requires the posting of zoning, land rates, neighborhood boundaries, and other information on the reviewer's maps and the property record forms. Manual valuation also requires calculation of base prices for land and improvements. The packs of property record forms given to the review appraiser should include all information needed in the field. A production control form for each pack, listing parcels with sales, will identify properties to be viewed first to establish benchmarks against which other properties in the neighborhood will be valued.

In a computer-assisted revaluation, the computer does many calculations and reports

for which office staff and appraisers would otherwise be responsible. For example, the computer can produce a valuation report and edit reports listing properties that should be checked for specific conditions. If several valuation techniques have been applied, reports summarizing the results and highlighting large differences can be prepared.

With a CAMA system, the appraiser can perform much of the review without making extensive calculations. A good CAMA system provides appraisers with essential information in an easy-to-use format, rather than overwhelming them with too much information. Computer listings can be bulky and unwieldy to use in the field; computer-generated reports on 8 1/2-by-11-inch paper are usually easier to handle.

Sales analysis, the first step in field review, helps the appraiser understand the local market and verify that the appropriate land influence factors (for size, shape, topography, and so forth) and quality grade and depreciation adjustments have been applied. Dates of sales and market appreciation or depreciation up to the valuation date are also taken into account.

The appraiser should not expect to match every sold property exactly but should strive for consistent values based on observable characteristics. Sales can also be analyzed to provide a basic per-square-foot (or per-unit) rate. Computer-generated value estimates expressed on a per-unit basis make comparisons easier. For rental property, gross rent multipliers and other benchmarks using available income data should be established.

Once the appraiser has completed a review of properties that have sold, a property-to-property review can verify data accuracy, es-

Figure 1. Partial Construction Completion Report

Parcel no. _____ Owner: _____

Property address: _____

Building permit no.: _____ Date issued _____

Contractor: _____ Appraiser: _____

Inspection dates: _____

Cumulative inspection percent: _____ Estimated completion cost: _____

CONSTRUCTION PHASE

Item	Percent of total	Cumulative percent	Cumulative percent complete
Excavation	2	2	
Forms set	2	4	
Foundation and/or blocks	8	12	
Basement floor	2.5	14.5	
Joists set	2	16.5	
Subfloor	2	18.5	
Framed	7	25.5	
Sheathed	5	30.5	
Roof shingled	4	34.5	
Windows set	4	38.5	
Siding on	5	43.5	
Heating installed	6	49.5	
Plumbing roughed in	6	55.5	
Wiring roughed in	3	58.5	
Insulated	2.5	61	
Walls roughed in	2	63	
Walls finished	5	68	
Interior trim & cabinets	6	74	
Doors hung	2	76	
Wiring finished	3	79	
Plumbing fixtures in	3	82	
Floors finished	5	87	
Finish hardware	1	88	
Interior decorating	4	92	
Outside painting	3	95	
Water and sewer connected	2	97	
Exterior concrete work	3	100	
Total percent complete			

Notes:_____

_____

pecially of subjective data critical to determination of value. The appraiser should look for exceptional conditions that data collectors may have missed.

If data collection and the modeling effort have been well done, very little may need correction. Overall consistency, not trivial value adjustments, is the goal.

In determining final values, review appraisers consider each of the three approaches to value on each property as applicable. Appraisers do not seek exact agreement among the approaches but judge which approach best estimates market value.

Time requirements for field review vary by type and density of properties, quality of data, and information available to the appraiser for reviewing data and making value judgments. In ideal situations, appraisers should be able to conduct drive-by reviews, leaving the vehicle only rarely to check apparent listing errors. Reports and documents should be routed to make this kind of review easier.

Many factors affect daily production rates. Figure 2 compares typical production rates for various property types under favorable conditions. In dense urban areas, a walking rather than drive-by review may be necessary because of traffic. In rural areas, production rates may be reduced by longer distances between properties and by the need to get off the public road, nearer the improvements, for an adequate review.

Office Review An office review, without a field review, may be sufficient if the property characteristics data are accurate and consistent and the valuation models are good. This option is most feasible in homogeneous areas. Sales ratios and other analytical reports produced by the CAMA system to draw attention to potential problem areas will also be helpful.

Jurisdictions with recent pictures of the properties may be able to conduct a particularly effective office review, especially if the pictures are accessed through a laser videodisk, or similar technology, that allows pictures to be retrieved randomly in a few seconds or less. Coupled with reports or inquiry screens listing sales in the neighborhood, the videodisk gives appraisers a tool for reviewing sales and conducting a quick subject-by-subject review of properties. The videodisk should increase production rates by 50–100 percent—more if driving time is considered.

Correcting Data and Updating Values

After the review, office follow-up procedures should process corrections to the property records. Clerical staff should log the work returned from the field or completed in the office and batched for data entry (if data are not being entered directly into the computer by review appraisers). If the review includes data changes, values will need to be generated for the updated parcels. These values should be checked against the original review document to make sure all changes were successfully applied.

Figure 2.   Field Review Production Rates

Typical medium-density urban property	100–150 per day
Suburban residential property	100–150 per day
Rural residential property	60–100 per day
Farm property	25–40 per day
Strip commercial property	20–40 per day
Heavier commercial property	10–25 per day

Some CAMA systems include a provision for the reviewer to estimate the value that will be generated by the system after a change in property characteristics is recorded. This estimate is entered at the same time as the changes. As long as the value produced as a result of the changes falls within a prescribed tolerance about the reviewer's estimate, the final computer-generated estimate is accepted. If the value falls outside the tolerances, the parcel record is reported. The appraiser again reviews the parcel to determine the source of the discrepancy (for example, a calculation error or omitted data change), corrects the problem, and, if necessary, enters a revised estimate.

Statistical Analysis   Statistical testing of final values is the part of quality control that measures the product against the standard, the product in this case being each final appraised value. Values may be measured against several standards, including performance against actual market sales and against the previous year's appraised values (stability). The tools for these measurements include audit trails, value change analysis, ratio analysis reports, and other reports.

Appraisers doing analysis will test computer-generated values throughout the modeling and valuation process. Modeling procedures that use sales data will probably produce biased statistics if the sales used in making the measurement were included in the analysis. Many modelers will set aside some sales as a control group, excluding them from the modeling process so they are available as an unbiased measurement of model performance.

Similarly, reviewers can set aside sales during review to help measure performance and to eliminate the appraisers' bias toward matching the sales prices of recently sold properties that are being reviewed. These control sales can be used to establish an unbiased measure of the reviewed values.

Reviewers' actions can be tracked to notify modelers about problem areas and to verify that reviewers are consistent. A value-change-reason code entered for all review changes allows tabulation of statistics on the value changes by reviewer, reason code, neighborhood, and so forth. It is also possible to track the amount of value change and the typical magnitude of overrides.

The more time spent ensuring that data and values are correct before notices go out, the better. Good data and accurate values help establish credibility with property owners and eventually with the general public.

Notification and Appeals

Notification and appeals are a key part of quality assurance and provide an opportunity to correct inventory and valuation errors. Unlike single-property appraisal, mass appraisal involves the property owner in the valuation process through the right of appeal. Because property owners often have strong feelings about the effect of value increases on their tax bills, public relations become important.

The assessment notice, with accompanying material, can do much to inform the individual taxpayer. Many assessors publish a brief brochure that explains the assessor's responsibilities and the steps taxpayers can take to appeal valuations. Inquiries can be answered on the phone by a well-prepared office staff. Finally, the assessor should use the news media as a vehicle for public information.

Taxpayer Contacts

The assessment office should conduct an open operation, explaining the assessment process and responding promptly to inquiries and complaints. Property owners are entitled to explanation of their assessments and should be notified of all changes in assessed values and assessable status. They should be told the reasons for a valuation increase, for example, cyclical revaluation, remodeling, or new construction. Taxpayers with questions should be encouraged to discuss them with the assessment office before lodging a formal appeal. Most questions can be resolved at this level — erroneous data corrected, concerns about taxes directed to more appropriate government agencies, and so forth.

Notices

The assessment notice may be the taxpayer's first contact with the appeals process. For many, it will be their first awareness that revaluation is going on in the community. The notice may include

- the owner's name and mailing address
- the purpose of the notice, that is, to inform a taxpayer that a property has been reappraised, and why, and that this value will be used in establishing an assessment for tax purposes
- the date of the notice
- the date and tax year on which the value is effective (assessment date)
- identification of the property to which the notice applies: address, parcel identification number, a brief legal property description
- other important identifying information, such as assessment class (especially if classification affects the assessment) and tax district number

- exemptions, if applicable
- the new appraised value of the property, the statutory level of assessment, and the corresponding assessed value, if not at 100 percent. (Statutes often prescribe the minimum information to be printed on the notice. Some statutes require that separate values be shown for land and improvements.)
- net change in assessment
- reason for the new assessment
- major characteristics of the property
- the prior assessed and appraised values of the property
- the taxpayer's appeal rights and the dates, times, and places for value review and filing of formal appeals
- tax relief programs available in the jurisdiction

Figure 3 is an example of an assessment notice. An accompanying brochure is often helpful in explaining in more detail the property tax system, the assessment process, and taxpayers' rights.

In addition, notices can be designed to respond to taxpayers' concerns about the effect of the reappraisal on taxes. An "impact" notice (figure 4) shows estimated taxes before and after a reappraisal, comparing last year's assessment and taxes against the new assessment and expected taxes (if total taxes levied do not change). The impact tax rate is calculated as

$$\text{Old tax rate} \times \frac{\text{Old tax base (total assessed value of all property)}}{\text{New tax base (total assessed value of all property previously assessed)}}$$

Even though the tax base may have increased two- or threefold due to revaluation,

Figure 3. Example of a Notice of Assessment

Town of Putnam

Pursuant to the provision of Sec. 12-55 of the General Statutes (Rev. 1958) of the State of Connecticut, you are hereby notified that the assessor has assessed your property in the Tax records for the year 1989 at $96,390. The change in the assessment is as follows:

Map/Lot	012/029-00		Map/Lot	012/029-00
1-1	dwelling lot	12,600	1-1 dwelling lot	6,475
1-2	excess acreage	350	1-3 dwellings	41,405
1-3	dwellings	82,810	1-4 outbuildings	315
1-4	outbuildings	630		

Property Loc: 356 SCHOOL ST R-20

DOE, JEANNE 1/2 INT,
DOE, JOHN & JANE 1/2 INT
356 SCHOOL ST
PUTNAM CT 06260

928-5376   ASSESSOR

at current value levels the tax rate will adjust to one-half or one-third of its previous level; additional taxes are not necessarily generated as a windfall from the revaluation. The impact notice should include the caveat that the impact tax rate is estimated from the previous year's tax levies and is no guarantee of the actual tax rate or the actual tax bill. The governing bodies of school districts, municipalities, and other taxing authorities set their levies and thus the eventual tax rate.

Because the new tax base is based on tentative assessed values that may be reduced as a result of informal review and appeals, some contingency can be built into the impact rate for these reductions. Also, the theoretical new tax base should include only parcels or improvements previously assessed. Value increases due to new construction, annexation, and changes in use resulting in an increase

in value usually are excluded from the computation.

Planning should always precede the preparation of notices. Design and printing of forms takes a minimum of six to eight weeks, longer if several agencies are involved or if the printing is put out to bid. The notice should conform to assessment law. Mass mailing requires lead time. If notices are to be computer printed, programs may need to be written or modified and tested.

Informal Reviews

When the notice of assessment is issued, the property owner has four valid reasons for requesting review:

• The face of the notice has an error; for example, the name, class, or property description is incorrect.

Figure 4.   Example of an Impact Notice

FOR INFORMATION ONLY—NOT A TAX BILL

OWNER INFORMATION: PARCEL INFORMATION:

HUGHES, HAROLD J. & MARY R.   3800-2400-155.13-3-1
BOX 304-A, RD #1   80 MAPLE AVENUE
BOZENKILL ROAD   2.10 ACRES
                                                PROPERTY CLASS: 210

YOUR PROPERTY AS DESCRIBED ABOVE HAS A FAIR MARKET VALUE AND TENTATIVE
ASSESSMENT OF $59,400 AS OF **DATE OF IMPACTS** WHICH IS AN INCREASE OF $53,600
AS COMPARED TO LAST YEARS ASSESSMENT.

IF YOU HAVE ANY QUESTIONS CONCERNING THE VALUE SHOWN ABOVE, YOU MAY
ARRANGE TO DISCUSS YOUR PROPERTY AT AN INFORMAL REVIEW BY
CALLING _____
BETWEEN THE HOURS OF 8:30 AM and 4:30 PM, MON.-FRI. WITHIN 10 DAYS OF THE RECEIPT
OF THIS NOTICE. IF YOU SCHEDULE A REVIEW, PLEASE BRING THIS NOTICE WITH YOU.

DATES OF INFORMAL REVIEWS: MARCH 10-28
TIMES: MON.-THURS. 11:00 AM-8:00 PM; FRI. 8:30 AM-4:30 PM
HEARING LOCATION: SHERMAN ELEMENTARY SCHOOL

	TAX PURPOSE	EXEMPT AMOUNT	TAXABLE VALUE	TAX
BASED ON YOUR 1985	SCHOOL	0	$5,800	$594
ASSESSMENT OF $5,800	COUNTY	0	$5,800	$232
YOUR TAXES, WERE	TOWN	0	$5,800	$151
	TOTAL TAXES WERE APPROXIMATELY			$977
USING THE TENTATIVE	SCHOOL	0	$59,400	$629
1986 MARKET VALUE OF	COUNTRY	0	$59,400	$246
$59,400 YOUR ESTIMATED	TOWN	0	$59,400	$160
TAXES WOULD HAVE BEEN				
	TOTAL TAXES WOULD HAVE BEEN APPROXIMATELY			$1,035

VILLAGE TAXES, IF ANY
ARE NOT INCLUDED   ESTIMATED NET TAX INCREASE | $58 |

- The value is not fair compared to other properties in the neighborhood or class.
- The property owner considers the actual valuation incorrect.
- The property owner claims an exemption from taxation.

None of these objections is an appeal at this time. Nevertheless, the appeals process can be said to begin with an informal consultation between the assessment office and the property owner to ensure that errors are corrected and new claims (for exemptions, changes in valuation data, and the like) reviewed.

This informal review may be handled by mail, in person, or by telephone (usually at the option of the property owner). The review allows for communication, and mutual understanding will reduce the number of formal appeals. Property owners who decide to lodge formal appeals should be required to state the grounds of the appeal in writing, as a prerequisite for further appeal, and the assessment office should also document its position. Informal reviews allow property owners to air grievances, obtain information, and, in many cases, resolve appeals at a low cost.

Logistics for the informal reviews should be planned. Will they be handled as part of the normal office operation or should appointments be scheduled or reviews held in a special location? With advance planning, this information can be printed on the notice. If a revaluation is being conducted for the first time in several years, the assessor should estimate a high volume of complaints and, if many calls are expected, set up a phone bank manned by employees trained in telephone etiquette, who can answer questions and schedule appointments for interviews with appraisers. Personnel planning should include sufficient time and staff to handle the review.

The hearing schedule should be planned so that property owners do not wait a long time. The schedule should allow at least 10–15 minutes per parcel for simple improved parcels, 20–30 minutes for farm parcels, and 20–30 minutes for commercial/industrial parcels. Owners of parcels with numerous improvements or major commercial/industrial parcels will require special and longer appointments. Hearing hours might be scheduled from 9 to 4 weekdays, with an hour free for lunch. Evening and Saturday hearings are a convenience to working property owners. Saturday might be used to schedule exceptional properties. The work flow can be better distributed if appointments are required. When appointments are required, property records and other documents needed for reviewing the appraisal can be ready when the property owner arrives.

The first step in the informal review is registration at the front desk and retrieval of the relevant file. The interviewer then determines the owner's concern and reviews property record information with the owner to verify accuracy. The informal reviews should incorporate the following steps:

1. Verify the parcel.
2. Exchange information.
3. Record nature of complaint.
4. Use sales to confirm property value.
5. Do not commit to any value change.
6. Clearly explain what action will be taken: office review, exterior review, interior inspection.
7. Explain appeal rights and procedures.
8. Record action taken.
9. Note changes to the property record in red.

After the informal review, the interviewer should complete an informal review form (figure 5) for documentation and to ensure that the action indicated to the property owner will be taken.

Formal Appeals

Formal appeals take place at several levels. The first recourse for the property owner is usually a local appeal board. Preparation for a board of appeal is more complex and time-consuming than the informal review process. Depending on the board's makeup and the manner in which it operates, additional reports may be necessary to describe the parcel under appeal and provide supporting documentation for the value established by the assessor. The board may require information on which to make an informed judgment as to the nature of the property and an independent estimate of its value. This information may include copies of tax maps, pictures of the property, information on the parcel, and comparable nearby sales.

The highest level of administrative review is usually a state or provincial property tax tribunal, which makes final decisions with respect to individual assessments or application of equalization factors. However, unresolved legal issues can be appealed to the courts. Issues of law or mixed law and fact, such as interpretations of statutes, applications of exemption privileges, and the jurisdiction of appellate boards and tribunals, are matters of appeal to the supreme court of the state or province.

Supporting Documentation for the Appeals Process

If understandable and convincing information is provided at the beginning of the ap-

peals process, and taxpayers recognize that the assessor has treated properties fairly and reasonably, time and money can be saved.

Property Inventories

In reviewing the property with the taxpayer, an understandable record of the property's characteristics is essential. The traditional property record form is usually a good document to work with if it lists the codes and descriptions for each of the important data elements used in the valuation process. With the proliferation of CAMA systems, however, the traditional card is no longer necessary. Many jurisdictions have designed data collection forms for field and office use, but not necessarily for taxpayer reviews. In such cases, the taxpayer review document is usually a computer-printed property record or inventory sheet (figure 6), a copy of which can be given to the taxpayer on request. Many assessor's offices have printers on public counters that property owners can use to print copies of their own property record data.

Valuation Models

A number of issues are related to the ease of explanation in CAMA (Gloudemans 1983), including simplicity of design, reasonability of the dollar values assigned to property attributes, consistency in these values between submodels, stability of these values over time, allocation of value among property components (especially land and improvements), and ease of explanation. Many of these are addressed in the context of the field testing of the model. The appraiser will ascertain that the values assigned to various attributes are reasonable and that these values are con-

Figure 5. Informal Review Form

INFORMAL REVIEW   No. _____

PARCEL IDENTIFICATION	FICHE	FRAME

PROPERTY OWNER: PROPERTY LOCATION (If different from owner's)

Name _____

Address _____

_____

INTERVIEWED BY: DATE:

NATURE OF COMPLAINT:

RECOMMENDED ACTION:

☐ None   ☐ Field review (no verification by owner needed)

☐ Clerical change   ☐ Field review (with interior inspection)

☐ Other _____

ACTION TAKEN:

☐ No change

☐ Change made by _____ date _____

☐ Maintenance completed by _____ date _____

Figure 6. Property Inventory Sheet

DATE: 870213

INVENTORY CONTENTS SHEET   MAS510   PAGE:000001

********** SKETCH FOR DWELLING **********

*********** PARCEL IDENTIFICATION ***********

CTY MAP SC S QT BL PARCEL O CD PARC-FIL
001 041 02 0 20 15 001.00 0 01

(010)
(060) MAPS: 041   (070) ROUTING:___
(101) NBHD: 100   (102) LAND USE: 111.0
(103) LVG UNIT: 001   (104) CLASS: RU
(105) ZONING: R4
(109) ADDRESS:3121   HOLLY LN   66600

************* SALES DATA *************

	MO	YR	TYPE	AMOUNT	SOURCE	VAL	DEL
(201)	08	85	2	10,000	4	9	
(202)	10	86	2	20,000	4	0	
(203)	02	87	2	30,000	1	0	

****** APPRAISAL PROCESS INFORMATION ******

	DATE	TIME	ID	CODE
(461)	102086	1115	005	5
(462)				
(463)				

(464) PERSON CONTACTED:
(465) CONTACT CODE:

********* BUILDING PERMIT RECORD *********

PRMT# DATE AMOUNT CODE PURPOSE
(471)
(472)

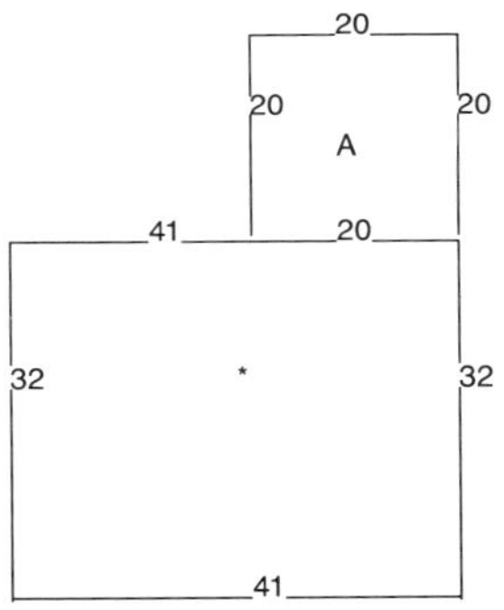

************ MAIN DWELLING DATA ************

(499) GROUP DELETE (FOR F.C.500-660)   0
(500) PROP. INDIC.
(505) STORY HEIGHT   10
(506) EXTERIOR WALLS   4
(507) STYLE   02
(508) ROOF MATERIAL   02
      YEAR BUILD AGE/EST REMODELED
(510)   1960   19
(515) FOUNDATION TYPE   2
(520) BASEMENT   4
(525) HEATING & COOLING   3
(526) HEATING FUEL TYPE   3
(527) HEATING SYSTEM TYPE   3
(530) TOTAL   BED   FAMILY
      ROOMS 07 ROOMS 03 ROOMS 0
(535) FULL   HALF   ADDN'L   TOTAL
      BATHS 1 BATHS 1 FIXT. 2 FIXT. 07
(540) ATTIC   1
(541) FLOOR COVERING   1
(542) INTERIOR WALLS   1
(545) PHYSICAL CONDITION   1
(560) GROUND FLOOR AREA   01312
(565) GRADE FACTOR C SIGN

********* COST & DESIGN FACTOR *********

(570) DESC.___ SIGN___ PCT.___
(575) CDU/DEPRECIATION AV

Figure 6. Property Inventory Sheet (cont.)

DATE: 870213   INVENTORY CONTENTS SHEET   MAS510   PAGE:000001

********** PROPERTY FACTORS & NOTES **********
(400) TOPOGRAPHY   1   (410) UTILITIES   1
(420) ACCESS   1   (430) FRONTING   4
(440) LOCATION   6
(451) NOTE-1
(482) NOTE-2   02DEACT 01/08/87
(483) NOTE-3
(450) PARKING   TYPE 3 QUANTITY 2 PROXIMITY 3

********** LAND DATA & COMPUTATIONS **********
(299) GROUP DELETE (for F.C. 300-330)
NONE #
(300)

LOTS	# ACT	EFF	DPT	UPRICE	IFACTOR	VALUE
(301)	1 120	020	171	11 100%		2,550
(302)	2 090	016	140	11 100%		2,230
(303)	1 010	010	100	120	COO%	1,100

SQ. FT. # SQUARE FEET UPRICE IFACTOR   VALUE
			%
(311)			%
(312)			%
(313)			%

ACREAGE # ACRES PG UPRICE IFACTOR VALUE
(321)		%
(322)		%
(323)		%
(324)		%
(325)		%
(326)		%
(327)		%
(328)		%

TOTAL ACRES
(329) GROSS #
(330) _ GROSS LAND VALUE

********** ADDITIONS & SKETCH VECTORS **********
(599) GROUP DELETE (FOR F.C. 601-608)
          LOW   1ST   2ND   3RD   AREA
(601)   10   400
(602)
(603)
(604)
(605)
(606)
(607)
(608)

(649) GROUP DELETE (FOR F.C. 651-660)
(651) AOCU32X41
(652) A1U32R21CU20X20H
(653)
(654)
(655)
(656)
(657)
(658)
(659)
(660)

********** APPRAISER'S FINAL REPORT **********
EFF. DATE RSN L/I +/- AMOUNT
(901)
(902)

********** MARKET VALUE/OVERRIDE **********
          VALUE   RSN   DATE   RVR
(960)   54,600   0   02/12/87 CST
(970)   ID TIEBACK 11110410205001000.002
TOTAL VALUE LAND   1,400
TOTAL VALUE BLDGS.   53,200

********** OTHER FEATURES **********
(551) BLT-IN GAR # OF CARS   1
(552) UNFINISHED AREA   001001000
(553) REC. ROOM AREA   12.X.030
       FINISHED BSMT LVG AREA
********** MASONRY FIREPLACE **********
(554) CHIMNEYS 1 UNITS 2
(555) PREFABRICATED FIREPLACE UNITS
(556) BASEMENT GAR # OF CARS ___
(557) MISC. ___ QTY. ___
       MISC. ___ QTY. ___

********** CONDOMINIUMS **********
(581) LEVEL ___   (582) UNIT TYPE ___
(583) AMENITIES ___

****** OTHER BUILDING & YARD IMPRVMTS ******
(699) GROUP DELETE (FOR F.C.701-711)

	TYPE	QTY	YR	SIZE	GR	CON	MA	MOC
(701)	RG1	01	00	000200	A		00	
(702)	RG1	01	76	10X020	C	A	00	
(703)	RG1	01	76	000200	C	A	02	
(704)	RG1	01	76	10X020	C	A	99	
(705)								
(706)								
(707)								
(708)								
(709)								
(710)								

(711) MISC. IMPROVEMENTS ___ MV

********* GROSS BUILDING SUMMARY *********
(800) DESCRIPTION
       TOTAL GROSS VALUE

sistent between the submodels used to value different segments of the market.

For the taxpayer, it is easier to understand a simple model, that is, one with few factors expressed in forms that reflect the taxpayer's perception of the factors' relation to property values.

Allocation of value to components of the property, especially land and improvements, is required in many states. Certain model structures lend themselves to this allocation better than others. Valuation using comparable sales, for example, does not automatically provide for explicit allocation of land and improvement values, although comparable sales provide excellent support for total property values.

Sales Comparison

The sales comparison approach has traditionally provided the main defense of appraised values in assessment appeals. If suitable comparables can be identified (or if the property itself has sold), and their sales prices support the assessor's value, there is no better defense. CAMA systems can readily provide comparable sales and produce reports that assessment offices can use when they review appraisals with property owners.

Comparables should be selected according to attributes property owners consider important in determining value. These include locational factors (neighborhood, community, and school district), construction factors (age, square footage, quality of construction, and so forth), and the property's style and other amenities. The sales prices of the comparables are then adjusted to account for differences from the subject property.

A comparable sales report (see figure 7) provides information about the subject property and the comparable sales that support its appraisal.

The Base Home Technique

Several techniques have been proposed for making valuation models understandable to the property owner. One is the base home concept, which uses simple tables to relate values to a typical, or base, home for each market segment. This concept allows techniques such as multiple regression analysis to be used in calibrating market models but expresses the results in an easy-to-understand format.

If multiple regression models were simple linear equations for property characteristics, the computations would not be difficult to understand. However, to adapt linear regression to the nonlinear interactive world, modelers introduce factors that better simulate the relationship between property characteristics and the market. For example, it is usual to introduce many terms that are expressed as per-square-foot adjustments, such as age, condition, and construction quality. When this is the case, a change in square feet results in a change in many different terms, not just one.

The base home valuation equation can be transformed into a table containing the base home value and adjustments to account for differences between the subject property and the base home. There are four steps in the base home approach. In the first, properties subject to the same valuation model are grouped into submodels based on location, type of property, or construction quality. This increases the similarity between the base home and subject properties and makes the process more understandable.

Figure 7. Comparable Sales Report

	SUBJECT	COMP 1	COMP 2	COMP 3	COMP 4	COMP 5
PARCEL-IDENTIFICATION						
ID	001-145-150-	001-145-150-	001-145-150-	001-142-090-	001-142-090-	001-142-040-
	30-05-006.000	30-05-006.000	30-08-001.000	30-14-001.000	30-11-001.000	10-01-009.000
CARD/OF CARD	0101	0101	0101	0101	0101	0101
STREET NUMBER	3458	3458	3858	3518	7112	6729
STREET NAME	SKYLINE DR	SKYLINE DR	SKYLINE PK	SWASHWORTH P	W SMITH PL	W 15TH ST
NGHBD ID/NGHBD GRP	461/004	461/004	461/004	561/005	561/005	241/002
MODEL #		1	1	1	1	1
CLASS	RU	RU	RU	RU	RU	RU
LAND DESCRIPTION						
TYPE	1	1	1	1	1	1
PRIMARY ACRES	0	0	0	0	0	0
TOPOGRAPHY	LEVEL	LEVEL	LEVEL	LEVEL	LEVEL	LEVEL
DWELLING DESCRIPTION						
NUMBER STORIES	1.0	1.0	1.0	2.0	1.5	1.0
EXTERIOR WALL	FRAME	FRAME	FRAME	FRAME	FRAME	FRAME
STYLE	SPLIT LEVEL	SPLIT LEVEL	RANCH	CONVENTIONAL	CONVENTIONAL	RANCH
YEAR BUILT/REMOD	976/00	976/00	979/00	977/00	971/00	957/00
BASEMENT	PART	PART	FULL	FULL	FULL	FULL
BED/FAM/TOT/BATH,HF	03/1/06/2/1	03/1/06/2/1	03/1/06/2/0	04/0/08/2/0	03/0/06/2/1	03/0/07/2/0
HEAT	CENTRAL/AIR	CENTRAL/AIR	CENTRAL/AIR	CENTRAL/AIR	CENTRAL/AIR	CENTRAL/AIR
FUEL/SYSTEM	G/WA	G/WA	G/WA	G/WA	G/WA	G/WA
PHYSICAL CONDITION	GOOD	GOOD	GOOD	GOOD	GOOD	AVERAGE
REC ROOM AREA	0	0	0	0	0	0
WBFP ST,OPN/METAL FP	1.2/	1.2/	1.2/	1.1/	./	./
BSMT GARAGE CAPACITY	2	2	0	0	0	0
FINISHED BASEMENT	400	400	870	0	0	960
GRADE	C +	C +	C +	B –	C +	C –
COST & DESIGN						
CDU	VG	VG	VG	VG	VG	GD
FIRST FLOOR AREA	1,760	1,760	1,740	972	1,408	960
SFLA	2,210	2,210	2,610	2,292	2,464	1.920
DETACHED GARAGE AREA	0	0	0	0	0	0
ATTACHED GARAGE AREA	0	0	572	552	0	312
POOL AREA	0	0	0	0	0	0
OPEN PORCH AREA	35	35	120	0	0	0
CLOSED PORCH AREA	0	0	0	0	0	0
PRICING DATA						
BASE PRICE	$73,570	$73,570	$72,920	$71,990	$80,910	$47,670
ADDITION PTS	21	21	87	175	19	42
OTHER FEATURES PTS	121	121	191	25	-21	168
RCN	$95,690	$95,690	$113,380	$112,580	93,060	$64,560
PERCENT GOOD	90%	90%	90%	90%	85%	65%
DWELLING VALUE	$86,800	$86,800	$102,700	$101,500	$79,200	$42,200
TOTAL OBCY	$700	$700	$700	$200	$100	$200
LAND VALUE	$5,200	$5,200	$5,200	$4,700	$4,100	$3,800
TOTAL VALUE	$92,000	$92,000	$107,900	$106,200	$83,300	$46,000
VALUATION						
SALE DATE		06/85	06/84	04/85	06/85	10/85
SALE PRICE		$99,950	$97,000	$106,000	$91,000	$50,300
MRA ESTIMATE	$95,190	$95,190	$94,937	$104,569	$96,754	$49,309
ADJUSTED SALE		$99,950	$97,253	$96,620	$89,436	$96,181
DISTANCE		0	122	130	132	142
WEIGHTED ESTIMATE	96,912					
MARKET VALUE	$96,600					
FIELD CONTROL CODE	1					
INDICATOR						

ADJ

The second step is specification of the characteristics of the base home for each model or submodel. The characteristics should include all characteristics used in the model development and can be computed as the mean, median, or other representative number. To simplify calculations, areas may be rounded to the nearest 100 square feet, ages to the nearest five years, and so forth.

The third step is the calculation of base home values, by simply applying the valuation equation to the characteristics of the base home. Because multiple regression analysis and other mathematical models tend to be reliable when the data are most typical, the base home value is estimated with a high degree of confidence.

The final step is the conversion of the model coefficients or factors into dollar amounts or percentages that indicate how much to add or subtract for differences between subject properties and the base home. These component adjustments represent the net change in value attributable to a unit change in a particular characteristic, such as a half-bath, fireplace, square feet of living area, or year of effective age. Depending on the model formulation, the component adjustments may be expressed as rates (dollars per square foot or other unit amounts), percentages, or flat dollar amounts. A spreadsheet program can be used to automate the conversion process.

Table 1 shows a multiple regression model, base home characteristics, and calculation of the base home value. This model includes several interactive terms that make the model a little more difficult to understand. The base home is defined as a five-year-old, 1,400-square-foot house of average quality construction (grade 4), with two full baths, a 200-square-foot porch, and a 300-square-foot carport on a 6,000-square-foot lot.

Tables are then created to provide adjustments for differences from the base home (table 1). This includes a size adjustment of $37.71 (for each square foot over or below the 1,400 square feet in the base home); per-square-foot adjustments for grade, age (five-year increments), and total square footage of the house, a deduction for lower-level living area (included in the square footage variable), and adjustments for one- and three-bath houses and for air conditioning. In addition, adjustments are made for patio, deck, and carport areas. Finally, an adjustment of $1.00 per $1.00 of depreciated cost is made for any miscellaneous other building and yard improvement values calculated from the cost approach.

Figure 8 shows the value calculations based on the tables in table 2 for a sample subject property. Note that the amount of adjustment for each physical difference from the base home is separately identified. Figure 11 shows the calculations for the same property based on the multiple regression analysis equation (except for rounding, the results are identical).

Use of Video Images in Hearings

Pictures of properties are helpful in defending assessments. The picture reassures property owners that someone was in the field and viewed properties and that appraisers had pictures available when doing appraisals even if not in the field themselves. A picture can also answer many questions about a property for the hearing officer. A property owner is less likely to make inaccurate statements about a property's condition and features if an accurate picture is available.

Table 1. Calculation of Base Home Value

MRA Model

Term	Coefficient	Base Home	Value	Comment
Total land size	4.00	6,000	24,000	
Grade factor × SF	$37.71	1,400	52,794	See note 1
Age × SF	− 0.3696	7,000	− 2,587	5 yrs. times 1,400 SF
Lower level living area	− 23.86	0	0	
Bathrooms	8,080.00	2	16,160	
Air conditioning	500.00	0	0	
Open porch area	7.45	200	1,490	
Enclosed porch area	8.41	0	0	
Deck area	1.00	0	0	
Carport area	17.50	300	5,250	
Other outbuilding	1.00	0	0	
Date of sale × SF	0.0036	51,800	186	See note 2
Constant	67,034	1	67,034	
Base home price			164,327	

Note 1: Grade factors multiply the square foot adjustment (3 = 0.85, 3 + = 0.90, 4 − = 0.95, 4 = 1.00, 4 + = 1.05, 5 − = 1.10, 5 = 1.15). Square feet (SF) include main floor and lower level living area.

Note 2: Date of sale is the number of months from the base date (12/84) to the effective valuation date of 01/88. This is multiplied times the square footage of living area. (37 × 1,400 = 51,800). In creating the base home tables this will be converted to a per square foot cost and added to the square footage adjustments by quality grade.

Even more can be done with video images. It becomes feasible to look at images of the subject property and neighboring properties without spending time retrieving pictures from the files. Laser videodisks provide maximum benefit, because images can be accessed in a few seconds or less, so that the appraiser or hearing officer can quickly step through pictures of neighboring or comparable sale properties. The discussion can return to the picture of the owner's property and a review of the characteristics immediately evident from the picture. If an on-line CAMA system is used, the attributes stored in the data base can also be reviewed while the picture is still displayed on the TV monitor. Demonstrating that such information is at the assessor's fingertips underscores the assessor's competence and the probable accuracy and fairness of the appraisal process.

Public Relations

Taxation is never popular, and the assessor is rarely a hero in the public eye. But a positive image for the assessor's office is still possible—and worth having. The most important requirement is fair, open, efficient ad-

Table 2. Base Home Example: Description and Adjustments

(a) Base home description

Characteristic	Value
Total land size	6,000
Grade factor × square feet	1,400
Depreciation	2,590
Lower level living area	0
Bathrooms	2
Air conditioning	0
Open porch area	200
Enclosed porch area	0
Deck area	0
Carport area	300
Other outbuilding value	0
Base home value	164,141

(b) Component adjustments

Land size adjustment
  Less than 6,000 — subtract 4.00
  Greater than 6,000 — add 4.00

Building size adjustment
  Less than 1,400 — subtract 37.71
  Greater than 1,400 — add 37.71

Per square foot (PSF) adjustments

Grade	Adjustment factor	Adjustment rate	Depreciation adjustments (PSF)						Deduct for lower-level living area
			0	5	10	15	20	25	
3	−0.15	−5.66	3.70	0	−3.70	−5.54	−7.40	−23.79	23.86
3+	−0.10	−3.77	3.70	0	−3.70	−5.54	−7.40	−23.79	23.86
4−	−0.05	−1.88	3.70	0	−3.70	−5.54	−7.40	−23.79	23.86
4	0.00	0	3.70	0	−3.70	−5.54	−7.40	−23.79	23.86
4+	0.05	+1.88	3.70	0	−3.70	−5.54	−7.40	−23.79	23.86
5−	0.10	+3.77	3.70	0	−3.70	−5.54	−7.40	−23.79	23.86
5	0.15	+5.66	3.70	0	−3.70	−5.54	−7.40	−23.79	23.86

Bathrooms
  For 1 — deduct 8,080
  For 3 — add 8,080

Air conditioning
  If present — add 5,000

Table 2.   Base Home Example: Description and Adjustments (cont.)

Unit adjustments

	Rate	Square footage					
		0	50	100	150	200	300
Open porch area	7.45	−1,490	−1,120	−745	−370	0	750
Enclosed porch area	8.41	0	420	840	1,260	1,680	2,520
Deck area	1.00	0	50	100	150	200	300
Carport area	17.50	−5,250	−4,375	−3,500	−2,625	−1,750	0
Other building and yard improvements dollar value	1.00						

Figure 8.   Base Home Pricing Work Sheet

Base Home Value   164,141

	Subject		Base		Difference		Adjustment		
Land adjustment	8,500	−	6,000	=	2,500	×	4.00	=	10,000

	Subject		Base		Difference		Adjustment		
Size adjustment	1,750	−	1,400	=	350	×	37.71	=	13,199

	Subject	Base	Difference	Subject square feet		
Grade adjustment	3 +	4	− 3.77	1,750	=	− 6,598

	Adjustment		Subject square feet		Subject depreciation		Base depreciation		
Age adjustment	− 3.70	×	1,750	=	− 6,475	+	2,590	=	− 3,885

		Adjustment		Subject LLLA		
Lower-level living area adjustment (LLLA)	deduct (−)	23.86	×	500	=	− 11,930

Other adjustments:	Subject	Base	
Baths	2	2	0
Air conditioning	none	none	0
Open porch	100	200	− 745
Enclosed porch	250	0	2,100
Deck area	0	0	0
Carport	200	300	− 1,750
Other building and yard improvements			500
Total			165,032

Figure 9. Calculation by Multiple Regression Formula

Constant			67,034
Land area	8500×4.00	−	34,000
Grade × square feet	$37.71 \times 1,750 \times .90$	=	59,409
Age × square feet	$-0.3696 \times 1,750 \times 10$	=	−6,468
Lower-level living area	-23.86×500	=	−11,930
Baths	$2 \times 8,080$	=	16,160
Air conditioning	500×0	=	0
Open porch area	7.45×100	=	745
Enclosed porch area	8.41×250	=	2,103
Deck area	1.00×0	=	0
Carport area	17.50×200	=	3,500
Outbuildings	1×500	=	500
Total			165,053

ministration of the assessment function. Individuals and agencies alike must know what the assessor does and that it is done well.

The assessor's public relations and information program can build on competent administration. A public relations program can be seen as a "first line of defense," so effective, it is hoped, that other defenses will rarely be used. Without a sound public relations program, the assessor may meet the public only through complaints and appeals. Even here, a firm, courteous staff can be effective, and informing taxpayers about their rights and obligations may prevent lengthy formal hearings.

The assessor's public includes not only individual taxpayers (who range from owners of modest single-family homes to major investors in commercial and industrial real estate), but also such groups as attorneys, appraisers, developers, title companies, real estate brokers, lending institutions, communications media, other units of government, civic and professional associations, and public institutions (such as schools) that benefit from the ad valorem property tax. The assessor's office must manage the information system so that these various publics have access to the large amount of useful and necessary information to be found in assessment records. These groups, in turn, can be a communications network that informs the general public about the assessor's office.

However, the most important parts of a public relations program are a well-run office with well-planned records and record storage, an office layout that makes public access easy, a courteous staff trained to deal with the public, and written rules of procedure. (See the IAAO *Standard on Public Relations* [IAAO 1988].)

Planning a Public Relations Program

A planned program of public relations will include well-thought-out responses to issues and inquiries, cooperation with other government agencies, and ways of getting information to the public—media contacts, printed information, and speaking engagements. One person should be designated to talk to the media, and, when possible, material such as press briefings should be prepared in advance.

Reviewing Needs The first step in planning good public relations is a review of needs. The assessor may ask such questions as:

- What is the assessing office's public image?
- How well informed is the general public? The real estate community?
- What is the political environment?
- What staff improvements are needed?
- What programs are already in place?
- What issues are likely to emerge?

This analysis of needs should be ongoing.

Responding to Inquiries and Issues

Taxpayers, real estate salespersons, and government officials often need information from the assessment office. Property information and maps are important resources for these and other groups. The assessor should find efficient means of responding to inquiries via telephone, computer screen, printed matter, or magnetic media (tapes and floppy disks). Fees may be charged to recover the costs of providing some forms of information.

Assessment is often controversial. Many issues surface, some in response to specific events, others repeatedly. Clear, well-defined responses to issues can increase public confidence in the assessment office. The office needs a way to predict emerging issues and to prepare responses to them. For example, adverse reaction to higher assessed values after reappraisal is likely. The assessment office can minimize taxpayers' displeasure by educating them about the reappraisal before value notices are sent and by providing opportunities to have questions answered. The media can be enlisted to cover the reappraisal

story from the assessor's perspective if they are given clear, well-written materials, and if the assessor has developed a cooperative relationship with the media. Press kits, graphics, and regular press briefings give the media the tools for telling the assessor's story.

Assessors who understand tax policy and the economic and political effects of assessment are in a good position to address recurring issues. Some of these issues are the following:

- *Rationale for implementing a new appraisal system.* Appraisal systems of the type advocated in this textbook are designed to permit more accurate and frequent reappraisals. Such systems ensure that tax liabilities are apportioned fairly. In addition, the tax base is stated more accurately, thereby strengthening the fiscal health of local governments. New systems also permit the assessor to do a better job with a given level of resources. A public information program should point out such advantages of improved assessment systems and procedures.

- *Impact of a reappraisal.* Many reappraisals result in overall increases in assessed values and, unless levies are held in check, in higher taxes. Reappraisals often result in shifts in tax burdens as well. The greater the elapsed time since the last reappraisal, the more dramatic the effects of the new appraisal are apt to be. The best response is to acknowledge such effects and point out that shifts in tax liabilities are an unavoidable consequence of correcting the inequities caused by infrequent reappraisals in the past. It is a good strategy to welcome inquiries about the new appraised values and to correct any mistakes made during the reappraisal. The issue of higher taxes can be addressed by focusing responsibility for the increase on those who set tax levies and rates. Higher assessments do not cause higher taxes.

- *Maintenance of property, new developments, and so on, discouraged.* In addition to general complaints about higher taxes, many specific complaints will be voiced—for example, that property maintenance will be discouraged, investment in new construction will be discouraged, farming will be uneconomical, and the poor and elderly will be driven from their homes. A number of things can be done to counter such arguments. In many states, of course, one or more property tax relief or incentive laws may be applicable. With respect to routine maintenance, clarifying which sorts of activities do not usually result in immediate reappraisal is helpful. (It might be pointed out that assessors do not lurk in paint and hardware stores in order to monitor maintenance activities.)

- *Assessment bias.* Reappraisals usually result in shifts in tax burdens. Often upper- and middle-class homeowners vocally oppose reappraisals on the ground that they are being discriminated against and business property is favored. Others may charge economic or racial bias. The frequency, pattern, and magnitude of assessment changes account for such suspicions. People may argue that equity is "equal" increases in assessed values. The best strategy is to demonstrate improvements in assessment uniformity with sales ratio data for different use classes and areas.

- *Incompetence.* Perhaps the most difficult public relations problem that assessing officers encounter is the pervasive view

that they are incompetent or that the property tax is administratively infeasible. Sales ratio statistics that show less than perfect congruence between appraised values and sales prices call into question the assessor's competence. The fact that sales are not perfect indicators of values is overlooked, or, if not, the fact is cited as evidence of administrative infeasibility. Such conclusions are not necessarily warranted.

Assessors, however, should not defend real or apparent failings on such grounds. Real shortcomings should be corrected; apparent ones usually disappear when the public and critics in particular are given sufficient information to understand what the assessment task is and how it is solved.

Cooperation with Other Public Agencies

The assessor, as a public servant, has a special relationship with other agencies of government. The legislature and the courts establish ground rules by which the office must operate. Other state agencies oversee the assessment operation. In the local jurisdiction, budgeting, purchasing, and even personnel may be done for the assessment office by another agency. Data may be cross filed with other agencies (sales data; court actions; land use planning; building permits and property splits; recording of deeds, titles, contracts, and so forth). In many jurisdictions, resources are shared with other units of government: mapping, equipment, publications, clerical services, computer facilities, and the like.

The assessor's need to work with other agencies and officials at all levels of government should lead to interdependent relationships that make the assessor's job easier. These relationships are sometimes difficult and time-consuming, yet they can save far more time and effort than they cost. And a poor relationship can be a continuing headache. Some guidelines for good relations with other public officials are:

- Avoid surprises, especially public ones. For example, discuss public statements in advance with officials who might be affected. (If another official issues a statement that affects assessment, the assessor should avoid premature comment. Get the facts first.)
- Avoid making unreasonable demands on others. Try to anticipate needs in advance so that others have time to prepare.
- Criticize directly—and in private. Don't use the media as a forum for interagency problems.
- Seek out advice. No one knows everything. It's important to let others know what you're thinking, especially when changes are being planned.
- Learn what other agencies do. Understand their functions as they relate to assessment.
- Keep other agencies informed.
- Share the glory; it makes everyone part of your team.

The many agencies of government are interdependent. And today's well-informed public expects the assessment office to relate the assessment function to government in general and tax policies in particular.

Means of Circulating Information

Media Contacts When an assessor must communicate with large numbers of people at once, the news media—radio, magazines, newspapers, and television—become part of the public relations team. Most media staff members appreciate relevant and accurate material. Remember, however, they often serve a public whose understanding of assessment is limited. It then becomes the responsibility of the assessor to translate technical information into meaningful material. Media staff may be willing to help prepare material for public consumption.

The information used by the media has traditionally been summarized as "who, where, what, why, when, and how." These essential facts should be presented in clear and simple language. Press releases should usually be limited to one page, often supplemented by a press kit giving further details, financial data, names of key people, and so forth. (Even after such efforts, what seems important to the assessment office may not always be treated as such by the media.)

Relationships with key media people and reporters should be established in advance whenever possible. If such people are informed before an issue becomes a public concern, they are likely to see the assessor as the best source of accurate information. Misquotation is minimized and useful publicity, maximized.

One warning: use whatever means possible to avoid being misquoted. Speak carefully, explain fully, ask for feedback before the reporter leaves, and, if possible, arrange to review the material before publication. Limit radio and television ad lib appearances to selected staff members only.

To be most effective with local media, the assessor should designate a staff member to meet with their representatives for recommendations on format, timing, special angles, preparation of material, and so forth. Contact with national media, or media contacts of a large jurisdiction, would call for professional guidance.

One communications medium, local public-access cable television, is fairly new, but can be effective for special occasions such as mass reappraisals and also for ongoing public education.

The print media may be especially important to an assessment jurisdiction because ad valorem taxation issues are so complex, making the relatively lengthy newspaper or magazine analysis more helpful than short radio and television spots. The effectiveness of print media can be increased by prompt responses on a day-to-day basis, background briefings before issues become public, carefully prepared press releases at the time of special events, and a planned, advance-appointment visit with the publisher or staff of each periodical in the area.

Printed Information Brochures can be as simple as a single typed sheet of paper or as complex as a professionally prepared, multipage, multicolor booklet. Whatever the cost or size, brochures must be neat, clear, accurate, and attractive.

Some brochures will cover general topics such as what the assessor does and routine assessment procedures. These will be available for distribution at all times. Other printed materials will be prepared before or during special activities such as a reappraisal.

Speaking Engagements Public speaking gives the assessor access to organized groups: civic clubs, associations, real estate organizations, and so forth. If the speech will end with an open question period, the speaker must know every aspect of the assessment process that might be of interest to the audience and, in addition, must have tact, sympathy, and discretion, for individual taxpayer problems may surface.

Standard speeches, charts and graphs, and films or slide shows can be prepared in advance so that the quality of the presentation does not suffer and last-minute invitations to speak need not be refused.

Summary

The nature of a business creates specific management problems. The assessment office must pay special attention to the areas of quality assurance and public relations.

Assessed values, the product of the assessment office, must be equitable. Achieving equity requires stringent quality-assurance measures in all areas of assessment work.

Even equitable assessed values, because they often mean higher taxes, are not popular with taxpayers, who also finance the office. The assessor is, therefore, doubly answerable to taxpayers, and to government leaders who supervise the assessment office on behalf of the taxpayers.

A well-administered office is the first step toward equity, quality, and effective public relations.

This book is the first in the assessment field to provide a comprehensive treatment of assessment administration. However, the technical systems that must be administered have not been neglected. Indeed, mass appraisal and new technology are important subjects in this book. The treatment of these topics, along with treatments of single-property appraisal and the economic principles underlying property appraisal, make this book the first comprehensive treatment of all the bodies of knowledge important in assessment administration.

Appendices

Appendices are arranged in the order they are referenced in the text. Appendix 1-1 is the first appendix referenced in chapter one, appendix 20-3 is the third appendix referenced in chapter 20, and so on. If the appendices are read as a group rather than singly, the following should be read in this order: 20-3, 20-5, 20-1, 20-8, and 18-1.

Appendix 1-1: Personal Property Ratio Studies

In many jurisdictions, personal property is a significant portion of the tax base. In such cases, it is important to ensure that personal property, like real property, is appraised accurately and in accordance with statutory requirements. In addition, in the United States it may be necessary to determine the assessment level for personal property in conjunction with discrimination suits brought under the federal Railroad Revitalization and Regulatory Reform Act of 1976 ("4-R" Act) or similar statutes.

As with real property, a sales ratio study is the preferred means of evaluating appraisal performance for personal property. With some exceptions, such as mobile homes, however, sales of existing (used) personal property items are often scarce or are not open market, arm's-length sales. Consequently, an appraisal ratio study or appraisal procedures audit will generally be required.

Because personal property is extremely diverse, the sample used in a personal property appraisal ratio study must be randomly selected. Either a random sample of all personal property accounts for the population under analysis or a stratified random sampling procedure may be used. Each account selected should constitute one record, akin to one parcel of real property, in the ratio analysis. The population from which the sample is drawn should include all personal property in the jurisdiction. For example, businesses operating from leased facilities should be included, even though such businesses will not be listed on the real property rolls.

Appraisal procedures used in a personal property ratio study should follow professionally accepted procedures. Usually, the cost approach will be the principal approach. Fortunately, widely recognized appraisal manuals, guides, or "blue books" are available for most types of personal property. Sales and lease data should also be used when available. See the IAAO *Standard on Personal Property* (1985) for additional guidance.

Personal property accounts selected for analysis should either be inspected on-site, or the taxpayer's personal property statements should be checked against business records, accounts, and ledgers. In some cases, income tax files also may be checked. Items that have not been reported or are otherwise not listed on the rolls should be included in the ratio study at a value of zero.

In addition to appraisal ratio studies, procedure audits can be conducted to evaluate whether personal property is being correctly appraised. If the jurisdiction is diligent in the discovery and listing of personal property, conducts regular audits and inspections, and follows state guidelines and professionally accepted procedures in valuation, then it can be assumed that personal property is correctly listed on the rolls. If not, only a ratio study as described above can uncover the full extent of the problem.

Appendix 5-1: Financing Adjustment Techniques

Sales prices must usually be adjusted for financing when the seller and lender are the same party, the buyer assumes an existing mortgage at a nonmarket rate of interest, the buyer assumes an existing lease at a nonmarket rent, the seller pays points, or the buyer pays delinquent taxes. Commercial properties and vacant land are more likely to require financing adjustments than residential properties. Note that the cash equivalency adjustments computed here may be smaller than those recognized by the market (see appendix 5-2).

Seller Financing

When seller and lender are the same, an arrangement known as a "seller carryback," the appraiser should analyze the down payment, interest rate, and other circumstances of the sale. If it appears that the seller has accepted no more than the usual degree of risk at approximately the market rate of interest, no adjustment is required. If the interest rate differs significantly from the market rate, an adjustment is required.

The size of the adjustment is determined by computing the present value of the difference in required monthly payments at the actual and market rates of interest. If the actual rate of interest is below the market rate, this amount should be subtracted from the sale price (the usual case). If, however, the actual rate of interest exceeds the market rate commensurate with the risk of the loan, then the present value of the difference in monthly payments should be added to the sale price. In such a case, the buyer and seller have apparently negotiated a lower purchase price in exchange for higher monthly payments.

Data for an example are shown in figure 1(a).

The monthly payments on the loan, under the contract and market rates of interest, are

$$\$90,000 \times 0.011278 = \$1,015.02$$
$$\$90,000 \times 0.009087 = \$\ \ 817.83$$

The difference is $197.19; 0.011278 is the monthly partial payment factor for twenty-five years at 13 percent, and 0.009087 is the monthly partial payment factor for twenty-five years at 10 percent. The present value of the monthly savings is

$$\$197.19 \times 88.668 = \$17,485;$$

88.668 is the present worth of 1 per period for 300 months (twenty-five years) at 13 percent, the current market rate of interest. Thus, the cash equivalent value of the sale is

$$\$120,000 - \$17,485 = \$102,515.$$

The cash equivalent value could also be computed as shown in figure 1(b).

Figure 1. Computation of Cash Equivalent Sale Price: Seller Financing

(a)

Sale price	$120,000
Down payment	$ 30,000
Term	25 years
Contract rate of interest	10 percent
Market rate of interest	13 percent
Amortization provisions	Equal monthly payments

(b)

Monthly payments	$817.83
Present worth of 1 per month for 25 yrs at 13 percent	× 88.668
Present worth of loan	72,515
Down payment	+ 30,000
Cash equivalent value	$102,515

Assumed Mortgages

An assumed mortgage at other than the current rate of interest is handled like a seller carryback. For example, a residence is sold for $99,500, with the buyer assuming the existing mortgage. The loan was originally issued for $50,000 for a term of thirty years at a 9.5 percent rate of interest, will mature in twenty-two years (264 months), has an unpaid balance of $46,484, and carries monthly payments of $420.42. The going rate of interest on home loans is 12 percent. The buyer pays cash for the balance of $53,016 ($99,500 − $46,484) to assume the loan. The cash equivalent sale price can be computed as shown in figure 2. The cash equivalent value then is $99,500 less $7,480, or $92,020. Another way to compute this is shown in the lower half of figure 2.

Figure 2. Computation of Cash Equivalent Sale Price: Assumed Mortgage

Method 1

Loan amount	$46,484
Monthly partial payment factor for 22 yrs at 12%	× .010779
Monthly payments at 12%	$501.05
Actual monthly payments	− $420.42
Monthly savings to buyer	$ 80.63
Present worth of 1 per month for 22 yrs at 12%	× 92.773
Present worth of savings	$ 7,480

Cash equivalent value:
$99,500 − $7,480 = $92,020.

Method 2

Buyer's monthly payments	$420.42
Present worth of 1 per month for 22 yrs at 12%	× 92.773
Present worth of payments	$39,004
Cash down payment	+ $53,016
Cash equivalent value	$92,020

If the monthly payments are not known, it may be possible to compute them in one of two ways when the interest rate and term of the loan are known. First, if the *original* amount of the loan is known, it is multiplied by the partial payment factor for the *entire* term of the loan. In the present example, the monthly payments are $420.42: the original loan amount times the monthly partial payment factor for thirty years at 9.5 percent ($50,000 × .0084085 = $420.42).

If the *remaining* balance and term of the loan are known, the *remaining* balance is multiplied by the partial payment factor for the remaining term of the loan to give the same result.

Remaining balance	$ 46,484
Monthly partial payment factor for 22 yrs at 9.5% ×	.0090445
Monthly payments	$ 420.42

Finally, if there is a loan assumption fee, it is added in calculating the cash equivalent sale price, because it negates part of the savings to the buyer. In this case, for example, if there were a $500 loan assumption fee, the cash equivalent value would be $92,020 plus $500, or $92,520.

Assumed Leases

Existing leases can affect sales prices. The proper adjustment can be determined by capitalizing the computed difference between market and contract rents. For example, assume the following:

Sale price	$250,000
Monthly market rent	$ 3,000
Monthly contract rent	$ 2,500
Years remaining on lease	5
Discount rate	14%

The difference between the market rent and contract rent is $500 per month, the present value of which is

$$\$500 \times 42.9770 = \$21,489;$$

42.9770 is the present worth of 1 per period for sixty months at 14 percent. Because the contract rent is less than the market rent, the value of the forgone income must be *added* to the sale price. That is, the negotiated price will be less than the market value because of the encumbering lease. Thus, in this example, the cash equivalent sale price is

$$\$250,000 - \$21,489 = \$228,511.$$

Where the contract rent exceeds market rent, the capitalized value of the difference in rents should be *subtracted* from the sale price, because the guaranteed above-market rent will result in sales prices that exceed market values.

Points

Points are a percentage (usually one percent each) of the loan amount. For example, two points on a $100,000 loan are $2,000. Many lenders charge points in exchange for somewhat lower rates of interest. When the buyer pays points to the lender, the sale price will be unaffected, because the points merely represent prepaid interest. However, when the seller pays points, as may be required in the United States on Federal Housing Authority or Veterans Administration loans, the buyer, in effect, receives a seller-subsidized interest rate. The seller must increase the sale price by the amount of the subsidy to obtain the same cash value as in a conventionally financed sale. The amount of any points paid by the seller therefore should be *added* to the sale price to determine the cash equivalent value of the sale.

Delinquent Taxes

Delinquent taxes constitute a lien against the property and, if paid by the buyer, should be *added* to the sale price. If the sale contract calls for the seller to pay delinquent taxes, the sale price will not be affected, and no adjustment should be made for the delinquency.

Appendix 5-2: Market Capitalization of Financing Adjustments

The market may not recognize or capitalize the full amount of cash equivalency adjustments derived from compound interest tables. That is, the difference between sales prices and cash equivalent values may *not* be as large as that obtained by computing the present value of savings to the buyer, using the methods presented in appendix 5-1. There are several reasons for this.

First, the buyer's intended holding period may be shorter than the term of the loan or the buyer may be unsure of the holding period, so that the monthly savings in loan payments will be capitalized over a shorter holding period than the term of the loan.

Second, income tax considerations come into play. In particular, the buyer is able to deduct interest payments, which reduces the effective payments associated with a higher (market) rate of interest. This in turn lowers the amount of after-tax savings associated with below-market financing.

Finally, creative financing tends to occur most frequently in periods of tight money, high interest rates, and reduced sales activity.

In such a buyer's market, sellers may not be able to command full premiums for favorable financing. Indeed, they may see creative financing more as a marketing tool and, unless particularly in need of cash, may not be averse to accepting an interest rate that although low by current standards may be favorable by other standards. Also, such sales can be treated as installment sales, with the gains partially deferred for income tax purposes.

Studies have been done to determine statistically the extent to which the market capitalizes below-market financing. In general, the results have shown that some, but not all, of the premiums are capitalized. The results show capitalization to be about 35–50 percent. For example, if, using the techniques presented in appendix 5-1, the computed value of below-market financing for a property were $10,000, the property may sell for only $3,500 to $5,000 above its cash equivalent value. The December 1985 and 1986 issues of the *Property Tax Journal* have several good articles on this topic.

Appendix 5-3: Time-Adjustment Methods

Four techniques of deriving time-adjustment factors from market data are paired sales analysis, resales analysis, sales ratio trend analysis, and multiple regression analysis. Time-adjustment factors can be developed and applied on either a compound or constant (straight-line) basis. Both produce highly similar results; for simplicity, the latter is used in the illustrations to follow.

Paired Sales Analysis

The technique of paired sales analysis to develop time-adjustment factors is rooted in the traditional sales comparison approach to value. Similar properties are identified that have sold at different times, the older sale is adjusted to the more recent sale to account for any physical differences between the properties, and then any remaining difference is attributed to time.

Assume, for example, that two nearby homes built by the same builder are sold within ten months of each other. Aside from landscaping and decorating, the homes are identical, except that the first includes a two-car garage and sells for $122,000, and the second has a two-car carport and sells for $123,000. Assume that appraisal models indicate a $3,800 difference in value between a two-car garage and a two-car carport.

Then the adjusted sale price of the first parcel can be computed as follows:

$122,000 Parcel 1 sale price (two-car garage)
−3,800 Value difference
$118,200 Adjusted sale price (two-car carport)

This leaves a residual difference in value attributable to time of $4,800, which equals 0.406 percent per month, or 4.87 percent per year:

$123,000 Parcel 2 sale price (two-car carport)
−118,200 Parcel 1 adjusted sale price (two-car carport)
$ 4,800 Value difference attributable to time

$4,800/10 = $480 per month
$480/$118,200 = 0.406 percent per month
0.406 × 12 = 4.87 percent per year

If a sufficient number of paired, comparable sales were analyzed in this way, an average rate of change could be extracted. Although several measures of "average" could be used, the median is preferable, because it discounts the influence of outliers. This rate of change, which should be expressed on a monthly or quarterly basis, could then be used to adjust sales to the assessment date as follows:

$$TAS = S\,(1 + rt), \qquad (1)$$

where TAS is the time-adjusted sale price, S is the unadjusted (original) sale price, r is the monthly (or quarterly) rate of change, and t is the number of months (or quarters) from the sale date to the assessment date. Assume, for example, that the monthly rate of inflation is 0.5 percent. Then a $100,000 sale occurring fourteen months before the assessment date would be adjusted as follows:

$$TAS = \$100,000\,[1 + (0.005)(14)]$$
$$= \$107,000.$$

For sales after the assessment or target date, the formula is

$$TAS = S\,(1 - rt'). \qquad (2)$$

In this case, t' is the number of months *after* the assessment date that the sale occurred. Again, assuming a 0.5 percent rate of inflation, a $100,000 sale occurring fourteen months after the assessment date would be adjusted as follows:

$$TAS = \$100,000[1 - (0.005)(14)]$$
$$= \$93,000.$$

If deflation occurs, r will be a negative number in the above formulas.

Resales Analysis

Resales can be analyzed like paired sales when extracting time-adjustment factors from the market. Using resales has the advantage of minimizing physical or locational adjustments. Nevertheless, physical changes in the property must be adjusted for.

A disadvantage of resales analysis is the limited number of such sales, particularly if separate adjustment factors are required in different areas. Resales can be supplemented with paired sales to obtain adequate samples.

Sales Ratio Trend Analysis

Trend analysis is an excellent technique for developing time-adjustment factors from the market. Consider figure 1, in which sale price-to-appraisal ratios (the reciprocal of appraisal-to-sale price ratios) are plotted against month of sale coded from 0 (oldest) to 24 (most recent). An analysis of the graph indicates that sale price-to-appraisal ratios have increased from an average of about 1.20 in the base period to an average of about 1.38 in the ending period. The increase of 0.18, or 0.0075 per month (0.18 divided by 24), from a base of 1.20 implies that property values have increased at the rate of approximately 0.625 percent per month (0.0075 divided by 1.20). Based on this, sales prices can be adjusted for time as usual. In this case,

$$TAS = S(1 + 0.00625t),$$

or

$$TAS = S(1 - 0.00625t'),$$

where t is the number of months by which the sale date precedes the target date and t' is the number of months by which the sale date exceeds the target date.

The rate of change can be extracted by visual inspection of the graph. More precise

Figure 1. Ratio Trend Analysis

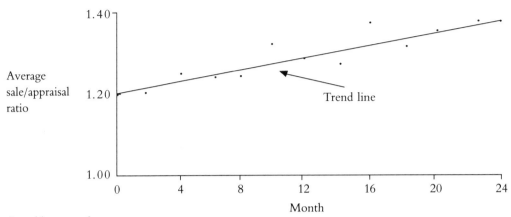

0 = oldest month;
24 = most recent month.

results can be obtained by mathematically fitting a line to the data with linear regression analysis (chapter 15), as in figure 1, to obtain the *amount* of change per month (0.0075) and the starting point, or intercept (1.20). To convert this to a *rate* of change, the first figure is divided by the second, as illustrated above.

The analysis of sales ratio data to derive time-adjustment factors has several advantages. First, unlike resales analysis, the technique can use most available sales, thereby greatly increasing sample sizes. Second, it is efficient, not requiring the analysis of paired sales and related adjustments for differences in physical characteristics. It implicitly considers such factors by expressing sales prices relative to appraised values, which should already reflect all relevant physical and locational factors.

Finally, market trends can be seen on a graph. If no pattern other than a horizontal band is apparent, then time adjustments are not necessary. If a nonlinear (other than

straight-line) pattern emerges, the pattern can be reflected through a series of adjustment factors. Assume, for example, that an analysis of sale price-to-appraisal ratios plotted over twenty-four months reveals that the rate of inflation averaged 1.00 percent per month for the first twelve months, and 0.50 percent per month for the next six months, and was flat for the final six months. A formula reflecting this trend in price levels is:

$$TAS = S(1 + 0.01t_1 + 0.005t_2), \quad (3)$$

where t_1 is the number of months (0–12) by which the sale date exceeds the base period and t_2 is the number of months (0–6) by which the sale date exceeds the base period by more than twelve months. A $150,000 sale occurring twenty months after the base period would be adjusted as follows:

$$
\begin{aligned}
TAS &= \$150,000\,[1 + (0.01)(12) \\
    &\quad + (0.005 \times 6)] \\
    &= \$150,000(1 + 0.12 + 0.03) \\
    &= \$150,000(1.15) = \$172,500
\end{aligned}
$$

Reliability of this approach requires an adequate sample representative of the underlying population. The appraised values should reflect a common assessment date.

Multiple Regression Analysis

Multiple regression analysis (MRA) is a tool for evaluating the influence of several independent factors, such as property characteristics, on a dependent factor, such as sale price. If time of sale is one of the independent variables, its effect on sales prices can be estimated and the rate of change in price levels extracted.

For example, if the regression analysis determines a value, or coefficient, for month of sale of $210, and the average sale price is $98,400, then the indicated rate of change is 0.21 percent per month ($210 ÷ $98,400), or 2.5 percent per year (0.0021 × 12).

Multiple regression can be used to develop nonlinear adjustments for time; also, separate models can be developed for different groups of properties. The technique is discussed in chapter 15.

Appendix 8-1: Observed Condition Breakdown Method

Description and Condition of Property

The subject property consists of two, three-story apartment buildings constructed forty-seven years ago. Each building contains forty apartment units with a gross floor area of 17,124 square feet (34,248 square feet total). The property is located in the peripheral older residential-commercial area surrounding the core of a larger city. The exterior walls are 10-inch, brick-faced masonry with concrete block backing. Casement, wood-sash windows account for approximately 16 percent of the wall area. The brick is of good quality but needs considerable pointing. The window sash has deteriorated. The ground floor, two upper floors, and the roof are all composed of wood joist and deck construction. The roofing is built-up tar, felt, and gravel on one-inch rigid insulation. There are no basements, but located in each building is a furnace room having a floor level five feet below that of the ground-floor level and about three feet below grade level. There is a crawl space below the ground floor for piping. The interior dividing walls are of concrete block, and the apartment partitioning is of wood studs and gypsum board plastered. The flooring is ⅜-inch strip hardwood, the ceilings are lathed and plastered and attached to the wood joists above, and the wall finishing is plaster. The doors and frames are of good-quality wood paneling, with good-quality hardware, and the baseboard and trim are of hardwood. The buildings are heated with hot-water furnaces using cast-iron radiators. Each apartment is furnished with electric stoves and refrigerators, with the exception of one building, in which the tenants are still using the old-fashioned built-in refrigerators connected to one central compressor. Apartment finishing also includes ceramic tiling in the bathrooms and built-in kitchen cupboards and counters.

Although the improvements are forty-seven years old, they are in fairly good physical condition, the maintenance is good, and the interiors are in fair condition. The effective age is thirty years. The remaining economic life is estimated to be thirty years. The roofing is ten years old; the furnaces were replaced ten years ago, but the radiators and piping are original, as are the plumbing fixtures and drains. The domestic hot-water system was replaced ten years ago in both buildings. The stoves are ten years old, the newer refrigerators, five years old.

Estimate of Reproduction Cost New

Summary of Building Costs

Grading and excavation	$ 1,883
Structural costs—foundation and foundation walls, interior masonry, bearing walls, floors, and staircases	131,854
Roofing	5,308
Exterior walls:	
Masonry	61,650
Pointing	6,850
Wood-sash windows	16,428
Entrances	2,383
Chimneys, brick with tile flues	9,619
Partition walls	61,911
Interior finishing ceilings, walls, and flooring	78,733
Electrical wiring and fixtures	27,013
Heating:	
Furnaces	10,000
Hot-water radiation	25,283
Drains	9,132
Plumbing fixtures, plus roughing in	93,139
Domestic hot water	7,448
Built-in cupboards and counter	19,200
Stoves	14,896
Refrigerators:	
Modern (personal property)	0
Built-in	5,320
Bathroom tiling	13,193
Fire escapes	1,170
	$602,413

Note: Contractor's overhead and profit and architectural fees are included in costs.

Depreciation

Summary of Cost and Physical Deterioration

Item	Cost	Class*	Effective age	Remaining economic life	Total economic life	Percent depreciated
Grading and excavation	$ 1,883	BS	30	30	60	50
Structural costs	131,854	BS	30	30	60	50
Roofing	5,308	SL	10	10	20	50
Exterior walls — masonry	61,650	BS	30	30	60	50
Exterior walls — pointing	6,850	SL	5	0	5	100
Wood-sash windows	16,428	SL	30	0	30	100
Entrances	2,383	SL	30	10	40	75
Chimneys	9,619	BS	30	30	60	50
Partition walls	61,911	BS	30	30	60	50
Interior finish	78,733	BS	20	10	30	67
Electrical wiring and fixtures	27,013	SL	20	10	30	67
Furnaces	10,000	SL	20	10	30	67
Hot-water radiation	25,283	SL	10	20	30	33
Drains	9,132	SL	10	10	20	50
Plumbing	93,139	SL	20	20	40	50
Domestic hot water	7,448	SL	10	10	20	50
Cupboards and counters	19,200	BS	30	30	60	50
Stoves	14,896	SL	10	10	20	50
Refrigerators — built-in	5,320	SL	30	0	30	100
Bathroom tiling	13,193	BS	30	30	60	50
Fire escapes	1,170	BS	30	30	60	50
Total	$602,413					

*BS = basic structure; SL = short-lived.

Physical Deterioration—Curable (Items That Are 100 Percent Depreciated)

Item	Amount of depreciation
Pointing — exterior walls	$ 6,850
Wood-sash windows	16,428
Built-in refrigerators	5,320
Total	$28,598

Physical Deterioration—Incurable: Short-lived Items

Item	Cost	Percent depreciated	Amount of depreciation
Roofing	$ 5,308	50	$ 2,654
Entrances	2,383	75	1,787
Interior finish	78,733	67	52,751
Electric wiring and fixtures	27,013	67	18,099
Furnaces	10,000	67	6,700
Hot-water radiation	25,283	33	8,343
Drains	9,132	50	4,566
Plumbing	93,139	50	46,569
Domestic hot water	7,448	50	3,724
Stoves	14,896	50	7,448
Total	$273,335		$152,641

Physical Deterioration—Incurable: Basic Structure

Item	Cost	Percent depreciated	Amount of depreciation
Grading and excavation	$ 1,883	50	$ 942
Structural costs	131,854	50	65,927
Exterior walls — masonry	61,650	50	30,825
Chimneys	9,619	50	4,810
Partition/walls	61,911	50	30,956
Cupboards and counters	19,200	50	9,600
Bathroom tiling	13,193	50	6,597
Fire escapes	1,170	50	585
Total	$300,480		$150,242

Physical deterioration—incurable: short-lived items	$152,641
Physical deterioration—incurable: basic structure	150,242
Total physical deterioration—incurable	$302,883

Functional Obsolescence—Curable

Removal of old refrigerators and compressors	$ 800
Salvage value	0
Installation of new electric refrigerators (personal property)	0
Total cost—functional obsolescence curable	$ 800

Functional Obsolescence—Incurable

As is typical in older apartment houses of this age group, there is inadequate closet space as measured by contemporary standards. Physically and economically, more closet space cannot be added to the apartments. It is a condition classified as incurable. From a survey of other rental apartment houses in the area, it is estimated there is a $7 per month per apartment rent loss attributable to inadequate closet space. A market analysis indicates that the local gross rent multiplier for this class of property is 6. Therefore:

Rent loss ($7 per apartment × 80 apartments × 12 months)	$ 6,720
Value loss (annual loss of $6,720 × 6)	$40,320

Economic Obsolescence

The subject property is an older type of apartment building, located in what was formerly a very harmonious neighborhood. Since then, a modern indoor arena has been erected on a nearby block, in which professional hockey, basketball, and traveling shows perform. This arena seats approximately 18,000 persons and is operated year-round. It has caused many old residences in the neighborhood surrounding the subject property to be demolished and replaced by vast stretches of parking lots. These are floodlighted at night, but, despite this, the intrusion of the crowds, the gas fumes, the noise, the loiterers, and the inevitable vandalism are causes of concern to the tenants. As a result, a rental loss of $10 per unit is attributed to the property, in addition to the $7 rent loss attributed to the lack of closet space. Because rent is low, vacancies have not as yet become a big factor. The subject building is situated on high-priced land, and the valuation split between land and buildings is approximately equal. Therefore:

Rent loss (80 apartments × $10 per month per apartment × 12 months)	$ 9,600
Indicated loss of value ($9,600 × 6)	57,600
Loss attributable to the building ($57,600 × 0.50) = total economic obsolescence	$ 28,800

Summary

Current cost of reproduction		$602,413
Less		
Physical deterioration—curable	$ 28,598	
Physical deterioration—incurable	302,883	
Functional obsolescence—curable	800	
Functional obsolescence—incurable	40,320	
Economic obsolescence	28,800	
Total accrued depreciation		$401,401
Value of improvements indicated by the cost approach		$201,012
Rounded to		$201,000

Note that all modern refrigerators were treated as personal property in this illustration. As such, they had no bearing on the calculation of accrued depreciation of the building.

The observed condition method, when performed by a skilled cost estimator, is a reliable method of estimating accrued depreciation. Its primary disadvantage is that it is not adaptable to mass appraisal because of the time required. Still, it is a tool that the appraiser should possess and use in those situations where other methods do not provide satisfactory results. The appraiser will find this method most applicable to larger, owner-occupied, special-use properties that rarely sell.

Appendix 15-1: Multistage Multiple Regression Analysis

Multistage multiple regression analysis (MRA) is a way of calibrating a hybrid model using linear and multiplicative MRA. One way to do this is:

1. Convert all the general, building, and additive qualitative variables to binary variables and specify an additive model structure of the form:

$$S = \Sigma GQ + \Sigma LQ + \Sigma LA + \Sigma BQ + \Sigma BA + \Sigma OA, \quad (1)$$

where S is estimated sale price; GQ, LQ, and BQ are general, land, and building qualitative binary variables, respectively; and LA, BA, and OA are land, building, and other additive variables. All qualitative variables must be binary variables coded 0 or 1. Such models may have a large number of variables. As a rule of thumb, the number of sales should be at least four times the number of variables, and each binary variable should have at least five cases coded 0 and at least five coded 1. Use additive MRA to solve the model and eliminate insignificant variables from further consideration.

2. Use the estimated coefficients for the binary variables significant in step 1 to create scalar variables centered on 1.00. For example, assume five construction grades with the following coefficients:

1 = −11,800
2 = −6,500
4 = 7,300
5 = 13,200 (3 = reference group)

Assume also that the average sale price is $94,260 and the average building value is approximately $75,408 (80 percent). The appropriate scalar weights are:

1 = (75,408 − 11,800)/75,408 = 0.844
2 = (75,408 − 6,500)/75,408 = 0.914
3 = 1.000
4 = (75,408 + 7,300)/75,408 = 1.097
5 = (75,408 + 13,200)/75,408 = 1.175

Land and general qualitative coefficients are converted to scalar variables in a similar manner, with land qualitative coefficients expressed as a percentage of the estimated average land value (0.20 × $94,260 = $18,852) and general qualitative coefficients divided by the average sale price ($94,260).

3. From the results of step 2 and the typical land-to-total value ratios, adjust sales prices to reflect standard qualitative characteristics:

$$S' = S \times \pi GQ' \times [LRATIO' \times \pi LQ' + (1 - LRATIO') \times \pi BQ'] \\ \pi GQ \times [LRATIO' \times \pi LQ + (1 - LRATIO') \times \pi BQ], \quad (2)$$

where S' is adjusted sale price; $LRATIO'$ is the typical land-to-total value ratio; $\pi GQ'$, $\pi LQ'$, and $\pi BQ'$ are products of the *standard* general, land, and building qualitative factors, respectively; and πGQ, πLQ, and πBQ are products of *actual* general, land, and building qualitative factors, respectively. Assume, for example, that S is $104,900, $LRATIO'$ is 0.24, $\pi GQ'$ is 1.056, $\pi LQ'$ is 1.083, $\pi BQ'$ is 0.961, πGQ is 1.150, πLQ is 1.250, and πBQ is 0.95. Then, S' equals

$$104,900 \times \frac{1.056 \times (.24 \times 1.083 + .76 \times .961)}{1.150 \times (.24 \times 1.250 + .76 \times .950)}$$

$$S' = 104,900 \times \frac{1.056 \times .990}{1.150 \times 1.022}$$

$$S' = 104,900 \times .8895 = 93,309$$

This is the estimated value of the house with *actual* additive characteristics but *standard* qualitative characteristics.

4. Use additive MRA to calibrate the model,

$$S' = b_0 + b_1 LA_1 + b_2 BA_1 + \ldots + b_p BA_p, \qquad (3)$$

where LA_1 is the land additive variable, for example, square feet of lot area, and BA_1, BA_2, ..., BA_p are the building additive variables, such as living area, basement area, and garage size. Variables for other additive features, for example, linear feet of block fencing, should also be included. This model isolates the effect of the additive components on sales prices.

5. Combine the qualitative components from step 2 and the additive components from step 4 into the general hybrid model:

$$ESP = \pi GQ \times [(\pi BQ \times \Sigma BA) + (\pi LQ \times \Sigma LA) + \Sigma OA], \qquad (4)$$

where ESP is the estimated sale price. Use this model for value estimation.

6. An optional sixth step can be added to refine the qualitative components estimated in step 2. From the values estimated in step 5, use multiplicative MRA to calibrate the model

$$S/ESP = Q_1^{b_1} \times Q_2^{b_2} \times \ldots \times Q_p^{b_p} \qquad (5)$$

where $Q_1, Q_2, \ldots, Q_p$ are the general, land, and building scalar variables from step 2. This model adjusts the scalar variables to the market after calibration of the additive components in 4 above. Because the model does not separate land and building components, the recomputed land and building scalar values must be adjusted for land-to-building ratios before incorporation into the general hybrid model (equation 4). For example, for the variable construction quality in step 2, assume that the computed coefficient (exponent) in the multiplicative model (equation 5) is 0.917. Assuming a land-to-total value ratio of 0.20, the scalar values would be adjusted as follows:

$1 = 1 + [(0.844^{0.917} - 1)/0.8] = 0.820$
$2 = 1 + [(0.914^{0.917} - 1)/0.8] = 0.901$
$3 = 1.000$
$4 = 1 + [(1.097^{0.917} - 1)/0.8] = 1.111$
$5 = 1 + [(1.175^{0.917} - 1)/0.8] = 1.199$

Adjustments for land-to-building ratios are necessary because, for example, with a land-to-building ratio of 4:1, a 10 percent increase in total value equals a 12.5 percent increase in building value. Land scalar variables should be adjusted in a similar manner. General qualitative variables do not require land-to-building ratio adjustments. Finally, the adjusted general, land, and building scalar values are inserted into the hybrid model (equation 4) and values recomputed.

Appendix 18-1: Testing for Equity between Property Groups

Often, measures of central tendency are computed for various property strata and compared visually for consistency. This is a good first step in the detection of inequities between property groups but does not answer the question of whether observed differences can be attributed to chance or actually indicate a systematic difference in appraisal practices.

There are two excellent nonparametric tests for equity between property groups: the Mann-Whitney test for two property groups and the Kruskal-Wallis test for three or more groups. Each has a logical appeal and is comparatively easy to perform. Being nonparametric, neither makes any assumptions about the distribution of the data. Parametric tests of equity between property groups are also available, but their validity is limited by the assumptions they make concerning the distribution of the data.

Mann-Whitney Test

The Mann-Whitney test is an excellent nonparametric test of the null hypothesis that two use classes, neighborhoods, or other property groups are appraised at the same percentage of market value. The rationale behind the test is straightforward. Individual ratios from the two groups being compared are pooled and ranked from smallest to largest. The Mann-Whitney test then determines at a specified confidence level whether the average ranks assigned to ratios from the two groups are approximately equal. If so, the null hypothesis, H_0 (see appendix 20-1), that the two property groups are appraised at equal percentages of market value is accepted. If, on the other hand, the difference in average ranks is too large to be attributed to chance, H_0 is rejected and the alternative, H_1, that the level of appraisal for the two groups is not equal, is accepted.

For example, to determine at the 95 percent confidence level whether vacant and improved parcels in a neighborhood are appraised at the same percentage of market value,

H_0 is: Vacant and improved parcels are appraised at equal percentages of market value;

H_1 is: Vacant and improved parcels are *not* appraised at equal percentages of market value.

Twenty-five recent arm's-length sales are available for the neighborhood, eleven for vacant parcels and fourteen for improved parcels. In Example A of table 1, ratios computed for these sales are arrayed and ranked in ascending order from 1 to 25. The average ranks of the two groups are 11.2 and 14.4, respectively.

Table 1. Mann-Whitney Tests

	Example A				Example B		
Vacant		Improved		Vacant		Improved	
A/S	Rank	A/S	Rank	A/S	Rank	A/S	Rank
0.302	1	0.374	4	0.659	1	0.753	3
0.340	2	0.419	7	0.698	2	0.894	7
0.358	3	0.428	8	0.795	4	0.929	10
0.378	5	0.437	10	0.831	5	0.934	11
0.402	6	0.446	11	0.862	6	0.953	13
0.430	9	0.452	13	0.907	8	0.970	15
0.449	12	0.455	14	0.924	9	0.983	17
0.477	17	0.465	15	0.948	12	0.996	19
0.492	19	0.475	16	0.956	14	0.999	20
0.556	24	0.486	18	0.974	16	1.041	21
0.614	25	0.494	20	0.992	18	1.073	22
		0.509	21			1.155	23
		0.524	22			1.129	24
		0.535	23			1.336	25
Total	123		202		95		230
Average	11.2		14.4		8.6		16.4

A is appraised value; S is sale price.

The Mann-Whitney test is based on the statistic, U, which may be calculated as either

$$U_1 = n_1 n_2 + \frac{n_1(n_1 + 1)}{2} - R_1 \,, \quad (1)$$

or

$$U_2 = n_1 n_2 + \frac{n_2(n_2 + 1)}{2} - R_2 \,, \quad (2)$$

where n_1 and n_2 are the number of ratios in the first and second groups, respectively, and R_1 and R_2 are the sum of the ranks assigned to ratios from the two groups. Although the two formulas will yield different values, the net result of the analysis will be identical. It is usually easier to compute U_1 if $n_1 < n_2$, and

to compute U_2 if $n_2 < n_1$. In the present example, however, both U_1 and U_2 are computed to illustrate that they produce identical conclusions.

Substituting from table 1 into equations 1 and 2 yields:

$$U_1 = (11)(14) + \frac{(11)(12)}{2} - 123 = 97;$$

$$U_2 = (11)(14) + \frac{(14)(15)}{2} - 202 = 57.$$

Now, as long as (1) both n_1 and n_2 are greater than 8 or (2) either n_1 or n_2 is greater than 20, the significance of the calculated value of U can be evaluated by the z-statistic,

$$z = \frac{U - (n_1 n_2)/2}{\sqrt{(n_1 n_2)(n_1 + n_2 + 1)/12}}. \quad (3)$$

Although this expression may appear complex, it is easy to compute by substituting values for U, n_1, and n_2. For U_1,

$$z = \frac{97 - (11)(14)/2}{\sqrt{(11)(14)(26)/12}} = 1.09.$$

For U_2,

$$z = \frac{57 - (11)(14)/2}{\sqrt{(11)(14)(26)/12}} = -1.09.$$

Hence, the choice of whether to calculate U as U_1 or U_2 affects only the sign of z, not its absolute value.

The significance of the calculated z-value is evaluated by reference to a table of z-values (appendix 20-6, table 1). For a two-tailed test at the 95 percent confidence level, the region of rejection consists of all values greater than 1.96 or less than -1.96. Because the calculated values do not fall in this region, the null hypothesis that vacant and improved parcels are appraised at equal percentages of market value cannot be rejected. Consider now a second set of sales ratios shown in Example B of table 1. Solving for U_1, in equation 1 yields

$$U_1 = (11)(14) + \frac{(11)(12)}{2} - 95 = 125.$$

To determine the significance of U_1 equals 125, calculate the corresponding z-value,

$$z = \frac{125 - (11)(14)/2}{\sqrt{(11)(14)(26)/12}} = 2.63.$$

Because 2.63 is greater than the critical z-value, namely 1.96, we reject H_0 in favor of H_1 at the 95 percent confidence level.

The reasonableness of the statistical acceptance of H_0 in Example A and rejection in Example B is borne out by a comparison of the average ranks assigned to vacant and improved parcels in the two examples. In Example A, the average ranks are 11.2 and 14.4, respectively. The Mann-Whitney test can be viewed as determining that this difference is not significant at the 95 percent confidence level, that is, it could simply be due to sampling error. In Example B, however, the difference in average ranks is much greater: 8.6 for the vacant parcels versus 16.4 for the improved parcels. This difference is significant at the 95 percent confidence level.

In the present example, no two ratios are the same. Ties can be avoided by computing ratios to at least three decimal places. When ties do occur, each of the tied ratios should be assigned the mean of the ranks for which they are tied. Thus, if the eleventh and twelfth ratios are identical, each should be ranked 11.5. Handled in this manner, ties will not affect the validity of the results.

Unfortunately, the significance of U cannot be evaluated by computing its z-value when the smaller sample is 8 or less *and* the larger sample is 20 or less. When this condition holds, one must first identify the smaller of U_1 and U_2. This can be done by calculating both U_1 and U_2 or, more quickly, by calculating U_1 and obtaining U_2 by the transformation,

$$U_2 = n_1 n_2 - U_1. \quad (4)$$

In any case, it is the smaller of the two values that is needed. When the larger sample is at least 9, critical values of U at the 95 and 98 percent confidence levels (two-tailed tests) can be found in the U-table (appendix 20-6, table 5). If the calculated value of U is equal to or less than the critical value from the table, H_0 is rejected. For example, if n_1 is 5 and n_2 is 12, H_0 can be rejected at the 95 percent confidence level whenever the calculated value of U is 11 or less.

When both n_1 and n_2 are 8 or less, detecting horizontal inequities becomes difficult. Appropriate tables based on the calculated value of U, however, are available (Owen 1962; Siegal 1956).

Kruskal-Wallis Test

The Kruskal-Wallis test is the appropriate nonparametric test of the null hypothesis that three or more property groups are appraised at equal percentages of market value. The rationale of the test is analogous to that of the Mann-Whitney test. Ratios from the three or more property groups are pooled and ranked in ascending order. The Kruskal-Wallis test determines at a predetermined confidence level whether differences in the average ranks of the groups are sufficiently large to indicate systematic differences in appraisal levels.

For example, to determine at the 98 percent confidence level whether residential properties in Neighborhoods A, B, and C are, on average, appraised at equal percentages of market value:

H_0 is: Residential properties in Neighborhoods A, B, and C are appraised at the same percentage of market value;

H_1 is: Residential properties in Neighborhoods A, B, and C are *not* appraised at the same percentage of market value.

In table 2, sales ratios corresponding to the ten most recent sales in each neighborhood are listed and ranked in order of magnitude. In this example no ties occur. Were ties to occur, as in the Mann-Whitney test, each of the tied ratios should be assigned the mean of the ranks for which they are tied. Average ranks for the three neighborhoods are 15.3, 18.3, and 12.9, respectively.

The statistic used in the Kruskal-Wallis test, H, is defined as

$$H = \frac{12 \times [\sum_{j=1}^{k}(R_j^2/n_j)]}{N(N+1)} - 3(N+1), \quad (5)$$

where k is the number of property groups, n_j is the number of ratios in the jth group; N is the total number of ratios in all groups, and R_j is the sum of the ranks for the jth group. Although it appears formidable, the statistic is not difficult to compute. In the present example,

$$H = \frac{12 \times [(153^2/10)+(183^2/10)+(129^2/10)]}{(30)(31)}$$

$$- 3(31) = 1.89.$$

As long as there are more than five ratios in each group, the significance of H can be evaluated from a chi-square table, (appendix 20-6, table 4). In this table, the critical chi-square value has $k-1$ degrees of freedom (d.f.), where k is the number of property groups under comparison. In the present example, k equals 3, so there are two degrees

Table 2.   Kruskal-Wallis Test

| Neighborhood A | | Neighborhood B | | Neighborhood C | |
A/S	Rank	A/S	Rank	A/S	Rank
0.556	1	0.680	4	0.598	2
0.720	6	0.769	8	0.641	3
0.751	7	0.850	12	0.693	5
0.812	10	0.900	16	0.784	9
0.891	15	0.933	19	0.844	11
0.905	17	0.940	20	0.856	13
0.946	21	0.963	22	0.868	14
0.984	23	1.000	24	0.927	18
1.022	26	1.060	28	1.017	25
1.048	27	1.324	30	1.095	29
Total	153		183		129
Average	15.3		18.3		12.9

A is appraised value; S is sale price.

of freedom. The region of rejection consists of all values greater than the critical values shown in the table. The critical value at the 98 percent confidence level (two-tailed test) is 7.82. Because the calculated value of H, 1.89, is less than this value, the null hypothesis that the neighborhoods are appraised at equal percentages of market value is accepted.

It should be emphasized that the Kruskal-Wallis test is designed to detect differences between *at least two* of three or more groups. Thus, if five property groups are being compared, a significant value of H could indicate, at one extreme, that appraisal levels differ between two of the groups, or, at the other extreme, that all five groups are appraised at different percentages of market value. In general, the more groups being compared, the more likely it is that a significant value of H at any given confidence level will be computed.

When any property group has five or fewer observations, the chi-square table can-

not be used to evaluate the significance of H. One solution, of course, is to combine or eliminate the small groups; another is to use supplemental tables for evaluating the significance of H for small samples (Owen 1962; Siegal 1956).

Parametric Tests

Parametric tests of equity between property groups are also available. When two groups are being compared and each contains thirty or more ratios, a z-test can be made of the hypothesis that the mean ratios of the two groups are equal. When one or both of the groups has fewer than 30 ratios, a t-test is appropriate. When three or more groups are involved, an F-test is appropriate. Each test is described in most introductory statistical texts (see, for example, Wonnacott & Wonnacott 1969; Neter, Wasserman & Whitmore 1978; Mendenhall & Reinmuth 1978).

The validity of these parametric tests rests on the assumption that the ratios from each property group being analyzed are normally distributed and have equal dispersion. This assumption often is not realistic. Nevertheless, when the assumption has been met, the parametric tests are slightly more efficient than their nonparametric counterparts. That is, they require slightly fewer observations (about 5 percent fewer) to reject H_0 at a given level of confidence.

Testing for Vertical Inequities

There are two types of systematic appraisal inequity: (1) horizontal, which relates to differences based on criteria other than value range, and (2) vertical, which relates to the value range of properties. Vertical inequities can be either regressive or progressive. Assessment regressivity occurs when high-value properties are underappraised relative to low-value properties; assessment progressivity is the opposite condition. The price-related differential (PRD), provides an index of vertical inequity.

Statistical tests for vertical inequity are difficult. At first glance, it would seem that properties could be stratified by sale price range and the tests described above applied. Although this approach is conceptually correct, it is complicated by the same technical problems that cause bias in the PRD. Specifically, when sales prices exceed market values, due to random market factors, sales ratios are biased on the low side. Similarly, when sales prices understate market values, sales ratios are biased on the high side. This results in a false negative correlation between sales prices and sales ratios.

Hence, stratification based on sale price will result in assigning some parcels to the wrong strata, for example, assigning a parcel with a market value of $105,000 that sold

for $98,000 to a strata with an upper bound of $100,000. If a similar parcel were to sell for $108,000, it would be assigned to the correct strata. Now, if both parcels are appraised equally, say at $100,000, it will appear that the first parcel is overappraised relative to the second: ratio of 1.020 ($100,000/$98,000) versus 0.952 ($100,000/$105,000). If the sample is large enough, such instances can lead to falsely concluding that appraisals are regressive at a specified confidence level. By the same token, stratification based on appraised values will create a bias in the direction of assessment progressivity.

The problem of measurement error inherent in using sales prices (or appraised values) as proxies for market values complicates other statistical tests for vertical inequities as well. For this reason, the rule of thumb for acceptable PRDs ranges from 0.98 to 1.03, rather than being centered on 1.00. Although similar adjustments can be incorporated into statistical tests for vertical inequity, they will not be presented here, because they are technically complex and arbitrary.

As a practical alternative, biases can be avoided by stratifying on variables other than sale price or appraised value. For example, one could test for differences in appraisal levels between neighborhoods of different price ranges. It will make little difference whether any resulting inequities are attributed to neighborhood or value range. The systematic inequity, whatever its underlying cause, will be revealed, and its correction will eliminate inequities between both neighborhoods and value ranges. Also, as a practical matter, if equity is achieved between key property criteria used in the appraisal process (neighborhood, property type, and age), vertical inequities are highly unlikely.

Appendix 19-1: Computer Applications

Computers make ratio studies faster and improve analytical capabilities. Mainframe computers, minicomputers, or microcomputers may be used for ratio studies. Except for large-scale studies, such as those conducted at the state level, modern desktop microcomputers easily possess the required storage and processing capabilities.

Ratio study software can be obtained from several sources. One option is the standardized programs sometimes included in commercially available mass appraisal software. Software can also be custom written, either in house or under contract. A third, increasingly attractive solution is to use general-purpose statistical software. In this case, selected features of the software package are adapted to the particular requirements of the agency performing the studies. This requires a working knowledge of the statistics and the chosen software package, but offers a means of developing customized software at low cost without "reinventing the wheel" (see Gloudemans 1958; and Gloudemans and Thimgan 1987).

A special consideration in programming sales ratio analyses relates to confidence intervals (appendix 20-4) and hypothesis testing (appendices 18-1, 20-1, and 20-8). From a programming viewpoint, these usually are the most difficult part of the ratio study, but are available in many general-purpose statistical packages. In addition, algorithms are available that enable the computer to calculate or approximate the information contained in standard statistical tables, such as the z-table and t-table (see Dornfest & Bluestein 1985).

Appendix 20-1: Hypothesis Testing

An hypothesis is a statement to be tested. Appraisers may need to test the hypothesis that the overall level of appraisal equals a specified percentage (appendix 20-8), that two or more property groups are appraised at equal percentages of market value (appendix 18-1), or that sales ratios are normally distributed (appendix 20-7).

Steps in Hypothesis Testing

Hypothesis testing involves the following steps:

1. *State the hypothesis.* The hypothesis to be tested, termed the null hypothesis, is abbreviated H_0. The null hypothesis is what one chooses to accept in the absence of sufficient evidence to the contrary. For example, the null hypothesis might state that property is appraised at market value.

2. *State the alternative hypothesis.* The alternative hypothesis, abbreviated H_1, is the conclusion made when H_0 is rejected. H_1 may be either two-tailed or one-tailed. When H_1 is two-tailed, the conclusion is simply that H_0 is not true, for example, that property is not appraised at market value. When H_1 is one-tailed, the conclusion states the direction of the relationship, for example, that property is appraised *below* market value.

3. *Choose a statistical test.* There are usually two types of tests available to test the same or similar hypotheses: one *parametric* and one *nonparametric*. The distinction between them is explained below. In addition, sample size sometimes influences the appropriate test.

4. *Specify a confidence level.* The confidence level is the degree of confidence required to reject H_0 in favor of H_1. Choice of the confidence level depends on the trade-off between "type I" and "type II" errors. A type I error occurs if H_0 is rejected when, in fact, it is true. Conversely, a type II error occurs when H_0 is accepted when, in fact, it is *not* true (see figure 1)

Figure 1. Type I and Type II Errors

	H_0 true	H_0 false
Accept H_0		Type II error
Reject H_0	Type I error	

Type I errors can create inequities through unwarranted value adjustments; type II errors will leave existing inequities unresolved. The higher the confidence level, the more likely a type II error, and vice versa. All things considered, a 95 percent confidence level is a reasonable choice for most ratio study applications.

5. *Perform the statistical test.* This generally involves computing a number or statistic using the chosen test.

6. *Determine whether the calculated number or statistic lies within the region of rejection.* The region of rejection is that area in which one has the specified degree of confidence that the calculated statistic will *not* fall when H_0 is true. If, for example, a 95 percent confidence level is specified, the region of rejection is that area in which there is only a 5 percent chance that the calculated test statistic will fall, provided that H_0 is true. The region of rejection is bounded by one or two *critical values*, depending on the test involved and on whether H_1 is one-tailed or two-tailed. These critical values are contained in statistical tables such as those in appendix 20-6. If the calculated value of the test lies within the region of rejection, H_0 is rejected in favor of H_1; otherwise H_0 is accepted.

Parametric and Nonparametric Statistics

Statistics can be divided into two basic types: parametric and nonparametric. Parametric statistics are based largely on assumptions concerning the distribution of data. The standard deviation and coefficient of variation are examples of parametric statistics. Parametric statistics also include the z-test, t-test, F-test, correlation analysis, and regression analysis. Nonparametric statistics, on the other hand, require no assumptions about the distribution of data. The coefficient of dispersion is an example of a nonparametric statistic. For the most part, nonparametric statistics are less well known than parametric statistics.

Despite their greater familiarity, however, parametric statistics have several limitations when applied to the measurement of appraisal performance. First, strict validity of parametric tests rests on the assumption that the ratios are normally distributed. Second, when ratios are being compared among two or more property groups (use classes, neighborhoods, and so on), strict validity of the parametric tests often requires the standard deviations to be approximately equal. Both of these assumptions are often unrealistic. Third, parametric tests generally involve the mean. However, for ratio data, the sample mean is a biased estimator of the population mean, further compromising the strict validity of most parametric tests.

In contrast, the validity of nonparametric tests does not rest on the distribution of the data. In addition, nonparametric tests are usually easier to understand and conduct than their parametric counterparts. For the most part, nonparametric tests involve ranking, sorting, and counting. The method and rationale of the tests are intuitive and do not require an understanding of broader statistical theory.

The one shortcoming of nonparametric statistics is that they are less efficient than parametric statistics. This means that whenever a nonparametric test is able to reject H_0, the corresponding parametric test will also be able to do so at the same confidence level on the basis of fewer observations. For the tests considered in appendices 18-1, 20-7, and 20-8, however, this difference is slight (about 5 percent).

Appendix 20-2: Evaluating Performance for Unsold Properties

The objective of ratio studies is to determine appraisal performance for the population of properties, that is, both sold and unsold parcels. As long as standardized schedules and formulas are used in the valuation process, there is little reason to expect any significant difference in appraisal performance between sold and unsold parcels. If, however, sold parcels are selectively reappraised based on their sales prices or other criteria, the appraised values used in ratio studies will not be representative and ratio statistics will be distorted. In all probability, calculated measures of central tendency will be artificially high and measures of dispersion will be artificially low.

Alternatives to sales ratio studies such as appraisal ratio studies have the advantage that they can be applied when sales are insufficient. When enough sales are available, however, sales ratio studies produce the most efficient and objective measures of appraisal performance, provided that unsold parcels are appraised in the same manner as sold parcels. Fortunately, there are several techniques for determining whether sold and unsold parcels are appraised similarly. These include (1) the two-study technique, (2) a comparison of average value changes, (3) a comparison of per unit values, and (4) ratio studies based on predicted values of unsold parcels.

Two-Study Technique

In this method, at least two ratio studies are performed upon values for a given tax year. The first uses only sales that occurred before appraisals were made. The second uses only later sales. Except for changes in market conditions and random sampling error, results of the two studies should be similar. When substantial appreciation or depreciation has occurred, sales used in the studies should be adjusted for time. Obtaining results that are consistently worse in the second study indicates selective appraisal of sold properties.

The degree of change between the two studies can be quantified by dividing key measures of performance in one study by the same measures from the other study. If measures of central tendency are being compared, results from the second study should be divided by results from the first study. A ratio of 0.85, for example, would indicate that the true level of appraisal was only 85 percent of that calculated in the first study. In the case of uniformity measures, such as the coefficient of dispersion, results from the first study should be divided by those from the second. An index of 0.50 would indicate that uniformity was twice as poor as indicated in the first study. A consistent pattern of low indices for several years in one jurisdiction would indicate a policy of selective reappraisal of sold parcels.

Comparison of Average Value Changes

If sold and unsold parcels are similarly appraised, they should experience similar changes in value over time. Accordingly, it is possible to compute the average change in value over a selected period for sold and unsold parcels and, if necessary, to test to determine whether observed differences are significant. If, for example, values for vacant sold parcels in an area have increased by 45 percent since the previous reappraisal, but values for vacant unsold parcels have increased only 10 percent, clearly sold and unsold parcels are not being appraised equally.

If an entire class of properties or the entire jurisdiction is being analyzed, additional insight can be gained by comparing relative frequency distributions based on value changes for sold and unsold parcels. This is particularly effective when various adjustment factors have been applied based on area or subclass of property. For instance, if increases of 15 percent or more were obtained for 20 percent of sold parcels but only 3 percent of unsold parcels, systematic biases would be evident.

In addition, statistical tests can be used to determine whether values for sold and unsold parcels have changed similarly. The chi-square test (appendix 20-7) is particularly well suited for this purpose. To apply the test: (1) Create class intervals based on percentage changes in value for the previous year, for example, −25 percent or less, −15 to −24.9 percent, −5 to −14.9 percent, −4.9 to 4.9 percent, 5 to 14.9 percent, and so forth.

(2) Then, from the percentage of unsold properties in each interval, calculate the expected number of sold parcels in each category and compare expected frequencies with actual frequencies. The chi-square test will determine whether differences are significant at a specified confidence level.

Monitoring value changes over time in this manner is easier if computerized data files for both the current and previous revaluation years are available. Also, particularly for unsold parcels, random samples can be selected rather than the entire population of properties.

Comparison of Average Unit Values

If sold and unsold parcels are appraised equally, average unit values for parcels of the same category should be similar. Properties can be stratified by class and area, and the average appraised value per square foot calculated for both sold and unsold parcels. The Mann-Whitney test described in appendix 18-1 provides an excellent test for significant differences between the two groups.

Ratio Studies Based on Predicted Values for Unsold Parcels

A technically sophisticated method of monitoring appraisal performance for unsold properties involves an appraisal ratio study using values generated from a mass appraisal model. Multiple regression analysis (chapters 14 and 15), for example, can be used to generate estimated sales prices for a random sample of unsold parcels. An appraisal ratio study is then conducted using the estimated sales prices as market value proxies, with measures of central tendency and dispersion calculated in the usual manner (see Gloudemans & Thimgan 1987).

The results of one such study are shown in tables 1 and 2. Table 1 shows sales ratio statistics for single-family sales in one jurisdiction. The data were then used to gener-

Table 1. Single-Family Sales Ratio Statistics

Category	Sales	Median	Mean	Aggregate mean	Coefficient of dispersion	Coefficient of variation	Price-related differential	Standard error of the mean
All single-family properties								
Single-family	684	0.978	0.991	0.986	10.9	14.1	100.5	0.005
Single-family properties by square-foot range								
800 square feet or less	71	0.886	0.899	0.878	10.7	15.8	102.4	0.017
801-1200	352	0.966	0.976	0.967	9.8	13.0	100.9	0.007
1201-1600	141	1.029	1.028	1.020	9.8	12.9	100.8	0.011
1601-2400	99	1.031	1.043	1.019	11.0	13.7	102.4	0.014
2401 or more	21	1.009	1.058	1.021	14.1	17.1	103.6	0.039
Single-family properties by construction quality								
Below average	70	0.924	0.949	0.925	13.2	18.6	102.6	0.021
Average	603	0.986	0.995	0.991	10.4	13.4	100.4	0.005
Above average	11	1.009	1.025	0.992	13.2	18.7	103.3	0.058
Single-family properties by year built range								
Built before 1945	38	0.931	0.929	0.913	13.4	16.4	101.8	0.025
1945-1959	206	0.933	0.959	0.947	11.1	14.8	101.3	0.010
1960-1974	188	1.012	1.022	1.015	10.1	13.1	100.7	0.010
1975 or later	252	0.993	1.004	0.996	10.0	13.3	100.8	0.008
Single-family properties by price range								
25,000-49,999	71	0.998	1.039	1.026	13.8	17.1	101.3	0.021
50,000-74,999	400	0.973	0.985	0.984	10.5	13.6	100.1	0.007
75,000-99,999	144	0.973	0.986	0.987	11.0	13.7	99.9	0.011
100,000-149,999	48	0.991	1.003	1.002	8.5	10.9	100.1	0.016
150,000 or more	21	0.949	0.959	0.946	13.5	18.3	101.4	0.038

ate a multiple regression model that was applied to a random sample of unsold parcels. Predicted values from the models were used in an appraisal ratio study (table 2). In this case, the results are very good and similar to those obtained for sold parcels, indicat-ing that unsold parcels are accurately appraised.

In addition to calculating measures of central tendency and dispersion, the tests of appraisal performance described in appendices 18-1 and 20-7 can be applied. Tests for ap-

Table 2. Single-Family Ratio Statistics: Unsold Properties

Category	Cases	Median	Mean	Aggregate mean	Coefficient of dispersion	Coefficient of variation	Price-related differential	Standard error of the mean
All single-family properties								
Total	622	0.987	0.993	1.001	8.9	11.8	99.2	0.005
Single-family properties by square-foot range								
800 square feet or less	29	0.880	0.897	0.901	8.2	12.3	99.6	0.020
801-1200	335	0.971	0.969	0.970	7.6	9.9	99.9	0.005
1201-1600	142	1.000	1.002	1.006	8.3	10.6	99.6	0.009
1601-2400	109	1.048	1.073	1.073	9.8	12.5	100.0	0.013
2401 or more	7	1.031	1.061	1.049	18.2	21.6	101.1	0.087
Single-family properties by construction quality								
Below average	34	0.811	0.842	0.847	12.1	15.1	99.4	0.022
Average	586	0.992	1.001	1.008	8.4	11.0	99.3	0.005
Above average	2	0.932	0.932	0.910	15.5	21.9	102.4	0.144
Single-family properties by year built range								
Built before 1945	2	0.876	0.876	0.879	8.6	12.1	99.7	0.075
1945-1959	121	0.918	0.936	0.942	11.1	13.5	99.4	0.011
1960-1974	213	1.005	0.997	0.998	6.8	9.6	99.9	0.007
1975 or later	286	0.987	1.014	1.020	9.1	11.8	99.4	0.007
Single-family properties by price range								
25,000-49,999	37	0.896	0.881	0.880	8.5	11.1	100.1	0.016
50,000-74,999	315	0.975	0.974	0.974	8.4	10.6	100.0	0.006
75,000-99,999	243	1.005	1.026	1.030	8.4	11.3	99.6	0.007
100,000-149,999	27	1.048	1.056	1.051	10.9	14.4	100.5	0.029

praisal level can be based on legal or administrative standards or on results achieved for sale properties. In the latter case, the tests would determine whether sold and unsold parcels were appraised at the same percentage of market value.

A ratio study for unsold parcels performed in this manner has several advantages. First, it explicitly quantifies appraisal performance for unsold parcels. Second, the approach is objective and rooted in the market. On average, predicted values should equal market values. Third, particularly if multiple regression is used, the statistical models can be evaluated for goodness of fit or reliability before being applied to the unsold parcels. This permits refinements of the models until satisfactory results have been obtained. If the goodness-of-fit statistics are poor, measures of appraisal uniformity for unsold parcels should either not be calculated or should be discounted. Measures of central tendency, however, can be interpreted in the usual manner. Fourth, and perhaps most important, the technique avoids the high costs associated with a traditional, narrative appraisal approach.

Appendix 20-3: Sample Size

As mentioned in the discussion of sampling, the reliability of ratio study statistics depends on the representativeness of the sample. Representativeness, in turn, is a function of several factors, particularly sample size. In general, the larger the sample, the more reliable the calculated statistics.

The relationship between sample size and statistical confidence, however, is also affected by the distribution of the data, that is, by the degree of normality and dispersion. When ratios are normally distributed and their dispersion is known, the statistical reliability of the measures of central tendency can be calculated.

Table 1 shows the 95 percent confidence interval for the mean and median ratios at various sample sizes and coefficients of variation (COV). For given sample sizes and COVs, one can be 95 percent confident that the true, but unknown, mean and median of the population lie within the indicated percentages of the calculated measures. For example, for a calculated mean of 0.926 and a COV of 20.0 based on a sample of 50 sales, one can be 95 percent confident that the true mean will lie within ± 5 percent of the calculated mean, that is, between 0.875 (0.926 − [0.055 × 0.926]) and 0.977 (0.926 + [0.055 × 0.926]).

For any given COV, the confidence interval narrows as the sample size increases.

Note, however, that the confidence interval does not narrow in proportion to the increase in sample size. For example, an increase in sample size from 50 to 100 does not cut the confidence interval in half, but by about 30 percent (for example, from 5.5 percent to 3.9 percent when the COV equals 20.0).

Also, the above relationships assume that the ratios are normally distributed. When they are not, the resulting confidence intervals will be narrower or larger, depending on the nature of the distribution.

If the ratios are normally distributed, it is possible to calculate the sample size required to estimate measures of central tendency of the population with a given degree of confidence. The appropriate formula is:

$$n = \sqrt{\frac{(t^2)(COV/100)^2}{h^2}} \ , \qquad (1)$$

where n is the required sample size, t is the t-statistic corresponding to the desired confidence level (table 2 in appendix 20-6) and h is the tolerance for error expressed as a percentage. Because t is a partial function of n, the equation can be solved only by trial and error, unless it is assumed that a sample of at least 30 will be required, in which case a t-value of 2.00 can be used.

If, for example, one wants to estimate the median and mean appraisal ratios for the

Table 1. Confidence Intervals and Sample Size

Sample size	95 percent confidence interval		
	$COV = 10.0$	$COV = 20.0$	$COV = 30.0$
5	± 12.4	± 24.8	± 37.2
10	± 7.2	± 14.3	± 21.5
50	± 2.8	± 5.5	± 8.3
100	± 2.0	± 3.9	± 5.9
300	± 1.1	± 2.3	± 3.4

COV = coefficient of variation

population with a margin of error of no more than 5 percent at the 95 percent confidence level, and in previous ratio studies the COV has been about 25.0, the required sample is:

$$n = \frac{(4)(25/100)^2}{0.05^2} = \frac{(4)(0.0625)}{0.0025} = 100. \quad (2)$$

Thus, with a sample of 100, one can be 95 percent confident that the true level of appraisal will be within 5 percent of the calculated level. If, for example, the calculated level were 0.80, one would be 95 percent confident that the true level is between 0.76 (0.80 − [0.05 × 0.80]) and 0.84 (0.80 + [0.05 × 0.80]).

Note that the formula for required sample size is *not* a function of the size of the population. That is, one does not require a larger sample for a population of 10,000 parcels than for a population of 2,500 parcels. This is true unless the size of the sample is unusually large relative to the population, in which case a somewhat smaller sample is required. In other words, the above formula assumes that the required sample is small relative to the population (less than 5 percent). Rarely will ratio studies violate this assumption. If they do, however, little harm is done, because the calculated sample size will be somewhat larger than required and thus provide slightly more accurate measures of appraisal performance.

Appendix 20-4: Confidence Intervals

A confidence interval is a range that contains a population parameter, such as the median level of appraisal, with a specified degree of confidence. The higher the specified level of confidence, the broader the confidence interval. The most common confidence levels are 90, 95, and 99 percent. A 95 percent confidence level is well suited to most ratio study analyses, although other levels can also be appropriate depending on the application at hand.

At any level of confidence, the size of the confidence interval is a function of the sample size and the distribution of the ratios. Larger samples and lower measures of dispersion are associated with tighter (narrower) confidence intervals, as illustrated by table 1 in appendix 20-3.

It is important to distinguish between statistics such as the mean and standard deviation, which are used to make inferences about *samples*, and confidence intervals, which are used to make inferences about *population* parameters. From the sample standard deviation, for example, one can determine the probability that a *single* parcel will be over- or underappraised by a given degree; from a confidence interval, one can determine the probable appraisal level for an *entire* class or category of property.

Confidence intervals can be calculated about the mean, median, and weighted mean ratios.

Mean Confidence Interval

The formula for the confidence interval about the mean assumes a normal distribution and is

$$CI(\overline{A/S}) \ = \ \overline{A/S} \ \pm \ \frac{(t)(s)}{\sqrt{n}} \ , \tag{1}$$

where $CI(\overline{A/S})$ is the abbreviation for the confidence interval about the mean, t is the t-value corresponding to the desired confidence level and sample size (see table 2 in appendix 20-6), s is the standard deviation, and n is the sample size. It should be noted that the t-value is based on *degrees of freedom*, which, in this case, is the sample size less one. The t-table can be used to verify that the correct t-value at the 95 percent confidence level for a sample of twenty-five sales is 2.064 (use the t-values shown for a two-tailed test).

The following example applies the formula and assumes that a sample of five sales yields a mean of 0.814 and a standard deviation of 0.132. The 95 percent confidence interval is

$$CI(\overline{A/S}) \ = \ 0.814 \ \pm \ \frac{(2.776)(0.132)}{\sqrt{5}}$$
$$= \ 0.814 \ \pm \ 0.164. \tag{2}$$

The lower confidence limit is 0.650 (0.814 − 0.164) and the upper confidence limit is 0.978 (0.814 + 0.164). Thus, despite the small sample size, one can be 95 percent confident that the mean level of appraisal for the population of properties is less than 100 percent.

Median Confidence Interval

Unlike the mean, the median confidence interval does not depend on the assumption of a normal distribution; nor is it as affected by outlier ratios. It is found by arraying the ratios and identifying the ranks of the ratios corresponding to the lower and upper confidence limits. The equation for the number of ratios (j) that one must count up or down from the median to find the lower and upper confidence limits is

$$j = \frac{1.96 \times \sqrt{n}}{2}, \qquad (3)$$

when n is odd, and

$$j = \frac{1.96 \times \sqrt{n}}{2} + 0.5, \qquad (4)$$

when n is even.

For example, the median confidence interval for the forty ratios in figure 2 of chapter 20 is

$$j = \frac{1.96 \times \sqrt{40}}{2} + 0.5 = 6.70. \qquad (5)$$

To find the upper and lower confidence limits, round this result up to the next largest integer and count *up* and *down* from the median ratio. In this case, the lower confidence limit is found by counting *down* seven ratios beginning with the twentieth largest ratio to obtain 0.890; the upper confidence limit is found by counting *up* seven ratios beginning with the twenty-first largest ratio to obtain 1.000. (If the number of ratios is odd, count up and down beginning with the ratios adjacent to the median ratio.) Thus, one can be 95 percent confident that the median level of appraisal falls between 0.890 and 1.000.

When the sample size is five or less, the 95 percent confidence interval for the median is nonexistent. When there are six to eight ratios, the lower and upper 95 percent confidence limits will equal the lowest and highest ratios in the sample, and caution is advised.

Weighted Mean Confidence Interval

The confidence interval for the weighted mean, $CI(\overline{A/S})$, can be approximated with the formula shown in table 1 (Cochran 1971, 30–34), where $\overline{A}$ is the average appraised value, $\overline{S}$ is the average sale price, and the other terms are as previously defined.

Table 1 applies the equation for a sample of twelve parcels. The weighted mean is 0.900 and the 95 percent confidence interval is 0.858 to 0.942. Appraised values and sales prices are expressed in thousands of dollars, which greatly eases the calculations.

Table 1.   Calculating a Confidence Interval for the Weighted Mean

Sale number	Appraised value (A)	(A^2)	Sale price (S)	(S^2)	$(A) \times (S)$
1	79.4	6,304.4	90.5	8,190.3	7,185.7
2	53.3	2,840.9	58.9	3,469.2	3,139.4
3	70.3	4,942.1	74.4	5,535.4	5,230.3
4	84.6	7,157.2	100.0	10,000.0	8,460.0
5	67.9	4,610.4	71.8	5,155.2	4,875.2
6	97.4	9,486.8	96.9	9,389.6	9,438.1
7	100.3	10,060.1	123.0	15,129.0	12,336.9
8	86.1	7,413.2	95.5	9,120.3	8,222.6
9	81.4	6,626.0	84.9	7,208.0	6,910.9
10	98.0	9,604.0	105.9	11,214.8	10,378.2
11	62.1	3,856.4	65.0	4,225.0	4,036.5
12	134.1	17,982.8	160.3	25,696.1	21,496.2
	1,014.9	90,884.3	1,127.1	114,332.9	101,710.0

$$\overline{A/S} = 1,014.9 \div 1,127.1 = 0.900$$

$$CI(\overline{A/S}) \simeq \overline{A/S} \pm t \times \frac{\sqrt{\Sigma \overline{A}^2 - 2\overline{A/S}\Sigma(A \times S) + (\overline{A/S})^2\,(\Sigma S^2)}}{\overline{S}\sqrt{(n)\,(n-1)}}$$

The following intermediate calculations are required:

$$2(\overline{A/S})\,\Sigma\,(A \times S) = 2(0.900)(101,710) = 183,078$$

$$(\overline{A/S})^2\,(\Sigma S^2) = (0.90)^2\,(114,332.9) = (0.81)(114,332.9) = 92,609.6$$

$$\overline{S} = 1,127.1 \div 12 = 93.9$$

Thus,

$$CI(\overline{A/S}) \simeq 0.900 \pm 2.201 \times \frac{\sqrt{90,884.3 - 183,078 + 92,609.6}}{93.9\sqrt{(12)(11)}}$$

$$CI(\overline{A/S}) \sim 0.900 \pm 2.201 \times .019 = 0.900 \pm .042 = \underline{0.858} - \underline{0.942}$$

Appendix 20-5: Combining Property Groups

The precision of measures of central tendency can often be improved by taking a weighted average of the results computed for individual groups or strata of properties. This ensures that each strata is properly weighted in the overall sample and provides a means of combining appraisals and sales in a ratio study.

The objective of the ratio study will determine the proper weighting scheme. If the objective is simply to monitor appraisal performance, the strata can be weighted according to the number of parcels. A strata that contained 13.4 percent of the properties in the population would, for example, receive 13.4 percent of the weight. If, however, the objective is the determination of market value, equalization, or the evaluation of a discrimination claim, then the strata should be weighted according to their assessed value. This ensures that any equalization actions will be based on "effective" discrimination and that after equalization all affected property groups will bear their fair share of taxes, that is, their effective tax rates will be equal (see Gloudemans & Scott 1980).

For example, to compute the total market value and overall assessment ratio of a jurisdiction, divide parcels into the following five categories: residential, commercial, agricultural, personal, and utility. A sales ratio study is conducted for the first three categories; personal property and utilities are assumed to be appraised at market value. The results are shown in table 1. The total estimated market value is $6,166 million, and the overall assessment ratio is 0.908 (the total assessed value, $5,600 million, divided by the total estimated market value).

Table 1. Weighted Average Assessment Ratio

Category	Total assessed value*		Weighted mean		Estimated market value*
Residential	$2,500	÷	0.900	=	$2,778
Commercial	1,200	÷	0.950	=	1,263
Agricultural	900	÷	0.800	=	1,125
Personal	300		NA		300
Utility	700		NA		700
	$5,600				$6,166
Overall ratio	= $5,600	÷	$6,166	=	0.908

*Millions of dollars

Note that in table 1 the weighted mean was chosen as the measure of central tendency for each stratum. As explained in chapter 20, the weighted mean gives equal weight to each dollar and is appropriate if the objective is determination of full market value. If an equalization action is being contemplated, however, then the median could be used, because it is less influenced by outlier ratios and thus tends to be the most stable measure of central tendency. In any case, as emphasized above, the results obtained for each class should be weighted according to their assessed values rather than parcel count.

Appendix 20-6: Statistical Tables

Table 1. Critical Values of z

				Second decimal place of z					
z	.00	.01	.02	.03	.04	.05	.06	.07	.08	.09
.0	.0000	.0040	.0080	.0120	.0160	.0199	.0239	.0279	.0319	.0359
.1	.0398	.0438	.0478	.0517	.0557	.0596	.0636	.0675	.0714	.0753
.2	.0793	.0832	.0871	.0910	.0948	.0987	.1026	.1064	.1103	.1141
.3	.1179	.1217	.1255	.1293	.1331	.1368	.1406	.1443	.1480	.1517
.4	.1554	.1591	.1628	.1664	.1700	.1736	.1772	.1808	.1844	.1879
.5	.1915	.1950	.1985	.2019	.2054	.2088	.2123	.2157	.2190	.2224
.6	.2257	.2291	.2324	.2357	.2389	.2422	.2454	.2486	.2517	.2549
.7	.2580	.2611	.2642	.2673	.2703	.2734	.2764	.2794	.2823	.2852
.8	.2881	.2910	.2939	.2967	.2995	.3023	.3051	.3078	.3106	.3133
.9	.3159	.3186	.3212	.3238	.3264	.3289	.3315	.3340	.3365	.3389
1.0	.3413	.3438	.3461	.3485	.3508	.3531	.3554	.3577	.3599	.3621
1.1	.3643	.3665	.3686	.3708	.3729	.3749	.3770	.3790	.3810	.3830
1.2	.3849	.3869	.3888	.3907	.3925	.3944	.3962	.3980	.3997	.4015
1.3	.4032	.4049	.4066	.4082	.4099	.4115	.4131	.4147	.4162	.4177
1.4	.4192	.4207	.4222	.4236	.4251	.4265	.4279	.4292	.4306	.4319
1.5	.4332	.4345	.4357	.4370	.4382	.4394	.4406	.4418	.4429	.4441
1.6	.4452	.4463	.4474	.4484	.4495	.4505	.4515	.4525	.4535	.4545
1.7	.4554	.4564	.4573	.4582	.4591	.4599	.4608	.4616	.4625	.4633
1.8	.4641	.4649	.4656	.4664	.4671	.4678	.4686	.4693	.4699	.4706
1.9	.4713	.4719	.4726	.4732	.4738	.4744	.4750	.4756	.4761	.4767
2.0	.4772	.4778	.4783	.4788	.4793	.4798	.4803	.4808	.4812	.4817
2.1	.4821	.4826	.4830	.4834	.4838	.4842	.4846	.4850	.4854	.4857
2.2	.4861	.4864	.4868	.4871	.4875	.4878	.4881	.4884	.4887	.4890
2.3	.4893	.4896	.4898	.4901	.4904	.4906	.4909	.4911	.4913	.4916
2.4	.4918	.4920	.4922	.4925	.4927	.4929	.4931	.4932	.4934	.4936
2.5	.4938	.4940	.4941	.4943	.4945	.4946	.4948	.4949	.4951	.4952
2.6	.4953	.4955	.4956	.4957	.4959	.4960	.4961	.4962	.4963	.4964
2.7	.4965	.4966	.4967	.4968	.4969	.4970	.4971	.4972	.4973	.4974
2.8	.4974	.4975	.4976	.4977	.4977	.4978	.4979	.4979	.4980	.4981
2.9	.4981	.4982	.4982	.4983	.4984	.4984	4985	.4985	.4986	.4986
3.0	.4987	.4987	.4987	.4988	.4988	.4989	.4989	.4989	.4990	.4990

Note—Entries in the table give the area under the normal probability curve for positive values of z. Areas for negative values of z are obtained by symmetry. Thus, for example, the probability of observing $0 \leq z < 1.41$ is 0.4207. Similarly, the probability of observing $-1.41 < z \leq 0$ is also 0.4207.

Table 2. Critical Values of t

Degrees of freedom	Confidence level for one-tailed test					
	.90	.95	.975	.99	.995	.9995
	Confidence level for two-tailed test					
	.80	.90	.95	.98	.99	.999
1	3.078	6.314	12.706	31.821	63.657	636.619
2	1.886	2.920	4.303	6.965	9.925	31.598
3	1.638	2.353	3.182	4.541	5.841	12.941
4	1.533	2.132	2.776	3.747	4.604	8.610
5	1.476	2.015	2.571	3.365	4.032	6.859
6	1.440	1.943	2.447	3.143	3.707	5.959
7	1.415	1.895	2.365	2.998	3.499	5.405
8	1.397	1.860	2.306	2.896	3.355	5.041
9	1.383	1.833	2.262	2.821	3.250	4.781
10	1.372	1.812	2.228	2.764	3.169	4.587
11	1.363	1.796	2.201	2.718	3.106	4.437
12	1.356	1.782	2.179	2.681	3.055	4.318
13	1.350	1.771	2.160	2.650	3.012	4.221
14	1.345	1.761	2.145	2.624	2.977	4.140
15	1.341	1.753	2.131	2.602	2.947	4.073
16	1.337	1.746	2.120	2.583	2.921	4.015
17	1.333	1.740	2.110	2.567	2.898	3.965
18	1.330	1.734	2.101	2.552	2.878	3.922
19	1.328	1.729	2.093	2.539	2.861	3.883
20	1.325	1.725	2.086	2.528	2.845	3.850
21	1.323	1.721	2.080	2.518	2.831	3.819
22	1.321	1.717	2.074	2.508	2.819	3.792
23	1.319	1.714	2.069	2.500	2.807	3.767
24	1.318	1.711	2.064	2.492	2.797	3.745
25	1.316	1.708	2.060	2.485	2.787	3.725
26	1.315	1.706	2.056	2.479	2.779	3.707
27	1.314	1.703	2.052	2.473	2.771	3.690
28	1.313	1.701	2.048	2.467	2.763	3.674
29	1.311	1.699	2.045	2.462	2.756	3.659
30	1.310	1.697	2.042	2.457	2.750	3.646
40	1.303	1.684	2.021	2.423	2.704	3.551
60	1.296	1.671	2.000	2.390	2.660	3.460
120	1.289	1.658	1.980	2.358	2.617	3.373
∞	1.282	1.645	1.960	2.326	2.576	3.291

Note — Table reports positive values only. The region of rejection consists of values more extreme than the indicated critical values. For example, the region of rejection for a two-tailed test at the 95 percent confidence level when degrees of freedom equals 10 is all values greater than 2.131 and less than -2.131.

Table 3. Critical Binomial Values

(95 Percent Confidence Level)

Sample size	One-tailed test Reject H_0 in favor of H_1 if the number of items supporting H_0 is less than	Two-tailed test Reject H_0 in favor of H_1 if the number of items in smaller group is less than
<5	NA	NA
5	1	NA
6	1	1
7	1	1
8	2	1
9	2	2
10	2	2
11	3	2
12	3	3
13	4	3
14	4	3
15	4	4
16	5	4
17	5	4
18	6	5
19	6	5
20	6	6
21	7	6
22	7	6
23	8	7
24	8	7
25	8	8

Table 4. Critical Values of Chi–Square

	Confidence level for one-tailed test					
	.90	.95	.975	.99	.995	.9995
	Confidence level for two-tailed test					
Degrees of freedom	.80	.90	.95	.98	.99	.999
1	1.64	2.71	3.84	5.41	6.64	10.83
2	3.22	4.60	5.99	7.82	9.21	13.82
3	4.64	6.25	7.82	9.84	11.34	16.27
4	5.99	7.78	9.49	11.67	13.28	18.46
5	7.29	9.24	11.07	13.39	15.09	20.52
6	8.56	10.64	12.59	15.03	16.81	22.46
7	9.80	12.02	14.07	16.62	18.48	24.32
8	11.03	13.36	15.51	18.17	20.09	26.12
9	12.24	14.68	16.92	19.68	21.67	27.88
10	13.44	15.99	18.31	21.16	23.21	29.59
11	14.63	17.28	19.68	22.62	24.72	31.26
12	15.81	18.55	21.03	24.05	26.22	32.91
13	16.98	19.81	22.36	25.47	27.69	34.53
14	18.15	21.06	23.68	26.87	29.14	36.12
15	19.31	22.31	25.00	28.26	30.58	37.70
16	20.46	23.54	26.30	29.63	32.00	39.29
17	21.62	24.77	27.59	31.00	33.41	40.75
18	22.76	25.99	28.87	32.35	34.80	42.31
19	23.90	27.20	30.14	33.69	36.19	43.82
20	25.04	28.41	31.41	35.02	37.57	45.32
21	26.17	29.62	32.67	36.34	38.93	46.80
22	27.30	30.81	33.92	37.66	40.29	48.27
23	28.43	32.01	35.17	38.97	41.64	49.73
24	29.55	33.20	36.42	40.27	42.98	51.18
25	30.68	34.38	37.65	41.57	44.31	52.62
26	31.80	35.56	38.88	42.86	45.64	54.05
27	32.91	36.74	40.11	44.14	46.96	55.48
28	34.03	37.92	41.34	45.42	48.28	56.89
29	35.14	39.09	42.56	46.69	49.59	58.30
30	36.25	40.26	43.77	47.96	50.89	59.70

Note—The region of rejection consists of all values greater than the indicated values.

Table 5. Critical Values of U

95 percent confidence level: two-tailed test

Number of ratios in the first group (n_1)												

Number of ratios in the second group (n_2)

(n_1)	9	10	11	12	13	14	15	16	17	18	19	20
1												
2	0	0	0	1	1	1	1	1	2	2	2	2
3	2	3	3	4	4	5	5	6	6	7	7	8
4	4	5	6	7	8	9	10	11	11	12	13	13
5	7	8	9	11	12	13	14	15	17	18	19	20
6	10	11	13	14	16	17	19	21	22	24	25	27
7	12	14	16	18	20	22	24	26	28	30	32	34
8	15	17	19	22	24	26	29	31	34	36	38	41
9	17	20	23	26	28	31	34	37	39	42	45	48
10	20	23	26	29	33	36	39	42	45	48	52	55
11	23	26	30	33	37	40	44	47	51	55	58	62
12	26	29	33	37	41	45	49	53	57	61	65	69
13	28	33	37	41	45	50	54	59	63	67	72	76
14	31	36	40	45	50	55	59	64	67	74	78	83
15	34	39	44	49	54	59	64	70	75	80	85	90
16	37	42	47	53	59	64	70	75	81	86	92	98
17	39	45	51	57	63	67	75	81	87	93	99	105
18	42	48	55	61	67	74	80	86	93	99	106	112
19	45	52	58	65	72	78	85	92	99	106	113	119
20	48	55	62	69	76	83	90	98	105	112	119	127

98 percent confidence level: two-tailed test

Number of ratios in the second group (n_2)

Number of ratios in the first group (n_1)	9	10	11	12	13	14	15	16	17	18	19	20
1												
2					0	0	0	0	0	0	1	1
3	1	1	1	2	2	2	3	3	4	4	4	5
4	3	3	4	5	5	6	7	7	8	9	9	10
5	5	6	7	8	9	10	11	12	13	14	15	16
6	7	8	9	11	12	13	15	16	18	19	20	22
7	9	11	12	14	16	17	19	21	23	24	26	28
8	11	13	15	17	20	22	24	26	28	30	32	34
9	14	16	18	21	23	26	28	31	33	36	38	40
10	16	19	22	24	27	30	33	36	38	41	44	47
11	18	22	25	28	31	34	37	41	44	47	50	53
12	21	24	28	31	35	38	42	46	49	53	56	60
13	23	27	31	35	39	43	47	51	55	59	63	67
14	26	30	34	38	43	47	51	56	60	65	69	73
15	28	33	37	42	47	51	56	61	66	70	75	80
16	31	36	41	46	51	56	61	66	71	76	82	87
17	33	38	44	49	55	60	66	71	77	82	88	93
18	36	41	47	53	59	65	70	76	82	88	94	100
19	38	44	50	56	63	69	75	82	88	94	101	107
20	40	47	53	60	67	73	80	87	93	100	107	114

Note—The region of rejection consists of values of U equal to or less than indicated critical values.

Appendix 20-7: Testing the Normality of Ratio Data

It is often important to determine whether ratio data are normally distributed. When ratios are normally distributed, the standard deviation and coefficient of variation provide very complete indicators of appraisal uniformity. When ratios are not normally distributed, however, they provide misleading measures of uniformity. In addition, the normality of ratios influences the choice between parametric and nonparametric tests of appraisal performance (appendix 20-1). When ratios are normally distributed, parametric tests are more efficient. When ratios are not normally distributed, only nonparametric tests are strictly valid.

Frequency distributions and histograms are good indicators of the normality of ratio data. In marginal cases, however, tests for the normality of ratios must be conducted. Two nonparametric tests can be used for this purpose: the chi-square test and the binomial test. The chi-square test is more powerful, although the binomial test is appropriate when sample size is less than 100. In both cases, the null and alternative hypotheses (see appendix 20-1) are:

H_0: Ratios are normally distributed.
H_1: Ratios are not normally distributed.

Chi-Square Test for Normality

The chi-square test compares the number of data items in two or more categories with the number expected to fall in each category when the null hypothesis is true. The test determines whether the differences between observed and expected frequencies are sufficiently large to reject the null hypothesis of normality at a specified confidence level, typically 95 percent.

The upper half of table 1 shows 114 ratios with a mean of 1.009 and a standard deviation of 0.167. In the lower half of the figure, the chi-square test is applied as follows:

1. *Choose class boundaries.* For the chi-square test to provide a valid test of normality, there must be at least six (preferably eight) class intervals, with no more than 20 percent having an expected frequency of less than five. There are eight class intervals in table 1; the class boundaries are 0.700, 0.800, 0.900, 1.000, 1.100, 1.200, and 1.300.

2. *Determine the expected percentage of ratios in each class.* This is done by reference to a z-table (appendix 20-6, table 1). The class boundary 0.700 lies 1.85 standard deviations below the mean:

$$(0.700 - 1.009)/.167 = -1.85.$$

The z-table shows that if the ratios are normally distributed, only 3.22 percent will be less than 0.700. Similarly, the class

617

Table 1. Chi-Square Test

A/S ratios in sample

0.500	0.845	0.922	0.950	0.995	1.030	1.066	1.120	1.200
0.550	0.867	0.930	0.951	1.000	1.031	1.066	1.125	1.220
0.611	0.870	0.930	0.954	1.010	1.031	1.069	1.127	1.245
0.656	0.875	0.930	0.960	1.010	1.033	1.072	1.133	1.250
0.699	0.900	0.935	0.964	1.015	1.035	1.075	1.133	1.260
0.726	0.900	0.937	0.966	1.017	1.037	1.080	1.150	1.270
0.765	0.900	0.939	0.966	1.018	1.040	1.085	1.165	1.300
0.790	0.903	0.940	0.970	1.020	1.050	1.090	1.170	1.350
0.795	0.910	0.942	0.975	1.022	1.055	1.093	1.180	1.500
0.800	0.912	0.944	0.980	1.023	1.056	1.093	1.182	1.700
0.811	0.917	0.945	0.982	1.025	1.058	1.097	1.185	
0.825	0.920	0.945	0.985	1.026	1.060	1.099	1.188	
0.833	0.922	0.947	0.990	1.030	1.062	1.115	1.199	

Mean = 1.009   Standard deviation = .167

Class interval at least	less than	Expected percent	Expected number (E)	Actual number (O)	(E − O)	(E − O)²/E
0.000	0.700	3.2	4	5	− 1	0.25
0.700	0.800	7.3	8	4	4	2.00
0.800	0.900	15.2	17	8	9	4.76
0.900	1.000	22.3	25	36	− 11	4.84
1.000	1.100	22.5	26	37	− 11	4.65
1.100	1.200	16.8	19	14	5	1.32
1.200	1.300	8.6	10	6	4	1.60
1.300		4.1	5	4	1	0.20
		100.0	114	114	0	19.62

boundary, 0.800, lies 1.25 standard deviations below the mean:

$$(0.800 - 1.009)/0.167 = -1.25.$$

If the data are normally distributed, 10.56 percent will lie below 0.800, thus leaving 7.34 percent in the interval 0.700 to 0.800 (10.56 percent − 3.22 percent). The percentage of the ratios expected to fall in the other class intervals can be found in a similar manner and is shown in the third column of table 1. The sum of the expected percentages must be 100 percent.

3. *Determine the expected frequency of each class.* This is done by simply multiplying the expected percentage of the data in each class by the sample size. In table 1, for example, if the ratios are normally distributed, four will be less than 0.700:

$$0.0322 \times 114 = 4 \text{ (rounded)}.$$

The expected frequencies (E) are shown in column 4 of table 1. The sum of the expected frequencies should equal the total sample size. If more than 20 percent of the class intervals have expected frequencies of less than five, the class boundaries should be redefined.

4. *Determine the actual frequency of each class.* This is done by simply counting the number of ratios falling within each class interval. Actual or observed frequencies (O) are shown in column 5 of table 1.

5. *Subtract the actual frequencies from the expected frequencies.* The total of the differences should equal zero, except for possible rounding errors if whole numbers are used to represent expected frequencies.

6. *Square the differences between the actual and expected frequencies.*

7. *Divide the squared differences by the expected frequencies.* This gives the relative squared differences (column 7).

8. *Add the relative squared differences.* This result is called chi-square and in table 1 is 19.62, the total of column 7.

The formula corresponding to the above steps is

$$\text{Chi-square} = \Sigma(O_i - E_i)^2/E_i, \quad (1)$$

where O_i and E_i are the observed and expected frequencies of each class, respectively. In this case,

$$
\begin{aligned}
\text{Chi-square} = {} & (5 - 4)^2/4 + (4 - 8)^2/8 \\
& + (8 - 17)^2/17 + (36 - 25)^2/25 \\
& + (37 - 26)^2/26 + (14 - 19)^2/19 \\
& + (6 - 10)^2/10 + (4 - 5)^2/5 \\
& = 19.62
\end{aligned}
$$

Critical values of chi-square are contained in table 4 of appendix 20-6. This application of the chi-square test is two-tailed with degrees of freedom (d.f.) equal to the number of classes less one, or 7 in the present case. The critical value of chi-square at the 95 percent confidence level is thus 14.07. Because the calculated value, 19.62, lies in the region of rejection, the null hypothesis that the ratios are normally distributed can be rejected.

Figure 1 summarizes the results in polygon form. Were the data normally distributed, the polygon would form the normal curve shown in the figure. Instead, the distribution is abnormally concentrated in the center and lacks the tails found in a normal distribution. In this case, relying on the standard deviation or coefficient of variation would result in a conclusion that appraisal uniformity was considerably worse than is actually the case.

Binomial Test for Normality

The median ratio always divides the ratios into two equal parts: half lie above the median and half lie below the median. In a normal distribution, the mean and median will be equal, so that half the ratios will lie on each side of the mean. The binomial test for normality determines whether the number of ratios that fall above and the number that fall below the mean are sufficiently different to conclude that the null hypothesis of normality can be rejected at a chosen confidence level.

The binomial test takes one of two forms, depending on sample size. If sample size is twenty-five or less, the observed distribution is evaluated directly from the binomial table (appendix 20-6, table 3; two-tailed test). Assume, for example, that an assessor wants to determine at the 95 percent confidence level whether a sample of twenty-five ratios can be regarded as normally distributed. Fifteen of the ratios lie below the mean and ten

Figure 1. Chi-Square Analysis of Distribution

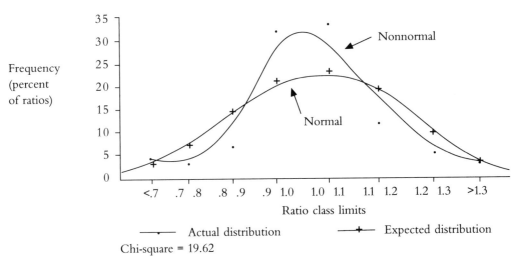

—•— Actual distribution   —+— Expected distribution

Chi-square = 19.62

above. The binomial table shows that there would have to be fewer than eight ratios in the smaller of the two groups to conclude with 95 percent confidence that the population of ratios is not normally distributed. Thus, in this case, the null hypothesis of normality cannot be rejected.

When the number of ratios is greater than twenty-five, the binomial test involves calculation of a z-value using the formula,

$$z = \frac{0.5(n - 1) - x}{\sqrt{(0.25n)}}, \qquad (2)$$

where n is the number of ratios and x is the number of ratios in the smaller of the two groups (above and below the mean). Assume, for example, that an assessor is interested in determining whether a sample of seventy-two ratios can be regarded as normally distributed at the 95 percent confidence level. Forty-four of the ratios lie below the mean and twenty-eight above. The value of z is calculated as

$$z = \frac{0.5(71) - 28}{\sqrt{(0.25)(72)}} = 1.77.$$

The significance of the calculated z-value is found by reference to a normal probability table (appendix 20-6, table 1). The region of rejection consists of z-values greater than 1.96. Because the calculated z-value does not lie in this region, the null hypothesis of normality cannot be rejected at the 95 percent confidence level (it could, however, be rejected with 90 percent confidence).

The binomial test is effective in detecting nonnormal distributions that lack symmetry, that is, those that are skewed either to the left or right, such as distributions (e) and (f) in the lower half of figure 8 of chapter 20. The test, however, is unable to detect nonnormal distributions that are attenuated in both directions or unusually concentrated toward the center, such as distributions (g) and (h) in the lower half of figure 8 of chapter 20. For example, the binomial test would not detect nonnormality in the data shown in table 1 and plotted in figure 1.

Appendix 20-8: Testing the Level of Appraisal

The IAAO *Standard on Ratio Studies* (1990) calls for an overall level of appraisal of at least 90 percent of the statutory level. In addition, many states and jurisdictions have established administrative standards for the level of appraisal. There are two tests of the null hypothesis (see appendix 20-1) that the properties in a jurisdiction, class, area, or other category are appraised at a specified percentage of market value: the parametric *t*-test and the nonparametric binomial test.

t-Test of the Level of Appraisal

The *t*-test can be used to test the null hypothesis that the mean level of appraisal equals a specified percentage, say, 100 percent. Thus,

$$H_0: \overline{A/V} = 1.000 \, ,$$

where $\overline{A/V}$ is the mean ratio of appraised value to market value for the population of properties. The alternative hypothesis is that the mean A/V ratio is not 100 percent, that is,

$$H_1: \overline{A/V} \neq 1.000 \, ,$$

Note that the alternative hypothesis is two-tailed. In other words, H_0 will be rejected in favor of H_1 if the level of appraisal is significantly above or below 100 percent. If one were specifically interested in testing whether the appraisal level were *at least* 100 percent, the alternative hypothesis would be one-tailed, namely,

$$H_1: \overline{A/V} < 1.000 \, .$$

The *t*-test is performed in the following four steps.

1. *Compute the mean and standard deviation.* For the data in table 1, these statistics are 0.964 and 0.161, respectively.
2. *Subtract the hypothesized mean from the calculated sample mean.* This gives 0.964 less 1.000, or −0.036.
3. *Compute the standard error of the mean.* This is done by dividing the standard deviation by the square root of the sample size. In the present case, this implies dividing 0.161 by the square root of 30 to obtain 0.0294.
4. *Divide (2) above by (3) above.* This gives −0.036 divided by 0.0294, or −1.22.

These four steps can be expressed by the formula,

$$t = \frac{\overline{A/S} - \overline{A/V}}{s/(\sqrt{n})} \, , \qquad (1)$$

where s is the standard deviation of the ratios and n is the number of ratios. In the present example,

$$t = \frac{0.964 - 1.000}{0.161/(\sqrt{30})}.$$

Table 1. *t*-Test of Appraisal Level

	Ratio	Mean	Difference	Squared difference
1	0.650	0.964	− 0.314	0.0986
2	0.721	0.964	− 0.243	0.0590
3	0.756	0.964	− 0.208	0.0433
4	0.798	0.964	− 0.166	0.0276
5	0.819	0.964	− 0.145	0.0210
6	0.834	0.964	− 0.130	0.0169
7	0.876	0.964	− 0.089	0.0079
8	0.888	0.964	− 0.076	0.0058
9	0.909	0.964	− 0.055	0.0030
10	0.916	0.964	− 0.048	0.0023
11	0.923	0.964	− 0.041	0.0017
12	0.938	0.964	− 0.026	0.0007
13	0.950	0.964	− 0.014	0.0002
14	0.958	0.964	− 0.006	0.0000
15	0.970	0.964	0.006	0.0000
16	0.972	0.964	0.008	0.0001
17	0.975	0.964	0.011	0.0001
18	0.984	0.964	0.020	0.0004
19	0.989	0.964	0.025	0.0006
20	0.996	0.964	0.032	0.0010
21	1.002	0.964	0.038	0.0014
22	1.011	0.964	0.047	0.0022
23	1.034	0.964	0.070	0.0049
24	1.039	0.964	0.075	0.0056
25	1.047	0.964	0.083	0.0069
26	1.053	0.964	0.089	0.0079
27	1.061	0.964	0.097	0.0094
28	1.074	0.964	0.110	0.0121
29	1.246	0.964	0.282	0.0795
30	1.538	0.964	0.574	0.3295
	28.927			0.7496

Mean = 28.927 ÷ 30 = 0.964
Standard deviation = $\sqrt{0.7496/29}$ = 0.161
Standard error = .161 ÷ $\sqrt{30}$ = 0.0294
t-value = (0.964 − 1.000) ÷ 0.0294 = − 1.22

Table 2 in Appendix 20-6 contains critical values for the *t*-test. In this application of the test, degrees of freedom (d.f.) equals the number of observations less one — 29 in the present example. The table shows that the critical *t*-value for a two-tailed test at the 95 percent confidence level with 29 degrees of freedom is ± 2.045. The region of rejection consists of all values outside of this range. Because the calculated *t*-value, −1.22, does not lie in the region of rejection, the null hypothesis that properties are, on average, appraised at market value cannot be rejected.

Because the *t*-test is parametric, its strict validity requires ratios to be normally distributed (see appendix 20-7 for a test of this assumption). In addition, the *t*-test suffers on the technical grounds that the mean *A/S* ratio provides a biased estimator of the mean *A/V* ratio.

Binomial Test of the Level of Appraisal

The nonparametric approach to testing the level of appraisal involves testing the hypothesis that the *median A/V* ratio equals a specified percentage. The appropriate test is the binomial test. In general, the binomial test determines at a specified confidence level whether the number of observations falling in each of two categories follows an hypothesized distribution. In the present context, it is hypothesized that one-half of the ratios lie below the specified median and one-half above.

When sample size is twenty-five or less, the binomial test can be performed at the 95 percent confidence level by simply counting the number of ratios above and below the hypothesized median and evaluating the result by reference to a binomial table (appendix 20-6, table 3).

Assume, for example, that an appraiser is interested in discerning at the 95 percent confidence level whether the median level of appraisal for residential properties in a neighborhood is at least 90 percent. The null and alternative hypotheses are

$$H_0: \widetilde{A/V} = 0.90.$$
$$H_1: \widetilde{A/V} < 0.90.$$

Analyzing twenty-two recent sales, the appraiser notes that sixteen of the sales resulted in ratios of less than 0.90 and six in ratios of 0.90 or more. The binomial table shows that the critical value for a one-tailed test for a sample of twenty-two is seven. That is, H_0 cannot be rejected if there are at least seven ratios equal to or above the hypothesized median. In the present case, however, with only six of the twenty-two ratios above the hypothesized median (0.90), the appraiser must reject H_0 at the 95 percent confidence level.

When sample size is greater than twenty-five, the binomial test requires calculation of a z-value using the formula,

$$z = \frac{0.5(n - 1) - x}{\sqrt{(0.25n)}}, \qquad (2)$$

where n is the sample size and x is the number of ratios above or below the median, whichever is less. For example, if the non-parametric binomial test, instead of the parametric t-test, is applied to the thirty ratios in table 1, the appropriate null and alternative hypotheses are:

$$H_0: \widetilde{A/V} = 1.000.$$
$$H_1: \widetilde{A/V} < 1.000.$$

Note that twenty of the observed ratios are less than 1.000 and ten are greater. Substituting into the formula for z yields

$$z = \frac{0.5(29) - 10}{\sqrt{(0.25)(30)}} = 1.64.$$

The critical values of z at the 95 percent confidence level for a two-tailed test are ± 1.96. This can be verified from a z-table (appendix 20-6, table 1) by noting that the combined probability of obtaining a value in this range is 95 percent. Because the calculated z-value (1.64) does not lie in the region of rejection, the null hypothesis that the overall level of appraisal is 100 percent cannot be rejected. If the test were one-tailed, the region of rejection would consist of z-values less than -1.645. If more than half of the ratios were above the hypothesized median, H_0 could be accepted automatically, because this situation will always result in a z-value greater than zero.

The binomial test is a more generally useful test of the level of appraisal than the t-test. Its validity does not rest on the assumption that the ratios are normally distributed and is not compromised by the problem of measurement error inherent in the t-test. One possible shortcoming of the binomial test is that it is based entirely on a simple determination of whether ratios lie above or below the hypothesized median. A ratio far above the hypothesized median would, for example, be offset by a ratio only slightly below the median. Nonetheless, such situations relate more to the distribution and variability of the ratios and can be discerned through an examination of frequency distributions and histograms.

Proving the Level of Appraisal

In some cases, it may be necessary to prove that the level of appraisal falls within a given range, for example, between 0.90 and 1.10. One way of doing this is to compute the confidence interval. If the upper and lower limits both fall within the range, the null hypothesis that the appraisal level is within the specified range can be accepted, and vice versa.

Alternatively, the *probability* that the level of appraisal falls within the specified range can be computed. Assume, for example, that an appraiser wishes to determine the probability that the true population mean is between 0.90 and 1.10 given the following:

Sample size (n) = 81
Sample mean = 0.94
Sample standard deviation = 0.18

The probability that the population mean is *less* than 0.90 is based on the z-statistic,

$$z = \frac{0.90 - 0.94}{0.18/\sqrt{81}} = -2.00 \; .$$

As the z-table indicates, there is only a 2.28 percent chance (0.5000 less 0.4772) of obtaining a z-value less than -2.00. Similarly, the probability that the population mean is *greater* than 1.10 is based on the z-value,

$$z = \frac{1.10 - 0.94}{0.18/\sqrt{81}} = 8 \; .$$

Because there is no probability of obtaining a value this extreme, the probability that the true level of appraisal is between 0.900 and 1.10 is 97.72 percent (1.0000 − 0.0228 − 0).

As in confidence interval testing, poor uniformity (large standard deviation) and small samples lessen the probability that the population mean lies within a given range of the calculated mean. Also, because a nonnormal distribution distorts the results, it is important to determine whether the ratios are normally distributed before performing the analysis.

Appendix 20-9: Legal Aspects of Ratio Studies in the United States

The design and use of ratio studies must conform to law. In the United States, certain fundamental protections for individual rights apply to the ad valorem taxation process. Equalization actions based on ratio studies are subject to provisions of the United States Constitution and state constitutions and statutes. These provisions may support and even require equalization and, on the other hand, also place limits on arbitrary action.

Federal Constitutional Protections

The protections affecting taxation found in the Constitution include the commerce clause, the Bill of Rights, and the Fourteenth Amendment. The commerce clause grants to Congress the power to regulate interstate commerce, preempting most state regulation in this area. The clause prohibits tax discrimination against taxpayers engaged in interstate commerce. The scope of commerce clause protection in state tax cases has been limited, however, by the Tax Injunction Act, 28 USC §1341. Complete Auto Transit, Inc., v. Brady, 430 U.S. 274 (1977), is the leading case on the balance between the taxation powers of the states and the federal protections afforded by the commerce clause.

A notable exception to the Tax Injunction Act, however, is the Railroad Revitalization and Regulatory Reform ("4-R") Act (49 USC §11503). This act has been the source of much litigation under commerce clause protections.

The Fifth Amendment in the Bill of Rights forbids the national government to deprive any person of "life, liberty, or property without due process of law." The Fourteenth Amendment extends the individual's due process protection to state government actions. It also forbids states to deny "the equal protection of the laws" to individuals.

Due process includes procedural protection, such as reasonable notice of an action and the opportunity for affected parties to be heard in defense of their interests (which may be financial or property interests, including taxes). Property owners affected by equalization actions have the right to appeal; the resulting valuations must be able to withstand scrutiny with respect to fairness and equity.

Interpretations of the Constitution vary. In the area of taxation, distinctions not involving protected areas are permissible if they have a rational basis. For example, personal and real property may be taxed at different rates, even though unequal tax burdens result. Tax exemptions also do not usually create equal protection problems. Similarly, the equalization of various property groups at market value based on any reasonable criteria (current use, location, age, and so forth) is entirely consistent with the Fourteenth Amendment. In fact, unless specifically authorized by state constitution or statute, unequal assessment or taxation among classes of property runs contrary to the equal protection clause.

Federal 4-R Act

A key federal statute relating to ratio studies is the 4-R Act, tax provisions of which are found at 49 USC §11503. Although federal jurisdiction with respect to most state taxes was curtailed by the Tax Injunction Act, Congress was concerned about perceived tax discrimination against railroads and created a sweeping exception for such property. Specifically, the 4-R Act requires rail transportation property to be equalized at no more than 105 percent of the assessment level of other commercial and industrial property in the same taxing jurisdiction and prohibits other tax and valuation discrimination against railroad property. Federal courts were invested with the power to enjoin taxes which violated these provisions. Also, the 4-R Act was quickly followed by tax discrimination prohibitions for air transportation property, motor carriers, and bus lines (49 USC §1513 & 11503a).

Although the 4-R Act permits railroads to compare their appraisal level to that of "other" commercial and industrial property, the act does not specify what this designation includes. Only owner-occupied residential and agricultural real property are clearly excluded. Railroads and states have contested inclusion and exclusion of vacant land zoned for commercial use, rental residential property, mines and utility property, and agricultural machinery and equipment. Another

consideration is whether the appraisal level should be compared separately for real and personal property or whether an aggregate level should be determined for both real and personal property.

Further classification problems have involved the status of totally or partially exempt property. Even where exempt property is excluded from the commercial and industrial class, exemptions may still constitute remediable discrimination if extensive or if transportation property is unfairly excluded.

The problems of proper classification are more than just academic. Consider the example in table 1. This appears to be a well-appraised and equalized jurisdiction. However, consider the potential for suit by a railroad car company, whose property has been held to be subject to 4-R Act provisions with the proper comparison class being commercial and industrial personal property. Although the reported level of personal property is 95 percent, the additional facts shown in table 2 change the appraisal image.

Hence, the total assessed value of commercial and industrial personal property is $4.6

Table 1. Example of Appraisal Levels: Exemptions Excluded

Classification	Value	Level
Commercial and industrial real property	$6 billion	95 percent
Commercial and industrial personal property	$2 billion	95 percent
Utilities	$2 billion	100 percent

Table 2. Example of Appraisal Levels: Exemptions Included

Classification	Value	Level
Inventory	$800 million	Exempt
Farm machinery and equipment	300 million	Exempt
Crops and livestock	500 million	Exempt
Timber machinery and equipment	100 million	50 percent
Timber	300 million	Exempt
Escaped personal property	500 million	0 Percent
Leaseholds on government land	50 million	Exempt
Commercial and industrial personalty subject to developer's exemption	50 million	Exempt
Total	$2.6 billion	

billion ($2.0 billion fully taxable plus $2.6 billion fully exempt, partially exempt, or escaped), the assessed value of which is $1.95 billion (0.95 × $2.0 billion + 0.50 × $100 million). The overall assessment level for commercial and industrial personal property, including exempt or escaped commercial and industrial personal property, is thus only 42.4 percent ($1.95 billion ÷ $4.6 billion).

Although the federal court may follow the explicit language of the 4-R Act and find that the exempt property is not in the commercial and industrial class, the car company could still have a remedy. If exemptions and missed property indicate pervasive discrimination, the court may reduce the personal property tax on the car companies.

The proper method of determining the level of assessment for purposes of the 4-R Act is also in dispute. That is, is the proper measure the median, mean, weighted mean, or some combination of these measures? The choice can alter the result markedly. If, as in the following example, utility property is appraised at 100 percent of market value, the weighted mean can differ significantly from the median (see table 3[a]). In this example, if the median is used, transportation prop-

erty would be entitled to a 6.9 percent reduction in taxes. However, the weighted mean is 95.3 percent, within the 5 percent tolerance allowed by the 4-R Act. Note also that in this example, taking a weighted average of the medians would give the same result (see table 3[b]). This underscores the crucial question of whether the classes should be weighted by number of parcels or value.

Another important question is the geographic area over which the level of appraisal should be determined. In some cases, taxing units have been used; in other cases, statewide figures have been allowed.

These and other problems inherent in ratio studies make determining the overall level of appraisal under the 4-R Act very complex. Of special note are the limited samples that usually comprise "other" commercial and industrial property groups.

State Constitutional and Statutory Provisions

In addition to federal constitutional rights to due process and equal protection, state constitutions offer their own versions of these

Table 3. Difference between Weighted Mean and Median for Measuring Level of Assessment

(a)

Classification	Parcels	Appraised value	Median	Weighted mean
Commercial and industrial real property	1,000	$6 billion	0.930	0.930
Utility	10	$3 billion	1.000	1.000
Total	1,010	$9 billion	0.931	0.953

(b)

Classification	Appraised value	Percent of value	Median		
Commercial and industrial real property	$6 billion	.667	× 0.930	=	0.620
Utility	$3 billion	.333	× 1.000	=	0.333
Total	$9 billion	1.000			0.953

provisions. Many states also add a uniformity clause to provide specific constitutional protection for property taxpayers. Uniformity clauses require property tax rates and appraisal level to be uniform by class of property within each taxing district. Some state constitutions define classes of property and impose limits on differences in assessment levels that their legislatures may enact. In other states, the legislature is free to make such determinations. At least one state has held its uniformity clause to require uniform level of appraisal statewide without regard to class (Idaho Telephone Co. v. Baird, 91 Idaho 425, 423 P.2d 337 [1967]).

All states permit some exemptions from ad valorem taxes. Some constitutions strictly limit exemptions to a few classes of property; others give the legislature unlimited discretion to grant exemptions. Regardless of the breadth of this delegation, exemption clauses do not authorize discrimination that is prohibited by the uniformity clause.

The protection afforded by state constitutions is often buttressed by state statutes establishing equalization programs. State supervision of local appraisal practices through equalization has a strong legal foundation. In BiMetallic Investment Company v. State Board of Equalization of Colorado, 239 U.S. 441 (1915), for example, Justice Holmes afforded local assessment officials little, if any, constitutional protection from statewide equalization authority, other than minimal due process protection. The strength of this opinion demonstrates a recognition by the courts that strong central authority to equalize is inherently necessary.

State equalization statutes have not been subject to as much judicial scrutiny as 4-R Act provisions. However, the trend appears to be to require proper sales screening and validation.

Glossary, Equations, and Readings

The glossary defines most technical terms used in the text. Additional definitions within the text may be found easily by using the book's index.

The list of equations pulls together equations from the text under the headings general models, sales comparison models, land valuation models, cost models, income models, statistics and statistical testing, equilibrium analysis, and miscellaneous. Equation 20.1 is the first equation in chapter 20, equation 14.3 is the third equation in chapter 14, and so on. Under each heading, equations are arranged from the simplest (or most general) to the most complex. All symbols used in equations are defined at the beginning of the list.

The additional readings will help readers who wish to pursue topics in more depth to find their way in the literature of the field.

Glossary

Words set in boldface within entries are defined elsewhere in the glossary.

Absolute value. The value of a number or expression regardless of its sign. For example, 3 and –3 (minus 3) both have an absolute value of 3. The mathematical symbol for absolute value is one vertical bar on each side of the number in question, for example, |3|.

Abstract. To reduce a **legal description** of a property to another form; also, to identify a property from its legal description.

Abstraction method. A method used to estimate the value of property from a knowledge of normal net income, discount rate, remaining economic life of the property, value of the building, income path attributable to the building, and income path attributable to the land. The method estimates total value by discounting the income stream attributable to the land and adding the result to an independent estimate of the value of the building. Also called land residual technique.

Accrued depreciation. The amount of **depreciation**, from any and all sources, that affects the value of the property in question.

Adaptive estimation procedure. A computerized procedure using properties for which **sales prices** are known to produce a **model** that can be used to value properties for which sales prices are not known. Also called feedback.

Additive model. A **model** in which the **dependent variable** is estimated by multiplying each **independent variable** by its coefficient and adding each product to a constant.

Address. (1) In a computer file, a specific juncture of circuits in computer machinery at which information is stored in the form of magnetic polarities. (2) Also, the name a programmer uses to refer to such a juncture. In a file of human-readable information, one must establish rules about whether and how to record various relevant addresses, including the situs address, owner's address, and mortgagee's address.

Adjusted sale price. The **sale price** that results from **adjustments** made to the stated sale price to account for the effects of time, personal property, financing, or the like.

Adjustments. Modifications in the reported value of a variable, such as sale price or gross income, such that the adjustments can be used to estimate market value; in the **sales comparison approach**, for example, by adjustments for differences between comparables and subject properties.

Ad valorem tax. A tax levied in proportion to the value of the thing(s) being taxed. Exclusive of exemptions, use-value assessment laws, and the like, the property tax is an ad valorem tax.

After-tax cash flow. *See* **cash flow**.

Age. *See* **chronological age; economic life; effective age.**

Age/life method. A method of estimating **accrued depreciation** founded on the premise that, in the aggregate, a neat mathematical function can be used to infer accrued depreciation from the age of a property and its **economic life**.

Agents of production. *See* **factors of production**.

Aggregate mean. *See* **weighted mean**.

Air rights. The rights to use space above real estate.

Algorithm. A precisely defined set of steps that, if followed exactly, will produce a prespecified result.

Allocation method. A method used to value land, in the absence of vacant land sales, by using a typical ratio of land to improvement value. Also called land ratio method.

Amortize. (1) To consider, for accounting and management purposes, one unusually large investment at a single time as really being a series of smaller expenses over a period of time. (2) To repay a loan, for example, a mortgage, by means of a series of small payments, usually a combination of principal repayment and interest charges, rather than one lump sum at the end of the term.

Annuity. A series of payments (often, but not necessarily, equal) receivable at regular intervals.

Anticipation. The principle that value depends on the expectation of benefits to be derived in the future.

Appeal. A process in which a property owner contests an assessment either informally or formally.

Appraisal. An estimation of **value**.

Appraisal date. The date as of which the assessments for a tax year are made. For example, if January 1 is the assessment date and a lot is vacant on that date, the property is appraised and assessed as vacant land even though a building is completed on it in April and the assessment roll may not be final and made public until May 15.

Appraisal principles. The economic concepts underlying appraisal: **supply, demand, change, balance, conformity, competition, contribution, anticipation, substitution, highest and best use, surplus productivity, and variable proportions.**

Appraisal ratio. (1) The ratio of the **appraised value** to an indicator of market value. (2) By extension, an estimated fractional relationship between the appraisals and **market values** of a group of properties. *See also* **level of appraisal**.

Appraisal ratio study. A **ratio study** using independent "expert" appraisals as indicators of **market value**.

Appraisal-sale price ratio. The ratio of the **appraised value** to the **sale price** (or **adjusted sale price**) of a property.

Appraised value. An estimate of the value of a property before application of any fractional **assessment ratio**, partial **exemption**, or other such adjustment.

Appreciation. Increase in value of a property, in terms of money, from all causes. For example, a farm may appreciate if a shopping center is built nearby, and property of any sort may appreciate as a result of inflation.

Arithmetic mean. *See* **mean**.

Arm's-length sale. A sale between two unrelated parties, both seeking to maximize their positions from the transaction.

Array. An ordered arrangement of data such as a listing of sales ratios in order of magnitude.

Assessed value. The monetary amount at which a property is put on the **assessment roll**. Assessed values differ from the assessor's estimate of **market value (appraised value)** for three major reasons: **fractional assessment** laws, partial **exemptions**, and decisions by assessing officials to override **market value** estimates.

Assessment-appraisal ratio. The ratio of the **assessed value** of a property to an independent appraisal.

Assessment equity. The degree to which assessments bear a consistent relationship to **market value**.

Assessment map. *See* **cadastral map**.

Assessment progressivity (regressivity). An appraisal bias such that high-value properties are appraised higher (lower) than low-value properties. *See also* **price-related differential**.

Assessment ratio. (1) The ratio of the **assessed value** to an indicator of **market value**. (2) By extension, an estimated fractional relationship between the assessed values and market values of a group of properties. *See also* **level of assessment**.

Assessment ratio study. Ratio study, sales ratio study, and appraisal ratio study are preferred.

Assessment review. The reexamination of assessments by a governmental agency that has the authority to alter individual assessments on its own motion. *See also* **appeal**.

Assessment roll. The basis on which the **property tax levy** is allocated among the property owners in a jurisdiction with taxing powers. The assessment roll usually lists an identifier for each taxable parcel in the jurisdiction, the name of the owner of record, the address of the parcel or the owner, the **assessed value** of the land, the assessed value of the improvement(s), applicable **exemption** codes if any, and the total **assessed value**. Synonyms include **cadastre**, list, grand list, abstract of ratables, and rendition.

Assessment-sale price ratio. The ratio of **assessed value** to **sale price** (or **adjusted sale price**) of a property.

Assessment year. The 365 days beginning with the **appraisal date**.

Assessor. The head of an assessment jurisdiction. Assessors may be either elected or appointed. The term is sometimes used collectively to refer to all administrators of the assessment function.

Audit trail. A set of records of the changes made to another set of records.

Average. The **arithmetic mean**.

Average absolute deviation. *See* **average deviation**.

Average deviation. The **arithmetic mean** of the **absolute** deviations of a set of numbers from a measure of **central tendency** such as the **median**. Taking **absolute values** is generally understood without being stated. The average deviation of the numbers 4, 6, and 10 about their median (6) is (2 + 0 + 4)/3, or 2.

Balance. The principle that markets tend to move toward **equilibrium** after a change in one of the **determinants of supply or demand**.

Balloon mortgage. A mortgage not fully **amortized** at maturity and requiring a lump sum or balloon payment.

Band-of-investment analysis. A perspective on (and a technique for estimating) the **discount rate**. The discount rate is viewed as being composed of two components, each weighted in proportion to typical financing terms for properties of the type in question. For example, if 75 percent loans are available at 9 percent interest and investors are known to seek a 14 percent return on **equity**, then the discount rate is 10.25 percent, that is, (0.75 × 0.09 = 0.0675) + (0.25 × 14 = 0.0350) = 0.1025 = 10.25 percent.

Base-lot method. A method of appraising land parcels whereby each parcel to be appraised is compared with a parcel of known value, called the base lot, and differences between the two in terms of location, size, shape, topography, and the like are analyzed by the appraiser in estimating the value of the lot to be appraised.

Before-tax cash flow. *See* **cash flow**.

Benchmark. (1) A term used in land surveying to mean a known point of reference. (2) In property appraisal, a property of known **value**, and of known **effective age** and **replacement cost**. (3) By extension, a model property to be used in determining by comparison the grade or **quality class** of other properties.

Bernard rule. A method of appraising corner lots whereby each lot is assumed to be two identical lots (one facing each of the streets), which are appraised using the appropriate average-unit-value rates. The values are summed to get the total value of the lot.

Bias. A **statistic** is said to be biased if the expected **value** of that statistic is not equal to the population **parameter** being estimated. A process is said to be biased if it produces results that vary systematically with some factor that should be irrelevant. In assessment administration, **assessment progressivity (regressivity)** is one kind of possible bias.

Binary variable. A variable for which only two values are possible, such as results from a yes-or-no question, for example, Does this building have any fireplaces? Used in **models** to separate the influence of categorical variables. Also called a dichotomous variable or a dummy variable. *See also* **discrete variable** and **continuous variable**.

Block face. The long edges of two city blocks that adjoin a street for the length of one block.

Breakdown method. *See* **observed condition breakdown method**.

Building residual technique. A technique uscd to estimate the value of a property from a knowledge of its **net operating income**, **discount rate**, **remaining economic life**, land value, the **income path** attributable to the building, and the income path attributable to the land. The technique estimates total value by discounting the **income stream** attributable to the building and adding the result to an independent estimate of the value of the land.

Bullet loan. Gap financing offered when a construction loan has expired but permanent financing has not yet been found.

Cadastral map. A scale map showing the dimensions of each parcel and related information such as **parcel identifier**, survey lines, and **easements**. Annotations on recent sales prices and land value are sometimes added.

Cadastre. An inventory of the land in an area by ownership, description, and value. *See also* **assessment roll**.

Calibration. The process of estimating the **coefficients** in a **mass appraisal model**.

Capital market. The interaction of buyers and sellers as they buy and sell long-term financial instruments, such as mortgages, bonds, and stocks.

Capitalization. The phenomenon whereby one or more events of economic consequence expected to happen in the future exert an economic effect on things in the present. Specifically, the conversion of expected income and rate of return into an estimated value in the income approach to value. Property taxes, anticipated changes, and land-related government services may also be capitalized. *See also* **yield capitalization**.

Capitalization of ground rents. A method of estimating land value in the absence of comparable sales; applicable to farmland and commercial land leased on a net basis.

Capitalization rate. Any rate used to convert an estimate of income to an estimate of market value; the ratio of **net operating income** to **market value**.

Cash-equivalent sale price. An indicator of **market value** that is a refinement over the raw sale price, in that the effects of unusual financing arrangements and extraneous transfers of personal property have been removed. *See also* **adjusted sale price**.

Cash flow. Amount of money left after subtracting operating expenses and **debt service** from rents collected. Before-tax cash flow (also called cash throw-off) signifies that income tax effect has not been considered; after-tax cash flow includes income tax savings generated by ownership.

Cash throw-off. *See* **cash flow**.

Central processing unit (CPU). The key part of a computer. Contains circuitry necessary to interpret and execute program instructions.

Central tendency. (1) The tendency of most kinds of data to cluster around some typical or central value, such as the **median** or **mean**. (2) By extension, any or all such **statistics**. Some kinds of data, however, such as the weights of cars and trucks, may cluster about two or more values, and in such circumstances the meaning of central tendency becomes unclear. This may happen in **ratio studies** when two or more **classes** of property are combined in a single analysis.

Central tendency, measure of. A single point in a range of observations, around which the observations tend to cluster. The three most commonly used measures of central tendency are the **mean**, **median**, and **mode**.

Certificate of deposit. A time deposit in a bank or savings institution that carries a fixed rate of interest and a penalty for withdrawal before maturity.

Change. The tendency of the social and economic forces affecting **supply** and **demand** to alter over time, thus influencing **market value**.

Check digit. An extra digit used for the purpose of performing a check. For example, using X and 0 to indicate divisibility or nondivisibility by 2 would result in the sequence of numbers 1, 2, 3, 4 being represented as 10, 2X, 30, 4X. Computer systems generally have a number of such checks built in to ensure that the machine made no errors in writing or reading data, the data entry clerk did not transpose digits or leave out records, and so on.

Chi-square. A particular **statistic**, and a particular **frequency distribution** associated with it, of interest in **inferential statistics**. (Chi, a Greek letter, is symbolized by X).

Chronological age. The number of years elapsed since an original structure was built. Synonyms are *actual age* and *historical age*. Contrast with **effective age**.

Class. A predefined category into which **data** may be put for further analysis. For example, ratios may be grouped into the following classes: less than .500, .500 to .599, .600 to .699, and so forth.

Classified property tax system. (1) A system intended by law to tax various kinds of property at different **effective tax rates**. Thus two different kinds of property worth the same amount of money have different tax bills. Although this could be done by applying different tax rates to different kinds of property that share a common **assessment ratio**, the usual approach is to apply a uniform tax rate to all properties and establish by law what the assessment ratio should be for each class of property. (2) Loosely, by extension, a set of assessment practices that has this result contrary to laws requiring uniformity.

COD. *See* **coefficient of dispersion**.

Coding. The act of reducing a description of a unique object, such as a parcel of real estate, to a set of one or more measures or counts of certain of its characteristics, such as square footage, number of bathrooms, and the like. *Encoding*, a related term, is usually used to refer to the act of translating coded descriptions useful to human beings into a form that can be processed by computers. Coding is sometimes also used to refer to the writing of instructions that direct the processing done by computers.

Coefficient. A number or quantity generally placed before and multiplying another quantity, as 5 in the expression $5x$, or a dimensionless **statistic**, useful as a measure of change or relationship; for example, **correlation coefficient**.

Coefficient of concentration. The percentage of observations falling within a specified percentage (say, 15 percent) of a measure of **central tendency**.

Coefficient of correlation. *See* **correlation coefficient**.

Coefficient of determination (R^2). A **statistic** that characterizes two or more sets of numbers. The coefficient of determination, when multiplied by 100, gives the percentage strength of the (linear) relationship between or among the sets of numbers. (*See also* **correlation**.) For two variables, the coefficient of determination and the square of the **correlation coefficient** are identical; for three or more variables, the coefficient of determination measures the strength of the relationship between the **dependent variable** and all the **independent variables** combined.

Coefficient of dispersion (COD). The **average deviation** of a group of numbers from the **median** expressed as a percentage of the median. In **ratio studies**, the average percentage deviation from the median ratio.

Coefficient of variation (COV). The **standard deviation** expressed as a percentage of the **mean**.

Commercial paper. Short-term promise to pay issued by a corporation.

Comparables; comparable sales. Recently sold properties that are similar in important respects to a property being appraised. The **sale price** and the physical, functional, and locational characteristics of each of the properties are compared to the property being appraised in order to arrive at an estimate of value. By extension, the term *comparables* is sometimes used to refer to properties with rent or income patterns comparable to a property being appraised.

Comparative unit method. (1) A method of appraising land **parcels** in which an average or typical value is estimated for each stratum of land. (2) A method of estimating **replacement cost** in which all the direct and indirect costs of a structure (except perhaps architect's fees) are aggregated and specified with reference to a unit of comparison such as ground area, floor area, or cubic content. Separate factors are commonly specified for different intervals of the unit of comparison and for different story heights, and separate schedules are commonly used for different building types and **quality classes**.

Competition. The attempt by two or more buyers or sellers to buy or sell similar commodities in the same market.

Complementary commodities. Goods related in such a way that an increase in the consumption of one increases the consumption of the other.

Computer-assisted assessment system. A system for assessing real and personal **property** with the assistance of a computer. A computer may be used, for example, in the appraisal process, in keeping track of ownership and exemption status, in printing the assessment roll, in coordinating the work load of real property appraisers and personal property appraisers with respect to the assessment of commercial and industrial properties, and in a number of other areas.

Computer-assisted mass appraisal (CAMA). A system of appraising property, usually only certain types of real property, that incorporates statistical analyses such as **multiple regression analysis** and **adaptive estimation procedure** to assist the appraiser in estimating value.

Condition. A judgment of the **depreciation** of an improvement.

Confidence interval. For a given **confidence level**, the **range** within which one can conclude that the population **parameter** (such as the **median** or **mean** appraisal ratio) lies. The reliability of confidence intervals depends on the extent to which any required statistical assumptions are met.

Confidence level. The required degree of confidence in a statistical test or **confidence interval**, commonly 90, 95, or 99 percent. A 95 percent confidence interval would mean, for example, that one can be 95 percent confident that the population **parameter** (such as the **median** or **mean** ratio of **appraised values** to **market values**) falls in the indicated range.

Conformity. The principle that the value of a property depends in part on its relationship to its surroundings.

Consideration. The amount of money and other valuable goods or services upon which a buyer and a seller agree to consummate a sale.

Contingency table. A table that shows how a **dependent variable** varies with respect to two **independent variables**.

Continuous variable. A **variable** for which it is conceivable that, given any two observed values, a value lying between them may occur. For example, temperature and finished living area are continuous variables; quality class and number of fireplaces are not. *See also* **binary variable** and **discrete variable**.

Contract rent. The amount of rent per unit of time specified in a contract. For very old contracts, the contract rent may be substantially less than the rent the property would bring today.

Contribution. The principle that the value of a particular feature is measured by its contribution to the value of the whole property, rather than by its cost.

Coordinate system. (1) A system for locating any geographic point by determining its north-south and east-west distance from some known base point. (2) By extension, a system for identifying each assessable **parcel** of real estate by means of coordinates, usually by recording the coordinates of the center of each parcel.

Correlation. A statistical phenomenon (and a technique for estimating its strength) whereby knowledge of one fact about a thing implies some knowledge of a second fact about that thing. For example, since the volume and weight of water are correlated, knowing that a quantity of water is 1 gallon tells you that its weight is 8⅓ pounds. Linear correlation, the kind most often encountered, means that an increase in one factor in some proportion (say, a doubling) changes the other in the same proportion. With curvilinear correlation, as between the radius and the area of a circle, this is not true, despite the fact that the correlation may be very strong in the sense that knowledge of one fact tells you precisely the other fact. These are examples of **variables** perfectly correlated or nearly so; more often correlation is only partial — for example, the correlation between the age and height of a child. The **correlation coefficient** gives the strength of the linear relationship between the two variables.

Correlation coefficient (r). A **statistic** that characterizes two or more sets of numbers and, when squared and multiplied by 100, gives the percentage strength of the (linear) relationship between the two sets of numbers. For example, if the coefficient of correlation between measures of the height and weight of a group of people were 0.9, then one would deduce that knowing the height of someone (loosely speaking) would explain (or account for) 81 percent of the weight.

Correlation matrix. The table of numbers used to display the **correlation coefficients** for each pair of **variables** when three or more variables are thought to be correlated.

Cost. The money expended in obtaining an object or attaining an objective; generally used in appraisal to mean the expense, direct and indirect, of constructing an improvement.

Cost approach. One of the **three approaches to value**, the cost approach is based on the principle of **substitution** — that a rational, informed purchaser would pay no more for a property than the cost of building an acceptable substitute with like **utility**. The cost approach seeks to determine the **replacement cost** of an improvement less **depreciation** plus land value.

Cost index. An index showing the variations in construction costs over time; sometimes, by extension, a set of similar numbers showing the relative costs of construction in different geographic areas.

Cost manual. A guide, containing pictures, specifications of structures, and **cost schedules**, used to help classify construction quality and estimate the cost of replacing a structure.

Cost-of-development method. A method of appraising undeveloped land, whereby an estimate is made of the probable proceeds to be obtained from selling the land as subdivided, developed parcels. The cost of so developing the raw land is subtracted from this estimate to obtain an estimate of the value of the raw land.

Cost schedules. Charts, tables, factors, curves, equations, and the like intended to help estimate the cost of replacing a structure from a knowledge of some other factors, such as its **quality class** and number of square feet.

Cost trend factor. A factor derived from a **cost index** used to estimate the contemporary cost of something based on its historical cost.

COV. *See* **coefficient of variation.**

Critical value. The value, found in a table, with which a computed statistic is compared to determine whether the **null hypothesis** is accepted or rejected at the specified **confidence level.**

Curable depreciation. That part of **depreciation** that can be reversed by correcting **deferred maintenance** and remodeling to relieve **functional obsolescence.**

Current-market-value appraisals. Appraisals that reflect contemporary market values rather than market values at some point in the past. Currency is commonly taken to be implicit in the term **market value.**

Data. Information expressed in any of a number of ways. *Data* is the general term for masses of numbers, codes, and symbols generally, and *information* is the term for meaningful data. Data is the plural of datum, one element of data.

Data edit. The process of examining recorded **data** to ensure that each element of data is reasonable and is consistent with others recorded for the same object, such as a **parcel** of real estate. Data editing, which may be done by human beings or by computer, is essentially a mechanical process, distinct from verifying the correctness of the recorded information by calling or writing property owners.

Data management. The procedures employed to ensure that no information is lost through negligent handling of records from a file, that all information is properly supplemented and up-to-date, and that it is easily accessible.

Date of sale. The date on which the sale was agreed to. The date of recording can be used as a proxy if it is not unduly delayed, as in a **land contract.** (Also date of transfer).

Debt service. The total payments of principal and **interest** on a mortgage.

Deed of trust. A document (or legal instrument) used to place the legal **title** to and control of a **property** in the hands of a trustee who is required under the conditions stated in the document to direct the use of the property for the benefit of some other person named in the document. A trust may be temporary, conditional, or permanent.

Deed recordation. The process of registering a sale of real property with the appropriate public body, usually the county recorder's office.

Deferred maintenance. Repairs and similar improvements that normally would have been made to a property but were not made to the property in question, thus increasing the amount of its **depreciation.**

Degrees of freedom (d.f.). The number of values, in a set of observations, that could be assigned arbitrarily within the specification of a system. For example, in stratifying a sample of n objects into k strata, there are $k - 1$ degrees of freedom, because, if $k - 1$ frequencies are specified, the other is determined by the total size n. The term is used in **statistics** in several slightly different senses but is important primarily only in connection with a certain aspect of **inferential statistics,** where it becomes a means of relating the value of a statistic calculated from a sample to a table of critical values for such statistics calculated for a wide range of potential sample sizes and amounts of information determined by the particular statistic of interest.

Demand. A schedule showing the amount of a good or productive service that would be purchased at various prices during a given period.

Denominator. In a fraction, the number by which another number (the **numerator**) is divided. For example, the denominator of 3/4 is 4.

Dependent variable. A **variable**, such as sale price, the value of which is predicted by the values of other variables, such as location and finished living area. Such a variable may be said to depend on the other (**independent**) **variables**.

Depletion. A decrease in land value due to the removal of trees, minerals, or other such resources.

Depreciation. Loss in value of an object, relative to its **replacement cost**, **reproduction cost**, or original cost, whatever the cause of the loss in value. Depreciation is sometimes subdivided into three types: **physical deterioration** (wear and tear), **functional obsolescence** (suboptimal design in light of current technologies or tastes), and **economic obsolescence** (poor location or radically diminished **demand** for the product).

Depth table; depth factor. A standard, mechanical technique for determining the value of a lot of urban land having a certain depth from the value of a base lot having different dimensions.

Descriptive statistics. (1) The branch of the science of statistics that is concerned only with characterizing or describing a set of **data** (numbers). (2) By extension, the measures used to characterize a particular set of data. *Contrast with* **inferential statistics**.

Determinants of supply and demand. Factors that cause supply and demand to change.

Dichotomous variable. *See* **binary variable**.

Differential assessments. Assessments in a system of laws that require that different **classes** of property be assessed with different **assessment ratios**. The term *differential assessments* is usually reserved for systems where the classes are broad and easily visible, such as classified property tax systems and **use-value** farmland assessment systems, although much the same effect is achieved by partial homestead exemptions, temporary exemptions to encourage rehabilitation or industrial location, and the like.

Discount rate. (1) The rate of return *on* investment; the rate an investor requires to discount future income to its present worth. It is made up of an interest rate and an equity yield rate. Theoretical factors considered in setting a discount rate are the safe rate earned from a completely riskless investment (this rate may reflect anticipated loss of purchasing power due to inflation) and compensation for risk, lack of liquidity, and investment management expenses. The discount rate is most often estimated by band-of-investment analysis or a sales comparison analysis that estimates typical internal rates of return. (2) In monetary policy, the rate that the Federal Reserve Bank charges member banks to borrow.

Discovery. The process whereby the assessor identifies all taxable property in the jurisdiction and ensures that it is included on the **assessment roll**.

Discrete variable. A **variable** for which it is not conceivable that, given any two observed values, a value lying between them may occur. For example, the number of rooms in a house is a discrete variable, but the living area of the house is not. *See also* **binary variable** and **continuous variable**.

Dispersion. The degree to which data are distributed either tightly or loosely around a measure of **central tendency**. Measures of dispersion include the **range, average deviation, standard deviation, coefficient of dispersion**, and **coefficient of variation**.

Dissimilarity function. An **algorithm** used to assign an index of dissimilarity (or similarity) to properties as compared to a subject.

Dummy variable. *See* **binary variable**.

Easement. A right held by one person to use the land of another for a specific purpose, such as access to other property.

Economic life. The period of time during which a given building or other improvement to property is expected to contrib-

ute (positively) to the value of the total property. This period is typically shorter than the period during which the improvement could be left on the property, that is, its physical life.

Economic obsolescence. Loss in value of a property (relative to the cost of replacing it with a property of equal **utility**) that stems from factors external to the property. For example, a buggy-whip factory, to the extent that it could not be used economically for anything else, suffered substantial economic obsolescence when automobiles replaced horse-drawn buggies.

Economic rent. In economics, the payment received by an owner of something being bought or rented in excess of the minimum amount for which he would have sold or rented it.

Edit. *See* **data edit; procedural edit**.

Effective age. The typical age of a structure equivalent to the one in question with respect to its **utility** and **condition**. Knowing the effective age of an old, rehabilitated structure or a building with substantial **deferred maintenance** is generally more informative than knowing its **chronological age**.

Effective gross income. **Potential gross rent** less vacancy and collection loss plus miscellaneous income.

Effective tax rate. The tax rate expressed as a percentage of **market value**; this will be different from the **nominal tax rate** when the **assessment ratio** is not equal to 1.

Emblements. Annual crops.

Equalization. The process by which an appropriate governmental body attempts to ensure that property under its jurisdiction is appraised equitably at **market value** or as otherwise required by law.

Equalized values. Assessed values after they have all been multiplied by common factors during **equalization**.

Equilibrium. A state of rest achieved by a balance of the forces that impel change. A **market** is said to be in equilibrium when the **factors of production** are used in the production of an array of consumer goods that maximize consumer welfare.

Equity. (1) The degree to which assessments bear a consistent relationship to **market value**. Measures include the **coefficient of dispersion** and **coefficient of variation**. (2) The net value of property after liens and other charges have been subtracted. *See also* **horizontal inequity** and **vertical inequity**.

Equity dividend. A synonym for before-tax **cash flow**.

Equity yield rate. *See* **yield rate**.

Error. The difference between the actual value of a **variable** and the expected value of the variable exclusive of sampling problems. Errors may be positive or negative, although in common speech taking the **absolute value** of the errors is sometimes implied. In **multiple regression analysis**, the term **error** is often used loosely to mean **residual**.

Escheat. The right to have property revert to the state for nonpayment of taxes or when there are no legal heirs of someone who dies without leaving a will.

Euclidean distance metric. A measure of distance based on the Pythagorean theorem; the distance between any two points as measured by the square of the length of the straight line connecting them.

Expense ratio. The ratio of expenses to gross income. A "typical" expense ratio is the relationship of normal expenses to **effective gross income**.

Exponent. A symbol usually written to the right and above an expression to indicate particular mathematical operations. For example, 6^2 means 6×6, or six squared. Fractional exponents indicate inverse operations; for example, an exponent of 1/2 signifies a square root. Exponents are also called powers. Valuation models make use of the following properties of exponents: A number raised to the exponent 0 is always 1.00; zero raised to any power is zero; any number raised to the power 1 is itself. Negative numbers cannot have exponents less than 1.

External diseconomies. Forces outside the activities of any single firm that cause resource prices to rise.

External economies. Forces outside the activities of any single firm that cause resource prices to fall.

Factor. (1) An underlying characteristic of something (such as a house) that may contribute to the value of a **variable** (such as its **sale price**) but is observable only indirectly. For example, construction quality is a factor defined by workmanship, spacing of joists, and materials used. Factor definition and measurement may be done subjectively or by a computer-assisted statistical **algorithm** known as factor analysis. (2) Loosely, any characteristic used in adjusting the sales prices of comparables. (3) The **reciprocal** of a rate. Assessments may be equalized by multiplying them by a factor equal to the reciprocal of the **assessment ratio**, and value can be estimated using the **income approach** by multiplying income by a factor equal to the reciprocal of the **discount rate**.

Factors of production. The four ingredients available for the production of goods and services that satisfy human wants: land, labor, capital, and management. Also called agents of production.

Federal rectangular survey system. A rectangular grid system, the basic elements of which are *townships* approximately 6 miles on each side. Each township is divided into thirty-six *sections*, nominally 1 mile square and containing 640 acres. Sections are further subdivided into quarter-sections, and so on.

Fee appraisal. Appraisal of properties one at a time for a fee.

Feedback. *See* **adaptive estimation procedure**.

Fee simple. In land ownership, complete interest in a property, subject only to governmental powers such as eminent domain. Also fee simple absolute.

Field canvass. The practice of collecting the **data** needed in assessment operations by systematically going from property to property coding the specified information.

Field review. The practice of reviewing the reasonableness of assessments by viewing the properties in question, sometimes by examining their interiors but more often by looking at their exteriors.

Fixed costs. Cost of fixed resources used by a firm that do not vary with production levels and cannot be changed in the short run.

Fixture. An item of equipment that, because of the way it is used, the way it is attached, or both, has become an integral part of a building or other improvement. A fixture, such as a bathtub, is classified as real property, but trade fixtures (fixtures used in the conduct of business) are classified as personal property.

Flowchart. Any of a number of kinds of graphic descriptions of an **algorithm**, showing the operations, data flow, equipment, and so on.

Fractional assessments. Assessments that by law or by practice have **assessment ratios** different from 1. Usually the assessment ratio is less than 1 and, if assessment **biases** are present, different **classes** of property may have different fractional ratios. Fractional assessments are often condemned as offering a way to obscure assessment biases.

Frequency distribution. A table showing the number or percentage of observations falling in the boundaries of a given set of classes. Used in **ratio studies** to summarize the distribution of the individual ratios. *See also* **class** and **histogram**.

Full-market-value assessment standard. Assessments for which a law or other standard requires that the **assessment ratio** equal 1.

Functional obsolescence. Loss in value of a property resulting from changes in tastes, preferences, technical innovations, or market standards.

Functional organization. A method of organizing personnel and practices under which the primary division is *what* is done to achieve the goals of the organization (such as producing the assessment roll) rather than *where* the activities are done. The latter method is called geographical organization. Functional organization of assessment usually means that special divisions are responsible for appraising properties by type: personalty, residential property, agricultural property, commercial property, industrial property, and vacant land. Improved land is generally the responsibility of the appraiser of the improvement.

Functional specialization. In assessment, appraiser specialization by type of property being appraised; sometimes also used to mean specialization by appraisal approach used, namely **cost**, **income**, or **sales comparison**. *See also* **geographical specialization**.

Future worth of 1. (Also called the compound amount of 1 or the amount of 1 at compound interest.) The amount to which one dollar will grow at compound interest over a specified number of years and at a specified interest rate.

Future worth of 1 per period. (Also called compound amount or accumulation of 1 per period.) The amount to which a series of equal periodic payments will accumulate at compound interest for a specified number of years and at a specified interest rate.

Gantt chart. A form of bar chart used in project management. Each element (task) of a project is represented by a horizontal bar. The bars are placed on the chart according to a time scale. The left end of each bar indicates when the task is to begin. The length of each bar indicates the duration of the task. The right end of each bar indicates when the task is to be completed.

General equilibrium. Simultaneous **equilibrium** of all individual economic units in the economy. Implies a condition in which consumers maximize their welfare given their income, producers maximize profits, and resources are used in their most productive use.

General equilibrium analysis. An economic analysis that attempts to understand how resources should be allocated to maximize a society's welfare.

Geocode. A code used to locate or identify a point, such as the center of a **parcel** of real estate, geographically. The code is composed of the east-west and north-south coordinates of the point relative to some standard point of reference.

Geodetic control network. A system of **monuments** that are used as reference points in calculating, through triangulation, the location of other points on surveys and maps.

Geographical specialization. Specialization of personnel, especially appraisers, by region rather than by type of property. *Contrast* **functional specialization**.

Geometric mean. A measure of **central tendency** computed by multiplying the values of all of the **observations** by one another and then taking the result to an **exponent** equal to one divided by the number of **observations**. The geometric mean is particularly appropriate when a typical rate of change is being calculated, such as an inflation rate or a **cost index**.

GIM. **Gross income multiplier**.

Goodness-of-fit statistics. Statistics used in **multiple regression analysis** and other kinds of statistical modeling to express the amount, and hence the importance, of the **errors** or **residuals** for all the predicted and actual values of a **variable**.

Government survey system. A general term referring to such surveys as the **federal rectangular survey system** in the United States.

Grade. *See* **quality class**.

GRM. **Gross rent multiplier**.

Gross income multiplier. The **factor** by which gross income is multiplied in order to obtain an estimate of value.

Gross leasable area. All area within the outside walls, including lobbies, washrooms, janitor's closets, and so on, but excluding building stairs, fire towers, elevator shafts, flues, vents, stacks, pipe shafts, and vertical ducts if they serve more than one floor.

Gross national product. The level of aggregated income of a country. The sum of consumer, investor, and government spending.

Gross rent multiplier. The **factor** by which gross rent is multiplied in order to obtain an estimate of **value**.

Heterogeneous. The opposite of **homogeneous**.

Heteroscedasticity. The opposite of **homoscedasticity**.

Highest and best use. A concept in appraisal and in assessment law requiring that each property be appraised as though it were being put to its most profitable use, given probable legal, physical, and financial constraints. The concept is most commonly discussed in connection with underutilized land.

Histogram. A bar chart or graph of a **frequency distribution** in which the frequencies of the various classes are indicated by horizontal or vertical bars whose lengths are proportional to the number or percentage of observations in each **class**.

Holding period. The length of time an investor expects to own a given property before selling it to someone else.

Homogeneous. Possessing the quality of being alike in nature and therefore comparable with respect to the parts or elements; said of **data** if two or more sets of data seem to be drawn from the same **population**; also said of data if the data are of the same type (that is, if counts, ranks, and measures are not all mixed in together).

Homoscedasticity. The quality of a **dependent variable** having constant **variance** for all values of the **independent variables**. For example, if regression **residuals** were plotted against living area, a band of uniform width would indicate homoscedasticity; a trapezoid would indicate **heteroscedasticity**.

Horizontal inequity. Differences based on criteria other than value range in the **levels of assessment** of groups of properties. For example, properties in one neighborhood may have a higher level of assessment than similar properties in another neighborhood. *See* **vertical inequity**.

Hotspot. A geographic area where sales activity is unusually strong and, usually, **market values** are rising and **assessment ratios** are declining.

Hybrid model. A model that incorporates both additive and multiplicative components. *See also* **additive model** and **multiplicative model**.

Hypothesis. A statement in inferential statistics the truth of which one is interested in determining. The usual procedure is to state what one chooses to accept in the absence of sufficient evidence to the contrary (the statement is called the **null hypothesis**), specify the relationship or statement to be proved (the alternative hypothesis), and analyze the available data to determine whether the null hypothesis can be rejected (and hence the alternative hypothesis accepted) at some confidence level.

Improper expenses. Expenses incurred in the ownership of income-producing property that are not used to calculate value in the **income approach**.

Improvement. Anything done to raw land with the intention of increasing its value. Thus a structure erected on the property constitutes one very common type of improvement, although other actions, such as those taken to improve drainage, are also improvements. Although such cases are rarely intentional, "improvements" can conceivably diminish the value of the land; note, however, that **easements** restricting the use and value of land are not considered improvements.

Income. The payments to its owner that a property is able to produce in a given time span, usually a year, and usually net of certain expenses of the property.

Income approach. One of the **three approaches to value**, the income approach uses **capitalization** to convert the anticipated benefits of the ownership of property into an estimate of present value.

Income path. The series of payments from an investment expressed as a percentage of the first year's payment; the plot or trajectory of the **income stream**.

Income stream. The series of payments (usually net income payments) receivable from an investment over the life of the investment. The series, of course, may be of any conceivable nature, including a constant series of equal payments (level), a series of decreasing payments that decrease by equal amounts each period (arithmetically decreasing), a series of increasing payments that grow larger each period at a constant rate (geometrically increasing), and so on.

Independent variable. A variable whose value is not determined by other (**dependent**) **variables**.

Indirect capitalization. *See* **yield capitalization**.

Inferential statistics. The branch of statistical studies concerned with making predictions about the values of a large number of **observations** of a **variable** on the basis of a small number of observations of that variable and related facts. (2) By extension, the **statistics** calculated in such predictions.

Inferior goods. Goods, the consumption of which decreases as consumer income increases.

Inputs. *See* **factors of production**.

Instrument. A formal legal document such as a deed, contract, will, or lease.

Intangible property. Evidence of ownership of value or the right to value, for example, notes, bonds, stocks, patents, mortgages, copyrights, insurance policies, and accounts receivable. A form of personal property that includes rights over **tangible** real and personal property, but not rights of use and possession.

Integrity. The quality of a **data** element or program being what it says it is; usually distinguished from **validity**, the quality of its being what it should be in terms of some ultimate purpose. After data are edited and encoded and programs are pre-

pared, their integrity is ensured by safeguards that prevent accidental or unauthorized tampering with them.

Interactive. Possessing the quality of being able to get reactions to proposals or instructions one at a time rather than merely all at once at the end of a session; usually said of a kind of computer system.

Intercept. Graphically, the point at which a line, such as a **regression line**, intersects the axis on which the **dependent variable** is represented; the value of the predicted **variable** when the value of all the other values in the **model** is zero; the constant b_0.

Interest (interest rate). The premium paid for the use of money; the **equilibrium** price in **money markets**. The interest rate usually incorporates a risk factor, an illiquidity factor, a time-preference factor, an inflation factor, and potentially others, too. *See also* **discount rate**.

Interest (interest transferred, interest acquired). The ownership rights of a person in a property. Complete ownership is called **fee simple** interest. It is possible to sell (transfer) and to own separately the component interests, such as mineral rights and air rights, that make up the fee interest.

Internal controls. The elements of a system for monitoring performance and ensuring **integrity** that are employed more routinely than **procedural edits** and are often performed automatically.

Internal rate of return. The rate that discounts all future **cash flows** to a present worth equal to the original investment. The internal rate of return is calculated, usually by trial and error, from a knowledge of the relevant cash flows.

Interquartile range (interquartile deviation). The result obtained by subtracting the first **quartile** from the third quartile.

Investment value. The worth of an investment property to a particular investor.

Iteration. One repetition or repeated cycle in an iterative process; a process of estimating values as close as possible to actual values by repeated approximations. The results of each approximation are used in the next one.

Kruskal-Wallis test. A test in **inferential statistics**, valid for all types of numerical data, that seeks to determine whether the **observations** in a **sample** came from one **population** as opposed to three or more distinct, homogeneous subpopulations. It is used in assessment to analyze **assessment ratios** from three or more **classes** of property to determine whether significant assessment **biases** are present among the classes of property. When only two classes are being compared, the appropriate test is the **Mann-Whitney test**.

Land contract. A contract for sale in which the seller retains title until the buyer completes installment payments for the property. The sale is not recorded until **title** passes to the buyer.

Land ratio. The ratio of land area to building area. The land ratio can be an important factor in grouping properties for **income approach** appraisal by means of direct sales comparisons.

Land ratio method. *See* **allocation method**.

Land residual technique. *See* **abstraction method**.

Leasehold. The interests in a property that are associated with the lessee (the tenant) as opposed to the lessor (the property owner).

Least cost combination of resources. A combination of resources at which the **marginal physical product** per dollar's worth of one resource is equal to the marginal physical product per dollar of every other resource.

Legal description. A statement in words or codes identifying land for all purposes of law.

Level of appraisal. The common or overall ratio of **appraised values** to **market values**. Three concepts are usually of interest: the level required by law, the true or actual level, and the computed level based on a **ratio study**.

Level of assessment. The common or overall ratio of **assessed values** to **market values**.

Levy. *See* **property tax levy**.

Lien date. The date on which an obligation, such as a property tax bill (usually in an amount yet to be determined), attaches to a property and the property thus becomes security against its payment. The term is usually synonymous with **appraisal date** but is not necessarily so.

Life estate. An interest in property that lasts only for a specified person's lifetime; thus the owner of a life estate is unable to leave the property to heirs.

Linear regression. A kind of statistical analysis used to investigate whether a **dependent variable** and a set of one or more **independent variables** share a linear **correlation** and, if they do, to predict the value of the dependent variable on the basis of the values of the other variables. Regression analysis of one dependent variable and only one independent variable is called simple linear regression, but it is the word *simple* (not *linear*) that distinguishes it from **multiple regression analysis** with its multiple independent variables.

Listing. The process by which the assessor ensures that records for the taxable property identified during **discovery** are preserved with **integrity**, available for use in **valuation** activities, and ultimately reflected in the **assessment roll**.

Locational obsolescence. A component of **economic obsolescence**; loss in value due to suboptimal siting of an **improvement**.

Location variable. A **variable**, such as the distance to the nearest commercial district or the traffic count on an adjoining street, that seeks to measure the **contribution** of locational factors to the total property value.

Logarithm; log. The number that, when used as an **exponent** for another number (called the base), results in a third number of some practical interest (called the antilogarithm). There are two bases that are used with any frequency; the base 10 produces what are called common logarithms, and the base 2.71828 (e) produces what are called natural logarithms. For example, $\log_{10} 100 = 2$; $10^2 = 100$. Logarithms were originally used to simplify complex calculations involving multiplica-

tions inasmuch as two numbers can be multiplied by adding their logarithms and taking the antilog of the result. Logarithms are also used as means of transforming variables in regression analysis.

Log-linear relationship. A **correlation** between two **variables** such that if the **value** of one variable changes by a certain percentage, the value of the other changes by a certain amount. (Recall that **logarithms** permit multiplication to be done by means of adding logs.) For example, there is a log-linear relationship between x and y in the following sequence:

x	5	6	7	8
y	20	30	45	67.5

Long run. A planning period long enough for a firm to be able to vary quantities of all resources it uses.

Macroeconomics. The economics of the economy as a whole—the forces causing recession, depression, and inflation together with the forces resulting in economic growth.

Mann-Whitney test. A test in **inferential statistics**, similar to the **Kruskal-Wallis test**, that seeks to determine whether the differences in values between two sets of observations from any population are statistically significant.

Map book and page system. A system for parcel identification in which a code (usually numeric) is used to identify each parcel, each code containing four elements: the volume or book of maps in which the parcel is to be found, the page on which it is to be found, the block, and the individual parcel on the block.

Marginal cost. The change in a firm's total costs per unit change in its output level.

Marginal physical product. The change in total output of a firm resulting from a one-unit change in the employment of a resource, holding the quantities of other resources constant.

Marginal revenue. The change in a firm's total revenue per unit change in its sales level. It is price in **pure competition** only.

Marginal unit. The last unit added to any economic process.

Marginal utility. The change in the total **utility** to a consumer that results from a one-unit change in the consumption level of an item.

Marginal utility theory. A theory of consumer choice that says that consumers will maximize welfare by allocation of their budget such that the **marginal utility** per dollar is equalized across all purchased goods.

Market. The "place" in which buyers and sellers interact. The collective body of buyers and sellers for a particular product.

Market price. The price a particular buyer and seller agree to in a particular transaction.

Market rent. The rent currently prevailing in the **market** for properties comparable to the **subject property**. Market rent is capitalized into an estimate of value in the **income approach**.

Market system. A type of economic system in which the questions of what to produce, for whom, and how are decided by the workings of an open and competitive **market**.

Market value. The most probable sale price of a property in terms of money in a competitive and open **market**, assuming that the buyer and seller are acting prudently and knowledgeably, allowing sufficient time for the sale, and assuming that the transaction is not affected by undue pressures.

Market-value standard. A requirement of law or practice that the **assessment ratio** of all properties be equal to 1. Two issues are implicit here: that fractional assessment levels be avoided and that all property be assessed on the basis of its **market value** and not on the basis of its value in some particular use—for example, agriculture—unless that use is the only use to which the property can legally be put (in which case its **use value** would be equal to its market value).

Mass appraisal. The process of valuing a group of properties as of a given date, using standard methods, and allowing for statistical testing.

Mean. The result of adding all the **values** of a **variable** and dividing by the number of values. For example, the arithmetic mean of 3, 5, and 10 is 18 divided by 3, or 6. Also called arithmetic mean.

Median. The midpoint or middle **value** when a set of values is ranked in order of magnitude; if the number of values is even, the midpoint or average of the two middle values.

Median absolute deviation. The **median** of the absolute deviations from the median. In a symmetrical distribution, the measure approximates one-half the **interquartile range**.

Median percent deviation. The **median** of the absolute percent deviations from the median; calculated by dividing the median absolute deviation by one hundredth of the median.

Mercator projection. Refers to one of several mathematical projections of the curved surface of the earth on an imaginary cylinder, which is then flattened. The original Mercator projection was on a cylinder the axis of which was in a north-south direction. Transverse Mercator projections are on imaginary cylinders with an east-west orientation. Transverse Mercator projections are more common than the original Mercator projection. In addition to the **universal transverse Mercator** (UTM) projection, there are the modified transverse Mercator system (MTMS), and the state transverse Mercator (STM) system.

Metes and bounds. Measurement of angles and distances; a description of a **parcel** of land accomplished by beginning at a known reference point, proceeding to a point on the perimeter of the property being described, and then tracing the boundaries until one returns to the first point on the perimeter, usually a corner. The angles are described by reference to points of the compass, and the distances are described in feet or chains; curves are treated as arcs on a circle.

Microeconomics. The economics of units, such as firms and neighborhoods, of an economic system (as opposed to **macroeconomics**, which studies the economy as a whole).

Mill, millage. One mill is one-thousandth of one dollar or one-tenth of one cent. In many states, the tax rate is expressed as mills per dollar. For example, a 2 percent tax rate is $2 per $100, $20 per $1000, or 20 mills per dollar.

Mineral rights. The right to extract ore, petroleum, or other minerals from a property.

Minkowski metric. Any of a family of possible ways of measuring distance. **Euclidean distance**, a member of this family, uses the straight-line distances (as the crow flies) squared. In mass appraisal model building, Minkowski metric usually refers to the sum of absolute differences (not squared) in each dimension, and resembles a "taxicab" or city block pattern. Other alternatives are possible, including the distance as calculated only for the dimension of greatest difference, but the city block distance is most common.

Mode. The value most often assumed by a **variable**. By extension for grouped **data**, the class in which a plurality of the observations fall.

Model. A representation of how something works. For purposes of appraisal, a representation (in words or an equation) that explains the relationship between value or estimated sale price and **variables** representing **supply and demand factors**.

Money market. The interaction of buyers and sellers of short-term credit instruments.

Monument. A term used in land surveying and geodesy to mean a permanent object placed in the ground marking a point, the location of which is known, on the surface of the earth. *See also* **geodetic control network**.

Mortgage coefficient. A component of the basic rate in the Ellwood variant of **mortgage-equity analysis**.

Mortgage constant. Annual **debt service** expressed as a percentage of the initial principal amount of the loan.

Mortgage-equity analysis. A technique used to estimate the value of a property from a knowledge of the equity **yield rate**, typical mortgage terms (including the interest rate, the loan-to-value ratio, the term of the loan, and the amortization provisions), the **holding period**, and the percentage by which the property will **appreciate** or **depreciate** over the holding period.

Moving average. A **statistic** used to smooth the values of a **variable** when those values are erratic over distance or time, as in the case of land values and mortgage commitments. For example, a five-block simple moving average of land values along a major street would assign to block 16 the average of the values for blocks 14–18; it would assign to block 17 the average of the values for blocks 15–19, and so on.

Multicollinearity. The phenomenon of two or more **variables** being correlated. If the two correlated variables are both **independent variables** (note that if they are correlated they are not truly *independent* in the relationship sense) used to predict the value of some other, dependent variable, then modeling problems will arise. If the multicollinearity is perfect, the **multiple regression** algorithms simply will not work; if the multicollinearity is serious but imperfect, the coefficients generated by the **algorithm** will be individually meaningless (although the **model** as a whole may still be useful).

Multiple regression, multiple regression analysis (MRA). A particular statistical technique, similar to **correlation**, used to analyze **data** in order to predict the value of one **variable** (the **dependent variable**), such as **market value**, from the known values of other variables (called **independent variables**), such as lot size, number of rooms, and so on. If only one independent variable is used, the procedure is called simple regression analysis and differs from correlation analysis only in that correlation measures the strength of relationship, whereas regression predicts the value of one variable from the value of the other. When two or more variables are used, the procedure is called multiple regression analysis. *See* **linear regression**.

Multiplicative model. A model in which the **coefficients** of **independent variables** serve as powers (**exponents**) to which the independent variables are raised or in which independent variables themselves serve as exponents; the results are then multiplied to estimate the value of the **dependent variable**.

Multiplicative transformation. A **transformation** of a set of **variables** accomplished by multiplying a variable by one or more other variables. For example, room area is a multiplicative transformation of length and width.

Multivariate statistical technique. Any of a number of statistical analyses in which **data** (such as the information on a single property record card) containing a number of **variables** (such as lot size, number of rooms, construction type) are analyzed to predict the value of some other variable. *See also* **multiple regression analysis**.

Municipal notes. Short-term promises to pay issued by local governments.

Natural logarithm. *See* **logarithm**.

Neighborhood. The environment of a subject property that has a direct and immediate effect on value. A geographic area (in which there are typically fewer than several thousand properties) defined for some useful purpose, such as to ensure for later multiple regression modeling that the properties are **homogeneous** and share important locational characteristics.

Neighborhood binary variable. A **binary variable** used in a valuation **model** to separate the effects on **value** of distinct neighborhoods.

Net operating income. Annual net income after **operating expenses** are subtracted from **effective gross income**. Does not include payments for **interest** or principal.

NOI. *See* **net operating income**.

Nominal. Pertaining to the named or stated value of something.

Nominal tax rate. The stated tax rate, which does not necessarily correspond to the **effective tax rate**.

Nonparametric statistic. A **statistic** whose interpretation or reliability does not depend on the distribution of the underlying **data**.

Normal distribution. A theoretical **frequency distribution** often approximated in real world situations. It is symmetrical and bell-shaped; 68 percent of the observations occur within one **standard deviation** of the **mean** and 95 percent within two standard deviations of the mean.

Normal goods. Goods, the consumption of which increases as consumers' income increases.

Null hypothesis. An **hypothesis** that one chooses to accept in the absence of sufficient evidence to the contrary.

Numerator. In a fractional expression, the number that is divided by some other number. For example, 3 is the numerator of the fraction 3/4.

Objective. The quality of being definable by specific criteria without the need for judgment. **Quantitative** variables are objective.

Observation. One recording or occurrence of the value of a **variable**, for example, one **sale ratio** among a **sample** of sales ratios.

Observed condition breakdown method. A method for estimating total **depreciation** by specifying the amount of each kind of depreciation, often for each major building component.

Observed depreciation method. A method for estimating total **depreciation** intuitively, in the aggregate by, for example, specifying **percent good**.

Obsolescence. A kind of **depreciation**. *See also* **economic obsolescence** and **functional obsolescence**.

Off-line equipment. Computing machinery not under the direct control of the computer's **central processing unit**.

On-line. *See* **interactive**.

Open market. A freely competitive market in which any buyer or seller may trade and in which prices are determined by **competition**.

Operating expenses. Expenses necessary to maintain the flow of income from a property. These are deducted from **effective gross income** to obtain **net operating income**, which is then capitalized in the **income approach** to obtain an indication of **market value**. Such expenses generally include the costs of property insurance; heat, water, and other utilities; repairs and maintenance; reserves for the replacement of such items as heat and air-conditioning systems, water heaters, built-in appliances, elevators, roofing, floor coverings, and other items whose **economic life** will expire before that of the structure itself; management; and other miscellaneous items necessary to operate and maintain the property. Not considered operating expenses are **depreciation** charges, **debt service**, income taxes, capital improvements, and personal or business expenses of the owner. In addition, for assessment purposes property taxes are usually treated as an adjustment to the **capitalization rate** rather than an expense item.

Opportunity cost. The principle that the cost of a resource for one use is the value of the resource in its best alternative use.

Optical character recognition. The ability of some kinds of computing machinery to translate a written symbol, such as a handwritten number or a letter typed on one of a few standard typewriters, into electrical pulses processable by the rest of the machinery, thereby avoiding the necessity for keypunching.

Outliers. **Observations** that have unusual values, that is, they differ markedly from a measure of **central tendency**. Some outliers occur naturally; others are due to **data** errors.

Outputs. (1) Goods produced by a firm. (2) The information returned by a computer to its user.

Overall rate. A **capitalization rate** that blends all requirements of **discount, recapture**, and **effective tax rates** for both land and improvements.

Parameter. Numerical descriptive measures of the **population**, for example, the **arithmetic mean** or **standard deviation**. Parameters are generally unknown and estimated from **statistics** calculated from a **sample** of the population.

Parametric statistic. A statistic whose interpretation or reliability depends on the distribution of the underlying data.

Parcel. A contiguous area of land described in a single description or as one of a number of lots on a **plat**; separately owned, either publicly or privately; and capable of being separately conveyed.

Parcel identification system. The scheme by which parcel identifiers are generated. Parcel identifiers are constructed from elements referring to surveying systems, map projection systems, map-page numbers, and geographic areas.

Parcel identifier. A code, usually numerical, representing a specific land parcel's **legal description**. The purpose of parcel identifiers is to reduce legal descriptions to a uniform and manageable size, thereby facilitating record-keeping and handling. Also called parcel identification number (PIN).

Partial equilibrium. Equilibrium of individual economic units or subsections of the economy in light of constraints imposed from outside the unit.

Partial equilibrium analysis. An analysis of one unit of the economy in light of constraints imposed by economic forces outside the unit. An example would be a **highest and best use** analysis of vacant land where the land use is limited by zoning.

Partial interest. An **interest** (in **property**) that is less complete than a **fee simple** interest.

Partial payment factor. (Also known as the amortization or periodic repayment factor.) The equal periodic payment that has a present worth of $1, for a specified number of periods and at a specified discount rate.

Percentage lease. A lease that provides for rent payments to be based on a percentage of income (gross or net), usually with a guaranteed minimum payment.

Percent good. An estimate of the value of a property, expressed as a percentage of its **replacement cost**, after **depreciation** of all kinds has been deducted.

Percentile. The values that divide a set of **data** into specified percentages when the data are arrayed in ascending order. The tenth percentile is the value of the observation below which the lowest 10 percent of the values fall, the twentieth percentile is the value below which the lowest 20 percent of the values fall, and so forth.

Perfect competition. The requirements of **pure competition** plus an additional condition of perfect knowledge on the part of buyers and sellers about all activity in the marketplace.

Performance bond. Insurance issued by a third party to guarantee the satisfactory completion of a contract.

Perimeter sketch. A graphic presentation of the boundaries of a **property**, either the land or the buildings on the land.

Personal property. *See* **property**.

Photogrammetry. The making of maps based on aerial photographs taken under rigidly controlled conditions.

Physical deterioration. Loss in value caused by wear and tear.

Pilot testing. Attempting to determine the workability of a system by testing it under realistic operating conditions before abandoning the former system.

Planimetric map. An accurate depiction on a flat surface of the size and shape of a **parcel** from a curved surface.

Plat. A map intended to show the division of land into lots or **parcels**. Upon recordation with the appropriate authorities, land included in the plat can thenceforth be legally described by reference to the plat, omitting a **metes-and-bounds** description.

Plottage value. The value of combined parcels in excess of the sum of individual values.

Points. Prepaid **interest** on a loan; one point is equal to 1 percent of the amount of the loan. It is common to deduct points in advance of the loan, so that an individual pays interest on 100 percent of the loan but gets cash on, say, only 99 percent.

Polygon. A line chart.

Pooled regression. Combining two or more **strata** to form one regression **model**.

Population. All the items of interest, for example, all the properties in a jurisdiction or neighborhood.

Potential gross income. The sum of **potential gross rent** and miscellaneous income, that is, the income from rent and other sources that a property could generate with normal management, before allowing for vacancies, collection losses, and normal operating expenses.

Potential gross rent. The total rent a property would produce if 100 percent occupied at **market rent**.

PRD. *See* **price-related differential**.

Present worth. The value of something after discounting future payments and receipts.

Present worth of 1. (Also called the reversion factor.) The lump-sum amount that would have to be set aside to accumulate with compound *interest* to $1 at the end of a specified number of years and at a specified rate of interest. Alternatively, it can be viewed as the present value of $1 receivable at the end of a specified number of years and discounted at a specified rate.

Present worth of 1 per period. (Also called the annuity factor, or Inwood **coefficient**). The present worth of a series of payments of $1, receivable at the end of each year, for a specified number of years and at a specified **interest** rate.

Price equilibrium. In a specific period, that price at which the quantity that buyers want is exactly equal to the quantity that sellers want to sell.

Price-related differential. The **mean** divided by the **weighted mean**. The **statistic** has a slight **bias** upward. Price-related differentials above 1.03 tend to indicate assessment regressivity; price-related differentials below 0.98 tend to indicate **assessment progressivity**.

Procedural edit. An audit, or review of operations, intended to discover erroneous and inefficient practices.

Production function. The physical relation between a firm's resource **inputs** and the **output** of goods and services per unit of time.

Progressivity. *See* **assessment progressivity (regressivity)**.

Property.   An aggregate of things or rights to things. These rights are protected by law. There are two basic types of property: real and personal. *Real property* is the rights to land and improvements to the land. *Personal property* is all property other than real property; it is not permanently attached and is, therefore, movable.

Property residual technique.   A technique used to estimate the value of a property from a knowledge of its **net operating income**, **discount rate**, **remaining economic life**, the amount of the **reversion**, and the **income path** attributable to the property over the **holding period** (generally the remaining economic life of the property). The technique estimates total value by discounting anticipated income and adding the result to the present worth of the reversion.

Property split.   A result of the sale of a piece of **property** held by a single owner such that different pieces of the property are owned by different owners. Splits may or may not occur along **plat** lines. Assessors need to monitor splits not only to ensure the correctness of the property listing but also to monitor the land and its adequacy as a lien against past and present tax liabilities.

Property tax levy.   (1) The total amount of property tax that a local government needs to raise. (2) Loosely, by extension, the **millage** rate or the property tax bill sent to an individual property owner.

Pure competition.   A market situation in which (1) individual buyers or sellers of an item buy or sell an amount too small relative to the market to be able to influence the price of the good and (2) the units of the item are homogeneous.

Qualitative.   Pertaining to the **subjective** nature of some **variable** of interest, that is, something that can be rated but not objectively reduced to an unambiguous scale. For example, view is a qualitative factor.

Quality class.   A **subjective** classification of a structure by an appraiser; intended to describe materials used, workmanship, architectural attractiveness, functional design, and the like. Quality class, or its synonym *grade*, is the key variable in most **cost schedules**.

Quantitative.   Pertaining to the **objective** nature of some **variable** of interest, that is, something that can be measured or counted with little ambiguity. For example, number of bathrooms is a quantitative variable.

Quantity survey method.   A method of estimating **reproduction cost** in which a complete itemization is made of all labor and material costs by component and subcomponent and all indirect costs; these are added to obtain an estimate of the cost of a structure or a reasonable bid for a contractor to submit on a proposed project.

Quartiles.   The values that divide a set of data into four equal parts when the data are arrayed in ascending order. The first quartile is the value below which the lowest quarter of the data falls, the second quartile is the **median**, and so forth.

Quasi rent.   *See* **economic rent**.

Quotient transformation. A **transformation** of two or more **variables** accomplished by dividing one by the other. For example, the length of a room is a quotient transformation of its area and its width. Like the **multiplicative transformation**, many useful quotient transformations are less intuitively obvious than the one in the example given.

Random sample. A **sample** in which each item of the **population** has an equal chance of being included and, by extension, each possible combination of n items has an equal chance of occurrence.

Range. (1) The maximum value of a **sample** minus the minimum value. (2) The difference between the maximum and minimum values that a **variable** may assume.

Rank. The order of a set of values according to the value of each in relation to the other. For example, the numbers 0.95, 0.87, 1.09, and 0.83 have ranks of 3, 2, 4, 1.

Rate of return. *See* **discount rate**.

Ratio study. A study of the relationship between **appraised** or **assessed values** and **market values**. Indicators of market values may be either sales (**sales ratio study**) or independent "expert" appraisals (**appraisal ratio study**). Of common interest in ratio studies are the level and uniformity of the appraisals or assessments. *See also* **level of appraisal** and **level of assessment**.

Read-and-write instruction. A kind of command embedded in a computer program that has the capability of both accessing a data file and altering it.

Read-only instruction. A kind of command embedded in a computer program that has the capability only of accessing the records in a data file, not of altering them.

Real estate transfer documents. The various kinds of deeds whereby real property is conveyed.

Real property. *See* **property**.

Real property transfer tax. The tax payable to a state (and sometimes to a locality) upon the sale of real estate and the recordation of the transfer. The payment is usually proportional to the sale price and is commonly used by appraisers in the absence of more accurate information to deduce the price for which the property sold.

Reappraisal. The **mass appraisal** of all property within an assessment jurisdiction accomplished within or at the beginning of an **reappraisal cycle** (sense 2). Also called revaluation or reassessment.

Reappraisal cycle. (1) The period of time necessary for a jurisdiction to have a complete reappraisal. For example, a cycle of five years occurs when one-fifth of a jurisdiction is reappraised each year and also when a jurisdiction is reappraised all at once every five years. (2) The maximum interval between reappraisals as stated in laws.

Reciprocal. The result obtained when 1 is divided by a given number. For example, the reciprocal of 4 is 0.25. Factors are reciprocals of rates.

Rectangular survey system. *See* **federal rectangular survey system**.

Rectify. To reconcile photographs or other representations of a curved surface, such as the earth, in order to form a single, two-dimensional representation, such as a map, of the surface features on the curved object.

Region of rejection. In tests of hypotheses, that range in which one has at least the specified degree of confidence that a calculated statistic will *not* fall when the **null hypothesis** is true.

Regression analysis. *See* **multiple regression analysis**.

Regression coefficient. The **coefficient** calculated by the regression **algorithm** for the data supplied that, when multiplied by the value of the **variable** with which it is associated, will predict (for simple regression) or help to predict (for multiple regression) the value of the **dependent variable**. For example, in the equation, Value = $10,000 + $5,000 × number of rooms, $5,000 is a regression coefficient.

Regression line. The line on a graph that represents the relationship defined by the regression coefficients. For example, the line from the relationship given in the definition of **regression coefficient** would cross the y-axis at the value $10,000 and would go up $5,000 for each movement of 1 to the right. This example illustrates one of the subtleties required in understanding regression analysis: in fact, there is no line, because the **independent variable** is not a **continuous variable**, but it is easier to talk about the relationship by pretending that the variable is continuous and represent the relationship by a line

rather than the more nearly correct series of vertical bars on a bar chart.

Regressivity. *See* **assessment progressivity (regressivity)**.

Regressivity index. *See* **price-related differential**.

Reject code. A flag applied to a record indicating that it should not be used for certain purposes.

Relationship. The phenomenon whereby knowledge of the value of one **variable** tells you something about the probable value of another. (*See* **correlation**.) Relationships may be positive (an increase in one value implies an increase in the other) or negative (a change in one value implies a change in the other direction for the other). Independence of two variables means that there is no relationship between them.

Remaining economic life. The number of years remaining in the economic life of a building or other improvement as of the date of the appraisal. This period is influenced by the attitudes of **market** participants and by market reactions to competitive properties on the market.

Replacement cost. The cost, including material, labor, and overhead, that would be incurred in constructing an improvement having the same utility to its owner as the improvement in question, without necessarily reproducing exactly any particular characteristic of the property.

Replacement reserve. An allowance in an annual operating statement for replacement of short-lived items that will not last for the **remaining economic life** of a property.

Representative sample. A **sample** of **observations** from a larger **population** of observations, such that **statistics** calculated from the sample can be expected to represent the characteristics of the population being studied.

Reproduction cost. The cost, including material, labor, and overhead, that would be incurred in constructing an improvement having exactly the same characteristics as the improvement in question.

Repurchase agreement. A short-term financing arrangement whereby those needing funds sell securities but agree to repurchase them at a fixed price at a specific time.

Required rate of return on equity. A component of the **discount rate**, as it is understood from the point of view of **band-of-investment analysis**, and a component of the **overall rate** developed according to **mortgage-equity analysis**.

Reserve requirement. The amount that a commercial bank that is a member of the Federal Reserve System must keep on deposit in the Federal Reserve Bank of its region.

Residual. The difference between an observed value and a predicted value for a **dependent variable**.

Revaluation. *See* **reappraisal**.

Reversion. The value of a property at the end of a **holding period**.

Review. *See* **assessment review**.

Sale price. The price for which a **property** was sold.

Sale ratio. The ratio of an appraised (or assessed) value to the sale price or **adjusted sale price** of a property.

Sales comparison approach. One of **three approaches to value**, the sales comparison approach estimates a property's **value** (or some other characteristic, such as its **depreciation**) by reference to **comparable sales**.

Sales data. Information about the nature of the transaction, the **sale price**, and the characteristics of a property as of the date of sale.

Sales file. A file of sales data.

Sales ratio study. A **ratio study** that uses **sales prices** as proxies for **market values**.

Sample. A set of **observations** selected from a **population**. If the sample was randomly selected, basic concepts of probability may be applied. *See also* **random sample** and **representative sample**.

Scale. The reduction ratio that characterizes a particular map. A ratio of 1:100, for example, is said to be a larger scale than 1:1,000.

Scatter diagram or scatterplot. A graphic means of depicting the relationship or **correlation** between two **variables** by plotting the values of one variable on the horizontal axis and the values of the other variable on the vertical axis. Often in **ratio studies** it is informative to determine how ratios are related to other variables. A variable of interest is plotted on the horizontal axis, and ratios are plotted on the vertical axis.

Schedules. Tables, equations, or some other means of presenting the relationship between the values of two or more **variables** that are functionally related. For example, **cost schedules** present the relationship between cost per square foot and living area for a number of **quality classes**, building heights, and other characteristics.

Secondary mortgage markets. A market in which the originator of a mortgage, such as a local savings bank, may sell it to another investor, such as a pension fund.

Short run. A planning period so short that a firm is unable to vary the quantities of some of the resources that it uses.

Significance. A measure of the probability that an event is attributable to a relationship rather than merely the result of chance.

Single-property appraisal. Appraisal of properties one at a time.

Sinking fund. A real or hypothetical fund or pool of money into which deposits are periodically made; these deposits, together with the compound **interest** they earn, are projected to accumulate to a given amount on a given date. Some sinking funds are dedicated to a particular purpose, such as replacing a heating system; others are simply convenient ways of thinking about flows of money.

Sinking-fund factor. The amount that must be periodically set aside to accumulate with compound interest to $1 at the end of a specified number of years and at a specified interest rate. The sinking-fund factor is sometimes known (in connection with **annuity** capitalization) as the capital recovery rate.

Site characteristics. Characteristics of (and **data** that describe) a particular property, especially land size, shape, topography, drainage, and so on, as opposed to location and external economic forces. By extension, any characteristics of either the site or the improvement.

Situs. The actual or assumed location of a property for purposes of taxation.

Skewed. The quality of a **frequency distribution** that makes it asymmetrical. Distributions with longer tails on the right than on the left are said to be skewed to the right or to be positively skewed; distributions with longer tails to the left are said to be skewed to the left or to be negatively skewed.

Slope. The change in the **dependent variable** associated with a change of 1 in the **independent variable** of interest. The slope is given by the **coefficient** of the independent variable.

Software. (1) Computer programs. (2) Those parts of a computer system that are not machinery or circuits; thus procedures and possibly documentation are included along with programs.

Spearman rank test. A standard nonparametic test useful in examining assessment **bias**, among other things. It is based upon the **correlation** of two sets of ranks.

Split. *See* **property split**.

Standard deviation. The **statistic** calculated from a set of numbers by subtracting the **mean** from each value and squaring the remainders, adding together these squares, dividing by the size of the **sample** less one, and taking the square root of the result. When the data are normally distributed, one can calculate the percentage of observations within any number of standard deviations of the mean from normal probability tables. When the data are not normally distributed, the standard deviation is less meaningful and should be used with caution.

Standard error. A measure of the precision of a measure of **central tendency**; the smaller the standard error, the more reliable the measure of central tendency. Standard errors are used in calculating a **confidence interval** about the **arithmetic mean** and the **weighted mean**.

Standard error of the estimate (SEE). An expression for the **standard deviation** of the observed values about the **regression line**; thus it provides an estimate of the variation likely to be encountered in making predictions from the regression equation.

Standardize. (1) To transform a **variable** to standard form; that is, to make the **mean** of the **frequency distribution** equal to zero and the **standard deviation** equal to one. (2) To adjust, for appraisal purposes, reported data such as income and expenses, so as to remove the effects of non-real estate factors, such as abnormally good or bad management, weather, and the like. The more common term for this adjustment process is normalization.

State plane coordinates. Geographic coordinates based on the **state plane coordinate system**.

State plane coordinate system. A mathematical projection of the curved surface of the earth on a flat surface over which a coordinate grid expressed in feet is laid. State plane coordinate systems have been established for all fifty states, and within each state there are one or more separate projections of areas known as *zones*. The boundaries of state plane coordinate zones are coterminous with county and state boundaries, an administrative advantage in that counties are never required to use more than one state plane coordinate zone.

State property tax tribunal. A quasi-judicial administrative review agency organized by at least one state (Michigan) to separate the state's **review** and **appeal** responsibilities from its administrative and equalization functions.

Statistics. (1) Numerical descriptions calculated from a **sample**, for example, the **median, mean**, or **coefficient of dispersion**. Statistics are used to estimate corresponding measures, termed **parameters**, for the **population**. (2) The science of studying numerical data systematically and of presenting the results usefully. Two main branches exist: **descriptive statistics** and **inferential statistics**.

Stepwise regression analysis. A kind of **multiple regression analysis** in which the **independent variables** enter the **model**, and leave it if appropriate, one by one according to their ability to improve the equation's power to predict the value of the **dependent variable**.

Straight-line capitalization. A means of estimating value whereby **net operating income** is divided by a capitalization rate composed of the **discount rate**, the **reciprocal** of **remaining economic life** as the recapture rate, and sometimes the effective tax rate. The method implicitly assumes that net operating income will decline by an equal dollar amount each year.

Straight-line method. A method of amortizing investments and other sources of **cash flows** so that equal amounts are attributed to each of several equal intervals of time.

Straight-line recapture. The recovery of capital invested in a wasting asset in equal periodic amounts over the **remaining economic life** of the asset.

Stratify. To divide, for purposes of analysis, a **sample** of **observations** into two or more subsets according to some criterion or set of criteria.

Stratum, strata (pl.). A **class** or **subset** that results from stratification.

Subject property. The **property** being appraised.

Subjective. Having the quality of requiring judgment in arriving at an appropriate answer or value for a **variable** (such as the **quality class** of a structure). *See also* **objective, qualitative,** and **quantitative**.

Subset. A group of properties within a **sample**, smaller than the sample, usually although not necessarily defined by stratification rather than by sampling.

Substitute goods. Goods related in such a way that an increase in consumption of one decreases consumption of the other.

Substitution. A principle stating that a property's value tends to be set by the cost of acquiring an equally desirable substitute.

Sum of squared errors. The sum of the squared deviations from the predicted values (rather than the **mean** value).

Sum of squares. The result obtained by adding all the squares of the individual deviations from some given value. Usually it is the sum of the squares of the deviations of the individual values of a **variable** from the mean value.

Summation approach. *See* **cost approach**.

Supply. A schedule showing the amount of a good or productive service that would be offered for sale at various prices during a given period.

Surplus productivity. The income remaining after the costs of labor, capital, and management have been paid.

Surplus value. The value of a commodity over and above the quantity of labor required to produce it.

Tangible property. Actual physical property (real or personal) in contrast to **intangible property**.

Task force. A kind of organizational unit, usually temporary, composed of employees from different functional areas whose assignment is usually some kind of nonroutine task, such as assisting in a system development effort.

Tax base. The total of all the **assessed values** in a given community.

Tax levy. *See* **property tax levy**.

Tax rate. The percentage of assessed value at which each property is taxed in a given district.

Terminal. The **on-line** device used to communicate with a computer.

Three approaches to value. A convenient way to group the various methods of appraising a property. The **cost approach** encompasses several methods for estimating **replacement cost** of an **improvement** less **depreciation** plus land value. The **sales comparison approach** estimates values by comparison with similar properties for which sales prices are known. The methods included in the **income approach** are based on the assumption that value equals the present worth of the rights to future income.

Time-adjusted sale price. The price at which a property sold adjusted for the effects of price changes reflected in the **market** between the date of sale and the date of analysis.

Time value of money. The principle that an amount of money receivable or anticipated as income in the future is always worth less than an equal amount actually in hand at the present time.

Title. The union of all elements constituting proof of ownership or the instrument that is evidence of ownership.

Tolerance. An acceptable margin of error or inaccuracy.

Transformation. The process of changing the values and definitions of one or more **variables** so as to make them more useful for further analyses. If **market value** changes with living area, for example, a valuable transformation would be to change length and width to area, and if market value does not change proportionally with area, a valuable transformation might be to use the logarithm of area.

Transverse Mercator coordinates. Geographic coordinates based on a transverse Mercator projection and usually expressed in meters. *See also* **Mercator projection; universal transverse Mercator**.

Treasury bills. Short-term debt obligations of the United States treasury.

Trended original cost. The cost of constructing an **improvement** at a particular time, adjusted to reflect inflation and deflation, as well as changes in construction costs, between that time and the present.

Trending. Adjusting the values of a **variable** for the effects of time. Usually used to refer to adjustments of assessments intended to reflect the effects of inflation and deflation and sometimes also, but not necessarily, the effects of changes in the **demand** for microlocational goods and services.

Triangular-lot table. A schedule of adjustments used to appraise a lot having a triangular shape (in whole or in part) by comparison with a **base lot** or a given unit factor, such as a front-foot rate.

t-statistic. A particular **statistic** important in **inferential statistics** for certain kinds of **hypothesis** testing of certain kinds of data.

t-test. A particular **parametric** statistical test useful, among other things, in testing the **level of assessment**.

Two-tailed test. A test in which the alternative **hypothesis** does not specify the direction of the relationship, as opposed to a one-tailed test, in which the direction of relationship is specified. For example, the alternative hypothesis that *a* does not equal *b* implies a two-tailed test, whereas *a* is greater than *b* implies a one-tailed test. *See also* **null hypothesis**.

United States Federal Reserve System. A governmental regulatory agency with responsibility for maintaining the health of the economy through its regulation of the money supply and rate of **interest**.

United States Public Land Survey. The land survey begun by the United States Congress in 1785 upon which the **federal rectangular survey system** is based.

Unit-in-place method. A method of cost estimating in which all the direct and some of the indirect costs of each individual construction component (such as the foundation walls) are specified in appropriate units (such as area, volume, or length), multiplied by an estimate of the quantity required by the particular structure, and added to obtain an estimate of the cost of the structure. *Compare* **comparative unit method** (sense 2) and **quantity survey method**.

Unit-value method. *See* **average-unit-value method**.

Universal transverse Mercator. The transverse Mercator projection used in the United States. Universal transverse Mercator projection zones are 6 degrees of longitude wide and cross civil boundaries. *See also* **Mercator projection**.

Unweighted mean. *See* **weighted mean**.

Usable area. The area of land that can be used, or the equivalent area after allowance for irregular topography.

Use class. (1) One of the following **classes** of property: single-family residential, multifamily residential, agricultural, commercial, industrial, vacant land, and institutional/exempt. (2) Any subclass refinement of the above—for example, townhouse, detached single-family, condominium, house on farm, and so on.

Use code. A code to indicate a property's **use class** or, less often, potential use.

Use value. The value of property for a specific use.

Use-value (farmland) assessment laws. Laws that require or permit assessors to appraise and assess property as though the property were subject to an enforceable restriction that forbade putting the land (or the entire property) to any use but the present one. Typically there is no such permanent enforceable restriction, but assessors may nevertheless be required to assess certain property types, especially agricultural land, and to a lesser extent historic properties, as though the restriction were real. In such instances the **sales comparison approach** may be inapplicable, and a version of the **income approach** may be required.

U-test. *See* **Mann-Whitney test**.

Utility. The satisfaction obtained from the goods and services that a consumer consumes.

UTM. Universal transverse Mercator.

Validity. The quality of a **data** element or procedure being what it should be in terms of some ultimate purpose or use. *See also* **integrity**.

Valuation. The process or business of appraising, of making estimates of the value of something. The value usually required to be estimated is **market value**.

Value. (1) Any number between positive infinity and negative infinity. (2) The monetary worth of something. (3) The estimate sought in a **valuation**. *See also* **market value**.

Value in exchange. The amount an informed purchaser would offer in exchange for a property under given market conditions.

Value in use. *See* **use value**.

Variable. An item of observation that can assume various values, for example, square feet, **sales prices**, or **sales ratios**. Variables are commonly described using measures of **central tendency** and dispersion.

Variable costs. The costs of the **variable resources** used by a firm in either the short run or the long run.

Variable proportions, law of. An economic principle stating: When the quantity of one productive service is increased in equal increments, while the quantities of other productive services remain fixed, the resulting increment of product will decrease after a certain point.

Variable resources. The resources used by a firm that can change in quantity in either the short run or the long run.

Variance. A measure of dispersion equal to the **standard deviation** squared.

Variation. (1) A general term meaning **dispersion**. (2) A reference to a particular **statistic** called the **coefficient of variation**.

Verify. To check the accuracy of something. For example, **sales data** may be verified by interviewing the purchaser of the property, and data entries may be verified by **check digits**.

Vertical inequity. Differences in the **levels of assessment** of properties related to the value ranges of the properties. That is, properties of higher value have assessment levels different from properties of lower value. *See* **horizontal inequity**.

Warranty deed. A deed conveying to the grantee **title** to the property free and clear of all encumbrances except those stated in the deed itself.

Wasting asset. A property or other thing of value whose value diminishes with the passage of time. For example, buildings are a wasting asset, but land and gold, traditionally, are not.

Weighted coefficient of dispersion. The **coefficient of dispersion** when the absolute differences between individual **assessment ratios** and the **measure of central tendency** (for example, **median** ratio) are weighted on the basis of sale price.

Weighted coefficient of variation. The **coefficient of variation** when the squared differences between individual **assessment ratios** and the **arithmetic mean** ratio are weighted on the basis of sale price.

Weighted mean; weighted average. An average in which the **observations** are weighted based on some criterion. In **ratio studies**, the weighted mean is calculated by weighting the ratios based on their sales prices. A shortcut method is to sum the appraisals or assessments, sum the sales prices, and divide the first result by the second.

Yield capitalization. Any of several methods used in the **income approach** to appraising. Yield methods involve certain subtleties and assumptions that vary according to the particular method employed, but include estimating such factors as the **required rate of return** on investment, the **remaining economic life** of the property, an investment **holding period**, the **income path**, anticipated **depreciation** or **appreciation**, and reversionary value. The yield methods stand in contrast to direct sales analysis methods, in which a typical relationship between incomes and sales prices is found by simply dividing observed incomes by sales prices for **comparable** properties, the fraction thus obtained then being applied (in the form of a **gross income multiplier** or an **overall rate**) to the properties being appraised. *See also* **building residual technique, discount rate, mortgage-equity analysis**, and **property residual technique**.

Yield rate. The required rate of return on equity capital; this is a component of the **capitalization rate** (or **discount rate** or mortgage-equity **overall rate**) that must be separately specified in **band-of-investment analysis** and **mortgage-equity analysis**.

z-statistic. The number calculated in a *z*-test, whose **significance** is evaluated by reference to a *z-table*.

z-table. A table of critical values associated with the *z-test*.

z-test. A test of any of a number of hypotheses in inferential statistics that has validity if sample size is sufficiently large and the underlying data are normally distributed.

List of Symbols and Equations

Symbols

Alphabetic

a. Consumer goods. Productive services (subscript).

a_n. Present worth of one per period.

A. Appraisal.

ADJ_c. Adjustments to comparable properties.

AGE. Age.

AGESQFT. Product of age and square feet.

AMENITY. Dollar value of unattached amenities.

AP. Adjusted price.

APC. Average absolute percent change.

app. Fractional increase in value over the holding period.

A/S. Appraisal-sale price ratio.

$\overline{A/S}$. Mean appraisal-sale price ratio.

$\overline{\overline{A/S}}$. Weighted mean appraisal sale-price ratio.

$\widetilde{A/S}$. Median appraisal-sale price ratio.

AUTO. Binary variable for auto sales or service business.

b. Consumer goods. Productive services (subscript).

b_0. Constant term in a regression equation.

b_i, b_j. Coefficients of variables in a regression equation.

B. Building.

BA. Building additive variable.

B_A. Building addition costs.

B_C. Constant building component costs.

BA_H. Horizontal building component costs.

BA_V. Vertical building component costs.

BATHS. Number of baths.

BeA. Adjustments for bedroom.

BED/UNIT. Bedrooms per unit.

BQ. Building qualitative variable.

BSIZE or *Bsize*. Building size.

BV. Building value.

c. Comparable (subscript).

C. (1) Cost. (2) Mortgage coefficient from *C* table.

CA. Adjustment for condition.

CLASS. Percentages of land in a soil classification.

COD, $\widetilde{COD}$, $\overline{COD}$, $\overline{COD}_w$. Coefficient of dispersion. $\widetilde{COD}$ means that it was calculated about the median, $\overline{COD}$ means that it was calculated about the mean, and $\overline{COD}_w$ means that it was calculated about the weighted mean.

COMPLEXn. Binary variable for a complex of properties.

COND. Scalar variable for condition.

CONV. Binary variable for convenience or fast food store.

CT. Constant building component (subscript).

d. Demand, demand factor.

d_F. Vector of demand factors.

D. Depreciation.

dep. Fractional decline in value over the holding period.

DF. Damping factor.

DISTCBD. Distance to central business district.

DS. Debt service.

e. Error.

E. Expected frequency.

EFFAGE. Effective age.

EGI. Effective gross income.

EGR. Effective gross rent.

ENDUNIT. End unit.

ESP. Estimated sale price.

ETR. Effective tax rate.

EXP. Expense.

f. Function.

F. (1) Cost trend factor. (2) Symbol for the *F*-statistic.

FF/GF. Ratio of front feet of land area to ground floor building area.

FINBASE. Finished basement area.

FRPL. Fireplace.

GA. Adjustment for garage type.

GARAGE. Number of garage stalls.

GARSQFT. Garage area.

GAR/UNIT. Garages per living unit.

GI. Gross income.

GIM. Gross income multiplier.

GOLF. Binary variable for golf course view.

GQ. General qualitative variable.

GRM. Gross rent multiplier.

h. Tolerance for error expressed as a percentage.

H. Statistic calculated in a Kruskal-Wallis test.

H_0, H_1. Null hypothesis and alternative hypothesis, respectively.

i. (1) The particular number of an observation (subscript). *See also j.* (2) Interest. (3) Annual rate of inflation.

I. Income.

I_b. Base index.

I_c. Cost index.

IA. Adjustment for inflation.

INSIDE. Aggregated variable for interior amenities.

IRREG. Binary variable for irregular topography.

IRRIG. Binary variable for irrigation.

ISIZE. Size of an improvement.

IV. Improvement value.

j. The particular number of an observation (subscript). *See also i.* When double subscripts are used, as in b_{ij}, *i* denotes the row and *j* denotes the column of the table in which the value of the variable of interest may be found.

k. (1) The rank of a particular variable. (2) A count of the number of observations in a sample, as in b_1, b_2, . . . , b_k (subscript or variable). *See also n; p.*

L. (1) Land. (2) Land value per square foot.

LA. Land additive variable.

ln. Natural logarithm.

LNAGE. Natural log of effective age.

LNLAND. Natural log of land area.

LOT. Lot.

LQ. Land qualitative variable.

LRATIO. Land-to-total value ratio.

LSIZE. Land size.

m. Loan-to-value ratio (Ellwood technique).

M. Building cost per square foot from cost manual.

MC. Marginal cost.

MPP. Marginal physical product.

MU. Marginal utility.

MV. Market value.

n. The count of the number of observations in a sample, as in $b_1, b_2, \ldots, b_n$ (subscript or variable). *See also k; p.*

NA. Adjustment for differences in neighborhoods.

NBHD. Neighborhood (usually a binary variable).

NOI. Net operating income.

O. Observed or actual frequencies.

OA. Other additions or improvements.

OAR. Overall rate.

OFFICE. Binary variable for office space.

OSIZE. Size of other additions.

OV. Value of other improvements or additions.

p. (1) Percentile. (2) A count of the particular number of variables or of observations in a sample (subscript or variable). *See also k; n.*

P. Price.

P_B. Building price.

P_I. Improvement price.

P_L. Land price.

PATSQFT. Patio area.

PERGOOD. Percent good.

PGR. Potential gross rent.

POOL. Pool area.

Q. Quantity.

QUAL. Qualitative scalar variable for construction quality.

QUALSQFT. Product of quality rating and square feet.

r. (1) Correlation coefficient. (2) Subscript for recalibrated value. (3) Monthly or quarterly rate of change.

R. Rate.

R^2. Coefficient of determination.

RCN. Replacement cost new.

RCNLD. Replacement cost new less depreciation.

REST. Binary variable for restaurant.

RM. Rate multiplier.

ROOMS. Number of rooms.

RP. Resale price.

s. (1) Supply or supply factor. (2) Standard deviation of a sample; in contrast, σ is used for standard deviation of a population.

s_F. Vector of supply factors.

s_j. Standard error of a regression coefficient b_j.

S. Sale price.

S^n. The future worth of one.

S_n. The future worth of one per period.

S/A. The reciprocal of the ratio of appraised value to sale price.

SB. Square feet of building area.

SEE. Standard error of the estimate.

SFF. Sinking fund factor at equity yield rate.

SFLA. Square feet of living area.

SIZE. Size.

SIZEADJ. Adjustment for size.

SL. Square feet of land.

SPC. Standard deviation of percent changes.

SQFT/UNIT. Square feet per unit.

SQFTZ. Square feet in thousands.

SQRTDIST. Square root of distance to a value influence center.

SQRTLAND. Square root of land area.

SQRTSF. Square root of square feet.

SSE. Sum of squared errors.

SSE_{EX}. Sum of squared errors explained by a model.

SSE_{UN}. Sum of squared errors unexplained by a model.

$STDSQFT$. Standardized square footage (actual divided by average).

t. (1) Time or a period. (2) Symbol for t-statistic.

TAS. Time-adjusted sale price.

$UNFBASE$. Unfinished basement area.

U-statistic. Statistic used in Mann-Whitney test.

V. Value.

V_c. Current value.

V_E. Present value of equity.

V_M. Mortgage balance.

V^n. Present worth of one factor.

V_O. Overall value.

V_p. Previous value.

$VIEWAV$ ($VIEWPR$, $VIEWGD$). Average (poor, good) view (qualitative variable).

w. A weight.

w_p. A weight assigned to previous year's value.

x. (1) Coordinate. (2) Any factor.

X. Any factor.

y. (1) Coordinate. (2) Any factor.

Y. (1) Any factor. (2) Equity yield rate.

Z. Symbol for the z-statistic.

Nonalphabetic

β Lower case Greek beta. Beta coefficient.

π Upper case Greek pi. Product sign.

σ Lower case Greek sigma. Standard deviation.

Σ Upper case Greek sigma. Summation sign.

$\ldots$ (ellipsis dots). And so on, that is, follow pattern established by values preceding and following the dots.

$\sim$ (tilde). Median or, loosely, calculated around the median.

$\hat{}$ (hat, or circumflex). An estimated or mathematically predicted value.

$\overline{}$ (overbar placed above a symbol). (1) Average, or arithmetic mean. (2) In $\overline{R}^2$, signifies that adjustments have been made for degrees of freedom.

$\#BATHS$. Number of baths.

$\%GOOD$. Percent good.

$\%D$. Depreciation factor.

General Models

The following models are applicable in all three approaches to value. The expansion of the simplest general model to the general hybrid model is shown in the text (pp. 317–19). The general hybrid model provides a framework for modeling value based on the underlying supply and demand factors in the relevant market.

The application of these models in the cost and sales comparison approaches is easy to understand. The box on p. 317 contains a proof of the income approach's reliance on supply and demand factors. The proof (for which additional equations are supplied below) provides a foundation for modeling market value, rates, rents, and expenses directly using the general hybrid model structure and relevant supply and demand factors.

Each equation is labeled with a number (or several numbers) that identifies the chapter and equation number. For example, (3.12) means chapter 3, equation 12. Several numbers signify that the equation is found in several places.

Expansion of Simple Model

$MV = IV + LV$ (4.10, 8.1, 13.1, 14.4, 15.1) additive, p. 105

$IV = P_I \times ISIZE$ (4.11, 14.5), p. 105

$LV = P_L \times LSIZE$ (4.12, 14.6), p. 105

$MV = P_I \times ISIZE + P_L \times LSIZE$ (4.13, 13.2, 14.7) additive, p. 105

$BV = (PB_1 \times BSIZE_1) + (PB_2 \times BSIZE_2) + \ldots + (PB_n \times BSIZE_n)$
(13.3, 14.8) additive, p. 310

$BV = BQ_1 \times BQ_2 \times \ldots \times BQ_n \times (PB_1 \times BSIZE_1 + \ldots + PB_n \times BSIZE_n)$
(14.9) multiplicative, p. 318

$LV = LQ_1 \times LQ_2 \times \ldots \times LQ_n \times (PL_1 \times LSIZE_1)$ (14.10) multiplicative, p. 319

$OV = (PO_1 \times OSIZE_1) + (PO_2 \times OSIZE_2) + \ldots + (PO_n \times OSIZE_n)$
(14.11) additive, p. 319

$MV = \pi GQ[(\pi BQ \times \Sigma BA) + (\pi LQ \times \Sigma LA) + \Sigma OA]$ (14.12, 15.2) hybrid, p. 319

Supply and Demand in the Income Approach

$$V = \frac{I - EXP}{R} \qquad \text{(p. 317)}$$

$$Rents = \int_{x=1,}^{n} \dot{s}_F \quad \overset{n}{d}_F \qquad \text{(p. 317)}$$

$$EXP = \int_{x=1,}^{n} \overset{n}{S_F}$$

$$V = \frac{\int s_F, \, d_F}{R}$$

$$V = \int RM \times s_F, \, d_F$$

Sales Comparison Models
Additive
General

$MV = S_c + ADJ_c$ (2.4, 6.1, 14.26), p. 34

$MV = b_0 + b_1 SFLA + b_2 \#BATHS$ (2.5), p. 34

$AP = S + BA + BeA + GA + IA + CA + NA$ (4.3), p. 85

$MV = IV + LV$ (4.10, 8.1, 13.1, 14.4, 15.1), p. 105

$MV = P_I \times ISIZE + P_L \times LSIZE$ (4.13, 13.2, 14.7), p. 105

$BV = (PB_1 \times BSIZE_1) + (PB_2 \times BSIZE_2) + \ldots + (PB_n \times BSIZE_n)$ (14.8), p. 318

$OV = (PO_1 \times OSIZE_1) + (PO_2 \times OSIZE_2) + \ldots + (PO_n \times OSIZE_n)$
   (14.11), p. 319

$MV = b_1 \times SQFT + b_2 \times QUAL$ (14.13), p. 324

$S = b_0 + b_1 X_1 + b_2 X_2 + \ldots + b_p X_p$ (14.16, 15.13), p. 325

$S = \$23,940 + \$34.20 \times SQFT + \$5,880 \times QUAL - 0.34 \times AGESQFT - \$3,100 \times NBHD1 + \$6,550 \times NBHD2 - \$2,480 \times NBHD4$ (14.17) example for 14.16, p. 326

$MV = b_0 + b_1 X_1 + b_2 X_2 + \ldots + b_p X_p$ (14.27), p. 339

$S = \$7,800 + \$32.10 \, X_1 - \$746 \, X_2$ (15.14) example for 15.13, p. 368

$S = b_0 + b_1 X_1$ (15.15), p. 369

$S_i = \$11,493 + \$47.90 \, X_i$ (15.17) example for 15.15, p. 370

$S = b_0 + b_1 X_1 + b_2 X_2$ (15.18), p. 370

$S = b_0 + b_1 (SIZE)$ (15.35), p. 379

$S = b_0 + b_1 (SIZE) + b_2 (ROOMS)$ (15.36), p. 379

Condominium/Townhouse

$MV = b_0 + (b_1 \times SQFT \times QUAL) + (b_2 \times GARSQFT) + (b_3 \times PATSQFT) + (b_4 \times AGE) + (b_5 \times COMPLEX1) + (b_6 \times COMPLEX2) + \ldots + (b_p \times COMPLEXn)$ (14.31), p. 343

$MV = b_0 + (b_1 \times SQFT) + (b_2 \times GARAGE) + (b_3 \times ENDUNIT) + (b_4 \times GOLF)$ (14.32), p. 343

Duplexes, Triplexes, and Fourplexes

$MV/UNIT = b_0 + (b_1 \times SQFT/UNIT) + (b_2 \times QUAL) + (b_3 \times GAR/UNIT) + (b_4 \times AGE) + (b_5 \times 3PLEX) + (b_6 \times 4PLEX) + (b_7 \times NBHD1) + \ldots + (b_p \times NBHDn).$ (14.34), p. 344

Land

$S = b_0 + b_1 SQRTSF + b_2 IRREG + b_3 VIEWPR + b_4 VIEWGD + b_5 NBHD01 + b_6 NBHD03 + b_7 NBHD04$ (7.3), p. 198

$MV/ACRE = b_0 + (b_1 \times SQRTDIST) + (b_2 \times IRRIG) + (b_3 \times CLASS1) + (b_4 \times CLASS2) + \ldots + (b_p \times CLASSn)$ (14.38), p. 346

$MV/ACRE = b_0 - \$1,050 + b_2 \times IRRIG + b_3 \times CLASS1 + b_4 \times CLASS2 + \ldots + b_p \times CLASSn$ (14.39), p. 346

Single-Family Residential

$MV = b_0 + (b_1 \times SQFT \times QUAL) + (b_2 \times FINBASE \times QUAL) + (b_3 \times UNFBASE) + (b_4 \times GARSQFT) + (b_5 \times PATSQFT) + (b_6 \times BATHS \times QUAL) + (b_7 \times LNAGE) + (b_8 \times SQRTLAND) + (b_9 \times NBHD2) + (b_{10} \times NBHD3) + (b_{11} \times NBHD4)$ (14.29), p. 341

Aggregated Variable

$INSIDE = BATHS + FIREPLACES + HEATING + COOLING$ (15.37), p. 385

Multiplicative

General

$BV = BQ_1 \times BQ_2 \times \ldots \times BQ_n \times (PB_1 \times BSIZE_1 + \ldots + PB_n \times BSIZE_n)$ (14.9), p. 318

$LV = LQ_1 \times LQ_2 \times \ldots \times LQ_n \times (PL_1 \times LSIZE_1)$ (14.10), p. 319

$S = b_0 \times SQFT^{b_1} \times QUAL^{b_2} \times PERGOOD^{b_3} \times b_4^{NBHD1} \times b_5^{NBHD2} \times b_6^{NBHD4}$ (14.18), p. 326

$\ln S = \ln (b_0 \times SQFT^{b_1} \times QUAL^{b_2} \times PERGOOD^{b_3} \times b_4^{NBHD1} \times b_5^{NBHD2} \times b_6^{NBHD4})$ (14.19) log transformation of 14.18, p. 326

$S = \$58.28 \times SQFT^{0.988} \times QUAL^{1.09} \times PERGOOD^{0.873} \times 1.133^{NBHD1}$
$\times 0.968^{NBHD2} \times 0.952^{NBHD4}$ (14.20) conversion of 14.19 to original units, p. 326

$MV = b_0 \times \pi b_i^{X_i} \times \pi X_j^{b_j}$ (14.28), p. 339

$S = b_0 \times X_1^{b_1} \times X_2^{b_2}$ (15.38), p. 388

$S = b_0 \times SQFT^{b_1} \times QUAL^{b_2} \times PERGOOD^{b_3} \times b_4^{NBHD1} \times b_5^{NBHD2} \times b_6^{NBHD4}$
(15.39), p. 388

$\ln(S) = \ln[b_0 \times SQFT^{b_1} \times QUAL^{b_2} \times PERGOOD^{b_3} \times b_4^{NBHD1} \times b_5^{NBHD2} \times b_6^{NBHD4}]$ (15.40) log transformation of 15.39, p. 388

$(S) = \ln(b_0) + b_1 \times \ln(SQFT) + b_2 \times \ln(QUAL) + b_3 \times \ln(PERGOOD) +$
$NBHD1 \times \ln(b_4) + NBHD2 \times \ln(b_5) + NBHD4 \times \ln(b_6)$ (15.41) log transformation of 15.39, p. 388

$\ln(S) = 4.065 + 0.988 \times \ln(SQFT) + 1.09 \times \ln(QUAL) + 0.873 \times \ln(PERGOOD)$
$+ 0.125NBHD1 - 0.033NBHD2 - 0.049NBHD4$ (15.42) example for
15.41, p. 388

$S = \$58.265 \times SQFT^{0.988} \times QUAL^{1.09} \times PERGOOD^{0.873} \times 1.133^{NBHD1} \times$
$0.968^{NBHD2} \times 0.952^{NBHD4}$ (15.43) conversion of 15.42 by antilog, p. 388

Duplexes, Triplexes, Fourplexes
$MV = b_0 \times b_1^{3PLEX} \times b_2^{4PLEX} \times QUAL^{b_3} \times GAR/UNIT^{b_4} \times SQFT^{b_5} \times$
$PERGOOD^{b_6} \times L/B^{b_7} \times b_8^{NBHD1} \times \ldots \times b_p^{NBHDn}$ (14.33), p. 343

Mobile Homes
$MV = b_0 \times SQFT^{b_1} \times QUAL^{b_2} \times PERGOOD^{b_3}$ (14.35), p. 344

Commercial
$MV = b_0 \times b_1^{STORE} \times b_2^{REST} \times b_3^{AUTO} \times b_4^{CONV} \times SQFT^{b_5} \times QUAL^{b_6} \times PERGOOD^{b_7}$
$\times L/B^{b_8}$ (14.37), p. 345

Hybrid
$MV = \pi GQ[(\pi BQ \times \Sigma BA) + (\pi LQ \times \Sigma LA) + \Sigma OA]$ (14.12, 15.2), p. 319

$S = [\$23,940 + (\$34.20 \times SQFT) + (\$5,880 \times QUAL) - (0.34 \times AGESQFT)]$
$\times [1.133^{NBHD1} \times 0.968^{NBHD2} \times 0.952^{NBHD4}]$ (14.21), p. 327

Single-Family Residential
$MV = [PERGOOD^{b_1} \times QUAL^{b_2}] \times [(b_3 \times SQFT) + (b_4 \times FINBASE) +$
$(b_5 \times BATHS) + (b_6 \times UNFBASE) + (b_7 \times GARSQFT) + (b_8 \times$
$PATSQFT)] + [b_8^{NBHD2} \times b_9^{NBHD3} \times b_{10}^{NBHD4} \times LAND^{b_{11}}]$ (14.30), p. 342

Apartments

$$MV/UNIT = (b_1{}^{NBHD1} \times b_2{}^{NBHD2} \times b_3{}^{NBHD3}) \times \{(PERGOOD^{b_4} \times QUAL^{b_5}) \times [(b_6 \times SQFT/UNIT) + (b_7 \times BED/UNIT)] + VIEW^{b_8} \times [(b_9 \times DISTCBD) + (b_{10} \times LNLAND)] + (b_{11} \times POOL)\} \quad (14.36), \text{ p. } 344$$

Land Valuation Models
General

$$LV = \frac{PGI - C}{R} \qquad (7.1), \text{ p. } 181$$

Abstraction Method

$$S - IV = LV \quad (7.2), \text{ p. } 195$$

Additive Sales Comparison

$$S = b_0 + b_1 SQRTSF + b_2 IRREG + b_3 VIEWPR + b_4 VIEWGD + b_5 NBHD01 + b_6 NBHD03 + b_7 NBHD04 \quad (7.3), \text{ p. } 198$$

$$MV/ACRE = b_0 + (b_1 \times SQRTDIST) + (b_2 \times IRRIG) + (b_3 \times CLASS1) + (b_4 \times CLASS2) + \ldots + (b_p \times CLASSn) \quad (14.38), \text{ p. } 346$$

$$MV/ACRE = b_0 - \$1,050 + b_2 \times IRRIG + b_3 \times CLASS1 + b_4 \times CLASS2 + \ldots + b_p \times CLASSn \quad (14.39), \text{ p. } 346$$

Multiplicative Sales Comparison

$$S = b_0 SQFT^{b_1} \times b_2{}^{IRREG} \times b_3{}^{VIEWPR} \times b_4{}^{VIEWGD} \times b_5{}^{NBHD01} \times b_6{}^{NBHD03} \times b_7{}^{NBHD04} \quad (7.4), \text{ p. } 199$$

$$S = \$327 \, (SQFT)^{0.44} \times 0.93^{IRREG} \times 0.84^{VIEWPR} \times 1.12^{VIEWGD} \times 1.04^{NBHD01} \times 0.90^{NBHD03} \times 1.18^{NBHD04} \quad (7.5), \text{ p. } 199$$

Cost Models
Additive

$$V = LV + IV \quad (2.1), \text{ p. } 33$$

$$V = LV + (IV - D) \quad (2.2), \text{ p. } 33$$

$$V = LV + BV \quad (4.5), \text{ p. } 85$$

$$V = (SL \times L) + (SB \times M) \quad (4.8), \text{ p. } 85$$

$$MV = IV + LV \quad (4.10, 8.1, 13.1, 14.4, 15.1), \text{ p. } 105$$

$MV = P_I \times ISIZE + P_L \times LSIZE$ (4.13, 13.2, 14.7), p. 105

$MV = LV + (RCN - D)$ (8.2), p. 205

$BV = (PB_1 \times BSIZE_1) + (PB_2 \times BSIZE_2) + \ldots + (PB_n \times BSIZE_n)$
(13.3, 14.8), p. 310

$OV = (PO_1 \times OSIZE_1) + (PO_2 \times OSIZE_2) + \ldots + (PO_n \times OSIZE_n)$
(14.11), p. 319

$MV = b_1 \times SQFT + b_2 \times QUAL$ (14.13), p. 324

$S = b_1 LV + b_2 IV$ (15.9), p. 360

$S = b_1 RCN - b_2 D + b_3 LV_1 + b_4 LV_2$ (15.10), p. 360

Multiplicative

$RCN = Bsize \times P_B$ (8.4), p. 218

$BV = BQ_1 \times BQ_2 \times \ldots \times BQ_n \times (PB_1 \times BSIZE_1 + PB_2 BSIZE_2 + \ldots + PB_n BSIZE_n)$ (13.4), p. 311

$LV = LQ_1 \times LQ_2 \times \ldots \times LQ_n \times (PL_1 \times LSIZE_1)$ (14.10), p. 319

Hybrid

$MV = GQ [LV + (RCN - D)]$ (8.3), p. 206

$MV = \pi GQ[(\pi BQ \times \Sigma BA) + (\pi LQ \times \Sigma LA) + \Sigma OA]$ (14.12, 15.2), p. 319

$MV = \pi GQ \times [(1 - BQ_D) \times RCN + LV]$ (14.23), p. 335

$RCN = [\pi BQ \times \Sigma(Bsize \times P_B)] + \Sigma OA$ (8.5), p. 219

$S = (LV^{b_1} + BV^{b_2}) \times b_3{}^{NBHD1} \times b_4{}^{NBHD2} \times b_n{}^{NBHDn}$ (15.11), p. 361

Depreciation

$D = RCN - (S - LV)$ (8.6), p. 223

$\%D = D/RCN \times 100$ (8.7), p. 223

$\%GOOD = \dfrac{S - (LV + OV)}{RCN}$ (15.7), p. 358

$D = 0.0335 \times EFFAGE^{0.6646}$ (15.8), p. 358

Replacement Cost New

$RCN = Bsize \times P_B$ (8.4) multiplicative, p. 218

$RCN = [\pi BQ \times \Sigma(Bsize \times P_B)] + \Sigma OA$ (8.5) hybrid, p. 219

$RCN = [\pi BQ \times (\Sigma BA_H + \Sigma BA_V + \Sigma BA_A + \Sigma BA_C)] + \Sigma OA$
(14.22) hybrid, p. 335

$RCN = [\pi BQ \times (\Sigma BA_S + \Sigma BA_I + \Sigma BA_A + \Sigma BA_C)] + \Sigma OA.$ (14.24) hybrid, p. 338

Size Adjustments

$SIZEADJ = b_0 \times SQFT^{b_1}$ (15.4), p. 355

$SIZEADJ = 8.284 \times SQFT^{-.29086}$ (15.5), p. 356

Cost-Trend Factor

$F = I_c/I_b$ (15.6), p. 357

Income Models

Relation of Income Model to Supply and Demand

$$V = \frac{I - EXP}{R} \quad \text{(p. 317)}$$

$$V = \frac{I - EXP}{R} \quad \text{(p. 317)}$$

$$Rents = \int_{x=1,}^{n} \overset{n}{s_F} \quad \overset{n}{d_F} \quad \text{(p. 317)}$$

$$EXP = \int_{x=1,}^{n} \overset{n}{s_F}$$

$$V = \frac{\int s_F, \, d_F}{R}$$

$$V = \int RM \times s_F, \, d_F$$

Direct

$V = I/R$ (2.3, 4.2, 9.1, 12.1), p. 33

$I = R \times V$ (4.1, 9.2), p. 84

$R = I/V$ (9.3), p. 231

$MV = NOI/OAR$ (14.40), p. 347

$MV = GI \times GIM$ (14.41), p. 347

Additive
Residential

$$GI/UNIT = b_0 + (b_1 \times QUAL) + (b_2 \times BED2) + (b_3 \times BED3) + (b_4 \times EFFAGE)$$
$$+ (b_5 \times AMENITY) + (b_6 \times NBHD1) + (b_7 \times NBHD2) + \ldots +$$
$$(b_p \times NBHDn) \quad (14.42), \text{ p. 347}$$

Commercial

$$OAR = b_0 + (b_1 \times OFFICE) + (b_2 \times REST) + (b_3 \times CONV) + (b_4 \times QUAL) +$$
$$(b_5 \times AGE) + (b_6 \times CBD) + (b_7 \times FF/GF) + (b_8 \times STDSQFT)$$
$$(14.45), \text{ p. 349}$$

Multiplicative
Commercial

$$EXP/GI = b_0 \times b_1^{REST} \times b_2^{CONV} \times b_3^{AUTO} \times QUAL^{b_4} \times COND^{b_5} \times SQFTZ^{b_6} \times$$
$$b_7^{CBD} \quad (14.43), \text{ p. 348}$$

Apartments

$$GIM = b_0 \times QUAL^{b_1} \times COND^{b_2} \times STDSQFT^{b_3} \times b_4^{NBHD1} \times b_5^{NBHD2} \times \ldots \times$$
$$b_p^{NBHDn} \quad (14.44), \text{ p. 348}$$

Yield

$$V = \frac{I_1}{1 + R} + \frac{I_2}{(1 + R)^2}$$

$$+ \frac{I_3}{(1 + R)^3} + \ldots + \frac{I_n}{(1 + R)^n} \quad (4.9), \text{ p. 86}$$

$$V = \frac{I_1}{1+Y} + \frac{I_2}{(1+Y)^2} + \frac{I_3}{(1+Y)^3}$$

$$+ \quad \ldots \quad + \frac{I_n}{(1+Y)^n}, \quad (12.2), \text{ p. 272}$$

Mortgage Equity Technique

$$V_O = V_M + V_E \quad (12.15), \text{ p. 292}$$

V_E = present worth of cash flow + present worth of reversion   (12.16), p. 292

V_E = $(NOI - DS) \times$ annuity factor + present worth of reversion factor $\times$ (value
realized at resale − mortgage at resale)   (12.17), p. 292

Ellwood Technique

$$R = Y - mC + dep\,(SFF) - \text{app}\,(SFF) \quad (12.18),\ \text{p. } 293$$

$$dep\,/\,app = \frac{RP - V}{V} \quad (12.19),\ \text{p. } 294$$

Statistics and Statistical Testing

Average Absolute Deviation around Median

$$AAD = \frac{\Sigma|A_i/S_i - \widetilde{A/S}|}{n} \quad (20.7),\ \text{p. } 533$$

Average Percent Error

$$\text{Average percent error} = \frac{100 \times \Sigma|S_i - \hat{S}_i|/S_i)}{n} \quad (15.30),\ \text{p. } 374$$

Beta Coefficient

$$\beta_j = b_j\,(s_j/s_S) \quad (15.34),\ \text{p. } 376$$

Coefficient of Determination

$$R^2 = \frac{SSE_{EX}}{SSE} = \frac{\Sigma\,(\hat{S}_i - \bar{S})^2}{\Sigma\,(S_i - \bar{S})^2} \quad (15.24),\ \text{p. } 372$$

$$R^2 = 1 - \frac{SSE_{UN}}{SSE} \quad (15.25),\ \text{p. } 372$$

Adjusted Coefficient of Determination

$$\bar{R}^2 = 1 - \frac{(n - 1)\,SSE_{UN}}{(n - p - 1)\,SSE} \quad (15.27),\ \text{p. } 373$$

Coefficient of Dispersion

$$COD = \frac{100\,(AAD)}{\widetilde{A/S}} \quad (20.8),\ \text{p. } 534$$

Coefficient of Variation

$$COV = \frac{(100)\,(SEE)}{\bar{S}} \quad (15.29),\ \text{p. } 374$$

$$COV = \frac{(100)\,(s)}{A/S} \quad (20.11),\ \text{p. } 539$$

Degrees of Freedom

degrees of freedom $= n - p - 1$ (p. 375)

F-statistic

$$\frac{\text{additional variance explained by } X_j}{\text{unexplained variance}} \quad (15.32), \text{ p. } 376$$

$F = t^2$ (15.33), p. 376

Means
Arithmetic

$\overline{A/S} = \dfrac{\Sigma(A_i/S_i)}{n}$ (20.3), p. 528

Weighted

$\overline{A/S} = \Sigma A/\Sigma S$ (20.4), p. 529

Geometric

$(\overline{A/S})_g = [A_1/S_1)(A_2/S_2), \ldots, (A_n/S_n)]^{1/n}$ (20.5), p. 530

Percent Error

$Percent\ error = \dfrac{S - A}{S} \times 100.$ (20.1), p. 525

Price-related Differential

$PRD = \dfrac{\overline{A/S}}{\overline{\overline{A/S}}}$ (20.12), p. 539

Rank
Computed from Percentile

$k = (p)(n) + p$ (20.6), p. 531

Median

$median\ rank = 0.5(n) + 0.5$ (20.2), p. 527

Regression Mean Square Error

$\dfrac{\Sigma(\hat{S}_i - \overline{S})^2}{p}$ (p. 378)

Residual Mean Square Error

$$\frac{\Sigma \ (S_i \ - \ \hat{S})^2}{n \ - \ p \ - \ 1} \quad \text{(p. 378)}$$

Standard Deviation—Sample

$$s \ = \sqrt{\frac{\Sigma(A_i/S_i \ - \ \overline{A/S})^2}{n \ - \ 1}} \quad \text{(20.9), p. 535}$$

$$s \ = \sqrt{\frac{\Sigma(A_i/S_i)^2 \ - \ \dfrac{[\Sigma(A_i/S_i)]^2}{n}}{n \ - \ 1}} \quad \text{(20.10), p. 535}$$

Standard Error of the Estimate

$$SEE \ = \ \left[\ \frac{\Sigma \ (S_i \ - \ \hat{S}_i)^2}{n \ - \ p \ - \ 1} \ \right]^{1/2} \quad \text{(15.28), p. 373}$$

Sum of Squared Errors

$$\Sigma e_i^2 \ = \ \Sigma \ (S_i \ - \ \hat{S}_i)^2 \quad \text{(15.16), p. 370}$$

$$SSE \ = \ \Sigma \ (S_i \ - \ \overline{S}) \quad \text{(15.19), p. 371}$$

$$SSE \ = \ SSE_{EX} \ + \ SSE_{UN} \quad \text{(15.22), p. 372}$$

$$\Sigma \ (S_i - \overline{S})^2 = \Sigma \ (\hat{S}_i - \overline{S})^2 + \Sigma \ (S_i - \hat{S}_i)^2 \quad \text{(15.23), p, 372}$$

Explained by Model

$$SSE_{EX} \ = \ \Sigma \ (\hat{S}_i \ - \ \overline{S})^2 \quad \text{(15.20), p. 372}$$

Unexplained by Model

$$SSE_{UN} \ = \ \Sigma e_i^2 \ = \ \Sigma \ (S_i \ - \ \hat{S}_i)^2 \quad \text{(15.21), p. 372}$$

$$SSE_{UN} \ = \ \Sigma e_i^2 \quad \text{(15.26), p. 372}$$

t-statistic

$$t_j \ = \ b_j/s_j \quad \text{(15.31), p. 375}$$

Equilibrium Analysis

Consumer Equilibrium

$$\frac{MU_a}{P_a} \ = \ \frac{MU_b}{P_b} \quad \text{(p. 43)}$$

Producer Equilibrium

$$\frac{MPP_a}{P_a} = \frac{MPP_b}{P_b} \qquad \text{(p. 63)}$$

$$\frac{MPP_x}{P_x} = \frac{MPP_y}{P_y} = \frac{1}{MC_a} = \frac{1}{P_a} \qquad \text{(p. 63)}$$

$$\frac{MPP_x}{P_x} = \frac{MPP_y}{P_y} = \frac{1}{MC_b} = \frac{1}{P_b} \qquad \text{(p. 63)}$$

General Equilibrium

$$\frac{MU_a}{P_a} = \frac{MU_b}{P_b} \qquad \text{(p. 73)}$$

$$\frac{MPP_x}{P_x} = \frac{MPP_y}{P_y} = \frac{1}{MC_a} = \frac{1}{P_a} \qquad \text{(p. 73)}$$

$$\frac{MU_a}{MU_b} = \frac{P_a}{P_b} = \frac{MC_a}{MC_b} \qquad \text{(p. 73)}$$

Miscellaneous

Adjusting *GIM* for Effective Tax Rate

$$GIM' = \frac{GIM}{1 + (GIM \times ETR)} \qquad \text{(15.12), p. 366}$$

Compound Interest Functions

Future Worth of One

$$S^n = (1 + i)^n \qquad \text{(12.3), p. 275}$$

Future Worth of One per Period

$$S_n = \frac{S^n - 1}{i} \qquad \text{(12.4), p. 276}$$

$$\frac{(1 + i)^n - 1}{i} \qquad \text{(12.5), p. 276}$$

Sinking Fund Factor

$$\frac{1}{S_n} = \frac{i}{S^n - 1} \qquad \text{(12.6), p. 277}$$

$$\frac{i}{(1 + i)^n - 1} \quad \text{(12.7), p. 277}$$

Present Worth of One

$$\frac{1}{S^n} \quad \text{(12.8), p. 278}$$

$$V^n = \frac{1}{(1 + i)^n} \quad \text{(12.9), p. 278}$$

Present Worth of One per Period

$$a_n = \frac{1 - \dfrac{1}{(1 + i)^n}}{i} \quad \text{(12.10), p. 278}$$

or

$$\frac{1 - V^n}{i} \quad \text{(12.11), p. 278}$$

$$a_n = \sum_{t=1}^{n} \frac{1}{(1 + i)^t} \quad \text{(12.12), p. 278}$$

Partial Payment Factor

$$\frac{1}{a_n} = \frac{i}{1 - V^n} \quad \text{(12.13), p. 279}$$

or

$$\frac{i}{1 - \dfrac{1}{(1 + i)^n}} \quad \text{(12.14), p. 279}$$

Correction Algorithms for Adaptive Estimation Procedure

$$\frac{S - \hat{S}}{\hat{S}} \times \frac{DF}{n} \quad \text{(15.44), p. 391}$$

$$\frac{S - \hat{S}}{\hat{S}} \times DF \times \frac{datum}{exponential \ smoothing \ average} \quad \text{(15.45), p. 391}$$

$$(SIGNIFICANT\% \times X) + (1 - SIGNIFICANT\% \times \overline{X}) \quad \text{(15.46), p. 391}$$

Euclidean Distance Metric

$$\sum_{j=1}^{k} = [w_j\,(x_{sj} - x_{ij}/\sigma_j)]^2 \qquad (6.2),\ \text{p. } 173$$

Inflation Adjustment

$$IA = ti(S) \quad (4.4),\ \text{p. } 85$$

Multiplicative Transformation

$$QUALSQFT = QUAL \times SQFT \quad (14.14),\ \text{p. } 325$$

Quotient Transformation

$$QUAL \times SQFT^{0.90} \quad (14.15),\ \text{p. } 325$$

Stability

$$APC = \frac{\sum |\,(V_c - V_p)/V_p\,|}{n} \quad (15.47),\ \text{p. } 396$$

$$SPC = \left[\frac{\sum [(V_c - V_p)/V_p]^2}{n-1}\right]^{1/2} \quad (15.48),\ \text{p. } 396$$

$$V_c = (w_p)\,(V_p) + (1 - w_p)\,(V_r) \quad (15.49),\ \text{p. } 398$$

Supply and Demand

$$Q_s = f\,(P,\, s_1,\, s_2,\, \ldots,\, s_n) \quad (14.1),\ \text{p. } 316$$

$$Q_d = f\,(P,\, d_1,\, d_2,\, \ldots,\, d_n) \quad (14.2),\ \text{p. } 316$$

$$P = f\,(s_1,\, s_2,\, \ldots,\, s_n,\, d_1,\, d_2,\, \ldots,\, d_n) \quad (14.3),\ \text{p. } 316$$

Additional Readings

Administration and Management

Anderson, Wayne F., Chester A. Newland, and Richard J. Stillman II. 1983. *The effective local government manager*. Washington, DC: Institute for Training in Municipal Administration.

Argyris, Chris. 1964. *Integrating the individual and the organization*. New York: John Wiley.

Ashton, D. 1976. Elton Mayo and the empirical study of social groups. In *Management thinkers*. ed. A. Fillell, T. Kempner, and G. Wills. Harmondsworth, England: Penguin.

Barnard, Chester L. 1960. *The functions of the executive*. Cambridge, MA: Harvard University Press.

Bennis, Warren. 1966. *Changing organizations*. New York: McGraw-Hill.

Bertalanffy, Ludwig von. 1968. *General system theory: Foundations, development, applications*. New York: George Braziller.

Buffa, E. S. 1968. *Operations management: Problems and models*. New York: John Wiley.

Carey, Alex. 1967. The Hawthorne studies: A radical criticism. *American Sociological Review* 32(3):403–13.

Chase, S. 1941. *Men at work*. New York: Harcourt, Brace, and World.

Churchman, C. West. 1968. *The systems approach*. New York: Dell Publishing Company, Inc.

Drucker, Peter F. 1954. *The practice of management*. New York: Harper and Row.

Eckert, Joseph K., and B. Jackson. 1984. How to do more with less: Systematic resource allocation. Presented at the National Association of Student Personnel Administrators, Nashville, TN.

Fayol, H. 1949. *General and industrial management*. London: Pitman.

Hampton, David. 1977. *Contemporary management*. New York: McGraw-Hill.

Kast, F., and Rosenzweig, J. 1974. *Organization and management: A systems approach*. New York: McGraw-Hill.

Katz, D., and R. L. Kuhn. 1966. *The social psychology of organizations*. New York: John Wiley.

Kirby, Warren E. 1966. *Long range planning: The executive viewpoint*. New York: Prentice-Hall.

Likert, R. 1967. *New patterns of management*. New York: McGraw-Hill.

Likert, R. 1967. *The human organization*. New York: McGraw-Hill.

Maslow, A. H. 1961. *Motivation and personality*. New York: McGraw-Hill.

McGregor, D. 1960. *The human side of enterprise*. New York: McGraw-Hill.

Mooney, J. D., and A. C. Reiley. 1931. *Onward industry*. New York: Harper and Row.

Reddin, W. J. 1970. *Managerial effectiveness*. New York: McGraw-Hill.

Tannen, Robert, and Warren H. Schmidt. 1958. How to choose a leadership pattern. *Harvard Business Review* 36(2):95–101.

Taylor, F. W. 1911. *Scientific management*. New York: Harper and Row.

Weber, Max. 1964. *The theory of social and economic organization*, trans. A. M. Henderson and A. Talcott Parsons. Glencoe, New York: Free Press of Glencoe.

Appraisal, General

American Institute of Real Estate Appraisers. 1987. *The appraisal of real estate*. 9th ed. Chicago: American Institute of Real Estate Appraisers.

Babcock, Frederick Morrison. 1924. *The appraisal of real estate*. New York: The Macmillan Company.

Bloom, George F., and Henry S. Harrison. 1978. *Appraising the single family residence*. Chicago: American Institute of Real Estate Appraisers.

Boykin, J. 1984. Development of value theory to its present state. *1984 Real Estate Valuation Colloquium*. Cambridge, MA: Lincoln Institute of Land Policy.

Eckert, Joseph K. 1984. *Principles of property assessment*. Chicago: International Association of Assessing Officers.

Friedman, Jack, and N. Ordway. 1981. *Income property appraisal and analysis*. Reston, VA: Reston Publishing.

International Association of Assessing Officers. 1978. *Improving real property assessment*. Chicago: International Association of Assessing Officers.

International Association of Assessing Officers. 1978. *Property assessment valuation*. Chicago: International Association of Assessing Officers.

Medici, Giuseppe. 1953. *Principles of appraisal*. Ames, IA: Iowa State College Press.

Ratcliff, Richard U. 1965. *Modern real estate valuation: Theory and application*. Madison, WI: Democrat Press.

Ring, Alfred A. and James H. Boykin. 1986. *The valuation of real estate*. 3d ed. Englewood Cliffs, NJ: Prentice-Hall.

Society of Real Estate Appraisers. 1984. *An introduction to appraising real property* (Course 101). Chicago: Society of Real Estate Appraisers.

Wendt, Paul F. 1956. Real estate appraisal: *A critical analysis of theory and practice*. New York: Henry Holt and Company.

Appraisal of Income Properties

Sources of Information

Building Owners and Managers Association International. *BOMA experience exchange report: Income/expense analysis for office buildings, data for calendar year*. Building Owners and Managers International, 1250 Eye Street, NW, Suite 200, Washington, DC 20005. Annual.

Dun & Bradstreet, Inc. *Key business ratios in 125 lines*. New York: Dun & Bradstreet, Inc., 430 Mountain Ave., New Providence, NJ 07974. Annual.

Hospitality Valuation Services. *Hospitality market data exchange*. Hospitality Valuation Services, Inc., 372 Willis Ave., Mineola, NY 11501.

Hospitality Valuation Services. *Rushmore on hotel valuation*. Hospitality Valuation Services, Inc., 372 Wilis Ave., Mineola, NY 11501.

Institute of Real Estate Management. *Income/expense analysis: Apartments, condominiums, and cooperatives*. Institute of Real Estate Management, 430 N. Michigan Ave., Chicago, IL 60611. Annual.

Institute of Real Estate Management. *Income/expense analysis: Office buildings*. Chicago: Institute of Real Estate Management, 430 N. Michigan Ave., Chicago, IL 60611. Annual.

Laventhol & Horwath. *U. S. Lodging Industry*. Laventhol & Horwath, 919 Third Avenue, New York, NY 10022. Annual.

Mortgage Bankers Association of America. *1987 Outlook and fact book*. Mortgage Bankers Association of America, 1125 15th Street, NW, Washington, DC 20005. Annual.

National Institute of Real Estate Brokers. *Percentage leases*. National Institute of Real Estate Brokers, *now* Realtors National Marketing Institute, 430 N. Michigan Ave., Chicago, IL 60611. Irregular.

National Retail Merchants Association. Controllers' Congress. *Department store and specialty store merchandising and operating results*. National Retail Merchants Association, 100 West 31st Street, New York, NY 10001. Annual.

National Retail Merchants Association. Department store lease study. 1983. New York: Financial Executives Division, National Retail Merchants Association.

National Retail Merchants Association. *Financial and operating results of department and specialty stores*. New York: National Retail Merchants Association, 100 West 31st Street, New York, NY 10001. Annual.

Pannell Kerr Forster. *Clubs in town & county*. Pannell Kerr Forster, 262 North Belt East, Houston, TX 77060. Annual.

Pannell Kerr Forster. *Trends in the hotel industry*. Houston: Pannell Kerr Forster, 262 North Belt East, Houston, TX 77060. Annual.

Rushmore, Stephen. 1983. *Hotels, motels, & restaurants: Valuations & market studies*. Chicago: American Institute of Real Estate Appraisers.

United States League of Savings Institutions. *Savings institutions sourcebook*. Annual.

Urban Land Institute. *Dollars and cents of off-price shopping centers*. 1986. Urban Land Institute, 1090 Vermont Ave., NW, Washington, DC 20005.

Urban Land Institute. *Dollars and cents of shopping centers*. Urban Land Institute, 1090 Vermont Ave., NW, Washington, DC 20005. Triennial.

Techniques and Principles

Blume, Marshall, and Jack Friedman. 1984. *The complete guide to investment opportunities*. New York: Macmillan/Free Press.

Boykin, James H., and Donald R. Epley. 1983. *Basic income property appraisal*. Reading, MA: Addison-Wesley.

Downs, James C. Jr. 1980. *Principles of real estate management*. 12th ed. Chicago: Institute of Real Estate Management, National Association of Realtors.

Friedman, Jack P., Waldo Born, and Arthur Wright. 1988. *Freestanding store development*. College Station, TX: Texas Real Estate Research Center, Texas A&M University.

Friedman, Jack P., and Nicholas Ordway. 1987. *Income property appraisal and analysis*. Englewood Cliffs, NJ: Prentice-Hall.

Graham, Benjamin. 1973. *The intelligent investor*. New York: Harper & Row.

Harris, Jack C. 1982. *The rent control controversy: Background, debate and alternatives*. Publication No. 333. College Station, TX: Texas Real Estate Research Center, Texas A&M University.

Kau, James B., and C. F. Sirmans. 1985. *Tax planning for real estate investors*. 3d ed. Englewood Cliffs, NJ: Prentice-Hall.

Kelley, Edward N. 1990. *Practical apartment management*. 3d ed. Chicago: Institute of Real Estate Management, National Association of Realtors.

Kinnard, William N., Jr. 1971. *Income property valuation: Principles and techniques of appraising income-producing real estate*. Lexington, MA: Heath Lexington Books.

Malkiel, Burton G. 1985. *A random walk down Wall Street*. 1985. 4th ed. New York: W. W. Norton & Company.

Messner, Stephen D., et al. 1982. *Marketing investment real estate*. 2d ed. Chicago: Realtors National Marketing Institute.

Wendt, Paul F., and Alan R. Cerf. 1979. *Real estate investment analysis and taxation*. 2d ed. New York: McGraw-Hill.

Wiedemer, John P. 1986. *Real estate finance*. Englewood Cliffs, NJ: Prentice-Hall.

Bibliographies

Assessment Digest. List of current publications in each issue. Chicago: International Association of Assessing Officers.

Clatanoff, Robert M. 1988. *A basic library for assessors*. Chicago: International Association of Assessing Officers.

International Association of Assessing Officers. Bibliographic Series. Various titles and on-line bibliographies for topics in appraisal and assessment. Write Library, International Association of Assessing Officers, 1313 East 60th Street, Chicago, IL 60637–2892.

Comparative Study of Various Real Property Taxation Systems

Hamilton, Stan. 1989. Comparative study of real property taxation systems in Canada. Presented at the *Real Property Taxation Conference*, Vancouver, BC. May 11–13.

Woolery, Arlo. 1989. *Property tax principles and practice*. Taiwan: Land Reform Training Institute.

Economics and Appraisal

Dilmore, Gene. 1971. *The new approach to real estate appraising*. Englewood Cliffs, NJ: Prentice-Hall.

Due, John F., and Robert W. Clower. 1966. *Intermediate economic analysis*. 5th ed. Homewood, IL: Richard D. Irwin.

Fisher, Irving. 1965 (originally published 1906). *The nature of capital and income*. New York: Augustus M. Kelley, Reprints of Economic Classics.

Kinnard, William N., Jr. 1984. *Real estate valuation colloquium: A redefinition of real estate appraisal precepts and process*. Cambridge, MA: Oelgeschlager, Gunn & Hain, in association with the Lincoln Institute of Land Policy.

Leftwich, Richard, and Ross Eckert. 1982. *The price system and resource allocation*. 8th ed. Chicago: Dryden Press.

Marshall, Alfred. 1950. *Principles of economics*. New York: Macmillan.

Mill, John Stuart. 1896 (originally published 1848). *Essays on some unsettled questions of political economy*. London: The London School of Economics and Political Science.

Ratcliff, Richard U. 1963. *A restatement of appraisal theory*. Madison: University of Wisconsin.

Ratcliff, Richard U. (ed.) 1963. *The Wisconsin colloquium on appraisal research, papers and proceedings*. Madison: Bureau of Business Research and Service, School of Commerce, University of Wisconsin.

Ricardo, David. 1917 (first published in 1817). *The principles of political economy and taxation*. New York: E. P. Dutton & Co., Inc.

Roll, Eric. 1947. *A history of economic thought*. New York: Prentice-Hall.

Smith, Adam. 1937. *An inquiry into the nature and causes of the wealth of nations*. New York: Modern Library.

Society of Real Estate Appraisers. 1980. *An introduction to appraising real property*. Chicago: Society of Real Estate Appraisers.

Stigler, George J. 1949. *The theory of price*. New York: Macmillan.

Watson, Donald S. 1972. *Price theory and its uses*. 3d ed. Boston: Houghton Mifflin.

Wendt, Paul F. *Real estate appraisal: A critical analysis of theory and practice*. New York: Henry Holt and Company.

Finance

American Council of Life Insurance. *Life insurance fact book*. Washington, DC: American Council of Life Insurance. Annual.

Britton, James A., Jr., and Lewis O. Kerwood. 1977. *Financing income-producing real estate*. New York: McGraw-Hill.

Brueggeman, William, and Leo Stone. *Real estate finance*. Homewood, IL: Richard D. Irwin.

Downs, Anthony. 1985. *The revolution in real estate finance*. Washington, DC: The Brookings Institution.

Lusht, K. 1985. Finance theory and real estate valuation. *1984 real estate valuation colloquium*. Cambridge, MA: Lincoln Institute of Land Policy.

Musgrove, Peggy B., and Richard A. Musgrove. 1984. *Public finance in theory and practice*. 4th ed. New York: McGraw-Hill.

Land Valuation

Chapin, F. Stuart, Jr. 1965. *Urban land use planning*. 2d ed. Urbana, IL: University of Illinois Press.

Harvey, Jack. 1987. *Urban land economics*. 2d. ed. London: Macmillan Education.

International Association of Assessing Officers. 1987. *Standard on urban land valuation*. Chicago: International Association of Assessing Officers.

Jensen, David. 1988. The use of multiple linear regression in residential land valuation. *Property Tax Journal* 7(3):215–40.

Kolacny, Bruce. 1988. *Commercial appraisal*. Unpublished narrative appraisal report. Chicago: International Association of Assessing Officers.

Rubinfeld, Daniel. 1973. *Urban land prices: Empirical and theoretical essays*. Working paper no. 13. Cambridge, MA. The Joint Center for Urban Studies of the Massachusetts Institute of Technology and Harvard University.

von Thünen, Johann Heinrich. 1966. *The isolated state: An English edition*, 1st ed., trans. Carla M. Wartenberg, Oxford and New York: Pergamon Press. Abridged from 2d Berman edition.

Mass Appraisal

Borst, Richard A., and John F. Thompson. 1987. Mathematical and computer system considerations related to the development of a generalized cost approach. *Property Tax Journal* 6(3):173–91.

Eckert, Joseph K. 1978. Modern modeling methodology. In *Introduction to computer assisted valuation*. Cambridge, MA: Lincoln Institute of Land Policy.

Eckert, Joseph K., and Jeffrey Epstein. 1987. The use of constrained regression as an updating method in Brookline, Massachusetts. *Property Tax Journal* 6(4):263–69.

Fruitman, Cecilia M. 1989. A feasibility study of CAMA for income-producing properties: Part 2. Presented at the Fourth Annual Technical Seminar of the International Association of Assessing Officers, Fort Worth, TX. September 28.

Fruitman, Cecilia M., and Robert J. Gloudemans. 1989. A feasibility study of CAMA for apartment and commercial property. *Property Tax Journal* 8(1):55–69.

Gilreath, Morgan B., Jr. 1990. Mass appraisal with general purpose software: Applying the income approach. *Property Tax Journal* 9(1):27–42.

Gloudemans, Robert J. 1978. Base home methodology. In *Introduction to computer assisted valuation*. Cambridge, MA: Lincoln Institute of Land Policy.

Gloudemans, Robert J. 1988. Using general purpose software in mass appraisal: Do your own thing. *Assessment Digest* July/August 10(4):11–12, 14–18.

International Association of Assessing Officers. 1974. *The application of multiple regression analysis in assessment administration*. Chicago: International Association of Assessing Officers.

International Association of Assessing Officers. 1983. *Standard on application of the three approaches to value in mass appraisal*. Chicago: IAAO.

International Association of Assessing Officers. 1984. *Standard on mass appraisal of real property*. Chicago: International Association of Assessing Officers.

Jensen, David L. 1987. The application of Bayesian regression for a valuation model update in computer-assisted mass appraisal. *Property Tax Journal* 6(4):271–83.

Landretti, Gregory J. 1986. Commercial/industrial property and the sales comparison approach: Selection, adjustments, confidence, and stability. *Property Tax Journal* 5(4):235–50.

Mathews, John P. 1987. The weighted-average estimator. *Property Tax Journal* 6(4):285–93.

Mendenhall, William, and James McClave. *Business statistics: Regression analysis*. San Francisco: Dellen Publishing Co.

Neter, John, William Wasserman, and G. A. Whitmore. 1979. *Applied statistics*. Boston: Allyn and Bacon, Inc.

O'Connor, Patrick M., and Jack Eichenbaum. 1988. Location value response surfaces: The geometry of advanced mass appraisal. *Property Tax Journal* 7(3):277–96.

Sauter, Bruce. W. 1987. Valuation stability: A practical look at the problems. *Property Tax Journal* 6(4):243–50.

Schreiber, Jan. 1978. A feedback primer. In *Introduction to computer assisted valuation*. Cambridge, MA: Lincoln Institute of Land Policy.

Thompson, John F., Jr., and Jack F. Gordon. 1987. Constrained regression modeling and the multiple regression analysis-comparable sales approach. *Property Tax Journal* 6(4):251–62.

Ward, Richard D. Apartment valuation model development. *Property Tax Journal* 8(1):43–53.

Ward, Richard D., and Lorraine C. Steiner. 1988. A comparison of feedback and multivariate nonlinear regression analysis in computer-assisted mass appraisal. *Property Tax Journal* 7(1):43–67.

Woolery, Arlo, and Sharon Shea. (eds.) 1985. *Introduction to computer assisted valuation*. Boston: Oelgeschleger, Gunn & Hain, in association with the Lincoln Institute of Land Policy.

Zangerle, John A. 1923. *Principles of real estate appraising*. Cleveland: Hampton-Keller.

Quality Control

Cochran, William G. 1971. *Sampling techniques*. 2d ed. New York: John Wiley.

Doering, Woerner W. 1972. Assessment ratio studies: Design and use. In *International property assessment administration*, vol. 4. Chicago: International Association of Assessing Officers.

Dornfest, Alan, and Sheldon Bluestein. 1985. Utilization of "z" and "t" distribution algorithms in determining compliance with ratio study standards. *Property Tax Journal* 4(3):197–206.

Gloudemans, Robert J., and Harold Scott. 1980. Sales ratio studies for equalization. *Proceedings of the 1980 Conference of the National Association of Tax Administrators*.

Gloudemans, Robert J., and Garth E. Thimgan. 1987. A statewide ratio study using microcomputers and generic software. *Proceedings of the Conference on New Developments in Hardware and Software Options to Support CAMA*. Lincoln Institute of Land Policy and International Association of Assessing Officers, Boston, MA. Nov. 10–11, 1987. Chicago: International Association of Assessing Officers.

International Association of Assessing Officers. *Analyzing assessment equity*. 1977. Chicago: International Association of Assessing Officers.

International Association of Assessing Officers. 1990. *Standard on Ratio Studies*. Chicago: International Association of Assessing Officers.

Jacobs, Thomas. Assessment quality control. *Assessment Digest*. July/August 9(4):8–14.

Mendenhall, William, and James Reinmuth. 1978. *Statistics for management and economics*. 3d ed. Belmont, CA: Duxbury Press.

National Association of Tax Administrators, Committee on Sales Ratio Data. 1954. *Report of the committee: Guide for assessment-sales ratio studies*. Chicago: Federation of Tax Administrators.

Owen, D. B. 1962. *Handbook of statistical tables*. Reading, MA: Addison-Wesley Publishing Co.

Property Tax Journal. 1985. December issue. Chicago: International Association of Assessing Officers.

Property Tax Journal. 1986. December issue. Chicago: International Association of Assessing Officers.

Siegal, Sidney. 1956. *Nonparametric statistics*. New York: McGraw-Hill.

Wonnacott, Thomas H., and Ronald J. Wonnacott. 1969. *Introductory statistics*. New York: John Wiley.

Standards

The Appraisal Foundation. 1987. *Uniform standards of professional appraisal practice*. Washington, DC: The Appraisal Foundation.

International Association of Assessing Officers. 1989. *Code of ethics and standards of professional conduct*. Chicago: International Association of Assessing Officers.

International Association of Assessing Officers. 1979. *Standard on certification of assessing officers and valuation personnel*. Chicago: International Association of Assessing Officers.

International Association of Assessing Officers. 1980. *Standard on property use codes*. Chicago: International Association of Assessing Officers.

International Association of Assessing Officers. 1981. *Standard on assessment appeal*. Chicago: International Association of Assessing Officers.

International Association of Assessing Officers. 1983. (Revised 1985.) *Standard on the application of the three approaches to value in mass appraisal*. Chicago: International Association of Assessing Officers.

International Association of Assessing Officers. 1984. *Standard on mass appraisal of real property*. Chicago: International Association of Assessing Officers.

International Association of Assessing Officers. 1985. *Standard on valuation of personal property*. Chicago: International Association of Assessing Officers.

International Association of Assessing Officers. 1986. *Standard on contracting for assessing services*. Chicago: International Association of Assessing Officers.

International Association of Assessing Officers. 1987. *Standard on urban land valuation*. Chicago: International Association of Assessing Officers.

International Association of Assessing Officers. 1988. *Standard on cadastral maps and parcel identifiers*. Chicago: International Association of Assessing Officers.

International Association of Assessing Officers. 1988. *Standard on public relations*. Chicago: International Association of Assessing Officers.

International Association of Assessing Officers. 1989. *Standard on facilities, computers, equipment, and supplies*. Chicago: International Association of Assessing Officers.

International Association of Assessing Officers. 1989. *Standard on education and training for assessing officers*. Chicago: International Association of Assessing Officers.

International Association of Assessing Officers. 1990. *Guide to assessment administration standards*. Chicago: International Association of Assessing Officers.

International Association of Assessing Officers. 1990. *Standard on ratio studies*. Chicago: International Association of Assessing Officers.

Index